SOCIAL WORK

IN THE 21ST CENTURY

*This book is about the helping impulse and the
wonderful profession of social work. My father and mother, Sam and Rose Glicken,
believed that helping others was the noblest thing we could do with our lives.
Their legacy is what prompted the writing of this book, and I dedicate it to them, with love.*

SOCIAL WORK
IN THE 21ST CENTURY

An Introduction to Social Welfare, Social Issues, and the Profession

Morley D. Glicken

Institute for Personal Growth:
A Research, Training, and Treatment Cooperative in Los Angeles

Professor Emeritus, California State University San Bernardino

SAGE Publications
Thousand Oaks ▪ London ▪ New Delhi

For information:

Sage Publications, Inc.
2455 Teller Road
Thousand Oaks, California 91320
E-mail: order@sagepub.com

SAGE Publications Ltd
1 Oliver's Yard
55 City Road
London EC1Y 1SP
United Kingdom

Sage Publications India Pvt. Ltd.
B-42, Panchsheel Enclave
Post Box 4109
New Delhi 110 017 India

Printed in the United States of America

Library of Congress Cataloging-in-Publication Data

Glicken, Morley D.
Social work in the 21st century : an introduction to social welfare, social issues, and the profession / Morley D. Glicken.
     p. cm.
Includes bibliographical references and index.
ISBN 1-4129-1316-0 (cloth)
   1. Social service—United States. 2. Social problems—United States. 3. People with social disabilities—Services for—United States. 4. United States—Social conditions—21st century. I. Title: Social work in the twenty-first century. II. Title.
HV91.G55 2006
361.973—dc22

This book is printed on acid-free paper.

06   07   08   09   10   10 9 8 7 6 5 4 3 2 1

Acquisitions Editor:	Kassie Graves
Editorial Assistant:	Veronica Novak
Typesetter:	C&M Digitals (P) Ltd.
Cover Designer:	Candice Harman

Contents

Preface

This book on social work covers three broad topics: (a) It describes a number of serious social problems in America such as poverty, youth violence, health and mental health problems, and substance abuse; (b) it helps you, the reader, understand the helping institutions we've developed to evaluate and hopefully treat those problems; and (c) it discusses the role of social work, the most significant helping profession in treating social problems, and explains how social workers resolve social problems within our social welfare and social service organizations, or wherever social workers are employed. It may surprise many of you to know that social workers serve in the military; are elected to local, state, and federal legislatures; and work in the business sector. Social work is a noble and exciting profession with a long history of professional service in America. Social work is a wonderful profession.

I hope that many of you will go on and earn your BSW and then your MSW degrees. For the three or four of you who don't jump on the social work bandwagon, I hope this book makes you much more aware of the many social problems facing America and the social workers who help treat these problems. As you will see, social workers are professionals who do great work with a range of people including gang members, substance abusers, felons, children at risk of having serious social and emotional problems, people who are very poor, people who have been the victims of terrorism, our fighting men and women in the armed service, and a host of people in difficult social and emotional situations. Even if you don't see yourself becoming a social worker, I hope you recognize the honor of doing social work and the good that results from it.

Maybe you've heard some things about social work that describe it as a profession handing out food baskets or taking children away from their homes. That's far from what we do. There just isn't another profession that has the ability to work with people's emotions and yet also strives to make our communities and institutions much healthier places. The coming together of help for what people feel and think, coupled with a strong emphasis on a clean, safe, and healthy environment, makes social work very unique among the helping professions.

I've been involved in university teaching for more than 35 years, and I know that an interesting and well-written book makes course material more relevant and your life less difficult. To make your job easier as a reader, I've included small sections in each chapter that summarize a great deal of information and statistics. The same information sometimes takes up a few pages in other books. I don't want you to get bored, and along with my easy style of writing and the interesting material I'm including, I'm also providing case studies that describe social work practice. When you read about what we do, I think you'll have a much better idea of how important our work is, and you will discover how interesting and meaningful social work can be. Because most of you are highly computer literate, suggested readings to supplement the material are provided at the end of most chapters as Internet sources.

I hope you also begin to recognize the need for a more sympathetic and caring society in America and that, as a result of this book and the educational process you are part of, you will develop what Bertrand Russell called the "unbearable sympathy for the suffering of others."

—Morley D. Glicken, DSW

Acknowledgments

During a professional career, you develop some very good role models. Sometimes you live up to their level of professional and personal integrity, but for the most part, you're lucky if you even come close. Arthur Katz, the former dean of the University of Kansas School of Social Welfare and my next-door office mate and critic of the mess and chaos of my office, is a wonderful man, a great social worker, and certainly one of the most outstanding people I've ever known. Dr. David Hardcastle, who followed him as dean, is another great person who supported and encouraged me even during times when my behavior was at its most infantile. Several early supervisors were people who helped change my professional direction, and the faculties in social work at the University of North Dakota, the University of Washington, and the University of Utah, where I received my various degrees, forgave me for being an ungrateful, childish lout and treated me with respect, encouragement, and dignity. These are the important people in my life who helped form the underlying basis of this book, and I want to acknowledge and thank them.

Arthur Pomponio, my editor at Sage, loved the idea of this book and not only accepted it immediately when I offered it to him but has been supportive throughout. His assistant, Veronica Novak, helped in many very important ways and worked closely with me during its production. Thanks, Art and Veronica. You're the best!

My many students over the years helped give me a voice for this book and a strong sense of how to write it. No one writes academic books without understanding that your teaching always influences your writing. Thanks to all my former students for teaching me more about life and the helping impulse than I taught them.

Professor Dan Huff of the Boise State University Department of Social Work discussed many aspects of this book and was very encouraging. His work on the history of social work, which is included in the book, is a creative and much appreciated addition.

Pat Fox, who offered encouragement and support at just the right moments, is a very special woman and I thank her for providing me with an emotional and creative safe haven.

Finally, my family has always been supportive of my work. My parents, Sam and Rose Glicken, and my daughter, Amy Glicken, are my rock and foundation for the sometimes lonely job of writing, and I thank them all from the bottom of my heart.

Part I

Social Problems, the Social Welfare System, and the Role of Professional Social Work

An Introduction to Social Problems, Social Welfare Organizations, and the Profession of Social Work

1

N o one we know starts out life wanting to be a substance abuser or to be poor. Most of us want to be lucky, cool, rich, and successful. Some of us are, but many of us aren't. Part of the reason for individual success and failure has to do with what we were given biologically in terms of intelligence and the ability to stick with projects and finish them. The other part of it has to do with the families we grow up in, the social and economic conditions of our lives, and the people who influence us, including parents, teachers, and friends. Some parents do wonderful things for their children and provide safe and happy homes. Other parents fight, use substances, and sometimes abuse and neglect their children. It doesn't take a genius to know that the child who grows up in a happy family has a better chance of being successful in life than the child growing up in a troubled family. Child abuse is everything it's cracked up to be and so are poverty, abandonment, unsafe neighborhoods, and poorly functioning schools. Some of us start life out on the right track, and some of us start out life on the wrong track. Often those people whose families function poorly overcome early life problems by the inner strength some people call resilience. But many children who grow up in difficult, unloving, and abusive homes suffer harm to the body and the spirit. It's difficult for them to be as successful as many of us who grew up in healthier homes. People sometimes pull themselves up by their bootstraps, but sometimes they don't, and in order to be more successful, they sometimes need professional help.

To help our most troubled families and the children who grow into adulthood having to cope with the burden of a great many early life problems, we've developed social programs and social service organizations to deliver those programs. We have organizations to help families when they lose the ability to work and to earn an income. We have other organizations to help families when the loss of work leads to the loss of their homes. We have organizations to help people who experience mental illness or physical disabilities brought about by accidents, war, and health problems. The organizations we have developed in America come from our concern that all Americans should have an equal chance to succeed in life. Sometimes our helping organizations work very well, but other times they don't. There's no question that helping organizations reflect the concerns of the society. When the concern is great, as it is when soldiers come back wounded from war or when people are hurt in terrorist attacks, the organizations often work extremely well. But when society is in a particularly blaming mood as it sometimes is about homelessness and poverty, then the organizations don't work as well because they've lost the support of citizens and funding is pulled back.

I'm not apologizing for organizations that don't work well. They need our help and support. Neither am I going to brag about our organizations that work very well. I'm just going to clarify what they do, what they cost, and how well they're doing the intended job of helping people resolve the social problems discussed in this book.

Social work is the profession originally developed to work with a number of these social problems. But it's not the only helping profession: Psychiatry, psychology, and counseling are also helping professions working with people in difficulty. The difference is that social work is concerned with the internal side of a person's behavior (his or her emotional problems and problem-solving skills) as well as the external side of a person's life (the quality of family life, the school the child attends, the safety of the neighborhoods, and the amount of money he or she has to live on). In a sense, social work sees people from a total perspective and works to resolve internal and external problems. But we use common sense. If a person is chronically hungry, social workers try to eliminate his or her hunger while at the same time resolving the reasons for this hunger. In this way, the immediate need for food is met and the likelihood of repeated need for food may be diminished.

I think all people who work in the helping professions are heroic because we give of ourselves daily to help others. But I believe that social workers are particularly heroic because we're on the frontline of all of the social problems that exist in our nation. We work with gangs, we care for the terminally ill, we help children who are battered and abandoned by parents and caretakers, we work with the homeless, and we provide help to families who need to learn to communicate with each other more effectively. We inspire, we cheerlead, and we advocate for millions of people every day and, in the process, many people who would otherwise suffer

InfoTable 1.1	Volunteering as a Social Responsibility by Amy J. Glicken

As the volunteer coordinator for a rural nonprofit program in Arizona, I've seen the generous nature of people when they're asked to volunteer. I think that people become volunteers as they begin to realize that someone else's tragedy can easily be their own, and while many of us feel a responsibility to give back to our communities, so often we feel powerless to make the changes that seem beyond our personal scope.

I believe we have the power to make those changes by using the skills we already have. Attorneys donate their time with legal services for the poor. Doctors provide services to the neighborhoods and communities with marginal health care. Helping professionals offer their time and expertise to the many social welfare organizations without professionals to supervise services and as board members and grant writers.

With all of the options for helping, some of us are gifted at what is sometimes called "impact work." Impact work is the attorney who chooses to represent 600 new immigrants from Mexico rather than simply representing the one immigrant who walked into her office. Impact work is going beyond providing shelter and counseling services to victims of domestic violence by looking at the causes of violence and finding new ways of preventing it. Impact work is building more low and no income housing rather than just providing temporary shelters for those without homes.

Many of us are overwhelmed with our daily workloads and feel unable to make long-term, far-reaching changes in our communities. But whether it's by peacekeeping, sculpting, growing corn, counseling, healing, or teaching children, each of us has a gift that we can use to make our communities much better than they are. The task is simply to discern what our gifts are and to utilize them. Because, in the end, we are each our own Tooth Fairies, taking what has been lost and giving gold in return. (Glicken, 2005, p. 310)

lives of quiet desperation and hopelessness have hope and succeed. We counsel people who want to end their lives far sooner than this should ever happen. We give hope to people facing a long struggle with terminal illness. We work with our political leaders to make our communities more livable and to offer opportunity where it didn't exist before. We are neither liberal nor conservative but believe that what we do from the heart is paid back in the wonderful feeling that our lives have been dedicated to helping others. My daughter, Amy Glicken (Glicken, 2005), wrote a piece on volunteering that describes what social workers do.

What Are Social Problems?

A social problem is an issue within the society that makes it difficult for people to achieve their full potential. Poverty and malnutrition are examples of social problems. So are substandard housing, employment discrimination, and child abuse and neglect. Crime and substance abuse are also examples of social problems. Not only do social problems affect many people directly, but they also affect all of us indirectly. The drug-abusing driver becomes the potential traffic accident that doesn't choose its victims by race, color, or creed, but does so randomly. The child of abusive parents all too often becomes the victim or perpetrator of family violence as an adult.

Social problems tend to develop when we become neglectful and fail to see that serious problems are developing. Between 1988 and 1993, for example, the United States saw a phenomenal increase in youth violence. In my book about children who commit violent acts (Glicken, 2004b), I documented that children younger than age 12 cause one-third of all fires resulting in death, and that the average age of children who sexually abuse other children is younger than age 10. According to Osofsky and Osofsky (2001), "The homicide rate among males 15–24 years old in the United States is 10 times higher than in Canada, 15 times higher than in Australia, and 28 times higher than in France or Germany" (p. 287). These are troubling examples of social problems that affect all of us.

Could these problems have been prevented if our social institutions had been working well? I think so, but this is where political philosophies are important to understand. Some people believe that the government should be very involved in providing services to people most at risk. I don't know if the labels *liberal* and *conservative* have much meaning anymore, but in times past, we might have called these folks liberals. Liberals believe that where our usual institutions fail, the government and the private sector should help out. Conservatives believe that intruding in people's lives often leads to a weakening of social institutions and the values that have served us well in the past. Conservatives might say that what we should be doing to reduce juvenile crime is to promote good family values and look to our traditional institutions (e.g., religious organizations and schools) to help prevent social problems from developing. They also believe that the more government has become involved in people's lives in the past, the more serious our social problems have become. And finally, although this is true of liberals as well, conservatives believe in the concept of social capital: "the good will, fellowship, sympathy, and social intercourse among the individuals and families who make up a social unit" (Hanifan, 1916, p. 130) will reduce social problems if used wisely. The tension between political philosophies is often the underlying reason why we respond to or neglect social problems.

Mahoney (2003) believes that several conditions must exist before an issue or situation is considered a social problem. They are as follows:

The condition or situation must be publicly seen as a social problem because of a public outcry. The conditions in New Orleans after the dikes broke and the city was flooded began a public outcry that focused on the slow response to the crisis by government, concerns about people in poverty who were left in the city to fend for themselves, concerns about the lack of law and order during the crisis, and, certainly, concerns about racism and feelings that the federal government had acted slowly because most of the people remaining in New Orleans after the flood were poor and black.

The condition must be at odds with the values of the larger society. Although people have varying degrees of concern about the poor, there was universal anger and grief at what happened to poor people in New Orleans and a growing recognition that government was potentially incapable of helping them if they found themselves in a similar crisis.

Most people must be in agreement that a problem exists. During a 10-year period from 1983 to 1993, America saw astronomical increases in juvenile crime. People were aware and concerned at the same time because their personal safety was at issue.

There must be a solution to a social problem. In the case of New Orleans and future disasters, most people must believe that government is capable of handling large-scale disasters, whether man-made or terrorist. If people don't believe this, they fall into apathy; and while the problem may still exist, they don't believe anything can be done about it.

Mahoney also notes that the more influential or powerful people are who might be affected by a social problem, the more likely there is to be a recognition of the problem and a response. The mass media also play a role in the recognition of social problems because it highlights problems in such a graphic way that many people are touched by it. I wonder how many people believed John Edwards when he spoke of two Americas during the 2004 presidential campaign. We are an affluent country, and many people have done very well. People who never thought they could afford a decent house now see initial investments of $100,000 worth many times that amount. It's hard to think about poverty when your net worth is skyrocketing. But pictures of poor people struggling to survive during the New Orleans flood had a devastating impact on the perceptions people had, after the flood, about poverty. The media were responsibility for informing us that, much as we might like to think that poverty is nonexistent in America, it does exist and its negative impact is substantial. But the media are not always unbiased or objective in the way they report the news. During the New Orleans' floods, for example, some networks focused on crime and violence whereas others focused on the plight of poor people and the slow and befuddled response by the government. There are many people who believe that the media reflect a liberal bias, and also many who think that the media are controlled by their corporate owners who, some think, skew the news to reflect a more conservative orientation.

InfoTable 1.2	Media Bias: Two Views

A Liberal View of the Media

Each year it is more likely that the American citizen who turns to any medium . . . will receive [80% of their] information, ideas, or entertainment controlled by the same handful of 5 corporations, whether it is daily news, a cable entertainment program, or a textbook. . . . One of the dangers in all this is that the new corporate ethic is so single-minded about extreme fast profits and expanded control over the media business that it is willing to convert American news into a service for the affluent customers wanted by the media's advertisers instead of a source of information significant for the whole of society. The rewards of money profit through market control by themselves and their advertisers have blinded media owners to the damage they are doing to an institution central to the American democracy. (Bagdikian, 2005, p. 1)

A Conservative View of the Media

Conservatives believe the mass media, predominantly television news programs, slant reports in favor of the liberal position on issues. Members of the media argue while personally liberal, they are professionally neutral. They argued their opinions do not matter because as professional journalists, they report what they observe without letting their opinions affect their judgment. But being a journalist is not like being a surveillance camera at an ATM, faithfully recording every scene for future playback. Journalists make subjective decisions every minute of their professional lives. They choose what to cover and what not to cover, which sources are credible and which are not, which quotes to use in a story and which to toss out.

   Liberal bias in the news media is a reality. It is not the result of a vast left-wing conspiracy; journalists do not meet secretly to plot how to slant their news reports. But every day pack journalism often creates an unconscious "groupthink" mentality that taints news coverage and allows only one side of a debate to receive a fair hearing. When that happens, the truth suffers. (Media Bias Basics, 2005, p. 1)

My Political Philosophy

What is my political philosophy? I like some liberal philosophies, yet I also like some conservative philosophies. Does this make me wishy-washy or, in the jargon of the 2004 presidential campaign, a flip-flopper? Maybe it does, but most of us in America are politically moderate and our beliefs don't neatly fit most labels. I grew up in a blue–collar, working-class family. My father was involved in the labor movement. I agree with Andrew Stern, president of the Service Employees Union, that "the idea that the rich get richer and wealth is going to trickle down is a bankrupt economic and moral theory" ("10 Questions," 2005, p. 6). Perhaps because of my early life experiences with the fight for fair wages and benefits for working people, I believe in many government programs that protect working people. Like what? Well, I believe in unemployment compensation for workers who have lost their jobs because of a poor economy. I believe in workman's compensation to protect workers who are injured on the job. I believe in Social Security and Medicare because they provide a safety net for older

InfoTable 1.3	Religion and Spirituality

According to George, Larson, Koenig, and McCullough (2000), a growing body of research points to the positive health benefits of religious involvement. Religious involvement was found to reduce the likelihood of disease and disability in 78% of the studies attempting to determine the existence of a relationship between religion and health. The positive health benefits of religion were particularly noted with certain medical conditions including coronary disease and heart attacks, emphysema, cirrhosis and other varieties of liver disease, hypertension, and disability. The authors also point to a relationship between religious observance and longevity, noting that "multiple dimensions of religion are associated with longevity, but attendance at religious services is the most strongly related to longevity" (p. 108).

Americans who would like to spend their later years enjoying the fruits of their hard labor. And I believe in public education, which means that all Americans, regardless of age, race, or gender, should have the opportunity to learn and benefit from a free, or reasonably inexpensive, but very high-quality educational system. Coming from a poor family, the quality of education I received helped me succeed in my life and was paid back many times in the work I've done, in the taxes I've paid, and in the mentoring I've done for a number of students who, like me, came from poor backgrounds and needed someone to cheerlead and offer a guiding hand.

On the other hand, I think that people who practice their religious beliefs are often better off because of it (see InfoTable 1.3). I also think that capitalism is a great economic system, but that its more predatory impulses need to be regulated and that people who are not competitive in our economic system because of physical or mental health reasons need to have alternative avenues of work. When they can't work, I think it's only humane that we help them by offering economic security.

I worry about what John Edwards called the "Two Americas" during the 2004 presidential campaign: one America for the wealthy and privileged and the other America for the rest of us. This book will continually return to the concern about two Americas and the belief that government needs to be the advocate for the majority of us who, after all, desire and deserve the same quality of health care, education, safety, and healthy environments as our more affluent fellow Americans.

This isn't to say that I'm not critical of our social institutions. That is not the case. This is an introduction to social problems and the institutions that guide us to the solution of those problems. I'm afraid that we have a long way to go before we can feel very happy about our ability to resolve many social problems. Money is often the issue. Even though we spend more money on health care than any other nation, the health of many Americans is not nearly as good as it is in many other countries. Part of the reason is that more than half of all Americans live in or near communities with substandard air quality, which dramatically increases the rates of asthma, emphysema, and lung cancer, particularly in very young children. Another reason is that many Americans either lack health insurance completely or have limited coverage. While we spend vast amounts of money on public safety, I'd venture a guess that most of you would not feel safe in many parts of urban America during the evenings or even in many parts of some communities during daylight hours. While we discuss family violence and child abuse and develop public education approaches to inform our citizens about the impact of family violence, it remains a serious problem affecting all too many American homes. You can legislate social change and develop organizations to reduce social problems, but you can't necessarily change people's behavior.

What Is Social Work?

This is where social workers come in. Social work has a long and glorious history, much of which is outlined in Professor Dan Huff's website found in Chapter 2. Professor Huff describes the early history of social work and explains our roots in charitable organizations that flourished in the United States in the 19th and 20th centuries. Out of this impulse to help people in need, the profession of social work developed with its unique emphasis on directly helping people as well as their environments. Social work is the only helping profession that deals with the internal aspects of the human condition (values, beliefs, emotions, and problem-solving capacities of people) and the external aspects of the human condition (the neighborhoods, schools, working conditions, social welfare systems, and political systems that affect us). By working with the internal and external aspects of the human condition, social work is able to provide a uniquely encompassing service to people in need. And by networking with other professionals, social work is able to help our clients receive needed medical, financial, and educational services that improve their physical, financial, and emotional lives. Because social workers act as advocates by helping our clients access services they may be unable to by themselves, we empower our clients. Our goal is to help make people self-sufficient by only doing for people what they may be unable to do for themselves.

We work in the organizations that help people with social and emotional problems. I think we're pretty terrific people because we work at demanding jobs with great conviction and dedication; and although we're paid well, nobody gets rich being a social worker. Like most Americans, social workers represent a range of political and religious beliefs. We come from different social, ethnic, and economic backgrounds. We have differences of opinions about how best to help people, and we can be as stubborn as any group of professionals in our beliefs. However, our core values have developed over the years and are apparent in all the work we do to help clients. The complete social work code of ethics is found in the appendix. These core values have been developed over the years by social workers through their experience and practice and are now part of the code of ethics of our professional organization, the National Association of Social Workers (1996).

Core Social Work Values

The following broad ethical principles are based on social work's core values of service, social justice, dignity and worth of the person, importance of human relationships, integrity, and competence. These principles set forth ideals to which all social workers should aspire.

I. SERVICE

Ethical Principle: A social worker's primary goal is to help people in need and to address social problems.

Social workers elevate service to others above self-interest. Social workers draw on their knowledge, values, and skills to help people in need and to address social problems. Social workers are encouraged to volunteer some portion of their professional skills with no expectation of significant financial return (pro bono service).

II. SOCIAL JUSTICE

Ethical Principle: Social workers challenge social injustice.

Social workers pursue social change, particularly with and on behalf of vulnerable and oppressed individuals and groups of people. Social workers' social change efforts are focused primarily on issues of poverty, unemployment, discrimination, and other forms of social injustice. These activities seek to promote sensitivity to and knowledge about oppression and cultural and ethnic diversity. Social workers strive to ensure access to needed information, services, and resources; equality of opportunity; and meaningful participation in decision making for all people.

III. THE DIGNITY AND WORTH OF THE PERSON

Ethical Principle: Social workers respect the inherent dignity and worth of the person.

Social workers treat each person in a caring and respectful fashion, mindful of individual differences and cultural and ethnic diversity. Social workers promote clients' socially responsible self-determination. Social workers seek to enhance clients' capacity and opportunity to change and to address their own needs. Social workers are cognizant of their dual responsibility to clients and to the broader society. They seek to resolve conflicts between clients' interests and the broader society's interests in a socially responsible manner consistent with the values, ethical principles, and ethical standards of the profession.

IV. THE IMPORTANCE OF HUMAN RELATIONSHIPS

Ethical Principle: Social workers recognize the central importance of human relationships.

Social workers understand that relationships between and among people are an important vehicle for change. Social workers engage people as partners in the helping process. Social workers seek to strengthen relationships among people in a purposeful effort to promote, restore, maintain, and enhance the well-being of individuals, families, social groups, organizations, and communities.

V. INTEGRITY

Ethical Principle: Social workers behave in a trustworthy manner.

Social workers are continually aware of the profession's mission, values, ethical principles, and ethical standards and practice in a manner consistent with them. Social workers act honestly and responsibly and promote ethical practices on the part of the organizations with which they are affiliated.

VI. COMPETENCE

Ethical Principle: Social workers practice within their areas of competence and develop and enhance their professional expertise.

Social workers continually strive to increase their professional knowledge and skills and to apply them in practice. Social workers should aspire to contribute to the knowledge base of the profession.

What Social Workers Do

The U.S. Department of Labor (2004) defines the functions of social workers as follows:

Social work is a profession for those with a strong desire to help improve people's lives. Social workers help people function the best way they can in their environment, deal with their relationships, and solve personal and family problems. Social workers often see clients who face a life-threatening disease or a social problem. These problems may include inadequate housing, unemployment, serious illness, disability, or substance abuse. Social workers also assist families that have serious domestic conflicts, including those involving child or spousal abuse.

Social workers often provide social services in health-related settings that now are governed by managed care organizations. To contain costs, these organizations are emphasizing short-term intervention, ambulatory and community-based care, and greater decentralization of services.

Most social workers specialize. Although some conduct research or are involved in planning or policy development, most social workers prefer an area of practice in which they interact with clients. For example, child, family, and school social workers provide social services and assistance to improve the social and psychological functioning of children and their families and to maximize family well-being and academic functioning of children. Some social workers assist single parents, arrange adoptions, and help find foster homes for neglected, abandoned, or abused children. In schools, they address such problems as teenage pregnancy, misbehavior, and truancy. They also advise teachers on how to cope with problem students. Some social workers may specialize in services for older adults. They run support groups for family caregivers or for the adult children of aging parents. Some advise elderly people or family members about choices in areas such as housing, transportation, and long-term care; they also coordinate and monitor services. Through employee-assistance programs, they may help workers cope with job-related pressures or with personal problems that affect the quality of their work. Child, family, and school social workers typically work in individual and family services agencies, schools, or state or local governments. These social workers may be known as child welfare social workers, family services social workers, child protective services social workers, occupational social workers, or geriatric social workers.

Medical and public health social workers provide people, families, or vulnerable populations with the psychosocial support needed to cope with chronic, acute, or terminal illnesses such as Alzheimer's disease, cancer, or AIDS. They also advise family caregivers, counsel patients, and help plan for patients' needs after discharge by arranging for at-home services—from meals-on-wheels to oxygen equipment. Some work on interdisciplinary teams that evaluate certain kinds of patients (e.g., geriatric or organ transplant patients). Medical and public health social workers may work for hospitals, nursing and personal care facilities, individual and family services agencies, or local governments.

Mental health and substance abuse social workers assess and treat individuals with mental illness or substance abuse problems, including abuse of alcohol, tobacco, or other drugs. Such services include individual and group therapy, outreach, crisis intervention, social rehabilitation, and training in skills of everyday living. They may also help plan for supportive services to ease a patient's return to the community. Mental health and substance abuse social workers are likely to work in hospitals, substance abuse treatment centers, individual and family services agencies, or local governments. These social workers may be known as clinical social workers.

Other types of social workers include social work planners and policymakers, who develop programs to address such issues as child abuse, homelessness, substance abuse, poverty, and violence. These workers research and analyze policies, programs, and regulations. They identify social problems and suggest legislative and other solutions. They may help raise funds or write grants to support these programs.

The Following Chapters

In the following chapters, I will discuss a number of social problems facing America. Many social problems, such as youth violence, child abuse, domestic violence, poverty, and racism, are of such a serious nature that they affect the way all Americans live. Social work organizations and social workers are on the front line in dealing with serious social problems. To show you what we do, most chapters will contain an actual case study demonstrating what social workers do in practice. To help you develop a sense of what you would do if you were a social worker, many chapters have a section that offers a short case vignette and then asks what you would do if you were the social worker. The websites you will find at the end of each chapter contain information that will add to your knowledge base. Some websites are government reports, some are articles written by authors for journals, and some provide historical overviews of the development of social programs.

I've tried, where possible, to give you many sides of each issue; but when it comes right down to it, I believe in helping people, and the side I've chosen is the side that seems humane, positive, and morally right. I believe that helping people always has a large payoff for society. It's what defines us as a caring nation. We are caring people in America, and social workers are highly caring professionals.

If, after reading this book, you absolutely want to be a social worker, I'll be very happy for you and feel that I've written it for the best possible reasons. If you think that helping people is a wonderful thing but that you'd do better as a volunteer, I'll also be very happy. And even if I simply move your attitudes and opinions a bit, that's equally wonderful. That's what I hope you'll do with this book. Give it a chance, think about the issues, talk to your friends and classmates about the problems discussed, and have a very good year! Social work is a terrific field, and I hope you think about making it your life career.

InfoTable 1.4	Political Correctness

There is a sad need to conform to ideas in America today and political correctness sometimes determines what can and what cannot be studied. Issues of race, ethnicity, gender and social class that should be very important to social scientists are often felt to be too risky, too likely to offend someone. I hope that you don't fall into the trap of political correctness and that the star you choose to shoot for is a star that may not blink as brightly for others. Dissent is the mother's milk of a democracy, and dissent born of rational analysis and objectivity is the most sublime form of dissent. (Glicken, 2003, p. 261)

Questions to Determine Your Frame of Reference

Many people believe that America is a divided nation and that this sharp division can be defined by political ideologies. Perhaps half the people are conservative and believe that government should have a limited role in people's lives. Many conservatives also believe that government should permit more religious observance in public settings, including schools, and that prayer in school should be permissible just as gay marriages should not. The other half have a more liberal ideology and believe that there is a significant role for government in people's lives: the role of protecting and offering succor and relief when help is needed. They point to the failure of government to function well and its consequences in Hurricane Katrina as an example of what happens when government becomes weakened. You are about to embark on a voyage into the world of social problems and the helping profession of social work. Given your current beliefs, please answer the following questions about your current ideological preferences.

1. Do you believe that prayer in school should not only be permissible but that it has a positive impact on children? A corollary might be whether you find it objectionable to mention "God" in the Pledge of Allegiance or whether you believe it begins a child's day with a strong sense of moral grounding.

2. Do you believe that most poor people are responsible for their situation and that if they worked harder or had more motivation, they'd be fine? Or is it more likely that most poor people are poor because they lack good education, healthy homes, and a safe environment?

3.   Do you believe that those who have the most income should pay the most taxes, or does it reduce incentive to work hard to have much of your income go to pay for taxes?

4.   Do you believe that most helping functions should be done by family, religious organizations, and other private charitable organizations, or do you believe that when people need help, it's good to have government there to provide it?

5.   Good citizens, whether they are liberal or conservative, take their vote seriously and vote in elections. Will you vote in the next election if eligible and, if not, why not?

6.   Social workers believe that all people should be treated with dignity. We have imprisoned many terrorists, some of whom have done awful things. Do you believe that they should be treated with dignity?

7.   Conservatives believe that in a country with high crime, high drug rates, dangerous sexual practices that sometimes lead to rape and unwanted pregnancy and then an astonishing number of abortions, that what we need in America is a moral rebirth through more religious involvement. What do you think?

8.   Liberals believe that poverty is increasing and that people often live lives of quiet desperation because we've become such an uncaring society. What do you believe?

9.   As you face your future, what excites you most? The amount of money you will make and accumulate, or the value of the work you do for yourself and others?

10. What would you do, if you had the power, to recognize our differences and help us become less divided and contentious as a nation?

Summary

This chapter explains the content of the book and provides an introductory discussion of the importance of one's own political philosophy in viewing social problems and their solution. Future chapters will discuss social problems in more detail, and the role of social service and helping organizations will be discussed as well as the function of social work within those organizations.

A Brief History of Social Work 2

From the Poor Laws to the Conservative Revolution

Social work, social problems, and the organizations that were developed in an attempt to cope with those problems have had almost a parallel history. This chapter discusses the dual development of organizations and the profession of social work. Some of the following discussion is taken with appreciation from Reich and Tannenbaum (2001).

The English Poor Laws: Regulating the Poor

The origins of American social welfare are found in the English Poor Laws. Although the laws were passed over a 400-year period and changed incrementally to reflect new thinking about poverty and work, a brief discussion of the poor laws follows with thanks to Peter Higginbotham (2004) for his wonderful website on the English Poor Laws.

The poor laws evolved and changed between 1601 and the new Act of 1834, but unlike the old poor laws of 1601, the new Act of 1834 differentiated between the deserving and the undeserving poor by a simple test: "Anyone prepared to accept relief in the repellent workhouse must be lacking the moral determination to survive outside it" (Higginbotham, 2004). The other principle of the new act was that of "less eligibility" or "that conditions in the workhouse should never be better than those of an independent labourer of the lowest class" (Higginbotham, 2004). These same ideas about the treatment of the poor are still with us today, as the chapter on social work with clients in poverty will attest.

InfoTable 2.1	A Slightly Edited 1536 Draft of the Poor Laws Explaining Who Is Poor and Why They Need Help

For as much as the king has full and perfect notice that there is within his realm a great multitude of strong valiant beggars [comprised of]: (1) vagabonds and idle persons, who might labor for their living but unlike your other loyal servants, live idly by begging, to the high displeasure of Almighty God, the hurt of their own souls, the evil example of others, and to the great hurt of the commonwealth of this realm; as are (2) the old, sick, lame, feeble and impotent persons not able to labor for their living but are driven of necessity to the charity of the people. And his highness (3) has perfect knowledge that some of them have fallen into such poverty (4) through sickness and other casualties, and some through their own fault, (5) whereby they have come finally to that point that they could not labor for any part of their living but are driven by necessity to live by the charity of the people. And some have fallen to such misery because they have been released from work by their employers because of sickness, leaving them without relief and comfort. Some have been neglected by friends and family and have developed idleness and the belief that they can live well without working. Some have even been taught to beg from childhood. And so for lack of good oversight in youth, many live in great misery as they age. And some have come to such misery through sloth, pride, negligence, falsehood and such other ungraciousness, whereby their employers, lovers and friends have been driven to forsake them until no one would take them to any service; whereby they have in process of time lain in the open streets and fallen to utter desolation. But whatever the reason is, charity requires that some way be taken to help them and prevent that others shall not hereafter fall into like misery. Therefore, his highness and the Parliament assembled [are asked to] provide certain remedies for the poor and miserable people, in the following manner . . . written by William Marshall (1536).

Under the 1601 Act, each parish (equivalent to a small county) was ordered to help the elderly and the infirm, to bring up needy children with a work ethic, and to provide work for others without a trade or those who were unemployed. The main objectives of the 1601 Act were:

The establishment of the parish as the administrative unit responsible for poor relief, with churchwardens or parish overseers collecting poor-rates and allocating relief.

The provision of materials such as flax, hemp, and wool to provide work for the able-bodied poor.

The setting to work and apprenticeship of children.

The relief of the "impotent" poor—the old, the blind, the lame, and so on. This could include the provision of "houses of dwelling"—almshouses or poorhouses rather than workhouses.

Any able-bodied pauper who refused to work was liable to be placed in a "House of Correction" or prison. (Higginbotham, 2004)

Much like current efforts to put those on welfare back to work, the workhouses were meant to stimulate a work ethic and to provide food, clothing, shelter, and medical care, but the reality of the workhouses were altogether different, as this description indicates.

InfoTable 2.2	The Workhouses

Whatever the regime inside the workhouse, entering it would have been a distressing experience. New inmates would often have already been through a period of severe hardship. It was for good reason that the entrance to the Birmingham Union workhouse was through an arch locally known as the "Archway of Tears." . . . The inmates' toilet facilities were often a simple privy—a cess-pit with a simple cover having a hole in it on which to sit—shared perhaps by as many as 100 inmates. Dormitories were usually provided with chamber pots or, after 1860, earth closets—boxes containing dry soil which could afterwards be used as fertiliser. (Higginbotham, 2004)

Under the 1834 Act, illegitimate children were the responsibility of their mothers until they were 16 years old. If mothers were unable to support themselves and their children, they usually entered the workhouse whereas the father was free of responsibility for his illegitimate children, a notion that continues to this day in America and is felt to be responsible for the feminization of poverty, even among legitimate children and mothers who have child support decrees from the court that are all too often ignored by fathers. Fortunately, this 1834 law on illegitimate children was unpopular and was replaced with a subsequent Act in 1844 (7&8 Vic. c.101) allowing an unmarried mother to order the father to pay maintenance of the mother and child, whether or not she was receiving poor relief.

The poor laws changed as times and the horrific conditions in the workhouses led the public to increasingly believe that the workhouses were shameful and that the British people deserved a much kinder and more humane approach to helping all people in times of economic and health concerns. As a result, Britain became one of the leading countries to institute free health care and other highly thought of social services, and became an important model for many social programs during President Roosevelt's New Deal (1933–1945).

InfoTable 2.3	A Criticism of the Poor Laws Written in 1817

The clear and direct tendency of the poor laws, is . . . not, as the legislature benevolently intended, to amend the condition of the poor, but to deteriorate the condition of both poor and rich. . . . If by law every human being wanting support could be sure to obtain it, and obtain it in such a degree as to make life tolerably comfortable, theory would lead us to expect that all other taxes together would be light compared with the single one of poor rates. The principle of gravitation is not more certain than the tendency of such laws to change wealth and power into misery and weakness. (Ricardo, 1817, par. 35-40)

The American Experience

Even before the American Revolution, services to the poor, to children, and to the mentally ill had been established in North America, many using the poor laws established in England to define who should receive services and the content of those services. By the early 19th century, states had begun providing relief through towns and counties. Because their efforts were often inadequate, private benevolent societies and self-help organizations began to supplement their efforts. These benevolent societies were the predecessors of modern social service agencies.

InfoTable 2.4	Dorothea Dix and the Condition of American Mental Institutions in 1840

In March 1841, Dorothea Dix entered the East Cambridge Massachusetts Jail, where she witnessed such horrible images that her life, from that point on, was changed forever. Within the confines of this jail she observed that prostitutes, drunks, criminals, retarded individuals, and the mentally ill were all housed together in unheated, unfurnished, and foul-smelling quarters (Viney & Zorich, 1982). When asked why the jail was in these conditions, she was told that the insane do not feel heat or cold.

Dix proceeded to visit jails and almshouses where the mentally ill were housed. She made careful and extensive notes as she visited with jailers, caretakers, and townspeople. Finally, she compiled all these data and shaped a carefully worded document to be delivered to the Massachusetts legislature. After a heated debate over the topic, the material won legislative support and funds were set aside for the expansion of Worcester State Hospital (Bumb, 2005).

InfoTable 2.5	Are We Doing Better Now?

Not according to the U.S. Justice Department in its 2005 review of California institutions treating the mentally ill, where a recent report noted that therapists and employees have been accused of sexually assaulting patients, patients are murdered by other patients, and "between January and June 20, 2003, one patient assaulted 20 other patients. Staff were afraid of this patient and failed to intervene to protect other patients" (Lopez, 2005, p. A1). The report continues to describe inadequate toilet facilities, patients dying for unknown reasons, unsupervised patients committing suicide, and, on the testimony of a physician, staff at one hospital bringing drugs to the faculty in exchange for cash. One wonders how Dix would view the progress made in even the past 30 years since the publication of "On Being Sane in Insane Places" (Rosenhan, 1973), where researchers at a state hospital faked being mentally ill and observed the maltreatment and lack of professional conduct of the staff to such an extent and to such a public outcry that American hospitals for the mentally ill were largely emptied and people began changing their location of being warehoused from the hospital to the streets and inner cities of America.

Those who worked or volunteered in benevolent societies were often upper-class women and men, often known as "friendly visitors," who used moral persuasion and personal example as helping devices. While I was a student social worker in the MSW Program at the University of Washington in 1963, my field placement in the Seattle public schools still used the term *friendly visitor* to designate who we were and what we did. How little things change.

As social work became more interested in the conditions that created social problems, "Organizations such as the Association for the Improvement of the Condition of the Poor and the Children's Aid Society began investigating social conditions in areas such as tenement housing and child welfare" (Reich & Tannenbaum, 2001).

The Origins of Modern Social Work

In the half-century after the Civil War, economic depressions, racism, and drastic increases in immigration from Southern and Eastern Europe prompted an awareness of the need for social programs and helping organizations to assist millions of people who were experiencing economic and social displacement. The recognition of serious social problems following the Civil War led to what was then called "scientific charity," an attempt to use concepts common to business and industry to cope with larger social problems. Reich and Tannenbaum (2001) note that although many clients receiving help from the first of these scientific charities, such as the American Charity Organization organized in Buffalo, New York, in 1877, benefited, many preferred the more personal approaches offered through self-help groups and community mutual aid. This distinction between large-scale efforts to resolve social problems and a more individualized approach sets the stage for the earliest notions of the helping process in social work—one that combines a personalized service with an understanding that environments and social policies need to be improved if individuals are to truly be served.

The more highly personalized approach to helping is noted in the development of the settlement house movement, begun in 1886 with the Neighborhood Guild in New York City, and made famous by the best-known of the settlement houses, Jane Addams and Ellen Gates Starr's much-admired Hull House in Chicago. Settlements focused on the causes of poverty and expanding jobs for the poor. They also "conducted research, helped develop the juvenile court system, created widow's pension programs, promoted legislation prohibiting child labor, and introduced public health reforms and the concept of social insurance" (Reich & Tannenbaum, 2001). By 1910, the settlement house movement had more than 400 individual settlements, many serving newly immigrated groups, which led to the creation of national organizations such as

> the Women's Trade Union League, the National Consumers' League, the Urban League, and the National Association for the Advancement of Colored People (NAACP). Settlement leaders were instrumental in establishing the Federal Children's Bureau in 1912, headed by Julia Lathrop from Hull House. Settlement leaders also played key roles in the major social movements of the period, including women's suffrage, peace, labor, civil rights, and temperance. (Reich & Tannenbaum, 2001)

The settlement movement put much of its efforts into what we now call macrosystem change. Macrolevel change reflects change at a community, state, and even national level. We would now call the approaches used by the settlement movement group work and community organization. The Charitable Organization Societies (COS) began to focus on individual work, or what became known in the profession as casework with individuals, families, and groups. Casework developed areas of specialization including medical, psychiatric, and child casework and led to the development of a formal training program created by the New York COS in 1897 in partnership with Columbia University. By 1919, there were 17 schools of social work identifying themselves collectively as the Association of Training Schools of Professional Schools of Social Work, the precursor of today's Council on Social Work Education (CSWE).

During and after World War I, the Red Cross and the Army gave social workers an opportunity to work with populations who were not impoverished but were suffering from war-related problems, including what was then called "shell shock." This new population of clients led to social workers interacting directly with individuals and families. By 1927, social workers were practicing in more than 100 guidance clinics with primarily middle-class clients in teams composed of social workers, psychiatrists,

InfoTable 2.6	Hull House

The Hull House community believed that poverty and the lack of opportunity bred the problems of the ghetto. Ignorance, disease, and crime were the result of economic desperation and not some moral flaw in the character of the new immigrants. Addams promoted the idea that if afforded a decent education, adequate living conditions, and reliable income, any person could overcome the obstacles of the ghetto; furthermore, if allowed to develop his skills, that person could not only make a better life for himself but contribute to the community as a whole. Access to opportunity was the key to successful participation in a democratic, self-governing society. The greatest challenge and achievement of the settlement was to help people help themselves (Luft, 2005).

and psychologists. At the same time, social workers were also employed in Community Chests, the organization that led the way to the United Fund and its Health and Welfare Councils.

The Great Depression and the New Deal

In October 1929, the stock market crashed, wiping out 40% of the paper value of common stock. Four years later, a common stock, if it were still negotiable, was equal to one-fifth of its worth before the Great Crash. Although politicians continued to issue optimistic predictions about the nation's economy, the Depression deepened, confidence evaporated, and many lost their life savings. Businesses closed their doors, factories shut down, and banks failed. Farm income fell 50% and, by 1932, one out of every four Americans was unemployed.

In 1933, Franklin Roosevelt introduced the New Deal, a social and economic program of recovery using the government as an instrument of change, an approach familiar to many Europeans for more than a generation. The New Deal ended laissez-faire capitalism and introduced the regulation of business activities, banking reform, and the ability of labor to organize and apply collective bargaining in its pursuit of fair wages and working conditions through passage of the National Labor Relations Act of 1935.

By 1933, millions of Americans were out of work, and bread lines were a common sight in most cities. An early attempt to reduce unemployment came in the form of the Civilian Conservation Corps (CCC), a program to reduce unemployment in young men aged 18 to 25 years. Paid a dollar a day, 2 million young men took part in the CCC during the decade, participating in a number of conservation projects that affect us today: planting trees to combat soil erosion and maintain national forests; eliminating stream pollution; creating fish, game, and bird sanctuaries; and conserving coal, petroleum, shale, gas, sodium, and helium deposits.

The New Deal years were characterized by a belief that greater regulation would solve many of the country's problems. With new agricultural policies in place, farm income increased by more than 50% between 1932 and 1935. Only part of the reason for the increase can be explained by new federal programs, however. A severe drought hit the Great Plains states, significantly reducing farm production. Violent dust storms hit the southern area of the Great Plains from 1935 to 1938 in what became known as the "Dust Bowl." Crops were destroyed, cars and machinery were ruined, and people and animals were harmed. Approximately 800,000 people left Arkansas, Texas, Missouri, and Oklahoma during the 1930s and 1940s. Most headed farther west to the land of milk and honey, California.

InfoTable 2.7	Problems Remain for the Social Security of Americans

We cannot be satisfied with the social security protection now provided to Americans. Retirement benefits in our old-age and survivors insurance system supply only one-third as much income, or less, to the workers no longer able to work than is enjoyed by older people still in employment. Although the benefits under state laws to unemployed and injured workers are greater, our unemployment insurance and workmen's compensation laws also are very much in need of liberalization and improvement. None of our social insurance programs is as broad in coverage as it should be. Great risks, like early disability and prolonged sickness, lack all governmental protection; and the voluntary forms of insurance we have, although most valuable, do not protect many of those who most need protection. The great objective of social security—assurance of a minimum necessary income to all people in all personal contingencies of life—has not been attained even in this great country in which the common man fares better than in any other (Witte, 1955).

The Works Progress Administration (WPA) provided work rather than welfare to the nation's unemployed. Under the WPA, buildings, roads, libraries, airports, courthouses, city halls, and schools were constructed. Actors, painters, musicians, and writers were employed through the Federal Theater Project, the Federal Art Project, and the Federal Writers Project. The National Youth Administration provided part-time employment to students and unemployed youth. By the time it was abandoned in 1943, the WPA had helped 9 million people.

Prior to the Great Depression, the social welfare system was a combination of local public relief agencies with some modest help from charitable organizations. Because the public now saw poverty as the result of economic problems rather than personal shortcomings, the Depression defined government's role in helping people whose economic situation was troubled. This change in the role of government prompted numerous government programs under the Roosevelt Administration, which ultimately led to our present social welfare system. Social workers such as Harry Hopkins and Frances Perkins, who were part of the Roosevelt Administration, enhanced the status of the social work profession.

The most significant program, and the centerpiece of dozens of social welfare programs that comprised the Roosevelt Administration's New Deal, was the Social Security Act of 1935. It gave recipients a social welfare net that provided retirement income and protection against catastrophic economic problems. As a result of the New Deal, social welfare went beyond relief to the poor to include housing, electricity, roads and dams for rural problem areas, health programs, child welfare programs, and many forms of social insurance for all Americans. This system of social programs comprise what is often referred to as the social welfare net, a series of programs that protect all Americans in times of serious social and economic upheavals. These programs led to a significant expansion of the profession and an increased role for social work in the many programs created by government. The number of social workers doubled from 40,000 to 80,000 within a decade and led to improved salaries and the need for increased educational requirements.

World War II and the Rise of Social Work Education

During World War II, many social workers were involved in war-related assignments, including work with war-impacted communities. As social work began to become a profession with a coherent and logical set of professional practices and objectives, there was a movement to standardize agency practices and create core MSW curricula. This movement to improve standards and increase the educational component of social work practice led to the formation of the CSWE in 1952 and the establishment of the National Association of Social Workers (NASW) in 1955.

Other changes during this period were the development of the Department of Health, Education, and Welfare (HEW) in 1953 and a shift from programs for the poor to programs serving middle-income white workers in the 1950s. This shift in who was served by social welfare programs caused the United States to lag behind other Western industrialized nations in the degree of social provision. "In a hostile political environment, social activism declined and openly anti-welfare attitudes reemerged" (Reich & Tannenbaum, 2001).

The "War on Poverty" and the "Great Society"

However, by the early 1960s, Americans rediscovered poverty as a social problem and the troubling fact that more than 40 million people, one-third of them children, lived lives that had been bypassed by modern economic and social progress. The shift in attention to the poor led to new types of social service organizations, such as Mobilization for Youth in New York, and resulted in President Johnson's proclamation of an "unconditional war on poverty" in January 1964.

The "War on Poverty" used the Economic Opportunity Act (EOA), which included the Job Corps, Upward Bound, the Neighborhood Youth Corps, Community Action, Head Start, Legal Services, Foster Grandparents, and the Office of Economic Opportunity (OEO). In 1965, the health programs Medicare and Medicaid were passed by Congress, the Department of Housing and Urban Development (HUD) was created, numerous services for the aged through the Older Americans Act were enacted, and the Food Stamp Program was created under the auspices of the Department of Agriculture. To equalize funding to less affluent schools, the Elementary and Secondary School Education Act directed federal aid to local schools. In 1966, the Model Cities Act provided comprehensive services to certain urban areas and stressed the idea of community control. Social workers played major roles in many antipoverty and community-action programs and helped train volunteers in newly formed organizations such as the Peace Corps and VISTA.

The 1970s

In 1972 and 1973, Congress passed the State and Local Fiscal Assistance Act and the Comprehensive Employment and Training Act (CETA), which established the concept of revenue sharing and direct aid to local communities for many social welfare programs. It also led to the dismantling of the Office of Economic Opportunity (OEO), which had by then become unpopular with many people for providing the poor with maximum feasible participation in many Great Society social welfare programs. Moynihan (1969), for example, portrayed the involvement of the poor in the governance of social programs as a chaotic adventure in radical democracy and called it a Maximum Feasible Misunderstanding, arguing that what sounded good in language had led to a form of radical activism in the late 1960s and early 1970s that resulted in social protests and the disruption of agencies providing services under OEO programs.

One of the more novel attempts to change the nature of poverty by developing a guaranteed annual income was introduced by Piven and Cloward (1971) in their attempt to destroy the public welfare system by encouraging everyone who qualified to apply. Only 25% of those in poverty were applying to an already overcrowded and badly functioning system in New York City. And although the increases in applications were modest, Pivan and Cloward were nearly able to make the welfare system stop functioning. The dream of a guaranteed annual income became reality and the public welfare system, perhaps a little wiser because of the experience, was felt to be more efficient and less discriminatory as a result of their efforts.

A significant social policy accomplishment of the Nixon Administration was the Social Security Amendments of 1972, which standardized aid to disabled people and low-income elderly and provided cost-of-living increases to offset the loss of income caused by inflation. Food stamps, child nutrition, and railroad retirement programs were also tied to cost-of-living increases. Title XX of the Social Security Act in January 1975 reinforced the idea of federal "revenue sharing," providing states with the flexibility to provide social services. Under Presidents Ford and Carter, Title XX focused attention on welfare dependency, child abuse and neglect, domestic violence, drug abuse, and community mental health.

Most social reforms stagnated by the mid-1970s because of a belief that many of the social programs of the Great Society had created social unrest in America. Despite a growing conservative and antigovernment attitude, there were significant changes in the social work profession. These changes included multicultural and gender awareness, which prompted new course content and minority recruitment; multidisciplinary joint degree programs with Schools of Urban Planning, Public Health, Public Policy, Education, and Law; the BSW as the entry-level professional degree; and the growth of private practice among social workers.

The Conservative Reaction: 1975 to the Present

Because of the increasing unpopularity of government intervention in the lives of people, even to help those who needed help, and an emphasis on cutting taxes, the Reagan years were a time when social welfare was placed on the back burner. Entire social welfare programs were reduced, frozen, or eliminated. "Consequently, during times of overall prosperity poverty rates soared, particularly among children, young families, and persons of color. By the early 1990s, the number of people officially listed as 'poor' had risen to 36 million" (Reich & Tannenbaum, 2001). This cutback in social welfare funding came at a time when America was experiencing serious problems with crack cocaine, the start of the AIDS epidemic, homelessness, domestic violence, and a crime epidemic from 1983 to 1994 among juveniles that would produce the highest crime rates experienced in America. Lack of attention to the changing needs of Americans and the desire to cut taxes and social programs had serious consequences that remain with us today.

The Clinton Years

Because of the antiwelfare sentiment that had become prominent in the 1980s under Presidents Reagan and Bush, emphasis under President Clinton was on limiting welfare to reduce what people were now calling welfare dependence, or the option to live off welfare benefits rather than work. The idea of welfare creating laziness is still prominent in American social welfare thinking, as is the notion that large bureaucracies serving the poor do a very ineffective job. These two ideas led to a welfare reform bill in 1996 that replaced Aid to Families with Dependent Children (AFDC) with block grants to states that included time limits and conditions on the receipt of cash assistance (now called

Temporary Assistance for Needy Families [TANF]). The legislation also increased the roles of private-sector and faith-based organizations in program implementation.

Under President Clinton, increasing numbers of social workers were affected by the decision to contract with agencies providing managed care to social work clients. The managed care movement came at a time when Americans believed that the private sector could do a better job of providing services than the government, and although the book is not closed on whether this concept has led to better social services and more effective social work practice, the unpopularity of managed health care is an indication that managed care may have run its course and that new ways of providing services may be evolving that place creative solutions in the hands of localities and states.

Remaining Social Problems

Problems that remain unattended are a national health care plan for all Americans, the increasing number of people without physical or mental health care coverage, increases in the number of people living in poverty, a rising juvenile crime rate, housing that is unaffordable for many working middle class and poor people, a serious backlash against illegal immigration, laws to protect us against terrorism that often limit our social liberties, and a potential shortfall in Social Security and Medicare funding. Although these challenges remain, social work continues to follow the lead set by the NASW *Code of Ethics* that we continue to meet basic human needs of all people and that special attention be given to empowering the vulnerable, the poor, and the oppressed.

Some Important Dates in Social Work and Social Welfare

The following dates are important ones in the history of social work and social welfare.

1536	The first draft of the English poor laws and what subsequently became the model for dealing with poverty, illness, and unemployment in England and later in America through the 19th century.

1841	Dorthea Dix begins her campaign for adequate services to the mentally ill after viewing horrible conditions in a hospital for the mentally ill in Cambridge, MA.
1877	American Charity Organization, organized in Buffalo, New York, in 1877 as one of the first attempts to help people with severe social problems in an organized and logical way.
1889	Jane Addams's and Ellen Gates Starr's much admired Hull House in Chicago. Settlements focused on the causes of poverty and expanding jobs for the poor. They also "conducted research, helped develop the juvenile court system, created widow's pension programs, promoted legislation prohibiting child labor, and introduced public health reforms and the concept of social insurance." Unions begin to grow in America representing the rights of workers for fair wages and better working conditions.
1898	Columbia University becomes the first school of social work in the Country.
1912	More than 400 guilds and settlement houses exist serving the poor and helping millions of new immigrants settle successfully in America. Fires in sweat shops in New York create a strong demand for safe working conditions and unions begin to flourish.
1914–1918	The First World War and the beginning use of social work with combat fatigue (PTSD) and war injuries.
1917	Mary Richmond wrote one of the defining books of social work, "Social Diagnosis" in which she lays the foundation for social work as a profession with a mission and a theoretical belief system.
1920	The American Civil Liberties Union (ACLU) is formed; The Child Welfare League of America is formed; Women exercise the right to vote; an early form of the Council on Social Work Education is formed calling itself, The Association of Training Schools of Professional Social Work. The beginning of the stock market rise and speculation which leads to conditions that cause the Great Depression.
1929	Overspeculation and manipulation of the stock market throws the country into the Great Depression which lasts almost to the start of World War II in 1941. Millions are unemployed and many businesses fail. The Dust Bowl, covering the Midwest, adds to problems and many people leave failing farms.
1933	The New Deal, a liberal set of social welfare programs is begun by newly elected president FDR and his liberal cabinet including social worker Frances Perkins who became Secretary of Labor.
1933–1941	A series of social programs that helped provide employment for unemployed men and women and which began the notion of the Safety Net including the Social Security Act which allows older adults to receive a pension after the age of 65.

(Continued)

(Continued)

1941–1945	America's involvement in WW II and the use of social workers to help soldiers and their families cope with war injuries and medical problems. Full use of social workers in the Veterans Administration, an organization begun with only a few social workers in 1926.
1952	The Council on Social Work Education is formed and begins its work to create high standards among existing and new schools of social work.
1956	The National Association of Social Work is formed, the profession's primary organization, with a mission to help and to create a better society and world.
1964	Civil Rights Act is passed; Title II and Title VII forbid racial discrimination in "public accommodations" and race and sex discrimination in employment. EEOC provides oversight and coordination of all federal regulation practices and policies affecting equal employment opportunity.
1965	The War on Poverty in which President Johnson pledges to overcome poverty; helps to pass the Voting Rights Act which makes discrimination in voting a federal crime; passes affirmative action which helps discriminated-against groups gain entry into schools, employment, housing and other areas of discrimination common in American life; passes the Older Americans Act which provides needed services to older adults and; creates the Administration for Children and Families to focus on the needs of children and to bolster the strength of families.
1966	The National Organization for Women (NOW) is founded.
1966–1972	A series of civil protests begin across American cities in which many lives are taken with the Watts Riots being the most widely known. These civil protests focused on frustration of minority communities with the conduct of the police and the lack of services and job opportunities available to people in the inner cities. Out of the riots began to develop a conservative approach to social welfare which some people called the "benign neglect of the poor."
1966–1972	A series of campus protests against the escalating war in Vietnam and the dem more power by students to shape curriculum and to include minorities in higher education. This may have led to the election of Richard Nixon as President and a further drawing back of liberal social welfare programs.
1972–1975	The break–in at Watergate and the turmoil in the presidency as Nixon is forced out of office.
1975–1992	Generally a conservative time when welfare programs were cut back and a conservative agenda moved the country away from concerns about civil rights and poverty. Significant rise in juvenile crime from 1982–1993. A period in social work where concerns are raised that social work is irrelevant and even unloved because we'd moved away from social action and social change and became too comfortable with small system change rather than large changes in the society.

1992–2000	Bill Clinton is elected president, but after an attempt to change our health care system, gives up and generally uses a conservative approach to social welfare programs; limits public assistance to 2 years and encourages retraining. Is thought to have "out–Republicaned" the Republicans.
1999	NASW adopts the current Code of Ethics.
2000	The election of George Bush and the beginning of a period of downgrading the social welfare net, a decrease in health care coverage and a war in Iraq with thousands of deaths and injuries. Social work helps with care of men and their families.
2005	A series of natural disasters tests the country's ability to cope with crisis and finds us badly unprepared. Decades of making poverty invisible show us that it is still pervasive as thousands of residents of New Orleans await help as a horrified nation watches after dikes break leaving the city under water.

Summary

This chapter discusses the history of social work and the social problems dealt with from the English Poor Laws to the current conservative view of social welfare. Many of the earliest attitudes about and the social problems that result from poverty are still with us today in our social policies and in the existence of what John Edwards called the two Americas: one for the wealthiest among us and the other for the rest of us.

Internet Sources

Peter Higginbotham's discussion of the English Poor Laws contains links to many interesting facets of the Poor Laws. Professor Dan Huff's social work history station has links to speeches, significant laws and people, and the train ride through social work history.

1. Higginbotham, P. (2004). *Poor Laws*. Retrieved August 6, 2005, from //users.ox.ac.uk/~peter/workhouse/poorlaws/poorlaws.html

2. Huff, D. (2005). *The social work history station*. Retrieved from http://www.idbsu.edu/socwork/dhuff/history/central/core.htm

The Social Work Process 3

S ocial workers traditionally use a series of steps or processes to help clients resolve their problems. These steps include collecting information about the client (assessment), making sense out of the information (diagnosis), collaborating with the client to develop a plan to change the problems being experienced (the treatment plan), and determining whether the process has been helpful (evaluation). We use two very powerful approaches to help the client change: (a) the helping relationship we develop with the client and (b) using one of the five or more helping approaches described in the prior chapter. This chapter discusses the social work process and the importance of developing a positive and cooperative helping relationship with clients.

Collecting Information About the Client: Assessment

Whereas medicine uses labels to describe conditions, social workers try not to use labels because they may fail to accurately describe the client's unique qualities or the historical reasons clients currently are having problems in their lives. Instead, we use a psychosocial assessment that summarizes the relevant information we know about a client into concise statements that allow other professionals to understand the client and the client's problem(s) at the same level that we understand them. Psychosocial assessments try not to use psychiatric labels or words that might create a biased perception of the client. They differ from the terms often used in the most commonly used diagnostic manual in mental health (the *Diagnostic and Statistical Manual of Mental Disorders* [*DSM-IV*]) because they provide brief historical information about the possible cause for the problem. Although they are problem-focused, they also provide an evaluation of the best evidence from the literature to support the assessment. The client's strengths are included in the assessment, as well as the problems that might interfere with the client's treatment. Van Wormer (1999) describes the need to include the positive behaviors of the client when doing an assessment:

> The first step in promoting the client's well-being is through assessing the client's strengths. A belief in human potential is tied to the notion that people have untapped resources—physically, emotionally, socially, and spiritually—that they can mobilize in times of need. This is where professional helping comes into play—in tapping into the possibilities, into what can be, not what is. (p. 51)

An Outline of a Psychosocial Assessment

SECTION I: BRIEF DESCRIPTION OF THE CLIENT AND THE PROBLEM

In this section of a psychosocial assessment, we include concrete information about the client such as age, marital status, family composition, what he or she is wearing, level of verbal and nonverbal communication, emotional affect, and anything of interest that may have happened in the interview. We should also include the defined problem(s) as stated by the client. We normally don't make interpretations here but just report the relevant information. Important information might be that the client cried throughout the interview, or he or she just stared off into space and answered questions in a flat monotone. We aren't certain exactly what this behavior means, but it tells us that the client isn't doing very well for reasons we have yet to discover.

SECTION II: HISTORICAL ISSUES

This section includes any past issues of importance in understanding the client's current problems. For example, if a client complains of memory loss, we might want to find out if he's been in an accident that caused minimal organic brain damage, if he has an illness that might be causing the symptoms, if he's using legal or illegal medications that might cause memory loss, or if he's had a traumatic emotional experience that has led to repressed memory loss. Many people who have experienced violence in their lives do not remember the violent situation and may have repressed (forgotten) it so that they don't reexperience the event and then feel anxious or depressed.

SECTION III: DIAGNOSTIC STATEMENT

The diagnostic statement is a brief overview of what we consider the most relevant problems experienced by the client and their potential causation. In the diagnostic statement, we combine material from the prior two sections and summarize the most relevant information into a brief statement.

A diagnosis often suggests a label defining what the client's problem is. However, words such as *schizophrenic* (mental illness) and *bipolar disorder* (manic-depressive behavior) have powerful negative meaning in our society, and it's important that we not think of a diagnosis as a negative label. Although labeling for diagnostic purposes may be relevant in medicine, diagnostic labels for mental health purposes are sometimes poorly defined and biased. Labels often harm people, and the most vulnerable among us—the poor, minority groups, women, immigrants, and the physically, emotionally, and socially disadvantaged—are those most harmed by labels. This may be particularly true of minority clients, where harm frequently occurs when labeling is used. Franklin (1992) says that African American men want to see themselves as "partners in treatment" and resent labels that suggest pathology because labels send signals to black clients who have had to deal with labels that subtly or overtly suggest racism. Franklin also states that African American men want to be recognized for their many strengths, and that clinicians should take into consideration that they may be doing well in many aspects of their lives. According to Franklin, African American men are particularly sensitive to male bashing and other sexist notions that berate men or negatively stereotype men in general and black men in particular. I think this is true of everyone. No one wants to be defined by a label that fails to include unique human qualities that make one person very different from another.

SECTION IV: THE TREATMENT PLAN

The treatment plan describes the goals of treatment during a specific period of time and comes from the agreement made between the worker and client in the contractual phase of treatment (see below). As an example of a treatment plan, let's assume that a client comes to see a social worker because he or she is experiencing marital problems and is feeling depressed. The treatment plan answers the following questions: How long might it take to resolve the problems in the marriage? How will we know if the problems are resolved? and Which approach will we use to help the client (see chapter 4)? It also implies a cooperative relationship between the social worker and the client and assumes that they will work together to achieve the same goals in ways that involve the client fully and focus on the client's strengths.

SECTION V: CONTRACT

This is the agreement between the worker and the client. It determines the problems to be worked on in treatment, the number of sessions agreed to, and other relevant rules related to being on time, payment, and the cancellation policies. Many workers have these rules in written form, with the client and the worker signing the contract.

You Be the Social Worker

This case was first presented in a book I wrote on evidence-based practice (Glicken, 2005, pp. 77–79) and is modified for this book. After reading the following material, try to conclude what exactly is wrong with the client. Some questions are posed after the case to help you decide what problem(s) the client is experiencing.

The Case

Jorge Rivera is 19-year-old Mexican National who came to the United States under the sponsorship of his maternal uncle to attend a California university. Jorge had been in the country a year and was doing well until signs of emotional change became apparent to his family. He was becoming increasingly aloof and secretive, had stopped attending school, and seemed to be a very different person from the happy, motivated young man he had been just a year earlier. Suspecting an emotional or physical problem, Jorge's uncle took him to see his family doctor, an American of Hispanic descent. The doctor was immediately struck by Jorge's aloofness, fearfulness, and social isolation. He did multiple tests and, unable to find anything physically wrong, urged the uncle to take Jorge to a Hispanic male social worker with whom the doctor had had prior positive experiences.

Because Spanish is Jorge's more proficient language and the one with which he can express his inner feelings with more accuracy, the first interview was conducted in this language. Jorge told the therapist that he was hearing voices at night when he tried to sleep and that the voices were telling him to do things that Jorge found repulsive and dangerous. These voices were new to Jorge, and he feared that he was going insane. Jorge began to talk about his fears that he was becoming psychotic and how this would place him in great jeopardy with his family. He said that being "muy loco" was what happened to people who were sinful, and that he would be punished by his family and friends with ostracism.

It was clear to the therapist that Jorge was in great distress, but pending additional information, the therapist deferred making a diagnosis. By using the major diagnostic tool of the helping professions, the *DSM-IV*, the therapist saw signs of schizophrenia. He decided to interview the uncle's family to determine the point of onset of Jorge's symptoms. Everyone confirmed that Jorge had been very outgoing, showing none of the signs of the mental illness he was now exhibiting. The onset was sudden, within the prior 3 months, and the symptoms had been rapid and worsening.

Below is a list of warning signs suggesting the onset of schizophrenia that was developed by families who have a relative with this disorder (World Fellowship for Schizophrenia and Allied Disorders, 2002, p. 1). Although some of the behavior would be considered normal, family members felt that there was a subtle yet obvious awareness that the behavior they were witnessing was unusual. Everyone noted social withdrawal as an important early sign that something was wrong. Most respondents believed that their relative had been a "good person, never causing any trouble"; however, seldom had the person been socially "outgoing" during his or her formative years. The warning signs of schizophrenia identified by family members were:

- excessive fatigue and sleepiness or an inability to sleep
- social withdrawal, isolation, and reclusiveness
- deterioration of social relationships
- inability to concentrate or cope with minor problems
- apparent indifference, even in highly important situations
- dropping out of activities (e.g., skipping classes)
- decline in academic and athletic performance
- deterioration of personal hygiene; eccentric dress
- frequent moves or trips, or long walks leading nowhere
- drug or alcohol abuse
- undue preoccupation with spiritual or religious matters
- bizarre behavior
- inappropriate laughter
- strange posturing
- low tolerance to irritation
- excessive writing without apparent meaning
- inability to express emotion
- irrational statements
- peculiar use of words or language structure
- conversation that seems deep but is not logical or coherent
- staring; vagueness
- unusual sensitivity to stimuli (e.g., noise, light)
- forgetfulness

As a way of comparing the subjective reports of family members of clients with a diagnosis of schizophrenia, the National Institute for Mental Health (NIMH) identifies the following diagnostic signs for early-onset schizophrenia:

The first signs of schizophrenia often appear as confusing, or even shocking, changes in behavior. The sudden onset of severe psychotic symptoms is referred to as an "acute" phase of schizophrenia. "Psychosis," a common condition in schizophrenia, is a state of mental impairment marked by hallucinations, which are disturbances of

(Continued)

(Continued)

sensory perception, and/or delusions, which are false yet strongly held personal beliefs that result from an inability to separate real from unreal experiences. Less obvious symptoms, such as social isolation or withdrawal, or unusual speech, thinking, or behavior, may precede, be seen along with, or follow the psychotic symptoms. (1999, p. 1)

In the next interview, the social worker asked Jorge to tell him about his life in Mexico and to provide the therapist with the client's theory about what was happening. Jorge had been romantically involved with a young woman who came from a highly affluent and influential family in Mexico. The couple were in love, but the young woman's parents were opposed to the marriage and had hired a *bruja* (literally, a witch) to cast a spell on Jorge so that he would become unattractive to the young woman and she would lose her feelings for him. The *bruja* was sending Jorge little totems that represented evil, which were frightening him and driving him into social isolation and withdrawal. He was convinced that the voices he heard were her doing and, as a result of the spells she had cast, that he would become insane, lose his beloved, and die a horrible death. He had known others who'd had similar fates in Mexico. *Brujas* were evil and caused immense harm, he told the therapist.

The therapist had grown up with stories of witches and spells, but wasn't a believer. Nonetheless, he contacted the uncle, told him what had happened, and wondered if he knew of some way to deal with the effects of the bruja. The uncle contacted a well-known *curandero* (remover of spells) he knew of in Mexico, paid his way to come to the United States, and had the *curandero* remove the spell in a ritual that lasted 24 hours. When the ritual was over, the *curandero* gave Jorge an amulet to wear around his neck to ward off future evil spells and urged him to break off the relationship with the young woman to cease the bruja's attacks on Jorge's mental health. The uncle again intervened, spoke to the young woman's family in Mexico, promised that Jorge would no longer be in contact with the young woman, and urged them to cease any more witchcraft on Jorge. Her family agreed, and a broken-hearted but functioning Jorge was able to return to school with his family's support and an occasional visit to the therapist.

Questions

1. Witches and counterwitches are pretty hard to believe. Couldn't Jorge have had a brief bout of mental illness brought on by the stress of school, loneliness, and his new life in the United States?

2. On the other hand, isn't it possible that Jorge was actually responding to his fear of witchcraft and that the fear (and nothing actually done by the bruja) was responsible for his psychotic-like condition?

3. The sudden onset on schizophrenia is a frightening thing for most clients and their families. Is it possible that, much like a disease or illness that comes and

goes, that schizophrenia is an opportunistic disease that often runs its course and, much like a severe virus, goes away in time?

4. You can see that a diagnosis of schizophrenia suggests a serious problem. What do you imagine most people believe are the chances of getting well again if someone is diagnosed with a mental illness?

5. Wouldn't most Anglo therapists assume that the story about witchcraft was just another indication of Jorge's mental illness? How can we protect against a misdiagnosis happening to people from other cultures?

Helping Relationships

Most social workers believe that the quality of the client-worker relationship is the key to whether clients will resolve their problems. In recognizing the importance of the helping relationship, Warren (2001) writes, "The relationship between the quality of the patient-therapist relationship and the outcome of treatment has been one of the most consistently cited findings in the empirical search for the basis of psychotherapeutic efficacy" (p. 357). Writing about the power of the therapeutic relationship, Saleebey (2000) says that "if healers are seen as non-judgmental, trustworthy, caring and expert, they have some influential tools at hand, whether they are addressing depression or the disappointments and pains of unemployment" (p. 131).

DEFINING THE CLIENT-WORKER RELATIONSHIP

Keith-Lucas (1972) defines the client-worker relationship as "the medium which is offered to people in trouble and through which they are given an opportunity to make choices, both about taking help and the use they will make of it" (p. 47). Keith-Lucas says that the key elements of the helping relationship are "mutuality, reality, feeling, knowledge, concern for the other person, purpose, the fact that it takes place in the here and now, its ability to offer something new, and its nonjudgmental nature" (p. 48).

In describing the significant elements of the relationship, Bisman (1994) says that therapeutic relationships are a form of "belief bonding" between the worker and the client, and that both parties need to believe that "the worker has something applicable for the client, the worker is competent, and that the client is worthwhile and has the capacities to change" (p. 77). Hamilton (1940) suggests that bonding takes place when the clinician and client work together and that "treatment starts only when mutual confidence is established, only when the client accepts your interest in him and conversely feels an interest in you" (pp. 189–190). I use the following definition for the relationship:

> It is a bond between two strangers and is formed by an essential trust in the helping process and a belief that it will lead to positive change. The worker facilitates communications, enters into a dialogue with the client about its meaning, and works with the client to decide the best way to change a life problem. (Glicken, 2004a, p. 50)

RESPONDING TO CLIENTS WITH WARMTH, GENUINENESS, AND EMPATHY

Many social workers believe that client-worker relationships are strongest when workers respond to the client with warmth, genuineness, and empathy. This means that the social worker is a real human being and not acting out a role. It also means that the worker is genuinely concerned about the client and can often sense, at a very significant level, how the client feels emotionally. As workers respond empathically to what clients say, clients are often able to continue discussing their problems at an increasingly introspective and accurate level without any prompting or questions from the worker.

You can determine your own level of empathy by using this simple 5-point scale and statements a client might say. First, I'll provide an example of how the scale works.

Empathy Scale

1.0: A response that actually makes the client feel much worse. Think of a response that blames the client for the problem or begins, "You always make the same mistakes and then complain that it's someone else's fault."

2.0: A response that is generally negative or critical. An example might be, "I know you were trying your best, but sometimes that's just not enough."

3.0: A neutral response. The client neither feels better nor worse (think of a response where the worker just restates what the client said but doesn't add to it).

4.0: A response that tells the client you understand and are sensitive to what the client is feeling (this response will bring about the client's desire to tell you more).

5.0: A response that so accurately captures what the client feels that it puts it into perfect words (this response will bring about a sort of epiphany in the client).

Example 1:

The client says, "Sometimes I really feel depressed."
The worker responds, "If you worked harder at your problems, you wouldn't feel that way."

Empathy Score: 1.5. The worker has said something hurtful and is blaming the client. This reduces trust and will stop the client from telling the worker anything significant.

Example 2:

The client says, "Sometimes I really feel depressed."
The worker responds, "It sounds like you feel really depressed sometimes."

Empathy Score: 3.0. The statement was neutral; it neither helped nor hurt the client's ability to progress with what he or she is feeling.

Example 3:

The client says, "Sometimes I really feel depressed."
The worker responds, "It must be painful for you on those days when you feel depressed."

Empathy Score: 4.0. The worker has said something that captures what the client feels inside.
The client might then say, "I feel so down on those days, I don't think I can make it."
The worker's brief statement has provided us with important information without a question being asked. We now know more about the depth of the depression.
The worker might then add, "And on those days when you don't feel you can make it, it must be a real struggle for you."
To which the client might say, "I think about how maybe it would be better if I just stopped living."
The worker could then say, "It must be painful to feel so depressed that you don't know you can go on, and yet something very positive and hopeful inside of you prevents that from happening."
And the client might respond by saying, "Yes, I just don't want to do that to my family. I think it would destroy them."

Discussion. In the above example, the worker has been able to find out a great deal about the client just by focusing on the client's feelings and responding empathically. The worker hasn't asked a single question, but has been empathic in responses by focusing entirely on the client's feelings. By doing so, the worker is able to determine that the client is not only depressed but that he or she is also experiencing serious thoughts of suicide, and that the only thing that stops him or her is an unwillingness to embarrass the family. Suicidal thoughts are serious and suggest an at-risk client. We might never have found this information out if we had just asked a number of direct questions.

Time to try it! Provided are five statements a client might give; write a worker response, then score yourself on the 1–5 scale. You must get a 3.0 or higher to allow the client to give you more information about his or her feelings and thoughts.

The client says:

1. "I hate my husband so much I just feel like packing up my bags, taking the kids, and leaving."

2. "School is so boring. I think I'll quit and get a job somewhere and make some money."

3. "Nobody likes me here. I'd be better off staying at home and reading a book."

4. "I can't concentrate on anything. My head just feels all over the place."

5. "I'm sick all the time and depressed. Why is God doing this to me?"

Evaluation of a Social Worker's Effectiveness

Determining if a social work client has improved isn't as easy as it might sound. In medicine, we think that if the patient feels better or if his or her blood work has improved that whatever is ailing him or her might have gone away. Of course, this often isn't true, and the same problem might just be hiding only to return and be even worse than it was originally. And though we think treatment may be the reason the patient recovers, we can't always be certain. Many times people heal on their own without medication or even seeing a doctor. In social work, it's even more complicated. How can we possibly prove that it was *our* treatment that led to a client getting better? There are many reasons people improve emotionally, and most are out of our control. A client might have met someone and fallen in love or inherited a great deal of money while seeing us for his or her depression. Was it the money/love or was it us that helped the client? Who can possibly tell? So to help us decide, researchers have devised the following guidelines to show whether it's our work that causes this change.

History. How long did the problems last before the client came for help? The longer a social or emotional condition lasted before the client came to see us for social work help, the less likely it is that the client recovered by chance. It's possible, of course, but less likely.

Baseline. When we saw them for the first time, we did a baseline reading of their problems. We found out how much they sleep, how much they weigh, their level of exercise, how much work or school they miss, and how often and how much they drink or take drugs. This is called a *baseline measure,* and it's similar to what doctors do when they see patients in their office. They check vital signs such as blood pressure and weight. If those vital signs improve during the course of our treatment, we usually feel confident that it was because of treatment and not some outside occurrence, although we can't be absolutely certain.

Outside verification. We can ask for outside verification to see if the client is doing well outside of our office. This helps give our evaluation a way of factoring out the tendency of clients to tell us that things are better or worse than they really are and makes our evaluation more valid and reliable. It doesn't necessarily tell us that change is because of our work, however.

Psychological tests. We can give the client a psychological test for any number of problems, including depression and anxiety. Although tests aren't completely accurate, they do give us a good idea about how well the client is doing and, if the test scores improve as we work together, we can often feel fairly certain that it's because of our work. Sometimes clients work with many professionals, and it might be better to assume that we're all helping.

Statistical tests. We can do some very simple statistical tests to tell us whether it was our work that led to change or some other chance occurrence.

Ask the client. We can ask the client directly whether it was our work or something else that caused his or her improvement. We can also give a satisfaction instrument that helps us know how happy the client is with our work. We hope being happy with our work translates into the client doing better. This isn't always the case, of course, but we think it's an important variable.

Ask other professionals. We can ask other professionals to evaluate the client before, during, and after treatment ends, and let them decide whether the client has improved and if it was due to our help.

Ask people in our client's life. We can ask important people in the client's life to provide feedback about the reasons he or she has improved, and if there were some reasons we don't know about. Sometimes people get better because they mature out of their problems. This is particularly true of adolescents, children, and adults going through a mid-life crisis. It is also true of people who have an undiagnosed illness that improves on its own.

Life changes. There are life changes that may have a profound effect on people's emotional health. Joining a church, becoming more spiritual, being a volunteer, and finding the right career are all quite separate from our work and may be more important variables in client change than the help we provide.

In the end, the client makes the judgment about whether he or she has improved. Our job throughout the helping process is to get feedback from the client that tells us honestly if what we're doing is helping and why or why not. Let's see if we can tell whether the following client has done better because of our work.

Evaluating a Client's Level of Improvement

Gerald Blake is a 21-year-old junior in college. He has sought social work help from the student counseling center because he's been depressed for longer than a year and has begun having suicidal thoughts. When Gerald came to see the social worker, he was sleeping 14 hours a day, missing half of his classes, and was close to failing school. After 12 one-hour sessions of cognitive therapy, he is sleeping 8 hours a day, is doing B-level work in school, and has stopped having suicidal thoughts. Gerald told the social worker throughout treatment that he didn't think he was being helped, and he was often sullen and angry with the social worker for not doing a better job; yet he improved. Gerald thinks he got better on his own because he started taking responsibility for his problems and doing something about them. The social worker believes that Gerald got better because of the help he was given.

Although we know that Gerald has improved, we don't know why. A check with his roommates and parents provides no other reasons for his improvement. A discussion with Gerald confirmed that although he had questions about the social worker, he admitted that she helped motivate him to seek solutions for his depression. He also thought the structure of having to come for help every week gave him an outlet to discuss his feelings and to solidify ideas concerning what to do about them. Was he satisfied with the help he received? No. Did he think he'd changed? Yes. Was it because of the work he did with the social worker? Probably. So, didn't the social worker help? Maybe she did, and maybe she didn't. The social worker didn't seem very concerned, but she did give Gerald some good advice. So didn't she help? Yes, maybe she did, but she could have been a lot better. And so it went. What do you think? Have you ever gone to a doctor who didn't seem very warm or concerned about you but was still a good doctor? Do you think it's important to be warm, sensitive, and empathic as a social worker? A lot of people think so.

Brent (1998), for example, finds a strong relationship between social workers who are warm and empathic (the ability to accurately sense how the client is feeling) and good treatment outcomes: "From the patients' points of view, provision of support, understanding, and advice have been reported as most critical to good outcomes" (p. 2). In further comments about empathy, Brent (1998) reports that empathy is a strong factor in successful treatment, even stronger than the therapy approach a worker might use. In successful therapy,

> The therapist is described as "helping and protecting, affirming and understanding," whereas the patient is seen as "disclosing and expressing." Not surprisingly, therapists tend to attribute success to technique, whereas patients attribute a good outcome to the therapist's support and understanding. (Brent, 1998, p. 2)

But Dr. Glicken, I suspect you might argue, the client told us that the social worker wasn't very empathic and he didn't respect the social worker's skills, yet he still admits that he got better. Why is empathy so important if the client improved and the social worker wasn't very empathic? Because, although the client may not experience the social worker as empathic, there may be issues that arise in treatment that confuse the picture. Such as? Well, what if the social worker reminds Gerald of his mother, with whom he had a love-hate relationship? What if the social worker is very empathic but Gerald is looking for a more personal relationship, perhaps a friendship or even a love relationship? It happens, and when it does and the social worker doesn't become the client's friend or lover (Freud called it *transference*), clients often become angry because certain basic needs aren't being met. Of course, the social worker is not ethically allowed to become a patient's lover because it would be a misuse of information the worker knows about the client. Being his friend would make it difficult to be his helping professional. And another thought: What if the client needs to feel that he resolved the depression on his own to save face? These are all good reasons, of course, but maybe the client is right and, in this instance, the client *did* get better in spite of the worker.

Why Clients Get Better

There are many reasons why clients improve. The following answers suggest most of the reasons:

1. Clients improve because they are motivated to and, even when the worker isn't competent, they do most of the work on their own.

2. Most problems resolve themselves. If you give them enough time, people can improve.

3. Sometimes the combination of the right worker, the right client, the right approach, and the right timing produce incredibly positive results.

4. Sometimes people don't improve while seeing a social worker, but if you give them time, many of the issues worked on in treatment begin to have an effect and clients improve as a result of treatment.

5. Sometimes people get better because of a combination of factors, including the help they receive, their support systems, their own self-work, and the biological changes that take place as they get well. This suggests that as the client is better able to cope with his or her emotional problems, subtle changes take place in the brain that lessen the biochemical reasons for emotional problems.

6. Sometimes medication taken for an emotional problem has a very positive effect, or the combination of help and medication together create change.

7. Sometimes people recover for reasons we can't explain, or situations in their lives that might be causing them emotional pain resolve themselves.

8. People get better because they have self-righting capabilities (resilience) and are able to cope with traumas and stressors in ways that are often quite unique and amazing.

Summary

This chapter discusses the social work processes used in helping people experiencing social and emotional problems. It includes the importance of the helping relationship and the ability to be empathic with clients. The chapter includes a discussion of evaluating change in clients and notes the difficulty in assuming that change is caused by social work intervention. A case example of a problem in diagnosis is provided.

Questions to Determine Your Frame of Reference

1. Doesn't using labels in medicine help doctors find appropriate treatments? How could we treat cancer if we never used the word to describe the patient's condition? Isn't there a danger in social workers not using labels because, although it may be politically incorrect, it's scientifically necessary?

2. People do awful things in their lives, such as physically and sexually abuse children. Why should we be sensitive to how they feel? Shouldn't we just tell it like it is and let them know how we feel about the awful things they've done?

3. If you're working with depressed clients, shouldn't you just come right out and ask them if they're suicidal? Why all this beating around the bush with being empathic?

4. I'm unclear about transference. Why would clients expect their social worker to love them? I don't feel that way about my doctor; why would clients feel that way about their social worker?

5. Isn't there a danger that if you're too nice and empathic to clients that they will misunderstand the relationship? If that's the case, what can social workers do to keep this from happening?

Internet Sources

First, Singer explains his model for practice, which was written while he was an MSW student. Next, Brodley's paper on relationships does an exceptionally good job of explaining why the helping relationship is so important in producing effective professional work. Finally, Tucker-Ladd states how clients effectively use help for social and emotional problems.

1. Singer, J. (1996). *Constructing a model for personal practice.* Retrieved November 27, 2004, from http://home.flash.net/~cooljazz/mssw/my_model.htm

2. Brodley, B. T. (1987). *Relationships: A client-centered psychotherapy practice.* Retrieved November 17, 2004, from http://lists.portents.com/~matt/cct.practice.html

3. Tucker-Ladd, C. E. (2000). *Methods of developing skill from psychological self-help.* Retrieved February 14, 2005, from http://www.mentalhelp.net/psyhelp/chap13/

Professional Social Work Practice

4

The Sophisticated Generalist

This chapter discusses generalist and specialized social work practice and the five primary ways we work with people to help them resolve problems in their lives: (a) the strengths perspective, (b) evidence-based practice, (c) cognitive practice, (d) the psychodynamic approach, and (e) solution-based practice. Social workers also work in communities and organizations (see Chapter 21 for a discussion of social work practice with larger client systems).

Let's begin with an explanation of the difference between the social work generalist (usually thought of as social workers with the BSW degree) and the social work specialist (often those with the MSW degree).

The Social Work Generalist

The following information describing generalist practice comes from an accreditation document prepared for Central Michigan University by members of the social work department and (a) the CSWE Educational Policy and Accreditation Standards (2001) and (b) Kirst-Ashman and Hull, Jr. (1999). Generalist practice in social work includes the following important elements:

Empowering people. Generalist social work practice focuses on empowerment of clients to solve problems and build on strengths. Empowerment of clients means that social work generalist practitioners work together with clients to promote social and economic justice, eliminate or reduce adverse environmental conditions, advocate for their clients, and influence social welfare policies and services. Clients include individuals, families, groups, organizations, neighborhoods, communities, and broader areas including the United States and other countries. We sometimes use the term client systems to signify that we are working with many different groups and organizations.

How generalists help others. Generalist practice usually takes place in a social agency under the supervision of an experienced social worker. Generalist practice includes the following elements: assessment, planning, implementing a treatment plan, evaluation, termination, and follow-up. Generalist practitioners collect and analyze information about clients, their social environments, and current practice research (see the discussion of evidence-based practice in this chapter). Assessment of information includes all information that may help us understand why the client currently is having a problem and includes biological, psychological, religious, social, family, economic, and cultural factors. Assessment data guide the social worker's treatment approach and are necessarily client-focused, research-based, and require ongoing evaluations of our work with clients.

Social work ethics and values. Social work generalist practice is guided by the ethics and values of the NASW Code of Ethics (1996), which can be found in its entirety in the appendix. The NASW Code of Ethics includes ethical principles such as service, social justice, dignity and worth of people, human relationships, integrity, and practitioner competence.

Diversity and cultural sensitivity. Generalist practice includes social work knowledge, skills, and values that respect the unique characteristics, needs, and resources of diverse, at-risk and multicultural groups, for example, people of color; women, children, and elderly people; immigrants; rural people; those with physical and emotional disabilities; and people with diverse religious affiliations and ethnic backgrounds, particularly those who are economically disadvantaged. Generalist practitioners recognize and use their professional skills to fight oppression and discrimination including racism, sexism, and group stereotypes. At the same time, generalist practitioners recognize that people are unique and that there are great differences within at-risk and multicultural groups.

How generalists develop relationships and communicate with others. Generalist practice includes a strong emphasis on positive relationships with clients, colleagues, community resource providers, and policy makers. Generalist practitioners communicate effectively with a wide range of people for the purpose of helping clients. Effective communication includes listening well; being empathic, warm, and genuine; and having an understanding of unclear or incongruent verbal and nonverbal communication. Communication with client systems includes collaboration and respect.

Professional skills. The generalist practitioner is not a specialist, although specialized training is available through graduate education or additional in-service training. The generalist is prepared to provide competent service to clients in settings that require a broad and nonspecialized provision of service. That level of service is appropriate to BSW-level social workers who may work in very rural and isolated settings or in large urban organizations, and who may see a large variety of clients with a broad range of problems. The generalist social worker understands the need to refer clients to other professionals when the limits of their training require more specialized service. Generalist practitioners also understand that specialized service is a function of advanced training and are prepared to seek more training as their needs and interests become apparent.

The Social Work Specialist

Social workers think of systems when we work with clients. Individual clients, for example, exist within families, groups, neighborhoods, communities, organizations, and so on. When we work with one system, all systems need to be considered and even intervened with. What makes generalist practice different from specialized practice is that whereas the generalist works within all systems at a basic level of competence, the specialist focuses on specific client problems, often within a specific client system. To explain this, some social workers specialize in grief work with children. This may require working with many other systems, but the core of their specialized work is with children who have lost a loved one and can't resolve their grief. To explain specialization even more fully, social work has developed into two broad practice areas: direct practice with clients who have social and emotional needs, and community and organizational practice with communities and organizations that are functioning poorly. Direct practice includes a number of specialties such as medical social work, clinical social work, industrial social work, school social work, and child welfare.

Sometimes the terms *counseling* and *psychotherapy* are used to describe clinical social work practice. Counseling generally refers to helping resolve client problems using advice, support, and other more superficial techniques that provide short-term and brief assistance. Psychotherapy usually refers to help that is more in-depth, may take a longer period of time, and tries to discover underlying reasons for a client's current difficulty. In reality, these terms are often used interchangeably.

Community and organizational practice includes work with organizations, communities, and groups with serious problems through the application of collaboration (helping diverse groups of people work well together), leadership development (developing leadership roles for people who represent a specific population of clients, citizens, and nonprofessionals), and facilitation (the ability to help people resolve large-scale problems by acting in a supportive and encouraging way until they develop the problem-solving skills unique to a specific group of people).

Five Approaches to Helping People Often Used in Social Work

The following discussion considers the five major theoretical approaches to helping people used in direct social work practice.

THE STRENGTHS PERSPECTIVE

Many social workers now understand that focusing on what's wrong with people doesn't help their clients get better; rather, it's focusing on what's right about them that really leads to change. The strengths perspective is a wellness model that tries to identify and then use the client's positive behaviors in the course of helping them cope with difficult situations. By helping them see that the successful strategies they use daily in their lives can be used to deal with areas of life that don't work as well, the focus of treatment is on their strengths.

The strengths perspective is based on resilience research, which tries to determine why people do so well in times of terrible stress. It's also based on the fact that people can change their life direction through a combination of "self-righting tendencies" and outside help in the form of good parental guidance, mentors, teachers, and professional helpers, including social workers. As an example of the resilience research that helped shape the strengths perspective, a longitudinal research study begun in 1955 by Werner and Smith (1992) found that one out of every three children evaluated by several measures of early life functioning to be at significant risk for adolescent problems (violence, mental illness, substance abuse) actually developed into well-functioning young adults by age 18. In their follow-up study, Werner and Smith (1992) report that two out of three of the remaining two-thirds of the children at risk had turned into caring and healthy adults by age 30. One of their primary theories was that people have "self-righting" capabilities. From their studies, the authors conclude that some of the factors that lead to self-correction in life can be identified. They also conclude that a significant factor leading to better emotional health for many children is a consistent and caring relationship with at least one adult. This adult (in a few cases, it was a peer) does not have to be a family member or be physically present all of the time. These relationships provide the child with a sense of protection and serve to initiate and develop the child's self-righting capacities. Werner and Smith believe that it is never too late to move from a lack of achievement and a feeling of hopelessness to a sense of achievement and fulfillment.

Elements of the Strength's Perspective

A few of those positive elements are noted in my book on the strengths perspective (Glicken, 2004a) as well as in the writings of others in the social work field (Goldstein, 1990; Saleebey, 1985, 1992, 1994; Weick, Rapp, Sullivan, & Kisthardt, 1989) and include the following:

1. The strengths perspective focuses on the coping mechanisms, problem-solving skills, and decision-making processes that work well for the client and result in an abundance of generally positive and successful behaviors. There is usually more about the client that is positive and functional than is negative or dysfunctional. Helpers must reassess the way they diagnose client behavior to recognize these largely positive behaviors (Turner, 2002).

2. Clients have the innate ability to resolve problems when the helper shows them that the majority of their life is successful. The focus on positive behaviors is very important in that it helps motivate and energize clients to effectively resolve problem areas in their lives and not to "give up" hope that their lives will improve.

3. Social workers can help by knowing the client's aspirations, dreams, hopes, and desires. Dreams are the hidden motivators that help clients cope with serious social and emotional problems and to continue on in life even when the path seems hopeless.

4. Social workers and their clients often experience a sense of newness and even astonishment when clients tell their stories. This sense of astonishment suggests that workers are openly and completely experiencing the client's stories. There are no assumptions made about the client's behavior. At this initial point in helping clients, the worker should feel a sense of newness and the client a sense of relief as they both struggle to understand the client's descriptions of his or her experiences in life that may have led to the problem for which help is sought.

5. The strengths perspective does not use labels that imply pathology because they are often misleading, pejorative, unhelpful in treatment, or provide an excuse for not helping the client. Some labels, such as mental illness, are excuses not to help people because the implication (untrue, of course) is that these clients won't recover even when help is provided.

Labels often stereotype people and fail to show the complex nature of their behavior. Someone isn't "just" mentally ill—they have a life history, talents, aspirations and dreams, and are, above all, human beings to be respected and loved.

6. The strengths perspective always views the client in a hopeful and optimistic way, regardless of the complexity of the problem, the length of time the client has experienced the problem, or the difficulty the client is having in resolving the problem. As Saleebey (2000) writes, "Healing, transformation, regeneration, and resilience almost always occur within the confines of a personal, friendly, and dialogical relationship. . . . The more the power of a caring relationship is actualized with those served, the better the individual's future" (p. 128).

7. The struggle to overcome life problems usually contains elements that are healthy and positive. In listening to clients discuss their attempts to change, we may find many examples of purposeful and adaptive behavior. Saleebey (2000) writes that "every maladaptive response or pattern of behavior may also contain the seeds of a struggle for health" (p. 129).

8. There must be recognition that the social and cultural environments of our clients are rich in opportunities for support, encouragement, and assistance from others. The worker's task is to help the client identify those people in his or her social and cultural environment who possess positive and reinforcing skills that can be used to help the client in times of need and to maintain gains made in treatment.

EVIDENCE-BASED PRACTICE

Much of this section on evidence-based practice (EBP) is based on my book on the subject (Glicken, 2005). EBP is about the use of research and critical thinking in determining the best ways of helping social work clients with social and emotional problems. The current practice of psychotherapy, counseling, and much of our work as helping professionals often relies on what is called *clinical wisdom*, or past experience, with little research evidence that what we do actually works. Clinical wisdom is often a justification for beliefs and values that bond us together as professionals but often fail to serve clients, because many of those beliefs and values may be comforting but inherently incorrect. O'Donnell (1997) likens this process to making the same mistakes, with growing confidence, during a long number of years. Issacs and Fitzgerald (1999) call practice wisdom "an effective technique for browbeating your more timorous colleagues and for convincing relatives of your ability" (p. 1).

In a review of the effectiveness of psychotherapy during a 40-year period, Bergin (1971) calls for an EBP approach when he writes, "It now seems apparent that psychotherapy has had an average effect that is modestly positive. It is clear, however, that the averaged group data on which this conclusion is based obscure the existence of a multiplicity of processes occurring in therapy, some of which are now known to be unproductive or actually harmful" (p. 263). Kopta, Lueger, Saunders, and Howard (1999) note that "researchers have repeatedly failed to find convincing evidence that different psychotherapies are differentially effective" (p. 441) and that when those differences are taken into consideration, the differences often have to do with researcher bias and personal beliefs rather than scientific evidence.

An argument is often made by helping professionals that what we do is intuitive, subjective, artful, and based on our long years of experience. However, as Gambrill (1999) points out, we often overstep our boundaries as professionals when we make claims about our professional abilities that we cannot prove. The following statement containing some of those over-stepped boundaries, followed by Gambrill's response, is a case in point:

> Professional social workers possess the specialized knowledge necessary for an effective social services delivery system. Social work education provides a unique combination of knowledge, values, skills, and professional ethics which cannot be obtained through other degree programs or by on-the-job training. Further, social work education adequately equips its individuals with skills to help clients solve problems that bring them to social services departments and human services agencies.
>
> These claims all relate to knowledge. To my knowledge, there is no evidence for any of these claims. In fact, there is counterevidence. In Dawes' (1994) review of hundreds of studies, he concluded that there is no evidence that licenses, experience, and training are related to helping clients. If this applies to social work and, given the overlap in helping efforts among social workers, counselors, and psychologists, it is likely that it does, what are the implications? (Gambrill, 1999, p. 341)

As a response to subjective and sometimes ineffective approaches to practice, EBP believes that we should consult the research and involve clients in decisions about the best helping approaches to be used, the issues in a client's life that need to be resolved, and the need to form a positive alliance with clients to facilitate change. This requires a cooperative and equal relationship with clients. EBP also suggests that we act in supportive ways to help clients gather information on their own and to rationally and critically process it. This differs from authoritarian approaches that assume the worker knows more about the client than the client does, and that the worker is the sole judge of what is to be done in the helping process.

What Is EBP?

Sackett, Richardson, Rosenberg, and Haynes (1997) define EBP as "the conscientious, explicit, and judicious use of current best evidence in making decisions about the care of individuals" (p. 2). Gambrill (2000, p. 1) defines EBP as a process involving self-directed learning which requires professionals to access information that permits us to (a) take our collected knowledge and provide questions we can answer, (b) find the best evidence with which to answer questions, (c) analyze the best evidence for its research validity as well as its applicability to the practice questions we have asked, (d) determine if the best evidence we've found can be used with a particular client, (e) consider the client's social and emotional background, (f) make the client a participant in decision-making, and (e) continually evaluate the quality of our practice with that specific client.

Gambrill (1999) says that EBP "requires an atmosphere in which critical appraisal of practice-related claims flourishes, and clients are involved as informed participants" (p. 345). Timmermans and Angell (2001) suggest that evidence-based clinical judgment has five important features: (a) it is composed of research evidence and clinical experience, (b) there is skill involved in reading the literature that requires an ability to synthesize the information and make judgments about the quality of the evidence available, (c) the way in which information is used is a function of the practitioner's level of authority in an organization and his or her level of confidence in the effectiveness of the applied information, (d) part of the use of EBP is the ability to evaluate the information used independently and to test its validity in the context of one's own practice, and (e) evidence-based clinical judgments are grounded in the Western notions of professional conduct and professional roles, and are ultimately guided by a common value system.

Gambrill (1999) points out that one of the most important aspects of EBP is the sharing of information with clients and the cooperative relationship that ensues. She believes that in EBP, clinicians search for relevant research to help in practice decisions and share that information with clients. If no evidence is found to justify a specific treatment regimen, the client is informed and a discussion takes place about how best to approach treatment. This includes the risks and benefits of any treatment approach used. Clients are involved in all treatment decisions and are encouraged to independently search the literature. As Sackett et al. (1997) note, new information is constantly being added to our knowledge base, and informed social workers and clients may often find elegant treatment approaches that help provide direction where none may have existed before. Gambrill (1999) believes that the use of EBP can help us "avoid fooling ourselves that we have knowledge when we do not" (p. 342).

Haynes (1998) writes that the goal of EBP "is to provide the means by which current best evidence from research can be judiciously and conscientiously applied in the prevention, detection, and care of health disorders" (p. 273). Haynes believes that this goal is very ambitious, given "how resistant practitioners are to withdrawing established treatments from practice even once their utility has been disproved" (p. 273).

Finally, in clarifying the type of data EBP looks for in its attempt to find best practices, Sackett, Rosenberg, Muir Gray, Haynes, and Richardson (1996) write, "Evidence based practice . . . involves tracking down the best external evidence with which to answer our clinical questions" (p. 72). The authors note that subjective research of treatment approaches (those without well-designed research designs) should be avoided because they often result in positive conclusions about treatment efficacy that are false. If randomized trials have not been done, "We must follow the trail to the next best external evidence and work from there" (Sackett et al., 1996, p. 72).

THE PSYCHODYNAMIC APPROACH

The psychodynamic approach developed by Sigmund Freud well more than 100 years ago affected social work practice for a very long time. This approach believes that all behavior is determined by forces that are often unknown to the client. Before clients can overcome their emotional problems, these unconscious forces, beliefs, and life experiences must be understood, explored, and resolved. An example of the unconscious might be adults who are molested as children, repress the experience so they can't remember it happening, but act in ways that suggest that something took place earlier in life that is now having a profoundly troubling effect on them. They may be depressed, drink too much, have many unsatisfying relationships, feel negatively about themselves, or are often anxious, depressed, and deeply unhappy. The psychodynamic approach would see the current behavior as a result of the molestation and would try and help the client remember the event, understand the reasons it happened, deal with the resulting guilt and shame, and hope that this process will lead to a happier and less anxious client who can now enter more successful relationships.

Unfortunately, this process often doesn't work, because knowing why something happened doesn't always make the damage go away. Nonetheless, the contribution of Freud to modern social work cannot be overstressed because many of us (myself included) still use the concept of prior events contributing to present events as a key way of understanding client behavior. We also believe that Freud made many helpful contributions that have remained part of the helping process, including his ideas about forming relationships with clients. We don't agree that he was always right, but his ideas were groundbreaking and developed psychotherapy and the helping process into a professional and respected practice.

THE COGNITIVE APPROACH

Unlike the psychodynamic approach that believes our behavior is determined by unconscious thoughts and motivations, which then lead to troubled emotions, social workers who use the cognitive approach believe that people think before they respond to situations and events. Those thoughts may be healthy and rational, or they may contain irrational ideas and perceptions of an event that often lead to troubled responses. The cognitive approach not only helps people see what's irrational about the way they perceive situations, but it also teaches people to view life situations more logically and accurately. Cognitive social workers therefore believe that it isn't what happens to us in life that causes us to be unhappy—it's how we view those events. If we can help clients see situations more rationally, we can then teach them to think and respond in healthier ways.

Let's first examine the idea of thinking before responding. Imagine yourself on the 18th floor of a building in a room with no other way out than one door. Through this doorway walks a cute little Cocker Spaniel. What is your response? Probably curiosity or affection, and a desire to pet it. Through the same door a 150-pound Doberman Pinscher walks into the room, foaming at the mouth. Remember, the only way out is to walk around the dog. Would I be wrong in assuming that your first emotion would be fear and that you'd be wondering how you'd get out the room with your head intact? In both instances, we've thought about the situation before we've had an emotional response. In the first instance, the response is affection; whereas in the second instance, it's fear. There is nothing unconscious about either response. We've correctly perceived both situations and responded accordingly. Some of the developers of cognitive therapy who often write about it include Albert Ellis, William Glasser, and Aaron Beck. (See "The ABCs of Cognitive Therapy" in Table 4.1, which provides our progression of thoughts that may lead to unwanted emotions and shows how cognitive therapy works.)

InfoTable 4.1	The ABCs of Cognitive Therapy

A. A situation or event occurs that leads to our becoming unhappy, even angry. Being turned down for a date might be an example.

B. We think about the situation. We might say to ourselves, "How dare anyone turn me down for a date! Who do they think they are?"

C. We become angry because our feelings are hurt.

D. With help, we learn to recognize that no one is obligated to go out with us and that while it doesn't feel good to be rejected, we can't control the feelings or actions of others. We chalk it up to a learning experience and immediately ask someone else out.

E. By immediately asking someone else out, we begin to learn successful approaches and, in time, someone accepts a date with us who is wonderful, sincere, kind, and intelligent and far superior to the first person who rejected us. The point is that *we* control our emotions, not the situation or other people.

F. Consequently, it isn't what happens to us in life that makes us upset, angry, or depressed, it's what we tell ourselves about what happens to us. We have absolute control over how we perceive situations and how we ultimately feel about them.

SOLUTION-FOCUSED THERAPY

In many ways, solution-focused therapy (SFT) applies elements of the strengths perspective, EBP, and cognitive therapy. The following describes the solution-focused approach:

1. SFT is a model that has evolved during years of thought, research, and experience.

2. It is a model that places the highest emphasis on respect for clients and their competence, strengths, and resources.

3. It is a model in which building a collaborative relationship with the client is key.

4. It is a systems-based model of therapy that recognizes that change is inevitable and ongoing.

5. It is a goal-directed model of therapy that focuses on working collaboratively with the client to build solutions.

6. SFT is an approach that challenges the assumption that learning all about the origins of the problem is the only way to find the solution to that problem.

7. SFT is a model which holds that there is no one single "correct" or "valid" way to live one's life; because this is so, it is the client's goals, not the therapist's, that should be identified and accomplished. (Suberri, 2004, p. 1)

In describing SFT, McKeel (1999) says that de Shazer (1988, 1994) encourages social workers to use the time spent with clients to talk about change. Examples might include expressing optimism that the client's situation will improve and exploring actions that the client can take to accomplish his or her goals. During a first session, solution-focused therapists usually ask clients what improvements in their problems have occurred since their call to request help (de Shazer, 1985, 1988). If the client reports any improvement, the therapist and client explore what the client did to accomplish that improvement. Exploring improvements also helps clients identify the steps that need to be taken to continue improvement. Identifying pretreatment changes may help clients feel encouraged because they realize their situation can improve. McKeel says that helping clients focus on what works for them in changing a situation is what workers should stress. Solution-focused therapists use questions to help clients recall and discuss information about their strengths, abilities, and successes.

Assuring Clients of Effective Social Work Practice

STATE LICENSURE

Many states require BSW- and MSW-level social workers to be licensed. This usually includes accumulating a certain number of supervised hours after graduating, taking a written test, and, in the case of the MSW worker, sometimes taking an oral examination as well. Social workers who plan on doing independent clinical work with clients are often called clinical social workers. They must provide evidence of their ability to perform independent clinical social work practice by not only accumulating sufficient hours under supervision, but also taking an examination and, in some states, an additional oral examination before a board of highly experienced licensed social work practitioners. The purpose of licensure is to protect clients by making certain that licensed social workers have the knowledge, skills, and values to perform effective and ethical social work practice.

ACCREDITATION

Many social work agencies are accredited by outside organizations. Accreditation generally suggests that the agency is operating at a very high level. Social work programs in universities and colleges are accredited by the Council on Social Work Education and must undergo a grueling series of challenges that include providing extensive written materials that conform to accreditation standards regarding curriculum, admissions, and faculty educational achievement, as well as library facilities and holdings and community acceptance. At some stage of the process, social work faculty representing CSWE come for a site visit and evaluate the program. They always speak to students, to social work faculty, to university administrators, and to directors of social welfare agencies in the community to obtain feedback. Most social work educational programs also have boards that represent the community made up of agency directors, clients, and students.

The accreditation process in social work assures students and employers that all accredited programs will have similar curriculums and experiences for student learning. This makes it possible for students to move around the country and apply for licensure, earn advanced degrees, or obtain social work jobs because the employer is certain that the education the student received from an accredited program elsewhere is comparable to what students in his or her area have also received. Accreditation is a great deal of work and sometimes more than an organization can handle, but most of us think it's worth it to get the sign of approval from an outside group of professionals that the job we're doing is a good one.

Accreditation also helps programs shore up what they aren't doing well. In the long run, accreditation, though demanding, provides for a healthy evaluation of what a social work educational program is doing. For this reason, the material provided to the accreditation organization is called a *self-study*.

THE USE OF SUPERVISION

Social work has always stressed the need for others to review our work and develop a professional relationship with a more experienced social work practitioner whom we consider our mentor and agency supervisor. This role has added importance in social work education, where students in the BSW program must do 400–500 supervised hours by an experienced MSW-level social worker in a social agency. MSW students must receive at least 900 hours of supervision. Supervisors review our work, take legal responsibility for the work we do, suggest ways of doing our work more effectively and efficiently, make recommendations for promotions and salary increases, do periodic reviews and evaluations of our performance, and act as the social agencies' assurance to the public that the quality of our work is at its highest possible level. But like any function, supervision sometimes doesn't work well. In the following case study (Glicken, 2005, pp. 300–303), you'll be asked to determine what you would do if you were the supervisor.

You Be the Social Worker

Julie Loren is an MSW level social worker with three years of experience who recently obtained her clinical license to practice independent social work. Julie was a very good student and did well in her classes but had problems in her two field placements. Both placements were in agencies providing services to fragile elderly and disabled clients. Julie has never been supervised in a setting providing intense psychotherapy services, and while she was able to receive her clinical license, her therapy skills are very minimal. In her MSW field settings, two MSW supervisors raised concerns about her people skills, her commitment to helping others, and about her ability to form relationships. Because she did so well in her classroom work, Julie was able to complete her field experience and receive passing grades even though two field instructors and two faculty-field liaisons had recommended failing grades in fieldwork.

Like many university settings, grade grievances are litigious affairs and Julie was able to challenge her grades and receive a passing grade in both field placements. In a system using pass/fail, this meant that no employer could actually know how

(Continued)

(Continued)

badly she'd done in her fieldwork. The agency she worked for after graduation had promised her supervision for her license. Although the overworked supervisor had strong concerns about Julie's abilities, she was aware that other supervisees had brought legal actions against supervisors who failed to support them at the point of licensure. Her supervisor wrote a mild and innocuous letter in support of Julie's licensure application which, if read carefully, would have confirmed the suspicion that Julie lacked the interpersonal and technical skills for clinical practice. Upon receiving her LCSW, Julie was hired by an agency with a severe shortage of clinical workers. The agency was under review by the state for it's poor level of work and was told to increase the number of LCSW's or face loss of certification for state payments for services. Julie was given a caseload of severely depressed clients, many of them suicidal. Her overworked supervisor, believing that Julie's license indicated the ability to work independently, provided very superficial supervision, usually on lunch breaks where the two often talked about the supervisor's troubled teenaged son.

Julie began seeing clients, recognizing that she had few actual skills for working with depressed clients. She was generally superficial, unsupportive, full of clichés about what clients should do about their depression, unknowledgeable about medications or potential for suicide, and uniformly disliked by her clients who called her "Miss Priss" in awareness of her condescending and uninformed attitudes about depression. One of the clients complained to Julie's supervisor and gave her a taped interview the client had made without Julie's knowledge or consent. The supervisor refused to listen to the tape and returned it to the client telling her that it was in violation of the federal law that mandated that people agree to be taped. The client pointed out Julie's flaws as a worker, but the supervisor, thinking that the client had relationship problems with Julie, refused to do anything about the complaint. Nonetheless, the supervisor began meeting with Julie for actual supervisory sessions and asked Julie to present cases. It was immediately clear that Julie knew nothing about depression, had a condescending attitude toward clients, and was likely to precipitate a suicide because of her incompetent work. A complicated grievance process in Julie's unionized agency led to a number of meetings and the supervisor was cautioned to use the contracted grievance procedure in future work with Julie. Nothing was done to Julie and the poor quality of work, followed by client complaints, continued.

In a highly agitated state, one of Julie's clients stabbed her after another condescending treatment session resulting in a punctured lung and a long-term disability claim by Julie. When she was well, she returned to the agency where she continues to provide poor level work and has now been assigned responsibility for training MSW students. One of the students complained to the university faculty field liaison that Julie calls her clients derogatory names like "Retard, bitch and queer." The university has decided to give up an otherwise excellent placement because Julie is too incompetent to supervise students. A meeting between the faculty field liaison and the agency director resulted in the following conversation:

Faculty Liaison (FL):   We've decided not to use the agency next year because we have strong concerns about the field instructor's competence (Julie).

Director (D): What does that mean?

FL: She's an incompetent practitioner.

D: How could that be? She was one of the top students to graduate in your program and she's licensed by the state to do advanced clinical work.

FL: I recognize that but still, she's not competent and her attitude toward clients is highly negative.

D: I'm confused. How would any of those things be possible if you were doing your job? How could someone you say is incompetent even get through your program, particularly the field segment of the program?

FL: You have a good point but our question is, knowing her level of incompetence, how can you keep her working with highly disturbed clients and, more to the point, how can you assign her to train students given the terrible attitude she has toward people in difficulty?

D: We hired her on the basis of her performance in your program and on the recommendation of another licensed social worker who did her supervision for licensure. Once having hired her, we have a difficult time firing her just because very troubled clients complain about her work. We tried to fire her but the union interceded. It would take hundreds of hours for us to develop a case against her and, even if we did, it's doubtful she'd be fired. So we assigned her the least dangerous role we could find: Training new students. We hope you'll counteract the harm she does with students, but that's where we are.

FL: It's a sad statement that the agency thinks training students doesn't result in harm to clients.

D: What would you do in our position?

FL: Fire her.

D: We tried. Talk to the union.

Questions

1. You've read the case and the dialogue that followed it. At what point in Julie's social work educational or employment experience would you have intervened, and what exactly would you have said and done?

2. You attend college and have many safeguards against an instructor grading unfairly. Is this case an example of instructors being too worried about the grievance

(Continued)

(Continued)

process and not worried enough about our clients? Look at the code of ethics in the appendix and find out whether Julie's supervisors acted unethically.

3. Regardless of what the union says, should there have been a concerted effort to fire Julie for her incompetent and seemingly unethical behavior? Again, see what the code of ethics has to say.

4. A client makes a complaint about Julie, which is discounted and kept secret. What would you have done if a client made a complaint about someone you were supervising?

5. The agency made Julie a supervisor of students rather than fire her or allow her to work with clients because they thought this was the least damaging thing they could do. But can't students who are poorly trained do considerable damage to clients? What do you think about making Julie a student supervisor?

Summary

This chapter discusses the various approaches to helping people used in social work practice and explains specialized and generalist practice. The chapter also discusses safeguards in social work practice, including accreditation, supervision, and state licensure. Finally, the chapter asks you to become a social worker by reviewing a case of an incompetent worker.

Questions to Determine Your Frame of Reference

1. Achieving client empowerment is a concept that is often used to describe professional social work practice. Give an example of how social work intervention might lead to client empowerment.

2. The strengths perspective asks us to focus on what's good and right about clients. How can we do that with clients who have very little that's good and right about them?

3. The cognitive approach sounds good until you ask yourself how reviewing irrational behavior can lead to more rational behavior in the future. Don't people tend to make the same mistakes in their thinking because of unconscious reasons better explained by the psychodynamic approach?

4. Professionals tend to make claims about the quality and effectiveness of their practice that are often not justified by the research evidence. When working with people, do you think it's ever entirely possible to prove that what you do works?

5. The idea that all behavior has meaning seems a little ludicrous. Can you think of behavior that has no meaning and tells us nothing about people?

Internet Sources

An article involving research on solution-focused brief therapy and an in-depth explanation of Sigmund Freud's work on the psychodynamic approach are presented here.

1. McKeel, J. (1999). *A selected review of research of solution-focused brief therapy.* Retrieved November 28, 2004, from http://www.enabling.org/ia/sft/Review%20McKeel.htm

2. Boeree, C. G. (1997). *Sigmund Freud.* Retrieved November 28, 2004, from http://www.ship.edu/~cgboeree/freud.html

Part II

Professional Social Workers Respond to Social Problems in Related Work Settings

The 5 Economically and Socially Disadvantaged

Professional Social Work in the Public and Private Social Welfare Systems

When I was growing up in the 1940s and 1950s, many of us in America were poor. Back then, the notion of poverty didn't mean that you would be locked into poverty for a lifetime. Many of us believed that with hard work and a good education, we would succeed in life. This is not to say that being poor was a pleasant or ennobling experience. It wasn't. That same optimism was not shared by people of color or by many women who had to fight the indignity of being locked out of the American Dream just because of their gender.

Because my mother was sick and there was no medical insurance for working-class people, my family struggled financially. This required my brother, sister, and me to work at jobs very early in life and to do the housework, shopping, and cooking or not eat. Because of my experiences with poverty from birth to age 22, I can tell you honestly that there is no romance in being poor. There is nothing honorable, intriguing, or inspiring about poverty. It immediately makes you a nonperson. While growing up, I was judged by the amount of money my family had (none) rather than my talents and abilities. There is nothing positive I can say about being treated like a third-class citizen. It still stings, and the thought of poverty in this wealthy land of ours makes me very angry. As you will see in this chapter, despite affluence as we've never known, there are millions of poor people in America. I think they feel the same way that I do about being poor: It's a hateful experience.

Poverty is more than a lack of money; it places you in a particular social class. As you will see in future chapters, poor people seldom go to college, have decent medical care, or achieve the American Dream of riches beyond anyone's wildest imagination. The truth is that once you're poor, the chances are that you'll continue to be poor. Poverty is shameful and unnecessary and we need to use our considerable talents to get rid of it.

Many of you think you're poor; perhaps some of you are. But how many of you could live at the poverty level of $9,300 (or the way many very poor people live, on half the poverty level) and still attend college, own a car, see films, go out for a meal, or experience any of the many pleasures we all should enjoy? Consider that when you read this chapter. Think about the term *poor but respectable* and imagine how respectable you'd feel if you had to live on the amount of money that defines poverty. Or if you were even less fortunate and had to live at half the poverty level of $4,660, imagine how many films, gallons of gas, excellent meals, drinks, clothing, or anything that we value you could afford.

As a definition, *poverty* is having insufficient resources or income to provide for anything other than a minimally secure life when it comes to housing, food, and health care. *Extreme poverty* is an annual income that is less than half of the official poverty level as determined by the U.S. Bureau of the Census. *Relative poverty* is having a family income of less than one-half of the median income for a similarly sized family in the United States. Relative poverty would then be an income level greater than the poverty line provided by the U.S. Census Bureau but still very low. Let's consider how poverty is defined in America (see Info Table 5.1) and some statistics about who is poor in America.

Who Is Poor in America?

The following information comes from the U.S. Census Bureau (2003). According to the official poverty measure, 35.9 million people were considered to be in poverty in the year 2003, or about 12% of the U.S. population. The poverty rate and the number of families in poverty increased from 6.8 million in 2002 (or 9.2% of all families) to 7.2 million (or 9.6%) in 2003. The number of people in severe poverty (people living at half the offical poverty level) increased from 13.4 million in 2002 to 14.1 million in 2003.

Among people who reported being black in 2003, 24.1% were in poverty, a higher number than the 22.7% for those who reported being black in 2002. The poverty rate for Hispanics in 2002 was 22%. Children younger than 18 had a poverty rate of 16.7% in 2003, whereas the poverty rate for people aged 65 and older was 10.4% in 2003. The rate for those aged 18 to 64 increased one-half a percentage point to 10.6% in 2003.

In terms of income, median income for black households of four was $29,000 in 2003 as compared to a median household income of Hispanics

InfoTable 5.1	2005 Poverty Guidelines (in dollars)		
People in Household	48 Contiguous States and D.C.	Alaska	Hawaii
1	9,570	11,950	11,010
2	12,830	16,030	14,760
3	16,090	20,110	18,510
4	19,350	24,190	22,260
5	22,610	28,270	26,010
6	25,870	32,350	29,760
7	29,130	36,430	33,510
8	32,390	40,510	37,260
For each additional person, add:	3,260	4,080	3,750

SOURCE: Adapted from the *Federal Register* (2005).

of $33,000 and for white families of four, $52,600. The median income of women in 2003 was $30,200 as compared to $39,500 for men, or 77 cents of female income for every dollar made by men. This continues the long-standing income inequity between men and women, discussed in greater detail in the chapter on the workplace.

InfoTable 5.2	The Feminization of Poverty

In the United States, typical family structures have changed significantly, with an increase in single-parent families, which tend to be poorer. Single-parent families, most often women with children, have a much more difficult time escaping poverty than do two-parent families, in which adults can divide and share childcare and work duties. In 1970 about 87 percent of children lived with both of their parents, but by 2000 this figure had dropped to 69 percent. The divorce rate in the United States more than doubled between 1960 and 1980, although it stabilized in the 1980s and fell somewhat in the 1990s. More importantly, perhaps, the proportion of children born to unmarried parents grew from about 5 percent in the early 1960s to more than 33 percent by 2000. ("Poverty," 2004)

The Culture of Poverty

Although there is considerable disagreement about Oscar Lewis and his work on the culture of poverty, Lewis says that not all people who are poor live in a culture of poverty. According to Lewis (1998), what distinguishes poor people from people who are part of the culture of poverty is the following:

1. The people in the *culture* of *poverty* have a strong feeling of marginality, of helplessness, of dependency, and of not belonging.

2. They are like aliens in their own country, convinced that the existing institutions do not serve their interests and needs.

3. Along with this feeling of powerlessness is a widespread feeling of inferiority, of personal unworthiness.

4. People with a *culture* of *poverty* have very little sense of history. They are a marginal people who know only their own troubles, their own local conditions, their own neighborhood, their own way of life.

5. Usually, they have neither the knowledge, the vision nor the ideology to see the similarities between their problems and those of others like themselves elsewhere in the world.

6. When the poor become class conscious or members of trade union organizations, or when they adopt an internationalist outlook on the world they are, in my view, no longer part of the *culture* of *poverty* although they may still be desperately poor.

7. Most people in the United States find it difficult to think of *poverty* as a stable, persistent, ever present phenomenon, because our expanding economy and the specially favorable circumstances of our history have led to an optimism which makes us think that *poverty* is transitory, but it is more widespread than has been generally recognized. (pp. 7–8)

Samuelson (1997) distinguishes people in the culture of poverty from people in poverty by splitting the poor into two groups. The first group lacks money because they are disabled, unemployed, or are single mothers who have been widowed, divorced, or abandoned. Even though they are poor, they have middle-class values and can benefit from a variety of government programs to help them out of poverty. The second group is what Samuelson refers to as the true lower class, those who see no value in working and no need for self-sacrifice or self-improvement. According to Samuelson, services to this group of poor are unlikely to change their condition even if their income were to be doubled. Samuelson points out that increased benefits to this second group of poor Americans will probably lead to welfare dependence and not appreciably improve their lives.

Social programs have raised the quality of life for many American children (see Table 5.3); "Unfortunately, these material improvements haven't translated into better social conditions. Crime has risen as have out-of-wedlock birthrates" (Samuelson, 1997, p. A21). In fact, juvenile crime rose in epidemic numbers in the peak years of 1987 to 1993, just as America was moving into one of our most affluent times and social welfare programs were showing significant positive gains for many poor people.

InfoTable 5.3	The Relationship Between Welfare Benefits and Improved Social Indicators

In 1970, about 26 percent of the poorest fifth of children hadn't visited a doctor in the past year; by 1989, the figure was only 14 percent. In 1973, about 71 percent of these children lived in homes without air-conditioning; by 1991, only 45 percent did. Unfortunately, these material improvements didn't translate into better social conditions. Crime rose; so did out-of-wedlock birthrates. The real test of any [welfare reform effort] is not reduced welfare caseloads. These have already dropped 21 percent since early 1994, mainly as the result of a strong economy. The real tests are less teenage pregnancy, more stable marriages and better homes for children. It's a tall order—perhaps an impossible one—for government to reengineer family life and human nature. (Samuelson, 1997, p. A21)

The Economic Safety Net

In 1996, Congress passed the Personal Responsibility and Work Opportunity Reconciliation Act. This legislation ended the program known as Aid to Families with Dependent Children and replaced it with a program called Temporary Assistance for Needy Families. Under TANF, welfare assistance is no longer an entitlement program. Welfare benefits are time limited and are closely tied to work requirements, which are intended to move welfare recipients off welfare and into the labor force. Pay particular attention to the discussion of unwanted pregnancies and adolescents who are not in school but have children. The major points of the TANF program are as follows (U.S. Office of Family Assistance, 2004):

The four purposes of TANF are:

- assisting needy families so that children can be cared for in their own homes;
- reducing the dependency of needy parents by promoting job preparation, work, and marriage;
- preventing out-of-wedlock pregnancies; and
- encouraging the formation and maintenance of two-parent families.

HIGHLIGHTS OF TANF

Work Requirements

- Recipients (with few exceptions) must work as soon as they are job-ready or no later than 2 years after coming on assistance.
- Single parents are required to participate in work activities for at least 30 hours per week. Two-parent families must participate in work activities 35 or 55 hours a week, depending upon circumstances.

- Failure to participate in work requirements can result in a reduction or termination of benefits to the family.
- States cannot penalize single parents with a child younger than age 6 for failing to meet work requirements if they cannot find adequate child care.
- States, in FY 2004, have to ensure that 50% of all families and 90% of two-parent families are participating in work activities. If a state reduces its caseload without restricting eligibility, it can receive a caseload reduction credit. This credit reduces the minimum participation rates the state must achieve.

Work Activities—(Counting Toward a State's Participation Rates; Some Restrictions May Apply)

- Unsubsidized or subsidized employment
- On-the-job training
- Work experience
- Community service
- Job search—not to exceed 6 total weeks and no more than 4 consecutive weeks
- Vocational training—not to exceed 12 months
- Job skills training related to work
- Satisfactory secondary school attendance
- Providing child care services to individuals who are participating in community service

Five-Year Time Limit

- Families with an adult who has received federally funded assistance for a total of 5 years (or less at state option) are not eligible for cash aid under the TANF program.
- States may extend assistance beyond 60 months to not more than 20% of their caseload. They may also elect to provide assistance to families beyond 60 months using state-only funds or social services block grants.

Teen Parent Live-at-Home and Stay-in-School Requirement

- Unmarried minor parents must participate in educational and training activities and live with a responsible adult or in an adult-supervised setting to receive assistance.
- States are responsible for assisting in locating adult-supervised settings for teens who cannot live at home.

Bonuses

- The law includes provisions for two bonuses that may be awarded to states and territories in addition to their basic TANF block grant.
- TANF's High Performance Bonus program provides cash awards to states for high relative achievement on certain measures related to the goals and purposes of the TANF program.
- The Department of Health and Human Services is required to award a Bonus to Reward Decrease in Illegitimacy Ratio to as many as five states (and three territories, if eligible) that achieve the largest decrease in out-of-wedlock births without experiencing an increase in their abortion rates above 1995 levels.

Homelessness

In 2004, an estimated 700,000 to 1 million adults were homeless in a given week (Substance Abuse and Mental Health Services Administration [SAMSHA], 2005). In the same year, an estimated 3 million adults were homeless during the course of a year. These numbers increased dramatically when children were included to 5 million. SAMSHA also estimated that about 2% to 3% of the U.S. population (5 to 8 million people) will experience at least one night of homelessness. For most of these people, the experience is short and often caused by a natural disaster, a house fire, or a community evacuation. As Hurricane Katrina taught us, the length of homelessness can be far longer than 1 or 2 days and can be perpetual. A much smaller group, perhaps as many as 500,000 people, have greater difficulty ending their homelessness. As Link et al. (1995) found, about 80% end homelessness within 2 to 3 weeks. They often have personal, social, and economic resources to draw on that people who are homeless for longer periods of time do not. About 10% are homeless for as long as 2 months, with housing availability and affordability adding to the time they are homeless. Another group of about 10% is homeless on a chronic, protracted basis—as long as 7 to 8 months in a 2-year period. Disabilities associated with mental illnesses and substance use are common reasons for homelessness within those who have protracted homelessness. On any given night, this group can account for up to 50% of those seeking emergency shelter.

SAMSHA (2005) suggests the following primary reasons why people become homeless:

Poverty. People who are homeless are the poorest of the poor. In 1996, the median monthly income for people who were homeless was $300, only 44% of the federal poverty level for a single adult. Decreases in the numbers of manufacturing and industrial jobs, combined with a decline in the real value of minimum wage because of inflation, have left large numbers of people without a livable income.

Housing. The U.S. Department of Housing and Urban Development (2001) estimated 5 million households in the U.S. with incomes below 50% of the local median who pay more than half of their income for rent or live in severely substandard housing. This is worsened by an increase in the cost of housing in some urban locations since 2001 of 200% to 300% and a significant increase in the cost of rentals.

Disability. O'Hara and Miller (2000) note that people with disabilities who are unable to work and must rely on entitlements such as Supplemental Security Income (SSI) find it virtually impossible to locate affordable housing. People receiving federal SSI benefits, which were $545 per month in 2002, cannot cover the cost of an efficiency or one-bedroom apartment in any major housing market in the country.

Mental illness. Untreated mental illness can so interfere with social and emotional functioning that it becomes difficult or impossible to maintain employment, pay bills, or keep supportive social relationships.

Substance abuse. Substance abuse can drain financial resources, erode supportive social relationships, and can also make exiting from homelessness extremely difficult.

Other reasons. People become homeless for a variety of other reasons, including domestic violence, chronic or unexpected health care expenses, release from incarceration, "aging out" of youth systems such as foster care, divorce, running away, or rejection by parents.

As you no doubt know from the poor performance of all sectors of government during the 2005 flood in New Orleans, we all have potential for homelessness. What should we do about it? The answers lie in our approach to a number of issues that center around poverty, but here are some thoughts:

1. We need a system of safe and comfortable emergency shelters for people displaced because of natural and man-made disasters, including terrorist attacks, staffed by helping professionals who can offer crisis counseling and supportive interventions.

2. We need safe and comfortable local shelters in every community for the displaced poor who should be permitted to stay for extended periods of time until they are emotionally and financially able to find their own housing. These shelters need to be staffed by social workers who can offer a variety of services to help people cope with

mental illness, substance abuse, and other social and emotional problems that leave them perpetually homeless.

3. We need to provide free or very inexpensive housing for people with disabilities who cannot work, and we need to increase the benefits we provide so that they can have normal lives within the limits placed on them by their disabilities.

4. We need to provide a livable income to the working poor in the form of a realistic minimum wage, health care, and other services that permit them to function as healthy family units.

5. We need to provide free or inexpensive long-term housing to adults with children. No child should be forced to live in a shelter for an extended period of time.

6. We need to be much more proactive to keep children from becoming homeless as a result of family disputes, abuse, and other preventable social and emotional problems.

7. We need to make homelessness a national concern and our private charitable and religious organizations need to provide services to the homeless as part of their mission.

8. Finally, as I suggest later in the chapter, we need to outlaw poverty. It may not eliminate all homelessness, but it would go a very long way to eliminate most of it.

A Social Worker Helps a Single Mother Move out of Poverty

Ethel Johnson is a 32-year-old mother of three whose husband abandoned the family. Ethel was a stay-at-home mother before her husband left, and she has no job skills. Because her children are all quite young (only one is in school), Ethel has had to apply for welfare benefits. The father's location is unknown. He has had no contact with either Ethel or the children and contributes nothing to the cost of their lives. Ethel was assigned a case worker by the welfare department with an MSW degree whose job was to help Ethel organize her life and begin the tough task of getting retrained and entering the workplace.

Through a program offered in her county, Ethel has become a part-time student at a local community college where she is studying to become a Licensed Practical Nurse (LPN). The welfare department pays for subsistence living, retraining, and child care while Ethel is in school. Many times she has found it difficult to make it on her benefits but always manages to figure out ways. When she is feeling down, Ethel sees her social worker for support and encouragement.

(Continued)

(Continued)

The social worker was on welfare herself when she was younger and knows exactly what Ethel is going through and how tough it is. She understands that Ethel has had to cope with the trauma of her husband leaving and the stress of raising three children on a fraction of the income she had before her husband left. She hasn't been in school for almost 14 years and initially found it difficult to compete with younger students who seemed a lot smarter than she was. In time, and with a lot of encouragement from the social worker, Ethel has begun to recognize that she is a great student and has a strong feeling for the work nurses do. Her field courses, in which she actually worked with patients, showed her that she has special skills with patients that everyone recognized. As a result, she was promised a number of well-paying jobs when she finished her degree. With the social worker's help, Ethel was able to obtain additional short-term funding to finish her degree full-time. She is now employed with a health maintenance organization (HMO) and loves her work. The job is well-paying, offers flexible hours, and has a day-care program on the campus of her facility that allows her to see her kids throughout the day.

While Ethel is lonely for companionship and would like to meet someone special, she has developed many friendships and has a rich social life. The feedback she gets at work makes her giddy. As a stay-at-home mother, she received little positive feedback. When she was asked about the role of the social worker, Ethel said, "Mollie really helped me when I was down. She has this 'can do' attitude, and she was there for me when I needed her. She always made time to see me when I had a crisis, and she is a loving person. She's been where I was, and she knows how tough it can be. She was my ally and best friend. When anyone ever says bad things about social workers, you know, how they keep people on welfare and stuff like that, I say that's not true at all and tell them about Mollie. And I see social workers on the job, and they're great. In fact, I'm sort of thinking I might go on, finish college, and then get my MSW. It seems like a great combination, being a nurse and being a social worker. You know about the physical reasons people have emotional problems as a nurse, and as a social worker, you know about the social and emotional reasons as well. Anyway, as soon as my kids are in school, I'm thinking about finishing my undergraduate degree and then going on to graduate school. I can't believe I'm feeling this way. Two years ago, I was down in the dumps and didn't think anything good would happen; now look where I am now. It's pretty amazing."

InfoTable 5.4   The Relationship Between Income and Academic Achievement

Understanding the consequences of growing up poor for a child's well-being is an important research question. Using a panel of over 6,000 children, our baseline estimates imply that a $1,000 increase in family raises math test scores by 2.1 percent and reading test scores by 3.6 percent. (Dahl & Lochner, 2005, p. 1)

InfoTable 5.5	The Relationship Between Academic Achievement and Reductions in Crime

One of the traditional ways of reducing poverty is through education, but education also has additional economic benefits to society. Lochner and Moretti (2002) calculate that a 1% increase in high school graduation rates would have led to nearly 400 fewer murders and 8,000 fewer assaults in 1990. In total, nearly 100,000 fewer crimes would have taken place for a savings of $1.4 billion. By comparison, hiring a single police officer would reduce crime costs by $200,000, while graduating 100 more students would have the same impact. Although increasing police forces is a cost-effective policy proposal, increasing high school graduation rates offers far greater benefits when both crime reduction and productivity are increased.

Why Don't We Outlaw Poverty?

I have an idea: Let's make poverty illegal. Nobody should be poor. Let's take the wealth that some people have and give it to poor people so they can live decent, safe, and healthy lives. Who needs $100 million? Wouldn't these people be just as happy with $50 million? When corporations give executives $140 million just as a payoff for doing a poor job, let's take $130 million and give it to poor people. Nobody should get $140 million for doing bad work because most of us who are fired either don't receive anything or we get 2 weeks' notice. And why should any CEO of a floundering company make $10 million a year? Wouldn't $1 million be more than enough?

Of course, this isn't an original idea. Schemes in many different forms to redistribute the wealth are common in all societies, and certainly in America. One way we redistribute wealth in America now is to tax the wealthy at a very high rate. In the 2004 presidential election, John Kerry suggested removing tax cuts for Americans who earn more than $200,000 a year and having them pay at the old higher rate.

The argument against redistribution of wealth schemes is that they remove the incentive for people to take chances in business that might lead to them becoming very wealthy. This argument is the operative one in America today and, judging by the conservative nature of our political class, it is the dominant argument: keep taxes low, encourage creation of new ideas and ventures, and remove as much of the social safety net as possible to discourage welfare dependence and force people to work.

These two arguments, liberal and conservative, are the dominant forces that either support or discourage redistribution of wealth schemes. Conservatives point to the dismal lives people had under communism as an example of a society with a redistribution of wealth philosophy. Incentives and initiative are discouraged in these systems, productivity is low, and the standard and quality of life is poor. Liberals, on the other hand, point to countries that encourage a redistribution of wealth and how well it has worked. Sweden is often given as an example. Conservatives might argue that Sweden is a very small, homogeneous country. Trying to have the state run many aspects of our lives in a large, diverse country like America would just not work because it would reduce incentives to create wealth and would, therefore, reduce productivity and the amount of money available. Without incentives to achieve wealth, people don't work as hard or take as many risks.

Liberals might respond by saying that's true, but why not make life a little easier for poor people? Why not have free child care, a negative income tax where people who earn less than the poverty level actually are paid an income, and other ways of helping poor people move out of poverty? To which the conservatives usually say that government involvement is costly and inefficient.

You can see that we have a long way to go before the idea of outlawing poverty becomes accepted, even though it's a good idea and we should all commit ourselves to outlawing poverty and making America a more comfortable place to live for all Americans. But what do you think?

What Social Workers Do to Help Clients Move out of Poverty

1. Social workers help clients in a financial crisis receive their full entitled financial, housing, child care, and medical benefits from public welfare programs.

2. Social workers help clients receive retraining and additional education so they can enter the workforce and go off public welfare. They also help clients prepare for the workplace and teach clients without prior work experience how to interview, write resumes, dress, and accomplish the other necessities of successful employment. And they prepare clients for the reality of receiving income with deductions for taxes and social security so that the initial check they receive isn't a disincentive.

3. Social workers provide support, encouragement, and more intensive counseling when needed to help clients who are too depressed or anxious to cope with children, retraining, and the other realities of life to move into the workplace just yet.

4. Social workers help clients learn to develop budgets and live on less income than they may be accustomed to.

5. Social workers help clients receive food stamps so they can purchase necessary food items and locate other food programs that provide enough basic quality food for a family to subsist on.

6.   They help clients learn to use public transportation and receive reduced monthly passes to use buses, subways, and trains in local communities.

7.   They help clients find support groups where other people in poverty provide support, encouragement, and ideas that help clients cope with and ultimately remove themselves from poverty.

8.   Social workers help clients find low-cost or publicly subsidized housing.

9.   They help clients with problems related to children. Poverty often has a negative impact on children and the data suggest that children in poverty are at much greater risk for social and emotional problems. By helping clients with children, social workers often prevent social and emotional problems experienced by some children in poverty.

You Be the Social Worker

Lilly Hanes is a 23-year-old single mother of three children. Lilly is addicted to crack cocaine and has had her children removed from the home. To get her children back, Lilly has undergone the arduous task of dealing with her addiction and has successfully completed treatment. After a year of being clean, Lilly has successfully applied to have custody of her children returned to her. By all indications, Lilly is a caring and nurturing mother, but Lilly wants to stay home and raise her children whereas the welfare department insists that she enter a job retraining program and become part of the workforce. The department believes that working mothers should provide their children with positive values about work and that the burden of caring for children should not exclusively be that of taxpayers. They also believe that mothers who fail to enter the workforce and instead become welfare mothers often begin a cycle of welfare dependence that may go on for many generations. In an effort to reduce welfare payments that have skyrocketed in many states, the welfare department sought child support from the children's father, who is now reluctantly paying $200 a month to the county welfare department. The father's portion is included as part of Lilly's public assistance allocation saving the state $200 a month.

Lilly insists that going to work will just mean that the negative influences of a child day-care center will be passed on to her children and that the cost of child care will outweigh the benefit of working. Lilly also points out that because she'll earn more than state guidelines allow, by working she'll lose her state medical insurance (Medicaid) and that it's unlikely an employer will offer Lilly a private medical plan she can afford. Lilly believes she is doing everything to raise her children in the correct way. As a stay-at-home mother she will do her children much more good than if she works. On the other hand, the welfare department believes it isn't responsible for the problems of Lilly's life and is only responsible to help Lilly get back on her feet. The department believes that many single mothers work, support their children, and do an excellent job of raising them with good values.

(Continued)

(Continued)

This problem would not exist, according to the local welfare rights organization, if America had a child assistance program similar to that of Canada. In the Canadian system, all families receive a stipend (called a child tax benefit) paid for by the federal government and based on income. Families need not declare poverty or sign up for welfare benefits. The stipend is based entirely on the family's past year's income as reported on their federal tax return. In Lilly's case, she would receive a child stipend for three children of $853 a month. Canada has universal health insurance, so Lilly wouldn't need to apply for Medicaid. If she needs more money, and she probably does, she can work or apply for temporary assistance and seek retraining or higher education. In this system it *does* pay to work, because Lilly can keep all of her benefits if she earns less than $23,000 a year (Canadian Revenue Service, 2005).

The Canadian system is somewhat similar to what has been called a negative income tax in America. In the negative income tax approach, anyone below a certain income wouldn't pay taxes but would actually have a tax paid to them. This redistribution of wealth approach has been very controversial because many people worry that it would encourage massive taxpayer fraud or put money in the hands of those who really don't need it. The Canadian system directly helps children. To qualify, you must have children and be below a certain income. The assumption of the plan is that the money given by the government to families will either be used directly for children or will pay for children to have clothing, books, and other benefits that have a positive effect on the country. Given Canada's low crime rate and high educational and health standards, they might be right. What do you think?

Questions

1. Whose argument do you think is stronger: Lilly's, that she stay home and raise her children, or the welfare department's, that Lilly enter the workforce and teach her children, through example, the value of working? Why do you feel this way?

2. The Canadian plan sounds awfully good. Why do you think America has failed to implement either a child tax benefit or free health insurance for everyone?

3. Lilly will always be at risk of becoming drug addicted if the stress in her life is too great. Which choice, raising her children and welfare dependence or working and raising her children without outside help is more stressful in your opinion?

4. How do you think multigenerational welfare dependence works, and who among welfare recipients do you think are most likely to become welfare dependent?

5. Welfare was originally developed to meet the temporary needs of people because of illness, disability, or unemployment. Can you anticipate a group of people who might have to be on welfare despite their desire not to be? Who are they, and why might they require long-term help?

Summary

This chapter discusses the cause and amount of poverty in America and the social programs developed to help poor people move out of poverty. Several case studies describe the ways social workers help clients out of poverty and the conflicting ideas clients and public welfare organizations have about the best way to do this. The chapter shows the role of social workers in helping clients cope with poverty and move out of it. There is also a discussion of the various ways people think about reducing poverty through redistributing wealth from the rich to the poor, and the approach used by Canada where child tax benefits are given to all Canadians with children whose income falls below a certain level as reported on their income tax returns.

Questions to Determine Your Frame of Reference

1. Many Americans believe that poverty is the fault of the poor person. If poor immigrants can come to America, work hard, and make a good living, then native-born Americans who are poor are usually too lazy to do anything about their situation. What do you believe and why?

2. The welfare system in America has been accused of treating poor people badly as a form of discouraging welfare dependence. What do you think?

3. Compassionate conservatives believe that the poor should be helped, but that all help should be provided by churches and private charities and that government should get out of the poverty business. What do you believe and why?

4. Welfare agencies are often cumbersome to deal with, slow, and make many errors. But they operate on rules set down by the government and are not supposed to discriminate against any group of people. This, many argue, is why government must be involved in poverty issues because churches and private organizations may discriminate against certain people because of race, religion, age, and other reasons. What do you believe?

5. What should be done to help people who are defined as being in the culture of poverty? Support your arguments with compelling evidence.

Internet Source

Hudson writes an intriguing and timely chapter (Chapter 8) on how to end poverty in the United States.

1. Hudson, W. (1996). *Economic security for all: How to end poverty in the United States.* Retrieved from http://inlet.org/esp//toc.htm

Children in Difficulty 6

The Child Welfare System and Professional Social Work With Abused, Neglected, and Emotionally Troubled Children and Their Families

The Serious Problems of Child Abuse and Neglect

Child physical and sexual abuse and neglect are very serious problems in America. Social work has been at the forefront of the movement to protect children from abuse. Most child protection workers in public child welfare agencies are social workers, many of them trained at the MSW level. To show the seriousness of abuse and neglect of children, the following data are a national summary of information provided by the National Clearing House on Child Abuse and Neglect Information, a program of the U.S. Department of Health and Human Services, Administration for Children and Families (2004).

The National Clearing House estimated that in the United States, 896,000 children were determined to be victims of child abuse or neglect in 2002. The rate of victimization per 1,000 children in the national population has dropped from 13.4 children in 1990 to 12.3 children in 2002, showing either some progress or fewer investigations. The report notes that 60% of child victims experienced neglect, almost 20% were physically abused, 10% were sexually abused, and 7% were emotionally maltreated. In addition, almost 20% were associated with "other" types of maltreatment based on specific state laws and policies. Children aged from birth to 3 years had the highest rates of victimization at 16.0 per 1,000 children. Girls were slightly more likely to be victimized than boys.

REPORTS OF CHILD ABUSE AND NEGLECT

In 2002, an estimated total of 2.6 million referrals concerning the welfare of approximately 4.5 million children were made to Child Protective

Services (CPS) agencies throughout the United States. Of these, an estimated two thirds (1.8 million) were accepted for investigation or assessment and one third were not accepted. Nonacceptance doesn't mean that abuse and neglect didn't exist, but the decision not to investigate may have been determined by agency policy or lack of staff.

More than half (56.5%) of all reports that alleged child abuse or neglect were made by professionals, including educators, law enforcement and legal personnel, social service personnel, medical personnel, mental health personnel, child daycare providers, and foster care providers. Nonprofessionals such as friends, neighbors, and relatives submitted approximately 43.6% of reports. About 30% of the reports included at least one child who was found to be a victim of abuse or neglect. Sixty-one percent of the reports were found to be unsubstantiated (including being intentionally false); the remaining reports were closed for additional reasons.

FATALITIES

In 2002, an estimated 1,400 children died because of abuse or neglect. Three fourths (76%) of the children who were killed were younger than 4 years old; 12% were 4 to 7 years old; 6% were 8 to 11 years old; and 6% were 12 to 17 years old. Infant boys (younger than 1 year old) had the highest rate of fatalities, nearly 19 deaths per 100,000 boys of the same age in the national population. Infant girls (younger than 1 year old) had a rate of 12 deaths per 100,000. The overall rate of child fatalities was 2 deaths per 100,000 children. One third of child fatalities were attributed to neglect. Physical abuse and sexual abuse also were major contributors to fatalities. Some researchers believe that the death rate would be much higher if the reason for death were indirectly related to abuse and neglect. Many poorly clothed and sheltered children develop illnesses which may be fatal, but the cause of death isn't directly attributable to abuse or neglect but to the illness itself.

PERPETRATORS

More than 80% of all abuse and neglect perpetrators were the parents. Other relatives accounted for 7%, and unmarried partners of parents accounted for 3% of the perpetrators. The remaining perpetrators included persons with other (e.g., camp counselor, school employee, etc.) or unknown relationships to the child victims. Female perpetrators, who were mostly mothers, were typically younger than male perpetrators, who were mostly fathers. Women also comprised a larger percentage (58%) of all perpetrators than men (42%). Of all parents who were perpetrators, less than 3% were associated with sexual abuse. Of all perpetrators of sexual abuse, nearly 29% were other relatives, and nearly one fourth were in nonrelative or non-child-caring roles.

SERVICES

Approximately 59% of the victims and 31% of the nonvictims received some type of service as a result of an investigation or assessment. Additional analyses indicated that children who were prior victims of maltreatment were more than 80% more likely to receive services than first-time victims. Children with multiple types of maltreatment were more than 80% more likely to receive services than children with only one type of recorded maltreatment. Services included both in-home and foster-care services. Almost one fifth of child victims of abuse or neglect were placed in foster care. About 4% of nonvictims also experienced a removal—usually a short-term placement during the course of the investigation.

TYPES OF VIOLENCE TO CHILDREN

In the National Family Violence Survey conducted by Straus and Gelles (1990), it was estimated that 110 out of every 1,000 children in the general population experience severe violence by their parents and that 23 in 1,000 experience very severe or life-threatening violence. Severe violence was defined as kicking, biting, punching, hitting, beating up, threatening with a weapon, or using a knife or gun (Sedlack, 1997, p. 178). Very severe violence results in serious bodily damage to a child. Because lower income families are much more likely to have abuse reported by an outside party than are more affluent families, it was estimated by Straus and Gelles (1990) that inclusion of potential abuse by more affluent families could raise the actual amount of abuse by 50%.

RUNAWAYS AS A RESULT OF ABUSE

When the home situation becomes extremely abusive, children may run away. A study by Finkelhor, Hotaling, and Sedlack (2000) indicates that about 133,000 children run away from home each year and, while away, stay in insecure and unfamiliar places. The same study reveals that almost 60,000 children were "thrown out" of their homes. Almost 140,000 abused and neglected children were reported missing to the police, whereas 163,000 children were abducted by one parent in an attempt to permanently conceal the whereabouts of the child from the other parent. These additional data suggest that the impact of abuse and neglect often leads to children being abandoned or running away to other unsafe environments where they may experience additional harm.

InfoTable 6.1 The Relationship Between Family Income and Child Abuse

In her study of the factors that influence multiple forms of child abuse and neglect, Sedlack (1997) reports that family income is a strong factor. She notes that

compared to children whose families had incomes of $30,000 a year or more, children from families with incomes below $15,000 per year were found to have:

1. 21 times greater risk of physical abuse.

2. More than 24 times the risk of sexual abuse.

3. Between 20 and 162 times the risk of physical neglect (depending on the children's other characteristics).

4. More than 13 times greater risk of emotional maltreatment.

5. 16 times greater risk of multiple maltreatment, and

6. Between 78 and 97 times greater risk of educational neglect. (Sedlack, 1997, p. 171)

Although child abuse is frequently reported against young children, the problem of adolescent abuse is often underestimated. Unfortunately, Child Protective Services (CPS), the public agency responsible for investigating child abuse and neglect, frequently bypasses adolescents because they are considered to be less "at risk" and have more options than younger children. Because it is believed that adolescents are able to leave the house until the parent/caretaker "calms down," they are not considered as helpless as younger children. However, many of the child prostitutes or children involved in alcohol and drug abuse are victims of physical or sexual abuse and neglect at home. Adolescents may have more options than younger children, but they are not necessarily positive ones. Adolescent abuse remains a serious problem that deserves much more attention and action.

Legal Definitions of Abuse and Neglect

Each state can develop definitions of child abuse and neglect by the agencies charged with protecting children at the local level. However, most states use the following federal guidelines of the Office of Child Development in the Department of Health and Human Services (Feller, 1992):

Physical Abuse and Neglect: An abused or neglected child is a child whose physical or mental health or welfare is harmed or threatened by the acts or omissions of his parent or other person responsible for his welfare. Harm to a child's health or welfare can occur when the parent or other person responsible for a child's welfare: 1) Inflicts, or allows to be inflicted upon the child, physical or mental injury, including injuries sustained as a result of excessive corporal punishment; 2) commits or allows to be committed, against the child, a sexual offense, as defined by state law; 3) fails to supply the child with adequate food, clothing, shelter, education (as defined by state law), or health care, though financially able to do so or offered financial or other reasonable means to do so. Adequate health care includes any medical or non-medical remedial health care permitted or authorized under state law; 4) abandons the child, as defined by state law; 5) fails to provide the child with adequate supervision or guardianship by specific acts or omissions of a similarly serious nature requiring the intervention of the child protective service of a court.

Sexual Abuse: Sexual abuse is defined as a sexual assault on, or the sexual exploitation of, a minor. Sexual abuse includes a broad range of behaviors and may consist of many acts over a long period of time (chronic molestation, for example) or a single incident. Victims range in age from less than one year through adolescence. Sexual assault includes: rape, incest, sodomy, oral copulation, penetration of genital or anal opening by a foreign object, and child molestation. It also includes lewd or lascivious conduct with a child under the age of 14 years which may apply to any lewd touching if done with the intent of arousing or gratifying the sexual desires of either the person involved or the child. Sexual exploitation includes conduct or activities related to pornography depicting minors and promoting prostitution by minors.

The Impact of Child Physical Abuse and Neglect

GENERAL INDICATORS

Laurence Miller (1999) reports the following indicators of Post Traumatic Stress Disorder (PTSD) in child victims of abuse who have been traumatized:

1) High levels of anxiety and hyper-vigilance causing the child's nervous system to constantly be on alert; 2) irritability, denial, intrusive thoughts which create panic attacks; 3) nightmares with similar themes of violence; 4) impaired concentration and memory lapses; 5) withdrawal and isolation; 6) acting-out, repetitive play and self-blame; 7) foreshortened future (where the abused child believes that they will live a short length of time); 8) regression; 9)

periods of amnesia; 10) turning the trauma into physical illnesses including headaches, dizziness, heart palpitations, breathing problems, and stomach aches. (p. 32)

Dodge, Bates, and Petit (1990) offer evidence that physical abuse in early childhood often leads to aggressive behavior in victims. The authors report a three-fold increase in the risk to become abusive in children who have witnessed abuse in their families and a significant increase in the way these children incorrectly view the hostile intent of others. Children who have been abused suffer from an inability to solve personal problems (Dodge et al., 1990). Widom (1989) notes that individuals who have been identified by juvenile courts as abuse victims as children are 42% more likely than controls to perpetuate the cycle of violence by committing violent acts as adults.

Glicken (2003, 2004b) reports that childhood victims of physical and sexual abuse are far more likely to enter into relationships with people who have themselves been abused or who will abuse them. This frequently ensures the continuation of violence in relationships. Physical abuse of adult partners and children often transitions into sexual abuse, particularly when substances are used and impulse control is at its lowest.

The emotional harm to children who have witnessed domestic violence or who have been victims of abuse includes severe life-long depression, rages that translate into panic and anxiety disorders, substance abuse, underemployment or difficulty working, sexual disorders, low self-esteem, prostitution, and continued rage reactions and difficulty controlling anger. Children who have been physically abused are sometimes likely to harm other children as well (Glicken, 2003).

Child Sexual Abuse

Sexual abuse of a child may surface through a broad range of physical, behavioral, and social symptoms. Some of these symptoms, taken separately, may not be caused by sexual abuse. They are listed below as a guide and should only be considered as being caused by abuse when there are no other reasons to explain the behavior.

A child may report sexual activities to a friend, classmate, teacher, friend's mother, or other trusted adult. The disclosure may be direct or indirect (e.g., "I know someone . . ."; "What would do you do if . . . "; "I heard something about somebody . . ."). It is not uncommon for the disclosure of chronic or acute sexual abuse to be delayed, or the child may wear torn, stained, or bloody underclothing that are discovered at school or a friend's home. The child may have an injury/disease (e.g., vaginal trauma, sexually transmitted disease) that is unusual for a specific age group and can only be contracted by sexual activity. This may have happened before, and knowledge of the child's medical history is very important (Brokenburr, personal communication, April 13, 1994; DePanfillis & Salus, 1992). These injuries or diseases often have discrepancies or are inconsistent with medical evaluation when parents or caretakers try to give explanations. Uneven teeth may also be a sign of sexual abuse, particularly in younger children, because it might suggest prolonged oral sex.

Another indicator of child sexual abuse is pregnancy. Pregnancy of a minor, regardless of age, does not constitute reasonable suspicion of sexual abuse because it may be the result of consensual sex between minors close in age. This activity might be considered a reason for prosecution of statutory rape, although consensual sex between minors is less frequently prosecuted in most states. However, when the pregnancy is the result of force or coercion, or when there is a significant age difference between the minor and her partner, it may suggest sexual abuse and it must be reported. All sexual abuse of minors must be reported. It is the responsibility of CPS and the courts to determine whether sexual abuse has taken place.

BEHAVIORAL INDICATORS OF SEXUAL ABUSE

Some specific behavioral indicators in children who have been sexually abused include the following (DePanfilis & Salus, 1992; Kessler & Hyden, 1991): (a) age-inappropriate understanding of sexual terms and inappropriate, unusual, seductive, or aggressive sexual behavior with peers and adults; (b) extreme curiosity about sexual matters or sexual areas of the body in self and others; (c) repeated concerns about homosexuality (particularly in boys who have been molested by a male perpetrator); (d) fear of the child's parents or caretakers as well as fear of going home; (e) eating disorders (e.g., overeating, eating too little, or aversion to certain foods); (f) school problems or significant changes in school performance (e.g., attitudes in class and/or grades); (g) false maturity or age-inappropriate behaviors such as bed-wetting and thumb-sucking; (h) sleep problems including nightmares, fear of falling asleep, fretful sleep patterns, or sleeping very long hours; (i) enuresis (bed wetting), which may be a defense against the perpetrator molesting the child at night; (j) significant changes in behavior that seem new and abrupt; (k) an inability to concentrate and withdrawal from activities and friends; and (l) a preoccupation with death.

The guilt and shame of the child victim and the frequent involvement of parents, stepparents, friends, or other persons caring for the child make it very difficult for children to come forward to report sexual abuse. Despite these problems, as public awareness develops and as children are taught more about sexual abuse in school, reports of sexual abuse made to CPS continue to increase.

Often a child who does seek help is accused of making up the story because people often cannot believe that a well-liked or respected member of the community is capable of sexual abuse. Because it is the word of the child against that of an adult, the child may give in to pressure from parents or caretakers and recant (take back) the accusation of sexual abuse. This happens because the child may feel guilty and frightened about turning in the abuser or breaking up the family and, consequently, might withdraw the complaint. This process leads many child protective workers and law enforcement officers to be skeptical about a child's complaint of sexual abuse, particularly in children who may appear manipulative or who have had prior disagreements with parents. Recanting an accusation of sexual abuse may leave the child feeling helpless and guilty about causing so much trouble for the family. The reality of sexual abuse is that without third-party confirmation or someone else reporting the abuse, the child often feels committed to keep the abuse secret. To reinforce the desire to keep the abuse secret, the abuser may use shame, fear, and actual threats with the child. If the abuser is a parent, the child may worry that reporting the parent will result in foster care and the abusing parent being sent to jail. These and other concerns are often repeatedly told to the victim by the perpetrator until the child victim is more concerned about the results of reporting the abuse than the actual abuse itself.

PROBLEMS RELATED TO SEXUAL ABUSE IN ADOLESCENTS

The following behavioral problems might be related to older children and adolescents who have been sexually abused: (a) poor hygiene or excessive bathing; (b) poor relations with friends and peers and poor interpersonal skills; (c) isolation, loneliness, withdrawn behavior, and depression; and (d) acting out, running away, and aggressive, antisocial, or delinquent behavior.

Children who have been sexually abused often have school problems that might include frequent absences, behavioral problems in the classroom, falling asleep in class, and drawings and stories told by the child that might suggest severe inner turmoil. Additional school-related problems might include a sudden and unusual decline in academic performance, the unwillingness to undress and shower in public for gym classes, or an unwillingness to be involved in sports or other activities requiring close physical contact with others. Prostitution or sexual acting out may also suggest sexual abuse. Children who have been sexually abused often suffer from school phobias and are afraid of coming to school for fear that the family may be broken up because of the abuse. Once home from school, the child may worry that he or she will be alone in the world. However, care must be taken not to assume sexual abuse just because any of the symptoms listed here may be noted in the child's behavior. Any of these symptoms may indicate other problems not related to sexual abuse (Brokenburr, personal communication, 1994; Kessler & Hyden, 1991).

Incest and Intrafamilial Abuse

The legal definition of *incest* is sexual activity between persons who are blood-related. Intrafamilial sexual activity refers to sexual contact between family members not related by blood (stepparents, boyfriends, etc.). In most reported cases, the father or another man acting as the parent are the initiators, with girls as the most frequent victims:

> The child's sex was significantly related to the risk of sexual abuse. However, after taking other important predictors into account, the child's sex was also related to risk in two other important categories (i.e., physical neglect and multiple maltreatment). In all cases, females were more at risk than males . . . and most at risk between ages 15–17. (Brown & Brown, 1997, p. 168)

However, boys are also victims much more often than previously has been believed. As Sedlack (1997, p. 168) notes, boys may be more at risk of multiple forms of abuse at a younger age than girls. There is reason to believe that the younger the age of onset of sexual abuse, the more harmful and long-lasting the impact of the abuse tends to be. The initial sexual abuse may occur at any age, from infancy through adolescence. However, the largest number of cases involve females aged 15 to 17. Sexual abuse may be followed by demands for secrecy and/or threats of harm if the secret is revealed. The child may fear disgrace, hatred, or blame for breaking up the family if the secret is revealed. Regardless of how innocent or trivial the first attempt to sexually approach a child may seem, sexual coercion tends to be repeated and escalates over time. The child may eventually accept the blame for the abuse, believing he or she somehow provoked it.

Repressed Memory Syndrome

For some victims of child sexual abuse, symptoms related to the abuse may carry forward into adulthood and can be very serious and require treatment. Symptoms related to child sexual abuse are particularly serious in adult victims who have been unable to confide in others about the abuse. Common adult symptoms of child sexual abuse include the following: (a) depression with suicidal attempts, (b) anxiety with panic attacks, (c) sleep and eating disorders, (d) generalized poor health and psychosomatic problems, (e) drug and alcohol abuse, (f) repeated failed relationships and multiple marriages by an early age, (g) sexual acting out, and (h) an aversion to sexual contact and severe intimacy problems.

Because a number of helping professionals in the late 1980s and early 1990s treating clients with many of these symptoms began to suspect child sexual abuse, even when their clients denied that it had taken place, many helping professionals began to believe that abuse had taken place and that the memory of the abuse had been repressed by the client. The concept of *repressed memory* suggested that the abuse was so highly traumatic that the child repressed any memory of it, even though the abuse may have occurred repeatedly and over a long period of time.

To support the belief that many adults who were seeking treatment for nonspecific emotional problems that didn't seem to improve with time or with multiple therapists had been sexually abused as children, a number of helping professionals began looking at the PTSD literature, particularly the reports of traumatic events that occurred during wartime and in workplace accidents (Glicken, 1986e). In these two situations, repression or memory loss were not uncommon, and therapists began to suspect child sexual abuse in their clients in ever-increasing numbers. Denials of abuse by parents were frequent and, in time, the idea of repressed memory began to decline in popularity as a reason for many of the symptoms noted in adult victims of child sexual abuse. In fact, a number of critics of the notion of repressed memory believed that therapists encouraged false memories of events that had never taken place. These critics pointed to the multiple reasons for serious adult problems, and stated that sexual abuse is such a powerful event in a child's life that the child was unlikely to repress the memory of the event.

Still, for a number of troubled adults in our society, child sexual abuse remains the reason for many serious emotional problems. Although we may never know the absolute reason for many of the problems that plague adults throughout their lives, it seems reasonable to believe that incest and other forms of child sexual abuse may be important reasons for continued difficulty. One maxim of therapy is that when a client sees a number of therapists and fails to improve, the underlying reasons for the problems are serious and often difficult to determine. Denial and repression are powerful mechanisms, and many people have repressed painful memories and events from their past to allow them to function reasonably well as adults. In time, the weight of these repressed events tends to have a negative impact, particularly when the adult is experiencing other forms of stress in his or her life. Although it is wise not to jump to conclusions regarding the cause of long-term adult unhappiness, it is also wise not to discount the possibility of sexual abuse in childhood. The trained and objective social worker always tries to collect information about a client's past in a way that doesn't permit the therapist to influence that information. However, the process of remaining objective is complex, and even

InfoTable 6.2	The Perpetrators of Incest

Brown and Brown (1997) report that incest has been attributed to many factors, including "dysfunctional relationships, chemical abuse, sexual problems and social isolation" (p. 336). They explain that men commit incestuous acts because they

> find sexual contact with a child emotionally gratifying, because they are capable of being sexually aroused by a child, because they are unable to receive sexual stimulation and emotional gratification from adults, and because they are not deterred by the social convention and the inhibitors against having sexual relations with a child. (p. 337)

Brown and Brown (1997) note further characteristics of men who sexually abuse children. These men often have poor impulse control, have low feelings of self-worth, have poor tolerance for frustration, and seek quick gratification of their sexual needs (p. 337). Furthermore, incest perpetrators are often described as angry individuals who do not learn from prior experience, have addictive personalities, experience low levels of guilt for their behavior, and tend to lie and be manipulative. Brown and Brown suggest that these men share three deviant attributes:

> 1) They tend to believe in the concept of male sexual entitlement, 2) perceive children as sexually attractive and motivated to experience sex, 3) and minimize harm caused by their sexual abuse. . . . [These characteristics] could prevent offenders from developing appropriate self-controls when presented with opportunities to offend. (p. 337)

very good social workers, out of concern for the client and frustration that treatment doesn't seem to be helping, may see child sexual abuse as a cause of an adult's emotional problems when it may not exist.

On the other side of the controversy are the professionals who point out that we should be studying the lives of adults who have been sexually abused as children but live reasonably normal, well-functioning, and productive lives. These resilient people, so the argument goes, can tell us a great deal about the way most people who have been abused deal with trauma. These professionals also suggest that the vast majority of adults abused as children live reasonably normal lives, and that by only studying the lives of adults with problems related to the abuse, we've developed an inaccurate notion of its impact. Furthermore, we've done too little to understand why one victim of abuse recovers whereas another may continually suffer its consequences. Some workers in the field believe that the resilient abuse victim experiences a combination of positive factors that might include very good coping skills, supportive families, a network of friends, spiritual and religious convictions, early intervention related to the abuse, and exceptionally good problem-solving skills. These notions remain to be tested, and we clearly need to do far more long-term research on the pervasive impact of child sexual abuse on adult victims. It stands to reason that most people, however resilient they may be, will suffer some ill effects of abuse, although the symptoms may be more subtle. It's difficult to believe that abuse victims will not experience intimacy problems or that their relationships will not suffer. (Resilience is more widely apparent in people than we may have initially thought, and the stories of those who display this quality are inspiring and touching [Glicken, 2006]).

The Organizations That Provide Services for Child Abuse

The primary organization working to investigate, treat, and prevent child abuse are the public sector organizations generally known as child protective services (CPS). These organizations are legal entities, often at the city or county level, with the right to remove children from their homes if abuse is found to exist and endangers the child. CPS agencies receive state and federal funding and must use standards of practice that meet state and federal guidelines. The following is taken from the 2005 State of Texas description of the investigation phase of protecting children where an accusation of abuse has been made:

> Child Protective Services caseworkers investigate reports of child abuse or neglect in order to determine whether any child in the referred family has been abused or neglected. In addition, caseworkers assess critical areas of individual and family functioning to determine whether any child in the referred family is at risk of abuse or neglect; and initiate protective services for children who need protection. To determine whether any child in the family has been abused or neglected and is still at risk of abuse or neglect, the investigative worker may interview family members and appropriate collateral sources. At the end of the investigation, staff must assign a disposition to each allegation identified for the investigation. (Texas Department of CPS, 2005, p. 1)

Law enforcement is often the first organization to note child abuse, either through contact with the public or because of domestic violence complaints that show evidence of child abuse or child endangerment. CPS would be called in if this were the case. Social workers often work for law enforcement and may do an initial investigation and help make appropriate referrals.

Hospitals and other health care facilities are key organizations where child abuse is found, and social workers working in emergency rooms or with doctor's groups often determine that child abuse may exist and contact CPS.

School social workers are often asked by teachers to help determine whether child abuse may have occurred, and are often the school personnel who contact CPS. Social workers, doctors, nurses, teachers, and psychotherapists in private practice are mandated reporters, which means that they are legally obligated to report child abuse.

The Role of Social Work in Treating and Preventing Child Abuse

Social work is the major field that investigates accusations of child abuse and neglect. Child protective workers are often trained social workers with advanced degrees. Their job consists of investigating complaints of child abuse, making recommendations regarding removal of children from the home, placing children in suitable foster homes until parents receive help and children can be returned, and testifying in court when child abuse is so severe that legal punishment is called for. Child protective workers supervise foster homes, find foster homes, and provide treatment to abused children and their families.

Social workers provide help to children who have been abused throughout their lives. The help can be in the form of psychotherapy, support, and help with social issues such as work and education. In many ways, social workers are the front line of help to children and adults who have suffered from childhood physical and sexual abuse and neglect.

Social workers serve in community- and state-wide programs to prevent child abuse. They also work in advocacy groups to protect the rights of children, help in the development of legislation, and are involved in research activities on a number of issues related to child abuse.

Social Work With a Female Child Victim of Sexual Abuse

The following case is based on one first reported in Glicken and Sechrest (2003, pp. 120–121), which also contains valuable chapters dealing with family violence and sexual abuse.

Joan is a 10-year-old Caucasian girl who was molested by a stranger on the way home from school. The molestation included oral sex and intercourse with ejaculation. Joan was taken to a hospital emergency room by a police officer, who was called to the scene by children who had found Joan naked in some bushes in a park near the school. Joan was highly agitated and unable to give a description of the perpetrator. She was immediately taken to a local emergency room, where personnel who were trained in working with sexual abuse examined Joan for signs of rape, sexually transmitted diseases, and pregnancy. A rape kit was used upon initial examination. The kit included the equipment to place hair, semen samples, and other physical evidence into an evidence box witnessed by an officer of the law. The rape kit has proven to be very useful in treating the physical aspects of rape and in providing DNA and other physical evidence against rapists.

(Continued)

(Continued)

Joan remained in the hospital for 3 days in a special unit for sexually abused children. She was given intensive crisis intervention by a hospital social worker and treated for damage to the vaginal area and cuts and bruises on her body. Test results indicated that she was HIV negative but that she was given syphilis by the perpetrator. Successful treatment with antibiotics was begun immediately in the hospital for the syphilis. She will be retested for HIV in 6 months because tests done soon after intercourse are not always accurate.

During her stay in the hospital, Joan received emergency crisis counseling from a hospital social worker. The focus of the treatment was on helping her understand that the molestation wasn't her fault and that there was nothing she could have done to prevent it. Her parents were told not to emphasize the molestation or to treat her differently because of the rape. Joan continued treatment with a clinical social worker in private practice after she left the hospital. During the first few weeks after the attack, Joan lost her appetite, was often depressed and tearful, and appeared very withdrawn to her parents. She returned to school, and although she was the object of some very mean-spirited ridicule and kidding from some of the boys, who said that she enjoyed the experience, Joan has begun to return to her old self. She is doing well again in school and her mood swings have subsided.

The social worker seeing her has been warm and supportive, allowing Joan to talk freely about any subject she wants to discuss. The social worker has also made certain that friends accompany Joan when she goes anywhere because she still has fearful moments. Hoping that she might benefit from a group experience, the social worker referred Joan to a self-help group for girls in her age group who have been molested. Joan feels that she is lucky to have survived her experience as well as she has, because many of the girls in the group seem far more troubled than she is for reasons that relate to their many years of violent molestation by family members. The girls have formed a bond with one another, and Joan continues going to the group because she feels that she can help some of the more troubled girls. Joan used to fantasize about marriage and to play games about love and romance with her friends, but she has stopped doing that. These things seem unachievable to her now and she would rather focus her energies on schoolwork and planning a career that will provide enough money for her to live without the help of a man. She thinks the physical things that were done to her were "disgusting" and doesn't think she will ever be able to do them again, even with a man whom she loves.

Discussion of the Case

Joan has suffered a serious trauma. Like most traumas, time, good parenting, and counseling may help heal some of the damage done. No one knows for certain if she'll ever be able to enjoy sexual intimacy or to trust a man in a loving relationship. Even one significant trauma can have a lifelong negative impact. She may be someone who is very successful in her career but much less successful in relationships. She may suffer periodic and unexplained episodes of depression that alternate with anxiety and panic attacks. These symptoms are often present as an aftermath of child molestation and rape.

Or she may come out of the experience, as some resilient children do, fairly unscathed. Continued treatment is certainly in order, and her parents must never subtly treat her as if she's fragile. Finally, work with the children in her school is important. Considerable harm is done to children like Joan when classmates mock her, ostracize her for what happened, or spread rumors about her.

We are still at the beginning stage of knowing what the most effective treatment approaches may be for children who have been sexually molested. Increasingly, the notion of early intervention with treatment approaches lacking evidence of effectiveness raises serious questions. There are some researchers who wonder if early intervention may even cause harm because it focuses attention on what happened to the child and forces the child to wonder if something is wrong with them. Tyndall (1997) suggests that the treatment goals for child sexual and incest survivors are the following: "Ameliorate the presenting symptoms; develop a realistic and factual understanding of the abusive experience; ventilation of feelings associated with the abuse; develop healthy physical, psychological and interpersonal boundaries; increase self-esteem; learn about healthy sexuality; prevent perpetration of sexual acting out" (p. 291). These seem like good goals, but the issue of when to intervene, when not to intervene, and to what extent one should intervene at all still seem to be key unresolved issues in the treatment of sexual abuse of children. Lacking convincing evidence of treatment effectiveness, social workers always need to be careful that the intervention is not overly intrusive or perpetuate a sense of "differentness" in the victim. This is admittedly a difficult task, but one that may be made with more ease if the child has a strong family who continue to treat the child as they have in the past: with support, respect, dignity, understanding, patience, and encouragement to do well in life.

InfoTable 6.3	Information About Sexual Abuse That Helps Treatment Efforts

The National Center for Child Abuse and Neglect (DePanfilis & Salus, 1992, p. 42) suggests that the following information must be obtained to assist in treatment efforts:

1. What are the names and ages of all the children in the household?

2. What are the names of the adults in the household?

3. What is the relationship of the adults to the children?

4. What incidents prompted this report?

5. Did the caller see abusive behavior firsthand?

6. Has this type of incident happened before and how often?

7. Which person is doing the abuse and against which child or children?

8. What is the relationship of the caller to the children?

9. Will the caller give their name and phone number if further information is necessary?

Social Work Intervention With Child Molestation

In the initial stage of intervention, when awareness of the molestation is made public, the child should be seen medically to determine if any physical harm has been done. Medical treatment should begin immediately and appropriate evidence gathering should take place to use in future testimony against the offender. Psychological testing and a very in-depth psychosocial history should be taken to determine emotional trauma and to plan short- and long-term treatment goals. Crisis intervention services to the child should include supportive intervention and consistent feedback assuring the child that the molestation was not the child's fault. Only very troubled people molest children. Fears of guilt or reprisal by the offender or family members need to be addressed, and the child needs to know that his or her safety is the ultimate concern of everyone providing treatment services. The perpetrator needs to be physically removed from the child's home, and contact should be stopped until the court determines that supervised contact might be resumed.

In their work for the National Center on Child Abuse and Neglect, a federal center that is part of U.S. Department of Health and Human Services, DePanfilis and Salus (1992) describe the treatment needs of children and their families. Treatment, they believe, is complex. Because the origins of the abuse have multiple explanations, many of them existing during a long period of time, the authors believe that "interventions need to address as many of the contributing factors [of abuse] as possible" (p. 61). They state that

> early research in child abuse and neglect treatment effectiveness suggests that successful treatment with maltreating families requires a comprehensive package that addresses both the intra-personal and concrete needs of all family members. . . . Recent research found that a broad range of therapeutic and other services for child sexual abuse exist including individual and group treatment, dyad treatment, family therapy, peer support groups, marital therapy, alcohol and drug counseling, client advocacy, parent's aides, education and crisis intervention. (pp. 61–62)

DePanfilis and Salus (1992, pp. 63–64) suggest that issues to be addressed in the family include: (a) the past history of abuse; (b) family attitudes toward violence; (c) problem-solving patterns; (d) anger and impulse control issues; (e) definitions of acceptable sexuality; (f) stress management, substance abuse, and patterns of abuse in families that may be historical and cross several or more generations; (g) impulse control and judgment problems within families; (h) conflicts with authority at work and in the community; (i) manipulative and self-indulgent behavior; (j) acting-out behavior with patterns of antisocial activities related to sexual and nonsexual matters; (k) demanding, controlling, and domineering behavior; and (l) a lack of the ability to trust and reduced degrees of intimacy.

Abused children still need to feel loved, and an affiliation with the family, even when the abuse is severe and prolonged, is often very important to the child. Also important is that social workers understand the following:

> It is essential to formulate specific and clear guidelines for treatment that center on survival abilities because gathering this information helps children to take pride in their accomplishments. Rebuilding self-esteem and pride is extremely important for children who have been sexually abused because the trauma permeates their identity and may leave them lacking in feelings of self-worth. (Anderson, 1997, p. 593)

You Be the Social Worker

Once again, it's time to consider yourself the social worker. In this case, you will be asked to work with a child who may have been sexually abused. The following is a short case study with some questions to help guide your answers.

Jean is a very high-functioning 9-year-old girl whose teacher noticed blood stains on her pants and, with the school nurse, discovered that Jean had blood on her panties that was not associated with menstrual bleeding but seemed to have had its origin in some type of sexual contact. Jean vigorously denied this and an interview with her serious and cooperative parents confirmed that no one in the family had been sexually molesting her. A doctor's evaluation failed to find any conclusive evidence of sexual abuse other than the doctor's suspicion that it was taking place. Lab tests and further evaluation by a specialist failed to disclose evidence of sexual abuse. There was no confirmed medical reason for the bleeding.

The social worker is at a loss. Jean is a very good student and is well-liked by her classmates and teachers. She shows no sign of the types of problems associated with sexual abuse. She is funny, has excellent social skills, has many friends, is a top-notch athlete, and was found to be emotionally healthy and stable on two psychological tests given during the evaluation. No one can find evidence of abuse, but the social worker is convinced that abuse is taking place and has promised herself to find out what's been happening to Jean. As the social worker followed Jean during the years with occasional interviews, the bright and cheerful girl turned into a sullen, rebellious, and low-achieving adolescent. She denies sexual abuse but complains that her parents are "morons who won't let me do anything. They think I'm out screwing everybody in sight when all I want is to be normal and have a good time. All this talk about being molested when I was a kid has ruined my life."

(Continued)

(Continued)

Questions

1. Is Jean right that the concern over a nonexistent molestation has made her parents overly strict and that their behavior has led to her becoming rebellious and unhappy?

2. Is there any possibility that Jean really *was* molested and that she's withholding information to protect someone, perhaps someone in the family or maybe even an older boyfriend?

3. How might we get to the truth because everyone seems to be denying that the molestation took place?

4. Changes in behavior in adolescence are common, and just because Jean seems sullen and rebellious, does this necessarily mean that she's been molested?

5. Is it possible that concerns over the years about Jean may have had a negative impact on her self-image by suggesting to her that there was something wrong when she was really quite normal?

Summary

Despite treatment efforts and more awareness of the impact of child abuse, much more must be done to correct this serious national problem. Prevention is one way to combat all forms of child abuse and neglect, and new programs must concentrate on prevention. The target population for prevention efforts includes schools, families, professionals, and communities. Far more research needs to be done in developing effective approaches to child intervention when abuse and neglect have been committed. We still know too little about effective interventions, and we may be using incorrect approaches and services that may cause harm.

Questions to Determine Your Frame of Reference

1. Why do some children experience child abuse and suffer severe problems throughout their lives, whereas other children seem to do reasonably well?

2. Can you give an explanation of why adults who have been abused as children develop abusive intimate relationships with other abuse victims?

It seems reasonable to assume that having experienced abuse, most people would be sensitive to the signs of abusive behavior in a partner and avoid those people.

3. It must be gratifying but also stressful work to help children who have been abused. Is this work you would like to do? Why or why not?

4. Do you believe it's possible for people to be so traumatized by repeated abuse that they actually can't remember it happening? Give reasons for your answer.

5. Why do you think that only some of the cases of child abuse and neglect referred to agencies are investigated?

Internet Sources

The first article, by the U.S. Department of Health and Human Services (2004), involves preventing child abuse and neglect. Next, Hopper (2004) has compiled information on child abuse with statistics and relevant data.

1. U.S. Department of Health and Human Services, National Clearing House for Child Abuse and Neglect. (2004, August 3). *Preventing child abuse and neglect.* Retrieved from http://nccanch.acf.hhs.gov/topics/prevention/index.cfm

2. Hopper, J. (2004). *Child abuse: Statistics, research and resources.* Retrieved from http://www.jimhopper.com/abstats/

Author's Note: The contribution of Ms. Doyle Brokenburr in the development of parts of this chapter is acknowledged.

The Education System in America and the Role of School Social Workers

7

> *It's no secret that the U.S. educational system doesn't do a very good job. Like clockwork, studies show that America's school kids lag behind their peers in pretty much every industrialized nation. We hear shocking statistics about the percentage of high-school seniors who can't find the U.S. on an unmarked map of the world or who don't know who Abraham Lincoln was.*
>
> —Gatto (2001, p. 1)

Schools are expected to do many things in our society. Certainly they're expected to teach children academic material that can be used to be successful in life. But additionally, schools teach children to get along, to be good citizens, to have a strong work ethic, and to help others. How well schools do is debatable because, if we know anything about schools, we know that they are not equal. The incomes of the parents whose children attend school can make a profound difference in the quality of the education these children receive and how it affects them in terms of future academic achievement and income. In 2004, only 4.5% of the children from the least affluent 25% of American families obtained a bachelor's degree, whereas 51% of the children from America's 25% most affluent families obtained this degree (Monteleone, 2004). Although public education is supposed to be an equal educational experience, as we all know, the schools in affluent American communities differ dramatically from the schools in America's poorest communities.

This difference in the quality of education places less affluent students, many of them minorities or newly immigrated, at risk educationally. Dropout rates are much higher in less affluent schools. Rates of learning are much lower. Often, teachers in less-affluent, overcrowded schools spend more time dealing with the behavioral problems of children who act out in class and less time teaching academic subjects. "No child left behind," the new aphorism of education in a field full of them, hasn't changed the equation at all. Children in affluent schools do well, whereas children in poor schools don't.

To show how race and income affect the educational experience, Coley (2001) reports the following: In 1998, 66% of Hispanic females and 60% of Hispanic males completed high school, as opposed to well more than 90% of Caucasian students. In terms of completion rate of college, usually thought to be an indicator of the quality of high school preparation, whereas 28% of Caucasian students who completed high school completed college, 16% of African American students completed college and only 10% of the Hispanic students completing high school received college degrees.

In a RAND Corporation report on factors influencing educational achievement, Lara-Cinisomo et al. (2004) found that the most important factors associated with the educational achievement of children were not race, ethnicity, or immigrant status, but rather the level of parental education, neighborhood poverty, parental occupational status, and family income. The authors also found that parents who use less discipline but greater parental warmth have children with fewer behavioral problems, regardless of ethnicity, immigrant status, or neighborhood. However, neighborhood poverty was a very strong predictor of behavior problems among young children—problems that impede school readiness. Children in poor neighborhoods, according to the researchers, are significantly more likely to exhibit anxious and aggressive behavior, regardless of parenting behavior. The authors note that living in a poor neighborhood is very stressful for young children and increases the stress levels of parents and older siblings, which indirectly increases stress in younger children. They conclude that "education policies intended to benefit racial and ethnic minorities can be more successful if policymakers focus less on racial and ethnic factors and more on socioeconomic ones. Education policies alone, when not combined with socioeconomic policies, will be less successful" (p. 1).

When schools need to function in so many different ways to make up for family problems and poverty, they often do badly. To help when children have problems in school, social workers are often available to help children and their families. The presence of social workers and other helping professionals offers children at risk an opportunity to be evaluated early in their lives so that physical, social, and emotional problems can be identified and treated. One of the problems that plagues schools in America is school violence. Because of the concern for bad behavior among some students, schools often spend an inordinate amount of valuable time making certain that violence doesn't occur. In general, they do a poor job.

InfoTable 7.1	A Parent's View of Public Education

I'm impressed with the dedication and concern of our teachers, but something is amiss. The dilution of true education and the introduction of "whole language" and "affective" curricula is not the result of grassroots efforts. Parents are not asking for values clarification and self-esteem therapy. They are not asking for kids to slowly learn on their own through osmotic "developmentally appropriate" programs. Parents and scientists are appalled with the failed New Math programs invading our schools. The problems seem to be coming from the top—from places like the NEA, the Dept. of Education, and the money-laden textbook publishers. Parents need alternatives. Some are home schooling, others are trying private schools or charter schools. But how I wish that more public schools would recognize that children can learn and gain true self-esteem in the process if only they are taught, challenged and motivated. (Lindsay, 2005, p. 1)

Sprague and Walker (2000) report that more than 100,000 students bring weapons to school each day and more than 40 students are killed or wounded with these weapons annually. The authors indicate that many students experience bullying and other behaviors that have a negative impact on how well they do in school. More than 6,000 teachers are threatened and more than 200 teachers are assaulted each year by students on school grounds, according to the authors. Schools are frequently used by gangs to recruit new gang members, and gang activities often disrupt normal classroom functioning and give students a sense of danger (Committee for Children, 1997; National School Safety Center, 1996; Walker, Colvin, & Ramsey, 1995). Crowe (1991) notes a National Institute of Education study revealing that 40% of the robberies and 36% of the assaults against urban youth took place on or near school grounds. Of the students who admit to bringing weapons to school, half say that the weapons are for protection against other youth with weapons.

The 2003 Youth Risk Survey (National Center for Injury Prevention and Control, 2004) summarized school-related violence by reporting the following data:

- 35.7% of high school students reported being in a physical fight in the past 12 months and 4% of students were injured in a physical fight seriously enough to require treatment by a doctor or nurse.
- 17.3% of high school students carried a weapon (e.g., gun, knife, or club) during the 30 days preceding the survey.
- 4.9% of high school students carried a gun during the 30 days preceding the survey.
- 14.2% of high school students had been in a physical fight on school property one or more times in the past 12 months.
- 7.7% of high school students were threatened or injured with a weapon on school property during the 12 months preceding the survey.

- 6.9% of high school students carried a weapon on school property during the 30 days preceding the survey.
- 5.4% of students had missed 1 or more days of school during the 30 days preceding the survey because they had felt too unsafe to go to school.

In a study by Peterson, Pietrzak, Speaker, and Kathryne (1998), 202 teachers, building administrators, and district administrators in 15 school districts of varying sizes from 12 states representing all geographical regions of the country shared their experiences with school violence. The authors report that most respondents had experienced some form of violence at least one or more times in the past 2 years. Of the respondents, 63% said that they had been verbally threatened or intimidated, 28% had been physically threatened or intimidated, 11% had been sexually threatened or intimidated, 68% had been verbally attacked, 9% had been physically attacked, and 55% indicated that their room, their personal property, or the school in which they worked had been seriously vandalized. Twenty-six percent of the respondents said violence was increasing or greatly increasing at the preschool level and 53% said violence was increasing or greatly increasing at the elementary level. Almost 65% of the respondents said violence was increasing at the middle school, junior high, and senior high level.

InfoTable 7.2	Invisible Kids Who Commit School Violence

Bender, Shubert, and McLaughlin (2001) suggest that most young adolescent children involved in school killings

are not the children who, traditionally, have been associated with violent acts within the schools; that is, they are not the school bullies or kids who have been previously identified as aggressive. [Instead, they are] the students who are easiest to ignore and they are using violence to offset and counteract their anonymity. They have internalized their aggression to such an extent that an explosion of violence is the result.

Bender (1999) initially used the term "invisible kids" to identify the group of kids who were the perpetrators in the random shootings in schools. This term was selected to underscore the fact that these students were generally unknown by many school personnel prior to the shooting incidents because they were not noted for overt behavior problems. On the other hand, because these perpetrators seem to be frequently identified as "nerds" or "geeks," other students may bully and pick on them rather than ignore them.

Emotionally wounded because of being shunned by other students, these students are essentially invisible to the adults in the school. Through an overtly violent act, these invisible kids seem to be demonstrating that they do have power in the school environment and that they will no longer accept a peer-imposed label of "nerd" or "geek." (p. 108)

The Reasons for Increased School Violence

In a study by Peterson et al. (1998), the primary reasons for the increase in school violence were the following:

> Lack of rules or family structure, 94%; lack of involvement or parental supervision, 94%; violence acted out by parents, 93%; parental drug use, 90%; student drug/alcohol use, 90%; violent movies, 85%; student poor self-concept/emotional disturbance, 85%; violence in television programs, 84%; nontraditional family/family structure, 83%; and gang activities, 80%. (p. 348)

In his study of school violence, Fitzpatrick (1999) came to the interesting conclusion that a major predictor of school victimization is how safe students assessed their school environments to be. He found that students in elementary and middle schools who had more negative views of the safety of their school environments were also victimized more often. Fitzpatrick (1999) believes that children who perceive dangerous environments often find themselves in the midst of those very environments and, as a result, experience a higher degree of violence. This is particularly true for elementary-aged children who may know that certain children in the school are dangerous but are unable to avoid them.

The Relationship Between Family Problems and School Acting Out

Studer (1996) writes that the family is thought to be the most violent institution in our society (Myers, 1993). Problems within the family, she notes, are often solved using aggression. Myers (1993) reports that 17% of all homicides in the United States occur within a family situation. Studer (1996) believes that when parents use harsh physical means to discipline their children, children learn that battering and physical aggression are normal ways of expressing frustration and resolving problems. Aggressive problem-solving techniques may frequently be practiced in the school setting and are reinforced when the child successfully resolves conflict through the use of aggression and intimidation. Griffin (1987) found that children who demonstrate physically aggressive and antisocial behaviors and have developmental and academic problems before age 9 display more aggressive tendencies as adults than individuals who do not demonstrate early behavioral and educational problems.

Herrenkohl and Russo (2001) suggest that child abuse and neglect reinforce a sense of distrust in children that may lead to aggressive interactions with peers and adults. The authors believe that abuse and neglect by parents model the way children are likely to interact with others. Eriksson's (1963) stages of psychosocial development include the development of trust. If a child experiences harsh physical punishment and neglect by a parent, it's possible that distrust related to hostile feelings toward the parent might result, which defines a child's interactions with others. Rutter (1987) believes that abuse and neglect by parents often lead to a sense of vulnerability in children that may cycle into aggression, and that vulnerable children sometimes use aggression as a way of coping with feelings of vulnerability and fear. Schools are one of the earliest social situations where children may feel vulnerable, inadequate, angry, less intelligent, ignored, and a host of other emotions that may result in early aggression.

In a study of teacher ratings of the causes of school violence, Petersen et al. (1998) found that the top four rated causes were: (a) lack of rules or family structure, (b) lack of involvement or parental supervision, (c) parental violence, and (d) parental drug use. Commenting on the changing structure of American families and what they consider to be the increasing deterioration of family life, the authors write:

> As the basic structure of the family disintegrates, violence among family members increases, and this domestic violence spills into the classroom (Lystad, 1985). The family must be committed to the educational process, whereas the educational structure must be committed to the family. Because the data indicate that schools need to take on roles previously played by family members, the roles of teacher and administrator must also evolve. It may be that schools will need to fill the gap in these areas for families who are unable or unwilling to become involved. (p. 353)

The idea that schools may need to fill the gap left by violent and/or deteriorating families is one frequently expressed in the literature but often criticized by educators. Educators complain that not enough training, time, or resources are available to teach academic subjects, let alone make up for deteriorating families. However, in their study of school violence, Bender et al. (2001) write, "Educators must be proactive and demand that some of the funds spent on school safety efforts be allocated to support educators' time to reflect on the emotional well-being of each student in an effort to identify the children who need some significant adult to reach out to them" (p. 109).

Petersen et al. (1998) call for a new definition of schools as "town centers" that offer a variety of services needed by deteriorating and dysfunctional families to reduce school violence. Because family life is so chaotic for many violence-prone children, the authors argue that schools must assume many of the roles previously played by family members and that the function of teachers and administrators must also change. Family disintegration, the authors argue, requires schools to take responsibility for teaching moral conduct. Education, they note, is more than "simply teaching the cognitive attributes of character development; it must also include the emotional attributes of moral maturity, such as conscience, self-respect, empathy, and self-control" (p. 350).

What Social Workers Do in Schools

The U.S. Department of Labor (2004) notes that school social workers

> provide social services and assistance to improve the social and psychological functioning of children and their families and to maximize the family well-being and academic functioning of children. Some social workers assist single parents; arrange adoptions; and help find foster homes for neglected, abandoned, or abused children. In schools, they address such problems as teenage pregnancy, misbehavior, and truancy. They also advise teachers on how to cope with problem students. (p. 1)

Social workers either work for school districts or mental health or family service agencies that contract out their services to school districts. Most school social workers receive referrals from concerned teachers and principals and are asked to assess a child's family functioning and emotional life to see if there is something outside of the school environment that may explain why a child is having trouble in school. Parents sometimes refer their children to social workers because they are concerned about the child's behavior at home. Most of the children referred for social work services at the elementary level are young boys who are either acting out in class or doing poorly academically. Sometimes children are referred because child abuse and neglect are suspected by teachers and principals. When we can, social workers see children and their families and work closely with teachers. It's a combination that has a tremendously positive outcome.

Social workers often work in special programs in schools, including programs for children who act out in class, have attention problems, or have learning difficulties. We now try and help all children with special needs in our public schools and to keep these children in regular classes (mainstreaming) so that they don't feel different from other students. Social workers are often members of a team that includes specially trained teachers, school psychologists, school counselors, and school nurses. In addition to offering social work interventions at a personal level to help children function better, social workers refer children to other agencies and make certain that services are provided in a timely and effective way. We usually also work directly with families and other social agencies.

I worked in a suburban Chicago school system and completed my first-year field placement for my MSW degree in the Seattle school system.

Without question, school social work was the most wonderful job I've ever had. My caseload was enormous—more than 400 children in the suburban Chicago area. It made me very creative in my treatment, from seeing children in groups to doing recreational work with less troubled children. Most of the children I saw improved because mobilizing families and schools to work together results in children responding positively. Of the more than 400 children I saw each year from kindergarten to eighth grade in the suburban Chicago area, I don't remember seeing more than a few girls. This is, in my opinion, because many girls don't start showing school-related problems until early adolescence. They may be having the same problems as boys, but it often isn't revealed in their school behavior. Only a few of the children I saw were truly emotionally disturbed. Most were unhappy, had low self-esteem, and had unsupportive families or teachers, and almost all of them loathed school because it was a place where, for the first time in their young lives, they experienced failure—failure in competing with others, failure to have others like them, and, worst of all, the sense that they would always be failures at whatever they did.

But they loved coming to see me because we played games, talked about nothing in particular, shot hoops when we felt like it, told jokes, and felt free to say what was on our minds. I didn't know it then, but I was practicing a positive approach to children I would later identify as the strengths approach. I thought my kids were terrific, and they thought the same thing about me. Every time I'd come to work in the morning, I'd have 10 kids hanging on my leg, begging me to let them come for social work. Being seen by a social worker had status; it meant something good, and it meant that a child was special. And they were. They got better, and many of them stayed better. A little supportive help and mentoring early in life can make all the difference in the world to a child with low self-esteem. Those of us who are lucky enough to help children in need have never had a better feeling at the end of the day than that.

I found that a few of the teachers were burned out. They would make any student feel awful. But most of the teachers were great, and I think we should be kind to teachers rather than blame them for the problems children have in school. I also think we should reward them with good salaries and give them more authority to teach in ways that inspire children. Good teachers make school social workers almost unnecessary. They handle classroom problems and have an intuitive way of knowing what troubled children need to feel better about themselves. Always? No, of course not, but much of the time. For the kids who just have too many problems because of family difficulties or other more serious issues that can't be resolved in the classroom, we have social workers and other helping professionals. If you want to have a very special time in your work and volunteer life, take the opportunity to work with the millions of children who lack a father, or have little stimulation in their lives, or who need a mentor to help them through the tough moments in life. You won't be sorry, I promise.

Reforming Public Education

In 1983, a presidential commission was formed to study the condition of education in America. The findings, *A Nation at Risk* (1983), include the following statements, many of which remain true today:

> If an unfriendly foreign power had attempted to impose on America the mediocre educational performance that exists today, we might well have viewed it as an act of war. As it stands, we have allowed this to happen to ourselves. We have even squandered the gains in student achievement made in the wake of the Sputnik challenge. Moreover, we have dismantled essential support systems which helped make those gains possible. We have, in effect, been committing an act of unthinking, unilateral educational disarmament.
>
> The people of the United States need to know that individuals in our society who do not possess the levels of skill, literacy, and training essential to this new era will be effectively disenfranchised, not simply from the material rewards that accompany competent performance, but also from the chance to participate fully in our national life. A high level of shared education is essential to a free, democratic society and to the fostering of a common culture, especially in a country that prides itself on pluralism and individual freedom. (p. 1)

Current data suggest that gains have been made in public education but that America still lags behind many industrial nations in overall student achievement. To improve the state of public education, the Public Agenda (2005) believes that five main problems need to be rectified before public education functions well:

Who controls education? Local control of education, although allowing creativity, often results in too many poorly funded, underachieving schools. Should education be controlled by the federal government, who would have uniform standards and a higher per capita child-to-teacher ratio? In countries such as France, the national government makes most of the decisions about education. "Local control means that good ideas spread more slowly and that voters may feel they can ignore problems in the community down the road" (Public Agenda, 2005, p. 1).

Improved standards. For many people, "The right strategy emphasizes higher standards for students and more accountability for schools. If a school is failing to produce results, the administration should be held accountable" (Public Agenda, 2005, p. 1). Supporters say that standardized tests motivate students and help improve academic performance, but critics believe that schools end up "teaching to the test" at the expense of other skills.

Improved critical thinking. Another set of reformers argue that children should be taught to think critically and that critical thinking, or the ability to think independently and to come up with elegant solutions to problems, is the way to make education exciting and challenging to children.

Make funding equitable. In California, a student attending the highest-poverty schools from the time of kindergarten through high school will have an estimated total of $135,654 less spent on all of his or her teachers than is spent on the K-12 teachers serving the most affluent students. A student attending the schools serving the highest numbers of Latino and African American students from kindergarten through high school will have an estimated $172,626 less spent on all of his or her teachers than is spent on the K-12 teachers in schools with the fewest Latino and African American students. This just covers salaries and doesn't include the significant difference in student-to-teacher ratio, quality of school environments, availability of computers, quality of teachers, and other resources or school safety (Education Trust West, 2005, p. 1).

Competition. A fifth approach suggests giving parents vouchers that could be used for students to attend either public or private schools. Parents could choose the school that's best for their child and, under a voucher system, public schools would be forced to improve to compete. Although this approach to improving the education of American children has many supporters, the National Education Association (NEA) takes a dim view of vouchers and says,

> Despite desperate efforts to make the voucher debate about "school choice" and improving opportunities for low-income students, vouchers remain an elitist strategy. From Milton Friedman's first proposals, through the tuition tax credit proposals of Ronald Reagan, through the voucher proposals on ballots in California, Colorado, and elsewhere, privatization strategies are about subsidizing tuition for students in private schools, not expanding opportunities for low-income children. (2005, p. 1)

In a publication of the National Parent Teachers Association (PTA), the organization notes that

> A study by the U.S. General Accounting Office (GAO) found that privately funded voucher programs do not significantly improve academic achievement for most recipients. The study examined 78 privately funded voucher programs, but focused on those in New York City, Washington, DC, and Dayton, Ohio. These findings reinforce those of an earlier study of publicly funded voucher programs in such areas as Cleveland, Milwaukee, and Florida, in which the GAO found little or no difference between the performances of voucher and public school students.
>
> Another cause of student attrition is dissatisfaction with the private schools themselves. Based on parents' reports, the private schools were less

likely than the public schools to have a nurse's office, a cafeteria, and to provide services and programs for those students with learning disabilities, or who are English-language learners. Parent satisfaction with private schools could be traced to the characteristics of the private schools that also exist in successful public schools, such as smaller class size, individual tutoring, and better communication between parents and teachers. (Connecticut PTA, 2005, p. 1)

However, Milwaukee has one of several court-approved voucher systems and the following suggests that the system has worked very well:

An analysis of the Milwaukee publicly-run voucher program by the officially appointed researcher shows the parents of "choice" kids are virtually unanimous in their opinion of the program: they love it. Parents are not only far more satisfied with their freely chosen private schools than they were with their former public schools, they participate more actively in their children's education now that they've made the move. Recently, a reanalysis of the raw data by statisticians and educational researchers from Harvard and the University of Houston found that choice students do indeed benefit academically from the program, showing significant gains in both reading and mathematics by their fourth year of participation. (Coulson, 2005, p. 1)

School Social Work With a Victim of Gang Violence in School

This case first appeared in modified form in my book concerning children who are violent at age 12 and younger (Glicken, 2004b, pp. 40–41), where I identified many of the reasons for school violence, including gang behavior in schools. The influence of gangs on younger children is significant and particularly noticeable in the school setting. Children join gangs for many reasons: a search for love; structure and discipline; a sense of belonging and commitment; the need for recognition and power; companionship, training, excitement, and activities; a sense of self-worth and status; a place of acceptance; the need for physical safety and protection; and because it's part of a family tradition when older brothers, cousins, and fathers are gang members (Glicken & Sechrest, 2003).

As dangerous as gang activity can be in schools, Schwartz (1996) writes that "gang activity at school is particularly susceptible to 'the Ostrich syndrome,' as administrators may ignore the problem. An unfortunate consequence of such denial is that opportunities to reduce violence are lost. This creates a situation where teachers do not feel supported when they impose discipline, students do not feel protected, and the violence-prone think they will not be punished" (p. 1). Schwartz (1996) offers the following suggestions for reducing potential gang activity in schools:

(Continued)

(Continued)

1. Make an accurate assessment of the existence of violence and, especially, gang activity.

2. Use all the resources in the community, including social service and law enforcement, and not just rely on school officials to deal with the problem.

3. Incorporate family services into both community and school programs.

4. Intervene early in a child's life.

5. Include not only anti-violence strategies but also positive experiences.

6. Create and communicate clearly defined behavior codes, and enforce them strictly and uniformly.

7. Prepare to engage in a long-term effort. (Schwartz, 1996, p. 5)

The Case

James is a sixth grader in a low-income area of an Eastern city of moderate size. There is a great deal of bullying and intimidation of students by classmates in James's school. Most of the children are too frightened to report the harassment and just accept it as part of the price they pay for being poor. Many of the children believe that the schools they attend are little more than warehouses—places to keep them off the streets and out of trouble. Little actual learning takes place, as a parade of new teachers present themselves weekly and then mysteriously disappear. Most of the day is spent disciplining boys who act out in class. Hardly anyone studies or takes school seriously. By age 12, many of the children believe their life path has been set and that nothing positive will ever happen to them. Their teachers reinforce this feeling of pessimism through attitudes that suggest to students that the teachers wish they were somewhere else.

James is a serious boy with serious aspirations. His parents, although desperately poor, have strong hopes for James. He thinks that if he does well in life, he can help his family leave the poverty and high level of crime in a neighborhood he has begun to despise and fear. James has a classmate by the name of Ronald who is being initiated into a gang. Ronald hates James because he represents everything that Ronald cannot be. He has decided to hurt James and has asked his older gang friends to help out.

One afternoon in school, the boys found James alone in the bathroom and severely beat him. James lay semiconscious in the bathroom for hours until he was found by a janitor who called 911. The police wondered why no one had gone looking for James and why the bathroom was unsupervised, but in a school as poorly functioning as his, these are daily occurrences and people have begun going to the restrooms in packs. The major criticism of James by his classmates was that he shouldn't have gone to the bathroom alone.

Ronald and his friends were sent to juvenile hall and were held until a hearing sent them to a juvenile facility in a different part of the state. James feels no comfort in this because he believes that he is marked for further violence by Ronald's gang friends. He feels so unsafe at school that he can hardly function, and his grades have begun to slip. James was referred to a school social worker, whose function is to be the liaison between James, his family, and the school. She also provides supportive help to James, family counseling, and advocates with the school for James and his family. With the help of the social worker, the school district is providing financial assistance to the family in lieu of a lawsuit. She has also helped the family receive money for victims of violence provided through the county attorney's office. Because of the ongoing threat to James and his family for further gang-related violence, his parents have decided to leave the community and move to a safer school for James. This has been a difficult decision but one that turned out to have a very positive impact on James. The actions of his parents and the support of the social worker touched him deeply. He has recommitted himself to school work and some of his prior feelings of optimism have returned. Like too many victims of violence, however, a core of James has been changed and he is hypervigilant and less trusting than he used to be. He knows he'll make it in life and help his family out of poverty, but he will never view the world as safe or fair. Cynicism in someone so young can go a long way to create unhappiness, even in the face of achievement, and James knows that he's changed and that he has to be tough and unsentimental about life.

Discussion

It's shameful that children most at risk for violence are often the same children who have the least protection from it. It's easy enough to blame the school district, but schools like James's former school are badly underfunded, and good teachers can't be forced to teach in schools where they feel unsafe. Many of the schools that are failing to provide either a safe environment or a sound educational experience are taken over by counties or states with little positive benefit. The fact is that like the inner cities of many urban areas of America, inner-city schools are violence-prone. Getting a sound education for the children who need it most is difficult when much of the day is spent dealing with serious acting-out behavior in the classroom. Although the solutions to school violence are varied and complex, children should not be in unsafe schools. Children showing early signs of violence need to be identified and provided services. Sometimes statistics fail to describe situations fully for children like James who grow up in high-poverty areas. In a book entitled *Kids Count Data Book* (2002), some figures might help describe the plight of children like James whose parents lack financial resources and whose lives are very much at risk as a result. In the United States in 1999, there were 12,844 deaths of children aged 1 to 14; 10,396 deaths from homicide and suicide in children aged 15 to 19; 1,514,000 teens who dropped out of school; 1,291,000 teens who dropped out of school and were not working; 18,000,000 children living with parents where no parent had full-time, year-round work; 13,500,000 children living in homes below the poverty level; and more than 9,000,000 families headed by a single parent (p. 179). These are data that beg for solutions, and until we can do a great deal better for children like James and his family, we can expect continued high levels of school violence and minimal academic standards in high-poverty, high-crime areas of the country.

You Be the School Social Worker

What would you do in the following situation? Once again, there are questions at the end of the case to help guide your thinking.

(Continued)

(Continued)

You have been placed in a school as part of your field experience in your undergraduate social work degree program. You've done well in class and you think you've learned something about human behavior and the helping process, but this is the first time you've ever seen a client. The client you get, Gary, is a sixth-grade boy, large for his age, who got into a fight with another boy during a baseball game in gym class and hit the boy over the head with a bat, causing the boy to have a concussion. Gary was immediately suspended for a month, and you've been asked to do an evaluation to determine if Gary can come back to school after his suspension. You set up a meeting with Gary and his father.

"Well, Gary," you ask, "why did you hit that boy with a bat?"

"'Cause he was bothering me," Gary replies.

"How was he bothering you?" you ask.

"Well, he kept calling me a *nigger* and telling me my mom was a *ho*."

"Oh," you say. "But shouldn't you have told the teacher?"

"Why?" Gary asks. "They say the same thing about us."

Gary's father is looking very sullen now and says, "How can you let this happen to my boy? He's a good boy. A white kid calls him names and it's my son who gets suspended? And those teachers. They just let it happen. They let them duke it out. The kid was an eighth grader and much bigger than Gary."

Now Gary looks sullen, too. "Are you ready to come back to school?" you ask.

"Yeah, I guess," he says, "but this ain't no school for black kids. They hate us here. What you gonna do about that?" *Very good question*, you think. What *are* you going to do about a school that sounds racist?

Questions

1. Gary and his father raise a very important question about a racist school. Is it your job to do something about it? Yes, absolutely. That's part of what social work does. But what? That's a question for you to answer.

2. Even though Gary was being baited by the older boy, hitting someone over the head with a bat is serious business. Should you do a much more in-depth evaluation of Gary's level of anger and use other professionals to help? And how about an in-depth psychosocial history to find out if this has happened before? How would the findings determine whether Gary can return to school and his potential for further violence?

3. To determine Gary's psychosocial history, create 10 questions you would ask Gary and his father to discover important issues in Gary's life that might help explain his response to the boy. You might also want to ask why this event happened now to find out if anything significant is going on in Gary's life that makes him likely to continue to be angry. What are some possible events in his life currently taking place that might precipitate his anger?

4. Might it also be a good idea to look at Gary's past grades and deportment and to talk to teachers who have known him prior to the incident happening? What might his past behavior tell us?

5. Did you have violence in your schools? Do you think an immediate suspension of Gary was called for without something being done to the boy who called him names, or is he the victim and it doesn't matter if he called Gary names because Gary should have restrained himself?

Summary

This chapter discusses the roles of social workers in the school system. A personal discussion of the work we do in schools is provided, as well as a case example. The chapter also discusses the problem of school violence, a problem that often affects the way students learn and victimizes a number of students. A short case is provided asking the reader to determine what they would do if they were the school social worker.

Questions to Determine Your Frame of Reference

1. Do you think it's fair to ask schools not only to teach students academic subjects but to discipline them, fill in where their parents won't or can't, teach them good citizenship and how to get along with others, monitor their use of drugs and alcohol, and do just about everything else that badly functioning families are unable or unwilling to do?

2. We blame schools for doing a bad job, but isn't the society we live in doing a bad job by not caring enough about kids from poor homes and troubled families?

3. In the case of James, who was forced to move to another school because of the behavior of gang members and the lack of supervision of the school, isn't this punishing the victim? How would you have dealt with the case differently?

4. How would you control school violence and yet protect the rights of students?

5. The statistics about income and completion of college suggest that lower income students fail to go to college because of their income levels and the quality of their academic preparation, but isn't the real

reason students go to college because parents encourage them to? Was that the case in your decision to attend college?

Internet Sources

The first article involves the nation's report card (2004), which evaluates how well we've done in teaching children to read and do math. Next, Simanek discusses the decline of education.

1. National Center for Educational Statistics. (2004). *The nation's report card (reading and mathematics)*. Retrieved from http://nces.ed.gov/nationsreportcard/

2. Simanek, D. (2004). *The decline of education.* Retrieved February 23, 2005, from http://www.lhup.edu/~dsimanek/decline1.htm

Troubled Families 8

*The Social Welfare Safety Net
and Professional Social Work
With Families Experiencing
Financial, Emotional, and Social Difficulties*

Americans have many inconsistent beliefs about family life. Although we treasure good family life and romanticize it in films, in novels, and on television, the fact is that many of us have had troubled experiences with our families and have physically and emotionally distanced ourselves from them. This process of removing ourselves from our families brings about an equally American condition: loneliness and a feeling of isolation. Bad as family life can be, the alternative, as some of you are now experiencing, can be just as bad or worse.

Why do we have such problems in American families, given our level of affluence and achievement as a nation? There are many reasons that this chapter explores, but social work's goal is very clear. Social work tries to keep families together, even very abusive families, because we know one thing for certain: Most children from abused families want to return to their families, regardless of the abuse. It's awful to be a child without a family and, although there are foster families and group homes as substitutes, not many children I know prefer them to their own families. And the terrible truth is that when we remove children from their homes and place them in state-provided homes or facilities, the very things that caused them to be removed from their original homes—abuse, neglect, and emotional maltreatment—often happen in the new homes provided by the state. It is a situation begging for a solution, and the solution for social work, when it's possible, is to work with families to stop abusive or neglectful behaviors so that children and parents can be reunited.

The desire to keep children in their homes and the removal of children from their biological parents often creates severe animosity toward social work and CPS agencies. On one hand, we shouldn't take children from their homes unless it is absolutely necessary, but if something happens in a home and we haven't prevented it, then we should have taken children from their homes sooner. You can see that CPS, the agency in most counties that handles child abuse and neglect, has a complex and challenging job.

As the following discussion will show, family life has been changing in America for better and for worse. Divorce rates, while declining, are still very high. All too many families lack medical insurance or suitable housing. Far too many children suffer from lack of food or abusive conditions and, more than ever, families are held to very high legal standards regarding their ability to care for children. Yet families are the system we believe should socialize children and teach them ethics and values. Families are expected to house and feed children and care for them when they suffer from physical and emotional problems. And families are supposed to promote education and teach children about citizenship and love of country and community. But when they can't or don't, we have a complex social service system to offer financial, housing, and counseling services often staffed by social workers. This safety net of services is in place to help families stay together and function well. This chapter explores the nature of those services and the way social work functions in the social welfare agencies and organizations most responsible for helping families in need.

The Changing American Family

Many aspects of family life in America have dramatically changed during the past 50 years. The *Journal of Pediatrics* (2003) reports the following data on family life in America: (a) the majority of families in America now have no children younger than 18 years of age; (b) people are marrying at an older age and the highest number of births occurs in women older than the age of 30; (c) from 1970 to 2000, children in two-parent families decreased from 85% to 69%; (d) 26% of all children lived with a single parent, usually their mother; (e) the rate of births to unmarried women has gone from 5.3% in 1960 to 33.2% in 2000, and the divorce rate, while slowing, is still twice as high as it was in 1955; (f) the median income of female-headed households is only 47% of the median income of married-couple families; (g) the number of children living in poverty is now five times higher for female-headed families than for married-couple families; (h) in 2001, 36% of all U.S. households with children had one or more of the following three housing problems—physically inadequate housing, crowded housing, or housing that cost more than 30% of the household income; (i) in 2002, about 5.6 million children, or 8% of the total, lived in a household that included a grandparent—the majority of these children (3.7 million) lived in the grandparent's home and two thirds had a parent present; and (j) children living in a grandparent's home with neither parent present were more likely to be poor (30%) than children living in their parent's home with a grandparent present (12%) or children living in a grandparent's home with a parent present (15%).

Although the concept of family is still well thought of in America, when social issues arise such as youth crime and lowering educational achievement, we tend to blame the family for problems experienced by children while at the same time looking to the family for solutions. The final report of the American Assembly (*Strengthening American Families*, 2000) suggests that changing social conditions in America have not only weakened but have overstressed many families, resulting in increasing numbers of troubled families and increasing numbers of malfunctioning children and adolescents. The idealized notion of the traditional family with one parent working and another staying at home and caring for the children has been replaced by families unable to succeed economically without both parents working, latch-key children who are home alone for long periods of time after school, increasing amounts of family violence, and poorly supervised children. Parents of poorly supervised children increasingly believe that as long as they clothe and provide housing for the child that anything that goes wrong is the result of malfunctioning social institutions. The malfunctioning social institutions most often blamed by parents of poorly supervised children are the schools, which they believe have the responsibility to modify poor social behavior, provide values, teach children about relationships and intimacy, and act as surrogates for missing, chaotic, and poorly functioning parents.

The social and economic pressures on American families have increased in many ways. Time, for example, which includes time to get to work and back, makes for a very long day for parents who might have to commute 2 to 4 hours per day plus an 8-hour workday. Child care complicates this very long day for parents by placing children in environments apart from their homes, where children respond to a number of forces that often compromise family values and result in incompatible approaches to discipline. The *Journal of Pediatrics* (2003) states that "in public opinion polls, most parents report that they believe it is more difficult to be a parent now than it used to be; people seem to feel more isolated, social and media pressures on and enticements of their children seem greater, and the world seems to be a more dangerous place" (p. 1541).

Healthy Families

In developing a list of the attributes of healthy families that help develop resilient children, the *Journal of Pediatrics* (2003) indicates that a well-functioning family consists of two married parents who offer children secure, supportive, and nurturing environments. Children have more life success when raised by caring and cooperative parents who have adequate social and financial resources. Defining parental attributes that lead to resilient children, Spock and Rothenberg (1985) write, "Good-hearted parents who aren't afraid to be firm when it is necessary can get good results with either moderate strictness or moderate permissiveness. . . . The real issue is what spirit the parent puts into managing the child and what attitude is engendered in the child as a result" (p. 8). Baumrind (1966) believes that parents who combine warmth and affection with firm limit-setting are more likely to have "children who are happy, creative, and cooperative; have high self-esteem; are achievement oriented; and do well academically and socially" (p. 887). Parents who are unresponsive, rigid, controlling, disengaged, overly permissive, and uninvolved jeopardize the emotional health of their children. These parental attributes consistently result in less emotionally strong and resilient children (Simons, Johnson, & Conger, 1994; Spieker, Larson, Lewis, Keller, & Gilchrist, 1999). Parents who supervise their children inside and outside of the home, encourage growth-enhancing activities, and then move toward shared decision-making and responsibility with children as they mature are likely to have the healthiest and most resilient children.

The *Journal of Pediatrics* (2003) also reports that religious or spiritual involvement offers important support for many families. A growing body of research shows a positive association between religious involvement/spirituality and health/well-being, with lowered risk markers among children for substance abuse and violence. Glicken (2005) reports similar findings but cautions that many research issues make this relationship a promising yet unproven one. Primary among the concerns about a relationship between religious involvement/spirituality and health/well-being is that only half the people who say they are attending religious services actually attend, and religious attendance is down one third since 1970 (Rauch, 2003). To further confuse the relationship between religious attendance and physical and mental health benefits, Rauch (2003) quotes theology professor John G. Stackhouse, Jr., as saying, "Beginning in the 1990's, a series of sociological studies has shown that many more Americans tell pollsters they attend church regularly than can be found in church when teams actually count. In fact, actual church going may be half the professed rate" (p. 34).

As an additional negative impact on children, Chatterji and Markowitz (2000) report the negative impact of parental substance abuse, noting that it affects the social, psychological, and emotional well-being of children and

InfoTable 8.1	Family Housing Data

The following data come from a 2003 report on the condition of America's children and families published by the Federal Interagency Forum on Child and Family Statistics.

1. In 2001, 36% of all U.S. households (owners and renters) with children had one or more of three housing problems: physically inadequate housing, crowded housing, or housing that cost more than 30% of household income.

2. The share of U.S. households with children that have any housing problems rose from 30% in 1978 to 36% in 1995 and has remained stable since.

3. In 2001, 7% of households with children had inadequate housing, compared with 9% in 1978.

4. Crowded housing, defined as housing in which there is more than one person per room, has also declined slightly among households with children, from 9% in 1978 to 6% in 2001.

5. Improvements in housing conditions, however, have been accompanied by rising housing costs. Between 1978 and 2001, the percentage of households with children with a cost burden—that is, paying more than 30% of their income for housing—rose from 15% to 28%. The percentage with severe cost burdens, paying more than half of their income for housing, rose from 6% to 11%. In an economic downturn, many of these people could lose their homes because of an inability to make their mortgage payments.

6. Households that receive no rental assistance and have severe cost burdens or physical problems are defined as having severe housing problems. In 2001, 11% of households with children had severe housing problems.

7. Severe housing problems are especially prevalent among very-low-income renters. In 2001, 31% of very-low-income renter households with children reported severe housing problems, with severe cost burden the major problem.

their families. The researchers indicate that 10% of American adults are addicted to substances that often cause them to be depressed and frequently result in family life that is chaotic, conflict-ridden, and may ultimately result in poverty, family violence, and divorce. Children in homes where one or both parents abuse substances are themselves at high risk of abusing substances and experiencing increased amounts of behavioral problems.

Yet resilient children often come from families that do, in fact, have many of the risk factors for social and emotional problems. How do they do so well? One reason is that we underestimate the strength of the family to survive in the midst of trauma and develop high levels of resilience in children. Early and GlenMaye (2000) suggest that to fully understand families, rather than looking at risk markers only, we should also consider the strengths of the families and their survival skills, abilities, inner resources, and emotional intelligence. Families with many risk markers often have elegant but unidentified strengths that lead to high levels of resilience in children. All children? Perhaps not, because it is true that some children growing up in malfunctioning families develop significant psychosocial problems whereas others are resilient, healthy, and survive family traumas. Perhaps resilient children also have the good fortune of reaching important developmental stages when family life may have provided a more positive and nurturing environment.

We also know that troubled families develop a type of triage where the children who can help the family are singled out for adult responsibilities that toughen them up and help them survive. These children are often found in immigrant families, families with severe emotional problems in parents, and substance-abusing parents. Often they are more the coparents of families than the children.

Family Poverty Data

The following data come from the 2003 report on the condition of America's children and families published by the Federal Interagency Forum on Child and Family Statistics.

1. The proportion of children living in families with incomes below the poverty threshold was 16% in 2001.

2. In 1993, 54% of children living in female-householder families were living in poverty; by 2001, this proportion had decreased to 39%.

3. In 2001, 18% of children younger than age 6 lived in poverty, compared with 15% of older children.

4. In 2001, 8% of children in married-couple families were living in poverty, compared with 39% in female-householder families.

5. In 2001, 10% of black children in married-couple families lived in poverty, compared with 47% of black children in female householder families. Twenty percent of Hispanic children in married-couple families lived in poverty, compared with 49% in female-householder families.

6. In 2001, 9% of white, non-Hispanic children lived in poverty, compared with 30% of black children and 27% of Hispanic children.

Health Care Data

The following data come from a 2003 report on the condition of America's children and families published by the Federal Interagency Forum on Child and Family Statistics.

InfoTable 8.2	Insufficient Food

The following data are from a 2003 report on the condition of America's children and families published by the Federal Interagency Forum on Child and Family Statistics.

1. Just less than half a million children (0.6%) lived in households with child hunger in 2001. In 2001, 4.1% of all children lived in households classified as food insecure with hunger.

2. Children living in poverty are much more likely than others to experience food insecurity and hunger. In 2001, about 2.6% of the children living in poverty were in households with hunger among children, compared with 0.3% of children in households with incomes at or above the poverty line. In 2001, nearly 45.9% of children living in poverty were in food-insecure households, compared with 11.5% of children living at or above the poverty line.

3. Children in families below the poverty level are less likely than higher income children to have a diet rated as good. In 1999–2000, for children aged 2 to 6, 17% of those in poverty had a good diet, compared with 22% of those living at or above the poverty line.

1. In 2001, 88% of children had health insurance coverage at some point during the year, maintaining the all-time high established in 2000. However, between 85% and 88% of all children have had health insurance in each year since 1987, leaving 12% to 15% of all children consistently without health insurance.

2. The number of children who had no health insurance at any time during 2001 was 8.5 million (12% of all children), which was similar to 2000.

3. The proportion of children covered by private health insurance decreased from 74% in 1987 to 66% in 1994, then increased to 70% in 1999, but dropped down to 68% in 2001. During the same time period, the proportion of children covered by government health insurance grew from 19% in 1987 to a high of 27% in 1993. Government health insurance decreased until 1999 and then began to climb again to 26% in 2001.

4. Hispanic children are less likely to have health insurance than white, non-Hispanic, or black children. In 2001, 76% of all Hispanic children were covered by health insurance, compared with 93% of White, non-Hispanic children and 86% of Black children.

Special Programs to Help Families

The following laws and policies have been enacted to help families. The Personal Responsibility and Work Opportunity Reconciliation Act of 1996 (PRWORA) (Pub. L. 104–193), as amended, is the welfare reform law that established the Temporary Assistance for Needy Families (TANF) program.

TANF is a block grant program designed to make dramatic reforms to the nation's welfare system by moving recipients into work and turning welfare into a program of temporary assistance. TANF replaced the national welfare program known as Aid to Families with Dependent Children (AFDC) and the related programs known as the Job Opportunities and Basic Skills Training (JOBS) program and the Emergency Assistance (EA) program. The TANF final regulations provide states with a clear and balanced set of rules for meeting the law's performance goals. They reflect a strong focus on moving recipients to work and self-sufficiency, and on ensuring that welfare is a short-term, transitional experience, not a way of life. The rules encourage and support state flexibility, innovation, and creativity to develop programs that can reach all families and provide support to working families. They do not tell states how to design their TANF programs or spend their funds. At the same time, the rules hold states accountable for moving families toward self-sufficiency (U.S. Department of Health and Human Services, Administration for Children and Families, 2004).

The Americans with Disabilities Act is a set of laws that protect family members, including children, from discrimination in housing, employment, education, and transportation and make it possible for all family members with disabilities to function without the fear of discrimination or unequal treatment. In Chapter 13 of this book, the Americans with Disabilities Act of 1990 (Public Law 101–336) is discussed in considerably more detail.

Social Security provides survivor benefits for children younger than age 18 or in other ways unable to care for themselves because of physical and emotional disabilities. Survivor benefits offer financial and medical protection to surviving children and spouses when a parent dies.

Medicare and Medicaid are federal and state medical programs that offer families medical care if they are indigent (poor) and younger than age 65 in the case of Medicaid, a state program. All workers who have paid into social security for 40 quarters (10 years) are eligible for Medicare benefits at age 65 and, depending on their date of birth, for social security benefits at age 65 or older.

Finally, families below a certain income level may be eligible for subsidized housing, low-interest loans to purchase houses, and free or low-cost lunches for children attending school.

How Social Workers Help Families

Working in family service agencies, Planned Parenthood agencies, mental health clinics, schools, forensic facilities, and numerous other agencies, social workers do many things for families. We try to reunite them when children have been removed from homes because of abuse and neglect, parental drug abuse, physical and emotional illness, and other factors which prevent families from being together. Social workers work in private practice and social agencies and provide family therapy for the purpose of helping existing families function better. We evaluate the ability of children to return home when the child has had problems with violence, mental illness, and other serious problems that require children to live in stable and supportive environments. Social workers help in family planning. This may include financial counseling by learning to spend more wisely or helping families to plan how large a family will be and when a couple might want to begin having children. We provide premarital counseling to help couples resolve problems that might interfere with the marriage and affect children. Couples who have had abuse in their backgrounds would be prime candidates for premarital counseling as a way of protecting the couple from family violence in their marriage, which could also affect the children. Social workers also do marital counseling as a way of strengthening family functioning. When marriages are in difficulty and it looks as if divorce is a possibility, social workers do divorce mediation, which helps the couple resolve divorce issues in a rational way rather than the usual abrasive and confrontational approaches used when two opposing attorneys fight for each partner in ways that often leave a great deal of animosity after the divorce. Social workers also do court-appointed evaluations of each parent to make recommendations to the court on child custody issues and work with the court to make certain that agreements regarding custody and visitation are maintained. We often work in public health agencies offering services to clients who have health-related problems that may have family repercussions. A pregnant 13-year-old girl might be an example, or a family member with a communicable sexual disease might be another. Finally, social workers help families where there are substance abuse problems and the parents or children are abusing alcohol or drugs.

Social Work With a Troubled Family

The Olson family has three children in school who exhibit numerous problems. Laura, the oldest child (10), is withdrawn and uncommunicative. Paul (8) acts out in class and is considered a bully. John (6) has delayed speech, is difficult to understand, and seems behind in his psychosocial development. A school social worker contacted the parents and asked if they could come to school and talk about their children. They readily agreed.

The parents, John (43) and Edna (37), both work at blue-collar jobs and told the worker that making ends meet financially is difficult because of the high cost of gas and the cost of housing, which kept increasing because they had an interest-only loan that saw their payments increase almost every month. They were now spending almost 60% of their income on mortgage payments and felt that instead of moving ahead in their lives, they were moving backwards. They recognized that they had little time for the

(Continued)

(Continued)

children and told the worker that just the time spent in driving to work (2 hours each way) left them both drained and too tired and irritable to do a good job of parenting. Any help the worker could offer would be appreciated. The worker brought the entire family in and asked anyone to describe the family. Paul said it wasn't a fun family and that he hated going home after school. His parents seemed very surprised. When asked if they also felt that way, the other two children agreed. During the course of 6 months with weekly hour-and-a-half sessions, the worker encouraged the family to problem-solve and develop a plan for making the family a more well-functioning unit. To the surprise of everyone, Laura came out of her shell and offered some concrete suggestions that included time to spend with their parents in exchange for the children doing some of the work around the house that the parents usually did. As the family experienced the giddy feeling of working together as a unit, the problems at school began to subside. John's delayed speech improved, Paul's bullying stopped, and Laura developed much better social skills and became much more outgoing.

Discussion

The worker explained that by helping the family develop its own strategy for problem-solving, he opened the door for the family to function better. It wasn't anything dramatic, he said, just a combination of people talking and learning to communicate feelings and ideas with one another, people feeling equal in their ability to help resolve the problems, and loving parents who felt overwhelmed but wanted to do better. "I see this all the time," he said. "These are very difficult times for families because financial pressures are extreme. Neither parent has insurance coverage, and any small medical problem creates extreme pressure. Often, rather than going to the doctor or dentist, the family does without and, because of ignoring problems that develop, all the children have dental and medical problems."

The worker was able to get a service club to help pay for dental and medical help. He also found out that the family qualified for special state coverage at a nominal fee under a program helping working parents who make more than the state coverage allows in income but have bills that make medical and dental expenses impossible to pay. He also helped the family secure a more stable loan that helps keep payments predictable. The combination of helping the family communicate and learn to share responsibility for problem-solving and the practical help the worker was able to arrange helped a family in growing difficulty become stable, responsive, and well-functioning.

In describing the help they received, Paul said it best when he told the worker, "You're really good at helping us talk. And you don't take sides or criticize. I feel a lot smarter now than I used to, and I'm not mad anymore when I go to school. And I like going home. It's hard work to keep the house clean and to do our chores, but it's worth it." Laura seconded Paul's assessment and told the worker, "I thought I was stupid or something, so I kept my mouth closed. But now I feel smart and I talk in class, and now I have friends. Everybody thought I was weird and, you know, people felt I was a little freaky. They don't anymore and my mom and dad, they're the best." John's parting words to the worker were, "Can't we come back anymore? I like talking about the family, but I don't like the chores. Well, they're OK, I guess, cause it's fun at home and helping my mom and dad makes us all happier."

Family Resilience

McCubbin and McCubbin (1993, 1996) believe that family resilience con-sists of two important family processes: (a) adjustment, which includes the strength of *protective factors* in mobilizing the family's efforts to maintain its integrity, function, and fulfill developmental tasks in the face of risk fac-tors; and (b) adaptation, which includes *recovery factors* that permit the family to effectively respond to a crisis. *Family resilience* is the ability of the family to deal with a crisis, to understand the potential risk factors associ-ated with this crisis, and to develop recovery strategies that permit family members to cope and adapt to crisis situations. Family crises might include financial problems, health problems, unemployment, marital problems, abusive behavior by a caregiver, social and emotional problems of children, loss of a home, and any number of problems that affect the entire family.

In additional studies of resilience in children, Baldwin, Baldwin, and Cole (1990) indicate the importance of parental supervision and vigilance. Conrad and Hammen (1993) emphasize the importance of maternal social support for children. In a study of 144 middle-class families, half of whom were divorced, Hetherington (1989) indicated the importance of structured parenting. Richters and Martinez (1993) found that low-income children living in a violent neighborhood did best when living in a stable and safe home environment. Wyman, Cowen, Work, and Parker (1991) report that children did best when the parenting style involved consistent discipline and an optimistic view of the children's future. Wyman et al. (1992) found that children who were most successful in grades 4 through 6 had nurtur-ing relationships with primary caregivers and stable, consistent family envi-ronments. Werner and Smith (1992) reinforce the importance of family environmental factors including self-confident mothers who value their children, supportive alternate caregivers, and supportive spouses.

In describing the factors that assist family recovery from a crisis, McCubbin, McCubbin, Thompson, Han, and Allen (1997) believe that the critical factors are the following:

1. Family integration: Parental efforts to keep the family together and to be optimistic about the future.

2. Family support- and esteem-building: Parental efforts to get com-munity and extended family support to assist in developing the self-esteem and self-confidence of their children.

3. Family recreation orientation, control, and organization: A family emphasis on recreation and family entertainment.

4. Discipline: Family life that includes organization, rules, and procedures.

5. Family optimism and mastery: The more families have a sense of order and optimism, the healthier the children.

Chatterji and Markowitz (2000) report that parental substance abuse negatively affects the social, psychological, and emotional well-being of children and their families. The researchers indicate that 10% of American adults are addicted to substances that often cause depression and frequently lead to family life that is disrupted, chaotic, and filled with conflict, and which may ultimately result in poverty, family violence, and divorce. Children in homes where one or both parents abuse substances are themselves more at risk of abusing substances and experiencing an increased amount of behavioral problems. In summarizing the concept of family resilience, Walsh (2003) writes,

> Building on theory and research, on family stress, coping, and adaptation (Patterson, 2002), the concept of family resilience entails more than managing stressful conditions, shouldering a burden, or surviving an ordeal. It involves the potential for personal and relational transformation and growth that can be forged out of adversity (Boss, 2001). Tapping into key processes for resilience, families can emerge stronger and more resourceful in meeting future challenges. A crisis can be a wake-up call, heightening attention to what matters. It can become an opportunity for reappraisal of priorities, stimulating greater investment in meaningful relationships and life pursuits. Members may discover or develop new insights and abilities. Many families report that through weathering a crisis together their relationships were enriched and more loving than they might otherwise have been. (p. 3)

The Story of an Immigrant Family

The following story of an immigrant family in America appears in a longer version in a book on resilience (Glicken, 2006, pp. 191–195) and shows the multiple levels on which families function and the types of problems that affect them, even those families with a great deal of resilience. Immigrants are often a forgotten group in the study of families, and hopefully this unusual family's story will identify the many pressures immigrant families face and their significant contribution to American life.

My father came to the United States in 1921 from a small rural town in the Ukraine called Beliazerkov. It means "White Church" in English. After the Second World War, there wasn't a single Jew left in Beliazerkov and the reality of the Holocaust became hopelessly apparent to my family in the endless Red Cross letters we received informing us that my father's 10 brothers and sisters in Russia were all dead and my mother's 8 brothers and sisters in Poland had died as well. Our assorted cousins and other members of both extended families had all perished, perhaps 200 or more people, many in the concentration camps of Dachau, Bergin-Belson and Auswitch. The news caused my mother to fall into a depression that lasted throughout her life.

Because my father was coming of age when the Communists came to power in 1918, he would have been forced into the military and certain death, an indignity since Jewish people in Russia were denied Russian citizenship. In the middle of the night he, my aunt, and grandmother left Russia. Perhaps he was 14. It took them three years of walking across Europe to earn enough money for their passage to America. When he saw the Statue of Liberty in New York Harbor, he and a thousand poor Europeans came up from steerage class at the bottom of the ship, stood on the deck, and wept.

My father went to work for the Great Northern Railroad when he was 17 and continued working as a blue-collar worker until he retired at 66. His job consisted of working outside in the freezing North Dakota cold, loading and unloading boxcars. Later, as he developed seniority, he had his pick of jobs and finally ended up working in the office where most of his coworkers were drunk by noon. He became secretary-treasurer of the railroad clerks union whose boundaries went somewhere from mid-Minnesota to mid-Montana. He was a deeply committed union man believing firmly in the rights of working men and women to have a secure and well-paid future. Together, on Sundays, we would take the milk train to small towns in North Dakota and Minnesota to preach the gospel of unionism to a largely drunk and disbelieving audience of railroad workers whom we met at the card halls and the pool joints, and who called my father the "Commie" and the "Jew Commie," but never-the-less had a love for him that I found exasperating.

It was these same men who would come to our house on Saturday nights after beating up their wives to ask my father for a few dollars of union money to get out of town for a while, or who caused drunken accidents that cost the railroad millions of dollars and then would hide behind my father who never failed to protect them. Later, these same men—bigoted, alcoholic, and wife beaters would meet me on the platforms of railroad stations across the northern part of America as I traveled from North Dakota to graduate school in Seattle and bring me sack lunches, or pastries, or buy me breakfast because my father had sent out smoke signals that his son was to be taken care of during the 2000 mile railroad odyssey through the prairies, Glacier National Park, and the Cascades of eastern Washington, to Seattle, and then back home. When they handed me little sacks of food, they would hide tears in their eyes and tell me stories about my father and how he'd saved them from being fired. They never knew my name and just called me by his name, Sammy.

He never gave up on anyone in the union. He believed in counseling for alcoholism and pushed for health benefits before either notion was popular. The well known liberal politicians of our time knew him and sometimes came to our home or stood with him on Labor Day celebration platforms. I sat with the future Vice President, Hubert Humphrey in 1948 and listened to the beauty of his language and felt chills run down my spine because of his passionate belief in democracy.

While I was in graduate school, he'd write to me in beautiful longhand about the way his boots sounded in the frozen snow, or how the smoke stood absolutely still in the 40 degree below North Dakota winter. His letters would go on for 30 pages with no punctuation marks and no logical progression. Page 1 had page 12 on the back and, "by the way," he'd add on page 19, "your mother is in the hospital again. I don't think she'll make it," and then the descriptions would begin again and he'd tell me that he saw a Robin one morning in mid-March and it made him cry because spring must be coming and maybe my mother would be able to come home from the hospital for a visit.

(Continued)

(Continued)

I remember eating breakfast with my father, listening to him describe the Cossacks and the retreat of the White Russian Army during the Russian Revolution. It was very early in the morning, well before the birds would start to sing. My father is dressed in his long underwear and has pieces of toilet paper covering cuts on his face from a very used, double-edged Gillette razor.

My mother, who used to be beautiful, lies in a hospital ward with an illness no one can explain. She is still a young woman but she looks old and wrinkled and I try not to think of her when my father talks about beautiful women. In a while, we will take a streetcar to see my mother in the hospital. I don't want to go.

I don't want to take this ride with my father. I'd rather sit at home and listen to his stories about Cossacks, but we board the streetcar anyway so that my father can see my mother before work begins. I never want to go with him and use every excuse I can muster. My father looks hurt when I tell him my excuses. Secretly, I think he doesn't want to visit her either. My little fibs just confirm his own feeling that my mother has given up and that the rides we take to the hospital on the streetcar are pointless. Often we ride together in brooding silence watching the people on the street and smelling the strange smells of foreign cooking that float through the open windows of the streetcar.

We walk in silence to the hospital. Inside, the hospital smells of disinfectant and I want to leave as soon as we walk into the lobby. But we climb up the dark old stairs to the third floor where my mother lies in a charity ward. I'm not sure what a charity ward is but it seems to me that all the women in the ward have sad looks on their faces, looks of hopelessness and despair.

My mother sits up in her bed waiting for us. She tries to smile, but the effort is so great that her body slumps. I know that she is 28-years old but she looks as old as my grandmother. Her hair has turned white. I hardly know what to say to her. She kisses me and I pull away, afraid, I guess, that I'll catch whatever she has. If she notices, I can't be sure. I have become an expert at reading the signs of hurt in people. It is a burden to be five years old and worry so much about other people's feelings.

My father gives her a perfunctory kiss and begins to tell her about work and the gossip from our street. I watch the ladies in the ward and notice a little girl sitting next to her mother. She is probably my age and has a very innocent look on her face. She is holding her mother's hand for all she is worth. Her mother, like the rest of the ladies on the ward, looks ill beyond repair. Little tears trickle down her mother's face, which the little girl wipes off with a tissue. The little girl has the same look of bewilderment I must have on my face.

I don't know why, but I start to cry just looking at the little girl. My father looks distraught and puts his finger over his lips, but I can't stop crying. The tears pour down my face and I feel ashamed to be causing such a scene.

One of the nurses comes over and speaks to me. She says that I'll have to leave if I don't stop crying, but the tears gush out of me and I sit on the chair next to my mother's bed and sob. The nurse takes me downstairs and makes me sit in the lobby next to the information booth. I want to stop crying, but I can't. The nurse tells the lady at the information booth that I'm a naughty boy and that if I can't stop crying, they won't let me see my mother anymore. I just want to be back home having a cream soda and eating warm pastries. I want someone to fuss over me and to treat me like I'm five instead of an adult.

On the way home, my father puts his head in his hands. I want to hug him, to give him a kiss, to let him know that I'm sorry his wife is sick and that he has to take care of us all by himself. But he just sits there in the streetcar with his head in his hands and says nothing. Maybe he's hurting, too, and we ride together, silently, keeping whatever is in our hearts to ourselves.

You Be the Social Worker

1. What impact do you think the mother's absence from the home will have on the little boy as a child and then, once he is grown, as an adult?

2. The boy blames his mother for the fate of the family. If you were seeing him in school, what type of problems do you think he would have? What would you focus on to help him deal with an absent mother?

3. Why does the little boy cry when he sees another child his age taking care of her ill mother?

4. The father in this story is a very complex man. He takes care of his son but also writes him long, poetic letters when the son is grown that only mention his wife's health in passing. How do you think having a father who is a poet and nurturing to his son, but seemingly dismissive of his wife's ill health, might affect the son in childhood and as an adult?

5. Immigrants are sometimes thought to be unconcerned about being Americans and come here primarily for financial reasons. But this is a story about an immigrant family who love America and believe America saved their lives. Does this story confirm or sway your opinion of immigrants to America, and why?

Summary

This chapter discusses the changing American family and the many pressures and stressors placed on family life. The role of social work and the programs often used to help families function more successfully are also discussed. Although we've made strides, far too many children are still without adequate medical care, housing, finances, or nutrition. A story noting problems in an immigrant family describes the impact of an ill mother without adequate medical insurance on family life.

Questions to Determine Your Frame of Reference

1. No society is perfect, and America, for all the criticism we hear about family life, seems to be offering a great deal of help to families with a good deal of success. Do you agree or disagree with this statement?

2. We've heard the term *two Americas*: one with all the benefits of wealth (good health insurance, housing, and opportunity) and the other with limited opportunity, poor health insurance, problems in housing, and insufficient income. Which America do you live in? Explain your answer.

3. It's difficult to believe that any American family goes hungry, but according to the data provided in this chapter, almost 5% of all children in America live in food-scarce homes. How could this happen in a country with so much excess food that a great deal of it is thrown away because of spoilage?

4. Divorce rates are declining but still constitute 40% of all marriages. Why do you think the divorce rate is so high and what do you think we can do to help marriages succeed?

5. Should our institutions take more responsibility for families to take some of the pressures off working parents who have limited incomes, energy, and time to do better jobs with their children? Who might those institutions be and what do you think they can do to help family life?

Internet Sources

First, Besharov (2001) discusses the future of the American family and his concerns about the current state of the family. Next, the U.S. Department of Health and Human Services (HHS) outlines what can be done to make families function more effectively. Finally, HHS describes the healthy marriage initiative.

1. Besharov, D. (2001). *Reflections on family*. Retrieved from http://usinfo.state.gov/journals/itsv/0101/ijse/besharov.htm

2. U.S. Department of Health and Human Services, National Mental Health National Information Center. (2005). *Psychoeducation*. Retrieved from http://mentalhealth.samhsa.gov/cmhs/community-support/toolkits/family/workbook/other.asp

3. U.S. Administration for Children and Families, Department of Health and Human Services. (2004). Retrieved from http://www.acf.dhhs.gov/healthymarriage/about/factsheets.html

Problems in the Workplace 9

Work-Related Helping Organizations and the Role of Industrial Social Work

> *To write about work is, by the very nature of the subject, to write about violence—to the spirit as well as to the body. It is about ulcers as well as accidents, about shouting matches as well as fistfights, about nervous breakdowns as well as kicking the dog around. It is above all (or beneath all) about daily humiliation. To survive the day is triumph enough for the walking wounded among the great many of us.*
>
> —Studs Terkel (1974, p. 1)

Few life experiences have more potential to give people pleasure or pain than their work. After years of concern for such workplace problems as low morale, un- and underemployment, job dissatisfaction, and worker burnout, we now have the culmination of these issues with the problem of workplace violence against coworkers.

The workplace is where we spend our day. It is the place that provides feedback about our worth. It rewards us for our labor and attaches a status that provides us with our identities. After being asked our names, we are usually asked what we do. Work suggests status and has a pecking order of importance. Above all, work allows us to schedule our time. Without work, we often lack direction and meaning. The unemployed tell us that, aside from the loss of pay, the worst thing about not working is being unable to organize time and the endless experience of boredom. Unemployment can literally drive normal and well-functioning people to acts of desperation and violence. The cause of many recent violent episodes in the workplace is explained by the insensitive and often mean-spirited ways workers have been laid off, downsized, given a temporary unpaid leave of absence, or any of the more creative words we use for being fired.

Without work, men and women lose status, income, the ability to organize their day, and their sense of self-worth. With work that is below their competency level or filled with conflict and tension, people often experience feelings of anxiety and depression that result in job-related stress and difficulties in their personal lives (Glicken, 1977, 1986a, 1986b, 1986c).

In its worst form, the workplace contributes to alcohol and drug abuse, anxiety, depression, marital discord, and violence within the workplace between workers (*Work in America*, 1973). That violence should move to the workplace is not difficult to understand. For years, researchers have seen the connection between spousal and child abuse and problems on the job. Researchers have also known of a connection between problems on the job and health problems including ulcers, headaches, back problems, and more severe forms of emotional trauma (*Work in America*, 1973). As workers are unable to resolve personal problems experienced in the workplace through the use of supervision, mediation, or union grievances, many workers have begun to show their anger at those whom they believe are the cause of their unhappiness at work: bosses, coworkers, customers, and the random innocent bystanders who are often in the wrong place at the wrong time.

One of the places where the workplace is the most unfair is in the minority and immigrant communities. Even when African American men begin to achieve in the workplace and incomes for middle-class black males are nearly equal to that of other middle-class Caucasian Americans, Akbar (1991) suggests that "as cruel and painful as chattel slavery was, the slavery that captures the mind and incarcerates the motivation, perception, aspiration, and identity in a web of anti-self images, generating a personal and collective self-destruction, is more cruel than the shackles on the wrists and ankles" (p. 7). This lack of a sense of freedom in the workplace prompts many African American men to question the value of their lives and the lives of others, regardless of their educational achievements or economic gain. Supporting this view of unhappiness in the workplace, Hochschild (1995) writes, "They [African American males] have grown disillusioned and embittered with the American dream" (p. 69). Houk and Warren (1991) believe that "marked economic and social disparities among Americans contribute to the etiology of violence [in the workplace] in fundamental ways. . . . Joblessness, and the lack of real employment opportunities promote violence by generating a sense of frustration, low self-esteem, and hopelessness about the future" (p. 228).

Another troubled area in the workplace is the existence of sexual harassment. Katz (2004) reports that studies of sexual harassment indicate that between 40% and 70% of women and 10% and 20% of men have experienced sexual harassment in the workplace. Almost 15,000 sexual harassment cases were brought to the attention of the Equal Employment Opportunity Commission (EEOC), indicating a tripling of complaints filed by men and representing 15% of all claims filed against female supervisors. A telephone poll conducted by Louis Harris and Associates on 782 workers revealed that 31% of the female workers claimed to have been harassed at work, whereas 7% of the male workers claimed to have been harassed at work. Sixty-two percent of the victims took no action. One hundred percent of the women polled claimed the harasser was a man, whereas 59% of the men claimed the harasser was a woman and 41% of the men said the harasser was another man. Of the women who had been harassed, 43% were harassed by a supervisor, 27% were harassed by an employee senior to them, 19% were harassed by a coworker at their same work level, and 8% were harassed by a junior employee. Whenever I ask my graduate classes about sexual harassment, virtually all of the women in the class claim they've been sexually harassed by men.

The workplace can often be physically dangerous to workers. When the catwalks over the main floor of the Kansas City Hyatt Regency collapsed during a dance and more than 100 people died, employees were severely traumatized by the accident (Glicken, 1986d). Wisely, the hotel corporation brought in crisis counselors to work with employees who had witnessed the accident, many of whom suffered symptoms of PTSD for months following the accident. From that experience and an earlier fire at the MGM Hotel in Las Vegas, it became evident that immediate mental health intervention was necessary or employees could experience many of the symptoms of PTSD so severely that it would affect their ability to continue to work in the organization. Many of the workers in the Hyatt Regency disaster felt guilty about what had happened and thought they were responsible for the accident, although there was no basis in reality for feeling that way. Significant numbers of workers had sleeping disorders, felt ill when they approached the worksite, experienced panic attacks, claimed they could hear the screams of dying people for months after the accident, had eating problems, or were often unable to work and experienced unemployment and relationship problems—classic symptoms of PTSD.

This chapter on the workplace will focus on the social and emotional problems related to work, including the importance of work, workplace conflict and violence, discrimination, low pay, job stress, underemployment, and unemployment. It will also describe the organizations and agencies available to help resolve workplace problems and the role of social work in the workplace.

Work-Related Stress

Job stress can be defined as the emotional and health-related problems that develop when a job requires work that is often at odds with a worker's abilities and the resources he or she has to complete the job.

In the past 20 years, many studies have evaluated the relationship between job stress and a variety of physical ailments. Mood and sleep disturbances, upset stomachs and headaches, and disturbed relationships with family and friends are examples of stress-related problems that often result when work-related problems exist. These early signs of job stress are usually easy to recognize, but the effects of job stress on chronic diseases are more difficult to determine because chronic diseases take a long time to develop and can be influenced by many factors other than stress. Nonetheless, evidence is rapidly accumulating to suggest that stress plays an important role in several types of chronic health problems, especially cardiovascular disease, musculoskeletal disorders, ulcers, and psychological disorders. Major emotional problems related to job stress include depression, anxiety, anger, violent behavior, family violence, alcoholism and drug addiction, burnout, and, in very severe cases of depression, suicide.

Unemployment

According to Avison (2004), there is considerable evidence that unemployment results in higher levels of psychological distress than is reported by workers who are employed. Unemployed workers also suffer from higher rates of depression, anxiety disorders, and substance abuse. Families of the unemployed experience increased emotional problems and children, especially teens, are at higher risk of emotional and behavioral problems. The literature also suggests that job loss increases financial strain and family conflict, resulting in serious self-esteem problems among unemployed workers and their families.

UNDERSTANDING THE UNEMPLOYMENT COMPENSATION LAW

When workers are terminated or laid off, the state they live in may give up to 26 weeks of unemployment compensation to help these workers manage financially until they can find new jobs. This may be increased if situations (such as 9/11) have affected the economy to such an extent that finding work is very difficult. The Almanac of Policy Issues (2002) notes that unemployment payments (compensation) are intended to provide an unemployed worker with the time to find a new job equivalent to the one lost without financial distress. Without employment compensation, many workers would be forced to take jobs for which they were overqualified or, perhaps, even end up on public assistance.

In the United States, each state administers a separate unemployment insurance program based on federal standards that must be approved by the U.S. Secretary of Labor. The employees who are eligible for compensation, the amount they receive, and the period of time benefits are paid are determined by a combination of federal and state law. To support the unemployment compensation systems, workers pay a combination of federal and state taxes. State employer contributions are normally based on the amount of wages they have paid, the amount they have contributed to the unemployment fund, and the amount that their discharged employees have been compensated with from the fund. Some states provide additional unemployment benefits to workers who are disabled.

Underemployment

Underemployment is a troubling situation where people are employed but not in the positions that they are trained for, could easily function well at, or desire to work in. Crown, Leavitt, and Rix (1996) describe two forms of underemployment: (a) workers who want full-time work can only find part-time employment, and (b) full- and part-time workers are employed at jobs below their education and skill level. As an indication of the growing discrimination against older qualified workers in our society, the authors found that the first type of underemployment for workers aged 50 to 64 grew 111% during the 1979–1993 period, and that 400,000 workers aged 50 to 64 were underemployed because they could not find full-time work. The second type of underemployment was found to be an even greater problem for older workers; preliminary estimates indicated that as many as 7.2 million workers aged 50 to 64 were employed in jobs below their skill or educational level.

Workplace Violence

Almost 2 million workers each year are victims of workplace violence, usually the result of the type of work they do. Police officers are understandably at high risk of violence. So are taxi drivers and convenience store clerks. But when the perpetrator of violence is a coworker, the impact of the violence can be even more serious. We often label this type of violence as "going postal" because of the high caseload of employee-to-employee violence in the U.S. Postal Service (USPS). The work of sorting mail is terribly stressful and monotonous, but the labor practices of the USPS have been roundly criticized for ignoring indications of violence and employing and continuing to employ workers who show increasing signs of emotional instability. I hope this doesn't affect my mail service, but why are more sales clerks available when there are no customers and why, during

InfoTable 9.1	Workplace Violence

According to the U.S. Department of Labor (2004), workers on the job in 2004 reported more than 51,000 rapes and sexual assaults, 400,000 aggravated assaults, more than 700 workplace homicides, and almost 7,000 fatal injuries. Workplace violence appears to be on the rise, according to Robinson (1996). Many of the perpetrators of workplace violence are disgruntled employees who were terminated, fired, or laid off. Twenty-five percent of the perpetrators of workplace homicide commit suicide after the violent act.

peak periods of business, are there fewer available clerks? One time at a Boise, Idaho, post office, there were 30 people in line and 2 clerks. "Why," I asked (fearing that my mail would be trashed for being so insolent), "are there so few people working?" The clerk responded, "Vacations." *Oh, I thought, what a fine answer,* because it begged the question of why there were no replacements for vacationing workers and why people were on vacation in such numbers that service was disrupted.

Regarding coworker-to-coworker violence, 500 managers were surveyed at an American Management Association (1994) Human Resources Conference. The managers surveyed reported that 43% of the workers they supervised experienced reduced morale as a result of workplace violence in the past 4 years, whereas 39% experienced lowered productivity. There was an 8% increase in workers filing disability claims, citing workplace violence as a contributor to stress and emotional difficulty, whereas companies with workplace violence experienced a 10% increase in litigation against companies for not containing workplace violence. Clearly, workplace violence has a negative impact on life at work.

HOW WORKPLACE VIOLENCE PROGRESSES

Dr. Steven Ino, a clinical psychologist at the University of California at Santa Barbara, and I (1997) have developed a series of progressively more violent stages in the development of violent behavior in the workplace. The workplace my colleague and I describe are university and college settings where a number of students and employees have been involved in workplace violence.

Level 1

A preoccupation with the feeling that the worker has been mistreated. A tendency by the worker to blame others for his or her own lack of success on the job and to obsessively complain about how badly he or she

InfoTable 9.2	Who Has Potential for Workplace Violence?

The following indicators of potential for workplace violence by coworkers have been identified by Rugala and Issacs (2003, p. 13) from members of the Federal Bureau of Investigation's National Center for the Analysis of Violent Crime, Profiling and Behavioral Assessment Unit:

1. Direct or veiled threats of harm to others in the workplace.

2. Intimidating, belligerent, harassing, bullying, or other inappropriate and aggressive behavior; numerous conflicts with supervisors and other employees.

3. Bringing a weapon to the workplace, brandishing a weapon in the workplace, making inappropriate references to guns, or fascination with weapons.

4. Statements showing fascination with incidents of workplace violence, statements indicating approval of the use of violence to resolve a problem, or statements indicating identification with perpetrators of workplace homicides.

5. Statements indicating desperation (over family, financial, and other personal problems) to the point of contemplating suicide.

6. Drug and or alcohol abuse; and, very erratic behavior with serious mood swings.

has been treated by others in the workplace. At this stage, the problem should be evaluated and an attempt should be made to try and resolve the concerns the worker has openly shared with supervisors, other workers, or personnel departments. These concerns, if voiced irrationally or if illogical, are particularly serious and need to be dealt with by encouraging counseling or by trying to help the worker develop a more accurate perception of the problem. Employee assistance programs or mediators can also be helpful at this early point in the worker's preoccupation with his or her mistreatment on the job. If the worker is unwilling to become involved in counseling, mediation, or some other form of dispute resolution, the worker needs to be clearly told about the organization's "no tolerance for violence" rules. There must also be an agreement from the worker to accept a "no-violence" contract so that any future concerns will be dealt with in a violence-free atmosphere. It may be wise to provide the worker with an advocate or an ombudsman to help in future disputes. The advocate represents the interests of the worker in any dealings with the organization and is recognized as the worker's ally.

Level 2

Obsessive thoughts develop, which include a plan to pay others back for the way the worker believes that he or she has been treated. The plan may be vague or elaborate. The plan is often shared with others on the job who may think that the person is just venting anger, and the plan isn't taken seriously by others. This is a considerable mistake because it is at this point in time that workers begin to obsess about revenge and when the plan they devise becomes more firmly fixed in their minds. The reason for the progression to this second level is that organizations often badly handle the worker at Level 1. The way the worker is dealt with initially can have significant meaning for the progression (or lack thereof) of violent impulses. All threats, plans, indications of payback, obsessive thoughts, and preoccupations with unfairness should be seen as being serious signs of potential violence by the organization, and every attempt should be made to deal with the problem through the use of an Employee Assistance Program (EAP), mediation, or some conciliatory process to logically resolve the problem. If the worker is being laid off, it should be done with notice, respect, and concern for the worker's long-term well-being. Stories of the way organizations lay off people, in cruel, insensitive, and often rude and disrespectful ways, suggest reasons for the development of anger in workers and dramatically increase the risk of violence.

Level 3

The worker's violent plan for payback is now articulated to those in the workplace who need to respond. Generally, previolent workers will share their plan with others or make specific threats to supervisors whom they trust or find sympathetic. At this stage, if threats are not taken seriously and if something isn't done to deal with them, the anger grows and workers become victims of their own inability to control feelings and emotions that are now clearly out of control. Most perpetrators of workplace violence have discussed their plan, to the extent that it is now clear, with others in a position of authority. Some managers act on this information, but all too many ignore it by thinking it best not to make problems for the worker. They may also worry that any report of the plan might end in a court action by the worker. For whatever reason, most workplace homicides have been articulated clearly by perpetrators to others, and it often doesn't come as a surprise when perpetrators actually harm or kill someone. When one hears about a workplace killing, it is almost always followed by statements from coworkers admitting that they didn't take the worker's threatened violence seriously or that they misjudged the degree of the worker's anger. This is the moment in time to make formal reports to the police or to company security so that action can be taken to protect other workers.

Level 4

Actual threats are made to people on the job. These threats may be made to those directly involved in the worker's obsessional system or to anyone nearby. The worker's anger is now increasingly more difficult to control because he or she has made the decision to confront others as a release for intense feelings of anger at the organization. At this point in time, the worker has clearly lost control. Coworkers begin to complain to superiors, who often do nothing to control the behavior or who may terminate the worker without necessary professional help or police involvement. The worker at Level 4 is now ready to commit an act of violence. In almost all cases of workplace violence, supervisors, personnel departments, and union stewards were forewarned about dangerous employees but did nothing to ensure that help would be given or that the problem would be resolved. When threats are made, it may be necessary to bring in the police and file charges against a violent employee. Although this may end in a trial or prison sentence, it may also end in mandatory treatment and the safety of a number of innocent people. Remember that many perpetrators of workplace violence injure innocent bystanders. They may also kill their own family members, often in despair over what they intend to do at work.

Level 5

The worker commits violent acts on the job. When workers say that they are going to kill someone or commit an act of violence to coworkers, take it seriously. Threats are more than words. They are acts about to take place and are often the worker's unconscious attempt to have the act stopped. When a threat is made and nothing constructive is done to help the worker, violence is very likely to follow. The violence may be directed at specific people, but more often than not it is random and affects people who have nothing to do with the worker's grievances against the organization.

Not surprisingly, many workers move to Level 5 in the development of violence. Far too many managers and supervisors worry about lawsuits or union actions if they intervene, and they become inactive when violent behavior begins to show itself. And it shouldn't surprise us if workers show none of the levels noted above and act out without seeming provocation. These are the anomalies of the workplace and the individual workers within the workplace. By and large, however, workers give advanced notice of potentially dangerous behavior. When that behavior is dealt with badly by organizations, violence is more likely to result.

Social Work Interventions: Employee Assistance Programs and Other Forms of Organizational Assistance

When problems in the workplace such as those affecting productivity and attendance, coworker relationships, use of substances, and personal problems begin to surface, managers often meet with workers to find out why the problem(s) are occurring. If the problem(s) are beyond their ability to resolve, social work help is often sought. Social workers in the workplace are sometimes called industrial social workers and may work in personnel departments of large organizations and businesses or in Employee Assistance Programs (EAPs). The function of an EAP is to work cooperatively with a company or organization to help workers resolve personal, work-related, and addiction problems that interfere with work and might, if not resolved, lead to their termination as employees. When workers have problems that cannot be resolved through the brief treatment provided by an EAP, longer term treatment might be necessary.

One task of the social worker in an EAP is to assess the problem to help understand its cause. Social workers in EAPs often use short-term crisis intervention approaches that offer advice, education, and homework assignments meant to help the worker practice new behaviors. Sometimes situations such as marital problems or problems with children can be dealt with in just a few sessions. Frequently, however, workplace problems exist because an organization has been unfair or treated a worker badly. It is the social worker's difficult job to help workers cope with the many destructive slights and attacks on their psyches in the workplace. Helping workers cope with painful work situations is difficult, particularly when the organization is unlikely or unwilling to change. But teaching people to cope does not imply that we help workers become passive. On the contrary, workers can be helped to develop strategies to change the way they interact at work so that they can more effectively control the outcomes of work-related problems.

Many problems of conflict and unhappiness in the workplace can be dealt with by the organization. Work assignments can be varied to prevent burnout. Promotional and salary decisions can be made equitably to ensure that all workers believe that they are treated with dignity and respect. References of workers can be checked carefully, with the added protection of having potential workers undergo careful screening and evaluation before they are hired to identify those applicants with obvious emotional problems or histories of troubled behavior on other jobs. Disputes between workers can be mediated informally before they become serious problems. Laying off workers should be done with care and concern for the individual and not in a heavy-handed, insensitive way. When workers feel diminished and no longer believe that the organization cares about them, the potential for workplace problems grows in severity. Imagine how a worker in a labor dispute with Caterpillar Company felt when stating, "I finally realized two years ago, when they threatened to replace us, that as far as they are concerned, I am nothing to them (after 24 years in the company)" (*Chicago Tribune*, 1994, p. 1).

When companies are responsive to their workers, many of the problems that lead to workplace violence can often be resolved. In these companies,

EAPs are used to offer workers an alternative way of resolving problems that may be difficult to resolve for managers and supervisors. Companies using EAPs offer a variety of alternatives to workers. Some EAPs are located in the organization and are readily available. In these organizations, managers, workers, and treatment personnel work closely together to resolve the problem. In other organizations, the worker might go to a social agency or counseling center with which the organization has contracted. The services provided may be time-limited and supportive, or they may be longer term and designed to meet the individual needs of the client (Glicken, 1988, 1996).

Workplace problems sometimes exist because of difficulties in the personal lives of workers. Resolving personal problems is important, but keeping the worker employed comes before resolution of a personal problem. Organizations often correctly complain that workers do not improve on the job after treatment is provided. This complaint is valid, but organizations also need to understand how long it may take for a worker to improve. Problems such as addictions to substances are slow to respond to treatment and may take months to improve, with the added possibility of a need for residential treatment. Just as employers give workers time to mend after an illness or surgery, employers need to give workers time to mend when they have emotional problems (Glicken, 1988, 1996).

Most workers have aspirations and dreams for the future. Far too many healthy and able people in America feel dead-ended in work much too early in their lives. The hopes and dreams of youth are replaced by cynicism and despair because workers often see that they have no opportunity to use their abilities. The stress and strain of work should not lead to workers who are burned-out in their 40s or to workers in their early 50s who have been permanently downsized because an organization feels so little about their contribution that it has stopped caring about a worker's future life. This discounting of older workers is one of the keys to the development of violence in the workplace. Imagine how someone in mid-life may feel when they've given 20 years of their life to an organization, only to be laid off. They will very likely never have the same opportunities in the workplace because age is now a negative factor in finding new and equally challenging work.

Some organizations use social workers in nontreatment roles to help reduce the threat of violence. Social workers may be used in ombudsman programs and may help in facilitation, mediation, and other methods of dispute resolution to identify and prevent potential workplace violence. These strategies are often most useful before the threat of violence becomes serious enough to require a formal workplace action. The following is a short description of some preventative techniques suggested by Robinson (1996) and others (NIOSH, 1992, 1993) that organizations have found useful in dealing with workplace violence problems in their early stages.

OMBUDSMEN

Ombudsmen are employed by an organization and use a variety of strategies to resolve workplace disputes including counseling, mediation, conciliation, and fact-finding. An ombudsman may interview all the parties involved in a dispute, review the history of the problem and the organization's personnel policies to see if they've been correctly applied, and offer suggestions and alternative ways of resolving the dispute to the workers involved in a disagreement. An ombudsman doesn't impose solutions but offers alternative strategies to resolve it. Workers involved in a dispute may refuse options offered by the ombudsman and are free to pursue other remedies or strategies, including legal ones.

FACILITATION

The facilitator focuses on resolving the dispute and is most helpful when the levels of emotion about the issues are fairly low. Facilitation is most effective when the people involved trust one another so that they might develop acceptable solutions.

MEDIATION

Mediation uses a third party who is not a member of the organization and is free of bias in the situation. The mediator can only recommend, although some organizations accept binding mediation as a way of resolving disputes with the mediator placed in the role of decision-maker. Mediation may be helpful when those parties involved in a dispute have reached an impasse and the situation is potentially dangerous. A mediator may offer advice, suggestions, and options to help resolve the problem. The authority mediators bring to the dispute is their neutrality and expertise. Hopefully, those involved in the dispute will accept suggestions made by someone in this capacity. Care must be taken to bring someone in with a very fair and unbiased track record in mediating disputes.

INTEREST-BASED PROBLEM SOLVING

Interest-based problem solving attempts to improve the working relationship between the parties in dispute. It attempts to help the parties use rational and focused ways of resolving problems and seeks to reduce emotions among the people involved. Techniques suggested for use in interest-based problem solving include brainstorming, creative alternative solutions to a problem, and agreed-upon rules to reach a solution.

PEER REVIEW

Peer review involves the evaluation and possible solution of a problem recommended by fellow employees. Because these suggestions come from coworkers, they may have more impact on the involved parties. However, there are concerns about peer reviews and their objectivity, composition, dual loyalties, and conflicts of interest. They are usually only helpful if done with the complete confidence of the parties involved. Again, review panels in sexual harassment cases might be a good model to explain this approach. Sexual harassment review panels have a mediocre to poor record of objectivity, and recommendations to upper management are often rejected because of due process issues and concerns regarding objectivity. On the other hand, courts have been reluctant to overturn decisions made by organizations when review panels are used in sexual harassment investigations and recommendations.

EMPLOYEE TRAINING

All employees should understand the correct way to report potentially or actively violent and disruptive behavior observed in other workers. Robinson (1996) suggests that the following topics be included in all workplace violence prevention training:

Discussion of the organization's workplace violence policy; a willingness of employees to report incidents; suggested approaches to preventing or coping with potentially violent and hostile behavior; conflict resolution training; training in managing stress and anger; training in the location and operation of alarm systems; personal security measures; and, understanding the various programs offered by organizations including employee assistance programs, the ombudsman, and mediation. (p. 6)

SUPERVISORY TRAINING

Special attention should also be paid to effective training of supervisors so that they know how to identify, evaluate, and resolve workplace problems that may lead to violence. This includes the use of personnel policies to provide accurate evaluations of performance and reports that correctly identify the worker's behavior with fair and organizationally correct disciplinary actions provided. Skills necessary to prevent workplace violence by managers may include the ability to screen applicants with potential for violence, crisis management and conflict resolution skills, and encouragement of other workers supervised by the managers to share incidents of observed violence or potential violence in coworkers.

SECURITY MEASURES

Workers need to feel safe on the job. Organizations can increase this feeling of safety by providing weapons checks, employee identification badges or cards with pictures, immediate response by the police if threats have been made, and assurance of the safety of workers who have been threatened or assaulted by coworkers. Organizations need to have a no-tolerance policy against all forms of weapons on the premises, with immediate suspension if a weapon is found on a worker. Reports of weapons must be immediately shared with the police.

PRE-EMPLOYMENT SCREENING

Before a worker is officially offered a position, the personnel department should be contacted to find out what pre-employment screening techniques (e.g., interview questions, background and reference checks, and drug testing) are permitted by federal and state laws and regulations for the position.

You Be the Social Worker

Parts of this case first appeared in a book I cowrote on workplace violence and the role of social work (Glicken & Sechrest, 2003, pp. 203–205).

Jim Kennedy is a 45-year-old Caucasian engineer working in the aerospace industry in Southern California. For the past two years, Jim and his supervisor have had a running battle over the quality of Jim's work. Jim thinks that his work is fine, as do his colleagues, but the supervisor believes that Jim doesn't follow directions and that his work wanders off into areas that aren't related to his assignments. On several occasions, they've almost come to blows.

Jim was referred to the company's Employee Assistance Program and was told by his supervisor that he either enter counseling or face termination. Jim is a difficult and unmotivated client. Although he comes for sessions, he seems unwilling to complete the homework assignments given to him by the social worker that might help him resolve conflict with others or to try to see the problem from the point of view of others. The social worker is supportive and positive, but Jim deeply resents this intrusion into his private life and tells the social worker that he's only coming for help because he has no choice.

Jim has a wife who doesn't work and two children in college. His salary barely covers his expenses and, many months, he lives on credit cards and loans. Quitting isn't a realistic option since a weak job market in the aerospace industry limits his work opportunities. The possibility of transferring to a different department at work is also limited since Jim's work is highly specialized. At 45, he doesn't want to stop contributing to a very good pension plan. He feels stuck and resents going for counseling. He believes that his problems at work are the supervisor's fault and thinks the supervisor should be in treatment, not him. He is becoming surly and difficult at work. On several occasions he's written derogatory things about the supervisor in the men's rest room and on the company elevator. While no one can prove that Jim is to blame, everyone knows he did it.

In the past six months, Jim has begun to deteriorate physically and emotionally. He often comes to work looking haggard and unkempt. People have begun to find his body odor offensive and wonder if he bathes. His EAP social worker suspects that Jim is drinking heavily and has ordered a random alcohol test.

Jim has made several indirect threats against his supervisor that coworkers have heard but have not reported. They believe that Jim has a legitimate grievance and feel obligated to protect him. The coworkers feel that Jim is just going through a mid-life crisis, but on closer examination, Jim is deteriorating badly. His thoughts, which he confides to his wife and family, have increasingly become violent. He purchased a gun and shoots it in the basement of his home and outside in the desert. The feel of the gun and the sound of the bullets give him a sense of power that he finds intoxicating. He has also begun to drink heavily and has a DUI charge that resulted in the removal of his license and the impounding of his car. He drives anyway, using a second car he purchased in his wife's name.

He feels invincible and doesn't think anything will happen to him. Because of his sophistication with the Internet, he has begun sending e-mail messages to everyone at work promising violence to certain people in upper management. He never mentions the name of the supervisor he hates so much and his e-mails are untraceable. In a company with thousands of people, it's difficult to pin-point who made the threats or how seriously they should be taken, but the messages unnerve everyone at work and there is a sense of foreboding in the company that something awful will happen.

Jim's EAP social worker believes that Jim's deteriorating condition is reason to worry about potential violence and has warned the company that he may be about to commit a violent act. The company fears a law suit if they fire Jim. They believe that he will do something serious enough, but not dangerous enough, to fire him. The EAP social worker disagrees. He sees concrete signs of potential for serious workplace violence. Those signs include a highly intelligent man who is emotionally deteriorating and who demonstrates increasing paranoia and an obsession for getting revenge. The drinking and fondness for guns add to the social worker's sense of potential violence. If the social worker knew of the verbal threats Jim has shared with his coworkers and the fact that Jim is the one making e-mail threats, the social worker would be absolutely certain that Jim's volatile behavior will end in a violent act.

Jim has always been eccentric. His aloofness from people, his disdain for others he considers to have lesser ability, and his angry feelings at management for not

(Continued)

(Continued)

recognizing his abilities provide a backdrop to his potential for workplace violence. As an unsupportive supervisor thwarts his ambitions, and as he suffers the indignity of having to go for counseling, Jim has begun to have fantasies of violence. They include going into the management side of the company building and randomly killing every manager in sight, starting with his own supervisor. The fantasy is so clear and appealing to him that it has almost taken on sensuous overtones. It is likely that while Jim seems troubled, but functional, that he is having moments of irrationality and severe emotional dysfunction that make him highly dangerous.

The EAP social worker is concerned about Jim's potential for danger and has warned the company. Unfortunately, he cannot pinpoint a specific threat or act to concretely suggest that Jim will be violent at work. While Jim seems to be going through a rough stretch, his coworkers aren't seeing the dangerous side of his behavior and believe that, like all eccentric people, Jim has a side of him that is different from the rest of the engineers he works with. That side; aloof, uncomfortable with people, egocentric, also makes him a good engineer, probably the best engineer in the group. For these reasons, his coworkers haven't accurately evaluated his level of increasing danger.

A day after a particularly degrading and offensive meeting with his supervisor where Jim was placed on administrative leave without pay because of the deterioration in his work, Jim took his guns to work and shot and killed three managers, including his supervisor. He wounded four others including several people who had nothing to do with the company and who were just there to deliver packages. The security guards assigned to the company shot and killed Jim in a struggle, and the company is left to sort out the reasons that it took them so long to take remedial action and to correctly determine his level of violence. Everyone interviewed believed that Jim was going through a patchy time and that he would snap out of it. No one other than the EAP social worker, whose warning to the company went unheeded, felt that he was excessively dangerous or that he showed potential for violence.

Questions

1. Do you believe that Jim's company should have taken earlier action to help Jim by suspending him with pay and referring him for counseling in a facility not connected to the company?

2. If you were the social worker, how would you have treated Jim's growing anger toward the company?

3. Do you think that companies have the right to fire workers who are not violent but have the potential for violence? How do you think this determination should be made to protect the rights of all parties involved?

4. Which of Jim's behaviors should the company have seen as possible predictors of violence? Do you think a program to help coworkers and colleagues identify potential for violence would reduce violence in the workplace, or might it contribute to increased paranoia and dismissals for potential violence that aren't warranted?

5. As a consequence of unfair dismissals, might a proactive policy actually lead to more violence by people who had no intention of doing anything violent but who now feel so badly treated that violence is now an option they might consider?

Summary

The workplace is a primary arena for crisis. Most problems can be resolved by managers who use fairness and good judgment. When managers fail to use good judgment, or when problems are more serious in nature, many companies refer workers to agencies who provide short-term crisis services to social workers. This chapter suggests a number of strategies for dealing with the potential for violence, including mediation and the use of an advocate. Many of these same strategies can be used for a variety of workplace problems that don't relate to violence, including addictions and family problems that affect work. The chapter also discusses the issues of un- and underemployment, the programs available for the unemployed, and the emotional impact of un- and underemployment on workers and their families.

Questions to Determine Your Frame of Reference

1. In your own work experiences, have you known workers who had serious problems on the job? What were the problems and how were they resolved, or were they?

2. Industrial social work involves the treatment of a number of social and emotional problems that are similar to all social work settings but also unique to the workplace. Identify the problems that are unique to the workplace.

3. I've been pretty tough on the workplace in this chapter, noting the insensitive and unfair conditions that exist in many organizations. My father was very involved in the labor movement. Do you think this might suggest a bias against management and one favorable to workers?

4. Would you rather represent workers or management in a dispute? Why?

5. Many of the problems affecting the workplace have to do with substance addictions. Do you think short-term help or referral to a substance abuse program would work, or should we have a no-tolerance to substances policy and fire substance abusers because they can endanger the lives of others on the job?

Internet Sources

1. The University of Iowa Injury Prevention Research Center. (2001, February). *Workplace violence: A report to the nation.* Retrieved from http://www.osha.gov/media/oshnews/may00/national-20000509 .html. This report summarizes the problem of workplace violence and the recommendations identified by participants at the Workplace Violence Intervention Research Workshop in Washington, D.C., April, 2000 The workshop brought together 37 invited participants representing diverse constituencies within industry; organized labor; municipal, state, and federal governments; and academia.

2. OSHA. (1998). *Workplace violence for health care and social service workers* (Publication 3148). Retrieved from http://www.osha-slc.gov/ Publications/Osha3148.pdf

3. DHHS (NIOSH). (1999). *Stress at work* (Publication No. 99-101). Retrieved from http://www.osha-slc.gov/OshDoc/Speech_data/SP19 980428.html. Job stress poses a threat to the health of workers and, in turn, to the health organizations. This booklet highlights knowledge about the causes of stress at work and outlines steps that can be taken to prevent job stress.

4. Common-sense recommendations to reduce workplace violence can be found at http://scripts.osha-slc.gov/PHP/redirect.php?url= http:// www.opm.gov/ehs/workplac/index.htm.

5. U.S. Office of Personnel Management. (1998). *Dealing with workplace violence: A guide for agency planners.* Retrieved from http:// scripts.osha-slc.gov/PHP/redirect.php?url=http://www.opm.gov/ehs/ workplac/ pdf/full.pdf. This handbook is the result of a cooperative effort of many federal agencies sharing their expertise in preventing and dealing with workplace violence. It is intended to assist those who are responsible for establishing workplace violence initiatives at their agencies.

6. U.S. Department of Justice. (1998, July 18). *Workplace violence, 1992-96.* Retrieved from http://scripts.osha-slc.gov/PHP/redirect .php?url=http://www.ojp.usdoj.gov/ovc/new/directions/pdftxt/ bulletins/bltn13.pdf.Analysis of workplace violence from a crime victimization survey from the Bureau of Justice Statistics.

7. DHHS (NIOSH). (1995). *Preventing homicide in the workplace* (Publication No. 93-109). Retrieved from http://www.cdc. The principal contributor to this Alert was Dawn N. Castillo, Division of Safety Research, NIOSH. Comments, questions, or requests for additional information should be directed to Dr. Thomas R. Bender, Director, Division of Safety Research, National Institute for Occupational Safety and Health, 944 Chestnut Ridge Road, Morgantown, WV 26505-2888; telephone: (304) 284-5700.

8. OSHA. (1996). *Workplace Violence Initiative.* Retrieved from http:// www.osha-slc.gov/workplace_violence/wrkplaceViolence.intro.html. National Institute of Occupational Safety, U.S. Department of Labor, Occupational and Health Safety Administration. (1999). *Stress at work* (Publication No. 99–101). Retrieved May 11, 2004, from http:// www.cdc .gov/niosh/ stresswk.html.

9. Legal Information Institute. (2004). *Unemployment Compensation Law: An overview.* Retrieved May 11, 2004, from http://www.law .cornell.edu/topics/unemployment_compensation.html.

Problems of Youth Crime and Violence

10

The Legal System and the Role of Forensic Social Work

> *During the Second World War, Jewish residents of Jedwabne, Poland were herded into a barn which was then torched by the townspeople killing over 1600 Jewish neighbors. How could such a thing happen? George Will (2001) believes that this terrible event took place, not because of political reasons or an affinity for the Nazi regime, but because the German authorities gave a hateful and deeply anti-Semitic people the opportunity to do so. Will writes, "Why in Jedwabne did neighbor murder their neighbor? Because it was permitted. Because they could" (p. 68). The lesson is that violence results when a society breaks down.*
>
> —Morley Glicken (2003, p. 239)

This chapter is about violent youth crime in America, a serious problem with a potentially harmful impact on all Americans. The chapter will discuss the helping organizations treating the victims and perpetrators of youth crime and the roles of social workers in the legal system. To show how serious the problem of violent crime is in America, by using comparative data from industrialized countries like Japan and Australia, Zimring and Hawkins (1997) report that U.S. violent crime rates are many times greater than other developed nations, whereas nonviolent crimes occur at about the same rates. For example, the U.S. homicide rate is 9.9 per 100,000, compared to countries such as England and Wales at 0.5, Japan at 0.6, France at 1.1, and Australia at 2.2. Even in countries that are in the highest 25% crime rate category (the United States, New Zealand,

Australia, Canada, and the Netherlands), the United States has four times the homicide rate.

Why should America have such a high rate of violence? Currie (1993) believes that our traditional institutions (e.g., the family, schools, and religious organizations) that teach people values and help control antisocial tendencies have weakened and no longer help control social and emotional problems that lead to violent behavior. In a more specific study of violence, Hawkins et al. (1992) analyzed 66 research studies that attempted to predict why people become violent. Five main reasons were identified: (a) individual factors (including medical, physical, and psychological), (b) family factors (parental criminality, child maltreatment, poor family management practices, poor bonding, parental substance use and violence, mobility, parent-child separation), (c) school factors (academic failure, low bonding to school, truancy and dropout, frequent school transitions, high delinquency rate), (d) peer-related factors (delinquent siblings, peers, and gang membership), and (e) community and neighborhood factors (poverty, community disorganization, drug and firearm availability, adult criminals, and exposure to violence and racial prejudice). The authors conclude that the greater the number of reasons for violence, the greater the probability that a person will become violent.

This is where social work comes in. Many people believe that treating childhood antisocial behavior, improving school performance, and helping children change negative peer influences are among the most successful ways of reducing the likelihood of violent behavior. Reducing family violence is another successful way of treating early signs of violence. When children come to the attention of the legal system because of their violent behavior, social workers are present in juvenile courts to help stop the cycle of violent behavior that, unless treated, will often lead to property damage, assault, rape, family violence, and, ultimately, homicide.

We can often identify the children who are most likely to become violent adolescents and adults. Wagner and Lane (1998) studied a sample of children and adolescents aged 10 to 17 years who had been referred to juvenile court in a large Oregon county whose arrest statistics were very similar to the nation as a whole. The authors discovered that 20% of the sample committed 87% of all new crimes. Sprague and Walker (2000) suggest that this small group of juvenile youth commit the most serious crimes and "are very likely to have begun their careers very early (i.e., before age 12)" (p. 369). Wolfgang (1972, 1987) reports that 6% to 7% of all boys in a given birth year will become chronic offenders, meaning that they will have five or more arrests before their 18th birthday. He also suggests that this same 6% to 7% will commit half of all crimes and two thirds of all violent crimes committed by all the boys born in a given birth year by age 18.

In another study, researchers looked at the relationship between violence and school disciplinary problems and found that 6% to 9% of the referred children were responsible for more than 50% of the total disciplinary

InfoTable 10.1	Homicide Data, 1976 to 2000

The demographic characteristics of homicide victims and offenders differ from the general population. Based on data for the years 1976 to 2000 (Fox & Zawitz, 2002),

- African Americans are disproportionately represented as homicide victims and are six times more likely to be victimized than are whites.
- Males represent three fourths of homicide victims and nearly 90% of offenders. In terms of rates per 100,000, males are three times more likely to be killed and almost eight times more likely to commit homicide than are females.
- Approximately one third of murder victims and almost half the offenders are younger than the age of 25. For victims and offenders, the rate per 100,000 peaks in the 18- to 24-year-old age group.
- About 924,700 adults were convicted of a felony in state courts in 2000. Of the felons convicted in a state court, more than two thirds were sentenced to prison or jail in 2000.

referrals and practically all other serious offenses including possession of weapons, fighting, and assaults on other children and teachers (Skiba, Peterson, & Williams, 1997). Early disciplinary problems in school are accurate predictors of future and more serious problems (Walker, Colvin, & Ramsey, 1995). According to Walker et al. (1995), students with 10 or more disciplinary referrals per year are seriously at risk for school failure and other, more serious life problems. Many of the children who are frequently referred to principals for disciplinary action are defiant and disobedient and may also be involved in bullying and intimidation of other students. They are, according to Sprague and Walker (2000), likely to move on to more serious offenses, including "physical fighting, and then ultimately rape, serious assault, or murder" (p. 370). Consequently, early identification and treatment of children at risk could significantly reduce the amount of violent crime in America.

Early and Late Starters of Violence

Moffit (1994) believes that children who develop early aggressive tendencies are much more likely to move on to more seriously violent behaviors than children who show no violent tendencies before adolescence. He calls these two groups *early* and *late starters*. Late starters show signs of violent behavior in late middle school and even high school. Early starters often show signs of disobedience, bullying, intimidation, and fighting when they begin kindergarten and elementary school.

According to Sprague and Walker (2000), "Early starters are likely to experience antisocial behavior and its toxic effects throughout their lives.

Late starters have a far more positive long-term outcome" (p. 370). Walker and Severson (1990) suggest that the behavioral signs of early starters include disobedience, property damage, conduct problems, theft, the need for a great deal of attention, threats and intimidation, and fighting. Mayer (1995) and Reid (1993) indicate that certain factors in a child's environment may predict potential for violent behavior. The most prominent of these factors include inconsistent and harsh parenting styles, disorganized or badly functioning schools, and the availability of drugs, alcohol, and weapons. Herrenkohl et al. (2001) note that

> individuals who initiate violent behavior in childhood are at particularly high risk for serious violent offending in adolescence and adulthood. . . . Risk for later violent offending typically diminishes with later ages of initiation, although initiation of violence at any age into adolescence is associated with an increased probability for violence at subsequent ages. (p. 45)

Elliott (1994) found that 45% of the preadolescents who began violent behavior by age 11 went on to commit violent offenses by their early 20s, whereas 25% of the children who began violent behavior between the ages of 11 and 12 committed violent offenses through adolescence and into adulthood. Thornberry, Smith, Rivera, Huizina, and Stouthamer-Loeber (1999) found similar patterns. The later the onset of violence, the less likely the child is to cycle into adult violence, whereas the earlier the violent behavior begins, the more likely it is to continue into adulthood. In a study of early onset violence, Herrenkohl et al. (2001) noted four indicators of future violent behavior in children aged 10: hitting a teacher, picking fights, attacking other children, and reports by parents indicating that the child frequently fights at home or in the neighborhood.

Catalano and Hawkins (1996) suggest that youth violence is the result of socialization into violent behavior that begins in early childhood and continues through adolescence. Violent behavior in elementary school increases the risk of violence in adolescence and adulthood. By socialization into violence, the authors believe that children have early experiences in antisocial behavior that are reinforced by peers and fail to be extinguished by adults monitoring the behavior. As the antisocial behavior continues with its particular rewards, the child seeks out others with similar behaviors that may accept, reinforce, and promote new antisocial behaviors that often lead to violence.

Gang Violence

Often, a significant connection exists between gang involvement, gang violence, and firearms. Quinn and Downs (1995, p. 15) studied 835 male

InfoTable 10.2	Gang Membership

1. It is estimated that more than 24,500 gangs were active in the United States in 2000, a decrease of 5% from the number estimated to be active in 1999. Despite this overall decrease in the number of gangs, cities with populations greater than 25,000 reported a very slight increase in the number of active gangs from 1999.

2. It is estimated that 772,500 people in the United States were members of gangs in 2000, a decrease of 8% from the number of active members in 1999, but again, cities with populations greater than 25,000 experienced an increase in the number of active gang members despite the overall drop.

3. In 1999 it was estimated that 47% of gang members were Hispanic, 31% were African American, 13% were white, and 7% were Asian. These percentages seem to remain fairly steady during the preceding years. (Egley, 2002)

inmates in six juvenile correctional facilities in four states. The authors found that movement from nongang membership to gang membership brought increases in most forms of gun-involved conduct. Of the sample, 45% described gun theft as a regular gang activity; 68% said that their gang regularly bought and sold guns, and 61% described "driving around and shooting at people you don't like" as a regular gang activity involving children as young as age 10.

The influence of gangs on younger children is significant and particularly serious in schools. Young people join gangs for a variety of reasons, which may include the following: a search for love; structure and discipline; a sense of belonging and commitment; the need for recognition and power; companionship, training, excitement, and activities; a sense of self-worth and status; a place of acceptance; the need for physical safety and protection; and part of a family tradition (Glicken & Sechrest, 2003).

Not all children who are living in poverty and adverse situations and are at risk of gang affiliation actually join gangs. The children who seem to be stress-resistant and avoid gang affiliation are those who: (a) are well-liked by peers and adults and have well-developed social and interpersonal skills, (b) are reflective rather than impulsive about their behavior, (c) have a high sense of self-esteem and personal responsibility, (d) believe they can influence their environment in a positive manner, (e) are flexible in the ways they deal with life situations, and (f) have well-developed problem-solving skills and intellectual abilities (Sechrest, 2001).

Although reasons for gang membership continue to be studied in considerable detail, there is relatively little information on the process of walking away from gang life. Hughes (1997) studied ex-gang members who successfully made the transition from gang life to more socially acceptable activities. She reports four reasons for leaving gang involvement: (a) concern for the well-being of young children, often their own;

InfoTable 10.3   Gang Violence in Los Angeles County, May 2005

	CRIME CATEGORY	THIS MONTH	PAST MONTH	YTD	PAST YTD	% CHG PAST YTD	5-YR AVG	% CHG TO 5-YR AVG
1	Homicide	17	17	114	137	−16.8	96.8	17.8
2	Attempted homicide	37	31	237	35	−24.8	242.4	−2.2
3	Felony assault	231	219	1164	1042	11.7	1013.8	14.8
4	Attack on police officer	5	1	32	30	6.7	34.4	−7.0
5	Robbery	155	191	856	1038	−17.5	846.0	1.2
6	Shots fired in inhabited dwellings	18	19	100	67	49.3	98.2	1.8
7	Kidnapping	4	3	28	17	64.7	21.4	30.8
8	Rape	1	4	14	27	−48.1	16.6	−15.7
9	Arson	0	0	4	1	300.0	2.0	100.0
10	Witness intimidation	48	61	258	311	−17.0	246.4	4.7
11	Extortion	2	1	9	7	28.6	5.8	55.2
12	Carjacking	8	5	49	58	−15.5	52.0	−5.8
	TOTAL	526	552	2865	3050	−6.1	2675.8	7.1

NOTE: YTD = year to date; CHG = change; AVG = average. These numbers are based on information input into a gang crime statistics database as of June 7, 2005. Data input into the system after this date will be reflected in the year-to-date total on the following month's report.

(b) fear of physical harm, incarceration, or both; (c) time to think about their lives, often done in prisons; and (d) support and modeling by helping professionals and volunteer community helpers.

According to Hughes (1997), the most promising reason for leaving gang life appears to be concern for the safety of young children. Many gang members have fathered children and, as their children begin to grow, fathers experience concern for their welfare. One of the major reasons for gang involvement, according to Sechrest (1991), is the family tradition of being in the same gang as a parent or sibling. Sometimes family tradition is used in the form of a "legacy" for early recruitment into gangs and may occur during elementary school when young recruits are given assignments to test their mettle as potential gang members. Such assignments may involve school violence and/or random violence involving the use of weapons.

In 1997, Father to Father, a national initiative supported by former Vice President Gore, was begun for the purpose of strengthening the bond between fathers and sons. Nationally, numerous programs have joined this initiative and have developed specific programs focused on fatherhood, an idea that could help gang members use their concern for the safety of children to leave gang life. Although these programs are promising, none has been well studied by researchers.

The Relationship Between Child Abuse and Violence

Many social workers believe there is a strong connection between child abuse and neglect and childhood, adolescent, and adult antisocial behavior and violence. Widom (1992) followed 1,575 cases from childhood through young adulthood, comparing the arrest records of children with reported and verified child abuse and neglect with children who had no recorded evidence of child abuse or neglect. The two groups were matched by age, race, gender, and approximate family socioeconomic status. The findings indicated the following: (a) the children who had been abused or neglected were 53% more likely to be arrested as juveniles; (b) the abused children were 38% more likely to be arrested as adults; (c) the abused children were 38% more likely to be arrested for a violent crime; (d) the abused children were 77% more likely to be arrested if they were female; (e) the children who had suffered abuse and neglect were arrested 1 year younger for their first crime; and (f) when compared to nonabused children, abused children committed twice as many offenses and were arrested 89% more frequently than children who were not abused. In follow-up interviews, Widom (1992) found serious problems in other areas of an abused child's life, including depression and suicide, poor problem-solving skills, extremely low IQs, poor reading skills, alcohol and drug problems, and un- and underemployment.

Are Childhood Bullies Likely to Be Violent Adolescents and Adults?

Natvig, Albrektsen, and Qvarnstrom (2001) found that about 10% in a population of youth aged 13 to 15 years were bullies. Pulkkinen and Tremblay (1992) report that bullies are typically aggressive, nonsocial, and hyperactive, but Olweus (1997) suggests that some bullies are insecure and anxious. On measures of self-esteem and self-views, Baumeister, Smart, and Boden (1996) found that youth with violent behavior often had unrealistically positive self-views that were not supported by feedback from teachers, classmates, and parents. If untreated, children who are bullied may develop depression, physical illness, and may even become suicidal. Borg (1998) notes that students who are bullies in elementary school may become involved in criminal and aggressive conduct during and after adolescence. Craig and Pepler (1997) believe that bullying is often tolerated by teachers and estimates that teachers intervene in only 4% of all incidents involving bullying behavior.

Natvig et al. (2001) report a significant relationship between bullying and increased feelings that school is "meaningless and unchallenging." The authors suggest that one way to deal with bullying is to find school activities that are more meaningful to these children. As an example, Ames (1992) suggests providing learning experiences that are less focused on memorization and repetition, the activities many students find boring and frustrating. These activities, which may not suit the learning style of children prone to bullying, may also increase stress. Consequently, the child who does poorly in school may take his or her failure out on other children in the form of hostile and aggressive behavior.

Cruelty to Animals Predicts Future Violence

Tapia (1971) discovered that in 10 of 18 case histories of children who were cruel and abusive to animals, bullying, fighting, fire-setting, and stealing were also commonly associated behaviors. Tapia (1971) also found that cruelty to animals suggests children who have problems of "aggression with poor control of impulses" (p. 76). Tingle, Barnard, Robbins, Newman, and Hutchinson (1986) determined that nearly half of the rapists and more than one fourth of the pedophiles they studied had been cruel to animals as children. In a study of serial killers, Lockwood and Church (1998) revealed that 36% of the serial killers reported killing and torturing animals in childhood. Ascione (1998) found that 71% of the battered women living in a shelter reported that their partners had harmed or killed at least one of their pets. One fifth of the women in Ascione's study delayed leaving their abusive partners because of their concern for the welfare of their pets. Arkow (1996) and Ascione (1993) suggest a connection between early childhood cruelty to animals and abuse of spouses and boyfriends/girlfriends in later life.

Fire Setting and Early Violence

The National Fire Protection Association (1999) reports that each year, fires set by juveniles account for a large amount of the property damage and deaths related to all fires in the United States. More than any other population, the fires set by children and adolescents are more likely to result in death (National Fire Protection Association, 1999). Fires set by children and adolescents resulted in 6,215 American deaths, 30,800 injuries, and billions of dollars in property damage in 1998 alone (National Fire Protection Association, 1999). The *Juvenile Justice Bulletin* (OJJPD, 1997) reports that juveniles younger than age 12 accounted for 35% of the arrests for arson in youth younger than age 18.

In a study of 186 juvenile fire setters, Showers and Pickrell (1987) found that 86% were male with an average age of 10. The authors note that juvenile fire setters often come from families whose parents abuse drugs or alcohol, and that the children were likely to have experienced emotional neglect and physical abuse. Juvenile fire setters, according to Showers and Pickrell (1987), are also more likely to have poor school performance. Kolko and Kazdin (1991) found that fire setters tend to have poorer social skills than non–fire setters and that they are more secretive, significantly more aggressive, yet also less assertive than non–fire setters. Raines and Foy (1994) note that typical juvenile fire setters have often experienced emotional neglect and/or physical abuse, have poor academic performance, and express more anger and aggressiveness than non–fire setters.

Sakheim and Osborn (1999) found that high-risk fire setters (children who had set more than five fires with the intent of harming others or doing property damage) gained sexual gratification from setting fires and often had fantasies about revenge and retaliation. A high number of serious fire setters had histories of acting in a sadistic way toward other children and animals. Few of the serious fire setters (27%) felt remorse or shame for the consequences of their fire setting, according to the authors.

Does Violence on Television and in Movies Lead to Violence in Real Life?

Simon (2001) reports that by the time a child completes elementary school, he or she has seen 8,000 murders on television. And although others may argue that if the home environment is right and the child is healthy then television violence doesn't greatly affect children, Simon doesn't agree. She says that when the aggressor in violent entertainment is admired by the child, the child begins to believe that violence will go unpunished if the reasons for such behavior are considered fair and correct by the child. She gives the example of her own child, who was sent home for fighting. He proudly told her that the other child didn't respect him and he had to be in charge. When she gave a disapproving look, her son shouted, "You don't understand! All the boys fight, mom" (p. 12).

InfoTable 10.4	Does Television Violence Cause Violence?

A great deal of concern has been raised about the relationship between early onset violence and a violent mass culture. On its national Web site, the American Psychological Association (2002) reports that

> children who watched many hours of TV violence when they were in elementary school tended to also show a higher level of aggressive behavior when they became teenagers. By observing these youngsters until they were 30 years old, researchers found that the ones who'd watched a lot of TV when they were eight years old were more likely to be arrested and prosecuted for criminal acts as adults. (p. 2)

Simon also cautions that young children are not socialized to understand transitions, subtle changes in behavior, or irony. What may be admirable to a child in a fictional character may be unacceptable to an adult. Furthermore, Simon argues that as children become desensitized to violence and their fear response becomes "muted," they may seek more gruesome shows and sights "to get the same thrill response and excitement, all in an attempt to master their fear" (p. 13). Finally, Simon notes that children believe that those who are victimized on television, in films, and in video games deserve to be victimized because they are bad or should be punished. "This increases the likelihood that children will act on aggressive impulses, with the confidence that they are right and that their actions are the way to resolve the conflict" (p. 15).

Simon (2001, p. 17) offers practical guidelines on ways of handling television violence at home. She suggests limiting total television for the family to 2 hours and watching television with the child to see what he or she is watching. She also suggests introducing children to different programming and to monitor the level of violence, even in cartoon shows. Discussing different ways in which a situation can be dealt with nonviolently can be helpful. Providing other alternatives to violent entertainment, such as outdoor activities, libraries, and sports, may be another alternative to a child watching violence in the media. Observe the adult's television viewing habits, she notes. Children will often watch what the adult watches. Keep the television out of the child's room and turn it off during meals. If children fight, unplug it.

Getting Tough on Violent Youth Crime

Horowitz (2000) believes that as a result of the increase in violence in America, many Americans are demanding harsher sentences for juveniles. In an opinion poll taken after the 1998 shootings in Jonesboro, Arkansas, in which four students were murdered by two classmates, Horowitz reports that half of the adults in America believed that the two killers should receive the death sentence even though they were only 11 and 13 years old. She says that increasing numbers of murders are committed by youth younger than age 18, and writes:

> Approximately twenty-three thousand homicides occur each year in the United States, roughly ten percent of which involve a perpetrator who is under eighteen years of age. Between the mid 1980s and the mid 1990s, the number of youths committing homicides had increased by 168%. Juveniles currently account for one in six murder arrests (17%), and the age of those juveniles gets younger and younger every year. For example, in North Carolina in 1997, seventy juveniles under eighteen years of age were arrested on murder charges. Thirty-five were seventeen, twenty-four were sixteen, seven were fifteen, and four were thirteen or fourteen. In 1999, for the first time in North Carolina's history, two eleven-year-old twins were charged with the premeditated murder of their father as well as the attempted murder of their mother and sister. (p. 133)

Horowitz (2000) argues that in this atmosphere of anger against juvenile violence that increasing numbers of states will pass legislation permitting the state to impose the death penalty on progressively younger and younger children, even though the U.S. Supreme Court has held that offenders must be at least 16 years of age before the death penalty can be imposed. As an alternative to the death sentence, which Horowitz believes is inhumane when applied to children, the easy road is to impose the death penalty on child killers; however, this approach will fail to address the underlying problems in our society that contribute to youth violence. She believes that focusing entirely on punishment will never end youth violence. What do you think?

Treating Youth Violence

Rae-Grant, McConville, and Fleck (1999) report that a number of programs have been tried with youthful offenders with some success. Among those programs are the following: school-based conflict resolution training programs, gun-free zones around schools, evening curfews, weekend and evening recreational programs, summer camps, job and training programs for youth at risk, and community policing (Ash, Kellerman, Fuqua-Whitley, & Johnson, 1996). Caplan et al. (1992) studied programs treating the early onset of drug use by teenagers. The outcomes of these programs resulted in better problem-solving skills, better control of impulsive behavior, and reduced alcohol use. Hansen and Graham (1991) found that fewer adolescents used alcohol and had better awareness of the risks of alcohol after drug and alcohol intervention. Mendel (1995) found that there was no relationship between the increase in guns obtained by the police and a decrease of violence in gun buy-back programs. Weil and Knox (1996), however, found programs limiting the flow of weapons across state lines to be effective.

Such popular but controversial programs as "boot camps" have not been shown to be effective (Henggeler, Schoenwald, Borduin, & Rowland, 1998). However, Borduin (1999) reports that multifocused diversion programs providing services to repeat youth offenders before they enter the court system have shown positive results. Greenwood, Model, Rydell, and Chiesa (1996) indicate that programs focusing on prevention of crime in youthful offenders were more cost-effective in lowering serious crime than mandatory sentences for adult repeat offenders. For children with multiple risk markers to develop violent and/or antisocial behavior, many programs target specific aspects of the child's family life.

Olds, Henderson, Tatelbaum, and Chamberlin (1988) provide an example of how an early infancy project for economically disadvantaged mothers with poor prenatal health, self-damaging behaviors, and poor family management skills can improve maternal diet, reduce smoking during pregnancy, result in fewer premature deliveries, increase the birth weight of babies, and result in significantly less child abuse. Johnson (1990) reports that providing social, economic, and health-related services to preschool children and their families with multiple risk markers improves academic success, reduces behavioral problems in at-risk children, improves parenting skills, decreases family management problems, and lowers the subsequent arrest rates for children. However, Johnson cautions that some of these positive outcomes are only effective for several years after follow-up. Johnson suggests that reasons for the lack of long-term effectiveness may be the result of diminished services to at-risk families, poor school experiences for children, and other problems in the lives of the families served. In a study of another preschool program, Weikart, Schweinhart, and Larner (1986) found similar results.

Rae-Grant et al. (1999) indicate that in elementary grade school children, "Interpersonal cognitive problem-solving programs gave rise to better problem-solving skills and fewer behavior problems in children with economic deprivation, poor impulse control, and early behavioral problems" (p. 338). Hawkins et al. (1992) report that a social development program in Seattle for similarly at-risk grade school children demonstrated positive results. Preschool and elementary school programs may be one proactive approach to preventing future delinquent and violent behavior.

Helping Organizations
Dealing With Youth Violence and Crime

The most frequently used helping organization for juvenile violence and crime is the juvenile court, an organization established in cities and counties whose dual purpose is to help youth who have committed a crime obtain necessary treatment and, if the court so deems it, to be placed in youth correctional facilities. Juvenile courts generally have an optimistic and positive view of children and believe that children should be treated in a gentler way when they get into difficulty than adults. This isn't always the case, however, and there is some truth in the belief that the older and more difficult the youth, the less lenient the court will be.

Juvenile courts also hold youth until the court has made a determination about the child, and are very different from adult courts because judges have great flexibility in the way a case might be handled. For this reason, some critics of juvenile courts point to less leniency for minority and poor youth and greater leniency for affluent youth or those with social and political connections. Conditions in juvenile facilities can be grim. I worked for King County Juvenile Court as a probation officer one summer during my MSW Program at the University of Washington in Seattle. My father came to visit me and groused about how kids get away with murder until he came to the court, saw how children were warehoused, smelled the institutional smells, went back to his hotel, and got sick.

Historically, the juvenile court was created nearly 100 years ago because it was recognized that children are developmentally different from adults and that these differences should be considered when legal issues involving children are discussed. But according to the Brookings Institution (2005), juvenile courts have "struggled to provide juveniles with the constitutional due process protections mandated by U.S. Supreme Court decisions of the 1960s and 1970s" (p. 1), and "political discontent with juvenile court outcomes has resulted in increasing numbers of juvenile offenders being transferred to adult court" (p. 1). The federal Adoption Assistance and Child Welfare Act of 1980 expanded the court's role in child abuse and neglect cases to include monitoring public child welfare agencies and ensuring that appropriate decisions about safe and permanent homes are carried out in a timely manner. In a further discussion of juvenile courts, the Brooking Institution notes that

> the juvenile court was created by and is governed by state law. In many jurisdictions, the court does not have adequate tools and capacity to meet the challenges before it: The court often suffers from low status and prestige within the state court system. Judges and attorneys frequently have little specific training for juvenile court work and rotate through the court for brief periods of time. Information systems are often rudimentary, and aggregate data about case outcomes and the court's handling of cases are in short supply. Promising trends that can help the court remain viable and meet the challenges before it include improved coordination of branches of the court addressing family issues and better use of alternative dispute resolution to reduce the number of formal court proceedings. (p. 1)

InfoTable 10.5	Juvenile Court

The juvenile court is a division of the superior court. It handles three types of cases: delinquency, status offense, and child abuse and neglect.

Juvenile delinquency: These cases involve children who have committed law violations that, if committed by an adult, would be considered crimes.

Juvenile status offenses: These offenses concern noncriminal behaviors that are illegal because of the child's age. These behaviors are not illegal for adults. For example, typical status offenses are truancy (cutting school) and running away from home.

Juvenile dependency: Abuse and neglect cases concern family situations where allegations of abuse or neglect have been made, and the juvenile court intervenes to protect the family's children.

The Court's Authority

The juvenile court has broad authority in juvenile delinquency and dependency cases. It can remove children from their homes, order their placement with relatives or in foster care or group homes, terminate parental rights, create new parental rights, and join various agencies to provide needed services. In delinquency cases, the juvenile court can also order children confined in locked facilities, such as detention halls, ranches, and the California Youth Authority.

Whenever the court decides to remove a child from his or her home, placement and responsibility for that child is given to a governmental agency. In delinquency and status offense cases, that agency is the probation department; in abuse and neglect cases, the agency is the county welfare department. The agency is responsible for meeting the health and educational needs of the child, as well as providing the care, treatment, and guidance the child may need. (Judicial Council of California, 2005)

A second helping organization is the child welfare system, which operates, in most places, on a county-wide level. Child welfare departments deal with child physical and sexual abuse and neglect and have the right to take children from homes and recommend prosecution of abuse and neglect to county attorneys. The child welfare system is very overworked in America, and few children actually are fully served because complete investigations of abuse and neglect are not made. Worker turnover rates of up to 100% have been reported in some agencies in 6 months because the work is tough. Deciding whether to take a child from his or her parents is always difficult, and not everyone can handle this demanding type of work. But no doubt, child welfare workers save lives and act as public defenders of children's rights.

The police are a third helping organization. Although we may not think of law enforcement as a helping profession, a cooperative relationship between the police and child welfare agencies often results in help to families at-risk early on because the police are called out on domestic disputes. When children are at risk of assault and molestation at home, the police try to ensure that these children will be safe.

Schools are often the first place abused, neglected, and children at risk of health and mental health problems are identified. School social workers, counselors, nurses, and teachers work very early on with troubled children and are often successful in identifying problems and making certain that treatment is provided. Schools are major referral sources to health, social welfare, and mental health agencies when children have problems too serious for the school to handle.

Health, mental health, and family service agencies are important organizations helping children at risk of violence. Physicians often see violent children because of fights that lead to physical injury and because schools are concerned that childhood violence may have a biological cause. They also see children who suffer from physical and sexual abuse and neglect, and they are mandated reporters of all forms of child abuse. Even though the communication between a client and a physician is confidential, when violence to children and adults is thought to be a problem, physicians must report suspicions of violence. Mental health and family service agencies often see adults whose emotional problems cycle over to the abuse of children. As mandated reporters, they are expected to report alleged child abuse to child welfare agencies. If the safety of a child is at risk, as in the case of sexual abuse or violent behavior by an adult to a child, these agencies are obligated by law to report the potential harm to the person at risk. In a child's case, the child welfare agency and the police would often be notified because they act in the interest of the child.

How Social Workers Help Violent Youth

Social workers have many responsibilities in the legal system. For this reason we are often called *forensic social workers* to indicate our responsibility for working with crime and violence in the legal system. Social workers help children with the potential for violent behavior or those who are currently experiencing violent behavior.

First, social workers are probation and parole officers in the state and federal court systems with juveniles and adults. Probation occurs when the court sentences a perpetrator to jail but opts instead to offer treatment in lieu of jail. Parole occurs after a perpetrator has been in jail or prison. In these capacities, social workers try and make certain that perpetrators of crimes do not reoffend. We do this by offering personal, group, and family counseling and by working with juvenile offenders to reenter school and receive training for work. We also work with the community to overcome biases about hiring people who have committed criminal acts. On a day-to-day basis, we keep tabs on perpetrators in our case loads and make certain that their living situations are suitable and they aren't breaking their probation or parole rules. Those rules include not associating with known felons, using substances, or committing crimes. Probation and parole officers have the right to order juvenile and adult offenders back to prison if there is evidence that these rules have been broken.

Many states require mental health services for people with emotional problems who are awaiting trial in county or city jails and juvenile detention facilities. Social workers provide these services either as public employees of the county or state or as employees of mental health agencies who contract their services out to local jails and prisons.

Social workers also work with police departments and are frequently used in hostage negotiations, domestic disturbances, profiling perpetrators in unsolved cases of violence, and working with police officers who have been traumatized by an aspect of their work or are suffering burnout or substance abuse problems.

In prisons and juvenile facilities, social workers provide treatment to prisoners. They also write recommendations to the court and parole boards regarding whether perpetrators should be allowed to leave juvenile or adult facilities on parole or receive probation instead of going to jail.

Social workers frequently work in mental institutions serving felons who have committed serious crimes but who have been judged to be mentally ill when the crime was committed. In this role, the social worker provides a range of services meant to help the person become well enough to stand trial for his or her offense.

In rape crisis centers and local and state victim assistance programs, social workers often help victims of crime. Social workers provide counseling and advocacy to victims of family violence and work with perpetrators to eliminate their violent behavior.

Social workers help prevent potential violent behavior by working with children at risk of becoming violent and their families in schools, recreational centers, and through community outreach programs such as Big Brothers, Big Sisters, and Al-Anon.

A great deal of individual, family, and group counseling to abused and neglected children at risk of violent behavior is provided by social workers. They do this in publicly funded child welfare agencies and in family service and mental health agencies. Many social workers are private practitioners and offer these services for a fee that may be paid by insurance companies as part of a medical insurance plan or by the state in the form of a contract for service. Many private, nonprofit agencies receive funding from city, county, and state grants to provide free services to abused children and their families.

Finally, abused and neglected and violent children are seen by school social workers. This is front-line work because children with serious problems that could lead to violence are almost always initially identified by their behavior in school. I've been a school social worker in Seattle and Chicago. It's the most glorious work, and I saw many angry and troubled children prone to future violence. My interventions, and those of my colleagues, at an early point saved thousands of children's lives from future problems. Being a helper to children is among the most important work any of us can perform. Almost every study shows that children at risk are mostly fine by age 18 when they have someone in their corner helping them out, and those who aren't do well by age 30 for the same reasons. It's never too late to make changes in life if you have a person you can trust who is helping and providing support.

You Be the Social Worker

Here's a case a student of mine worked with. What would you do if you were the social worker?

Xavier Brown is a 16-year-old African American high school student who was arrested for beating a homeless man after Xavier had spent the day drinking with friends. He claims that he blacked out and that the next thing he remembered was being placed in the patrol car by a police officer. He has no memory of assaulting the homeless man. He says that he comes from a religious family where violence is not permitted. This is the third time in 4 months that Xavier has assaulted someone after a bout of drinking. He is currently in a county juvenile detention facility where he is awaiting a 9-month placement in a residential facility specializing in the treatment of juvenile offenders with drug and alcohol problems.

There is a history of drinking problems in Xavier's family, although no one has been involved in violence. Xavier was introduced to liquor at age 10 by an uncle and has been frequently using it since he was 13. He says that he can go for weeks without a drink, but then something happens and he just can't stop drinking. He doesn't understand the blackouts and is never sick afterwards. He doesn't know why he assaults people when he's been drinking. He considers himself to be a religious person and has a personal code that doesn't allow violence. He does well in school, where he is seen as a quiet and respectful student earning average grades. He is a skilled athlete, and many people at his high school think he has the ability to play major league baseball. His future seems bright, except for his drinking and the violence it precipitates.

I was the field liaison (similar to a mentor for a student teacher) for the juvenile court forensic (mental health) unit, a division of the county mental health department and unaffiliated with the juvenile court. The presence of mental health in juvenile court is unpopular with court personnel but is required to meet a state law

(Continued)

(Continued)

that offenders with emotional problems should be provided with mental health services while incarcerated. I met with the graduate social work student assigned to work with Xavier and his supervisor, a licensed clinical social worker. Xavier has been seen three times in 4 months by the student because of arrests for assaults. Because the relationship between the forensic unit and the probation department is strained, plans are made for Xavier that often fail to include the recommendations of the mental health workers.

I wondered why Xavier blacked out and then committed crimes rather than pass out the way many people do when they have had too much to drink, but the supervisor said that this was common among many adolescent alcoholics and that it was the way many of them came into the system. The student believed that Xavier may have had some other problems, perhaps neurological in nature. Xavier was hit by a car at age 7 while walking across the street. He spent a number of weeks in the hospital. Xavier has no memory of the event and, because he was living with grandparents out of state at the time, the entire affair is sketchy. It raises the issue, however, of minimal organic brain damage and the possibility that the blackouts may be more the result of a neurological problem induced by alcohol and less the result of alcohol addiction.

The graduate social work student felt that placing Xavier in a drug and alcohol facility was a mistake without first obtaining a complete medical workup. Because the decision is the probation officer's, who has never actually met Xavier and who carries a caseload of 200 juvenile offenders, the student has accepted that the forensic unit is present in juvenile detention but is not expected to provide any meaningful treatment or to be involved in discharge planning. As the graduate student said when the conference ended, "Dr. Glicken, these people think social work is a joke. They figure the only way to treat offenders is to be even meaner than the juvenile. I don't know, but it seems to me Xavier's going to kill someone soon with his blackouts, and here I am trying to warn people and no one wants to listen."

Questions

1. Why would there be such a difference of opinion about Xavier between the mental health and the probation departments? Do you think the two approaches, mental health and probation, have very different philosophies about the way to deal with violent behavior? What do you think those philosophies might be?

2. How do you feel about people blacking out after drinking and committing crimes for which they say they have no memory? Do you think it actually happens, or do you think it's just a way of manipulating the legal system by removing blame for violent behavior from the perpetrator? Have you or anyone you know blacked out after drinking, done something out of character, and then had no memory of the event?

3. In addition to neurological reasons for blacking out, are there other medical/psychological reasons to explain selective amnesia in the commission of a crime?

4. The graduate student is opposed to sending Xavier to a facility treating substance abuse and thinks the client needs a complete medical and psychological workup before any treatment decision is made. Do you agree with this assessment? What if a neurological problem were found? Doesn't Xavier still have a substance abuse problem that needs to be treated?

5. Why would someone who is gentle when they are sober become violent when they drink? Do you think that alcohol releases inhibitions and the violence that results is a reflection of the anger people feel inside but can't express when they're sober?

Summary

This chapter on juvenile violence presents material on the causes of juvenile violence and the youth most likely to commit offenses. A number of scholars believe that the earlier violence starts in a child's life, the more likely he or she is to commit violent offense throughout life. Effective treatment approaches, the agencies dealing with violent children, and the role of social work are identified. A case study of a violent youth and questions are presented.

Questions to Determine Your Frame of Reference

1. Juvenile crime decreased from 1993 to 2000 but has been gradually increasing since then. Why do you think violent youth crime is on the increase?

2. Gang violence seems to be escalating in many urban and rural communities. Why do you think so many youth joins gangs?

3. The concept of early and late starters of violence suggests that early starters have more problems over their life span than late starters. Do you think this is necessarily true?

4. Do you think curfews and random checks for guns and substances in school and elsewhere will reduce violent youth crime? Might there be some unwanted consequences of these action? What might they be?

5. Children who have been repeatedly abused at an early stage in life are often full of rage. What would you do to help an abused child better cope with his or her anger?

Internet Sources

First, Satcher (2001) reports on youth violence. Next, the Center for Disease Control argues that violence is a public health problem. Finally, Dunn and Frost (2004) report the findings and recommendations of the bipartisan working group of the U.S. House of Representatives on preventing youth violence.

1. Satcher, D. (2001). *Youth violence: A report to the U.S. Surgeon General.* U.S. Department of Health and Human Services. Retrieved from http://www.surgeongeneral.gov/library/youthviolence/toc.html

2. Thornton, T. N., Craft, C. A., Dahlberg, L. L., Lynch, B. S., & Baer, K. B. (2002). *Best practices of youth violence prevention: A sourcebook for community action.* Center for Disease Control (CDC). Retrieved from http://www.cdc.gov/ncipc/dvp/bestpractices.htm#Download

3. Dunn, D., & Frost, N. (2000). *Preventing youth violence.* Bipartisan Working Group of the U.S. House of Representatives. Retrieved from http://www.house.gov/dunn/workinggroup/wkg.htm

The Graying of America 11

Helping Organizations
With Older Adults and the Role
of Social Workers in Gerontology

Older adults increasingly make up the population of the United States. In growing numbers, their issues and life experiences influence social policies and health and social welfare services. For the year 2003, the U.S. Census Bureau (2005) reported that 12.4% of the population consisted of Americans aged 65 and older constituting 36,000,000 Americans. The population of older Americans is getting older, with the number of Americans older than age 85 increasing faster than any other group. Since 1900, the proportion of Americans aged 65 and older has more than tripled, with current life expectancy for men at 73 years and for women, 80 years. Some demographers are predicting at least 600,000 to 4,000,000 Americans older than age 100 by 2020, and that 35% of the total population will be composed of Americans older than age 65.

Of all Americans aged 65 and older, 42% suffer from disabilities that affect their daily functioning whereas 10% of the total number of people in the population below the poverty line are older than age 65, with many living on an average social security pension of $12,500 a year and no other source of income.

As the number of older Americans grows, so does the realization that many have serious social, emotional, health, and financial problems that make aging a joyless and sometimes anxious and depressing experience. Many older adults with social and emotional problems go undiagnosed and untreated because underlying symptoms of anxiety and depression are thought to be physical in nature, and health and mental health professionals frequently believe that older adults are neither motivated for therapy nor find it an appropriate treatment. This often leaves many older adults trying to cope with serious emotional problems without adequate help. As this chapter will describe, the number of older adults dealing with anxiety and depression is considerable and growing as the number of older adults increases in America. Health problems, loss of loved ones, financial insecurities, lack of a support group, a growing sense of isolation, and a lack of self-worth are common problems among the elderly that lead to serious symptoms of anxiety and depression, problems that often coexist among many older adults. A case study presented in this chapter provides added information about the cause and treatment of depression and anxiety in the elderly.

Common Emotional Problems Experienced by Older Adults

The following data about common emotional problems experienced by older adults come from the website of the American Psychological Association (2004):

1. For adults, 5% to 7% of those aged 65 or older and 30% of those aged 85 or older suffer from dementia, an irreversible deterioration of cognitive abilities accompanied by emotional problems including depression, anxiety, paranoia, and serious problems in social functioning.

2. Six percent of older adults experience problems with anxiety for a period of 6 months or longer.

3. Older adults have much higher suicide rates than other age groups. Caucasian men who live alone suffer the highest suicide rates.

4. Sleep problems often increase with age, and roughly half of all older adults older than the age of 80 have problems sleeping.

5. Although rates of alcohol problems are lower than for other age groups, 2% to 5% of all men older than the age of 65 and 1% of all women in this age group experience alcohol problems.

6. Drug abuse is a common problem among older adults, who use 25% of the medication taken in the United States. The drug addiction problem is complicated by the fact that older adults are prescribed too many medications.

7. Older adults experience high rates of depression, which is often characterized by feelings of sadness and helplessness. Depression may come on quickly in older adults who are experiencing physical problems or have had prior emotional problems and may result in complaints about memory loss.

8. Adults experience the onset of Alzheimer's Disease, which affects memory and produces symptoms of disorientation. The symptoms of Alzheimer's are often gradual and may take 8 to 20 years from onset to complete deterioration and memory loss. The symptoms are profound

| InfoTable 11.1 | Taking the Car Keys From Elderly Is Tough: I Know First Hand |

The toughest thing I've ever done was to tell my dad he had to stop driving. He was 82 at the time. His memory was fading. His reflexes were slowed. It was a conversation we should have had long before he became a hazard to himself and others on Cleveland's highways. But it was a conversation no one in the family wanted to have. So we put it off until we could no longer ignore the obvious. Dad, like some of the nearly 19 million drivers age 70 and older in the United States, was a hazard on the highways.

We confronted him on a Sunday afternoon in 1997. My mom was in the hospital with two broken arms. The hospital's social worker had approached my brother Jim and me. "We're concerned about your dad's driving," she told us. "Several people here at the hospital are worried about how he pulls into and out of the hospital parking lot. He's going to kill someone, including himself. It's simply a matter of time. Today, tomorrow, but soon," she said.

So, we devised a foolproof plan. First we'd talk to Mom. And she agreed. "Your father should not be driving," she told us. We decided to meet in Mom's hospital room to talk to dad. According to our plan, the social worker would open the conversation in a nonthreatening way. We'd second her concerns. Mom would agree with us. And dad would hand over the keys. Simple. Do-able. Right? We rehearsed the meeting several times. Mom was fabulous. Jim, a psychologist, was excellent, too.

Dad arrived at noon. While he chatted with Mom, Jim and I went over the plan with the social worker. And then we walked into Mom's room. "Saul," the social worker began, "we're worried about your driving. We care about you. We don't want you to hurt yourself or anyone else." Jim and I jumped in at that point, echoing her words.

Dad looked like a kid who'd been cornered by bullies on the playground. His back literally against the wall, he looked from me to Jim, at the social worker and then at Mom who'd said nothing so far. "What are you talking about?" he whispered. "I'd be the first to know if I had a problem driving. I've been driving for more than 60 years. I'm a good driver." There were tears in his eyes. In mine, too. That's when Mom jumped in. "Your father's a wonderful driver," she said. "The best. I should know, I've driven with him for more than 50 years." And that was it.

Dad drove for another year or so until dementia made it impossible for him. At some point, he couldn't even remember how to start the car. We were lucky he didn't hurt himself or anyone else. But it was just dumb luck.

The fact is, people over 70 have a disproportionate number of accidents per miles driven, according to the National Highway Traffic Safety Administration. Indeed, their statistics show that not only do older drivers have more accidents; they are more likely than any other age group to kill themselves or others in an accident. We knew Dad should have stopped driving long before he did. My guess is most family members know. But there's a long way from knowing to doing something about it.

We need tough new laws to require annual driving tests, eye exams and other physical tests for older people. It's in their best interests and ours. What did we learn from our experience? Dad died in February 2000. Mom was still driving then, at 84. But we talked to her about our concerns and she agreed to sell the car. She's not happy about it, but today, at 87, she's alive and doing quite well.

Strict new laws could keep other older people safe, too. (Aaron, 2003, p. 3K)

and memory loss may be so severe that victims of the disease may not recognize family members and are often unable to function without help from others whom they may not even recognize.

Social Programs to Help Older Adults

SOCIAL SECURITY

This is the primary pension fund for older adults, paid for by a payroll tax of 7.75% for the employee and 7.75% for the employer. Social security not only provides a monthly benefit dependent on how long a worker has contributed to the fund and how much (the longer and more you've contributed, the greater your monthly benefit), but social security also provides monthly income if a worker becomes disabled and monies to the children of workers younger than age 18 if a worker dies. Social security is under a great deal of discussion currently because of fears that the social security fund will run out of money in the next 30 to 50 years. An article on the website (see Chapter 23) discusses options to fund social security and questions at the end of the chapter ask how you, as an employee, want the fund to proceed so that you will have income available when you retire.

MEDICARE

In 1965, the Social Security Act established both Medicare (a federal program) and Medicaid (a state program partially paid for by federal funds). Currently, Medicare provides coverage to approximately 40 million Americans. Medicare is the national health insurance program for:

- people aged 65 or older;
- people who choose to begin their social security benefits at 62 but at a reduced amount with limits on how much you can earn and still retain your benefits;
- some people younger than age 65 with disabilities; and
- people with End-Stage Renal Disease (ESRD), which is permanent kidney failure requiring dialysis or a kidney transplant.

ELDER ABUSE PROGRAMS

The abuse of older Americans is a very serious problem. The first National Elder Abuse Incidence Study estimated that a 551,011 elderly persons aged 60 and older experienced abuse, neglect, and/or self-neglect in domestic settings in 1996 (Rennison, 2000). Of this total, 115,110 (21%)

were reported to and substantiated by adult protective service (APS) agencies, with the remaining 435,901 (79%) not reported to APS agencies (National Center on Elder Abuse, 1998).

Neglect of the elderly was the most frequent type of elder maltreatment (48.7%); emotional/psychological abuse was second (35.5%), physical abuse was third (25.6%), financial/material exploitation was fourth (30.2%), and abandonment was least common (3.6%). Adult children comprised the largest category of perpetrators (47.3%) of substantiated incidents of elder abuse; spouses followed second by 19.3%, other relatives were third at 8.8%, and grandchildren were last with 8.6%.

Three out of four elder abuse and neglect victims suffer from physical frailty. About half (47.9%) of the substantiated incidents of abuse and neglect involved elderly persons who were not physically able to care for themselves, whereas 28.7% of the victims could marginally care for themselves.

Some experts estimate that only 1 out of 14 domestic elder abuse incidents (excluding self-neglect) comes to the attention of authorities. Based on these estimates, somewhere between 820,000 and 1,860,000 elders were victims of abuse in 1996, indicating that the majority of cases went unreported to state protective agencies (Tatara, 1997). From 1986 to 1996, there was a steady increase in the reporting of domestic elder abuse nationwide, from 117,000 reported cases in 1986 to 293,000 reported cases in 1996—a 150.4% increase.

SENIOR CENTERS

Public and private senior centers offer older people a place to go for nutritious meals, social activities, and a range of programs such as health screenings, flu shots, creative arts, exercise, and special events unique to individual centers. One special purpose for senior centers is to reduce feelings of loneliness and isolation that may exist because friends have passed on, a spouse may be ill or have died, and support systems have weakened with time.

MEALS ON WHEELS

Meals on Wheels (MOW) is a term to define organizations that provide meals to seniors in their homes. They are loosely affiliated organizations (usually staffed by volunteers) that are run by churches, civic-minded individuals, senior residence homes, and some locally funded agencies. At a local level, these organizations are highly efficient in providing meals for seniors who need some nutritional help at home, and many offer the chance for a personal visit as well. Each local organization is run independently and has its own rules, though most are very similar. Each local MOW sets its own prices and many have a "pay if or as you can" policy, whereas others have a minimum charge and each is responsible for finding new volunteers to deliver meals.

ASSISTED AND LOW-INCOME LIVING

Many communities offer older adults a needs-based option to live in subsidized housing. To qualify for subsidized housing, older adults must pass a needs test to determine their level of income and whether health problems limit their ability to safely live alone. Many communities also have publicly and privately supported assisted living options where a person may live alone but under the supervision of a qualified staff member who regularly checks to see if residents are free of emotional and health problems or have any personal needs that are unmet. Assisted living also offers residents hot meals to make certain nutritional needs are met.

NURSING HOMES

When older adults become too ill or disabled to utilize assisted living, nursing homes are available, but they are very costly. It's not unusual for nursing homes to charge a resident $5,000 a month or more. For this reason, many communities try to maintain older adults in independent or assisted living arrangements through the use of homemakers who do light house cleaning, volunteers who help older adults who don't drive to get needed food and medical care, and low-cost or free busing. I was the executive director of a family service agency in Tucson, Arizona. We were proud to say that our average client receiving homemaker services was older than 90. This meant that our agency was able to help keep people in their own homes for a very long time and that the move to assisted living and nursing homes only happened as an absolute last resort. People are happiest when they live in familiar surroundings. The move from one's home to an unfamiliar place is often very traumatic and, for some older adults, it is accompanied by depression and anxiety.

How Social Workers Help Older Adults

Social workers help older adults in the following ways:

1. By providing counseling and psychotherapy where indicated for emotional problems.

InfoTable 11.2	Future Growth of Older Adults

The older population will continue to grow in the future. This growth will slow somewhat during the 1990's because of the relatively small number of babies born during the Great Depression of the 1930's. The most rapid increase is expected between the years 2010 and 2030 when the "baby boom" generation reaches age 65.

By 2030, there will be about 70 million older persons, more than twice their number in 1996. People 65 and older are projected to represent 13% of population in the year 2000 but will rise to 20% by 2030.

Minority populations are projected to represent 25% of the elderly population in 2030, up from 13% in 1990. Between 1990 and 2030, the white nonhispanic population 65 and over is projected to increase by 91% compared with 328% for older minorities, including Hispanics (570%) and nonhispanic blacks (159%), American Indians, Eskimos, and Aleuts (294%), and Asians and Pacific Islanders (643%). (American Association of Retired Persons [AARP], 1997)

2. By helping older adults with problems related to finances, food, and shelter.

3. By helping older adults receive necessary social, legal, and medical services.

4. By working in nursing homes and ensuring that older adults are taken care of properly, medically and emotionally, and that families stay in contact with nursing home residents.

5. By working in agencies that protect older adults from elder abuse by caretakers and others.

6. By advocating for older adults in the political system and with other social and health-related agencies.

7. By providing case management assistance that assures older adults that someone is managing the case so that they receive the best care possible. Case management is an approach that is usually associated with "case identification and outreach, assessment and service planning, service linkage, monitoring of service delivery, and advocacy" (Rubinbach, 1992, p. 139). The purpose of case management is to provide a complete range of services to clients and to "bind" the case manager to the client and the community by assuring both groups that all services needed by the client will be delivered in a timely, effective, and coordinated manner.

8. By assuring families that older adults living in their own homes are in good physical and emotional health.

9. By helping with retirement planning and, once retired, by helping older adults with the sometimes difficult transition from work to retirement.

Social Work Intervention With Problems of Older Life Anxiety and Depression

InfoTable 11.3	Suicide in Adults Older Than 65

1. Although adults aged 65 and older comprise only 13% of the U.S. population, they accounted for 18% of the total number of suicides that occurred in 2000.

2. The highest rate of suicide (19.4 per 1,000) is among people aged 85 and over, a figure that is twice the overall national rate. The second highest rate (17.7 per 100,000) is among adults aged 75 to 84.

3. Older adults have a considerably higher suicide completion rate than other groups. While for all age groups combined there is one completed suicide ending in death for every 20 attempts, there is one completed suicide ending in death for every four attempts among adults who are 65 and older. (Older Women's League, 2004)

Anxiety in Older Adults

Older adult anxiety may be suggested by the following symptoms: chest pains, heart palpitations, night sweats, shortness of breath, essential hypertension, headaches, and generalized pain. Because physicians often fail to diagnose the underlying reasons for anxiety in elderly patients, the emotional aspects of the problem are frequently not dealt with. Definitions and descriptions of anxiety used in diagnosing younger patients often fail to capture the unique stressors that older adults must deal with or the fragile nature of life for older adults as they attempt to cope with limited finances, failing health, the death of loved ones, concerns about their own mortality, and a sense of uselessness and hopelessness because their roles as adults have been dramatically altered with age and retirement.

Smith, Sherrill, and Celenda (1995) report symptoms of anxiety in 5% to 30% of older primary care patients and believe that intense late-life anxiety results from "feelings of loneliness, worthlessness, and uselessness. Ill health, the loss of friends and loved ones, and financial problems all can contribute to the development of anxiety symptoms" (p. 5). Lang and Stein (2001) found that women have higher rates of anxiety across all age groups and that older adults who have experienced anxiety problems in the past are more at risk of the problem worsening as they age. Agoraphobia, or the fear of leaving home, may also be more likely to have a late-life onset as a result of physical limitations, disabilities, unsafe neighborhoods, and other factors that make some older adults fearful of leaving home. Because anxiety in the elderly may have a physical cause or may realistically be connected to concerns about health, Kogan, Edelstein, and McKee (2000) provide the following guidelines for distinguishing an anxiety disorder in the elderly from anxiety related to physical problems.

PHYSICAL CAUSES OF ANXIETY

A physical cause of anxiety is more likely if the onset of anxiety comes suddenly, the symptoms fluctuate in strength and duration, and if fatigue was present before the symptoms of anxiety were felt. The authors identify the following medical problems as reasons for symptoms of anxiety: (a) medical problems that include endocrine, cardiovascular, pulmonary, or neurological disorders; and (b) the impact of certain medications, most notably stimulants, beta-blockers, certain tranquilizers, and, of course, alcohol and some nonprescription medicines.

EMOTIONAL CAUSES OF ANXIETY

An emotional cause of anxiety is more likely if the symptoms have lasted 2 or more years with little change in severity and if the person has other coexisting emotional symptoms. However, anxiety may cycle on and off, or a lower level of generalized anxiety may be present that causes the elderly client a great deal of discomfort. Obsessive concerns about financial issues and health are realistic worries that trouble elderly clients. These concerns may be situational or they may be constant but not serious enough to lead to a diagnosis of anxiety. Nonetheless, they cause the client unhappiness and may actually lead to physical problems including high blood pressure, cardiovascular problems, sleep disorders, and an increased use of alcohol and over-the-counter medications to lessen the symptoms of anxiety.

Depression in Older Adults

Wallis (2000) suggests that older adults may express depression through such physical complaints as insomnia, eating disorders, and digestive problems. They may also show signs of lethargy, have less incentive to do the activities they did before they became depressed, and experience symptoms of depression while denying that they are depressed. Mild and transient depression brought on by situational events usually resolve themselves in time, but moderate depression may interfere with daily life activities and can result in social withdrawal and isolation. Severe depression may result in psychotic-like symptoms, including hallucinations and loss of touch with reality (Wallis, 2000). Clearly, however, older adults have intrusive health and mental health issues that may cause depressed feelings and lead to changes in functioning.

To determine whether there are factors other than health problems or issues of isolation that cause depression, Mills and Henretta (2001) found significant differences along racial and ethnic lines. Many more Hispanics and African Americans older than age 65 report that their health is only fair or poor, as compared to non-Hispanic white elderly. Axelson (1985) reports that Mexican Americans tend to see themselves as "old" much earlier in life than other groups (e.g., at about age 60, as compared with age 65 and 70 for black and white Americans). Axelson believes that attitudes and expectations about aging "may put the Hispanic elderly at increased risk of what has been called psychological death, meaning a giving up or disengagement from active involvement in life" (Mills & Henretta, 2001, p. 133).

While socioeconomic status (SES) has often been thought to predict life span and overall health, Robert and Li (2001) found evidence of a relationship between levels of community health and individual health. Lawton (1977) believes that older adults experience the community as their primary source of support, recreation, and stimulation rather than family or a core of friends. Lawton and Nahemow (1973) suggest that healthy community environments are particularly important for older adults who may have emotional, physical, or cognitive problems. To understand the concept of healthy communities, Robert and Li (2001) define healthy communities as having (a) a physical environment with limited noise, manageable traffic, and adequate lighting; (b) a social environment with low crime rates, safe environments to walk in, and easy access to shopping; and (c) a service environment that includes easy and safe access to inexpensive transportation, senior centers, medical care, and meal sites.

Social support networks for older adults are also a factor in positive health and mental health. Tyler and Hoyt (2000) studied the emotional impact of natural disasters on older adults who had predisaster indications of depression and found that participants with consistent social supports had lower levels of depression before and after a natural disaster than depressed participants without social supports. In a study of successful aging, Vaillant and Mukamal (2001) found that one can predict longer and healthier lives before the age of 50 by considering the following indicators: family cohesion, preexisting major depression, ancestral longevity, childhood temperament, and physical health at age 50. Negative variables affecting physical and emotional health that we have control over include alcohol abuse, smoking, marital instability, lack of exercise, obesity, unsuccessful coping abilities, and lower levels of education.

Vaillant and Mukamal (2001) suggest that we have considerable control over our health after retirement. They believe that successfully aging older adults (a) see themselves as healthier than their peers, even though their physicians may not agree; (b) plan ahead and retain intellectual curiosity and involvement with their own creative abilities; (c) believe that life is meaningful; (d) use humor as a way of coping with life; (e) remain physically active and continue physical activities that were used at an earlier age, including walking, tennis, and aerobic exercises; (f) have a more serene and spiritual approach to life than those who age less well; (g) continue to have friendships, positive interpersonal relationships, and satisfaction with spouses, children, and family life; and (h) are socially involved in civic and volunteer work.

Depression in an Older Adult

This case study first appeared in modified form in my book on evidence-based practice (Glicken, 2005, pp. 227–229).

Jake Kissman is a 77 year-old widower whose wife, Leni, passed away a year ago. Jake is emotionally adrift and feels lost without Leni's companionship and guidance. He has a troubled relationship with two adult children who live across the country and has been unable to turn to them for solace and support. Like many older men, Jake has no real support group or close friends. Leni's social circle became his, but after her death, her friends left Jake to fend for himself. Jake is a difficult man who is prone to being critical and insensitive. He tends to say whatever enters his mind at the moment no matter how hurtful it may be, and then is surprised that people take it so badly. "It's only words," he says, "what harm do words do? It's not like smacking somebody." Before he retired, Jake was a successful salesman and can be charming and witty but, sooner or later, the disregard for others comes through and he ends up offending people.

Jake's depression shows itself in fatigue, feelings of hopelessness, irritability, and outbursts of anger. He doesn't believe in doctors and never sees them. "Look what the jerks did to poor Leni? A healthy woman in her prime and she needed a surgery like I do. They killed her, those butchers." Jake has taken to pounding on the walls of his apartment whenever noise from his neighbors upsets him. Complaints from surrounding neighbors have resulted in the threat of an eviction. Jake can't manage a move to another apartment by himself and someone from his synagogue contacted a clinical social worker in the community who agreed to visit Jake at his apartment. Jake is happy that he has company, but is angry that someone thought he needed help. "Tell the morons to stop making so much noise and I'll be fine. The one next door with the dog, shoot her. The one on the other side who bangs the cabinets, do the same. Why aren't *they* being kicked out?"

The social worker listens to Jake in a supportive way. He never disagrees with him, offers advice, or contradicts him. Jake is still grieving for his wife and her loss has left him without usable coping skills to deal with the pressures of single life. He's angry and depressed. To find out more about Jake's symptoms, the social worker has gone to the literature on anger, depression, and grief. While he recognizes that Jake is a difficult client in any event, the data he collected helped him develop a strategy for working with Jake.

(Continued)

(Continued)

The social worker has decided to use a strengths approach (Weick, et al., 1989; Saleebey, 1992; Glicken, 2004) with Jake. The strengths approach focuses on what clients have done well in their lives and uses those strengths in areas of life that are more problematic. The approach comes from studies on resilience, self-healing, and on successful work with abused and traumatized children and adults.

Jake has many positive attributes that most people have ignored. He was a warm and caring companion to Leni during her illness. He is secretly very generous and gives what he has to various charities without wanting people to know where his gifts come from. He helps his children financially and has done a number of acts of kindness for neighbors and friends, but in ways that always make the recipients feel ambivalent about his help. Jake is a difficult and complex man and no one has taken the time to try and understand him. The social worker takes a good deal of time and listens closely.

Jake feels that he's been a failure at life. He feels unloved and unappreciated. He thinks the possibility of an eviction is a good example of how people, "do him in" when he is least able to cope with stress. So the social worker listens and never disagrees with Jake. Gradually, Jake has begun discussing his life and the sadness he feels without his wife who was his ballast and mate. Using a strengths approach, the social worker always focuses on what Jake does well and his generosity, while Jake uses their time to beat himself up with self-deprecating statements. The social worker listens, smiles, points out Jake's excellent qualities, and waits for Jake to start internalizing what the social worker has said about him. Gradually, it's begun to work. Jake told the social worker to go help someone who needed it when Jake's anger at the social worker became overwhelming. Jake immediately apologized. "Here you're helping me and I criticize. Why do I do that?" he asked the social worker. There are many moments when Jake corrects himself or seems to fight an impulse to say something mean-spirited or hurtful to the social worker, who recently told him, "Jake, you catch more flies with honey than you do with vinegar." To which Jake replied, "So who needs to catch flies, for crying out loud? Oh, I'm sorry. Yeah, I see what you mean. It's not about flies, it's about getting along with people."

Gradually, Jake has put aside his anger and has begun talking to people in the charming and pleasant manner he is so capable of. The neighbors who complained about him now see him as a "doll." Jake's depression is beginning to lift and he's begun dating again, although he says he can never love anyone like his wife, "but a man gets lonely so what are you supposed to do, sit home and watch soap operas all day? Not me." The social worker continues to see Jake and they often sit and quietly talk about Jake's life. "I was a big deal once. I could sell an Eskimo an air conditioner in winter. I could charm the socks off people. But my big mouth, it always got in the way. I always said something that made people mad. Maybe it's because my dad was so mean to all of us, I got this chip on my shoulder. Leni was wonderful. She could put up with me and make me laugh. When she died, I was left with my big mouth and a lot of disappointments. You want to have friends, you want your kids to love you. I got neither, but I'm not such an "alte cocker" (old fool) that I don't learn. And I've learned a lot from you. I've learned you can teach an old dog new tricks, and that's something. So I thank you and I apologize for some things I said. It's hard to get rid of the chip on the shoulder and sometimes it tips you over, that big chip, and it makes you fall down. You're a good person. I wish you well in life."

Discussion

Most of the treatment literature on work with older depressed adults suggests the use of a cognitive approach. Jake's clinical social worker felt that the oppositional nature of Jake's personality would reject a cognitive approach. Instead, a positive and affirming approach was used that focused on Jake's strengths because, "Most depressed patients acutely desire the social worker's approval, and it is an effective therapist who gives it warmly and genuinely" (O'Connor, 2001, p. 522). While much of the research suggests the positive benefits of cognitive therapy, the social worker found the following description of cognitive therapy to be at odds with what might best help Jake. Rush and Giles (1982) indicate that cognitive treatment attempts to change irrational thinking through three steps: 1) Identifying irrational self-sentences, ideas and thoughts; 2) developing rational thoughts, ideas and perceptions; and, 3) practicing these more rational ideas to improve self-worth and ultimately, to reduce depression. While this approach might work with other older clients, the social worker believed that Jake would take offense and reject both the help and the social worker, finding them preachy and critical.

Instead, the social worker decided to let Jake talk, although he made comments, asked questions to clarify, and made connections that Jake found interesting and oddly satisfying. "No one ever said that to me before," Jake would say, shaking his head and smiling. "You learn something new everyday, don't you." The social worker would always bring Jake back to the positive achievements in his life, which Jake would initially toss away with comments like, "That was then when I paid taxes, this is now when I ain't gotta penny to my name." Soon, however, Jake could reflect on his positive achievements and began to use those experiences to deal with his current problems. In discussing the conflict with one of his neighbors, Jake said, "Maybe I should bring flowers to the old hag. Naw, I can't bring flowers, but she's no hag. I've seen worse. What about flowers? Yeah, flowers. Down at Vons, I can buy a nice bunch for a buck. So it costs a little to be nice. Beats getting tossed out on my keester." Or he would tie something he had done when he was working to his current situation. "I had something like this happen once. A customer complained to my boss, so I go over and ask her to tell me what she's mad about so I can fix it, and she does, and it gets fixed. Sometimes you gotta eat a little crow." As Jake made connections and as he began to trust the social worker, this process of self-directed change reinforced his sense of accomplishment and led to a decrease in his depression. It also led to a good deal of soul searching about how he had to make changes in his life now that his wife was gone. "So maybe I should stop feeling sorry for myself and take better care. What do you think?" (Glicken, 2005, pp. 229–230)

You Be the Social Worker

Linda Johnson is a 68-year-old retired executive assistant for a large corporation. Linda had a long, successful, and happy career moving up the ladder in her company to one of its most important and highly paid positions. She retired at age 65

(Continued)

(Continued)

in good health and wanted to travel and spend more time with her grown children and her grandchildren. A year earlier, still in good health and happy with her decision to travel, Linda experienced the beginning signs of depression. Alarmed because she had never experienced prolonged depression before, she saw her gynecologist during her annual physical examination and shared her symptoms with him. He immediately referred her to a psychiatrist, who placed her on an antidepressant medication and urged her to consider therapy. Because she had no idea what was causing the depression and thought that it might be something biochemical related to aging and the discontinuation of hormone therapy for symptoms of menopause, she decided against therapy and stayed with the antidepressant. There was little relief from the medication, and a second visit with the psychiatrist confirmed the need for therapy and a change in medication. The second medication made her fatigued and lethargic. After an additional month of feeling depressed, she saw a clinical social worker who worked with a group of physicians recommended by her psychiatrist.

Linda was very pessimistic about seeing a social worker. She had known many people in her company who had gone for therapy and who had come back, in her opinion, worse than before they'd entered treatment. She also thought therapy was for weak people and refused to see herself that way. When she began seeing the social worker, she was very defensive and kept much of the problem she was having to herself. The social worker was kind and warm and didn't seem to mind at all. This went on for four sessions. On the fifth session, Linda broke down, cried, and described the awful feeling of depression and her confusion about why someone who had never been depressed before would experience such feelings. The social worker asked her if she had any ideas about why she was experiencing depression now. She didn't. All she could think that might be relevant was that she had been an active woman all of her life and since her divorce at age 55, she had put all of her energies into her work and her children but now felt as if she was of little use to anyone. She was bored and thought it had been a mistake to retire.

The worker thought this was a very good theory and suggested that she might want to explore the possibility of going back to work, perhaps part-time at first, to see if she liked it. She returned to her old company, worked part-time in a very accepting and loving department where people were genuinely happy to have her back, and found that, if anything, the depression was increasing. Alarmed, she contacted the social worker and they began the work that ultimately led to an improvement in her depression.

The social worker felt that Linda had put many of her intimacy needs aside when she divorced her husband. She had not had a relationship since her divorce and felt bitter and angry with her ex-husband for leaving her for a younger woman. She had no desire to date or to form intimate relationships and repeatedly said that her good female friends were all she needed in her life. It turned out, as the clinical social worker helped Linda explore her past, that Linda was given large responsibilities to manage her dysfunctional family when she was a child. Never having learned about her own needs, Linda took care of people and now wondered who would take care of her as she tried to deal with depression and aging. Her very good friends found it difficult to be around her when she spoke about her depression. Increasingly, she felt alone and unloved. Her children were busy with their own lives, and she didn't feel it was right to ask for their help. The social worker arranged for several family meetings. Her children were, as Linda had predicted, sympathetic but unwilling to help in more than superficial ways. The recognition that her family didn't care about her as fully as she cared about them validated feelings she had not expressed to the social worker that her family and friends were not the supports she imagined them to be and that, in reality, she was alone in life.

This recognition of being alone led to a discussion of what Linda wanted to do in treatment. Improving the depression was foremost in her mind, but she also wanted to make some changes in her life. She expressed interest in social activities and accepted the social worker's suggestion that she join a self-help group for depressed older people going through an adjustment to retirement. Going to the group made Linda realize that she was a much more healthy and optimistic person than many of the severely depressed people in the group. She also made several friends who turned out to be true friends, one of whom was male. Although the relationship didn't become intimate, they were able to have companionship, travel together, and attend events. Linda found his company very comforting and supportive. She joined a dance group and, through the group, also made several friends. She began to date and experienced a type of intimacy with the man she was dating that she hadn't known in her marriage. In treatment, she focused on what she wanted in her life and how to use her highly advanced skills to achieve those goals. The depression began to lift as her social and personal life improved.

There are moments when she is still depressed. The social worker believes that these are more biochemical and situational than serious signs of depression. She continues to work with the psychiatrist on finding a better way to manage her depression biochemically. After 6 months of trial and error, they found a medication and dosage that worked well for her. She continues to work part-time, recognizes the primary reasons for her depression, and works on those reasons with her clinical social worker.

Discussion

Linda is like many older adults who find that retirement brings with it the painful realization that they are often alone in life. Depression isn't an unusual end result of this realization. Linda is a highly successful woman with many advanced strengths. The one thing that she could not easily do is to seek help, a common condition in people who have cared for others throughout their lives with little thought to being cared for themselves. The social worker stayed with Linda during her moments of denial and rejection of help and allowed Linda to go at her own pace.

(Continued)

(Continued)

Once Linda confirmed her painful depression and explained why she thought it was happening, the social worker supported her theory, which led to a helping agenda Linda could accept. Like many parents, the recognition that her children were only marginally involved in her life was a difficult one for Linda to accept, and it felt hurtful to her in the extreme. However, Linda now recognizes that her children have resented her intrusiveness into their lives since her divorce. The reaction of her children made Linda realize that she had been using her children for intimacy needs, both before and after her divorce, and that they resented it.

Once again, Linda feels in control of her life and, highly intelligent and insightful woman whom she is, sees the rebuilding of her life as a primary goal to ensure health and happiness. She has moved to another self-help group of more highly functioning people and feels a kinship with them. Her relationships with her male friends have blossomed and she realizes that the anger she had for her husband limited her ability to allow men into her life. The new feeling of comfort with her male friends has made her aware that many men find her interesting and attractive, and she is experiencing the pleasant sense of being in demand as a friend and companion. She values her male friends and sees in them the true friendships she wasn't always able to have before therapy began.

I spoke to Linda about her experiences in treatment. "I think I'd been a bit depressed since my marriage started to fail," she told me. "To cover it up, I was busy every second of the day. I'd work all day and then went to every play, musical event, and function I could find, usually with friends. My relationships were very superficial and it came as no real surprise that my friends weren't there for me when I became really depressed. The first thing I realized after retirement was that I had free time that I'd never had before. I filled it with everything I could find but still had time on my hands, and at some point, I didn't know what to do with myself. It was clear to me that my children felt confused about having me around so much, but I talked myself into thinking they needed me. I certainly didn't pick up the signs of their unhappiness over my frequent calls and visits. When the depression hit, I knew I needed help but I talked myself into believing it was hormonal. I knew better, of course, but I just didn't want to accept that I was depressed because I was living a depressing life.

"My social worker was pretty amazing. She let me babble on and not ever get to the point until I finally had nowhere to go with my feelings and just fell apart in her office. She involved me in determining the issues we would work on. She was very supportive and encouraging and always seemed to be able to see things in a positive way. In time, I guess I began to see things more positively. The groups I went to, run by other depressed people, really made a difference in my life. I've made some very good friends through the people I've met in group. They're not superficial people and they care about me. I've stopped bugging my family and I don't need to be busy every minute of the day. I have moments when I'm depressed, but it's not like the depression I had when I began therapy. That depression felt like I was falling down a black hole and I'd never get out. My social worker made me realize that I had lots of skills to manage my depression. The discussions about my life gave me an opportunity to see that I had never really asked anyone to give back to me emotionally. I think my husband got tired of my always giving even when he didn't need anything. He'd ask what he could do for me and I'd never know what to say. I think he started to feel irrelevant. I have a relationship in which we give equally, and while it sometimes feels wrong to even ask, I'm getting a lot better at it. Would I have gotten better without treatment? I doubt it very much. Medication helps a little, but it's no magic cure. My social worker pretty much saved my life."

Questions

1. I often hear from women of a certain age that they'd rather be with their female friends than with a man because they've had so many bad experiences with men. They frequently say that their friends are more supportive than any man could ever be. Do you think this is true, and do you know older women who feel this way? Do you think their relationships with other women are true friendships or are they more the superficial acquaintances described by Linda?

2. It's painful to think that Linda's children are unsupportive and even resentful of their mother and believe that she's been too involved in their lives as a way of not dealing with her own. Do you have any suggestions for the social worker to bring the family closer together, or do you think it should be left alone while Linda develops other areas of intimacy and friendship?

3. Do you think Linda retired too early, or is this a problem that would have occurred anyway?

4. It's too early for you to be thinking about retirement, but can you imagine suddenly stopping school and work and not having anything to do during the day? Many people at 65 are in excellent health but are bored and burned out with their jobs. What would you tell them about retiring?

5. Linda may be codependent, which means that she was trained by her biological family to care for others and not to think about her own needs. How is it possible for codependent people to ever gain real happiness when they have no idea of what it takes to be happy? Do you know anyone like this? How do they deal with having their own needs met?

Summary

This chapter discusses problems experienced by older Americans, particularly anxiety and depression in older adults, and the programs available to assist older Americans with health and financial problems.

Because older adults are often not thought to be open to using therapy, underlying symptoms of anxiety and depression may be ignored and medication or other nontherapy approaches may be used instead. Research data suggest that older clients are as positively affected by treatment as younger clients but are more susceptible to suicide, recurrence of depression, and other serious problems resulting from untreated symptoms. A case study and the You Be the Social Worker section gave examples of how social workers assist older adults experiencing anxiety and depression.

Questions to Determine Your Frame of Reference

1. Wouldn't the amount of anxiety and depression in an older population be eliminated if we had free health care, low-cost housing, decent pensions and important roles for older adults?

2. How can counseling and psychotherapy possibly help older adults deal with deteriorating health and the diminished capacity to do physical activities that were so easy for them to do when they were younger but are now so difficult?

3. There is great concern that the social security system will run out of money just about the time you will retire. Which of the following ways of keeping the system solvent do you support, and why or why not: (a) raising the payroll deduction tax from 7.75% to 8.5%, (b) not providing full benefits to anyone retiring before the age of 70, (c) not permitting people with good pensions from their employers or incomes greater than $50,000 to receive social security benefits, (d) allowing people to put aside some of their social security tax into private accounts managed by mutual funds or other financial instruments separate from government, or (e) decreasing benefits at the time of retirement from their current levels.

4. Why do older people have such a negligible role in American society when in other countries they play such an important role in government, family life, and business?

5. In a small group, discuss the following questions: (a) What age do you think you'll be when you retire? (b) Do you think you'll be sexually active at that age? (c) Do you think you'll be married? (d) What will you do with your time? (e) Will you have a close relationship with your extended family? (f) Will you have health problems? and (g) Do you think you'll be involved in community (volunteer) work?

Internet Sources

A discussion of aging is available from the Federal Interagency Forum on Aging (2004). Next, check the discussion of the silent epidemic of substance abuse among older adults (2004). The final article focuses on poverty among older women (1998).

1. Federal Interagency Forum on Aging. (2004, September 9). *Older Americans 2000: Key indicators of well-being.* Retrieved from http://www.agingstats.gov/chartbook2000/listoftables.html

2. U.S. Department of Health and Human Services. (2004). Substance abuse among older adults: An invisible epidemic. In *Substance abuse among older adults: Treatment Improvement Protocol (TIP)* (Series 26). Retrieved from http://www.health.org/govpubs/BKD250/ 26d.aspx

3. Poverty among older women. (1998). *Family Economics and Nutrition Review, 11* (3), 71–73. Retrieved from http://www.usda.gov/cnpp/ FENR%20V11N3/ fenrv11n3p71.PDF

Serious Emotional Problems and Mental Illness

12

Helping Organizations and the Role of Clinical Social Work

S ocial workers are very involved in the treatment of a range of emotional problems and their more serious form, mental illness. Many people in America have emotional problems that often interfere with schoolwork, jobs, and relationships. These problems include minor and major forms of depression and anxiety. The most serious forms of emotional problems are known as mental illnesses. This chapter will discuss the amount of emotional problems and mental illness experienced by Americans and their impact, the organizations that have major responsibility for helping people with emotional problems, the role of social work, and the best evidence of treatment effectiveness. A case study will discuss the symptoms, progression, treatment, and prognosis of a form of mental illness. Questions about whether mental illness is a life-long condition and the stigma attached to mental illness will also be discussed and, once again, you will again be asked to help resolve some serious problems in a case.

Definitions of Emotional Problems and Mental Illness

MENTAL ILLNESS

This category of serious emotional problems includes the various forms of schizophrenia and other mental disorders characterized by hallucinations, disorganized speech and thought processes, and grossly disorganized behavior including catatonia, flattened affect, and other symptoms that may so impair the client that meaningful work, relationships, and self-care are seriously affected (American Psychiatric Association [APA], 1994, p. 285).

MOOD DISORDERS

The fourth edition of the *Diagnostic and Statistical Manual of Mental Disorders (DSM-IV)* (APA, 1994) indicates that mood disorders include major depressive disorders lasting 2 weeks or longer with evidence of symptoms of depression; dysthymic disorders, in which depression has lasted longer than 2 years with more depressed days than nondepressed days; bipolar disorders, where depression and mania may be even at a severe level and where one or both symptoms may cycle back and forth; and cyclothymic disorders, where depression and mania cycle back and forth, but not at the same levels associated with bipolar disorders (APA, 1994, p. 317). The common bond among these various disorders is an impact on mood that suggests intermittent to long-term depression, or cycling between very high manic stages and very severe depressions. It is also possible that some mood disorders may have psychotic features, as is sometimes the case with bipolar disorder or very severe depressions. However, this is often not evident, and psychosis is only suggested for those clients demonstrating psychotic behavior and not by the term *mood disorders.*

The Extent of Serious Emotional Problems

The following data were found in a National Institute for Mental Health report (2001c):

> *General data.* An estimated 22.1% (44 million) of Americans aged 18 and older—about 1 in 5 adults—suffer from a diagnosable mental disorder in a given year. In addition, 4 of the 10 leading causes of disability in the United States and other developed countries are mental disorders—major depression, bipolar disorder, schizophrenia, and obsessive-compulsive disorder. Many people suffer from more than one mental disorder at a given time.

> *Depression.* Approximately 18.8 million American adults, or about 9.5% of the U.S. population aged 18 and older in a given year, have a depressive disorder. Nearly twice as many women (12.0%) as men (6.6%) are affected by a depressive disorder each year. These figures indicate that 12.4 million women and 6.4 million men in the United States suffer from depression in any given year. The average age of onset of depression is in the mid-20s but much earlier onset is common and might be seen in young children.

Bipolar disorder. Bipolar disorder affects approximately 2.3 million American adults, or about 1.2% of the U.S. population aged 18 and older in a given year. Men and women are equally likely to develop bipolar disorder. The average age at onset for a first manic episode is the early 20s.

Suicide. In the year 2000, 29,350 people died by suicide in the United States. More than 90% of the people who kill themselves have a diagnosable mental disorder, commonly a depressive disorder or a substance abuse disorder. The highest suicide rates in the United States are found in white men older than age 85. In 2000, suicide was the third leading cause of death among 15- to 24-year-olds. Four times as many men as women die by suicide; however, women attempt suicide two to three times as often as men.

Schizophrenia. Approximately 2.2 million American adults, or about 1.1% of the population aged 18 and older in a given year, have schizophrenia. Schizophrenia affects men and women with equal frequency. Schizophrenia often first appears earlier in men, usually in their late teens or early 20s, than in women, who are generally affected in their 20s or early 30s.

Anxiety disorders. Approximately 19.1 million American adults aged 18 to 54, or about 13.3% of people in this age group in a given year, have an anxiety disorder. Twice as many women as men suffer from panic disorder, post-traumatic stress disorder, generalized anxiety disorder, agoraphobia, and specific phobias, although about equal numbers of women and men have obsessive-compulsive disorder and social phobia.

Post-traumatic stress disorder (PTSD). Approximately 5.2 million American adults aged 18 to 54, or about 3.6% of people in this age group in a given year, have PTSD. About 30% of Vietnam veterans experienced PTSD at some point after the war. The disorder also frequently occurs after violent personal assaults such as rape, mugging, or domestic violence; terrorism; natural or human-caused disasters; and accidents.

InfoTable 12.1	Why We Have So Much Unhappiness

Martin Seligman (2002) worries that Americans have become so caught up in a personal sense of entitlement that even helping professionals have gone along with, in fact encouraged, "the belief that we can rely on shortcuts to happiness, joy, rapture, comfort, and ecstasy, rather than be entitled to these feelings by the exercise of personal strengths and virtues, which results in legions of people who, in the middle of great wealth, are starving spiritually" (ABCNews.com, 2002). Seligman goes on to say that "positive emotion alienated from the exercise of character leads to emptiness, to inauthenticity, to depression, and, as we age, to the gnawing realization that we are fidgeting until we die" (ABCNews.com, 2002).

Although the quality of life in America has dramatically improved during the past 50 years, Seligman (2002) reports that depression rates are 10 times higher now whereas life satisfaction rates are down substantially, suggesting widespread levels of unhappiness, depression, and more serious emotional disorders.

The Impact of Serious Emotional Problems

Druss et al. (2000) reports that about 3 million Americans have an emotional condition that affects their ability to work or to seek educational opportunities. NIMH (2001a) estimates that more than 2 million Americans experience the symptoms of bipolar disorder each year. The symptoms of bipolar disorder include distorted views and thoughts, a lack of will to live, labile emotions that often seem out of control, difficulties with cognition, and symptoms that affect the ability to work, attend school, have successful relationships, and live fulfilling lives (Jamison, 1995). In depressive phases of the disease, the suicide rate for bipolar disorder is very high.

Of clients diagnosed with mood disorders, 15% commit suicide and fully two thirds of all suicides are preceded by episodes of depression (Bostwick & Pankratz, 2000). Clients with depressive disorders had three times the number of sick days in the month before the illness was diagnosed than coworkers who weren't depressed (Parikh, Wasylenki, Goerung, & Wong, 1996). Depression is the primary reason for disability and death among people aged 18 to 44 years (Murray & Lopez, 1997). Pratt et al. (1996) followed 1,551 participants without a history of heart disease for 13 years. Participants with major depressions were 4.5 times more likely to have serious heart attacks than those without major episodes of depression (Pratt et al., 1996).

Markowitz (1998) found that people with mental illness are "more likely to be unemployed, have less income, experience a diminished sense of self, and have fewer social supports" (p. 335). According to Markowitz, much of the reason for this finding may be a function of the stigma attached to mental illness: "Mentally ill persons may expect and experience rejection in part because they think less of themselves, have limited social opportunities and resources, and because of the severity of their illness" (p. 343). Markowitz also suggests that clients with histories of mental illness anticipate rejection and failure because they've experienced social and employment-related discrimination. Understandably, this compounds feelings of low self-worth and depression (Markowitz, 1998). And although the quality of life in America has dramatically improved during the past 50 years, Seligman (2002) reports that depression rates are 10 times higher now whereas life satisfaction rates are down substantially, suggesting widespread levels of unhappiness, depression, and more serious emotional disorders.

The Mental Movement in the United States

The following information comes from the National Mental Health Association's (2005) history of mental health movement in the United

InfoTable 12.2	The Burden of Mental Illness

The *Global Burden of Disease* study developed a single measure to allow comparison of the burden of disease across many different disease conditions by including both death and disability. This measure was called Disability Adjusted Life Years (DALYs). DALYs measure lost years of healthy life regardless of whether the years were lost to premature death or disability. The disability component of this measure is weighted for severity of the disability. For example, disability caused by major depression was found to be equivalent to blindness or paraplegia whereas active psychosis seen in schizophrenia produces disability equal to quadriplegia.

Data developed by the massive *Global Burden of Disease* study conducted by the World Health Organization, the World Bank, and Harvard University, reveal that mental illness, including suicide, accounts for over 15 percent of the burden of disease in established market economies, such as the United States. This is more than the disease burden caused by all cancers.

Using the DALYs measure, major depression ranked second only to ischemic heart disease in magnitude of disease burden in established market economies. Schizophrenia, bipolar disorder, obsessive-compulsive disorder, panic disorder, and post-traumatic stress disorder also contributed significantly to the total burden of illness attributable to mental disorders. (NIMH, 2001b)

States. In the 17th and 18th centuries, individuals with mental illnesses underwent great suffering at the hands of American society. Viewed as demon-possessed or characterized as senseless animals, they were subject to deplorable treatment. Physical and mental abuse was commonplace, and the widespread use of physical restraints—straight-jackets and heavy arm and leg chains—deprived patients of their dignity and freedom. Nineteenth-century reformers, such as Phillip Pinel in France and Dorothea Dix, made great strides in promoting humane treatment of those with mental illness.

In 1900, Clifford Beers, a Yale graduate and young businessman, suffered an acute breakdown brought on by the illness and death of his brother. Shortly after a suicide attempt, Beers was hospitalized in a private Connecticut mental institution. At the mercy of untrained, incompetent attendants, he was subjected to degrading treatment and mental and physical abuses. Beers spent the next few years hospitalized in various institutions, the worst being a state hospital in Middletown, Connecticut. The deplorable treatment he received in these institutions sparked a fearless determination to reform care for individuals with mental illnesses in the United States and abroad.

In 1908, Beers changed mental health care forever with the publication of *A Mind That Found Itself* (1910), an autobiography chronicling his struggle with mental illness and the shameful state of mental health care in America. The book had an immediate impact, spreading his vision of a massive mental health reform movement across land and oceans. The actualization of the movement began that same year when Beers founded the Connecticut Society for Mental Hygiene. The Society expanded the following year, forming the National Committee for Mental Hygiene. The Society, in Connecticut and then nationally, set forth the following goals:

- to improve attitudes toward mental illness and the mentally ill,
- to improve services for the mentally ill, and
- to work for the prevention of mental illness and promote mental health.

The National Committee began fulfilling its mission of change immediately, initiating successful reforms in several states. In 1920, the Committee produced a set of model commitment laws which were subsequently incorporated into the statutes of several states. The Committee also conducted influential studies on mental health, mental illness, and treatment, prompting real changes in the mental health care system. The First International Congress for Mental Hygiene in 1930 was, perhaps, the pinnacle of Beers's career. The Congress convened 3,042 officially registered participants from 41 countries—with many more actually in attendance—for constructive dialogue about fulfilling the mission of the Mental Health Movement. The Movement was well established when Beers died in 1943.

In a historic merger, three organizations—the National Committee for Mental Hygiene, the National Mental Health Foundation, and the Psychiatric Foundation (an offshoot of the American Psychological Organization primarily concerned with fund-raising)—banded together on September 13, 1950. The National Association of Mental Health (NAMH) continued to educate the American public on mental health issues and promote mental health awareness.

In 1979, the NAMH became the National Mental Health Association (NMHA). In 1980, NMHA's 3-year leadership role in raising grass-roots support and cooperation with the federal government resulted in the development and passage of the Mental Health Systems Act of 1980. The Act fostered the continued growth of America's Community Mental Health Centers, which allow individuals with mental illnesses to remain in their home communities with minimal hospitalization.

NMHA created commissions on the insanity defense, the mental health of the nation's unemployed and homeless, the mental health of rural Americans, and the prevention of mental-emotional disabilities. These commissions examined the status of each issue and directed future reform efforts. In 1990, NMHA played a leading role in the development of the Americans With Disabilities Act, which protects mentally and physically disabled Americans from discrimination in such areas as employment, public accommodations, transportation, telecommunications, and state and local government services.

NMHA continues to strive to fulfill Clifford Beers's goals, spreading tolerance and awareness, improving mental health services, preventing mental illness, and promoting mental health. Its massive National Public

Education Campaign on Clinical Depression, begun in 1993, continues to inform Americans on the symptoms of depression and provide information about treatment. NMHA is also involved in the struggle for parity of mental health benefits with other health coverage. The Mental Health Parity Act of 1996 was a great victory, barring insurance companies and large self-insured employers from placing annual or lifetime dollar limits on mental health support, and cooperation with the federal government resulted in the development and passage of the Mental Health Systems Act of 1980. The Act fostered the continued growth of America's Community Mental Health Centers, which allow individuals with mental illnesses to remain in their home communities with minimal hospitalization.

Deinstitutionalization

In the 1970s, concerned that large numbers of people who were either not truly mentally ill or who could function well in communities with supervision and treatment were being warehoused in state mental institutions, hundreds of thousands of patients from state hospitals were released. Many reports of mistreatment of the mentally ill or the complete absence of any treatment led to the emptying of state hospitals which today are generally used only for those who are dangerous to others, who have committed a crime, who have been found to be insane when the crime was committed, or who are unable to involve themselves in an affirmative defense and await a court hearing when and if they are sane enough to stand trial. This leaves a large number of untreated mentally ill who often have few places to receive treatment, although county mental health facilities and group homes are sometimes available and a certain amount of day programming may be provided by city, county, and state governments offered through existing community agencies.

Unfortunately, the warehousing of the mentally ill in large mental institutions soon became the warehousing of the mentally ill in urban and rural downtown areas, where many mentally ill patients are often the homeless and destitute of urban and rural America. Commenting on the results of deinstitutionalization, Torrey and Zdanowicz (1999) write:

> The images of these gravely ill citizens on our city landscapes are bleak reminders of the failure of deinstitutionalization. They are seen huddling over steam grates in the cold, animatedly carrying on conversations with invisible companions, wearing filthy, tattered clothing, urinating and defecating on sidewalks or threatening passersby. Worse still, they frequently are seen being carried away on stretchers as victims of suicide or violent crime, or in handcuffs as perpetrators of violence against others.

While Americans with untreated severe mental illnesses represent less than one percent of our population, they commit almost 1,000 homicides in the United States each year. At least one-third of the estimated 600,000 homeless suffer from schizophrenia or manic-depressive illness, and 28 percent of them forage for some of their food in garbage cans. About 170,000 individuals, or 10 percent, of our jail and prison populations suffer from these illnesses, costing American taxpayers a staggering $8.5 billion per year.

Torrey and Zdanowicz (1999) go on to note that deinstitutionalization leads to delayed treatment, with a worsening of the problem and victimization. They report that more than 500,000 mentally ill people are being held in prisons in the United States, that 22% of women with untreated schizophrenia have been raped, and that suicide rates for those with untreated mental illness are 10 to 15 times higher than for the general population. They estimate that 5% to 10% of the 3.5 million people suffering from schizophrenia and manic-depressive illness require long-term treatment and hospitalization, something not often available since we've lost 93% of our state psychiatric hospital beds since 1955.

Treating Mood Disorders and Mental Illness

TREATMENT EFFECTIVENESS

In a study of why people drop out of out-patient mental health treatment, Edlund et al. (2002) found a dropout rate of 10% by the 5th visit, 18% by the 10th visit, and 20% by the 25th visit. Reasons for dropping out included concerns about treatment effectiveness and discomfort with the mental health treatment process. Commenting on these two issues, Edlund et al. write, "A large proportion of respondents believed that mental health treatments are not effective. Patients who held such a belief were significantly more likely to drop out of treatment" (p. 850).

Manfred-Gilham, Sales, and Koeske (2002) report that clients whose mental health workers prepared them for realistic vocational and community barriers were more likely to continue on with their treatment programs. The authors write, "We have some evidence from Kazdin, Holland, Crowley, and Bretan (1997) that therapists' perceptions of barriers predicted client treatment continuation more strongly than did the client's own self-report" (p. 220). In a very negative view of treatment effectiveness with severely depressed clients, O'Connor (2001) says that most depressed people receive care that is "superficial, inadequate, and based on false information" (p. 507). He also argues that close examination of most treatments for severe depression suggests that they are inadequate (Mueller et al., 1999; Solomon et al., 2000) and that most assumptions about the treatment of depression turn out to be untrue. Those assumptions include the belief that newer antidepressants are effective, that cognitive psychotherapy helps most patients, and that most patients can recover from an episode of depression without lasting damage (O'Connor, 2001, p. 507).

Remick (2002) found psychotherapy to be as effective as antidepressant medications in treating mild to moderate depression. The author found little support for a commonly held belief that a combination of drug treatment and psychotherapy was more effective than the use of either approach alone (Remick, 2002, p. 1260).

Powell, Yeaton, Hill, and Silk (2001) studied the effectiveness of treatment with clients experiencing long-term mood disorders. They concluded that self-help groups are very important providers of positive management of mood disorders. "Social support (information, encouragement, and advocacy) provided in a self-help context may be especially effective because it is offered by people who have experienced (and may be still experiencing) the illness" (p. 9).

InfoTable 12.3	Detection of Mood Disorders in Children and Adolescents

Writing about early detection and treatment of severe mood disorders in children and adolescents, Duffy (2000, p. 345) suggests several important predictors of mood disorders:

- A family history of major affective disorder is the strongest, most reliable risk factor for a major affective illness. Other factors associated with affective disorders include female gender (risk factor for unipolar illnesses), severe life events and disappointments, family dysfunction, poor parental care, early adversity, and personality traits.

- Based on the current state of knowledge, emphasis on identifying and treating mood disorders as early as possible in the course and particularly early-onset (child and adolescent) cases and youth at high risk (given a parent with a major mood disorder) is likely to be an effective strategy for reducing the burden of illness on both the individual and society.

CASE MANAGEMENT

One widely accepted approach to the treatment of mental illness is the use of case management, an approach that is usually associated with "case identification and outreach, assessment and service planning, service linkage, monitoring of service delivery, and advocacy" (Rubinbach, 1992, p. 139). The purpose of case management is to provide a complete range of services to clients with persistent and severe mental illness and to "bind" the case manager to the client and the community by assuring both groups that all services needed by the client will be delivered in a timely, effective, and coordinated manner. In a study of the published articles on the effectiveness of case management in work with the mentally ill, Rubinbach (1992) writes:

Do the foregoing studies justify current claims that case management has been shown to be effective with seriously mentally ill individuals? These studies' mixed results and the uneven quality of their research designs leave plenty of room for cognitive dissonance factors to influence different reviewers to draw different conclusions. In this reviewer's interpretation, the answer is no. (p. 145)

SELF-HELP GROUPS

Edmunson, Bedell, Archer, and Gordon (1982) report that after 10 months of participation in a patient-led support group, half as many former psychiatric inpatients required rehospitalization as those not participating in the support group. Members of patient-led groups had average hospital stays of 7 days as compared to 25 days for nonparticipants. Kurtz (1988) reports that 82% of 129 members of the Manic Depressive and Depressive Association coped better with their illness after becoming members of a self-help group. Of the sample, 82% required hospitalization before joining the support group, but this number fell to 33% after becoming members of the group. Kennedy (1990) studied the benefits of a self-help group for 31 participants with chronic psychiatric problems and found that members of the self-help group spent far fewer days in a psychiatric hospital during a 32-month period than did 31 former psychiatric patients matched by similar age, race, gender, marital status, number of previous hospitalizations, and other factors. Group members also experienced an increased sense of security and self-esteem and an improved ability to accept problems in their lives without blaming others. Galanter (1988) studied 356 members of a self-help group for former mental patients. Although half of the members of the self-help group had been hospitalized before joining the group, only 8% of the group leaders and 7% of the recent members had been hospitalized since joining.

Is Mental Illness a Lifetime Condition?

One commonly held belief is that most clients with a diagnosis of some form of mental illness will very likely suffer throughout their life span with chronic, recurring episodes of mental illness. However, Carpenter (2002) reports that most people with a diagnosis of schizophrenia or other serious mental illness experience "either complete or significant remission of symptoms, and work, have relationships, and otherwise engage in a challenging and fulfilling life" (p. 89). In a study of more than 500 adults diagnosed with schizophrenia, Huber, Gross, and Schuttler (1975) found that more than 20% of the sample experienced complete remission and more than 40% experienced significant remission of symptoms. In a 40-year follow-up study, Tsuang, Woolson, and Fleming (1979) found that 46% of those diagnosed with schizophrenia had no or only nonincapacitating symptoms. The Vermont Longitudinal Study (Harding, Brooks, Ashikaga, Strauss, & Breier, 1986a, 1986b), a 20- to 25-year follow-up study of former state hospital patients, found that 72% of the people diagnosed with schizophrenia had only slight or no psychiatric symptoms. Despite these very optimistic findings, Carpenter (2002) believes that the long-term impact of mental illness as an intractable disease is a widely accepted concept in the mental health field and that this pessimistic view of mental illness continues to be communicated to people with psychiatric disabilities and to their families (Kruger, 2000). A pessimistic view of the chronic nature of mental illness "leaves little room for a sense of hope on the part of those labeled with mental illness and, as such, may become a self-fulfilling prophecy" (Carpenter, 2002, p. 89).

InfoTable 12.4	A Personal Account of Bipolar Disorder

It's impossible for me to determine when my mania began, but I was certainly aware of my first depression . . . an event that altered my life shortly after the age of 29. The experience left me paralyzed. I was unable to cope with even the simple tasks of living. It took a long time for me to find out what was happening to me. During the months and months of not knowing, I spent most of my days in bed, unable to communicate with anyone.

Mental illness caused me to lose my husband, children, my upper east side apartment and its contents, and, eventually, found me living with my aging mother. Within days after arriving at her apartment in Queens, I was in a deep depression which lasted for more than three years. The downward swing of my mood was paralyzing. I was unable to have a clear thought. I spent every day reading the same newspaper over and over again. My mother, always in denial, did little to help, and was probably battling her own demons.

I've had a very turbulent life and would have preferred to read about most of the events than to have had the experience. Yet, I remain very optimistic about the future and watching the growth of my business. Being an entrepreneur is risky, but then . . . so is being alive. (Albert, 1998)

THE CONSUMER-SURVIVOR RECOVERY MOVEMENT

One of the positive new approaches to the treatment of mental illness is the consumer-survivor recovery movement. Carpenter (2002) states that the consumer-survivor recovery movement assumes that people with psychiatric disabilities can and will recover. Recovery is defined as a process of achieving self-management through increased responsibility for one's own recovery. This process is aided by a sense of hope provided by the person's professional, family, and peer support systems. Carpenter (2002) writes that "the consumer-survivor definition of the experience of psychiatric disability is as much about recovery from the societal reaction to the disability as it is about recovery from the disability itself" (p. 90). Anthony (1993) believes that recovery from mental illness is aided by what he calls "recovery triggers" that include sharing the research with patients, families, and communities indicating that many people with psychiatric problems *do* recover. Another recovery trigger involves information about the availability of services and treatment options such as self-help groups and alternative treatment approaches.

In a further discussion of the consumer-survivor recovery movement, Chinman, Weingarten, Stayner, and Davidson (2001) suggest that a significant way of improving treatment results and decreasing recidivism is through the mutual support of other mentally ill clients. According to the authors, mutual support groups reduce hospitalization rates, the amount of time spent in hospitals, symptoms, and days spent in the hospital. Additionally, they improve quality of life and self-esteem, and contribute to better community reintegration of clients with severe psychiatric disorders (Davidson et al., 1999; Kyrouz & Humphreys, 1996; Reidy, 1992). Mutual support groups provide acceptance, empathy, a feeling of belonging to a community, necessary information to help with management of social and emotional problems, new ways of coping with problems, and role models who are coping well. Chinman et al. (2001) indicate that "mutual support also operates through the 'helper-therapy' principle that suggests that by helping one another, participants increase their social status and self-esteem (Riessman, 1965)" (p. 220).

Beyond mutual support groups, Chinman et al. (2001) suggest that there is growing evidence that consumer-run services may prove to be very effective in helping clients with mental illnesses (Davidson et al., 1999) because consumer providers are often more empathic than professionals; see clients' strengths that professionals might miss; are tolerant, flexible, patient, and persistent; and know how to respond to clients' needs. These skills help to create a supportive environment that serves as a catalyst for faster recovery and an earlier return to community life (Dixon, Krauss, & Lehman, 1994; Kaufman, 1995). According to the authors, studies have found that consumer-led case management is as effective as conventional case management (Felton et al., 1995; Solomon & Draine, 1995).

The Organizations That Help People With Emotional Problems and Mental Illness

There are a number of organizations that respond to severe emotional problems and mental illness. They are the following:

1. Community mental health agencies that provide, through publicly funded services, therapy, management of medications, case management,

and referral to other resources, including self-help organizations. The following is a statement of the services offered in a rural Michigan community mental health center, Ionia Community Mental Health (2005):

Ionia County Community Mental Health is here to serve your needs in the areas of mental health, substance abuse, and developmental disabilities. We have a strong commitment to serving you and want you to be completely satisfied with the care that you receive.

Our office is located at 375 Apple Tree Drive in Ionia, Michigan. Our hours of operation are Monday through Friday, 8:00 A.M. to 5:00 P.M. and evenings by appointment. To receive services, call 616–527–1790. We have an additional office located at 4771 Storey Road in Belding, Michigan. Also, check our *Support/Treatment Groups*. Our toll-free crisis line is available 24 hours a day at 1–888–527–1790.

Adolescent Services are supportive services offered to schools and students and may include a peer-listening program, facilitating groups for youth, short-term individual sessions with adolescents, and crisis planning and intervention.

The **Assertive Community Treatment (ACT) Team** serves people with severe and persistent mental illness in the community. Multiple issues, such as health, hospitalizations, legal problems, homelessness, employment issues, and social isolation as a result of mental illness are used as criteria for providing services from the ACT Team.

Case Management/Support Coordination are therapeutic services for adults and children with developmental disabilities and/or serious mental illness/emotional disabilities.

Community Supports promote natural supports and community inclusive opportunities for individuals.

Crisis Services—emergency appointments are available during regular office hours. A 24-hour crisis line (1–888–527–1790) is available for mental health related emergencies.

The **Employabilities Team** strives to connect the work needs of area businesses with the work skills of individuals with disabilities. Many ICCMH consumers have found meaningful employment through this program.

The **Family Intervention Team (FIT)** offers intensive, family-based therapy services to families in Ionia County. This service operates by a "whatever it takes" philosophy which reflects the need for flexibility and creativity in designing services to meet the needs of families. Families are viewed as partners in both the design and delivery of services.

Family Support Services are family-focused services provided to families of individuals with serious mental or emotional disturbance for the purpose of assisting the family in relating to, caring for, or maintaining the family member. Other services may include, but are not limited to, education and support, assistance in accessing financial entitlements, respite care, and mentoring.

Infant Mental Health is an intensive, home-based prevention program for at-risk mothers in their third trimester of pregnancy and/or families with infants and toddlers. This service focuses on the bonding and attachment process. Services and supports may include counseling, ongoing infant assessment, parent and child development education, crisis intervention, and development of community resources.

Jail Diversion is a program designed to keep those with mental illness out of jail. This program works in close collaboration with the county legal system and provides ongoing training to police officers in identifying mental health related behaviors.

Prevention Initiatives are designed to be responsive to the community's needs for physical and mental wellness education. Services may include collaborating with groups, agencies, or schools to create and/or present programs focused on specific topics, such as stress management, conflict resolution, body image, and/or bullying.

Older Adult Services focus on providing mental health services to older adults living in nursing homes, adult foster care homes, and private homes.

Out-Patient Therapy provides short-term, solution-based therapy to children, adolescents, and adults who are experiencing significant symptoms that interfere with their ability to function in more than one life area. Patients are seen in individual, group, and/or family counseling. Psychological testing and assessment are also offered.

2. State mental hospitals are primarily used for people who suffer from mental illness and are dangerous to themselves or others, and people who have committed serious violent crimes and are judged to be mentally ill at the time. This group receives services until they are well enough to stand trial, and then the justice system determines future treatment or punishment, including either jail or a return to a locked state treatment facility.

3. Private social workers, psychologists, or psychiatrists who provide ongoing therapy and supportive care through inpatient or outpatient agencies and facilities, which are usually private facilities offering services for a fee or that bill a patient's insurance company.

4. Family service agencies that provide low-cost social work assistance through donations, public and private grants, and fees for services. Family agencies are nonprofit, or what some people call charitable agencies.

5. Self-help and consumer advocacy groups that offer support and specific help to people with lesser and more serious emotional problems.

How Social Workers Help

Social workers provide a number of important services to people experiencing emotional problems and mental illness. We provide most of the inpatient and outpatient counseling and psychotherapy in America to people experiencing emotional problems and mental illness. Social workers work in treatment teams in in- and outpatient facilities treating serious emotional problems and mental illness. Our expertise is in understanding the social context of the person's problems, his or her family life, and the historical reasons the client is experiencing emotional difficulty. We provide case management services, which means that we act as the manager of the various services received by clients and make certain those services are being offered in an effective and efficient way. Social workers make certain that social issues are cared for, including adequate housing, work, food, clothing, and sufficient finances on which to live. We often write psychosocial assessments that help identify the early onset of emotional problems and their cause. The social assessment would also determine if there were other family members who have experienced emotional difficulties and any diseases that might be causing the problem. It is well known that thyroid problems cause depression and lethargy as well as hypermania and anxiety. Certain medications also affect moods and, of course, a history of illicit drugs would certainly make one suspect drug-related mood disorders, some of them even suggesting psychotic-like behavior. A health history might also suggest minimal organic brain damage consistent with

InfoTable 12.5	Recovery From Mental Illness: Developed Versus Undeveloped Countries

The evidence from 2 studies by the World Health Organization (WHO), one in 1979 and the second in 1992, comparing the recovery rate, mostly from schizophrenia, in developing countries with the recovery rate in industrialized countries indicates that the recovery rate was roughly twice as high in the developing countries compared with the industrialized.

The implications are profound. It shows that schizophrenia is more pronounced and prolonged in industrialized countries. I've started to gather information from developing countries about how they approach treatment and healing. They have a completely opposite approach from Western countries. They're very socially oriented, and they instinctively recognize the importance of keeping people connected to the community. We have ceremonies of segregation and isolation, which is really what our labeling and our hospitalization process is. They have ceremonies of reintegration and connection. (Fisher, 2005)

child abuse or an accident. Social workers act as patient advocates, making certain that the civil rights of hospitalized or institutionalized patients are not violated. Finally, social workers conduct research on many nonmedical aspects of mental illness and other emotional problems.

Social Work With an Emotionally Troubled 17-Year-Old

This case first appeared in my book on the strengths perspective, in which the way this approach to treatment works with serious emotional problems is defined in greater detail (Glicken, 2004a, pp. 174–175).

Robert Byers is a 17 year old with beginning signs of Bi-Polar Disorder. Robert walks around downtown Palm Springs, California with his face painted like a mime and has several friends he hangs out with who accompany him on his walks. Robert curses a great deal and many people find his behavior upsetting. The police, who know that warm weather communities have many mentally ill people in residence, try to handle Robert gently. Each encounter with the police to modify his behavior brings torrents of abuse and curse words directed at the police and anyone else within hearing distance. Robert often walks through the streets and obsesses about his "hassles" with the police for days.

Robert's parents are wealthy enough to allow Robert to live in an apartment in Palm Springs and to see a private therapist and psychiatrist. They briefly had Robert hospitalized, but the experience was so stigmatizing for the family that they prefer the illusion of telling friends that Robert is attending a good private school and doing well. In fact, Robert is doing badly. He uses illicit drugs, doesn't take his medications, misses his therapy sessions, and is very close to being in legal trouble because of his confrontations with the local police. Robert's parents seldom see him and, even though he is under age, the police have found the parents uncooperative and unwilling to come to Palm Springs to help develop a plan to help Robert. Instead, they refer the police to his therapist.

After a particularly bad encounter with the police where Robert assaulted a police officer, he was involuntarily committed to a psychiatric unit of a local general hospital for a mandatory 72-hour observation period. He was diagnosed with Bi-Polar Disorder with increasing signs of psychosis and was sent, by the court, to a residential facility in Palm Springs with a day program, which he was required to attend or be remanded to court and charged with assault of a police officer, a Class "A" Felony in California.

Robert was initially a very hostile and uncooperative patient. Visits with friends were withheld because of fear of drug exchanges. His medication needs were met by giving him shots since it was believed he wouldn't take his medication orally. Over a two-week period, his behavior began to moderate and he was integrated into the day program while still under close observation in the clinic's in-patient unit. Initially uncooperative and belligerent in the day program, within a month Robert began cooperating. His behavior moderated so that the Bi-Polar symptoms were almost unnoticeable. He attended high school in the facility and turned out to be a highly intelligent young man with very strong math and science skills. The patients in the residential facility were accepting and positive, and Robert began feeling that he was part of a family, a unique experience for him. He contacted his parents by phone and, astonished by the change, they began to come for visits. In time, his parents agreed to begin family therapy with

Robert and to be part of a parent's group to learn more about the management of Bi-Polar Disorder. Robert is very involved in the patient managed day program and helps determine the program schedule for field trips. He is also on the committee that meets to consider violations of the patient rules of conduct, developed and enforced by the patients. Robert feels that it is a privilege to be in the day program and sees the changes in his life as a direct result of his involvement in the day program.

Discussion

Robert spoke to me about a year after his initial involuntary hospitalization. "Jan, the social worker on staff, helped me in every way I can think of. She helped me especially during my first month when I was really uncooperative and belligerent. I got into a couple of fights and she helped me resolve the problems. She helped me change roommates because the one I had didn't get along with me. When we found out that I had math and science skills, she helped me get a special tutor and to attend classes at a local university. She had faith in me and it really helped me deal with being in a locked facility.

"I don't think I even understood how disturbed I was before I was hospitalized. I was angry and using drugs, and I thought the problem was with other people, not with me. When I was sent to the facility, I was very angry and uncooperative. The medication certainly helped calm me down but more than that, the people in the program were wonderful. I'd never really felt that I was part of a family before since mine is so dysfunctional. Being in the program at the clinic, I started to feel loved and valued by the other patients and the staff. These were new feelings for me and I began to respond to other people in the same way. During my drug years, I thought that being nice to people would result in a knife in my back, but being nice to others and having them be nice to me was like a wonderful experience. And the people in the clinic program, I mean we were all pretty wacky, but most of us are working or going to school. I thought wacky people sat around and vegetated. Not in this program. In this program you work hard, you go to school, you do your job, and you help others. There are days I feel pretty crazy, but others see it and I feel protected. No one is going to let me fall apart and do the things I did before I came here.

"Jan helped me get back with my family and now I see my family every weekend and, you know, we're a lot better. I've gone for weekend furloughs, and while we don't always click, we do better than before. It isn't a good place for me to be since it's too close to all the things that got me into trouble, but I love my family and I'm pretty happy that things in that area have improved. I'm doing really well in school and they tell me I have ability in math and science. I'm sort of surprised since I always thought I was pretty stupid. And you don't find any B.S. here. They're very honest about my medical problems and how I have to stay on top of them. Bipolar disorder is something you have to be intelligent about. When I start feeling hyper or down, I talk to the staff and they make certain I get some changes in my medications. It's not rocket science. It's knowing how your body is operating and making sure you don't let it go bonkers. The big difference is that I used to medicate myself with uppers and downers and every drug I could find. The staff knows a lot more about medication and I know a lot more about my body. We work together and we trust that we'll do the right thing. It's pretty great. When I get ready to leave high school and go to college, I intend to stay with the program and live here in the clinic. Jan helped me choose a university and went with me to see if I'd like it there and if they'd like me. I know I can't do that forever, but it's home now and you shouldn't leave home until you're ready, at least that's what I think."

You Be the Social Worker

Rebecca Larson is a freshman at a private college in the Midwest. She has been complaining of depression since the end of her first semester of classes. This is a new problem for Rebecca, because she has always been a vivacious and upbeat person. Rebecca was referred to the college counseling center by her advisor and was seen by a female clinical social worker. In doing an assessment of Rebecca's case, the worker began to get the clear idea that Rebecca had been sexually assaulted at a campus party. Rebecca admits that she had been drinking heavily and can't remember the details or who was responsible, but she woke up the next day with bruises on her body and vaginal soreness. She immediately saw a doctor at the student health service who took a rape kit and did lab work for sexually transmitted diseases, AIDS, and pregnancy. She was given the "day after" pill to eliminate the possibility of pregnancy and a pregnancy test was taken as a precaution. All of her lab work came back negative. Although Rebecca enjoys good health, she has begun to slip into a deep depression. She feels that the rape was something she allowed to happen because she drank too much, and now she feels powerless to do anything about it. Asking around, she found out who the young man was, and a meeting with him revealed that they had consensual sex. They had both been binge drinking and were very drunk at the time. The young man was very apologetic and offered to see the social worker with Rebecca to apologize in front of her, but Rebecca declined. It was her problem, she said, and it was her responsibility to do something about it.

One evening while Rebecca was studying, she experienced strong suicidal impulses and took a bottle of pills her doctor had given her for depression. The dose would have killed her had her roommate not found her in time and called 911. Rebecca was brought out of a deep coma after 2 days in the hospital. Her parents were immediately called and when Rebecca was released from the hospital, they held a family meeting with the social worker to decide if Rebecca should stay in school and get treatment or take time off, go home, and receive treatment under the supervision of her parents.

Questions

1. Do you think the binge drinking leading to sex is what is causing Rebecca to be so depressed, or might there be other reasons? What might the other reasons be?

2. Isn't it common for some freshman students to experience depression? Dropout rates among new college students have been reported as high as 50% during the first year of college. Might this just be a short-term situational problem rather than serious depression?

3. Do you think binge drinking is an indication to men and women that sex is probably going to happen and that it's acceptable?

4. If you were the social worker, would you advise Rebecca to stay in school or go home?

5. Having read this chapter, what issues would you focus on to help Rebecca deal with her depression?

Summary

This chapter discusses the prevalence of mental illness and mood disorders in America and the often stigmatizing effect the label of mental illness can have on patients. Stigma toward the mentally ill frequently affects employment opportunities and in many ways creates the impression that once someone is diagnosed with mental illness, the problem and the label will remain indefinitely. A case study suggests the positive way people benefit from treatment and a short case asks you to decide on treatment.

Questions to Determine Your Frame of Reference

1. This chapter argues that most mentally ill people improve and stay improved over time. Do you think this happens because of advances in treatment or because most people just get better over time, and that mental illness is no different in that respect from other illnesses?

2. Why do you think people experience emotional problems, some of them very serious and long-term? Do you think it's because of inherited reasons or because of the traumatic things that happen to be people as they develop?

3. If you live in a large city, you often see people whose behavior is like that of Robert in the case study. Isn't it possible that people who live alternative lifestyles are perfectly sane but that our tolerance for their behavior is low?

4. In the case study you were asked to work on, is sex really consensual when two people have been binge drinking?

5. Do you think there is far too much use of substances in our colleges and universities? Do our schools do anything to control it? Do you see outcomes of binge drinking similar to that of Rebecca?

Internet Sources

The Surgeon General of the United States, David Satcher (1999), discusses common and severe forms of emotional difficulty and mental illness. Next, the discussion of common and severe forms of emotional difficulty and mental illness is reported by the National Institute of Mental Health (2004). Finally, there is a report on recovery programs that emphasize the consumer recovery movement and its effectiveness. All three reports consider the amount of emotional difficulty in the United States and suggest appropriate responses by friends, family members, and professionals.

1. Satcher, D. (1999). *Mental health: A report of the U.S. Surgeon General.* Retrieved from http://www.surgeongeneral.gov/library/mentalhealth/home.html

2. National Institute of Mental Health. (2004). Home page. Retrieved from http://www.nimh.nih.gov/

3. SAMSHA. (2000). *Review of recovery programs.* Retrieved from http://www.nasmhpd.org/general_files/publications/ntac_pubs/reports/ralphrecovweb.pdf

Health Problems, Disabilities, Death and Dying, and Access to Care

13

The Many Roles of Medical Social Workers

After having diabetes for fourteen years, it has become more than a chronic disease for me, more than a steady companion; diabetes is very much a part of who I am. Diabetes is not a burden, nor is it a crutch. It is just a disease that I, and millions of others, live with every moment of every day. When we face the fact of surviving with diabetes, as many have to face the fact of surviving with cancer, or HIV, or heart disease, we find strength in our uniqueness and in our ability to control our illness rather than letting it control us. I live with diabetes as though it were my troubled child—a lot of work and occasionally painful, but in the end, oddly beautiful and uniquely mine.

—Amy Glicken (2002)

While Americans believe that we have the best health care in the world, the reality is that not only do we spend much more for health care than any other nation, but because of poverty, race, gender, and ethnicity issues, many people receive marginal or no health care at all. In fact, many industrialized nations far surpass the United States in the quality and effectiveness of their health care systems. An editorial in the University of Pittsburgh Faculty Newspaper, *The University Times* (2004), reports that the United States has higher infant mortality rates and shorter longevity than almost any other developed country including Australia, Canada, England, France, Germany, Israel, Italy, and Spain—countries which, like the United States, have multiethnic populations. The same editorial notes that a World Health Organization (WHO) report for the year 2000 found that the United States spent a far greater proportion (14.1%) of its gross domestic product on health care than any other country but goes on to say that "it is distressing to learn that despite being the world's richest country, WHO ranked the overall performance of the American health care system at 37th among the 191 U.N. member countries, just between Costa Rica and Slovenia" (p. 1). In fact, the United States fails to meet the standards of health care available in almost all of the rest of the developed world. And finally, the editorial notes that "the United Kingdom, oft criticized for long waits for medical procedures, ranks 18th when measuring overall health system performance, compared to the U.S. ranking of 37th" (p. 1).

Why these troubling health statistics, given the amount of money we spend on medical care? Some of the reason, of course, has to do with the way we take care of ourselves. Obesity, lack of exercise, far too much substance abuse, stressful lives, and too many expensive medications that have dubious if not negative effectiveness are partly to blame. But for the most part, the medical care system doesn't work well because so many people aren't a part of it. Poverty causes people to wait until their medical conditions are very serious and then use emergency rooms, the most expensive form of health care, for medical attention. Many less affluent people can't afford the cost of medication, which in the case of very common illnesses is far less expensive when purchased in Canada or Mexico. But many people distrust the medical care system for reasons of culture, gender, and race, and because they've been treated badly in the past by doctors, insurance companies, and other aspects of the health care system.

This chapter will consider the reasons we pay so much for medical care but receive less than we should in return. It will also provide a case study of a woman being treated by a social worker for prolonged grief after the unexpected death of a spouse, and it will explain the various functions of social work in the health care system. Finally, it will discuss some of the laws and policies that provide for health care and protect the disabled from discrimination. But before reading this chapter, take the following short test about your approach to health. You should know where you stand on your personal health care before considering the state of health care in America and your role in it.

Race and Health Care: Unequal and Troubling

Members of ethnic and racial minority groups often experience unequal health care. In an article on black and white differences in health care, the

InfoTable 13.1	Questions About Your Health Care

These are questions you should ask yourself about your own health because they may affect you later in life:

1. Do you smoke? If you do, the likelihood is that you'll die sooner than you should and possibly develop one of the most serious, painful, and untreatable forms of cancer: lung cancer.

2. Are you overweight? If you are, you will very likely begin to suffer from cardiovascular problems much earlier in life than you should. You may also experience pain in your joints and difficulty breathing.

3. Do you exercise? If you don't, you may experience all of the problems related to being overweight.

4. Is your diet full of junk food or high-calorie foods? If it is, see number 2, and don't believe any diet fads. The way to keep your weight even is to not put more calories into your body than it can burn off.

5. Are you a binge drinker? If you are, you have a high probability of becoming a substance abuser and having a serious accident. Binge drinking is one of the primary reasons for rape on American campuses.

6. Do you never see doctors because you don't like bad news? If so, you'll miss the early stages of serious problems that could have been treated early but may be difficult or impossible to treat in their later stages.

InfoTable 13.2	Health Insurance Woes

- 43,000,000 people are without any form of health insurance, or 15% of the total U.S. population.
- Of households earning less than $25,000 annually, 23% lacked health insurance.
- Adults aged 18 to 24 were least likely of any age group to have coverage, with 28% lacking coverage.
- Hispanics were less likely than non-Hispanic whites to be covered by health insurance, with 66.8% having insurance, compared with 90% of whites. Among blacks, the coverage rate of 81% was the same as that for Asians.
- Families with incomes above $75,000 made up nearly 58% of the increase in the uninsured, although they make up only 30% of the population. Experts said that income group is most likely to have coverage and, therefore, in times of recession or job cutbacks, most likely to lose it. (Epstein, 2004, pp. 603–605)

authors (Council on Judicial Affairs, 1990) found that "despite improvements in health care for African Americans over the last three decades, African Americans have twice the mortality rate of Caucasian Americans

InfoTable 13.3	The Tuskegee Syphilis Experiment

For forty years between 1932 and 1972, the U.S. Public Health Service (PHS) conducted an experiment on 399 black men in the late stages of syphilis. These men, for the most part illiterate sharecroppers from one of the poorest counties in Alabama, were never told what disease they were suffering from or of its seriousness. Informed that they were being treated for "bad blood," their doctors had no intention of curing them of syphilis at all. The data for the experiment were to be collected from autopsies of the men, and they were thus deliberately left to degenerate under the ravages of tertiary syphilis—which can include tumors, heart disease, paralysis, blindness, insanity, and death. "As I see it," one of the doctors involved explained, "we have no further interest in these patients until they die." By the end of the experiment, 28 of the men had died directly of syphilis, 100 were dead of related complications, 40 of their wives had been infected, and 19 of their children had been born with congenital syphilis. (The Tuskegee Syphilis Experiment, 2004)

and have a significantly shorter life expectancy, 6 years less" (p. 2344). This disparity in health care is similar to the differences between black and white Americans in education, housing, income, and other factors that may explain the reason African Americans receive fewer specific surgeries for cardiac problems, kidney transplants, and other high-cost medical procedures that prolong life. To make the medical care issue more poignant, about 25% of all African Americans in the United States and 37% of all Hispanics lack health insurance (Satcher, 2001).

Because African Americans have experienced nonconsensual experimentation (e.g., the Tuskegee Experiment), Randall (1996) believes that there is a great deal of distrust of the medical care system in America. This fear helps explain why African Americans tend not to use the medical care system to the same extent as other racial and ethnic groups.

This disparity in care is even more pronounced when it comes to African American and Hispanic citizens who experience mental health problems. The Surgeon General's report (Satcher, 2001) finds that African Americans are overrepresented in populations at high risk for developing mental illness, primarily the homeless, prisoners, and children in foster care where the need for mental health treatment is generally higher. Yet black Americans are more likely than whites to receive mental health treatment for the first time in emergency rooms and psychiatric hospitals because they delay seeking treatment until their symptoms are very serious, the report said.

Although overall rates of mental illness among Hispanics roughly equal those of whites, young Hispanics have higher rates of depression, anxiety disorders, and suicide. The Surgeon General's report also found that Hispanics born in the United States are more likely to suffer from mental illness than those born in Mexico or living in Puerto Rico. American Indians and indigenous Alaskans living in isolated, rural communities have "severely" limited mental health treatment options, the report said, and notes that these groups have a suicide rate 50% higher than that of the general U.S. population. A lack of research into mental health issues surrounding Native Americans makes it difficult to design and evaluate appropriate mental health care, the study concluded (Satcher, 2001).

Gender Differences in Health

In reporting data from the University of Michigan's Institute for Social Research, Gupta (2003) notes that "men outrank women in all of the 15 leading causes of death, except one: Alzheimer's. Men's death rates are at least twice as high as women's for suicide, homicide and cirrhosis of the

InfoTable 13.4	Gratitude

I am so lucky! I am the one who found my cancer.

I found it one spring evening, while nursing my son. A perfectly round lump, the size of a small marble, smooth and hard and anchored deep within.

I went to two different doctors and consulted a surgeon. I had a mammogram, and an ultrasound. Each time, I was pronounced "healthy." "It's just a cyst, nothing to worry about."

I am so lucky. It didn't go away. I insisted on its removal.

After my biopsy, the surgeon assured my husband, "It's nothing. Looks like a cyst."

I am so lucky. The lab report was conclusive.

I had cancer.

I am so lucky to learn, early on, not to rely on "experts" to divine my body and its intelligence.

I am so lucky to have rediscovered my own voice, whose insistence and volume saved my life.

I am so lucky to learn that "they," the outside voices, could not save me or even help very much. In this disavowal, I found the power to engage life and death, loss and gain with an expanded range of freedom and fascination.

They said, "How sad she has to lose a breast, a terrible sacrifice she has to make to live."

I observed, "What a relief it is to lose a body part and yet still feel completely whole. I understand now, I am not a body, but something more."

They said, "She's going to lose her active lifestyle, her professional tenure."

I observed, "What a privilege it is to stare out the window, for hours, at trees dancing in an autumn storm. See how they embrace their destruction with grace and guile, knowing spring waits just beyond its bluster."

They said, "She's bald, one-breasted, she can't think, she can't even care for her children. How tragic."

I observed, "Years of striving to obtain worldly power, to maintain appearances and to craft an identity, never even got me in the neighborhood of 'happy.' I found it lying alone in a bathtub, bald, maimed and brain-dead. It was a feeling of being held and loved beyond measure. Because I had nothing to give the world, I could at last hold it and something else beside."

They said, "Thank God it isn't me!" I giggled and thought, "Thank God it is me!" I am so lucky. (Glicken, 2006, pp. 127–128)

liver" (p. 84). The principal researcher on the study of men's health, David Williams, says that men are twice as likely to be heavy drinkers and to "engage in behaviors that put their health at risk, from abusing drugs to driving without a seat belt" (Gupta, 2003, p. 84).

Gupta goes on to report that men are more often involved in risky driving and that SUV rollovers and motorcycle accidents largely involve men. Williams blames this behavior on "deep-seated cultural beliefs—a 'macho' worldview that rewards men for taking risks and tackling danger head on" (Gupta, 2003, p. 84). Further examples of risky male behavior leading to injury and death are that men are twice as likely to get hit by lightning or die in a flash flood, and are more likely to drive around barricades, resulting in more death by train accidents and drowning in high water.

In further examples of gender differences and health, Gupta reports that women are twice as likely as men to visit their doctor once a year and are more likely to explore broad-based preventive health plans with their physician than men. Men are less likely to schedule checkups or to follow up when symptoms arise. Men also tend to "internalize" and "self-medicate" their psychological problems, notes Williams, whereas women tend to seek professional help. Virtually all stress-related diseases—from hypertension to heart disease—are more common in men. Saunders (2000) notes that a poll by Louis Harris and Associates in May and November 1998 indicated that 28% of the men as compared to 8% of the women had not visited a physician in the prior year. Although 19% of the women didn't have a regular physician, 33% of the men didn't have one either. More than half of the men surveyed had not had a screening test for cholesterol or a physical examination in the prior year. Waiting as long as possible to receive needed medical care was a strategy used by one fourth of the men surveyed. Only 18% of the men surveyed sought medical care immediately when a medical problem arose.

Additional health data paint an equally troubling picture of male health. Drug Store News (1998) reports the following information for American pharmacists: (a) women still outlive men by an average of 6 to 7 years, despite advances in medical technology; (b) the death rate from prostate cancer has increased by 23% since 1973; (c) oral cancer, related to smoking, occurs more than twice as often in men; (d) three times as many men suffer heart attacks before the age of 65 than women, and nearly three in four coronary artery bypasses in 1995 were performed on men; (e) bladder cancer occurs five times more often in men than women; (f) nearly 95% of all DWI cases involve men; and (g) in 1970, the suicide rate for white men was 9.4 per 100,000, as compared to 2.9 for white women. By 1986, the rate for white males had risen to 18.2, as compared to 4.1 for women. And by 1991, the rate for white male suicide was 19.3 per 100,000, as compared to a slight increase to 4.3 for women. In 1991, suicide rates for black and Latino men were 11.5 per 100,000, or almost six times the rate of suicide for black and Latino women, whose rate was 2 per 100,000.

Regarding male vulnerability to other diseases, Kraemer (2000) reports that men are more physically vulnerable than females. Although there are more male than female embryos, the male embryo is much more at risk of being terminated before conception than the female embryo. After conception, the male fetus is at greater risk of death or damage and "prenatal brain damage, cerebral palsy, congenital deformities of the genitalia and limbs, premature birth, and stillbirth are commoner in boys. By the time a boy is born, a newborn girl is the physiological equivalent of a 4 to 6 week old boy" (p. 1611). Kraemer indicates that after the male child is born, a pattern sets in and he is more prone to developmental disorders. Hyperactivity, autism, stammering, and Tourette's syndrome are three times more prevalent in boys than girls and conduct disorders (e.g., acting out, fighting, and illegal behavior) are twice as prevalent among boys. Kraemer believes that to cope with the variety of problems faced by boys, "Males are attempting something special all through life" (p. 1609).

The Reasons for Male Health Problems

In covering sessions on men's health at the American Psychological Association's 2000 Annual Convention, Kogan (2000) reports that panelists all agreed that the pressure men feel to maintain a strong image of masculinity is literally making them sick. She notes that many men do not get regular check-ups because the feelings of vulnerability and passivity in the role of the patient are incompatible with their view of male behavior. Men shy away from psychotherapy and counseling because talking about their feelings is often felt to be feminizing and inconsistent with male roles. Because men let their health slide, they place themselves at particular risk for preventable diseases and illnesses.

Kraemer (2000) reports that males are more vulnerable to health problems from the beginning of life but caregivers assume that a boy should be tougher than a girl. However, cultural expectations about the way boys should react to social and emotional stressors shape the experience of boys as they grow up. Kraemer believes that the boys most at risk of developing serious health-related problems are "the boys who don't talk. They become ashamed of being ashamed, and try to stop feeling anything. This makes them seem invulnerable, even to themselves. This is not a safe strategy" (p. 1610). Kraemer believes that male patterns of mismanagement of risk lead to dangerous behaviors, including drug and alcohol abuse and violence. The author notes increasing rates of male suicide, death by violence, and death by avoidable accidents, which he attributes to "poor motor and cognitive regulation in developing males" (p. 1610).

Harrison, Chin, and Ficarrotto (1988) suggest that as much as three fourths of the 7-year difference in life expectancy between men and women is attributable to socialization. Although parents often believe that boys are tougher than girls, they may be far more vulnerable to illness and disease than female children. Male children are more likely to develop a variety of behavioral difficulties such as hyperactivity, stuttering, dyslexia, and learning disorders. There seems to be little evidence that these behavioral health problems experienced by boys are genetically determined. In explaining the difference in health data between men and women, Harrison et al. (1988) write, "Male socialization into aggressive behavioral patterns seems clearly related to the higher death rate from external causes. Male anxiety about the achievement of masculine status seems to result in a variety of behaviors that can be understood as compensatory" (p. 306).

In explaining some of the reasons for poor health care by men, Harrison et al. (1988) believe that the impact of certain health choices made by men are associated with strongly defined masculine roles:

> Men's basic needs are the same as women's: all persons need to be known and to know, to be depended upon and to be dependent, to be loved and to love, and to find purpose and meaning in life. The socially prescribed male role, however, requires men to be non-communicative, competitive and nonliving, and inexpressive, and to evaluate life success in terms of external achievement rather than personal and interpersonal fulfillment. All men are caught in this double bind. If a man fulfills the prescribed role requirements, his basic needs go unmet; if these needs are met, he may consider himself, or be considered by others, as unmanly. (p. 297)

InfoTable 13.5	Compensatory Masculinity

One way children cope with anxiety derived from sex-role expectations is the development of compensatory masculinity (Tiller, 1967). Compensatory masculinity behaviors range from the innocent to the insidious. Boys naturally imitate the male models available to them and can be observed overemphasizing male gait and male verbal patterns. But if the motive is the need to prove the right to male status, more destructive behavioral patterns may result, and persist into adulthood. Boys are often compelled to take risks that result in accidents; older youth often begin smoking and drinking as a symbol of adult male status (Farrell, 1974); automobiles are often utilized as an extension of male power; and some men find confirmation of themselves in violence toward those whom they do not consider confirming their male roles (Churchill, 1967). (Harrison et al., 1988, p. 298)

HIV/AIDS

The following information is summarized from a report by the U.S. National Institutes of Health (2003).

More than 830,000 cases of AIDS have been reported in the United States since 1981. As many as 950,000 Americans may be infected with

HIV, 25% of whom are unaware of their infection. The epidemic is growing most rapidly among minority populations and is a leading killer of African American males aged 25 to 44. AIDS affects nearly seven times more African Americans and three times more Hispanics than Caucasians.

HIV can infect anyone who practices risky behaviors such as the following:

- sharing drug needles or syringes,
- having sexual contact with an infected person without using a condom, or
- having sexual contact with someone whose HIV status is unknown.

Symptoms often experienced months to years before the onset of AIDS include:

- lack of energy,
- weight loss,
- frequent fevers and sweats,
- persistent or frequent yeast infections (oral or vaginal),
- persistent skin rashes or flaky skin,
- pelvic inflammatory disease in women that does not respond to treatment, or
- short-term memory loss.

The diagnosis of AIDS is given when HIV-infected people have fewer than 200 CD4 positive T-cells per cubic millimeter of blood. Healthy adults usually have CD4 positive T-cell counts of 1,000 or more. In addition, the diagnosis of AIDS includes 26 clinical conditions that affect people with advanced HIV disease. Most of these conditions are opportunistic infections that generally do not affect healthy people. Symptoms of opportunistic infections common in people with AIDS include the following:

- coughing and shortness of breath;
- seizures and lack of coordination;
- difficult or painful swallowing;
- mental symptoms, such as confusion and forgetfulness;
- severe and persistent diarrhea;
- fever;
- vision loss;
- nausea, abdominal cramps, and vomiting;
- weight loss and extreme fatigue;
- severe headaches; or
- coma.

A small number of people first infected with HIV 10 or more years ago have not developed symptoms of AIDS. Scientists are trying to determine the reasons for their lack of progression to AIDS. Reasons might include special characteristics of their immune systems, being infected with a less aggressive strain of the virus, or their genes may protect them from the effects of HIV. Scientists hope that understanding the body's natural method of controlling infections may lead to ideas for protective HIV vaccines and the use of vaccines to prevent the disease from progressing.

During the past 10 years, researchers have developed drugs to fight both HIV infection and its associated infections and cancers. Many people infected with HIV have no symptoms. Therefore, there is no way of knowing with certainty whether a sexual partner is infected unless he or she has repeatedly tested negative for the virus and has not engaged in any risky behavior. People should either abstain from having sex or use male latex condoms or female polyurethane condoms, which may offer partial protection, during oral, anal, or vaginal sex. Only water-based lubricants should be used with male latex condoms.

SOCIAL WORK AND AIDS

Social workers help people with HIV/AIDS in a number of ways. We help arrange for medical care. We work with people who are too ill to be employed and help them obtain adequate housing, food, and clothing. We arrange for home care when it is needed. We help educate AIDS patients about the disease and treat periods of high depression and anxiety, which are common to AIDS patients. We help families cope with their anguish over the disease and their first knowledge that their child is gay, if this is the case. We try and overcome the initial perception that everyone who gets infected is gay, which is often not the case. We do community intervention to make certain that HIV/AIDS patients are not discriminated against in jobs, housing, or in any other way. We are involved in community and political action to make certain that anyone with HIV/AIDS is receiving needed medications and high-level medical care. We often work internationally with the victims of AIDS in countries in the sub-Sahara who suffer high rates of AIDS. And social workers are involved in social research efforts to find better ways of helping AIDS patients deal with the social and psychological aspects of the disease.

Disabilities

Finn (1999) reports that there are as many as 24 million Americans with a severe disabling condition and "an estimated 1.7 million people with

InfoTable 13.6	The Impact of Disabilities

In a study of the impact of physical and emotional disabilities, Druss et al. (2000) write that

> combined mental and general medical disabilities were associated with high levels of difficulty across a variety of functional domains: bad days, perceived stigma, employment status, disability payments, and reported discrimination. These findings may best be understood by the fact that co-morbid conditions, unlike either mental or general medical conditions alone, are most commonly associated with deficits spanning several domains of function. In turn, respondents with deficits across multiple domains have few areas of intact function available to make up for their existing deficits. The uniquely high levels of functional impairment associated with combined conditions speak to the potential importance of integrated programs that can simultaneously address an individual's medical and psychiatric needs. (p. 1489)

disabilities who are homebound and an additional 12.5 million who are temporarily homebound. There also are many caretakers of disabled and elderly people who are essentially homebound as a result of their responsibilities at home" (p. 220). Finn (1999, p. 220) goes on to note that a number of social and emotional problems develop from being "alienated" or "socially quarantined" from the larger society, including depression, loneliness, alienation, lack of social interaction, lack of information, and lack of access to employment (Braithwaite, 1996; Coleman, 1997; Shworles, 1983).

Finn (1999) studied the content of messages sent by people with disabilities who were using the Internet as a form of group therapy. He found that most correspondents wanted to talk about their health and specific issues of treatment and quality of care but that overall, the correspondents acted as a support group helping others cope with emotional, medical, and social issues. These issues ranged from "highly technical descriptions of medications, procedures, and equipment to subjective accounts of treatment experiences. There also was considerable discussion of interpersonal relationship issues such as marital relationships, dating, and sexuality" (p. 228). Finn reminds us that many disabled people are homebound and that the Internet becomes an important part of the communicating they do each day. This is particularly true for homebound people who may also have difficulty speaking or hearing.

THE AMERICANS WITH DISABILITIES ACT

The reasons for the Americans with Disabilities Act of 1990 (Public Law 101–336) are as follows: unlike individuals who have experienced discrimination on the basis of race, color, gender, national origin, religion,

InfoTable 13.7	Congressional Findings: Disabilities and Their Impact

(1) 43,000,000 Americans have one or more physical or mental disabilities, and this number is increasing as the population as a whole is growing older; (2) historically, society has tended to isolate and segregate individuals with disabilities, and, despite some improvements, such forms of discrimination against individuals with disabilities continue to be a serious and pervasive social problem; (3) discrimination against individuals with disabilities persists in such critical areas as employment, housing, public accommodations, education, transportation, communication, recreation, institutionalization, health services, voting, and access to public services. (Americans with Disabilities Act, 2004)

or age, individuals who have experienced discrimination on the basis of disability often have no legal way to address such discrimination. Individuals with disabilities continually experience discrimination, including outright intentional exclusion; the discriminatory effects of architectural, transportation, and communication barriers; overprotective rules and policies; failure to make modifications to existing facilities and practices; exclusionary qualification standards and criteria; segregation; and relegation to lesser services, programs, activities, benefits, jobs, or other opportunities. Many studies have documented that people with disabilities often occupy an inferior status in our society and are severely disadvantaged socially, vocationally, economically, and educationally. Individuals with disabilities are a group of Americans who have been faced with restrictions and limitations, subjected to a history of purposeful unequal treatment, and relegated to a position of political powerlessness in our society. This behavior is based on issues that are beyond the control of the disabled and occur because of stereotypical assumptions about disabilities that fail to evaluate the true ability of an individual to participate in, and contribute to, society. The nation's proper goals regarding disabled Americans are to ensure equality of opportunity, full participation, independent living, and economic self-sufficiency.

The purpose of the Americans with Disabilities Act is to (a) eliminate discrimination against the disabled, (b) provide standards with teeth that deal with discrimination against the disabled, (c) ensure that the federal government enforces the standards established in this Act, and (d) use congressional authority, including the power to enforce the 14th Amendment and regulate commerce to address day-to-day discrimination faced by the disabled.

Medicare and Medicaid

Some of the material for this discussion was found on the Internet through a site maintained by the Center for Medicare and Medicaid Services (2004).

In 1965, the Social Security Act established both Medicare and Medicaid. *Medicare* is a federally funded program offering medical care to virtually all Americans older than age 65 and some Americans with disabilities younger than age 65. Medicare is the responsibility of the Social Security Administration (SSA). In 2002, 40,500,000 people received Medicare assistance at a cost to the federal government of more than $225 billion. *Medicaid* is a program that pays for medical assistance for certain individuals and families with low incomes and resources. This program became law in 1965 and is jointly funded by the federal and state governments (including the District of Columbia and the Territories) to assist states in providing medical long-term care assistance to people who meet certain eligibility criteria. Medicaid is the largest source of funding for medical and health-related services for people with limited income. Within certain limits, Medicaid programs differ between states, and many poorer states have very limited programs for economically disadvantaged Americans and their children. For the year 2003, there were more than 50,000,000 recipients of Medicaid, half of them children younger than age 18, at a cost of more than $200 billion to the federal and state governments.

The first U.S. president to propose a prepaid health insurance plan was Harry S. Truman. On November 19, 1945, in a special message to Congress, President Truman outlined a comprehensive, prepaid medical insurance plan for all people through the social security system. The plan included doctors and hospitals, as well as nursing, laboratory, and dental services, and was dubbed National Health Insurance. Medical insurance benefits for needy people were to be financed from federal revenues.

In determining who should receive national health insurance, a national survey found that only 56% of those aged 65 years or older had health insurance. President John F. Kennedy pressed legislators for health insurance for the aged. However, it wasn't until 1965 that President Lyndon B. Johnson signed H.R. 6675 (the Social Security Act of 1965 [PL 89–97]) to provide health insurance to the elderly (Medicare) and the poor (Medicaid).

Medicare does not cover all the medical requirements of older people, nor is it free. Social security recipients must pay a quarterly premium for Medicare and then a supplemental fee to cover those aspects of care that are not included under Medicare. Depending on the type of coverage one chooses to supplement Medicare, the cost for insurance alone can be several hundred dollars a month. Furthermore, because some recipients cannot afford a supplemental plan and Medicare does not cover the cost of medication, Congress passed a drug plan in 2003 to offer reduced costs on medication, which is partially funded by the federal government and American drug companies. In many cases, the cost of medication under this plan is still appreciably more than buying the same medication in Canada or Mexico and has been very unpopular with many older Americans, who believe that drug companies inflate the cost of medication to Americans and then sell the same drug to other countries at a lower cost. It's not unusual for older Americans on very low fixed incomes to pay many thousands of dollars for medication even with the new drug plan.

The Role of Medical and Rehabilitation Social Workers

Medical and rehabilitation social workers work in hospitals, clinics, HMOs, and rehabilitation centers, where we provide supportive services and sometimes longer and more in-depth services to patients who have serious and sometimes terminal illnesses that require work with families and patients as they struggle with their health problems. We arrange for after-hospital care so that patients can be seen medically and for social work help once they leave a medical facility. We help with the emotional aspects of ill health and disabilities. Social workers help with prolonged grief after the loss of a loved one (see the case at the end of the chapter). We are members of the rehabilitation team that helps patients while they're in a medical or rehabilitation center (see the short piece on my experiences working in a rehabilitation center). Finally, because of our familiarity with Medicare and Medicaid and our personal contacts within both programs, we are often able to help patients receive benefits from these programs that they may have been denied or aren't aware of.

A Personal Story About Rehabilitation Social Work

Early in my career as a social worker, I worked for the Sister Kenny Foundation in Minneapolis, a rehabilitation center. Quite without knowing why, I would buy ice cream after work and go from room to room, visiting my clients in the evening when the facility suddenly became empty and quiet and my clients were left with their own thoughts. Many of my clients had serious disabilities brought on by strokes, polio, or accidents. There was a rawness to these evening visits, and my clients would often despair about their lives as we sat together in their rooms. I was too young to know what a disability was like, physically, but my patients would struggle through their daily regimens of physical therapy and sometimes collapse in exhaustion and despair. The physical therapists had a way about them I could only admire as I watched them coax my clients on. It was tragic, and it was also wonderful.

During my evening visits, my clients would tell me about their fears, their sorrows, and their deepest anguish, and something in me reached out to them as we held hands in the night and comforted one another. I was wise enough to listen and remain silent for the most part, but the urge to be a cheerleader was very strong and sometimes I would say something so palpably optimistic and positive that my clients would smile and nod their heads as if to say, in that way clients have of telling you how off-base you've been, "Bravo for trying, but maybe you don't quite know what you're talking about." The impulse to say something positive is strong in most of us, and it may help, but I've come to realize that just listening and sitting with a client can do wonders.

Like most of us, I cannot imagine a life of immobility and pain, or the terminal illness that takes a life before anyone can possibly be ready for death. And like most of us, I don't think I could cope, and it makes me very humble when I work with people who are not only coping well but are, in a real sense, evolving. The process of evolving in the midst of pain, disability, and possible death seems quite beautiful to me, and I am in wonder of it.

Clients whom I have worked with ask me my notion of death. I haven't a very firm one, and I can never give them a very good answer. Instead, I wonder about their idea of death. Often, like for me, death bewilders them. They haven't thought about it and admit that it's a subject they've always avoided. But often, they want to see to unfinished business with family, some of it painful and disturbing. Frequently, they want to remember the good moments in their lives and have someone confirm that they're good people. Often, they want to talk to a religious figure and share their worries about the afterlife. And quite frequently, they are angry. Why shouldn't they be? And I listen to their anger, some of it directed at me because I represent someone healthy when they are not, and I think it's a small price to pay for what they're enduring.

In the end, death isn't clean, or pleasant, or uplifting. It is often filled with pain, misery, and fear. The one thing you realize when you work with dying patients is that they want to make their time with you meaningful. What they talk about, the empathic way you respond, and the gentle listening you do can help them move gracefully from this place to the next. As one of my clients wrote me as he faced the end of a long and painful illness:

> I will go to the river and I will lie in peace.
> And when the sun sets, I will sleep the peaceful sleep
> of a child.
> And when it is dark and night comes,
> I will go from this place to the next.
> And I will be with God, and I will know
> His tender mercies.

Death and Dying

TERMINAL ILLNESS

Hardwig (2000) reports that patients with terminal illnesses are often unable to deal with a number of important emotional issues because they feel "cast out" and abandoned by friends, family, their bodies, and God. "Many [dying patients] find that the beliefs and values they have lived by no longer seem valid or do not sustain them. These are the ingredients of a spiritual crisis, the stuff of spiritual suffering" (Hardwig, 2000, p. 29).

Hardwig (2000) believes that for a number of reasons, dying patients have difficulty resolving long-standing personal and family concerns. Those reasons include the fact that the medical care system often makes important treatment decisions without actually consulting the terminally ill patients, and that the use of pain-killing drugs often limits the dying patient's ability to think clearly or effectively problem-solve. Hardwig is concerned that no one listens to terminally ill patients or helps them resolve important life issues. Because we live in a death-denying society, loved ones may interfere with the patient's need to find closure on long-standing family issues. The lack of closure may affect the family's ability to cope with the patient's death and often complicates and prolongs bereavement. Because a family may find it difficult to let a loved one die naturally, they may ignore the patient's wishes and prolong life by using intrusive life supports and treatments.

Although Caffrey (2000) believes that there is a role for social work with terminal illness, he thinks that the reduction of anxiety and depression in dying patients (palliative care) is narrow-minded. In considering palliative care versus help with unfinished life issues, McClain, Rosenfeld, and Breitbart (2003) found that low levels of spirituality in terminally ill patients were highly related to "end-of-life despair, providing a unique contribution to the prediction of hopelessness, desire for hastened death, and suicidal thoughts even after controlling for the effect of depressive symptoms and other relevant variables" (p. 1606). The authors report that high levels of spirituality in dying patients lead to hopefulness, which results in a more cooperative relationship with the treatment team, improved resolution of long-standing emotional problems, and the desire to live longer. As Kubler-Ross (1969, 1997) wrote, "We can help them die by trying to help them live" (Caffrey, 2000, p. 519).

Lloyd-Williams (2001) found depression in 25% of the terminally ill patients he screened and cautions that depression seriously affects the success of medical treatment to prolong life and help the patient complete important unfinished business. Lloyd-Williams (2001, p. 35) suggests the following treatment strategies for depression in terminally ill patients: (a) establish good rapport, (b) diagnose and treat emotional problems, (c) treat underlying physical problems that may be contributing to the depression, (d) differentiate normal sadness and grief from serious depression, (e) provide supportive therapy and reduce the patient's level of isolation from others, (f) provide family treatment and support if called for, and (g) use antidepressives in selective cases.

Blundo (2001) believes that social workers must make a substantial shift in their work with terminally ill patients in crisis. This shift requires that we engage clients in a highly collaborative dialogue, which begins without any preconceived ideas of underlying emotional difficulty. Greenstein and Breitbart (2000) report that collaborative relationships with terminally ill patients often result in "patients reordering their priorities, spending more time with family, and experiencing personal growth through the very fact of having had to cope with their traumatic loss or illness" (p. 486).

Commenting on the environment in which patients who are terminally ill reside, Richman (2000) notes the need for an empathic and caring approach to terminal illness and reports that a study of empathy found that 40% of the patients whose physicians were described by patients as nonempathetic had symptoms of depression, whereas 27% of the patients who described their physicians as empathic reported depression. Patients with nonempathic physicians "were more likely to consider euthanasia or doctor-assisted suicide" (p. 485).

BEREAVEMENT

Balk (1999) writes that *bereavement* is the loss of a significant person in one's life that can result in long-lasting physical and emotional problems, including fear and anger, sleeping disturbances, substance abuse, cognitive difficulties, and uncharacteristic risk-taking that may significantly affect relationships with others (p. 486). Jacobs and Prigerson (2000) warn that bereavement sometimes develops into a complicated or prolonged grief lasting more than a year. The symptoms of complicated grief include intrusive thoughts about the deceased, numbness, disbelief that a loved one has passed away, feeling confused, and a diminished sense of security. Prolonged grief may not be responsive to interpersonal therapy or the use of antidepressants.

Stroebe (2001) points out a number of problems with the grief work usually done to treat prolonged bereavement by suggesting that there is limited empirical evidence that resolving grief is a more effective process than letting it resolve naturally. Stroebe believes that resolving prolonged bereavement is complicated because of cultural, religious, gender, and socioeconomic differences, and writes, "There is no convincing evidence that other cultural prescriptions are less conducive to adaptation than those of our own" (p. 654). Stroebe is also concerned that traditional treatment for grief work seems to be primarily concerned about complicated grief and lacks precise definitions useful for research studies. The researcher must thus ask, "What is being worked through? In what way?" (Stroebe, 2001, p. 655).

To resolve this problem, Stroebe (2001) suggests that the following issues be studied in more detail: (a) What are the coping skills that allow some people to cope with loss whereas others don't? (b) What are the differences between normal and prolonged grief? (c) What are the primary reasons that some people resolve their grief in natural ways whereas others experience complicated and prolonged bereavements? (d) Is an existential approach to grief work where meaning-of-life issues are dealt with any more effective than focusing on removal of grief-related symptoms? and (e) Do those who resolve their grief naturally and in a normal period of time experience their grief later and, if so, is it a more severe grief than those who experience prolonged grief?

To help provide social workers with some guidance for the assessment of prolonged grief, Jacobs and Prigerson (2000) suggest that the following symptoms lasting more than 2 months and having significant negative impact on social functioning do suggest prolonged grief:

1. Frequent efforts to avoid reminders of the deceased (e.g., thoughts, feelings, activities, people, and places)

2. Purposelessness or feelings of futility about the future

3. Subjective sense of numbness, detachment, or absence of emotional responsiveness

4. Feeling stunned, dazed, or shocked

5. Difficulty acknowledging the death (e.g., disbelief)

6. Feeling that life is empty or meaningless

7. Difficulty imagining a fulfilling life without the deceased

8. Feeling that part of oneself has died

9. Shattered worldview (e.g., lost sense of security, trust, or control)

10. Assumes symptoms or harmful behaviors of, or related to, the deceased person

11. Excessive irritability, bitterness, or anger related to the death. (p. 496)

You Be the Social Worker

As you've probably noticed throughout this book, I'm very interested in why some people cope with social and emotional problems well, even heroically, and why others fall into depression and other troubling emotional states. The death of a loved one generally creates intense emotional states which we call grief. Because we often dislike talking about death and feel that grief should be a fairly short state, perhaps a few months, we might wonder what happens when people continue to experience grief many months, even years after a loved one has passed away. This case describes social work with a client who is experiencing prolonged grief. As you read the case, think about people you've known who have lost a loved one and how well they've handled the grieving process. If you've lost a loved one, why not analyze your response to the loss, including how long it took to recover from your grief and whether you think you dealt with it in a healthy way.

This case is from my book on resilience (Glicken, 2005, pp. 210–212).

The Case

Edna Stern is a 47-year-old mother of three children aged 10, 7, and 5 whose husband suddenly passed away following a major heart attack. Edna's husband, Frank, was a health fanatic who worked out daily, often in preference to spending time with his family. Frank thought he was experiencing chest pains in the middle of the night. As is the case with some heart victims in extreme denial, he went to the gym at 4 a.m. and began exercising until he passed out and was pronounced dead at the scene. Edna was left with a large number of debts, no insurance, and no benefits because Frank was self-employed and trying to save money. She and the children receive a social security survivor's pension, but it isn't enough to cover basic costs and she's had to apply for welfare to cover medical expenses.

Frank passed away more than a year ago, but Edna has traumatic grief as noted by severe depression, high levels of anxiety, very angry and intrusive thoughts about Frank and the condition he left them in, and obsessive thoughts about what she wished she'd said to him before he died——uncomplimentary and angry remarks that convey her depth of despair over her current situation. Her physician referred Edna to a licensed clinical social worker when she continued to complain of the symptoms of prolonged grief more than a year after Frank's death. Edna's social worker met with her and they immediately began a discussion about what was keeping Edna from resolving her feelings of grief.

Edna is stymied, so the social worker suggested that she make a list of everything that came to mind and do a literature search into the typical causes of prolonged grief and the best evidence of how to treat it so that they might continue the discussion during the next session. Edna was initially angry that she was asked to do the work that her social worker should be doing for her. She complained to her referring physician, who encouraged her to give it a little more time. She half-heartedly did what the social worker had asked of her and came only slightly prepared for further discussions at the next meeting.

When asked why she wasn't better prepared, Edna became angry and confrontational. "You haven't even said you're sorry about my loss," she said, and angrily confronted the social worker for doing what her husband always did: leaving decisions up to her. The therapist said she appreciated the feedback and *did* feel badly about Edna's loss. Still, she wondered why Edna was unprepared and explained that only by working together could they resolve Edna's painful and extended grief.

(Continued)

(Continued)

Questions

1. How would you help the client deal with the anger she feels for her dead husband and the fact that she's blaming him for her current life problems?

2. Have you known anyone who continued grieving for the loss of a loved one for more than several months? Describe their loss and why you believe they continued to grieve so long. Do you think a parent might grieve for the death of a child for a prolonged period of time? What might be some of the reasons of prolonged grieving for a child?

3. Why is Edna being so uncooperative with the social worker? She feels stymied in life and depressed. Shouldn't she be more than willing to work hard to resolve the problems she's experiencing after the death of her husband?

4. Why would anyone experiencing a heart attack and the terrible pain associated with it go to a gym early in the morning and exercise?

5. Perhaps Edna was a bit passive in her marriage. Do you think people who are more in control of their lives when they are married and less dependent on others would be less likely to experience prolonged grief? Explain your answer.

Summary

This chapter discusses the health problems of Americans with an emphasis on disabilities and the troubling finding that although we spend more on health care than any other nation, the end result is that Americans are ranked 37th in health and suffer from many preventable health and emotional problems that are often diagnosed and treated too late. Many Americans lack health insurance and cannot afford health care. Older Americans have difficulty paying for many health problems because Medicare, the program of medical coverage for those older than 65, doesn't cover all costs associated with illness. The chapter also discusses the health problems of minority group members and men and suggests that the health care system may be discriminatory in the way it provides services and treats patients. Two case studies are offered, one showing my work in a rehabilitation center and another discussing the treatment of prolonged grief.

Questions to Determine Your Frame of Reference

1. Do you believe the health care you receive is high-quality care? Explain your answer.

2. The treatment of minority group members and men by the health care system points to some troubling problems. What do you think the reasons are for those problems?

3. Social security and Medicare place an enormous burden on younger workers to provide benefits to older workers. Do you think you'll receive the same benefits when you're eligible? Explain your answer.

4. How long do you think it should take for someone who has lost a loved one to recover? Explain your answer.

5. The Americans with Disabilities Act does not permit the field of social work education to ask anyone about a physical or emotional problem that may interfere with them doing social work. Consequently, it's possible for some inappropriate people to enter the profession who could do harm to clients. How should we address the problem, or is there a problem? Explain your answer.

Internet Sources

The CDC (2002) reports the 10 leading causes of death by age group. Next, a highly informative discussion of alternative medicine is provided; you may be surprised to know that the government offers information on the effectiveness of many alternative approaches to health care. Finally, a national health care plan that would cover all Americans with health needs is summarized.

1. *10 leading causes of death.* (2002). Retrieved from http://webapp.cdc .gov/cgi-bin/broker.exe

2. National Institute of Health. (2005). *Get the facts: What is Complementary and Alternative Medicine (CAM)?* Retrieved September 16, 2005, from http://nccam.nih.gov/health/whatiscam/

3. National Institute of Health. (2005). *Health Security Act: Summary.* Retrieved September 16, 2005, from http://www.ibiblio.org.nhs/ summary.html

CAPITALISM PLUS DOPE
EQUALS GENOCIDE
By Michael "Cetewayo" Tabor (Political Prisoner, NY 21)
BLACK PANTHER PARTY, U.S.A.

A Society With Serious Substance Abuse Problems

14

*The Helping Organizations and
the Role of Social Workers in Treating
and Preventing Alcohol and Drug Abuse*

We all know people who abuse alcohol and drugs. Perhaps we're a little reluctant to classify them as true substance abusers, even when something inside of us wonders if they have a problem. But you've seen people who abuse substances in your dorms, at parties, and maybe in your own or friends' families. They often have a beer in their hand, even when it's early in the morning. They love to talk about drinking and drugs. They seem nicer or meaner when they drink or use drugs (it's a mystery why some of us are happy drinkers whereas some of us are mean). Some people drink when you just can't imagine that happening, like when they're playing sports. I'm a chatty drinker, but after a few drinks, the lights go out and I stare into space. Playing sports while drunk astonishes me.

Although we talk about drug and alcohol abuse as addictions and diseases, the fact remains that many Americans believe that substance abuse problems are signs of a weak character or moral weakness. Our laws have become very strict in response to traffic accidents and crimes committed while under the influence of drugs and alcohol. Drug use is punishable by severe penalties in many states, and some people believe that the emphasis on punishment rather than treatment has produced a system that blames victims for their addictions while allowing alcohol and illicit drug sales to skyrocket. This approach has been heavy on legal solutions but weak on treatment and prevention. Consequently, our policies toward substance abuse are very confused. Many insurance companies don't pay for substance abuse counseling, and public agencies treating addictions are frequently underfunded and overloaded with clients who receive minimal services.

To help explain the important social problem of alcohol and drug abuse, this chapter will discuss the extent of the problem of substance abuse in America, the organizations that treat substance abuse and how successful they are in reducing substance dependence, and the role of social work in the treatment of substance abuse. This chapter will also ask you to think about some very important issues that affect your life and the lives of friends and loved ones.

Prevalence of Substance Abuse in America

How bad a problem is substance abuse in America? Let's consider the 2004 data provided by the U.S. Department of Health and Social Services (2005) in a national survey.

ALCOHOL USE

- An estimated 120 million Americans aged 12 or older reported being current drinkers of alcohol in the 2004 survey (51.0%). About 54 million (22.9%) participated in binge drinking at least once in the 30 days prior to the survey, and 15.9 million (6.7%) were heavy drinkers.
- The prevalence of current alcohol use increased with age in 2004, from 2.0% at age 12 to 6.5% at age 13, 13.4% at age 14, 19.9% at age 15, 29.0% at age 16, and 36.2% at age 17. The rate reached a peak of 70.9% for persons aged 21 years old.
- About 10.7 million persons aged 12 to 20 reported drinking alcohol in the month prior to the survey interview in 2004 (28.8% of this age group). Of these, nearly 7.2 million (19.3%) were binge drinkers and 2.3 million (6.2%) were heavy drinkers.
- About 1 in 7 Americans aged 12 or older in 2002 (14.2%, or 33.5 million persons) drove under the influence of alcohol at least once in the 12 months prior to the interview.

ILLICIT DRUG USE

- In 2004, an estimated 19.5 million Americans, or 8.3% of the population aged 12 or older, were current illicit drug users. *Current drug use* means use of an illicit drug during the month prior to the survey interview.

- Marijuana is the most commonly used illicit drug, with a rate of 6.2%. Of the 14.6 million past-month marijuana users in 2004, about one third, or 4.8 million persons, used it on 20 or more days in the past month.
- In 2004, an estimated 2.0 million persons (0.9%) were current cocaine users, 567,000 of whom used crack. Hallucinogens were used by 1.2 million persons, including 676,000 users of Ecstasy. There were an estimated 166,000 current heroin users.
- An estimated 6.2 million persons, or 2.6% of the population aged 12 or older, were current users of psychotherapeutic drugs taken non-medically. An estimated 4.4 million used pain relievers, 1.8 million used tranquilizers, 1.2 million used stimulants, and 0.4 million used sedatives.
- Among youth aged 12 to 17, 11.6% were current illicit drug users. The rate of use was highest among young adults (aged 18 to 25 years) at 20.2%. Among adults aged 26 or older, 5.8% reported current illicit drug use.
- Among pregnant women aged 15 to 44 years, 3.3% reported using illicit drugs in the month prior to their interview. This rate was significantly lower than the rate among women aged 15 to 44 who were not pregnant (10.3%).
- The rates of current illicit drug use were highest among American Indians/Alaska Natives (10.1%) and persons reporting two or more races (11.4%). Rates were 9.7% for blacks, 8.5% for whites, and 7.2% for Hispanics. Asians had the lowest rate at 3.5%.
- Among youth aged 12 to 17, the rate of current illicit drug use among American Indians/Alaska Natives (20.9%) was significantly higher than the rate among all youth (11.6%), and the rate among Asian youth (4.8%) was significantly lower compared with the overall rate for all youth.
- Of the 16.6 million illicit drug users aged 18 or older in 2004, 12.4 million (74.6%) were employed either full- or part-time.
- In 2004, an estimated 11.0 million persons reported driving under the influence of an illicit drug during the past year. This corresponds to 4.7% of the population aged 12 or older. The rate was 10% or greater for each age from 17 to 25, with 21-year-olds reporting the highest rate of any age (18.0%). Among adults aged 26 or older, the rate was 3.0%.

Alcohol Alert, a publication of the National Institute of Alcohol Abuse and Alcoholism (2000), reports that more than 700,000 Americans receive alcoholism treatment alone on any given day. Kann (2001), who uses HHS data, writes that the use of alcohol and drugs continues to be one of the country's most pervasive and serious health and mental health problems, and their use is among our nation's most pervasive health and social concerns. Kann emphasizes that substance abuse is a leading cause of car accidents, homicide, suicide, and HIV infection and AIDS, and contributes to crime, poor workplace productivity, and lower achievements educationally.

How Do We Know if Someone Is Abusing Substances?

People in the mental health field use the *DSM-IV* (APA, 1994). This manual was compiled by a group of social workers, psychiatrists, and psychologists. I'm happy to say that one of the editors of the current manual is a social worker. According to the *DSM-IV*, a dysfunctional use of substances causing impairment or distress within a 12-month period is determined by one of the following: (a) frequent use of substances that interfere with functioning and the fulfillment of responsibilities at home, work, school, and so forth; (b) use of substances that impair functioning in dangerous situations, such as driving or the use of machines; (c) use of substances that may lead to arrest for unlawful behaviors; and (d) substance use that seriously interferes with relations, marriage, child rearing, and other interpersonal responsibilities (p. 182). Substance abuse may also lead to slurred speech, lack of coordination, unsteady gait, memory loss, fatigue and depression, feelings of euphoria, and lack of social inhibitions (p. 197).

The important thing to understand is that substances affect behavior. Too much of them affect behavior badly. Some people have no tolerance for alcohol or drugs. Just a little may affect behavior, so you can't always determine a substance abuse problem by how much you drink or use drugs—what they do to you is the key factor. Most illicit drugs are just dangerous and shouldn't be taken at all. Crack cocaine, for example, is addictive and kills. So do cocaine, heroin, and especially methamphetamine (speed), which is known to cause brain damage. Alcohol is dangerous as well. Too much alcohol during too long a time period causes irreversible health problems including liver, kidney, and cardiovascular problems. Many of you will experiment with alcohol and illegal drugs, and I want to caution you. Most date rape and auto accidents occur when people have been drinking or using illicit drugs, and the consequences of bad judgment with substances affect them for the rest of their lives.

InfoTable 14.1   Attitudes of Youth Aged 12 to 17 Toward Drug and Alcohol Use

In a 2002 survey by the Department of Health and Human Services (HHS), 32.4% of youth indicated that smoking marijuana once a month was a great risk. A higher percentage of youth perceived a great risk in using cocaine once a month (50.5%). Smoking one or more packs of cigarettes per day was cited as a great risk by 63.1% of youth. About three fifths of all youth (62.2%) thought that having four or five drinks of an alcoholic beverage nearly every day was a great risk.

Tests to Determine the Extent of a Substance Abuse Problem

Are there ways to determine if a person has a substance abuse problem? Yes. Miller (2001) reports that two simple questions asked to substance users have an 80% chance of diagnosing substance abuse: (a) "In the past year, have you ever drunk or used drugs more than you meant to?" and (b) "Have you felt you wanted or needed to cut down on your drinking or drug abuse in the past year?" Miller says that this simple approach has been found to diagnose substance abuse in three controlled studies using random samples and laboratory tests for alcohol and drugs in the blood stream following interviews.

Stewart and Richards (2000) and Bisson, Nadeau, and Demers (1999) suggest that four questions from the Cut, Annoyed, Guilty, and Eye-Opener (CAGE) questionnaire predict alcohol abuse. The four questions are:

1) **Cut:** Have you ever felt you should cut down on your drinking?
2) **Annoyed:** Have people annoyed you by criticizing your drinking?
3) **Guilty:** Have you ever felt guilty about your drinking?
4) **Eye-Opener:** Have you ever had a drink first thing in the morning (Eye-opener) to steady your nerves or get rid of a hangover? (Bisson, Nadeau, & Demers, 1999, p. 717)

Stewart and Richards (2000) write, "A patient who answers yes to two or more of these questions probably abuses alcohol; a patient who answers yes to one question should be screened further" (p. 56). However, tests for substance abuse are often not as valuable as a simple social history focusing on the use of substances. Perhaps this lack of a substance abuse history is why Backer and Walton-Moss (2001) found that 20% to 25% of all patients with alcohol-related problems were treated medically for the symptoms of alcoholism rather than for the condition itself, and that a diagnosis of alcohol abuse was never made in almost one fourth of all alcoholics seen for medical treatment.

InfoTable 14.2   Alcohol Use at the Office

In a study of workplace alcohol problems done at the University of Buffalo and reported by the *Los Angeles Times* (Cromley, 2006), of 2,805 employed adults, almost 2% of the workforce consumed alcohol at least once before coming to work, 7% consumed alcohol at least once during the workday, and more than 9% come to work with hangovers. Additionally, 15% of the workforce had at least one incident of taking a drink before coming to work, drinking on the job, or having a hangover at work at least once during 2004.

OLDER ADULTS DON'T GET NEEDED HELP

Another problem caused by the lack of a complete psychological and social history is that services are often withheld from certain populations of people, notably, elderly patients with substance abuse problems. Pennington, Butler, and Eagger (2000) report that older patients referred to a psychiatric service with a diagnosis of alcohol abuse failed to receive the clinical services recommended by the American Geriatrics Society. Rather than being treated for alcoholism as a primary problem, most elderly clients abusing alcohol (4 out of 5) were treated for depression or associated medical problems. The authors believe that the reason elderly patients are not adequately treated for alcohol abuse is that "some health professionals harbor a misguided belief that older people should not be advised to give up established habits or they may be embarrassed to ask older patients personal questions about alcohol use" (p. 183), even though those behaviors may be self-injurious and possibly dangerous to others.

FEMALE SUBSTANCE ABUSERS

Writing about female alcohol abuse, Backer and Walton-Moss (2001) report that "unlike men, women commonly seek help for alcoholism from primary care clinicians" (p. 13). Furthermore, the development and progression of alcoholism is different in women than in men. Women with alcohol problems have higher rates of dual diagnoses (drinking and a mental health problem such as depression), childhood sexual abuse, panic and phobia disorders, eating disorders, PTSD, and victimization. "Early diagnosis, brief interventions, and referral are critical to the treatment of alcoholism in women" (p. 13).

InfoTable 14.3	How Do Female Substance Abusers Differ From Male Substance Abusers?

Backer and Walton-Moss (2001) report the following information about female alcoholics: because women metabolize alcohol differently than men, women tend to show signs of becoming intoxicated at a later age than men (26.5 vs. 22.7), experience their first signs of a recognition of alcohol abuse later (27.5 vs. 25), and lose control over their drinking later in life (29.8 vs. 27.2). The death rate for female alcoholics is 50% to 100% higher than it is for men. Liver damage occurs in women in a shorter period of time and with a lower intake of alcohol. Backer and Walton-Moss report that "female alcoholics have a higher mortality rate from alcoholism than men from suicide, alcohol-related accidents, circulatory disorders, and cirrhosis of the liver" (p. 15). Use of alcohol by women in adolescence is almost equal to that of male adolescents, and whereas men use alcohol to socialize, women use it to cope with negative moods and in response to specific stressors in their lives (Backer & Walton-Moss, 2001).

ADOLESCENT SUBSTANCE ABUSE

Kuperman et al. (2001) report that the risk factors for adolescent alcoholism include home problems, personal behavioral problems, and early use of alcohol. Home problems are defined as problems with parental use and acceptance of alcohol and drugs, problems with family bonding and family conflict, ease in obtaining alcohol, a high level of peer use of alcohol, and positive peer attitudes toward alcohol and drug use. Personal behavioral problems include rebellious behavior against parents, gaining peer acceptance by drinking and other risky behaviors meant to impress peers, and self-treatment through the use of alcohol and drugs for mental health and/or academic problems. Early use of alcohol and drugs may occur in elementary school and is usually a confirmed addiction by early adolescence. Grant and Dawson (1997) report that 40% of young adults aged 18 to 29 years who began drinking before the age of 15 were considered to be alcohol-dependent, as compared to roughly 10% who began drinking after the age of 19.

MEDICAL PROBLEMS RESULTING FROM SUBSTANCE ABUSE

Stewart and Richards (2000) believe that a number of medical problems begin with heavy alcohol and drug use. Head injuries and spinal separations as a result of accidents may have been caused by substance abuse. Because heavy drinkers often fail to eat, they may have nutritional deficiencies that result in psychotic-like symptoms including abnormal eye movements, disorganization, and forgetfulness. Stomach disorders, liver damage, and severe heartburn may have their origins in heavy drinking because alcohol destroys the stomach's mucosal lining. Of all heavy drinkers, 15% develop cirrhosis of the liver (a fatal disease), and many develop pancreatitis (potentially a fatal disease if not caught early). Weight loss, pneumonia, muscle loss because of malnutrition, and oral cancer have all been associated with heavy drinking. Stewart and Richards indicate that substance abusers are poor candidates for surgery. Anesthesia and pain medication can delay alcohol withdrawal for up to 5 days postoperatively. "Withdrawal symptoms can cause agitation and uncooperativeness and can mask signs and symptoms of other postoperative complications. Patients who abuse alcohol are at a higher risk for postoperative complications such as excessive bleeding, infection, heart failure, and pneumonia" (Stewart & Richards, 2000, p. 58).

| InfoTable 14.4 | How Do You Know if You've Had Too Much to Drink? |

Stewart and Richards (2000) provide the following blood alcohol levels as measures of the impact of alcohol in screening for abuse:

0.05% (equivalent to one or two drinks in an average-sized person)—impaired judgment, reduced alertness, loss of inhibitions, euphoria.

0.10%—slower reaction times, decreased caution in risk-taking behavior, impaired fine-motor control. Legal evidence of intoxication in most states starts at 0.10%.

0.15%—significant and consistent losses in reaction times.

0.20%—function of entire motor area of brain measurably depressed, causing staggering. The individual may be easily angered or emotional.

0.25%—severe sensory and motor impairment.

0.30%—confusion, stupor.

0.35%—surgical anesthesia.

0.40%—respiratory depression, lethal in about half of the population.

0.50%—death from respiratory depression. (p. 59)

Helping People With Substance Abuse Problems

We have a number of ways to help people with substance abuse problems, including outpatient mental health and drug counseling therapy, inpatient therapy, medicines that help abusers with underlying problems of depression, and self-help groups such as Alcoholics Anonymous (AA). Most treatment for substance abuse is offered through community drug and alcohol treatment centers paid for by state and federal funds, family service agencies paid for through public and private grants, and fee-for-service hospitals and outpatient treatment centers specializing in treating substance abuse.

Of all the ways of helping, self-help groups such as AA seem to be the most effective. According to Humphreys and Ribisl (1999), "Self-help groups can provide benefits that the best health care often does not: identification with other sufferers, long-term support and companionship, and a sense of competence and empowerment" (p. 326). Riessman (1997) identifies the following principles, function, and purpose of self-help groups: (a) members share a similar condition and understand each other; (b) members determine activities and policies that make self-help groups very democratic and self-determining; (c) helping others is therapeutic;

(d) self-help groups build on the strengths of the individual members, the group, and the community while charging no fees and not being commercialized; (e) self-help groups function as social support systems that help participants cope with traumas through supportive relationships between members; (f) values are projected that define the intrinsic meaning of the group to its members; (g) self-help groups use the expertise of members to help one another; (h) seeking assistance from a self-help group is not as stigmatizing as it may be when seeking help from a health or mental health provider; and (i) self-help groups focus on the use of self-determination, inner strength, self-healing, and resilience.

How Effective Are We in Treating Substance Abuse?

SELF-HELP GROUPS

A psychologist named Seligman asked readers of *Consumer Reports* to provide feedback on the effectiveness of many types of counseling and psychotherapy. Seligman (1995) concluded that "Alcoholics Anonymous (AA) did especially well . . . significantly bettering mental health professionals [in the treatment of alcohol- and drug-related problems]" (p. 10). Humphreys and Moos (1996) found that during a 3-year period of study, alcoholics who initially chose AA over professional help had a 45% ($1,826) lower average per-person health care cost than those receiving professional treatment. Even with the lower costs, AA participants had reduced alcohol consumption, had fewer numbers of days intoxicated, and achieved lower rates of depression when compared to alcoholic clients receiving professional help. In follow-up studies, these findings were consistent at 1 year and 3 years after the start of the study.

Humphreys, Mavis, and Stoffelmayr (1994) report that African Americans (253 participants) in Narcotics Anonymous and AA showed improvement during 12 months in six problem areas (employment, alcohol and drug use, and legal, psychological, and family problems). African American group members had much more improvement in their medical, alcohol, and drug problems than did African American patients not involved in self-help groups. In an analysis of more than 50 studies, Emrick, Tonigan, Montgomery, and Little (1993) report that AA members who were also professionally treated alcoholic patients were somewhat more likely to reduce drinking than those who did not attend AA. Membership in AA reduced physical symptoms and improved psychological adjustment. Alemi et al. (1996) assigned two groups of pregnant women with substance abuse histories to either a self-help group meeting biweekly or to self-help groups operating over a bulletin board accessed by telephone.

Bulletin board participants made significantly fewer telephone calls and visits to health care clinics than did the group assigned to participate in the face-to-face group. Both groups had similar health status and drug use at the end of the study.

Hughes (1997) studied adolescent members of Alateen, a self-help group for children with an alcoholic parent, and noted that Alateen members had significantly fewer negative moods, much more positive overall moods, had higher self-esteem than adolescents who were not members and didn't have an alcoholic parent. McKay, Alterman, McLellan, and Snider (1994) reported on African American participants in self-help groups for substance abuse after a 7-month follow-up. Participants with high rates of attendance at group meetings reduced their use of alcohol and drugs by half as much as those who had poor attendance records. Both groups were similar in their use of substances prior to the start of their group involvement. Pisani and Fawcett (1993) studied alcoholic patients admitted for a short hospital treatment program who were referred upon release to AA. In an 18-month follow-up study, the more days group members attended AA meetings, the longer their abstinence lasted. Interestingly, AA involvement was seen as a more powerful way to continue abstinence than use of medication to treat the addiction.

SHORT-TERM TREATMENT

Bien, Miller, and Tonigan (1993) found that two or three 10- to 15-minute counseling sessions are often as effective as more extensive interventions with older alcohol abusers. The sessions include motivation-for-change strategies, education, assessment of the severity of the problem, direct feedback, contracting and goal-setting, behavioral modification techniques, and the use of written materials such as self-help manuals. Brief interventions have been shown to be effective in reducing alcohol consumption, binge drinking, and the frequency of excessive drinking in problem drinkers, according to Fleming, Barry, Manwell, Johnson, and London (1997). Completion rates using brief interventions are better for elder-specific alcohol programs than for mixed-age programs (Atkinson, 1995), and late-onset alcoholics are more likely to complete treatment and have somewhat better outcomes using brief interventions (Liberto & Oslin, 1995).

Fleming and Manwell (1998) report that people with alcohol-related problems often receive counseling from primary care physicians, nursing staff, or in emergency rooms in five or fewer standard office visits following an accident. The counseling consists of information about the negative impact of alcohol use as well as practical advice regarding ways of reducing alcohol dependence and the availability of community resources. Gentilello, Donovan, Dunn, and Rivara (1995) suggest that 25 to 40% of the trauma patients seen in emergency rooms may be alcohol dependent.

InfoTable 14.5	Key Components of Brief Treatment for Substance Abuse

Miller and Sanchez (1994) summarize the key components of brief intervention using the acronym FRAMES: feedback, responsibility, advice, menu of strategies, empathy, and self-efficacy:

1. *Feedback.* Includes an assessment with feedback to the client regarding the client's risk for alcohol problems, his or her reasons for drinking, the role of alcohol in the patient's life, and the consequences of drinking.

2. *Responsibility.* Includes strategies to help clients understand the need to remain healthy, independent, and financially secure. This is particularly important when working with older clients and clients with health problems and disabilities.

3. *Advice.* Includes direct feedback and suggestions to clients to help them cope with their drinking problems and with other life situations that may contribute to alcohol abuse.

4. *Menu.* Includes a list of strategies to reduce drinking and help cope with such high-risk situations as loneliness, boredom, family problems, and lack of social opportunities.

5. *Empathy.* Bien et al. (1993) strongly emphasize the need for a warm, empathic, and understanding style of treatment. Miller and Rollnick (1991) found that an empathetic counseling style produced a 77% reduction in client drinking as compared to a 55% reduction when a confrontational approach was used.

6. *Self-efficacy.* This includes strategies to help clients rely on their inner resources to make changes in their drinking behavior. Inner resources may include positive points of view about themselves, helping others, staying busy, and good problem-solving coping skills.

The authors found that a single motivational interview, at or near the time of discharge from the hospital reduced drinking levels and re-admission for traumas during 6 months of follow up. Monti et al. (1999) conducted a similar study with 18 and 19 year olds admitted to an emergency room with alcohol-related injuries. After 6 months, all participants had decreased their alcohol consumption, however, "the group receiving brief intervention had a significantly lower incidence of drinking and driving, traffic violations, alcohol-related injuries, and alcohol-related problems" (Monti et al., 1999, p. 3).

LONGER-TERM TREATMENT

Baekeland and Lundwall (1975) report dropout rates for inpatient treatment programs of 28%, and that 75% of the outpatient alcoholic patients in their study dropped out of treatment before their fourth session. Leigh, Ogborne, and Cleland (1984) report that of 172 alcoholic outpatients studied, 15% failed to attend their initial appointment, 28% attended only a session or two, and 19% attended only three to five times. In studying 117 alcoholism clinic admissions, Rees (1986) found that 35% of the clients failed to return after their initial visit and another 18% terminated treatment within 30 days. These studies suggest what many people believe is a lack of motivation to stop abusing substances.

To try and reduce the number of dropouts in alcohol treatment programs, Walitzer and Dermen (2002) randomly assigned 126 clients entering an alcohol treatment program to one of three groups to prepare them for the treatment program: a role induction (RI) session, a motivational interview (MI) session, or a no-preparatory session control group (CG). They found that clients assigned to the MI "attended more treatment sessions and had fewer heavy drinking days during and 12 months after treatment relative to control group" (p. 1161). Clients assigned to the MI went without using substances in the first 3 months following treatment more often than the CG but the difference, unfortunately, did not last for the remaining 9 months of follow-up. Clients assigned to the RI group did no better than the CG in any of the variables studied.

In describing the MI, Walitzer and Dermen (2002) indicate that it consists of the following:

> (a) Eliciting self-motivational statements; (b) reflective, empathic listening; (c) inquiring about the client's feelings, ideas, concerns, and plans; (d) affirming the client in a way that acknowledges the client's serious consideration of and steps toward change; (e) deflecting resistance in a manner that takes into account the link between therapist behavior and client resistance; (f) reframing client statements as appropriate; and (g) summarizing. (p. 1164)

TREATMENT STRATEGIES

Herman (2000) believes that the primary strategy in the treatment of substance abuse is to initially achieve abstinence. Once abstinence is achieved, the substance abuser can begin to address relationship problems that might interfere with social and emotional functioning. Merrill claims that the key to treatment is to match the client with the type of treatment most likely to help. He suggests that the following phases exist in the treatment of substance abuse:

Phase 1. Abstinence.

Phase 2. Teaching the client coping skills to help prevent a relapse through cognitive-behavioral techniques that help clients manage a stressful situation likely to trigger substance abuse. These techniques may include recognizing internal cues that lead to substance abuse (depression and feelings of low self-esteem); managing external cues (responses by others and interpersonal relationships); avoiding peers who are likely to continue to abuse substances and encourage the client to do the same; and alternative behaviors that help the client avoid drug use (substituting substance abuse with exercise, or attending social events where alcohol isn't available).

Phase 3. Because the underlying problems that contribute to substance abuse are often feelings of low self-worth, depression, and self-loathing, therapy should help the client deal with negative feelings and beliefs that are likely to lead to relapse.

NATURAL RECOVERY (RECOVERY WITHOUT PROFESSIONAL HELP)

Granfield and Cloud (1996) estimate that as many as 90% of all problem drinkers never enter treatment and that many end their alcohol abuse without any form of treatment (Hingson, Scotch, Day, & Culbert, 1980; Roizen, Cahalan, Lambert, Wiebel, & Shanks, 1978; Stall & Biernacki, 1989). Sobell, Sobell, Toneatto, and Leo (1993) report that 82% of the alcoholics they studied who terminated their addiction did so by using natural recovery methods that excluded the use of professional treatment. As an example of the effectiveness of natural recovery techniques, Granfield and Cloud (1996) report that most ex-smokers discontinued their tobacco use without treatment (Peele, 1989), and many addicted substance abusers "mature out" of a variety of addictions, including heavy drinking and narcotics use (Snow, 1973; Winick, 1962). Biernacki (1986) reports that people who use natural methods to end their drug addictions use a range of strategies, including discontinuing their relationships with drug users, avoiding drug-using environments (Stall & Biernacki, 1989), having new goals and interests in their lives (Peele, 1989), and using friends and family to provide a support network (Biernacki, 1986). Trice and Roman (1970) believe that self-help groups with substance-abusing clients are particularly helpful because they develop and continue a support network that assists clients in maintaining abstinence and other changed behaviors.

Granfield and Cloud (1996) studied middle-class alcoholics who used natural recovery alone without professional help or the use of self-help groups. Many of the participants in their study felt that some self-help groups were overly religious, whereas others believed in alcoholism as a disease that suggested a lifetime struggle. The participants in the study believed that some self-help groups encouraged dependence on the group and that associating with other alcoholics would probably complicate recovery. In summarizing their findings, Granfield and Cloud report that many [research participants] expressed strong opposition to the suggestion that they were powerless over their addictions. These respondents saw themselves as efficacious people who often prided themselves on their past accomplishments. They viewed themselves as being individualists and strong-willed. One respondent, for instance, explained that "such programs encourage powerlessness" and that she would rather "trust her own instincts than the instincts of others." (p. 51)

Waldorf, Reinarman, and Murphy (1991) found that many addicted people with jobs, strong family ties, and other close emotional supports were able to "walk away" from their very heavy use of cocaine. Granfield and Cloud (1996) suggest that many of the respondents in their study had a great deal to lose if they continued their substance abuse, and their sample consisted of people with stable lives, good jobs, supportive families and friends, college educations, and other social supports that gave them motivation to "alter" their drug-using behaviors.

The Organizations That Provide Assistance to Substance Abusers

Because substance abuse is such a widespread problem in American society, we have made a number of efforts to develop programs to help people become less addicted to alcohol and drugs. The following information shows where people have received help for substance abuse problems (HHS, 2002):

1. An estimated 3.5 million people aged 12 or older (1.5% of the population) received some kind of treatment for a problem related to the use of alcohol or illicit drugs in the 12 months prior to being interviewed in 2002. Of these, 1.34 million received treatment for alcohol and illicit drugs, 0.7 million received treatment for illicit drugs but not alcohol, and 1.1 million received treatment for alcohol but not illicit drugs.

2. Among persons aged 12 or older in 2002, males were more likely than females to receive treatment for an alcohol or illicit drug problem in the past year (2.1% vs. 0.9%, respectively). Among youth aged 12 to 17, males also were more likely to receive treatment than females (1.7% vs. 1.2%, respectively).

3. Among persons aged 12 or older in 2002, the rates of alcohol or illicit drug treatment during the 12 months prior to the interview were highest among American Indians/Alaska Natives (4.8%), blacks (2.2%), and persons reporting two or more races (2.1%). The lowest rate of treatment was among Asians (0.2%).

4. Among the 3.5 million persons aged 12 or older who received treatment for alcohol or illicit drugs in the past year, more than half (2.0 million) received treatment from a self-help group. There were 1.5 million people who received treatment at a rehabilitation facility as an outpatient; 1.1 million at a rehabilitation facility as an inpatient; 1.0 million at a mental health center as an outpatient; 859,000 at a hospital as an inpatient; 523,000 at a private doctor's office, including nonphysicians who offer therapy; 469,000 at an emergency room; and 259,000 at a prison or jail. Does the fact that people receive help for substance abuse in jail surprise you?

5. More than half (2.2 million) of the 3.5 million persons who received treatment for a substance in the past year received treatment for alcohol during their most recent treatment. An estimated 974,000 persons received treatment for marijuana, 796,000 for cocaine, 360,000 for pain relievers, and 277,000 for heroin.

The Role of Social Work in Treating Substance Abuse

Social workers perform a number of functions when working with substance abusers. Some of these many functions include providing in- and outpatient clinical services to substance abusers and their loved ones aimed at reducing the amount of substance use and improving functioning at work, in school, and in their families. We organize and are often coleaders in self-help groups dealing with substance abuse. Self-help groups use the helping impulses and knowledge of group members to help each other stop drinking or using drugs. Social workers help substance abusers cope with social issues including work, school, housing, finances, health insurance, and other necessities of life. They may help in finding housing and jobs after a substance abuser has been hospitalized or in a long-term decline.

We advocate for substance abusers when their behavior involves legal issues, such as suspension of licenses, and accidents that may be drug- or alcohol-related. This doesn't mean that we excuse the behavior, but when life isn't going well, we act as mentors, teachers, friends, and advocates, which may involve writing letters of support and encouragement and going to bat for people.

Social workers refer people to appropriate professionals and act as case managers to make certain that clients receive the proper help they need to overcome their addictions. We offer support and encouragement to families and help with problems of family codependence, which involves family members who enable or allow the substance abuser to maintain their substance abuse by excusing it. Social workers write assessments of substance abusers that help to explain their reasons for abusing substances, and we provide information about early family life, health issues, early life behavior, and anything of importance that might help others understand why a person is abusing substances.

Social workers help to educate and prevent substance abuse through community education efforts. We are involved in research efforts to find out more about substance abuse and how best to treat it. Finally, social workers are employed by the judicial system and may provide helping services to individuals and families of substance abusers as a condition set down by the court where crimes or traffic accidents have been committed while under the influence of a substance.

You Be the Social Worker

This case study first appeared in my book (Glicken, 2005, pp. 175–178) that presents a research-oriented approach to counseling and psychotherapy for substance abuse called evidence-based practice.

The Case

Jake Anderson is a 17 year-old high school student who was taken to the emergency room after his car spun out of control and hit an embankment. Three passengers in the car were slightly injured. Jake and his friends had been drinking "Ever Clear," a 180% proof alcoholic beverage they purchased through an older friend. All four friends were very intoxicated and had walked a block and a half from a party to their car wearing tee-shirts in 40 degree below zero weather. Jake sustained minor injuries. After he became sober enough in the emergency room to recognize the seriousness of the accident and that his blood alcohol level was in excess of .25%, three times the allowed drinking and driving level of .08%, he became antagonistic and withdrawn. His parents rushed to the hospital and were very concerned about Jake's behavior. His drinking was unknown to them, although Jake had begun drinking at age 10 and was regularly becoming intoxicated at weekend parties by age 13. Jake thought he was doing social drinking and felt that he was no different from his other friends. The accident, however, seemed to be a wake up call to do something about his risky behavior.

A hospital social worker and nurse met with Jake and his parents 3 times over the course of a two-day stay in the hospital. They gave out information about the health impact of drinking and did a screening test to determine Jake's level of abusive drinking. They concluded that Jake was at very high risk of becoming an alcoholic since his drinking impaired his judgment, affected his grades, and was thought to be responsible for high blood sugar readings consistent with early onset diabetes and moderately high blood pressure. A psychosocial history taken by the social worker revealed that Jake had begun experimenting with alcohol at age 10 and was frequently using it at home and with friends from age 13 on. He was drinking more than a quart of alcohol a week, some of it very high in alcohol content.

Jake's drivers license was revoked by the court and, on the basis of the report made by the emergency room personnel, Jake was sent for mandatory alcohol counseling to a family service agency in his home town where he was seen by a clinical social worker.

Jake is a reluctant client. He discounts his drinking problem, claiming that he drinks no more than his friends. Were it not for the accident, he argues, he would not be in counseling since he was not having any serious problems in his life. That isn't altogether true, however. With an IQ of over 130, Jake's grades are mostly in the "D" range. He misses classes on a regular basis and often misses class in the mornings because of hangovers. His parents are having marital and financial problems and fail to supervise Jake closely. Furthermore, Jake has been fantasizing about harming his friends whom he thinks have been disloyal to him for reasons he can't validate. "Just a feeling, ya know?" he told the social worker. Was the accident really an accident? "Sure," Jake says, "what else?" His social worker isn't so sure. He has hints of Jake's antagonism toward other students and has heard Jake talk about dreams in which Jake harms others. Jake spends a great deal of time on the Internet and has assumed various identities, many of them demonstrating anti-social and violent intentions. The social worker believes that Jake is a walking time bomb of emotional distress and that his alcoholism, while robust, is just one way of self-medicating himself for feelings of isolation, low self-esteem, and rejection by his parents and classmates.

After months of treatment during which time Jake would often sit in silence and stare at the therapist, he has begun to talk about his feelings and admits that he has continued drinking heavily. He also drives, although his license has been revoked. He is full of self-hate and thinks that he is doomed to die soon. He feels strong when he drinks, he told the social worker, and loves the peaceful feeling that comes over him as he gets drunk. Like his parents, he romanticizes his drinking and can hardly wait to have his first drink of the day. Sometimes he drinks when he wakes up and often drinks rather than eats. He is aware that this cycle of drinking to feel better about himself can only lead to serious life problems, but doesn't think he is capable of stopping.

Consistent with the evidence-based practice approach in which the social worker and the client work together to resolve emotional problems, the social worker asked Jake to help him do an Internet search to find the best way to help Jake with his drinking problem. It seemed like a silly request to Jake since the social worker was suppose to be the expert, but Jake was intrigued and did as he was asked. When he met next with the therapist, Jake had printed out a number of articles suggesting ways of coping with adolescent alcoholism that seemed reasonable to him and to the therapist. From the work of Schlosser, Kramer, Bucholz et al. (2001), they agreed that Jake had a number of problems that should be dealt with including problems at home, with friends, and with his alcohol abuse. They decided that a cognitive-behavioral approach would work best coupled with homework assignments. Jake was intrigued with an article he found on the strengths approach and showed the therapist an article by Moxley and Olivia (2001) they both found quite useful. Another article on self-help groups by Humphreys (1998) convinced them that a self-help group for adolescent alcohol abusers might also be helpful. Finally, Jake brought up the issue of working with his parents and it was decided

(Continued)

(Continued)

that the family would be seen together to work on some of the problems they were having and to develop better communication skills.

Jake has been seeing the clinical social worker for over a year. He is applying himself in school and has begun talking about going to college. His drinking has modified itself somewhat. Although he still drinks too much at times, he won't drive when he is drinking or engage in risky behavior. He feels much less angry and has developed new friendships with peers who don't drink or use drugs. The changes seem very substantial, but it's too early to know if the alcoholism is likely to become problematic when he deals with additional life stressors. Jake is unsure and says that, "Yeah, it's all helping me but my head isn't always on straight and sometimes I do dumb stuff. I'm more aware of it now but I still do it. I'm getting along with my folks a lot better and my new friends are real friends, not drinking buddies. I don't know. I looked at some studies on the Internet and it looks like I have a pretty good chance of becoming a drunk. I like booze. It makes me feel good. That's not a good sign, is it. And I'm still pretty mad about a lot of things. I spend time on the Internet in chat rooms and it's pretty bizarre, sometimes, the things I say. But yeah, I know I'm better. I just hope it lasts."

Jake's social worker told me, "Jake has a good handle on himself. I wouldn't argue with anything he said. He has lots of potential but he also has enough problems to make me unwilling to predict the future. What I *will* say is that he works hard, is cooperative, and seems to be trying to work on some long standing issues with his family and his perception of himself. I think that addictions are transitory and you never know when his desire to drink will overwhelm his desire to stay sober. The self-help group he's in keeps close tabs on his drinking, and his new friends are helpful. I'd caution anyone who works with adolescents not to expect too much from treatment. I do want to applaud the professionals he worked with in the hospital. Even though the treatment was brief, it made a lasting impact on Jake to hear that he was considered an alcoholic, and it did bring him into treatment. That's exactly what you hope for in serious alcoholics who are in denial."

Questions

1. How is it possible that Jake's parents didn't know about his drinking problem? Would you have concluded that they were too aloof from their son to know what was actually going on in his life, or are parents who don't know about their child's substance abuse more the norm?

2. Jake is making some headway, but do you think Jake might resume his drinking? Explain your answer.

3. Friends who let other friends drive when they are very drunk are, in a way, allowing the drinking to progress as a problem. What should his friends have done to prevent Jake from driving and having an accident? Do you think most people your age would have done what Jake's friends did?

4. Focusing on what's right about Jake rather than on his drinking problem might be a bit risky. Do you think that a positive approach is more likely to help rather than one that utilizes tough love with limit-setting and serious consequences if Jake keeps drinking?

5. There appears to be little information explaining why Jake began drinking at such an early age. What might be some possible reasons, based on people you know who began drinking at a fairly early age?

Summary

In this chapter on substance abuse, research findings are reported on the prevalence of substance abuse in America and the effectiveness of various types of treatment, particularly brief treatment with high-risk abusers. Promising research on natural recovery and self-help groups suggests that treatment effectiveness may be consistently positive with these two approaches. A case study is provided that asks you to be the social worker with an adolescent substance abuser following a car accident, and questions are posed about the nature of substance abuse and the effectiveness of treatment with addictions.

Questions to Determine Your Frame of Reference

1. Binge drinking is epidemic on many university campuses in the United States. Do you feel that binge drinking is a sign of potential for alcoholism?

2. Brief treatment of substance abuse flies in the face of what many people believe about the long-term addictive nature of alcohol and drug dependence. What is your view about the effectiveness of brief treatment?

3. The idea that people will walk away from their addictions when they're ready is contraindicated in studies of weight loss. In these studies, people cycle back and forth and fail to sustain weight loss. Might not the same thing be said about addictions to substances?

4. Why do you think America has such a problem with substance abuse? Do you think substances make up for feelings of emptiness in people's lives, or might they just be a quick way to feel happy that becomes addicting?

5. The fact that children of alcoholics are at high risk of becoming alcoholics suggests either a genetic reason for alcoholism or that alcoholism is a learned behavior and that, in subtle ways, alcoholic parents teach their children to drink. Which theory do you support, and why?

Internet Sources

The results of a national survey by the Department of Health and Human Services (2002) on substance use in the United States are provided. Next, the National Institute for Health (2004) reports on preventing substance abuse among children and adolescents. Finally, binge drinking and campus use of substances is addressed (Task Force of the National Advisory Council on Alcohol Abuse and Alcoholism, 2002).

1. Department of Health and Human Services, Substance Abuse and Mental Health Services Administration Office of Applied Studies. (2002). *National Survey on Drug Use and Health: National findings.* Retrieved from http://www.oas.samhsa.gov/NHSDA/2k2NSDUH/Results/2k2results.htm#chap3

2. National Institute on Drug Abuse, National Institute for Health. (2004). *Preventing drug abuse among children and adolescents.* Retrieved from http://www.nida.nih.gov/Prevention/Prevopen.html

3. Task Force of the National Advisory Council on Alcohol Abuse and Alcoholism. (2002). *A call to action: Changing the culture of drinking at U.S. colleges.* Retrieved March 2, 2005, from http://www.collegedrinkingprevention.gov/Reports/TaskForce/TaskForce_TOC.asp

Part III

International Issues and the Roles of Social Work

Immigration 15

Xenophobia, the Organizations Helping New Immigrants, and Social Work's Role in Smoothing Transitions to the United States

Give me your tired, your poor, your huddled masses yearning to breathe free.

—Emma Lazarus (wording on the Statue of Liberty welcoming new immigrants to America)

The United States has been described as a melting pot where many cultures and ethnic groups come together and live in peace yet retain their own identity. However, many people believe that the expectation of assimilation is so strong in American life that newly immigrated groups soon lose the strength of their cultures and become Americanized, creating a homogenized society in which different cultures have little importance other than the addition of new foods and music. Which argument is more correct is difficult to say, but what we do know is that America goes through periods of anti-immigration sentiment (xenophobia) and that many groups experience overt discrimination. Two immigrant groups who certainly experience discrimination are Latinos and Asians, and much of this chapter will discuss ethnically sensitive social work practice with both groups. Chapter 18 discusses ethnically sensitive practice with another discriminated-against group, African Americans.

We also know that immigrants play a vital role in the American economy. In fact, in his book *The Sibling Society,* Robert Bly (1996) writes that Americans have developed such a sense of entitlement that were it not for legal and illegal immigrant labor, we would lack the labor pool to sustain our economy. Many of these immigrant groups come to America because of political conflicts that threaten their survival. Others come to America for the economic prosperity we enjoy and to raise families in a more positive political and economic climate. This chapter is about two immigrant groups who come to America and their cultures and traditions, culturally sensitive social work practice, problems of discrimination that affect people's lives, and the organization that help immigrants adjust and cope with American life.

InfoTable 15.1	Undocumented Immigrants

The U.S. Census Bureau in its 2000 census report estimated that in 2000, there were about 7 million illegal immigrants in the United States up from 5.6 million just 4 years earlier. Projections for 2006 increased that number to 11–12 million, 70% of whom come from Mexico. The increase in undocumented aliens is estimated to be roughly 600,000 a year. While California is home to most undocumented workers, the greatest increases have occurred in Arizona, Georgia and North Carolina. It is estimated that between 4,000 and 7,000 people enter the U.S. illegally each day. (Center for Immigration Studies, 2003)

InfoTable 15.2	Undocumented Workers and Wal-Mart

250 undocumented workers were arrested by the INS in a sweep of Wal-Mart stores. Although none of the employees were Wal-Mart employees and worked for separate contractors, Wal-Mart officials knew the practice was being used and insiders said that the use of undocumented workers paid at much lower rates without benefits lowered labor costs for Wal-Mart substantially. The penalty for hiring illegal workers can run as high as $10,000 per worker although the practice is so common and prosecution so unlikely that much of the less desirable labor in America is done by undocumented workers living on substandard wages, often not protected from industrial accidents and illness by health insurance or workman's compensation. (CNN.Money, 2003).

The Cost to Taxpayers of Illegal Immigration

Many of us believe that the immigrants who enter the United States are among our hardest workers and best citizens. With immigration controls tight, where can poor, hard-working, and ambitious people like my parents go in the world where they can experience freedom and unlimited economic opportunity other than the United States and a few other developed nations? And yet, there is a downside to illegal immigration: very low wages for dangerous work; the possibility of being deported at any time (repeat violators can spend up to 2 years in prison); living in unsafe houses and apartments where rents are outrageously high because illegal immigrants have little legal protection and complaining means they may be deported;

many people may share a small room or apartment, increasing the probability of child abuse, rape, and lethal fights; and although illegal alien workers increase profits for employers and some say keep prices of goods low, they are costly to the American taxpayer.

The Federation for American Immigration Reform (2004) estimated that the cost of providing social services, education, roads, prisons, and other services to illegal immigrants is about $45 billion after sales taxes are factored in. The cost of incarceration of illegal aliens in state prisons has also risen rapidly. In fiscal year 2002, the Department of Justice's State Criminal Alien Assistance Program (SCAAP) distributed $550 million to the states to help defray their expenses, but this was estimated to cover only a part of the actual expense of $2.5 billion, costs picked up by local and county governments. Between 1999 and 2002, alien detention increased by 45% (from about 69,300 inmate years to more than 100,300 inmate years), and that trend is continuing. These expenses do not include the costs of illegal aliens incarcerated in federal prisons, public safety expenditures, detentions pending trial, expenses of trial proceedings, interpreters, public defenders, or the incarceration expenses of immigrants for minor offenses that do not meet the standards of the SCAAP reimbursement program (Federation for American Immigration Reform, 2004).

Some argue that these data are patently false (Barkan, 1996) and that Mexican workers returning to Mexico, after working in the United States, claim they have paid social security and state and federal taxes through employer deductions but have received no benefits. They also argue that illegal immigrants are law-abiding but that local police abuse them or pick them up on false charges. Crime is not done only by illegal immigrants but has been increasing in America because its own native population has become more violent and drug-addicted. Finally, they argue that the low wages illegal immigrants are paid more than offset the cost to taxpayers of certain services, a savings that makes it possible for Americans to purchase homes built by and agricultural goods picked by illegal aliens at a much lower price than they would pay in other countries.

The Helping Organizations Assisting Immigrants

Family service agencies, private and faith-based, are among the organizations that help immigrants the most by providing emergency clothing, shelter, legal assistance, work, family support, educational opportunities, and counseling when needed. As an example of the type of work done by faith-based organizations, the Catholic church has developed a program called Bridging Refugee Youth and Children's Services, which is a technical clearing house to other agencies providing services to immigrant children and their families. The purpose is to pool resources and develop collaborative efforts among various private-sector organizations.

The U.S. Immigration and Naturalization Service (INS) provides the following benefits to immigrants: citizenship, asylum, lawful permanent residency, employment authorization, refugee status, intercountry adoptions, replacement immigration documents, family- and employment-related immigration, and foreign student authorization. In addition to administering the programs that provide these benefits, the INS also answers questions and finds solutions to problems brought to our attention by the public, special interest groups, other government agencies, and the U.S. Congress regarding immigration concerns.

Schlosberg (1998) notes that illegal aliens are allowed to receive emergency medical care through state Medicaid programs if they otherwise qualify. An emergency medical service is defined by Schlosberg as

> a medical condition (including labor and delivery) manifesting itself by acute symptoms of sufficient severity (including severe pain) such that the absence of immediate medical attention could reasonably be expected to result in— (A) placing the patient's health in serious jeopardy, (B) serious impairment to bodily functions, or (C) serious dysfunction of any bodily organ or part.

Social Work's Role in Immigration

Social workers assume a number of roles with legal and illegal immigrants. The most frequently assumed are the following: helping immigrants with housing, finances, clothing, work, legal documentation, and, in time of difficulty with the law, helping to provide legal resources with which to defend themselves. Social workers help immigrants understand their legal rights and act as advocates. We provide crisis services when immigrant clients have been evicted from housing or lose jobs and are in financial crisis. Social workers work in health departments and hospitals where serious communicable or life-threatening diseases are treated. We work in child protective service agencies, schools, and other facilities where child problems, including abuse and neglect, are investigated and treated. When immigrant clients are unfamiliar with abuse and neglect laws, social workers help them understand new and sometimes confusing laws. Finally, social workers help unify families and often work in social and family agencies that assist clients from other countries in family unification and essential documentation.

Culturally Sensitive Social Work Practice With Two Immigrant Groups

The following two examples of work with clients from two distinctly different countries, Mexico and Asia, will hopefully help you understand both the cultures and the way social work approaches culturally sensitive work.

CULTURALLY SENSITIVE
SOCIAL WORK WITH LATINO CLIENTS

Counseling and the idea of sharing confidential information with a social worker are not well-accepted ideas in traditional Latino culture. As increasingly strict control on issues pertaining to child abuse, domestic violence, and substance abuse affect the Latino client, many newly immigrated Latinos find themselves involved in some form of treatment, often against their desire for help or their understanding of how this help will make a difference in their lives. The following are culturally relevant guidelines social workers use in assisting the newly immigrated or culturally traditionally Latino client:

Latino Clients Process Information Indirectly

The emotional problems related to a crisis will usually not be discussed directly by the client. Rather, there will be a long period of talking around the problem. This is partly done as a way of gauging the worker's competence, but it also serves as a way of processing the problem in a manner that is familiar to the client. Social workers are often prepared for a longer and more indirect way of gathering vital information from the newly immigrated Latino client than is customary for the Anglo or more assimilated Latino client in crisis. The client may also be very suspicious of the worker's motives. Indirectness helps the client maintain control over the interview until the worker can be better evaluated for his or her competence and level of kindness.

The Importance of Strength in a Crisis

There is a considerable imperative to be strong, even in the midst of a crisis. The act of discussing feelings or complaining about inequities in life may make the client feel weak. This feeling of weakness in the midst of a crisis is complicated by its incompatibility with role expectations. Women, in particular, are expected to be strong or the family may not function well without their guidance and direction. The emphasis on strength has its emotional impact on immigrant Latino women. Salgado de Snyder (1990) found that immigrant Mexican women have a much higher level of generalized distress and psychological stress than immigrant men. Salgado de Snyder believes that immigrant Latino women are more likely to develop long-term psychological problems, particularly depression and anxiety, than non-Latino clients in crisis.

InfoTable 15.3	Latino Women

Latino women have been portrayed as being weak and ineffectual. It is not true. Latino women are the glue that holds the family together. They often work and care for large families. They manage the finances and set standards for the children. They keep going even while they are sick or emotionally drained. There is tremendous emphasis in Hispanic families for the mother to be above the commonplace crises of the day. She cannot get sick or emotionally down or the family may fall apart. Men may be given respect and admiration, but love is almost always the domain of the Latino woman. In a crisis, it is usually the woman who is the change agent for the family. But who takes care of her when she has a crisis? Why, she does. (Glicken, 2004a, p. 108)

Focusing on Positive Behavior

Latino clients like to be respected for their accomplishments. One technique social workers use is to praise accomplishments, particularly those related to the extended family. Although the client, particularly a female client, might appear shy in the midst of such praise, it serves the purpose of building trust and gives the client confidence in the worker as well as self-confidence.

Latino clients view their family as an extension of themselves. If children do well or poorly, it reflects on the client. One way to permit clients to discuss inner feelings is to pose the following question: "I know that you've experienced much heartache and may not feel that your family appreciates you. How would you like your family to treat you differently?" This discussion might touch on core reasons for the crisis. Another useful question is to ask how the client taught his or her children to handle the issue of respect for a parent, because this issue is key to how parents view their children and, ultimately, how successful they have been with their children.

Many Latino clients, particularly male clients, have a strong belief that respect is the core issue of achievement in one's life. With respect, they are people of accomplishment and acceptance. Without respect, they are people of little consequence. When economic factors create underemployment or poverty, absence of respect from family is a sign of failure, and Latino clients may be more crisis-prone as a result.

The Use of Therapeutic Metaphors, or Dichos

In Latino culture, wise sayings, or *dichos*, assume considerable importance in guiding the client toward solutions to problems. Zuniga (1992) notes that dichos are actually metaphors that have been traditionally used in treatment and consist of the following:

InfoTable 15.4   What Is *Machismo?*

One widely misunderstood term to describe the need for respect is *machismo*. In describing the commonly defined way machismo is thought of, Baca Zinn (1980) writes,

> The social science literature views machismo as a compensation for feelings of inadequacy and worthlessness. This interpretation is rooted in the application of psychoanalytic concepts to explain both Mexican and Chicano gender roles. The widely accepted interpretation is that machismo is the male attempt to compensate for feelings of internalized inferiority by exaggerating masculinity. At the same time that machismo is an exaggeration of power, its origin is ironically linked to powerlessness and subordination. (p. 20)

Baca Zinn (1980) notes that traditional views of male roles in the Latino culture include such exaggerated masculine behaviors as dominance, aggressiveness, an emphasis on physical prowess, and other highly stereotypic masculine behaviors that may be characteristic of many lower socioeconomic men. This view of machismo sometimes leads Americans to believe that Latino males are too proud to accept help in a crisis situation, but as Goff (1994), an American anthropologist who lives in Mexico, suggests,

> Mexican men are often described as being very macho which, in the minds of some, translates into being stubborn and unwilling to accept help or advice from others. But we should understand that machismo is a way of providing men who have very little social esteem with self-importance and self-worth. There are bragging rights implied here. The best way to approach a Mexican male when help is needed in the family is to focus on his accomplishments, to praise him for his efforts to provide for the family, and to respect him for his hard work in difficult times. You will then get someone who is willing to work hard in treatment in the service of his family. (Glicken, 2004a, p. 109)

1. major stories that address complex clinical problems

2. anecdotes or short stories focused on specific or limited goals

3. analogies, similes or brief figurative statements or phrases that underscore specific points

4. relationship metaphors, which can use one relationship as a metaphor for another

5. tasks with metaphorical meanings that can be undertaken by clients between sessions

6. artistic metaphors which can be paintings, drawings clay models or creations which symbolize something else. (p. 57)

Several dichos that are commonly used by social workers are as follows. *Sentir en el alma* translates literally as "to feel it in your soul," but the real meaning is to be terribly sorry. *Con la cuhara se le queman los frijoles* translates literally as "even the best cook burns the beans"—in other words, everyone makes mistakes. *Entre azul y buenos noches* translates directly as "between blue and good night," but its popular meaning is to be undecided. *A la buena de Dios*, or "as God would have it," has the common meaning of as luck would have it. *No hay mal que por bien no venga* translates as "there is nothing bad from which good does not come," meaning that it is a blessing in disguise. Another dicho used by social workers is *La verdad no mata, pero incomoda*, which means that the truth doesn't kill but can hurt. Yet another is *Al que no ha usado huaraches, las correas le sacan sangre*, which loosely means, "he who has never worn sandals is easily cut by the straps," or it's difficult to do things you're not used to. And finally, as Zuniga notes for the client in a deteriorating relationship that might end in termination, the dicho *Mejor sola que mal acompanada* might work. Roughly translated, this dicho means that it's better to be alone or unmarried than to be in a bad relationship.

InfoTable 15.5	Distant Neighbors

For the United States, "understanding" Mexico—its "distant neighbor"—has become a matter of self-interest and even of national security. To avoid policies that could prove counterproductive, the United States must learn to look beyond the surface crisis to the inner subtleties of an ancient, complex, and unpredictable nation. To gain insight into Mexico's future, it must sift through the country's entire past and present for clues. The task is not easy. Mexico does not surrender its secrets willingly, because they are the secrets to its survival. It is fierce in its judgment of itself, but resents the probings of foreigners as assaults on its defenses. Yet Mexico is of such importance to the United States that it cannot be permitted to remain permanently shrouded in mystery. (Riding, 1989, p. 1)

The Importance of Feelings

Feelings are highly valued in Latino culture. One approach used by social workers is to tell the client that they will communicate *de corazon a corazon*, or heart to heart. In Mexico, this concept of a close personal relationship in which true feelings can be communicated has various levels of meaning. It is sometimes associated with the process called *el desague de las penas*, or unburdening oneself. It is what social workers might call venting or getting something off your chest. It might also be a part of the process of opening one's soul to a *compadre* or a close personal friend so that the friend can see inside a person's heart and therefore feel his or her sorrow and despair. Allowing Latino clients to unburden themselves often improves the quality of social work with reluctant clients in crisis.

InfoTable 15.6	Hate Crimes Against Latinos

People from Latin America are increasingly targets of bias-motivated crimes. Of 814 hate crimes in 1995 motivated by bias based on ethnicity or national origin, the FBI found that 63.3% (or 516) were directed against Hispanics, often because of their immigration status. Attacks on Hispanics have a particularly long history in California and throughout the Southwest where, during recurring periods of strong anti-immigrant sentiment, both new immigrants and long-time U.S. citizens of Mexican descent were blamed for social and economic problems and harassed or deported en masse. (American Psychological Association, 1998)

Confusing Aspects of Life in America

It is important for us to remember that many problems experienced by newly immigrated Latinos are created by feelings of not being welcome in this country, even when the client has a legal right to be here. This immediate sense of alienation and the unfamiliar rules and regulations common to American life often place the client in situations that lead to crisis. Unfamiliar child care laws and arguments within the family that sometimes become loud and spill onto the streets may bring the client into immediate contact with the judicial system. Prevention of these unnecessary situations can be made by a process of socialization that is a necessary but often neglected function of the social and educational institutions of America. Emphasizing this sense of alienation, Gonzalez (2000) argues that Latinos are the largest minority group in America and that

> mental health problems of Hispanics living in poverty and undocumented Hispanic immigrants are often exacerbated by socioeconomic stressors, racism, and political oppression. Effective mental health treatment for this segment of the Hispanic population must encompass case advocacy, community outreach, and the mediating of complex social systems. Mental health clinicians who treat poor and/or undocumented Hispanics should be skilled in the implementation of multiple interventive roles such as that of advocate, mediator, broker, and teacher.

Commenting on the anti-immigrant attitudes that often exist among North Americans toward Hispanics, Brooks, an American journalist living in Mexico, says that

> Mexican immigrants come to the United States to work and to help their families. What meets them is hesitant acceptance of their need to be in the country and cultural stereotypes that they are lazy, even when they work hard at cruel and dangerous jobs. If the United States wants the best of its neighbor's labor and the commitment to good citizenship, it should recognize the Latino as a worthy and proud person capable of grace and beauty.

If it did that, Latinos would respond as immigrants have always responded: with hard work and love of country. (Glicken, 2004a, p. 113)

InfoTable 15.7	The Need to Be Culturally Sensitive

The Surgeon General's Report on Mental Health (Satcher, 2001) notes that although Latinos and other members of racial and ethnic minority groups are an increasing part of America's population, many racial and ethnic minority group members find the mental health system to be

uninformed about cultural context and, thus, unresponsive and/or irrelevant. It is partly for this reason that minority group members overall are less inclined than whites to seek treatment (Sussman et al., 1987; Gallo et al., 1995), and to use outpatient treatment services to a much lesser extent than do non-Hispanic whites. In the interim, culturally competent services—that is, services that incorporate understanding of racial and ethnic groups, their histories, traditions, beliefs, and value systems—are needed to enhance the appropriate use of services and effectiveness of treatments for ethnic and racial minority consumers.

CULTURALLY SENSITIVE SOCIAL WORK WITH ASIAN CLIENTS

Parts of this section were cowritten with Dr. Steven Ino, a clinical psychologist with the University of California, Santa Barbara, Counseling Service, and have appeared in greater detail in Glicken (2004a) and Ino and Glicken (1999, 2002).

Understanding Asian Clients

Hsu (1983) describes the core American national character as "rugged" individualism that values self-containment, autonomy, self-reliance, and self-determinism, implying that the person takes self-responsibility before taking responsibility for others. The Asian worldview, on the other hand, values social collectivism: a social order that is essentially family-based and interpersonally or collectively oriented. This worldview is principally explained by versions of Confucianism, Buddhism, and Taoism that have been incorporated into the various Asian cultures.

In Asian thought, pragmatism is valued over idealism, and the focus of life activity is in the present time. Unlike Western notions of being the master of one's own fate, Asian belief is that one is not in ultimate control but is always an integral part of the larger encompassing universe that has authority over the individual.

Taoism differs from Confucian pragmatism by its concern with the mystical: the cosmic process of *Tao*, or the Way. The person, an integral part of the cosmos, follows the principle of *Wu-Wei*, or nonaction, which means that he or she should always act in accordance with nature rather than against it. The notion that "nature heals, and man (medicine) assists" suggests the belief that nature, not the person, has ultimate authority over the course of one's existence (Chang, 1982). Taoism therefore believes that the person is not in complete control of nature, nor of his or her destiny.

Buddhism concerns itself with the four noble truths: (a) the truth (or fact) of suffering, (b) the origin of suffering, (c) the end of (or the possibility of ending) suffering, and (d) the path that leads to the end of suffering. Enlightenment is attained by following the Noble Eightfold Path, including accurate knowledge and correct actions that lead to the effective or "right" development of the mind. Concentration and meditation are mental processes that help lead to the development of the "right" mind. Buddhism stresses seeking enlightenment through the avoidance of desires and ignorance and teaches the idea of eternal life through rebirth. Proper deportment and social conduct, ancestor worship, emotional restraint, loyalty, and respect for others in the present life have implications for the quality of one's next life (Chang, 1982; Gaw, 1993).

Dynamic social harmony is the major social rule governing all meaningful interpersonal relationships (Ho, 1987). It requires varying degrees of social cooperation, adaptation, accommodation, and collaboration by all individuals in the social hierarchy. In the Asian social hierarchy, social roles are based more on family membership and position, gender, age, social class, and social position than on qualification and ability. However, there is a basic belief that age, training, and life experience are associated with wisdom and competency, although deference and respect from an individual in a subordinate role requires that the person in a superior social position look after that individual.

The formal idea of family in Asian society extends family identity and membership backwards in time through all of the ancestors in the male family line, continuing on in the present time, and then on to those future descendants who have yet to appear (Lee, 1996). One's sense of family is not time-bound or limited to only those important kin who are living. Although the father is the head of the nuclear family household and is responsible for the family's economic and physical well-being, he still shows deference and loyalty to his father and older brothers, as well as to his mother and older sisters. Elders in the father's extended family are also respected. The mother becomes included in the extended family of her husband. As a mother, she is the "emotional hub" of her nuclear family of creation, responsible for nurturing her husband and their children. Although wielding tremendous emotional power and often acting as the relational and communication link between father and children, she nevertheless has little public power and authority and defers to her husband, his mother, and the elders in the husband's extended family.

Self-restraint and stoicism, inhibiting disruptive emotional expression, conscientious work to fulfill one's responsibilities, heightened social sensitivity, and other-directedness all contribute to maintaining social harmony. However, a person's breach of social obligation or duty can potentially damage the social harmony of the family, group, or larger community. Significant others will condemn their loss of confidence in that individual's ability to fulfill obligations to the family or group through the mechanism of shaming that person.

From an Asian perspective, the prescribed forms of interpersonal interaction are intended to preserve social harmony by minimizing direct conflict and social discord. Communication tends to flow downward from superior to subordinate, often in the form of directives. Both verbal and written communications are indirect, are in the passive tense, and at times may appear convoluted. Furthermore, much of the communication is nonverbal, where the conduct of the superior and not the content of the message is most meaningful. These principles of Asian communication styles serve to maintain social harmony and cooperation in all interpersonal interaction.

The Asian socialization process develops adults with mature levels of deep emotional interdependency and strong feelings of role responsibility and obligation. But physical distress may signify emotional distress (Root, 1993). A stomach disorder can be viewed as an expression of psychological stress over an intense interpersonal conflict and is not necessarily seen as a "symptom" or indicator of the client's inability to cope with conflict. To alleviate the physical symptom may be an appropriate treatment for conflict over which one has no control.

When Asian Clients Seek Social Work Assistance

Asians tend to seek help from mental health professionals only when all other more familiar coping strategies, interpersonal resources, and safer avenues of help have been exhausted. Despite the limited use of existing services, many Asian mental health professionals believe that there is a significant unmet need for appropriate mental health care (e.g., Furuto, Biswas, Chung, Murase, & Ross-Sheriff, 1992; Gaw, 1993; Sue & Morishima, 1982; Uba, 1994). In a study of nonpatient Southeast Asian Americans, Gong-Guy (1987) estimates that 14.4% of the sample needed inpatient mental health services and 53.75% could benefit from outpatient care, in comparison to corresponding 3% and 12% rates in the general population.

Several reasons explain the discrepancy between perceived need and overall service usage. They include the following: the Asian conception of mental health/mental illness and their management, the strong Asian stigma and shame attached to seeking "out-of-the-family" assistance for mental illness, the inappropriateness of Euro-American mental health care approaches for Asians, shortages of culturally sensitive mental health professionals, and socioeconomic barriers (Sue & Morishima, 1982; Uba, 1994).

Asians will often initially seek mental health services only after they are in serious emotional crisis. They will first exhaust their usual and then their atypical coping strategies and will have sufficiently overridden their sense of shame and humiliation at breaching family privacy and "loss of face" by seeking help from outside the family. The Asian client who is experiencing the emotional disequilibrium of a crisis situation is most responsive to outside assistance (Golan, 1978; Roberts, 1990). However, the same client is also very vulnerable to outside influences, leaving the client concerned about the possibility of miscommunication and misinterpretation of the need for mental health services by the client's family, friends, and the Asian community.

When an Asian client seeks mental health services, the client is already emotionally disengaged from family and significant others because the usual Asian social support system has failed to remedy the problem. Because of strong feelings of shame or the need to protect the family and/or significant others, the client may typically be withdrawn and isolated. On the other hand, if the family seeks help for one of its members, then the family has exhausted its own helping strategies and must now seek outside assistance and risk considerable shame. The emotional danger for the client is that the family may be prepared to "save face" by disowning or abandoning the client.

InfoTable 15.8	The Stigma of Emotional Problems in Asian Cultures

The high level of stigma associated with intractable emotional problems and mental disturbance has its origin in the strong Asian belief-set that an individual can endure hardship and overcome personal problems through individual perseverance, hard work, stoicism and the avoidance of morbid and disturbing thoughts and feelings. If the client is unable to benefit from these belief-sets, then he or she is felt to have a weak character, be biologically defective, or is the unfortunate victim of bad luck, a curse, vengeful spirits, or fate. (Glicken, 2004a, p. 120)

In discussing the concerns of Southeast Asian refugees, Gong-Guy, Cravens, and Patterson (1991) note that mental illness might also be interpreted as the consequence of past family transgressions. Contributing to its stigma is also a great fear of deportation, loss of government support, and the spread of damaging gossip throughout the ethnic Asian community. A family member's serious mental illness can make all eligible family members unmarriageable in the eyes of the community.

The Asian client experiencing unmanageable emotional pain may assume very passive-dependent behaviors as he or she seeks a wise worker to act as an authority figure who can advise and assist them. If the client has confidence in the worker's wisdom and respects the worker's authority, timely intervention can provide significant emotional support and guidance, which may lead the client to make corrective life changes.

Asian clients should have considerable say in selecting the worker, because this can strengthen client motivation. However, it is the responsibility of the worker to sensitively inquire about this because the client may not wish to insult or embarrass anyone by making such a request. There may also be a natural preference for the client to work with an Asian worker who has a similar ethnic and sociocultural background. Leong (1986) notes the tendency for Asian clients to "describe their therapists as more credible and competent if they are Asian" (p. 198).

InfoTable 15.9	Discrimination Against Asians

Bias against Asian Pacific Americans, which is increasing today, is long-standing. The Chinese Exclusion Act passed in 1882 barred Chinese laborers from entering this country. Along with trepidation that these workers would take jobs away was the feeling expressed by one Senator during the Congressional debate and reported in Chronicles of the 20th Century, that members of this group "do not harmonize with us." (APA, 1998)

Working with an older, professionally trained, and credentialed male or female worker can create immediate trust in the client. In some cases, however, the client may be very threatened by an Asian therapist sharing a similar background. There is great fear of gossip in which the client's family or community finds out about the client's need for treatment. In this case, the client may feel more comfortable with a culturally aware Asian worker who is "removed" from the client's family and community by virtue of coming from a different ethnic background. On the other hand, both first-generation and highly acculturated Asians may wish to work with a mainstream Caucasian worker, believing that they are best-trained and most competent to help. Whatever the background of the worker, he or she must be prepared to be a "culture broker" negotiating between multiple social worlds.

The client's feelings about the effectiveness of the initial encounter with the worker will determine the success of that first session and whether there will be further meetings. A substantial amount of material must be covered in the first session as the worker attempts to establish rapport, clarify the problem focus, evaluate the client, and develop a treatment plan. This treatment effort must balance the Asian client's natural reluctance to self-disclose intimate life details to the therapist-as-stranger. Because time and interpersonal activity have a different meaning and pace to the Asian client, the worker must be more flexible in allowing sufficient time—both in terms of session length, frequency, and number of sessions—to accomplish a successful intervention. First and foremost, the worker must be able to ensure that the Asian client feels respected and is able to maintain personal dignity.

If possible, the initial session should last as long as necessary for the client to feel a completion in the disclosure of relevant life issues and the basic establishment of a trusting therapeutic relationship. This may take 30 minutes or 3 hours. The client may be adamant that this is to be a one-session meeting, which means that the worker must be prepared to provide the entire sequence of interventions in that single session (Ewing, 1990). If it appears that the client is willing to return, it is the worker's responsibility to outline an understandable schedule of further sessions and clear and reasonable goals asking, of course, for feedback and clarification from the client to determine if the proposed plan is acceptable.

The worker should not expect Asian clients to readily explain what brought them in for treatment. Fear of losing face, mistrust because of experiences with racism and discrimination, and/or suspiciousness of the therapist and mental health services can make the client reluctant to self-disclose personal and family information. When asked, the client may initially focus on physical symptoms. Consequently, physical complaints must be seen as valid problems to be treated in a competent and respectful way. Explaining the physical symptoms as having an emotional base may alienate the client and can create unmanageable conflict. Sometimes, the client may begin by seeking help for a "minor" or less pertinent problem as a way of testing the skill and trustworthiness of the worker. If the experience is felt to be helpful, the client may then proceed to disclose the real reason for coming.

Treatment Issues Involving the Collective Self

The American definition of mental health assumes that treatment restores emotional health and the ability to solve emotional problems. But the Asian American client is strongly influenced by the way his or her individual conduct will affect family. And here, family takes on a very broad level of importance because family in many Asian countries provides the client with a sense of identity that may affect every aspect of life from birth to death. Family includes an extended nuclear group. What an individual does in Asian societies has heavy consequences, for it may affect the way the family may be viewed by the entire community. All social work must therefore consider the impact of change on the extended family, recognizing that changes in the client may affect all members of the family in ways that are often unpredictable.

Asian Americans may face up to six common life circumstances that may develop into problems serious enough to warrant intervention: bicultural identity development, significant non-Asian relationships, significant loss, serious loss of face, expulsion from the family, and dysfunctional families of origin.

Case Example of Social Work With a Traditionally Asian Client

James is a 41-year-old Sansei (third-generation Japanese American) who has been married for about 2 years to Lisa, a 35-year-old Anglo American. Lisa is very unhappy with the marriage and frustrated that they have not been able to communicate effectively with each other about her unhappiness. Whenever she tries to initiate a conversation about the marriage, James avoids discussing their problems, saying only that their marriage is good and that they just have to work harder at it. He has consistently rejected her earlier requests that they talk to a counselor. James feels very embarrassed about sharing their marital problems with a stranger. Although Lisa's family is aware of their marital problems and tries to be supportive, James does not want to disclose their marital problems to his family. As Lisa has become more adamant about separating and as James has become more desperate to save the marriage, he has finally agreed to join Lisa for five treatment sessions.

When they came to see a social work marital counselor, Lisa was friendly, self-assured, worried, and verbally expressive. James, on the other hand, looked tired, disheveled, tense, constricted, and depressed, and seemed to be on the verge of tears. Separately, both denied any serious physical risk to either James or Lisa, although Lisa continued to worry about James. Both acknowledged to the social worker that they still cared very deeply for each other, despite the serious marital stress, and that there was more disappointment than animosity in their feelings about the marriage. The short-term goal of the marital counseling, agreed upon by the couple, was to help James better deal with the stress of their marital problems and to do some preliminary exploration to help identify the reasons for their conflicts.

In the course of the five sessions, James began to feel more emotionally stable. He was getting considerable support from his older brother and his wife, as well as from two close friends. Major sociocultural differences were uncovered that neither James nor Lisa thought were present. Although James identified himself as "all-American" and highly assimilated into mainstream America, his core self was collective rather than individualistic in origin. His own Nisei parents, who seemed as "American as apple pie" and only spoke English at home, had nevertheless raised James and his older siblings in a more traditional Japanese way. Even though James had had mostly non-Asian friends throughout his life, he developed a thick layering of individualistic self which he actualized in his social relationships but which concealed a core collective self base. With Lisa, as he settled into a secure married life, he began to relax his defenses, allowing his collective needs to emerge and seek fulfillment. James had a very traditional view of marriage and was critical of Lisa for not understanding, even though he had failed to explain the traditions of his culture sufficiently for Lisa to recognize that James expected Lisa to defer to him and place his needs above hers. There were many other unspoken expectations of Lisa that James had not explained but felt Lisa should understand and respect just because she was his wife.

By the end of the five sessions, both Lisa and James realized that they had entered into a much more complex marriage than either had imagined. James left treatment feeling much more in touch with the traditions of his culture and ready to enter into a dialogue with Lisa to explain and process those traditions. Lisa left treatment recognizing their cultural differences and agreeing to learn much more about the traditions that had shaped James, but uncertain that she could meet all of James's needs. Both were impressed with the process, which they described as not only positive but, which James noted, "helped me understand not only the problems my cultural heritage created in our marriage, but many of the positives in those traditions which I have a deep appreciation for. It also confirmed my feelings for Lisa and helped me realize the hard work she had done to maintain our marriage. What I thought would be an embarrassing experience turned out to be very touching, and I'm grateful to Lisa for not giving up on me."

You Be the Social Worker

Keiko is a 32-year-old Japanese permanent resident of the United States. She was brought to the community mental health clinic by two younger Japanese female friends. A Nisei bilingual older female social worker received them. Keiko appeared severely depressed and withdrawn and would only give monosyllabic replies to questions when directly pressed. For the most part, she appeared to allow her friends to speak on her behalf. Her friends told the social worker that her 38-year-old Japanese husband, Masao, a naturalized American citizen, had just died a week ago in a tragic car accident. The funeral had already taken place. They said that Masao was everything to Keiko and that he was a devoted and caring husband. The two of them appeared to have developed an intense enmeshment.

The friends were very worried about Keiko's lack of social responsiveness or emotion during and after the funeral and by the fact that she often looked vacantly out into space, oblivious to others around her. Neither Keiko nor Masao had any close family in the United States, and Masao had no contact with his family in Japan. Also, Keiko had once mentioned to a friend that she had left Japan for the United States 4 years ago against her family's strong wishes in order to marry and live with Masao in the United States. Another friend mentioned a second personal tragedy: A few months ago, Keiko and Masao were expecting their first child when she had a miscarriage early in her second trimester. They were trying once again to have a baby when Masao died.

The social worker spent the session with Keiko and her two friends, whom Keiko indicated she wanted present. Keiko was diagnosed with major depression, and there was serious concern about suicidal risk. Keiko refused to discuss her actively suicidal thoughts, but she was able to disclose to the therapist that all she felt was a "nothingness," an "empty black hole" inside.

(Continued)

(Continued)

Questions

1.   Keiko is certainly suicidal. What would you do at this point to make certain she doesn't kill herself?

2.   Given the importance of family in the lives of Asian clients, do you think it would be a good idea to contact Keiko's family in Japan and alert them to Keiko's condition? What do you think this would accomplish?

3.   There is no mention of Keiko's late husband's family. Might they be contacted as well? What might this accomplish?

4.   The extremely close relationship between Keiko and her late husband, described as being enmeshed (or pathologically close, removing most other people from the relationship), might be considered a sign of a very dysfunctional relationship. What do you think?

5.   Do you think people who are suicidal are as passive as Keiko, or are there variations in the way suicidal people behave? What might those variations be, and what could they mean?

Summary

This chapter suggests the need to understand the cultural differences and traditions of immigrant groups. Two immigrant groups, Latinos and Asians, are discussed in detail. New immigrants often face discrimination, which may increase the possibility of crisis. A case and a vignette asking the reader to provide answers to questions are included, along with a discussion of culturally relevant social work practice with Latino and Asian immigrants.

Questions to Determine Your Frame of Reference

1.   The notion of people entering the country illegally and using free social service and medical help makes many people angry. How do you feel about the issue, and why?

2.   We certainly are ambivalent about immigrants. We value their hard work but discriminate against them in many ways. Can you think of some ways we discriminate against illegal aliens?

3. The case of James and Lisa points out the complexity of interracial marriage. Do you feel interracial marriage suggests more potential problems than marriage between people of the same race and ethnic backgrounds? Isn't marriage risky at best? How can we ever know how two people are going to work out in a relationship?

4. The two sections on culturally sensitive practice assume that all Latinos and Asians are unassimilated or have traditional beliefs. Hasn't international television and film pretty much made us a people, worldwide, who think and act alike?

5. Do you think you could work well with immigrant clients? Explain your answer.

Internet Sources

First, the U.S. Congress presents a report on illegal immigration (2000). Next, some concerns about U.S. Immigration policy are raised (1998), followed by a response to the suugestion that the country use a national ID system to determine if anyone is here illegally (2004).

1. *Illegal Immigration Issues Hearing before the Subcommittee on Immigration and Claims of the Committee on the Judiciary.* (2000). Retrieved from http://commdocs.house.gov/committees/judiciary/hju62494.000/hju62494_0f.htm

2. The Close Up Foundation. (1998, July). *U.S. Immigration policy.* Retrieved March 3, 2005, from http://www.closeup.org/immigrat.htm

3. The Cato Institute. (2004). *A national ID system: Big Brother's solution to illegal immigration.* Retrieved March 3, 2005, from http://www.cato.org/pubs/pas/pa237.html

Natural Disasters, Terrorism, and Random Violence

16

Helping Organizations and the Role of Social Work in Treating Victims

Many Americans worry that a terrorist attack like the ones we experienced in the 1995 Oklahoma City bombing of a federal building and the September 11, 2001, bombings of the World Trade Center and the Pentagon, or that devastating natural disasters such as the Gulf Coast hurricane and the New Orleans flood in late summer 2005, will occur once again and that the impact on their lives will be devastating. If they do happen, who will care for the injured and traumatized, and will a condition related to reliving the experience known as PTSD affect a number of victims? This chapter discusses random violence, including natural disasters and terrorism, the organizations that help when these events take place, the definition of PTSD and its relationship to acts of violence and disasters, major ways of helping people with PTSD symptoms following a serious trauma, and the role of social work in helping people who are the victims of random traumatic events.

There are many acts of random violence that affect Americans, including assaults, rapes, muggings, carjackings, and gang violence. Natural and manmade disasters also account for a certain amount of PTSD, but not in the numbers attributable to acts of random violence. Although disasters and other forms of violence are mentioned in this chapter, the primary emphasis is on understanding the characteristics of PTSD, the probability of developing PTSD symptoms, the people most at risk, and the most effective treatment approaches. Not everyone who experiences an act of violence develops PTSD. The research on resilience may help us understand why some people develop PTSD and others don't.

What Is PTSD?

DESCRIPTION OF PTSD

According to the *DSM-IV* (APA, 1994, pp. 427–429), the core criteria for PTSD include distressing symptoms of: (a) reexperiencing a trauma through nightmares and intrusive thoughts; (b) numbing by avoiding reminders of the trauma, or feeling aloof or unable to express loving feelings for others; and (c) persistent symptoms of arousal as indicated by two or more of the following—sleep problems, irritability and angry outbursts, difficulty concentrating, hypervigilence, and exaggerated startle response lasting more than a month and causing problems at work, in social interactions, and in other important areas of life. The *DSM-IV* considers the condition to be acute if it has lasted less than 3 months and chronic if it has lasted more than 3 months. It is possible for the symptoms to be delayed. The *DSM-IV* says that a diagnosis of delayed onset is given when symptoms become apparent 6 months or later after the original trauma (APA, 1994, p. 429).

We think PTSD is caused by highly traumatic experiences or life-threatening events that produce troubling thoughts related to a very disturbing aspect of the original event. Those thoughts are difficult to dislodge once they reach conscious awareness. In many cases of PTSD, the client physically and emotionally reexperiences the original traumatic event and is often in a highly agitated state as a result. Symptoms of PTSD usually begin within 3 months of the original trauma. In half of the cases of PTSD, complete recovery occurs within 3 months of the onset of symptoms, but many cases last longer than 12 months (APA, 1994, p. 426). Ozer, Best, Lipsey, and Weiss (2003) describe the symptoms associated with returning Vietnam veterans that led to a recognition of PTSD as a distinct diagnostic category: "Intrusive thoughts and images, nightmares, social withdrawal, numbed feelings, hypervigilance, and even frank paranoia, especially regarding the government and vivid dissociative phenomena, such as flashbacks" (p. 54). The authors believe that the complexity of the symptoms often led to a misdiagnosis of schizophrenia. There are numerous reports of people entering catatonic states after a trauma only to return to normal functioning within days or weeks of the trauma because of the natural cycle of healing.

Stein (2002) indicates that another symptom of PTSD is physical pain and writes, "Patients with PTSD are among the highest users of medical services in primary care settings. Ongoing chronic pain may serve as a constant reminder of the trauma that perpetuates its remembrance" (p. 922). Asmundson, Coons, Taylor, and Katz (2002) report that patients with

PTSD present a combination of physical and mental health problems, including increased alcohol consumption and depression. In a study by White and Faustman (1989), 20% of military veterans with PTSD developed chronic pain.

Gist and Devilly (2002) are concerned that PTSD is being predicted on such a wide scale for every tragedy that occurs that we have watered down its usefulness as a category of emotional distress. The authors suggest that many early signs of PTSD are normal responses to stress that are often overcome with time and distance from the event. Victims often use natural healing processes to cope with traumatic events, and interference by professionals could make the problem more severe and prolonged. In determining whether PTSD will actually develop, people must be given time to cope with the trauma on their own before we diagnose and treat PTSD.

To emphasize this point, Gist and Devilly (2002) report that the immediate predictions of PTSD in victims of the World Trade Center bombings turned out to be almost 70% higher than actually occurred 4 months after the event. Susser, Herman, and Aaron (2002) note that 2,001 New Yorkers were interviewed by telephone between January 15, 2002, and February 21, 2002. The interviews found a significant decrease in the stress-related symptoms participants experienced during and after the World Trade Center bombings only several months earlier, prompting the authors to write, "Many affected New Yorkers are clearly recovering naturally, a tribute to the resilience of the human psyche" (p. 76). Although symptoms of PTSD may develop much later than 4 months after a trauma, people often heal on their own and a diagnosis of PTSD made too early may be inaccurate.

InfoTable 16.1	The Impact of Terrorism

Terrorism erodes—at both the individual level and the community level—the sense of security and safety people usually feel. Terrorism challenges the natural need of humans to see the world as predictable, orderly, and controllable. Studies have shown that deliberate violence creates longer lasting mental-health effects than natural disasters or accidents. The consequences for both individuals and the community are prolonged, and survivors often feel that injustice has been done to them. This can lead to anger, frustration, helplessness, fear, and a desire for revenge. Studies have shown that acting on this anger and desire for revenge can increase rather than decrease feelings of anger, guilt, and distress. (Hamblen, 2004)

Who Develops PTSD?

In explaining the potential for developing PTSD, the *DSM-IV* (APA, 1994) notes that "the severity, duration and proximity of an individual's exposure to the traumatic event are the most important factors affecting the likelihood of this disorder" (p. 426). Additional factors that may contribute to PTSD, according to the *DSM-IV*, include the absence of social support networks, traumatic family histories or childhood experiences, and preexisting emotional problems. There may be other factors determining whether PTSD develops following a trauma. A review of studies determining the impact of traumatic experiences found in the *Harvard Mental Health Letter* suggests that "the people most likely to have symptoms of PTSD were those who suffered job loss, broken personal relationships, the death or illness of a family member or close friend, or financial loss as a result of the disaster itself" ("What Causes," 2002, p. 8). Several additional studies reported in the *Harvard Mental Health Letter* indicate that a person's current emotional state may influence the way he or she copes with the trauma. Environmental concerns (e.g., living in high crime areas) and health risks (e.g., disabilities that make people vulnerable) raise the likelihood of repeated traumatization that may increase the probability of developing PTSD. Stein (2002) suggests that one significant event influencing the development of PTSD is exposure to violence, including serious fights, domestic violence, child abuse, muggings, sexual molestation and rape, and other forms of traumatic violence. Stein believes that vulnerability to repetitive acts of violence greatly increases the probability of developing PTSD.

InfoTable 16.2	The Trauma of Sexual Assault and Rape

In studies of women who have been sexually assaulted or raped, women particularly at risk of developing PTSD are those who were injured in the assault, were threatened by the perpetrator with death or injury if they reported the rape, had a history of prior assault, or experienced negative interactions with family, peers, or law enforcement officers after the assault (Regehr, Cadell, & Jansen, 1999). In further studies of women who had been sexually assaulted or raped, a significant proportion of women experienced symptoms of PTSD within 2 weeks following the assault (Resnick, Acierno, Holmes, Kilpatrick, & Jager, 1999). PTSD continued to persist in survivors of rape and sexual assault at lifetime rates of between 30% and 50% (Foa, Hearst-Ikeda, & Perry, 1995; Meadows & Foa, 1998; Resnick et al., 1999).

How Prevalent Is PTSD?

The National Vietnam Veterans Readjustment Study (Kulka et al., 1990; Weiss et al., 1992) estimated that 9% of the men and 26% of the women serving in Vietnam have experienced PTSD at some point since their Vietnam service. Current prevalence of PTSD among Vietnam veterans is 2% for men and 5% for women (Schlenger et al., 1992). Combining the estimates for all current full and partial veterans with a diagnosis of PTSD results in an estimate of approximately 830,000 Vietnam theater veterans who continued to experience significant posttraumatic distress or impairment 20 years after their exposure to one or more traumatic stressors (Weiss et al., 1992). We may expect similar rates of PTSD among returning veterans from Iraq and Afghanistan.

Studies of civilian populations have found lifetime PTSD prevalence rates of between 2% and 10% (Breslau, Davis, Andreski, & Peterson, 1991). The National Co-morbidity Study (NCS) (Kessler, Sonnega, Bromet, Hughes, & Nelson, 1995) found that women had twice the lifetime prevalence of PTSD of men (10.4% for women vs. 5.0% for men). Although 50% to 60% of the U.S. population is exposed to traumatic stress, only 5% to 10% develop PTSD (Ozer et al., 2003).

The *Harvard Mental Health Letter* ("What Causes," 2002) reports on a study done at the University of California, San Diego, in which 132 randomly selected patients seen by family doctors completed an interview and questionnaire describing traumatic events in their lives including combat, natural or manmade disasters, violent rape, abusive behavior, and assault. Almost 70% of the sample had experienced at least one traumatic event. Of the sample, 20% currently had PTSD, 29% had major depressions, and 8% had both. Of the patients with current or lifetime PTSD, 70% said that an assault was their worst traumatic experience.

Resilience: The Ability to Cope With Traumas

Many people believe that the notion of resilience explains why some people do not experience symptoms of PTSD after very traumatic events. Henry (1999) defines resilience as "the capacity for successful adaptation, positive functioning, or competence despite high risk, chronic stress, or prolonged or severe trauma" (p. 521). Abrams (2001) indicates that resilience may be seen as the ability to readily recover from illness, depression, and adversity. Walsh (1998) defines resilience in families as the "capacity to rebound from adversity, strengthened and more resourceful" (p. 4). She continues in her definition by saying that "we cope with crisis and adversity by making meaning of our experience: linking it to our social world, to our cultural and religious beliefs, to our multigenerational past, and to our hopes and dreams for the future" (p. 45).

Werner and Smith (1982) identify the following factors that reduce the risk of stress: an easygoing disposition, strong self-esteem and sense of identity, intelligence, physical attractiveness, and supportive friends and loved ones. Seligman (1992) believes that resilience exists when people are optimistic; have a sense of adventure, courage, and self-understanding; use humor in their lives; have a capacity for hard work; and posses the ability to cope with and find outlets for emotions. In their 32-year longitudinal study, Werner and Smith (1982) found a strong relationship between the ability to problem-solve, good communication skills, and a belief that they had control of their lives in resilient children who had suffered abuse.

The Impact of Natural Disasters

In reviewing the studies of emotional responses to natural disasters, Norris (2002) found that one third of these studies found significant distress, with the most frequently reported condition being PTSD, followed by depression and then other anxiety disorders. Many survivors reported health problems, chronic problems in living, and anxiety about lost homes and jobs. Risk factors in adults for adverse reactions to natural disasters included more severe exposure, female gender, middle age, ethnic minority group membership, secondary stress, prior psychiatric problems, and weak or deteriorating psychosocial resources. Consistent support from others has been found to help people cope and to predict whether people will suffer emotional consequences of natural disasters.

Although most people improve in time, a minority continue to be distressed long after an event. In major disasters including Hurricane Hugo, Hurricane Andrew, and Hurricane Mitch, Norris (2002) reports that in one study of 400 highly exposed residents of southern Dade County, 25% of the sample met criteria for PTSD 6 months after the hurricane. Symptoms of depression and avoidance remained high as long as 30 months after the hurricane struck. Lasting symptoms were particularly likely when people experienced other forms of life stress in addition to the hurricane such as health problems, or had poor self-esteem or weak social ties. Long after Hurricane Andrew, many people felt less positive about the quality of their social relationships than they had felt before the disaster, suggesting that perceptions of social support are also harmed by disaster experiences.

InfoTable 16.3	The Political Reasons for the Lack of Preparation for Hurricane Katrina

There was last week an immediate and furious debate about the racial implications of the tragedy since most victims we saw on TV were black. There were recriminations about the lack of preparedness and the corroded infrastructure. . . . Since the 1960's the Republicans exploited southern opposition to integration. This implicit racism evolved into a tacit unwillingness to rethink problems of poverty and race and to plan for the future. This new philosophy of government was said most crudely by former British Prime Minister Margaret Thatcher: "There is no such thing as society. . . . There are individual men and women and there are families." (Klein, 2005)

Norris (2002) reports that in a study of the effects of Hurricane Andrew, Latinos, especially less acculturated Latinos, appeared to have more severe emotional problems than did non-Hispanic whites and blacks, a finding that may be partially explained by the fact that Latinos suffered greater exposure and loss to the storm. Norris also suggests that Latino reactions to the storm can be explained because Latinos had a low-level perception of their control of life (also called locus of control) after the disaster and were particularly vulnerable because of a lack of support systems.

There are three factors that contribute to long-term problems following a natural disaster, according to Norris: (a) when victims believe they are not cared for by others, (b) when they believe they have little control over what happens to them, and (c) when they lack the physical and/or emotional ability to deal with stress.

You Be the Social Worker

As part of your university's volunteer project to help victims of the New Orleans flood in late summer 2005, you've been sent to Houston, Texas, to work with victims of the flood. One of your assigned clients is Albert Green, age 31, one of the thousands of displaced victims of the New Orleans flood who lived in the Superdome for almost 6 days before being transported to Houston, where he now lives in the Astrodome with 12,000 other victims of the flood. Albert suffers severe symptoms of PTSD, which were complicated by the violence in the Superdome as hungry and frightened people waited for days before help came. "I lost everything," he tells you. "And they was rapin' and beatin' people and weren't nothin' done about it. I cain't sleep, I worry all the time, I feel sick, my life is over with." Albert's elderly parents are thought to be victims of the flood, but Albert isn't certain. "It's been 2 weeks now and most of us, we still don't know if our kin is alive. We get food, and they give us some money and clothes, and we thank the people who have been generous, but it feels like we was abandoned. It feels like the government don't care if some poor black people get killed, or if their kin is alive. How else you gonna explain something like this, but that the government don't care about black folks? We work, we pay taxes, but then something like this happens, we called refugees like we ain't no part of America, like we foreigners."

You offer support and encouragement, but Albert doesn't seem to be improving, although many of the other people you work with have made amazing recoveries and are doing well. You try and convince Albert to see some of the positives of his situation, but it feels wrong to you to try and be supportive when Albert and those around him have suffered so much.

(Continued)

(Continued)

A month later, Albert tells you that "they finally tell me my folks, they dead. It hurt to go a month not knowin' nothing. And now I can see we ain't goin' back to New Orleans for a long time. I lost my job, and I don't have no real skills and just 6 years in school. When I left school, nobody from the school ask why and nobody care. I had to work to support my folks and now look where I am. Yesterday, they come around and ask if we have computer skills, they's jobs for us in Texas. Well, hell, I cain't even spell and I cain't hardly write. What they think? New Orleans' schools like white schools? They teach folks about computers? That a joke. When I was in school it was mainly about not getting cut up with knives by gangs. I ain't feelin' so good. I just don't care much. I figure what the point of worryin'? It don't help none. I just make myself sick, so now I go on welfare. What kind of life is that for me?"

Questions

1. Why do you think others who are very similar to Albert in education and the loss of loved ones are doing so much better than Albert? Go to the literature on resilience and see if you can find the conditions that lead to or take away from resilience after a natural disaster.

2. All you've done is offer Albert support and encouragement. What services might the government offer at this point to help Albert?

3. If you were in charge of the Federal Emergency Management Agency (FEMA) and knew the high probability of the dikes in New Orleans breaking from a Category 3 hurricane like Katrina, what would you have done immediately to help the people on the Gulf Coast and in New Orleans?

4. Many African Americans believe that the poor response by the government was an indication of the lack of care about poor people, particularly people of color. What do you believe?

5. In your view, how do natural disasters and terrorist attacks differ in terms of their impact on people, or do they? Justify your response with material from the research literature.

The Impact of Recent Acts of Terrorism in America

From data evaluated by Galea (2002) in 1,008 telephone interviews with Manhattan residents, the rate of PTSD in those living close to the World Trade Center was 20%. Sprang found that 7.8% of 145 city residents in Oklahoma City who were not near the building after the bombing developed PTSD, whereas North found PTSD in 34% of 182 survivors who had been in or near the building (Galea, 2002). Using statistical analysis to estimate the number of New Yorkers traumatized by the World Trade Center bombings, Susser et al. (2002) write: "The bottom line: even when making the most conservative estimates based on available data, we concluded that a minimum of approximately 422,000 New Yorkers experienced PTSD as a result of September 11" (p. 73). Galea (2002) only reported on PTSD and clinical depression and not on related conditions such as anxiety and low-level depression. Untold millions who witnessed the attacks through the media were surely shaken and experienced distress. Susser et al. (2002) also state that "in addition, the effects of terrorism on those already suffering from psychological conditions must be assumed to have been especially profound" (p. 74).

In another study of the impact of 9/11, Hoff (2002) reports a survey of 8,266 public school students in New York regarding their reactions to the New York City attacks. The data indicate that 10.5% of the city's 710,000 public school students experienced PTSD. Hoff also notes that the survey found high numbers of other disorders related to the bombings, including the fear of open places.

InfoTable 16.4	The Impact of the Oklahoma City Terrorist Attack

Almost half of the survivors directly exposed to the blast reported developing problems with anxiety, depression, and alcohol, and over one third of these survivors reported posttraumatic stress disorder (PTSD). Over a year after the bombing, Oklahomans reported increased rates of alcohol use, smoking, stress, and PTSD symptoms as compared to citizens of another metropolitan city. Children who lost an immediate family member, friend, or relative were more likely to report immediate symptoms of PTSD than children who had not lost a loved one. Two years after the bombing, 16% of children and adolescents who lived approximately 100 miles from Oklahoma City reported significant PTSD symptoms related to the event. (Hamblen, 2004)

You Be the Social Worker

John Martin is a 51-year-old office worker in one of the buildings hit in the 9/11 attack on the World Trade Center. John not only escaped from one of the floors immediately below the bombing, but he helped a number of coworkers leave the building safely. John was burned on the legs and hands in the process of helping other people. After his medical convalescence, John developed severe symptoms of PTSD. He was unable to sleep at night, complained of headaches and symptoms that had no medical cause, was in constant pain even though his doctor assured him that his burns had healed, couldn't go back to work, and began locking himself in his home, preparing himself for an emergency evacuation in the event of

(Continued)

(Continued)

another terrorist attack. John's problems alienated his family, who left him, and John now lives alone. He attends therapy twice a week and is in a weekly recovery group, but for reasons that are unknown to John or to his medical and social work professionals, John continues to experience severe symptoms of PTSD. John is taking a number of antianxiety and depression medications, which also fail to help. His social worker wonders if John had an emotional problem before the attack or if he had childhood problems that he may be reexperiencing, but John steadfastly denies either.

Because of the monies paid by the government and private donations to victims of the attack, and because John has been deemed unable to work, he receives social security disability payments and is comfortable financially. He is also presuicidal and his social worker worries that if some breakthrough in his treatment isn't forthcoming, John will commit suicide. He experiences severe anxiety attacks when he sees pictures of any Middle Eastern person on television and obsesses that someone from a terrorist cell will come and kill him. He cannot help himself, and obsessively watches fiction programs on television with terrorism as themes. After each program he feels more and more convinced that another terrorist attack will take place and that he will perish. God is cruel, he says, and his good fortune in escaping 9-11 will only result in another attack and his eventual and horrid death.

Questions

1. Review this chapter and the reasons people have prolonged PTSD experiences. Does anything suggest the need for more information regarding John's current and prior life?

2. Does the fact that he's financially stable enough not to work suggest a reason for him to stay at home instead of working? This is an argument made about people on public welfare. Do you think it applies here?

3. Are we sure he has PTSD? Is it possible that something else is wrong, something that may have existed before the terrorist attacks but has been overlooked? What might that be?

4. Does doing heroic acts mean that you always feel heroic? Is it possible that he felt afraid or that he failed to help someone because of fear, and now he feels ashamed? Why would he feel that way?

5. Might the experience of being in a burning building serve as a catalyst for a prior trauma and he's now reacting to that trauma and the way he felt during that event? What might some of those prior events and experiences be?

Helping Interventions With PTSD

EXPOSURE THERAPY

Rothbaum, Olasov, and Schwartz (2002) describe a type of treatment which believes that PTSD develops as a result of fearful memories. To reduce the number of thoughts that elicit fear, the client must have his or her "fear network" activated so that new information can be provided that interrupts the fear network. This is done by (a) repeated reliving of the original trauma to reduce anxiety and correct a belief that anxiety will necessarily continue unless the person avoids memories of the traumatic event, (b) discussing the traumatic event to help the client see it in a logical way that corrects misperceptions of the event, (c) speaking about the trauma to help the client realize that it's not dangerous to remember the trauma, and (d) speaking about the trauma to provide the client with a sense of mastery over his or her PTSD symptoms. The authors call this type of treatment exposure therapy.

Hensley (2002) provides an explanation of exposure therapy as it might be given to a rape victim:

1. Memories, people, places, and activities now associated with the rape make you highly anxious, so you avoid them.

2. Each time you avoid them you do not finish the process of digesting the painful experience, and so it returns in the form of nightmares, flashbacks, and intrusive thoughts.

3. You can begin to digest the experience by gradually exposing yourself to the rape in your imagination and by holding the memory without pushing it away.

4. You will also practice facing those activities, places, and situations that currently evoke fear.

5. Eventually, you will be able to think about the rape and resume your normal activities without experiencing intense fear. (p. 338)

Effectiveness studies on using exposure therapy for PTSD have been quite positive. In the annual review of important findings in psychology, 12 studies found positive results using exposure therapy with PTSD. Eight of these studies received special recognition for the quality of their methodology and for the positive nature of their outcomes (Foa & Meadows, 1997). Several of the studies were done with Vietnam veterans and showed a significant reduction in the symptoms of PTSD following exposure therapy (Keane, Fairbank, Caddell, & Zimering, 1989). The same positive results were found in studies with rape victims when exposure therapy was used (Foa et al., 1999; Foa, Rothbaum, Riggs, & Murdock, 1991). Exposure therapy has been used with a variety of PTSD victims, including victims of combat traumas, sexual assaults, child abuse, and other forms of violence. Exposure therapy has the most consistently positive results in reducing symptoms of PTSD when compared to other forms of treatment (Rothbaum, Meadows, Resick, & Foy, 2000).

DEBRIEFING

In this approach, people who have experienced a trauma are seen in a group session lasting 1 to 3 hours within a week to a month of the original traumatic event. Risk factors are evaluated, and a combination of information and opportunity to discuss their experiences during and after the trauma are provided (Bisson, McFarlane, & Rose, 2000). Most debriefing groups provide educational information to group members about typical reactions to traumas, what to look for if group members experience any of these symptoms, and where to seek professional assistance if additional help is needed. Debriefing groups may also attempt to identify group members at risk of developing PTSD (van Emmerik, Kamphuis, Hulsbosch, & Emmelkamp, 2002).

Despite the appeal of this approach, there is little evidence that debriefing works (van Emmerik et al., 2002). In fact, debriefing may be less effective than no treatment at all following a trauma (van Emmerik et al., 2002). Gist and Devilly (2002) support these findings and write, "Immediate debriefing has yielded null or paradoxical outcomes" because the approaches used in debriefing are often those "kinds of practical help learned better from grandmothers than from graduate training" (p. 742).

The authors report that although still high, the estimates of PTSD after the 9/11 bombing dropped by almost two thirds within 4 months of the tragedy and concluded the following: (a) debriefing interferes with natural healing processes and sometimes results in bypassing usual support systems such as family, friends, and religious groups (Horowitz, 1976); (b) upon hearing that PTSD symptoms are normal reactions to trauma, some victims of trauma actually develop the symptoms as a result of suggestions provided in the debriefing session, particularly when the victim hasn't had time to process the various feelings he or she may have about the trauma (Kramer & Rosenthal, 1998); and (c) clients seen in debriefing include both those at risk and those not at risk. Better results may be obtained by screening clients at risk through a review of past exposure to traumas that may have served as catalysts for the current development of PTSD (Brewin, Andrews, & Valentine, 2000).

The Organizations That Help Victims of Violence

One of the primary organizations helping people who have been in traumatic situations is the police. They are front line and the unsung heroes who are often the first ones on the scene when a traumatic event takes place. Social workers often work for police departments as crisis workers.

The Red Cross, the Salvation Army, and many religious charitable organizations often provide immediate help to people experiencing traumatic events. Social workers are often paid employees or volunteers in these agencies and organizations. During the initial days of the Gulf Coast hurricane in Mississippi, Alabama, and Louisiana, the Salvation Army was serving meals to more than 150,000 people a day.

The Department of Homeland Security, whose task it is to defend America from terrorist attacks, has the following function: to make America more secure by preventing, disrupting, and responding to terrorist attacks. This function doesn't directly include help to victims, something that is done at the local level by emergency and crisis workers in state and local government and by FEMA, an arm of Homeland Security that was strongly criticized after the New Orleans flood of late summer 2005 for its delayed response to victims of the flood.

Victim assistance programs are state-level programs. An example from California includes a discussion of restitution from perpetrators of crime to victims and states, "Restitution fines are paid to the State Board of Control (BOC), Victims Restitution Fund. The BOC, Victims of Crime Program is the state agency responsible for administering the Victims Restitution Fund. The restitution fund is for victims of violent crimes who suffer out-of-pocket losses and who may be eligible to apply for financial reimbursement. The fund reimburses eligible victims for lost wages or support, medical or psychological counseling expenses and other related costs" (California Department of Corrections, 2004).

What Social Workers Do to Help Victims of Traumas

In times of natural disasters, terrorist acts, assaults, rapes, and other forms of violent traumatic events, social workers provide immediate help and support, including food, shelter, clothing, and crisis counseling. We make certain loved ones are contacted and involved. We also help in evaluating the client's need for more long-term services. When services are needed, social workers arrange for clients to see other professional or service providers. Referring people to others is an important aspect of what social workers do and requires that we have a large network of contacts and that we advocate for needed client services with social, medical, and financial organizations.

Social workers help with relocation (if needed), contact employers, provide supportive services to loved ones, and provide needed supportive and counseling services to clients with persistent social and emotional problems resulting from a traumatic event. When additional services are needed and do not exist, social workers advocate with the political system to develop those services. Through helping organizations such as the Red Cross and the National Association of Social Workers, we offer our services by volunteering. Many social workers were on the front line of 9/11 and Oklahoma City, offering help to victims and the families of victims. Finally, we work in agencies (e.g., Catholic charities) that provide food, shelter, and other services when people experience traumas.

Recovering From PTSD

In describing the recovery process of women who had experienced sexual assault and rape, Hensley (2002) indicates that although treatment research suggests good results, the recovery process can be long and difficult. "Survivors are vulnerable to victim-blame, self-blame, unwillingness to disclose the rape to others, and an overall lack of support in addition to PTSD symptoms and other significant negative psychological and physiological outcomes" (p. 342). Hensley reports that women who survive sexual assaults need validation for their experiences and positive reinforcement for their attempts to deal with the traumas they've experienced. Instead, they must often deal with limited support and even skepticism from family, friends, professionals, and the legal system. This concern for the limited support of PTSD victims as they try and recover from the traumas they've experienced is true of many other victims of traumas.

Rothbaum et al. (2002) believe that many people think that clients suffering from PTSD will recover in time without help, but prolonged suffering suggests that this may not be the case. Help in prolonged symptoms of PTSD should be introduced when client symptoms are intrusive and the client voluntarily seeks help. The authors also suggest that a trauma doesn't need to be current to require help with recovery. Many clients who have experienced child abuse and other early life traumas benefit from therapies such as exposure therapy by focusing on their worst memory of a trauma. Reducing stress involved with that memory has carry-over benefits to other traumas. The authors report that exposure therapies are often useful in treating non-PTSD symptoms that occurred before the traumatic event causing PTSD and help to provide a more complete recovery by reducing "feelings of depression, rage, sadness, and guilt [in addition] to reducing related problems, such as depression and self-blame" (Rothbaum et al., 2002, p. 71). Many of these symptoms may predate the trauma. Therapy can be very effective in speeding up the rate of recovery.

A Case of Repeated Violence

Anna Ramirez is a 26-year-old woman who was repeatedly raped during her travels from Guatemala to the United States. Anna is one of a number of men, women, and children who seek a better life by entering the United States illegally. This is her story.

"My family is very poor and they asked me to go to America so I could work and send money back. Many people in my village do that, but to get to America, I needed to hire a guide, or what they call a 'Coyote' in America. My family had little money, so the guides felt that they could have me sexually whenever they wanted to. Up to that time I was a virgin. I was also beaten and humiliated before large numbers of men. Many times I was raped by many men at the same time. I caught a sexual disease, which wasn't treated until I came to America, and now I'm told I can't have babies. Some of the men used objects inside of me and I still have much pain in my woman's organs. I can't stand it when men touch me now, even if I like them or they do it innocently. I get scared and very nervous most of the time. I see a social worker who speaks Spanish and I'm in a group of women who have had this same thing done to them. That's helped, but not being able to have babies has made me very depressed. I have a good job in the United States and I send money home. I always worry about getting caught and being sent back, but what can I do? I feel most Americans hate people like me even though we work hard, our intentions are good, and we cause no trouble. I'm happy for my family, but it's hard for me to sleep at night because I dream about what happened to me, and the sad feelings make me cry a lot. I think my boss is getting mad at me about my crying.

"The social worker lets me talk and is always encouraging. She helped me get medical care and medicine for my infections and my depression. She also helped me talk to Immigration, and I may get a Green Card. She's wonderful, and I guess she went through the same thing 20 years ago. But she got her education and now she does social work for poor Latinas like me. I really respect her and I wish to be like her someday. She says I'm smart, but I feel very stupid now. I don't know. You never think life will be so cruel and that people can do such things to another human being, but they do. Maybe it'll get better. I hope so, anyway."

Anna's Social Worker Talks About the Case

"It saddens me to see women like Anna. She has great spirit, but how long can it last? I find women like Anna to be amazing. We use the word *resilient*, but it has no meaning. Anna just keeps going no matter what. It's easy to work with her. She's very motivated. She wants us to talk in English so that she can learn the language. She has a wonderful family and they write long, supportive letters. She has friends now in America and they are her support, as is her church. She has made the best of things. Although I have helped in small ways by getting her medical care and helping with clothing and food and with immigration, it's people like Anna who are the backbone of America . . . the poor immigrants who offer us everything and ask for little in return except the right to work and make something of themselves. You wish your children could all be like the Annas I see every day. They are wonderful people with so much to give and such great joy and love.

(Continued)

(Continued)

"I weep for Anna. She will never have children and most men, when they find out what was done to her, will never marry a woman like Anna. It's shameful. I thank God I'm an American and can help Anna. And social work is a wonderful profession because we help people when they most need it. We help in all areas of life and believe that people are able to do most of what needs to be done to get along by themselves with just a little of our help. We like to say in social work that we help people help themselves. Who would have thought that a poor girl like me who went through what Anna did could now be a professional? It makes me very proud and happy that I endured the trip to America. God bless this country because, for a lot of us who want to love a country and be as successful as we can be, America is our safe haven."

Summary

This chapter on PTSD includes the symptoms, prevalence, and best evidence of treatment effectiveness. Data from two recent terrorist attacks in the United States is also included. Assaults are one of the primary reasons for the development of symptoms of PTSD. Data from studies on a form of brief therapy known as debriefing suggest that its use following a trauma may actually increase the probability that PTSD symptoms will develop. A case study is provided showing the impact of a terrorist attack and an effective form of treatment. The presence of resilience is thought to be one of the primary reasons some people cope well with severe traumas.

Questions to Determine Your Frame of Reference

1. Why would so many people who were not directly affected by a terrorist attack (e.g., people watching the events on television) develop symptoms of PTSD?

2. Talking about a trauma until it no longer creates anxiety seems an inefficient and painful way to treat PTSD. Can you think of other, commonsense approaches that might lessen the symptoms of PTSD more quickly?

3. Don't you think we make too much out of stressful life experiences in the United States? Many people in other countries suffer from devastating natural disasters, hunger, and malnutrition and seem to cope well. Isn't there a point at which the culture encourages people to experience PTSD because it believes that most people are too psychologically fragile to cope with extreme stressors?

4. During 9/11, American television focused on the bravery of countless men and women. Do you think that helped reduce the impact of the tragedy for many people with potential for developing symptoms of PTSD?

5. The notion that debriefing may actually lead to an increase in PTSD seems entirely wrong-headed. Can you give some examples of the positive impact of debriefing in cases of trauma?

Internet Sources

The U.S. Justice Department provides a report on violent crime statistics in the United States. Also, there is an article for Congress on terrorism, the future, and how the United States should conduct foreign policy in response to terrorism, and an article from the University of Michigan evaluating America's war on terror. Lastly, a troubling article is presented on rape and the criminal justice system, and the poor job we do in bringing rapists to trial and then sentencing them.

1. U.S. Department of Justice, Bureau of Justice Statistics. (2002). *Crime and victim statistics.* Retrieved from http://www.ojp.usdoj .gov/bjs/cvict.htm

2. *Terrorism, the future and U.S. foreign policy: Issue brief to Congress.* (2003). Retrieved from http://www.fas.org/irp/crs/IB95112.pdf

3. Koss, M. (2004). *Rape and the criminal justice system.* Retrieved April 13, 2004, from http://vip.msu.edu/theCAT/CAT_Author/MPK/ justicecritique.html

4. The University of Michigan Document Center. (2004). *America's war against terrorism.* Retrieved April 13, 2004, from http://www.lib .umich.edu/govdocs/usterror.html

International Social Problems 17

*The Helping Organizations
and the Roles of International
Social Workers*

International Social Work

We live in a global economy where many of the goods and services we purchase every day are made in foreign countries. This global dependence suggests that we should know more about the cultures of other countries and that we involve ourselves in helping developing countries with high rates of poverty and health problems. These are social work's traditional areas of involvement, and it is natural that a chapter on international social work should be included in this book. International social work is larger than just culturally sensitive work with clients from other cultures and is, in Sanders's view (1977):

1. A way to increase our understanding of other cultures, political systems, and different ways of dealing with social problems. By doing so, we gain added understanding into values, diverse groups, and culturally different outlooks on life in our own country.

2. We can test social work ideas, theories and practice approaches in different societies and cultures. This could have importance for the way we practice social work in our own country.

3. Ideas from other countries could have a positive impact on the way we provide social services in America.

4. At a time of increasing antagonisms between countries, international social work could open the way for cooperative efforts to cope with our differences and to resolve human problems such as hunger; lack of work; low wages; the mistreatment of women and children; child

labor and sweat shops; the slave trade in women for sexual purposes; genocide; and other serious social problems that are common internationally and could be helped by a more international perspective by social workers. (Estes, 1992)

Estes (1992) indicates that social work has had a distinguished history of professional involvement in international issues by helping with the resettlement of refugees and other people displaced by war; by operating emergency field relief services for victims of natural and man-made disasters in foreign countries; through active advocacy for the rights of vulnerable populations; by organizing groups of oppressed people into effective political entities; through advocacy efforts to provide material and social assistance to populations in need of such services; and by pointing out social injustices wherever they have existed in the world. Social workers have also worked for world peace, an effort that earned Jane Addams the profession's first Nobel Prize.

Americans often forget that there is a great deal to be learned from other cultures. Because we often think that America is supreme in all areas of health and mental health treatment, it's interesting to note that the World Health Organization compared the outcomes of treatment for schizophrenia in developing third-world countries with that of developed industrialized countries, including the United States. The findings showed that people in developing countries had a 73% recovery rate, showing the best possible outcome, and only a 13% rate of the worst possible outcome, as compared to a 53% best outcome in developed countries and a worst possible outcome of 24% (Lauriello, Bustillo, & Keith, 1999; Sartorious, Jablensky, Ernberg, Korten, & Gulbinat, 1987). In developing countries, mentally ill people live with their families, have assigned work and social responsibilities, care for children, and are an accepted part of the community. In developed countries, the mentally ill are often stigmatized by their illness and find that the label of mental illness often creates bias in work, relationships, and community involvement.

Much of the treatment of the mentally ill in developing countries is what we in America might call *alternative medicine*, relying on the use of herbs, diet, meditation, spirituality, dream therapy (dreams are often considered messages from ancestors that have profound meaning), and simple supportive counseling that focuses on the person's strengths. In most developed countries, the treatment of mental illness includes very powerful psychotropic medications that often distance clients from their surroundings and leave them feeling highly fatigued and disoriented. In this instance, a great deal can be learned from other cultures. Involvement with other cultures creates a two-way learning experience for the social worker and the international society he or she works in.

International Social Problems Affecting the United States

THE INTERNATIONAL SEX TRADE

Landesman (2004) estimates that of the many hundreds of thousands of kidnapped or bartered women and children sold into the international sex trade worldwide, 50,000 end up in the United States, where they are often forced into prostitution, child pornography, or sweat shop labor as a way of repaying debts. Landesman estimates that the international sex trade is a $7 billion per year business and so lucrative that only drugs and arms trading bring in more money. Bertone (2000) reports that victims of the international sex trade live in conditions that are akin to slavery and are often beaten into submission, undergo severe physical and psychological abuse, and are made to understand that if they misbehave or resist their captors, serious harm will be done to their families.

In another example of the mistreatment of women internationally, the World Health Organization (2002) reports the following disturbing data:

- At least 1 out of every 3 women in the world is beaten, forced into having sex, or abused during her lifetime.
- Domestic violence is the major cause of death and disability for women aged 16 to 44. Domestic violence causes more deaths to women than cancer and traffic accidents combined.
- Approximately 60 million women are missing as a result of gender-selective abortions and infanticide (the killing of female infants because a male is preferred).
- Up to 70% of female murder victims are killed by their male partner.
- In studies in the United States and Kenya, one fifth of women with HIV/AIDS reported domestic violence because of their health status.

FOOD AND HUNGER: DEFINITIONS AND DATA

Malnutrition is a general term that indicates a lack of some or all nutritional elements necessary for human health. There are two basic types. The first and most important is protein-energy malnutrition (PEM)—the lack of enough protein (from meat and other sources) and food that provides energy (measured in calories) which all of the basic food groups provide. The second, also very important, is micronutrient (vitamin and mineral) deficiency.

PEM is by far the most lethal form of malnutrition/hunger and the one referred to when world hunger is discussed. Approximately 850 million people worldwide are malnourished. Children are the most visible victims

InfoTable 17.1	World Hunger

More than 800 million people in the world go hungry. In developing countries, 6 million children die each year, mostly from hunger-related causes. In the United States, 13 million children live in households where people have to skip meals or eat less to make ends meet. That means one in ten households in the U.S. are living with hunger or are at risk of hunger. (World Hunger Facts, 2004)

of malnutrition. Malnutrition plays a role in at least half of the 10.9 million child deaths each year—5 million deaths.

The World Produces Enough Food to Feed Everyone

World agriculture produces 17% more calories per person today than it did 30 years ago, despite a 70% population increase. This is enough to provide everyone in the world with at least 2,720 kilocalories (kcal) per person per day. The principal problem is that many people in the world do not have sufficient land to grow or income to purchase enough food.

Poverty Is the Principal Cause of Hunger

There are an estimated 1.2 billion poor people in developing countries that live on $1 a day or less. Of these, an estimated 780 million suffer from chronic hunger, which means that their daily intake of calories is insufficient for them to lead active and healthy lives. Extreme poverty remains an agonizing problem in the world's developing regions, despite the advances made in the 1990s. Progress in poverty reduction has been concentrated in Asia and, especially, East Asia. In all the other regions, the number of people in extreme poverty has increased. In sub-Saharan Africa, there were 58 million more poor people in 1999 than in 1990.

Hunger Is Also a Cause of Poverty

Hunger causes poor health, low levels of energy, and even mental impairment, conditions that lead to even greater poverty. The causes of poverty include poor people's lack of resources and extremely unequal income distribution in many countries.

Conflict as a Cause of Hunger

Worldwide, there were some 19.8 million refugees and displaced persons in 2002—largely as a result of wars, political turbulence, civil conflict, and social unrest (e.g., Sudan, Liberia, Colombia, Afghanistan, Burundi, Bosnia, and Herzegovina). In such emergencies, malnutrition seriously increases the risk of disease and death.

Progress in Reducing the Number of Hungry People

There has been some progress in reducing the number of hungry people, but it has been slow. Most current data show that the number of undernourished is increasing by 15 million a year, reflecting a serious deterioration in the battle against hunger.

Vitamin A Deficiency

This can cause night blindness and reduces the body's resistance to disease. In children, Vitamin A deficiency can cause growth retardation; an estimated 79 million preschool children suffered from Vitamin A deficiency in 1995. In South Asia and Africa, approximately 30% of children suffer from Vitamin A deficiency.

Iron Deficiency

This is a principal cause of anemia. Two billion people—more than 30% of the world's population—are anemic, mainly due to iron deficiency, and, in developing countries, this is frequently exacerbated by malaria and worm infections. For children, health consequences include premature birth, low birth weight, infections, and elevated risk of death. Later, physical and cognitive development is impaired, resulting in lowered school performance. For pregnant women, anemia contributes to 20% of all maternal deaths.

Iodine Deficiency Disorders

Iodine deficiency disorders (IDD) jeopardize children's mental health—often their very lives. Serious iodine deficiency during pregnancy may result in stillbirths, abortions, and congenital abnormalities such as cretinism, a grave, irreversible form of mental retardation that affects people living in iodine-deficient areas of Africa and Asia. IDD also causes mental impairment that lowers intellectual prowess at home, at school, and at work. IDD affects more than 740 million people, 13% of the world's population. Fifty million people have some degree of mental impairment caused by IDD.

GENOCIDE

The following discussion of genocide is summarized from the work of Fein (2004). Genocide, according to Fein, is the crime of murdering massive numbers of people because of their ethnic, national, racial, or religious identity. In the 20th century, mass killing has increasingly become part of the national policies of many countries. During World War I (1914–1918), the Ottoman Empire killed between a million and a million-and-a-half Armenians through starvation, massacres, rape, and dehydration. The genocide by Nazi Germany during World War II resulted in the deaths of an estimated 6 million Jews, 500,000 Roma (Gypsies), and millions of other people considered subhuman by the Germans. Croatia, in the former Yugoslavia, also was responsible during World War II for killing 200,000 to 340,000 of its Serbian citizens as an act of ethnic cleansing.

In Cambodia, the Communist Khmer Rouge killed close to 1.7 million Cambodians between 1976 and 1979. During Guatemala's civil war from 1960 to 1996, an estimated 200,000 people were killed and Guatemala's right-wing military government specifically targeted the indigenous Maya people, killing 85,000 to 110,000 people. In 1994 in Rwanda, between 500,000 and 1 million people, mostly of the Tutsi tribe, were killed following the takeover of the government by extremist Hutus. In all of these cases, virtually nothing was done by other countries or political organizations such as the United Nations (UN) to prevent the genocide.

Fein says that there are four main types of genocide: (a) ideological, (b) retributive, (c) developmental, and (d) despotic. However, any genocide may have characteristics of more than one of these types.

Ideological. The Nazi Holocaust, the Armenian massacres, and the Cambodian genocide are examples of ideological genocide. This type of genocide is committed to achieve a society where all members of society are alike or hold the same beliefs.

Retributive. Retributive genocide is undertaken when one group dominates another group and fears its rebellion or when the other group actually rebels.

Developmental. This is genocide undertaken for economic gain, such as killing people living in certain areas to gain control of mining or water rights.

Despotic. Despotic genocide is intended to terrorize real or potential enemies. During the 1970s and early 1980s, Ugandan presidents Idi Amin and Milton Obote killed hundreds of thousands of Ugandans who had opposed or who could oppose their dictatorial rule.

In 1948, the UN passed the International Convention on the Prevention and Punishment of the Crime of Genocide. This act made genocide a crime under international law. In 1993 and 1994, the UN established an international tribunal to investigate and prosecute people involved in war crimes, crimes against humanity, and genocide in the former Yugoslavia and in Rwanda, convicting a number of people.

| InfoTable 17.2 | Genocide in the 20th Century: The Roll Call |

1–1.5 million Armenians killed by the Ottoman Empire. 5–6 million Jews and 20% of all Russian prisoners taken by the Nazi's in WW II killed by the Nazi's. Forty thousand Americans killed in WW II during and after the Bataan Death March. Hundreds of thousands of innocent civilians killed in indiscriminate and militarily non-essential air raids by the Germans, Japanese and the Allies during WW II. Over 100,000 Japanese died in one fire bombing of Tokyo late in WW II. 1.7 million people killed by the Khmer Rouge in Cambodia. Five hundred thousand to one million Tutsis in Rowanda killed by the Hutus. (Fein, 2004)

| InfoTable 17.3 | The Technology of Genocide |

In the following report of the gassing of Kurds by Saddam Hussein from La Monde Diplomatique (1998), one gets another view of technologically advanced genocide:

> The town of Halabja, with 60,000 inhabitants, is located a few miles from the border with Iran. On March 16, 1988, continual waves of Iraqi MiGs and Mirages dropped chemical bombs on the city, covering it with a stench of rotten apples. In the morning, the streets were covered with corpses, many of them babies still being held by their mothers. In just a few hours, 5,000 people were killed. The 3,200 without families were buried in a mass grave.

A Social Worker Helps a Surviving Victim of the German Death Camps

Igor Rubin is a 74-year-old Jewish survivor of the German death camps during the Second World War and is originally from the Ukraine area of Russia. He saw his entire family perish in the gas chambers and was able to stay alive because he was liberated by Jewish partisans organized to save the inmates of the concentration camps in Poland during the war. Igor suffers from a number of physical and emotional problems, most notably an ongoing depression. Igor is sickened by the continuation of genocide in so many parts of the world. For many years, Igor was a successful physician in Israel and then in the United States, but with the death of his wife and the seeming lack of concern shown by his two grown children, Igor has fallen into a deep depression. He is being seen by an MSW-level clinical social worker from Jewish Family Service who visits him in his home twice a week.

(Continued)

(Continued)

Igor is talking about suicide, always a sign of a very serious depression. The social worker did a threat evaluation and concluded that Igor had the capacity and motivation to kill himself. She was able to convince Igor to give her a pledge not to kill himself and to agree that he would call the agency's 24-hour crisis hotline if he felt the urge to kill himself was too great to overcome. She also arranged for several older volunteers from the agency to visit Igor every day to make certain he was OK.

As a retired physician licensed in his state to practice medicine, Igor hasn't worked in several years. Feeling it would be good for him to get out of the house, the social worker got Igor to agree to volunteer as a physician at a local group facility for homeless children. Something about the experience so touched Igor that he began volunteering so many hours that the group home asked him to join the staff as a paid physician. Believing that part of Igor's depression related to the death of his wife, the social worker encouraged Igor to attend book clubs and other functions where he might meet and interact with other older adults. In the course of one of the functions, which to his surprise Igor enjoyed, he met a highly educated widow who had been a professor of biology before she retired, and they now provide each other with companionship and support. Most of all, the worker had Igor focus on his many accomplishments in life and helped him think about important "meaning of life" issues. Although he was highly suicidal, he hadn't made an actual attempt on his life. The fact that he hadn't acted on his impulse to kill himself suggested, as their talks progressed, that he was frightened of what killing himself would mean in the afterlife and that he didn't want a successful life to end on such a note of resignation and failure. This discussion, and others like it, surprised Igor and helped him to see the many reasons for continuing a life that still offered so much opportunity and pleasure.

A year later, Igor has his sad days and thinks that the experience he had in the death camps did terrible harm to him. He misses his extended family, but he survives and is much happier and involved in life than before. His children were contacted by the social worker, who told them about their father's depression. They have become much more involved, call many days, and see him often. Igor says that just being with his children gives him great joy. In discussing his social worker and the help she provided, Igor said, "She came into my life when I had given up, this little girl, no more than 25. To me she seemed like a little girl. At my age everybody does. She brought wisdom to my life, and kindness, and tenderness, and it made such a difference. I've been a doctor since I was 24 and I know that only special people can do what she did because she's a true healer. I think people with that ability are touched by God, and how wonderful and appropriate that she works for an agency like Jewish Family Service. For an old man who suffered because he was a Jew, how lovely that I'm now being helped by a Jewish agency, and how wonderful, after those dark days when so many Jews were murdered, that we have come so far that we have Jewish agencies that can help people who suffer. I'm on the board of the agency now and I thank God for what they did for me and for other older people like me. In our language we call it a 'mitzvah' or good deed to help others. Returning to work and being on this board are mitzvahs, and they've made me whole again when I was nearly broken."

WORLD POVERTY

World poverty is an increasingly serious problem as the economic distance between developed and nondeveloping/developing countries continues to grow. Consider some of the data provided by Shah (2004): (a) half the world, or about 3 billion people, live on less than $2.00 a day; (b) the gross domestic product for a quarter of the world's poorest countries, a measure of wealth, is less than the wealth of the world's three richest countries; (c) nearly a billion people can't read or sign their names; (d) less than 1% of the money spent on weapons worldwide would have put every child in the world in school, and yet it didn't happen; (e) a few of the richest people in the world have more money than 1 billion people worldwide; (f) a mere 12% of the world's population uses 85% of the water, and these people do not live in arid places where water needs to be consumed in greater quantities; (g) 20% of the world's population in developed countries consume 86% of the world's goods; and (h) almost 800 million people in Asia and Africa are chronically undernourished because of poverty.

InfoTable 17.4	Poverty and Health

1. Every year, more than 500,000 women die from complications of pregnancy and childbirth—99 percent occur in the developing world.

2. Almost 4 million babies die annually in the developing world during their first week of life. These deaths are often the result of limited prenatal health care and births spaced closely together.

3. Diarrhea kills about 2.2 million people each year, most of them children under 5.

4. By the end of 2001, an estimated 40 million people were infected with HIV, with over 95 percent of those living in developing countries. Approximately 18.5 million people with HIV are women and 3 million are children under age 15.

5. Malaria threatens the lives of more than 2.2 billion people in over 100 countries, about 40 percent of the world's population. Each year, an estimated 300 million to 500 million clinical cases of malaria are recorded. (CARE, 2004)

WORLDWIDE HIV/AIDS EPIDEMIC

The overwhelming majority of people with the human immunodeficiency virus (HIV), some 95% of the global total, live in the developing world. The number will grow even more as infection rates continue to rise in countries where poverty, poor health care systems, and limited resources for prevention and care fuel the spread of the virus. By December 2004, 37.2 million adults and 2.2 million children were living with HIV. This is more than 50% higher than the figures projected by World Health Organization in 1991. In 2004, almost 5 million people became infected with HIV, which causes AIDS. In the same year, AIDS caused 3.1 million deaths. About half the people who acquire AIDS do so younger than age 25 and typically die before they are 35, leaving behind 15 million AIDS orphans who are vulnerable to poverty, exploitation, and themselves becoming infected with HIV. They are often forced to leave the education system and find work, sometimes to care for younger siblings or head a family.

The area in Africa south of the Sahara desert, sub-Saharan Africa, has just more than 10% of the world's population but is home to more than 60% of all people living with HIV. An estimated 3.1 million adults and children became infected with HIV during 2004. This brought the total number of people living with HIV/AIDS in the region to 25.4 million by the end of the year. African women are at least 1.2 times more likely to be infected with HIV than men. To stop the worldwide AIDS epidemic, AVERT (2005), a worldwide AIDS Charity Organization, notes the following:

> People need to challenge the myths and misconceptions about human sexuality that translate into dangerous sexual practices.
>
> Work and legislation are needed to reduce prejudice felt by HIV+ people around the world and the discrimination that prevents people from "coming out" as being HIV positive.
>
> HIV prevention initiatives need to be increased, people across the world need to be made aware of the dangers, the risks, and the ways they can protect themselves.
>
> Condom promotion and supply needs to be increased, and the appropriate sexual health education needs to be provided to young people before they reach an age where they become sexually active.
>
> Medication and support needs to be provided to people who are already HIV+, so that they can live longer and more productive lives, support their families, and avoid transmitting the virus onwards.
>
> Support and care needs to be provided for those children who have already been orphaned by AIDS, so that they can grow up safely, without experiencing poverty, exploitation, and themselves falling prey to HIV. (p. 1)

You Be the International Social Worker

Hank Thoreau just graduated with his BSW and took a position with a world hunger organization in a drought-stricken part of the sub-Sahara in northern and middle Africa, an area plagued by war, AIDS, starvation, and extreme poverty. Hank feels strongly about his role coordinating food and water supplies to starving people. He can see the change in the people he serves and is thrilled to notice their improved health, particularly that of the children and infants. But Hank is overwhelmed by the enormity of the problem. He feels like quitting and going back to Idaho, where he had a wonderful life and where he can find a job in local social welfare agencies or pursue his graduate degree in social work. Many nights he puts himself to sleep thinking about rafting wild rivers or fishing and hiking mountain trails in pristine areas of Idaho near the Canadian border.

His supervisor has had many talks with Hank and can see that Hank is conflicted, but he also knows that Hank is a natural and does his job very well under difficult circumstances. This is the conversation he and Hank had when Hank's burnout became severe:

Hank (H): I'm so homesick I can hardly get up in the morning and, yeah, I know I do my job well and it's the most important work I'll ever do, but the problem is endless. For everyone we help there are 50, 100, 1,000 people in need. The wars keep going, no one pays any attention, and all we do is put on band-aids while the real problems of poverty, weather change, and war just get worse.

Supervisor (S): I know how you feel, Hank. I feel the same way, but God, Allah, Buddha, or someone has chosen us to do the work. Even if the need is overwhelming, we help, Hank, we do. People live because of us, and it's complicated work. You know that. There are so many political, religious, and cultural issues we deal with, and we deal with well, that you have to be proud of our skill, and, I mean, we save lives, Hank, we do.

H: Yeah, but how long before I get malaria or some other disease, some crazy person kills me with a hatchet, or some warring tribal outbreak takes place right here where we are?

S: I know, but still, we've been able to keep that from happening so far. You, me, and our wonderful assistants from right here. These are great and noble people.

H: But I just want a normal life again. I want to have a beer and pizza and go to clubs, and just rock. I have no life here. I can't even think

(Continued)

(Continued)

about a love life here because so many women have AIDS. I'm a young guy and this job is making me old.

S: Really, is it? Will you ever have another experience like this in your life where you live in such a strange and wonderful area and you do work that matters so much? Do you think work in some large office in the United States will be as challenging or allow you so much freedom?

H: No, but I'm just 23 and all I can think about is going home. I've been here a year. How can you ask me to stay longer?

Questions

1. If you were Hank, what would you do and why?

2. Do you think the supervisor's arguments about never being able to have such an exciting experience are true? Explain your answer.

3. If you go to a developing country in great turmoil, how long should you commit yourself to stay?

4. Is Hank burned out, scared, homesick, or just lonely? Which of these is the most significant in Hank's desire to go home, and why?

5. Saving lives is something most of don't do unless we're in the medical profession, but Hank is saving lives by feeding starving people. Do you think that's the most important work any of us can ever do?

Summary

In this chapter on international social work, some major problems of an international nature that affect the United States are discussed. A case study is provided to help the reader better understand the impact of genocide and the work we do as social workers to help victims cope with life-long problems. Finally, you are asked to be the social worker in a decision to stay or leave a job distributing food to starving people in Africa.

Questions to Determine Your Frame of Reference

1.   Do you think it's ethical for American social workers to go to countries very different from our own and to try and change the lives of people

without a substantial understanding of their culture, traditions, and history? Isn't this what gets us into difficulty all over the world?

2. What is your position on illegal entry of very poor people into this country for the purpose of working?

3. Isn't the major reason countries continue to be poor their corrupt political systems and politicians who rob people of resources and wealth?

4. Is it the fault of developed countries that underdeveloped countries are so poor?

5. Why does genocide exist in a world that is supposedly so philosophically, medically, and technologically advanced?

Internet Sources

A disturbing United Nations Report (2004) is provided on world hunger. Next, Dutton argues that the economies of many third- and fourth-world countries are improving and with that improvement, hunger is decreasing. Finally, the United Nations (2004) reports on worldwide rates of AIDS and HIV.

1. *United Nations World Hunger Programme: Facts and figures.* (2004). Retrieved from http://www.wfp.org/index.asp?section=1

2. Deaton, A. (2002, June). Is world poverty falling? *Finance Development, 39*(2). Retrieved from http://www.imf.org/external/pubs/ft/fandd/2002/06/deaton.htm

3. *United Nations Report on worldwide AIDS/HIV epidemic.* (2004). Retrieved from http://www.unaids.org/bangkok2004/report.html

Some International Social Welfare Organizations

American Association
  for World Health
2001 S Street NW
Washington, DC 20009
(202) 265-0286

Amnesty International, USA
322 8th Avenue
New York, NY 10001

American Friends Service
   Committee
1501 Cherry Street
Philadelphia, PA 19102–1479

CARE
660 First Avenue
New York, NY 10016
(212) 686-3110

Council of International
   Programs
1101 Wilson Boulevard
Suite 1708
Arlington, VA 22209–2504
(703) 527-1160

Inter-American Foundation
1515 Wilson Blvd
Arlington, VA 22209
(703) 841-3813

International Council on
   Social Welfare
U.S. Committee
Council of International
   Programs
1101 Wilson Boulevard,
   Suite 1708
Arlington, VA 22209–2504
(703) 527-1160

International Development
   Foundation
P.O. Box 70257
Washington, DC 20024
(202) 723-7010

International Labor Office
Publications Center
49 Sheridan Avenue
Suite WD
Albany, NY 12210
(518) 436-9686

International Monetary Fund
Publications Division
700 19th Street NW
Suite 700
Washington, DC 20005
(202) 393-0150

Inter-University Consortium for
   International Social
   Development
San Jose State University
School of Social Work
San Jose, CA

Organization of American States
1889 F Street NW
Washington, DC 20006

Overseas Development Council
1717 Massachusetts Avenue, NW
Washington, DC 20036
(202) 234-8701

Panos Institute
(Sustainable Development)
1717 Massachusetts Avenue NW
Suite 301
Washington, DC 20036
(202) 529-3210

Society for International
   Development
Washington Chapter
1401 New York Avenue NW
Suite 1100
Washington, DC 20005
(202) 347-1800

Society for Intercultural
   Education, Training, and
   Research
733 15th Street NW
Suite 900
Washington, DC 20005

United Nations Childrens Fund
  (UNICEF)
3 United Nations Plaza
New York, NY 10017
FAX (212) 326-7768

U.S. Agency for International
  Development
Department of State
Washington, DC 20523
(202) 647-1850

U.S. Institute of Peace
1550 M Street
Suite 700-S92
Washington, DC 20005–1708

Women's Foreign Policy Council
9th Floor
1133 Broadway
New York, NY 10010

Women's International Policy
  Action Committee
845 Third Avenue
15th Floor
New York, NY 10022
(212) 759-7982

World Bank
1818 H Street NW
Washington, DC 20433
(202) 477-8825

World Education, Inc.
210 Lincoln Street
Boston, MA 02111
(617) 482-9485

WorldWatch Institute
1776 Massachusetts Avenue NW
Washington, DC 20036
(202) 452-1999

World Resources Institute
1735 New York Avenue NW
Suite 400
Washington, DC 20006
(202) 638-6300

Medical, Social, and Emotional Problems in the Military

18

The Veterans Administration and Military Social Work

The War on Terror and the Role of Social Work in the Military

With wars in the Middle East and the threat of terrorism continuing to affect Americans, military social work has become an increasingly important aspect of life for many military personnel and their families experiencing such common war-time problems as PTSD, substance abuse, financial concerns, marital problems (e.g., domestic violence), and a variety of other social and emotional problems that affect us in times of stress. PTSD is a significant problem for those in combat zones. Combining the estimates for all current full and partial veterans with a diagnosis of PTSD resulted in an estimate of roughly 830,000 Vietnam theater veterans who continued to experience significant posttraumatic distress or impairment approximately 20 years after their exposure to one or more traumatic stressors (Weiss et al., 1992).

In a study of emotional problems related to combat in Iraq and Afghanistan, *USA Today* (Elias, 2004) reports a study appearing in the *New England Journal of Medicine* estimating that almost 20% of returning servicemen and servicewomen will suffer from emotional problems including PTSD, anxiety, and depression. "The military should fully integrate mental health care into medical clinics instead of having some separate offices for therapy; train soldiers to recognize the signs of mental disorders; and use more therapists who are independent of the military" (Elias, 2004, p. 10D),

315

the study states. One year later, these concerns were realized when a 2005 study of returning soldiers from Iraq indicated that "30% of the returning troops from Iraq have developed stress-related mental health problems 3 to 4 months after coming home, according to the Army's Surgeon General" (Manske, 2005, p. A4). The problems included anxiety attacks, depression, nightmares, anger, and an inability to concentrate. A smaller but significant number of soldiers also suffer from PTSD, according to the report. The bad news is that a 2004 *New England Journal of Medicine* study of "6200 Marines in the Iraq and Afghanistan wars found that veterans with mental help problems did not seek counseling because they didn't want to be seen as weak" (Zucchino, 2005, p. A25).

SOCIAL WORKERS IN THE MILITARY

According to Tallant and Ryberg (2004), social workers have been serving in the military since World War I. Harris (1999) indicates that a Red Cross social worker reported for duty at the U.S. Army General Hospital Number 30 at Plattsburgh, New York, on September 1, 1918. From 1918 until 1945, the U.S. Army relied upon enlisted social workers to provide an array of services. In 1945, commissioned status for social workers was achieved in the U.S. Army. Since that time, there has been a growing number of both military and civilian social workers.

At present, the U.S. Army has 150 commissioned officers serving on active duty (Lockett, 1999). The U.S. Air Force presently has 225 civilian social workers and 215 commissioned social work officers (Tarpley, 1999). The U.S. Navy employs 400 civilian social workers and 31 commissioned social work officers (Kennedy, 1999). Excluding civilian social workers employed by the U. S. Army, this represents more than 1,000 social workers, and a much higher number would be likely since 2002. Social workers in the military focus on improving conditions that cause social problems, such as drug and alcohol abuse, racism, and sexism. According to the U.S. Department of Defense (2004), the purpose of social work in the military is to sustain military readiness by enhancing the quality of service members, military families, units, and communities, and to do the following:

- Counsel military personnel and their family members
- Supervise counselors and caseworkers
- Survey military personnel to identify problems and plan solutions
- Plan social action programs to rehabilitate personnel with problems
- Plan and monitor equal opportunity programs
- Conduct research on social problems and programs
- Organize community activities on military bases

Specific Functions of Military Social Work

DeAngelis (2004) believes that one of the important functions of social work in the military is to reunite soldiers with their families. Long absences and changing family circumstances sometimes require social work intervention through family support programs and mental health counseling. Jill Manske, the director of social work services in the Veterans' Affairs (VA) headquarters in Washington, D.C., says that social workers are "the liaisons between the families and the VA, between the families and communities—we're the resource people." Manske reveals that in VA hospitals and military installations across America, thousands of social workers are helping military personnel adjust to civilian life by offering the following services:

1. Family and parent support groups and centers. For the first time in our history, many women with children are serving in war zones, which means a great deal of anxiety by families about the welfare of their mothers. Social workers try and keep mothers in contact with children and when problems arise with children, to provide the necessary help.

2. Marriage and family counseling and therapy for people prone to domestic violence, child abuse, and neglect. Soldiers about to be deployed are often more prone to abuse, particularly when they aren't ready to go to war.

3. During wartime, services to help an increasing number of soldiers experiencing stress from war-time duty.

4. Evaluating and treating drug and alcohol problems. These problems were epidemic in Vietnam and seem to be serious problems in the wars in the Middle East.

5. Working with soldiers who have been wounded or disabled and helping in finding housing that will accommodate their disabilities.

6. Working with solders who have developed PTSD and are in need of long-term treatment.

7. Working with soldiers who have witnessed the death of friends and colleagues and are suffering from depression and prolonged grief.

8. Working with soldiers who have committed military or legal offenses and are in the stockade or are about to get dishonorable discharges for breaking military codes of conduct and policies.

Ethical Dilemmas in Military Social Work

Loewenberg and Dolgoff (1996) define a dilemma as "a problem situation or predicament which seems to defy a satisfactory solution because the decision-maker must choose between two options of near or equal value." Tallant and Ryberg (2004) identify four ethical dilemmas for social workers in the military: (a) military social workers can and often are ordered to perform a task by either a nonsocial worker or an individual within their chain of command who is not their immediate supervisor, (b) military social workers are held responsible and punished for not following legal orders, (c) military social workers must work within the boundaries of civilian and military law, and (d) military social workers cannot quit their jobs because they disagree with their immediate boss or the chain of command. Tallant and Ryberg provide the following example of an ethical dilemma for military social workers, asking you how to handle each situation.

You Be the Social Worker

You are an Army social worker dealing with issues of family violence. As the base family advocacy officer, you know the base commander very well. He has written you several key endorsements on your yearly officer performance report. You are a captain up for promotion this year and you believe the base commander will support you for promotion.

The base commander calls you at home on a Saturday evening around 11:30 P.M. and tells you that his wife and he just hosted a party for several couples at his home. During the course of the evening, his executive officer became drunk and verbally abusive to his own wife. The couple left the commander's house in an argument. An hour later the commander's wife telephoned the wife to see if everything had settled down. The executive's wife was crying and clearly upset. She reported that her husband had hit her several times and had left the house for the rest of the evening. She did not know where he had gone.

The base commander orders you to do the following. First, go to the home of the executive officer to check on the condition of the wife. Second, conduct an assessment on Sunday morning with the executive officer to determine if this is an abusive situation. Third, he tells you to not talk to anybody about the situation. Finally, he tells you to phone him Sunday afternoon with an update on the situation.

As ordered, you go to the executive's house. The wife has been hit several times in the face, but refuses to go to the hospital. She reports that the abuse has gone on for years and she wants her husband to get help. She asks for your help. The next morning you meet with the executive officer and he admits he hit his wife, but denies he "has a problem" with abusive behavior. He blames the incident on having too much to drink. He refuses treatment and says to you, "Captain, I am a Colonel—get out of my life!"

After conducting your assessment, you come to the conclusion that this couple needs immediate help. You believe the incident should be opened as an active family advocacy case. You report this to the base commander. He orders you to keep this case "off the record" and not to discuss the situation with anyone. The commander says he will take care of the situation. He assures you that he will get this couple some help. In fact, he tells you that he will "order" his executive officer to get help. But you're not sure that your commanding officer will do anything. As the officer in charge of abuse among enlisted men and soldiers, what would you do? (Tallant & Ryberg, 2004)

Questions

1. Do you think the base commander will order his executive officer to get treatment, or will he commiserate with him about how demanding wives can be and let the whole thing go? Explain your answer.

2. When you sign on for a job in the military, you accept the rules. Even though the social worker is bound by professional ethics to do what he believes is right, he is also bound by military rules to do as he is told. Which set of rules outranks the other in this case?

3. The executive officer's wife doesn't want to go to the hospital. Should the social worker have agreed with her decision or should he have called for medical help? What if the executive's wife is more seriously injured than she at first imagines herself to be? Would the social worker be held liable?

4. The commanding officer's behavior seems consistent with many reported incidents of sexual harassment and sexual assault in the military, where commanding officers fail to act. Do you think the military really cares about the victims of sexual abuse and harassment?

5. Because the military is dominated by a warrior culture, do you think social work and its belief system are really welcomed or appreciated?

The Veterans Administration (VA)

The Veterans Bureau was established on June 16, 1926, with 14 social workers. Currently, there are 3,788 social work staff (VA Workforce Statistical Data Report, 2001) located in 163 medical care facilities (U.S. Department of Veterans Affairs, 2004).

Early social work involvement at the VA was centered exclusively on the psychiatric and tuberculosis patients but has evolved in the VA into treatment approaches that address individual social problems and work with acute/chronic medical conditions, dying patients, and bereaved families. VA social workers ensure continuity of care through the admission, evaluation, treatment, and follow-up processes and by coordinating discharge planning and providing case management services.

Social work coordinates the Community Residential Care (CRC) program (U.S. Department of Veterans Affairs, 2004), which provides basic room and board, as well as limited personal care and supervision, to veterans who do not require nursing home or hospital care but are not able to live independently and may not have family to provide the needed care. These veterans would otherwise be among our homeless population. The Department of Veterans Affairs is affiliated with more than 100 Graduate Schools of Social Work that train 600 to 700 students per year (VA Office of Academic Affairs, 2002).

The mission of the VA is to provide benefits and services to veterans and their families in a responsive, timely, and compassionate manner in recognition of their service to the nation. Those benefits and services include the following: disability benefits, medical care, counseling, home loans, education, retraining and helpfinding jobs, vocational rehabilitation, burial rights, life insurance, and dependent and survivor benefits. Social workers are involved in most of these areas. A service provided to veterans with direct relevance to social work is the National Center for Post-Traumatic Stress Disorder, created within the Department of Veterans Affairs in 1989, in response to a Congressional mandate to address the needs of veterans with military-related PTSD. Its mission is "to advance the clinical care and social welfare of America's veterans through research, education, and training in the science, diagnosis, and treatment of PTSD and stress-related disorders" (Veterans Administration, 2004).

The VA is a huge organization providing very diverse services to millions of former and returning vets, many with very serious physical and emotional problems. Yet the VA has received considerable criticism for being unfriendly to veterans, inefficient, slow to respond to the changing needs of veterans (it was the VA that incorrectly diagnosed PTSD in early returning Vietnam War vets as a form of schizophrenia), outdated in its treatment, highly bureaucratic, and mistake-prone. Some support for this can be noted in the controversy over Agent Orange, a defoliant that was used to kill jungle growth during the Vietnam War. Many veterans suffered from Agent Orange poisoning for years before the VA even recognized it as a problem or did anything about it. The same can be said for soldiers serving in the Gulf War in 1991 who suffered from a variety of serious illnesses known as Gulf War Syndrome without the VA responding well. Not that this was entirely the fault of the VA alone, because it was the military that denied the existence of both medical problems and suggested that anyone suffering from either problem had emotional problems. Funding for the VA has not always been adequate, and the political nature of the organization, with many pressures placed on it by politicians, is often a problem to administrators in many VA settings. I supervised a number of students receiving MSW training at the VA and always found the social work departments forward-looking and effective. The clients seen in social work were very diverse and included the severely chronically mentally ill; many clients with PTSD who were having problems readjusting to life after combat; veterans who had become drug and alcohol addicted as a way of coping with the stress of combat; homeless veterans whose families had become estranged from them after returning home with multiple medical and emotional problems; clients who had serious medical problems and disabilities and were being provided transportation and supportive services through the social work department; veterans who needed basic help with clothing, housing, and food; veterans who needed an advocate within the VA system; and a range of other problems often seen by social workers in a number of social agencies in America.

| InfoTable 18.1 | Persian Gulf Syndrome |

Walking, never mind running, made Paul E. Perrone wheeze and gasp for breath. He was groggy, like he just woke up, except he could never make the feeling go away. His knees, hips and ankles ached. His stomach hurt.

"It was unusual pain, especially for a 26-year-old," said Mr. Perrone, describing how he felt as an Air Force sergeant during the Persian Gulf War.

For years, Mr. Perrone fought government officials who refused to believe his pain was caused by serving in the war. He testified before Congress. He drove to medical appointments in Maryland. He was scanned, X-rayed and pin-pricked dozens of times. Today, on the 10th anniversary of the start of the Gulf War, Mr. Perrone said the government is finally recognizing Gulf War Syndrome and trying to figure out why veterans are sick. "You don't hear Gulf War Syndrome being called 'stress' anymore," Mr. Perrone said.

The most damaging effect of the war, however, emerged as soldiers returned home complaining of vague physical problems such as fatigue, muscle and joint pain, headaches, memory loss, skin rash, diarrhea and sleeping problems. They raised questions about the experimental drugs they received and the chemicals they may have been exposed to, including biological weapons from Iraq and depleted uranium used in some American weapons.

"The government bungled it," said Phil Budahn, a spokesman for the Department of Veteran Affairs in Washington, D.C. "There's a clear consensus the government did not handle these problems when they started arising." (Crowley, 2001)

An Example of Social Work in a VA Hospital

Kenneth Jackson is a 27-year-old Staff Sergeant who was severely wounded in the Iraqi war. Kenneth lost part of one leg and an arm and has severe burns to his face and neck from a bomb explosion, which set his vehicle on fire. Although he has had skin grafts for his burns, the burns have left notable scars that are quite disfiguring. Ken won't go out during the day and lives alone without work or friends. Before the war, he was very outgoing and a promising athlete whose baseball career had progressed to within one step of a major-league baseball career. As a member of the National Guard in his home state, he entered combat for which he had minimal training, and is bitter that he was sent to the front lines in the war without being adequately prepared.

Ken is in the local VA hospital being treated for an infection in his leg wound. The supervising physician referred Ken for social work services because Ken is depressed, isn't working, and refuses all attempts to help him resume a social life. The medical social worker tried to interview Ken in the hospital, but he was unresponsive and uncooperative. The worker *did* make a home visit after Ken was discharged and found Ken with his side arm in hand, ready to shoot himself. The social worker was able to talk Ken down from doing anything, took his side arm away, and drove Ken to the VA psychiatric ward, where he was placed on a suicide watch.

Ken is frightened of killing himself and is equally frightened of life with his disabilities and scars. He feels like a "freak" and has a hateful attitude toward the military. During his time in the psychiatric ward, Ken joined an ongoing group therapy session of men who had various injuries, many more disfiguring than Ken's. He listened to the men talk about drinking themselves into stupors every night and the harmful things they were doing to themselves. Many of the men were even younger than he was. As a result, he asked to see the social worker who had prevented his suicide, and together they began a long-term plan to help Ken become fully rehabilitated, socially and physically. Ken agreed to get fitted for a leg and arm and to talk to a cosmetic specialist about covering his facial wounds. Much to his surprise, he discovered that certain cosmetics did a very good job of hiding scars. Ken is a very handsome and athletic man. Once his arm and leg were fitted and he could use them properly, it was difficult to tell that he'd had an injury. The cosmetics helped restore his confidence to go out during the day. He could also see that women were looking at him in the same way that they did before his injury, and he felt much more confident. The social worker helped Ken reunite with his family, who were heartbroken that Ken had chosen to isolate himself from them. He also reunited with his former girlfriend, who was happy to have Ken back in her life and had been very hurt by his unwillingness to see her.

The social worker also helped Ken return to the workplace. Although he no longer can play baseball, the team he was on before he went to Iraq had always found Ken to have a very keen baseball mind and hired him as a coach with a promise of becoming a small-town manager if the coaching job worked out. Ken exercised every day with the strengths coach of his team to return to his former level of strength. Being outdoors in a game he loved among many players 10 years younger than he was, and being called the "old man," Ken realized that he had teaching skills he never knew he had. He mentioned this to the social worker and was told about the VA's educational programs and his military benefits to seek retraining or additional education. Ken is enrolled in a local university, where he thinks he's going to become a teacher if his baseball career doesn't work out.

Ken found the apartment he lived in hard to maneuver. The social worker had a list of apartments that were more easily accessible for anyone with a disability, and together they found an ideal place with no steps to climb, wide hallways, and an easy-to-use shower. Ken continues to see the social worker on a fairly consistent basis because the depression he thought he'd eliminated is still there. Sometimes he feels so depressed it's hard for him to function, but with the help of the social worker and many other professionals at the VA, Ken has been able to progress rapidly. Two years after his suicidal episode, he was given his first managing job. Halfway through the season, his team is in second place. The year before they were dead-last. Ken is a very inspirational speaker and is well-liked in his community. He continues to work on his teaching degree but also wants to prepare himself for a possible career in business, and is doing a joint degree in education and business. He and his girlfriend were married last year, and although there have been many bumps along the way, they seem to be happy.

In discussing the social worker who helped him at the VA, Ken said, "He saved my life. He took the gun out of my hand and he drove me to the VA. He was there to give me encouragement when I was about as down as anyone could be. He helped me get my life together and to use my anger to do good things for myself and others instead of doing bad stuff to myself. He had faith in me and I felt it. And it wasn't a job to him, it was a calling. The time I tried to commit suicide was late one Sunday evening. I'd been drinking and I was going to 'off' myself. I know he doesn't work on Sundays and he told me later that he had a feeling something was wrong and just came over to my place on an impulse. See, that's the kind of guy he is. When we started this journey together of my getting my life in order, it was him who was there every step of the way encouraging me and being my cheerleader. I can't say enough about how much he helped me. After all the things he did and the things other people did to help, I stopped feeling my country had let me down and I'm proud that I fought and helped stop terrorism. I speak out against that war these days, but I'm proud that I served and that I did so willingly. It seems to me service to country and to others is the noblest thing any of us can do."

Summary

This chapter discusses the role of social work in the military and the function of social work in the VA. Because social workers in the military work in a setting far different than that of a social agency, there are ethical concerns that exist. Those concerns are discussed and two examples are provided. The role of the VA in working with veterans of America's wars is discussed, and a positive example is given of social work with a badly disabled veteran of the Iraqi war.

Questions to Determine Your Frame of Reference

1. When men and women serve in harm's way, isn't it an affront to the role of being a soldier to complain about physical and emotional health

problems? General Sherman in the Civil War said that "war is all hell." Shouldn't everyone who serves voluntarily in the military be prepared for some type of problem as a result of combat and not complain about it?

2. Concerns about ethical dilemmas in the military are really no different than ethical problems in social agencies, where social workers are asked to bend the rules for politicians who owe someone a favor. Isn't this just another example of how the code of ethics sometimes bumps into situational ethics?

3. Do you think that helping soldiers deal with emotional problems experienced during combat so they can be sent back into battle (where their problems might get worse or they could be killed) is a noble function for social workers?

4. If you were in a National Guard unit and were trained as a social worker but were told to be a prison guard in a highly violent and volatile prison housing suspected terrorists, would you feel obligated to report abuses of prisoners by members of your unit?

5. The VA is an example of the quality of patient care when big government is the provider of services. Do you think private hospital care is better than that received at VA hospitals? Go to the Internet and find studies comparing the care at private hospitals with that of the VA.

Internet Sources

VA benefits are summarized to help you understand the long-term medical and service benefits in one the country's largest medical and social service systems. An outstanding article follows on treating PTSD in returning Iraqi veterans, which was written for the Department of Veterans Affairs. Finally, the famous scientist Noam Chomsky, who has done much of the cutting-edge work on the development of speech in children, discusses the war on terror in a very controversial way which will hopefully encourage discussion and thought.

1. Veterans Benefits Administration. (2004, February). *A summary of VA benefits.* Retrieved from http://www.vba.va.gov/bln/21/summary VAbenefits.pdf

2. National Center for PTSD: A Program of the U.S. Department of Veterans Affairs. (2005). *The Iraq War clinician guide* (2nd ed.). Retrieved from http://www.ncptsd.org//war/iraq_clinician_guide_ v2/iraq_clinician_guide_ch_4.pdf

3. Chomsky, N. (2001). *The new war against terror.* Retrieved January 12, 2006, from http://www.zmag.org/GlobalWatch/chomskymit.htm

Part IV

Key Elements
in Combating
Social Problems
and Achieving
Social Justice

The Problems Faced by Diverse Populations 19

The Helping Organizations and Culturally Sensitive Social Work Practice

I've seen too much hate to want to hate, myself, and every time I see it, I say to myself, hate is too great a burden to bear. Somehow we must be able to stand up against our most bitter opponents and say: We shall match your capacity to inflict suffering by our capacity to endure suffering. We will meet your physical force with soul force. Do to us what you will and we will still love you. . . . But be assured that we'll wear you down by our capacity to suffer, and one day we will win our freedom. We will not only win freedom for ourselves; we will appeal to your heart and conscience that we will win you in the process, and our victory will be a double victory.

—Martin Luther King, Jr. (from "A Christmas Sermon on Peace," December 24, 1967)

America has come a long way in its attempt to treat all people fairly regardless of race, creed, or gender. But we still have a long way to go, which is made clear by the continuing debates over gay marriage, minority un- and underemployment, sexual harassment concerns by women, and a general preference in society for people based largely on their racial and ethnic backgrounds. In the 2003 U.S. Census, for example, the average salary for Caucasians was $45,572 compared to an average for Hispanics of $32,997 and for African Americans, $29,689. Although there are many factors involved in these figures, including level of education, the fact is that in two minority groups, income is substantially less than the dominant Caucasian group, raising concerns about equity and satisfaction of life for many black and Hispanic Americans.

Discrimination

One of the ways we know discrimination is still alive and well in America is through numerous and serious hate crimes. On its public affairs website, the American Psychological Association (APA) (1998) defines hate crimes as "violent acts against people, property, or organizations because of the group to which they belong or identify with" (p. 1). Although many people believe that hate crime perpetrators are neo-Nazis or "skinheads," fewer than 5% of the offenders are members of organized hate groups (APA, 1998). Individual offenders often believe that they have societal permission to commit hate crimes. In 1996, the Federal Bureau of Investigations (FBI) reported 8,759 bias-motivated criminal offenses. Data collected by private organizations show a higher prevalence of hate crimes than do federal statistics (APA, 1998). However, by 2002, the 7,462 hate crime incidents reported to the FBI represented a drop of nearly 25% from the 9,730 reported in 2001. The number also was below the 8,063 incidents recorded in 2000 (CNN.COM, 2003).

InfoTable 19.1   An Example of a Hate Crime

Extreme hate crimes tend to be committed by people who have a history of antisocial behavior. One of the most heinous examples took place in June 1998 in Jasper, Texas. Three men with jail records offered a ride to a black man who walked with a limp. After beating the victim to death, they dragged him behind their truck until his body was partially dismembered.

InfoTable 19.2   Hate Crime Legislations

The Hate Crimes Prevention Act of 1998, introduced in both the House (H.R. 3081) and Senate (S. 1529), seeks to expand federal jurisdiction over hate crimes by (1) allowing federal authorities to investigate all possible hate crimes, not only those where the victim was engaged in a federally protected activity such as voting, going to school, or crossing state lines; and (2) expanding the categories that are currently covered by hate crimes. (APA, 1998)

HATE CRIMES AGAINST RACIAL, RELIGIOUS, GENDER, AND ETHNIC GROUPS

FBI statistics released in October 2004 for the year 2003 indicate that there were 7,489 reported hate crimes (U.S. Federal Bureau of Investigation, 2004). Racial bias, the most prevalent type of hate crime and largely directed against African Americans, accounted for more than 50% of all reported hate crimes in America. Hate crimes aimed at religious groups, primarily Jews and Muslims, accounted for 18% of all hate crimes, whereas sexual orientation accounted for 18% of all hate crimes and ethncicity/national origin accounted for 13%. These data differ very little from a similar report made in 1996, which noted that the largest number of hate crimes were against African Americans. In 1996, 4,831 of the 7,947 such crimes reported to the FBI, or 60%, were committed because of race, with close to two thirds (62%) targeting African Americans (APA, 1998). Ethnic minorities are often the victims of hate crimes because they are considered new to the country or they are seen as different. Ethnic minorities are often the victims of anti-immigrant bias, which includes resentment when they succeed and anger when they act against established norms. Most religiously motivated hate crimes are directed against Jewish people, but acts of discrimination against Muslims have been on the rise since 9/11 and the war in Iraq.

The most widespread form of hate crime is against gays and lesbians, who suffer more serious psychological effects from it than they do from other types of criminal injury. Of nearly 2,000 gays and lesbians surveyed in Sacramento, California, roughly one fifth of the women and one fourth of the men reported being the victim of a hate crime since age 16. Within the past 5 years, 1 woman in 8 and 1 man in 6 had been victimized. More than half the respondents reported antigay verbal threats and harassment in the year before the survey (APA, 1998).

Human Rights Watch (2001) indicates that there are media and research reports that gay, lesbian, bisexual, and transgender (GLBT) individuals experience high levels of antigay harassment, abuse, and violence. *Transgender* refers to those individuals who are male or female but regard themselves as actually being of the opposite gender. These reports may lead people to believe that only GLBT people experience antigay harassment, but adolescents targeted for harassment in public schools are often incorrectly assumed to be homosexual. In fact, of the 5% of a school population in Seattle (Seattle Youth Risk Survey Results, 1995) who experienced antigay harassment, only 20% of the students were actually gay, demonstrating how homophobic behavior can affect even heterosexual adolescents.

SAMSHA (2001), a branch of National Institute of Mental Health, writes, "Gay, lesbian, and bisexual youth experience significantly more violence-related behaviors at school and have higher rates of suicide attempts" (p. 1). The report continues, "Active homosexual and bisexual adolescents had higher rates of suicide attempts in the past year (27%) compared to youth with only heterosexual experience (15%). Students with same-sex experience were significantly more likely to be threatened with a weapon, to have property stolen or deliberately damaged, and to not go to school because of feeling unsafe" (p. 1). Bidstrup (2000) describes the harm done by homophobia:

> There are the obvious murders inspired by hatred. In the U.S., they number in the dozens every year. But there are other ways in which homophobia kills. There are countless suicides every year by gay men and lesbians, particularly youth, which mental health professionals tell us are not the direct result of the victim's homosexuality, but is actually the result of how the homosexual is treated by society. When one lives with rejection day after day, and society discounts one's value constantly, it is difficult to maintain perspective and realize that the problem is *others'* perceptions, not one's own, which is why gay youth commit suicide at a rate of about seven times that of straight youth. Yet it is surprising how often homophobes actually try to prevent intervention by teachers in the schools!

According to Elizur and Ziv (2001), GLBT youth are at much greater risk than the general population of youth for "major depressions, generalized anxiety disorders, conduct disorders, substance abuse and dependence, suicidal behaviors, sexual risk-taking, and poor general health maintenance" (p. 125). The authors indicate that estimates of suicide attempts, for example, are far above adolescent norms, ranging from 30% to 42%.

Theuninck (2000) describes two primary sources of stress in the lives of GLBT individuals. External stressors include events that are largely independent of a person's perception of them, such as physical and verbal insults and abuse. Internal stressors include internalized homophobia and the perception of a society that discriminates against gay people. Through internalized homophobia, Theuninck suggests that some GLBT individuals come to believe that homosexuality is illegitimate, a sickness, a moral weakness, a defect, or a deformation of self. This belief may lead to intense self-loathing, according to the author. Theuninck also believes that because of stigma, people come to fear that their sexuality will become known and that the ever-present possibility of being attacked or discriminated against in the course of daily life will increase.

Laws Governing Discrimination

There are a number of state and federal laws that attempt to protect citizens from acts of discrimination. The primary federal laws are the following:

- Title VII of the Civil Rights Act of 1964 (Title VII), which prohibits employment discrimination based on race, color, religion, sex, or national origin;
- the Equal Pay Act of 1963 (EPA), which protects men and women who perform substantially equal work in the same establishment from sex-based wage discrimination;
- the Age Discrimination in Employment Act of 1967 (ADEA), which protects individuals who are 40 years of age or older;
- Title I and Title V of the Americans with Disabilities Act of 1990 (ADA), which prohibit employment discrimination against qualified individuals with disabilities in the private sector, and in state and local governments;
- Sections 501 and 505 of the Rehabilitation Act of 1973, which prohibit discrimination against qualified individuals with disabilities who work in the federal government; and
- the Civil Rights Act of 1991, which, among other things, provides monetary damages in cases of intentional employment discrimination.
- The U.S. Equal Employment Opportunity Commission (EEOC) enforces all of these laws. EEOC also provides oversight and coordination of all federal equal employment opportunity regulations, practices, and policies. (U.S. Department Equal Opportunity Employment Commission, 2004)

HAVE ANTIDISCRIMINATION LAWS WORKED?

Although a number of state and federal laws protecting Americans from discrimination in housing and education also exist and were passed because of perceived acts of discrimination based on bias against specific groups, questions arise about their effectiveness in stemming descrimination. Women were discriminated against in education for a very long time, requiring a number of laws to be passed, some of which have helped women achive equity with men and many that have not been helpful at all. Although almost 200,000 more women than men graduated from college in 2003 and did appreciably better academically (Conlin, 2003), women still earned much less than men for doing the same work. For example, female physicians earn 40% less than male physicians (Hojat et al., 2000). In 1990, women's average weekly pay was equal to approximately 77% of men's average weekly pay (Davidson & Cooper, 1992), but by 1997, Caucasian women earned approximately 75% of Caucasian men's weekly earnings, a 2% decrease over 1990 (Keaveny & Inderrieden, 2000). In the 2003 U.S. Census, the average salary for women was $30,724, compared to an average male salary of $40,668. Furthermore, a comparison of men and women with the same Census occupational codes found women in lower paying positions (Firestone, Harris, & Lambert, 1999). The salary disparity is so obvious for women that Hojat et al. (2000) found that even among first-year medical students across a 28-year period (1970–1997), women expected to earn 23% less than men, and these differences were fairly stable over time. Even when provided with current salary information, women continued to estimate lower starting salaries for themselves than men (Martin, 1989). One of the problems with discrimination that laws can't erase is that the victims sometimes accept discriminatory practices because they don't believe that it can or will improve.

Much more needs to be done to deal with inequity in the lives of groups that are typically discriminated against: women, the disabled, older adults, the less educated, racial and religious minorities, and the socially and economically disadvantaged. Social workers are often employed in organizations that help change laws and then do follow-ups to see if those laws have worked. Social workers are employed as policy analysts, as aides to state and federal legislators, as independent researchers, as administrators in programs designed to help at-risk populations, as politicians, and as community organizers, where we act as change agents advocating for groups at risk of discrimination. Much of our work is done with individuals and their families. Social work is committed to knowledgeable, respectful, and effective practice with culturally diverse people. We call this *culturally* or *ethnically sensitive* practice.

Ethnically Sensitive Social Work Practice

This section is about social work practice with clients whose diverse backgrounds make it particularly important to recognize that their cultural, racial, and gender differences need to be recognized and valued by the social worker. I've chosen one group to discuss in this section, African Americans (for ethnically sensitive social work practice with Asian and Latino clients, refer to the discussions on immigration in Chapter 15).

People sometimes complain that we've become too politically correct in America and that talking about differences ignores the fact that we're all Americans with only slight differences between us. I wish that were the case. If it were, we'd never have to talk about ethnically sensitive practice again. All clients would live their lives as well-accepted members of society and we would never have to deal with the sting of racism. Were that only so. When I was growing up in a small town in North Dakota immediately after we discovered that 6 million Jewish people had died in the German death camps, some of them members of my extended family, don't think it didn't hurt to go to school and have kids I'd grown up with, who had played at my house, ask if we drank the blood of our dead or buried them on top of one another. Where did they get those ideas, anyway? The word *kike* hurts as much now as it did then, and being told that someone will "Jew" me down, meaning they'll get a better price because Jews are supposedly cheap and always haggle, hurts very much. I thought then and still think that Jewish people are the most generous on earth. Racial, religious, ethnic, and gender slurs still exist, and it hurts a gay person to be called a *fag* or an African American person to be called a *nigger* as much as it hurts a Jewish person to be called a *kike.* So, no—America, wonderful place that it is, still has a problem with the way people out of the mainstream are treated. As long as that exists, we absolutely do need ethnically sensitive practice.

Ethnically sensitive practice is social work practice that (a) is sensitive to cultural, racial, ethnic, gender, and class differences; (b) treats all people with respect and dignity; (c) makes a conscious effort never to use stereotypes of people or personal biases in the helping process; (d) tries to find out as much about the person's unique qualities as possible; and (e) always views people in the most positive, accepting, and optimistic ways possible.

Ethnically Sensitive Practice With African American Clients

RACIAL PROFILING

A number of studies have examined the relationship between racial bias and psychiatric diagnoses. Laszloffy and Hardy (2000), found that a high number of African American patients were misdiagnosed as schizophrenic, a finding the authors also note in studies of Latino patients. According to the authors, even though the symptoms were the same, African American and Latino patients were often diagnosed as schizophrenic whereas white patients were almost always correctly diagnosed with less serious emotional problems (Garretson, 1993; Rogler & Magaldy, 1987; Solomon, 1992). Laszloffy and Hardy (2000) believe that underlying the misdiagnosis is a "subtle, unintentional racism" (p. 35). In defining *racism*, the authors write that "all expressions of racism are rooted in an ideology of racial superiority/inferiority that assumes some racial groups are superior to others, and therefore deserve preferential treatment" (p. 35), a definition that makes unintentional or subtle racism difficult to imagine.

Flaherty and Meagher (1980) found that among African American and white male schizophrenic inpatients who were diagnosed as schizophrenic, "African American patients spent less time in the hospital, obtained lower privilege levels, were given more medications, and were less likely to receive recreation therapy and occupational therapy. Seclusion and restraints were more likely to be used with black patients" (p. 679).

In a report on the importance of ethnically sensitive practice in the mental health field, the U.S. Surgeon General (Satcher, 2001) writes that "while not the sole determinants, cultural and social influences do play important roles in mental health, mental illness and service use, when added to biological, psychological and environmental factors" (p. 1). In trying to understand barriers to treatment that affect ethnic and racial minorities, the Surgeon General says that the mental health system often creates impediments that lead to distrust and fear of treatment and stop racial and ethnic minorities from seeking and receiving needed services. Importantly, the Surgeon General adds that "mental health care disparities may also stem from minorities' historical and present day struggles with racism and discrimination, which affect their mental health and contribute to their lower economic, social, and political status" (Satcher, 2001, p. 1). In an earlier report on mental health, the Surgeon General (Satcher, 1999) wrote that "mental illness is at least as prevalent among racial and ethnic minorities as in the majority white population. Yet many racial and ethnic minority group members find the organized mental health system to be uninformed about cultural context and, thus, unresponsive and/or irrelevant" (p. 4).

Whaley (2001) is concerned that Caucasian clinicians often see African Americans as having paranoid symptoms that are more fundamentally a cultural distrust of Caucasians because of historical experiences with racism. He believes that helping professionals discount the negative impact of racism and make judgments about clients suggesting that they are more disturbed than they really are. Whaley argues that cultural stereotyping by clinicians who fail to understand the impact of racism leads to "more severe diagnoses and restrictive interventions" (p. 558).

Ethnically Sensitive Practice Guidelines With African American Clients

In supporting the need for cultural and racial sensitivity, Pena, Bland, Shervington, Rice, and Foulks (2000) write that "in work with African-American patients, the therapist's skill in recognizing when problems do or do not revolve around the condition of being black could have serious implications for the acceptability of treatment" (p. 14). The authors believe that helping professionals with limited awareness of the significance of race may experience problems in "listening empathically" and actually understanding client conflicts that are directly related to race.

Franklin (1992) believes that all therapy must recognize the invisible factor of racism, which provides messages from childhood that black males "lack value and worth and deny Black males full access to life's amenities and opportunities" (p. 353). Franklin also states that the African

American male's sense of invisibility damages self-esteem because of constant messages that he is unacceptable and of little worth:

> Constant assaults on his self-esteem lead, in turn, to feelings of anger and internalized rage. To cope with these indignities, African American men devise various strategies and behaviors [including] immobilization, chronic indignation, acquiescence, depression, suicide or homicide, and/or internalized rage. (p. 353)

To deal with these complex issues, Franklin (1992) suggests that helping professionals must go slowly with black males, allowing them to gradually develop trust. He also suggests that therapists must keep in mind the need to see black male clients in a positive way by approaching them with respect and positive reinforcement. Insights into the client's behavior should be approached gently and should not appear magical or outrageous, but should convey "knowledge, understanding, and empathy, all of which will strengthen the client's sense of trust in the therapist's humanity and competence" (p. 354).

Williams (1992) provides the following guidelines for effective work with black men:

Confronting negative and acknowledging positive behaviors. This guideline suggests that black males must be recognized for their many strengths. Although distorted or negative behavior needs to be confronted, it must be remembered that the client is doing well in many aspects of his life, so the positive behavior must be considered when confronting the negative behavior.

The influence of labels. Williams notes that African American men want to see themselves as "partners in treatment." They resent labels that suggest pathology because labels send up signals to black men who have already had to deal with labels that subtly or overtly suggest racism.

Addressing sexism and racism. Williams believes that black men are particularly sensitive to sexist notions that berate or bash men, and they are likely to increase violence. We must be particularly careful not to generalize male behavior and must be aware that black men are very sensitive to racist notions that may include negative attitudes toward black men.

Cultural congruence. Williams suggests that we need to value the black experience and approach black men with respect, concern, and awareness of the many unique factors that create tension in the lives of black men.

Working with the black community. Williams argues that as important as treatment is, it is equally important to work with black institutions, including the church and the family unit, to prevent and treat abuse. Black institutions are particularly powerful in the lives of black males, and they can be used effectively to deal with domestic violence.

Poussaint (1993, pp. 88–89) suggests the following guidelines for working with African American clients: (a) the importance of acknowledging sexist behaviors, including lack of respect for women and the need for psychological and physical dominance, and acknowledging the reverse sexism of viewing black men as losers; (b) the need to explore the reasons for competitive feelings toward one another and making certain to avoid one-upmanship; (c) the need to analyze attitudes toward interracial romance and, painful though the subject might be, understand that everyone has a right to select his or her own mate; (d) the need to be more empathic toward shared concerns about racial discrimination affecting both black men and women; (e) the ability to listen to one another and hear mutual concerns about life; (f) the importance of emphasizing the positive qualities of blacks and identifying black couples who model positive behaviors that black men and women may emulate; (g) the need to control anger, put-downs, and verbal and psychological abuse; (h) the need to treat one another with respect and dignity; and (i) the avoidance of using sex and money to manipulate or control partners.

Lawson and Sharpe (2000) propose similar guidelines for helping African American men following a divorce or, more broadly, with a range of social and emotional problems. The authors propose a culturally sensitive practice that does the following:

1. Promotes a culturally competent relationship in which clinicians need to be aware of the discrimination and economic inequities that divorced black men face.

2. Develops compassion and awareness for the emotional issues that African American men may not openly show but which are deeply felt feelings of grief over the loss of a relationship. This also suggests screening for symptoms of depression and anger.

3. Respects the ambivalence African American men feel for the helping process and remembers the many past and present examples of how badly black men have been treated by the medical and psychiatric communities.

4. Encourages alternative approaches to practice that utilize spirituality, family, support networks, and client strengths.

5. Promotes community education and encourages public concern for the vitality of the black family and for black men.

6. Provides services in alternative locations, including churches, employment benefits programs, sports arenas, and community health centers.

7. Utilizes self-help groups for the purpose of mutual support and acceptance by other black men experiencing divorce.

8. Influences social policy changes by training more culturally competent practitioners who are sensitive to the needs and concerns of black men.

9. Works to encourage legislation that permits flexible property division, child custody, and economic support policies.

A Social Worker Helps an African American Man Reunite With His Father

I had a wonderful African American student who is now a close friend. Art and I play racquetball together and work out in the gym when I need help keeping in shape, which seems to be always. Art is a former football player and in such great shape that he exudes health.

Some years ago, Art took a course from me in crisis intervention. He was testing the waters to further his career, not sure if he wanted to remain in education or if the larger arenas of life (such as public administration, social work, and policy work) were more suited to him.

As is my practice whenever I teach a class, I asked for a volunteer to role play the type of therapy I do, which is very active. Arthur asked to role-play a problem he was having with his father. In Arthur's opinion, his father was an alcoholic. I did what one would normally do: I asked Arthur on what he based this judgment. He said, "My father drinks all day long and I'm afraid that he won't be alive when I need him the most."

"All day long?" I asked.

"Pretty much," Arthur responded.

"How many drinks would that be?" I wondered.

Arthur shook his head. "I really don't know," he replied. "I never counted."

"But you're sure that he's an alcoholic," I said.

Arthur just sat and stared at me. No one had ever questioned his view of his father. It just was a fact in his mind that his father was an alcoholic. I asked Arthur to role play a confrontation with his dad. He was to tell his dad that he worried about his drinking and that he was afraid that his father wouldn't be alive when Arthur needed him most. Mind you, this was all done in front of a class of 25 other students. In responding to the confrontation, Arthur said the following:

"Dad, I worry that you drink too much and that your health will suffer. I want you to be part of my life, to see me when I'm successful in life, to see my kids grow up. I don't want you to die early like so many black men."

In my response (in the role of Arthur's father), I took a chance and said, "Arthur, where did you get this idea that I drink too much? I worked for 40 years. I went to work every

(Continued)

(Continued)

day. I provided for everyone. We had a good life. I'm retired now, Arthur, and I have a nip or two with the boys, with my friends, does that make me an alcoholic?"

Art's head snapped back, literally. He looked at me for a long time and then said, "But that's what Mom says about you, that you drink too much."

In the role play, I leaned over and touched Arthur on the arm and then said, "But Arthur, your mother is a very religious woman. Any drink is too much for her, you know that. Why shouldn't I enjoy these retired years and have some fun? And if I take a drink or two, so what? I'm a healthy man, I've worked hard, and I'm not irresponsible. Aren't I entitled to enjoy these years after working so hard? You have your dad alive and well. There aren't many black sons who can say that. Why not enjoy me instead of criticizing me?"

Tears were forming in Arthur's eyes. Like most men who have been given permission to see their fathers as compatriots and friends, he was overwhelmed by the experience. It was liberating not to carry the burden of a father who had somehow failed his son.

When Arthur composed himself, he turned to the class and said that no one had ever given him the opportunity to talk about these things. He thought it wasn't masculine for black men to discuss problems. Now he knew how wrong that was and that it was clear he wanted to be in social work, if this was what we did to help people. "How many black boys and men would benefit from a similar discussion?" he asked the class. And then he answered his own question. "All of them," he said. "All of us."

Six months after that initial interaction with Arthur, he asked me out for dinner to a nearby Cajun restaurant to meet his father. That night stands out in my mind. It was such great fun because, much as I had guessed, his father was a man of great joy. A cut-up and a storyteller, charismatic and generous, his father reminded me of my own, now passed away. I never told this to Arthur, but that night was like being with my own father at a point in time when I would have appreciated him all the more for his ability to make an ordinary event so much fun.

Arthur has gone back to Louisiana with his father to meet relatives and discover his roots. He sees his father often, and they share in the ways adult men can share when the conflicts between them have been lessened. Arthur now sees his father as a man with flaws and with goodness; a complex person, too complicated to easily categorize. And it's been freeing for him. In addition, Arthur was admitted to the MSW program, won many awards, and is currently deciding where to earn his doctorate. Because I mentor him, I know it will be somewhere very good, and his career will be very successful.

One afternoon after seeing a movie, Arthur and I were having coffee and he reminded me of the time in class when he was able to work out those issues about his dad. He used the words of an old spiritual to describe how he felt: "Free at last. Lord Almighty, thank God, I'm free at last."

You Be the Social Worker

Jeff Langer is a 19-year-old unemployed Caucasian high school dropout. He lives with his parents in an uneasy alliance and spends much of his time with friends who abuse alcohol and drugs. Jeff hates gays and lesbians. When he was 6 years old, he was sexually abused by an older male relative. He never told anyone about the abuse, but he has developed an overwhelming level of homophobia that startles his family and even worries his friends. He sees homosexuality everywhere and frequently accuses straight people of being gay. The accusations have resulted in fights, with Jeff usually getting the worst end of the fight. He is filled with a rage against gay people that has a toxic effect on his life.

Because Jeff is physically weak and can only show his homophobia when he is high on drugs or alcohol, he has taken to parking his car outside of known gay or lesbian bars and clubs. He waits until someone comes out of the club or bar who appears to be drunk and defenseless. He then gets out of the car with a baseball bat and beats the person to the point of unconsciousness. He has done this six times and has gotten away with all six beatings. When he is done with the beatings, he feels empty and cries. What he's done is wrong and he knows it, but his remorse and calmness last only weeks before they are displaced with his growing rage toward gay people.

In a final act of extreme anger, Jeff beat and killed an elderly man who left a bar frequented by gay men after most of the other patrons had left. It turned out to be a janitor who was straight. When Jeff read about it in the paper the next day, he cried in his room, went to the bathroom, and slit his wrists. Although he lost a considerable amount of blood, his parents found him and his life was saved in the emergency room by, ironically enough, a gay doctor. Jeff is in jail now waiting for his trial. His fellow inmates have decided to have sex with him as much as they can, and he has been anally raped eight times. Because he is on a suicide watch, he is unable to kill himself. The guards are aloof during the rapes, thinking he's getting what he deserves.

Discussion of the Case

Like most hate crimes, there is usually a reason, but homophobia is so rampant in our society that it exists, like racism, often without logical explanations. It's a shame that Jeff wasn't able to discuss his molestation with someone and obtain appropriate help. The inability to resolve the emotions related to the experience have surely created deep feelings of humiliation and anger, which are now directed against all gay people.

Jeff was sentenced to 25 years to life after a court trial attended by many gay people. The audience in the trial brought signs into the courtroom, which humiliated Jeff. They called him a "Closet Queer," suggesting that Jeff's anger toward gays was really a form of denial of his own leanings toward homosexuality. Secretly, Jeff had found himself attracted to men and wouldn't admit it, but in prison, Jeff has come out of the closet. He is the "wife" of one of the prisoners who, in exchange for sex, protects Jeff from some of the more brutal inmates.

In a treatment group for perpetrators of hate crimes that Jeff is required to attend, Jeff has admitted to being attracted to men but denies that he's gay. He says that his relationship in prison is based upon the need to survive but that he doesn't enjoy the sexual parts of the relationship. The other men snicker and laugh at

(Continued)

(Continued)

Jeff. They've been involved in similar hate crimes. One man hates black people but admits to having had a secret love affair with a black woman before going to jail. All the men know that their hate is ambivalent and that their behavior is inconsistent. Most of the men have had serious physical and sexual abuse in childhood. As one inmate told his therapist, "You got to hate somebody for what your pa did to you. I hate niggers. I blame them for everything. My pa drunk hisself to death, but there are plenty of niggers out there to hate, and I hate every one. Every time I think about my pa and what he done to me, I hate another nigger worse. They never did nothin' to me that I can think of but when I was a kid, I started seeing that they were the reason my pa beat me and done the other stuff to me. He lost his job to a nigger so I started feeling that it was their fault that he beat me. I got so that I can't be around them at all, I hate them so much."

This tendency to displace anger onto others is very common among perpetrators of hate crimes and is one of the best explanations we have for anti-Semitism and other historical forms of mass bigotry. Unfortunately, we live in a society of bigotry where even "good" people tell jokes about minorities and gays. It forms a backdrop for hate crimes because it frees those who act out their anger to do terrible things to others. It is a situation with great potential for harm to all too many people.

Questions

1. People who are molested as children suffer severe traumas because of the experience, but few of them develop the degree of rage shown by Jeff. What other factors might have contributed to Jeff's severe homophobia?

2. Jeff's anguish at being sexually attracted to men seems to be a key reason for his homophobia. Had he been helped to share these feelings with a social worker, could it have saved the lives of the people he attacked, or do you think men are so defensive about hidden attractions to other men that he would have been unable to discuss it?

3. Are there groups of people to whom you feel superior? Identify who they are and explain your reasons for feeling superior. Can you work through those feelings without old beliefs and stereotypes entering into your thinking?

4. For a free country, we certainly have many misconceptions about a range of people because of their race, religion, ethnic origin, and gender. Why do you think that's so when all of us interact and know many groups of people who represent diversity in America?

5. Do you think there comes a time when people are so assimilated that they no longer think of themselves as being African Americans or Latinos or Asian Americans but just Americans? If that's the case, would we even need to practice social work in an ethnically sensitive way?

Summary

This chapter discusses the problems experienced by diverse groups in America including unequal salaries, discrimination, and insensitivity when people need personal help. Ethnically sensitive practice is described using African American clients. The issue of whether ethnically sensitive practice is really needed, given the fact that we are all American, is discussed, and concerns about ongoing racial and gender discrimination is provided as an answer.

Questions to Determine Your Frame of Reference

1. What can we do as a nation to reduce the obvious discrimination against certain diverse groups of people?

2. Ethnically sensitive practice sounds ideal for all clients. Why even call it ethnically sensitive practice rather than practice that is sensitive to all differences in people?

3. There are many reasons why certain groups earn higher salaries than others. Some women may not want to put salary ahead of the needs of their children. Some minorities might value family life over demanding and intrusive work. Can you think of other reasons for wage differences, and do you accept them as good reasons?

4. If you examine your feelings about a number of minority groups, can you identify areas of prejudice? What are they?

5. Do you think you've had privileges many minorities your age have never had, or do you believe you are on par with other people and that focusing on differences just makes us all the more unable to get along? Do we make too much of social, ethnic, religious, and gender differences?

Internet Sources

The Centers for Disease Control and Prevention (2006) reports on the prevalence of HIV/AIDS among African Americans and what we might to do lower the rate of the disease. Next, the U.S. Census Bureau (2003) provides insight into black history, and Lewis (2005) discusses hate crime statistics. Finally, Bistrup (2005) examines homophobia and its irrational premises.

1. Centers for Disease Control and Prevention. (2006). *HIV/AIDS among African Americans.* Retrieved from http://www.cdc.gov/hiv/topics/aa/index.htm

2. U.S. Census Bureau. (2003, February). *African American history month.* Retrieved from www.census.gov/Press-Release/www/2003/cb03ff01.html

3. Lewis, T. (2005, December). *FBI releases 2004 hate crime statistics.* Retrieved January 16, 2006, from http://www.civilrights.org/issues/hate/details.cfm?id=38513

4. Bidstrup, S. (2005). *Homophobia: The fear behind the hatred.* Retrieved from bidstrup.com/phobia.htm

The Role of Social Work and Social Welfare Organizations in Developing Healthy Community Life

20

The community stagnates without the impulse of the individual.
The impulse dies away without the sympathy of the community.

—William James (1842–1910)

S ocial work has a long history of creating healthy community life. Many of us in social work believe that healthy communities create emotionally and physically healthier people. Although much has been made of the condition of American communities with their high rates of traffic congestion, pollution, crime, and lack of adequate transportation, the Chicago heat wave of 1995 is a graphic example of how unhealthy community life leads to disaster. In the 1995 heat wave, 739 older and less mobile people died in Chicago. One of the main reasons for this very large death rate was that many elderly and less mobile people were afraid to leave their homes and be exposed to environments that they felt were even more dangerous and unsafe (Gladwell, 2002). In explaining why she was afraid to leave her home even though she was literally dying of heat prostration, one elderly lady said, "Chicago is just a shooting gallery" (Gladwell, 2002, p. 80). Furthermore, Chicago had no emergency system for helping elderly and less mobile people; so many people died during the heat wave that callers to 911 were put on hold. . . . The police took bodies to the Cook County Medical Examiner's office, and a line of cruisers stretched outside the building. The morgue ran out of bays in which to put the bodies. The owner of a local meat-packing firm offered the city his refrigerated trucks to help store the bodies. The first set wasn't enough. He sent a second set. It wasn't enough. (Gladwell, 2002, p. 76)

Healthy Community Life

Saleebey (1996) believes that "in communities that amplify individual resilience, there is awareness, recognition, and use of the assets of most members of the community" (p. 298). In these healthy communities, informal networks of people provide "succor, instruction, support, and encouragement" (p. 298). Saleebey challenges helping professionals to work with communities because so many of the problems common to social work clients can be avoided. "In communities that provide protection and minimize risk," he writes, "there are many opportunities to participate, to make significant contributions to the moral and civic life of the community, and to take on the role of full-fledged citizen" (p. 298).

To demonstrate how we are all at risk when communities develop problems, Putnam (2000) reminds us that violence exists in even the most affluent communities: "The shooting sprees that affected schools in suburban and rural communities as the twentieth century ended are a reminder that as the breakdown of communities continues in more privileged settings, affluence and education are insufficient to prevent collective tragedy" (p. 318).

What is a healthy community? Kesler (2000) provides a model of communities that defines social connectedness, civic virtue, and the social responsibilities of its members. In healthy communities, there is "a sophisticated, integrative, and interconnected vision of flourishing of the individual and the human collective in an environmental setting" (p. 272) that involves all sectors of the community, including the disenfranchised. People in healthy communities connect intimately with one another and are aware of special issues that need to be addressed with sensitivity and creativity. In healthy communities, a dialogue exists among people to help formulate public policy agendas that function with consensus among all community groups and political persuasions. Healthy communities are caring, mature, and aware; seek alliances with other community-based movements; and "encourage all concerned to rise to higher integrative levels of thinking, discourse, research, policies, programs, institutions, and processes, so that they might truly begin to transform their lives, their communities, and the greater society" (p. 271).

Writing about the strengths perspective and the importance of healthy community life, Saleebey (1996) suggests the following:

> Membership [in a community] means that people need to be citizens—responsible and valued members in a viable group or community. To be without membership is to be alienated, and to be at risk of marginalization and oppression, the enemies of civic and moral strength (Walzer, 1983). As people begin to realize and use their assets and abilities, collectively and individually, as they begin to discover the pride in having survived and overcome their difficulties, more and more of their capacities come into the work and play of daily life. These build on each other exponentially, reflecting a kind of synergy. (p. 297)

Robert and Li (2001) believe that although most researchers think there is a relationship between income and health, research actually suggests a limited relationship between the two variables. Rather, there seems to be a relationship between community levels of health and individual health. Lawton (1977) suggests that older adults may experience communities as their primary source of support, recreation, and stimulation, unlike younger adults, who may find it easier to move about in search of support and recreation. Lawton and Nahemow (1973) believe that positive community environments are particularly important for older adults with emotional, physical, or cognitive problems. The need for healthy and vital communities is particularly relevant to older adults with health problems that limit their mobility.

Robert and Li (2001) suggest three indicators of healthy communities that relate directly to individual health: (a) a positive physical environment that provides an absence of noise, traffic, inadequate lighting, and other features of a community that may lead to functional loss in older adults; (b) a positive social environment that includes an absence of crime, the ability to find safe environments to walk in, and easy access to shopping; and (c) a rich service environment that includes simple and safe access to rapid and inexpensive transportation, the availability of senior centers, and easy access to meal sites.

In studying the impact of natural disasters on a population of elderly adults demonstrating predisaster signs of depression, Tyler and Hoyt (2000) report that elderly adults indicating high levels of social support (e.g., friendships, concerned neighbors, church involvement, and volunteer activity) had lower levels of depression before and after a natural disaster. They also report that "older people with little or no social support, perhaps due to death of a spouse and/or loss of friends, may have a more difficult time dealing with life changes and, as a result, are particularly vulnerable to increases in depression" (p. 155).

In an early attempt to define healthy community life, Lindeman (1921, p. 1) said that an ideal community should furnish people security of life and property through an efficient government, economic security through productive industries, physical well-being through public health agencies, constructive use of leisure time though public health agencies, a system of morality supported by the organized community, intellectually stimulating education through free and public institutions available to everyone, free expression of ideas by everyone in the community, free information and public forums to discuss issues, democratic discussion involving the entire community to express ideas and see that those ideas have been applied, and spiritual and religious associations that show concern for issues related to the meaning of life.

Writing about the purest form of community outreach, the natural helpers who define the most elegant aspects of social responsibility, Waller and Patterson (2002) note that "informal helping sustains and extends resiliency in individuals and communities . . . and [is] consistent with the growing body of research suggesting that informal social support buffers the effects of stress on adaptational outcomes" (p. 80). In their study of natural helping in a Navajo community, Waller and Patterson interviewed community members who were noted for their willingness to help others. One of the women whom they interviewed defined the sense of social responsibility we hope would exist in most Americans. In explaining her desire to reach out to others, she said,

> Giving peace to somebody, calming somebody down. It's just something that I . . . it's just an intuition. And throughout my whole life, with my father and mother doing that. . . . So I think it's just something that comes, and if I know how to do it then I will offer IT . . . out in something good and knowing that somewhere along the line you will get rewarded with something . . . and I receive the reward back in that way, but not expecting or looking for it. (p. 78)

In another example of social connectedness and reaching out, a 30-year-old female helper describes helping her 27-year-old sister-in-law:

> She had been left by her husband . . . so she had no place to go and she brought her kids here. And on top of that she had a handicapped child. She was carrying more load than we were so we accepted her in and we did our part. We would help her pull some of the load she was carrying. We spent the whole winter with her and about half of the summer. I think we did pretty good with that. And we really gave her a lot of strength to be a single parent. As of last year she graduated and she's been promoted to a higher paying job. So she got what she wanted and it makes us feel proud. A lot of times it's just like a teamwork that keeps us together, working together and understanding each other. Then we know that we have to pull together and just challenge what we're facing. (Waller & Patterson, 2002, p. 77)

What Happens When Communities Are Unhealthy?

AIR POLLUTION

According to the National Institutes of Health (2004), children who live in polluted communities are five times more likely to have less than 80% of the lung function expected for their age, and pollutants from cars and fossil fuels burned to produce electricity reduce lung development and limit breathing capacity for a lifetime. As an example of how pollution affects children, when children with lower lung function have a cold, they often develop more severe lung symptoms or wheezing, and the symptoms last longer than in children whose lung functioning is normal.

By using a rating that includes a combination of the five most toxic and dangerous air pollutants, AIRNow (2004), a cross-governmental series of agencies concerned with issues of pollution, allows you to check the air quality in any location in America you wish. In the most polluted community in America, Los Angeles (my favorite because I live there), 50% of the summer days had pollution readings of 100–150, serious enough to affect children with asthma. How many children have asthma in this city? An astonishing 224,657. In the third most polluted city, New York City (which has a much larger population), 188,596 children suffer from asthma. Riverside and San Bernardino Counties, also in California and the second most polluted areas in America, experienced pollution readings between 100 and 150 on 70% of all summer days.

InfoTable 20.1	Understanding Air Quality: The Air Quality Index (AQI)

- Good: The AQI value for your community is between 0 and 50. Air quality is considered satisfactory, and air pollution poses little or no risk.
- Moderate: The AQI for your community is between 51 and 100. Air quality is acceptable; however, for some pollutants there may be a moderate health concern for a very small number of people. For example, people who are unusually sensitive to ozone may experience respiratory symptoms.
- Unhealthy for Sensitive Groups: When AQI values are between 101 and 150, members of sensitive groups may experience health effects. This means they are likely to be affected at lower levels than the general public. For example, people with lung disease are at greater risk from exposure to ozone, while people with either lung disease or heart disease are at greater risk from exposure to particle pollution. The general public is not likely to be affected when the AQI is in this range.
- Unhealthy: Everyone may begin to experience health effects when AQI values are between 151 and 200. Members of sensitive groups may experience more serious health effects.
- Very Unhealthy: AQI values between 201 and 300 trigger a health alert, meaning everyone may experience more serious health effects.
- Hazardous: AQI values over 300 trigger health warnings of emergency conditions. The entire population is more likely to be affected. (AIRNow, 2004)

TRAFFIC CONGESTION

According to the Federal Highway Administration Office of Operations (2002), the following data indicate how serious a problem traffic congestion has become in our communities, nationwide:

1. Congestion results in 5.7 billion hours of delay annually in the United States.

2. Of our daily travel, 32% occurs within congested conditions—and the trend continues to climb. In small urban areas alone with less than 500,000 people, congested travel increased 300% between 1982 and 1997.

3. The annual delay from traffic congestion in America per person was 36 hours per year. The delay is 41 hours per person per year in cities with more than 3 million people. In the metropolitan area with the worst delay problems, Los Angeles, the delay was 56 hours per person per year and, living in that city, I can tell you it's much worse than that! Between 1982 and 1999, the annual delay per person in the 68 metropolitan areas increased at a compound rate of 7% (from 11 to 36 hours).

4. The individual cost of congestion exceeded $900 per driver in 1997, resulting in more than $72 billion in lost wages and wasted fuel. Given the much higher prices for gas, that amount increases to more than $3,000 per driver in lost wages and wasted fuel.

5. If you've experienced road rage because of traffic congestion (there were almost 30 shootings on Los Angeles freeways in the summer of 2005, resulting in 5 deaths), you know that traffic congestion increases assaults, dangerous driving, heart attacks, and the serious consequences of ongoing stress. My tennis partner in the eastern part of the L.A. metropolitan area told me that he had to leave his home at 3:00 a.m. to make a 7:00 a.m. meeting only 50 miles away because of traffic congestion. He almost missed the meeting until he realized that his hybrid car allowed him to use the carpool lanes reserved for those with two or more people in the car.

The same report called for state and local partnerships and leadership to establish, enhance, and nurture strategies to lessen the impact of congestion. Partnerships need to be formed with the right people at the table, including representatives from both transportation and public safety communities. But even when partnerships are formed, it's interesting how difficult it is to make public officials responsive. A good friend of mine lives in the quiet and lovely suburb of Claremont, about 30 miles east of downtown Los Angeles. A new highway was built near his home to decrease traffic congestion. Part of the highway is below ground but comes to ground level four blocks from his house, and the noise level is deafening. He has tried for 2 years to convince CalTrans, the public department charged with highway construction and maintenance, to rubberize the surface to reduce noise. Even though 4,500 people signed a petition to change the surface of the road and numerous meetings were held, many conciliatory with promises made to fix the problem, in the end, nothing was done and a civil lawsuit is in progress. It's not always easy to get change, but my friend is now deeply involved in community issues and realizes that a healthy community can become a troubled one without the constant involvement and awareness of its citizens.

VIOLENCE

Although violent crime has shown a significant decrease since the peak years of 1985 to 1993, homicide victims and offenders have been getting younger and, according to Zimring and Hawkins (1997), there is a trend toward an increase in the severity (if not the prevalence) of violence. Fagan (1997) says that absolute violence rates in America continue to increase, with violence ranging from everyday violence, such as youth and domestic violence, to the increased use of weapons that produce lethal results. Zimring and Hawkins (1997) conclude that crime is not the factor that sets America apart from other nations—it is the existence of lethal violence, especially a preference for crimes of "personal force and the willingness and ability to use guns" (p. 2).

Increases in violence have affected the way we often live our lives, with many Americans choosing to live in "safe havens" within otherwise dangerous communities where gates, guards, and limited access to outsiders provide the illusion of safety. Currie (1993) attributes much of the increase in violence to the weakening of traditional socializing institutions of the community—the family, the schools, and the churches—and to the lack of care and concern of citizens who often believe that the best way to deal with violence is either to run away from it and live in suburbia or to deny it by ignoring the evidence of violence in decaying and crime-ridden inner cities.

Although rates of violence have been decreasing across the country, gang violence is on the increase. Compton, California, an economically disadvantaged and primarily African American community of 95,000 in metropolitan Los Angeles, had 45 murders by July 2005, a rate that threatens the record of murders set in Compton in 1993 of 80 (*Los Angeles Times*, 2005, p. A1). A woman waiting for a bus at 2 p.m. was killed by crossfire from warring gangs. Not a day goes by that a similar story isn't reported. Although crime in Los Angeles is down from 10 years ago, minorities and the economically disadvantaged consider Los Angeles to be a shooting gallery.

The Tools of Community Change

The following professional responses are used when social workers are employed to help communities cope with dysfunctional problems affecting community life.

ADVOCACY

Advocacy is the help provided by social workers and others to assist individuals and groups with business, political, educational, and social service leaders and organizations to resolve issues of concern. One example of advocacy is an organization called Mothers & More (2004), whose goal is to recognize and support the critical social and economic work all mothers perform as primary caregivers. Mothers & More has three primary goals for its advocacy programs, which are achieved through lobbying efforts, public education, public relations, and private meetings with public and private leaders of large organizations:

- Broad acceptance that the work of caring for others is valuable and essential to families, communities, and society as a whole.
- Mothers, fathers, and others who care for their families, whether they work for pay, merit access to basic public and private protections from economic risk.
- Reshaping the workplaces so that mothers, fathers, and others who need to care for their families have more and better options for combining achievement on the job with a successful home life.

COMMUNITY ORGANIZATION

Walls (1994) notes that community organizing consists of following well-tested and successful techniques: protest, which includes rallies, marches, demonstrations, and boycotts; political action, which might include voter registration, lobbying, and electoral campaigns; mutual aid, such as co-ops and credit unions; organizational development, including house meetings and conventions; fundraising, door-to-door canvassing and phone banks; and media access through press conferences and publications. Writing about the history of community organization, Walls says that

> the label "community organizing" has been attached to a variety of activities drawing on disparate traditions and historical periods. The turn-of-the century settlement house movement, exemplified by Jane Addams's Hull House in Chicago, continues to influence social workers with its example of

neighborhood improvement and social uplift. Saul Alinsky was more attracted to the militant alternative modeled by the CIO industrial union drives and the radical neighborhood organizing of unemployed councils in the late 1930s. Tactics of nonviolent direct action were refined from the mid-1950s through the 1960s by the civil rights movement in the South, which, as sociologist Aldon Morris has shown, mobilized networks of local black churches, NAACP chapters, and black colleges—with assistance from such movement catalysts as the Highlander Center and the Fellowship for Reconciliation.

Rothman (in Brager & Specht, 1973, pp. 26–27) identified three distinct types of community organizing:

Locality development. This is used to achieve community building and includes a cross-section of the community. Social workers help enable the community to reach consensus through determining common interests. Developing leadership and educating participants are important aspects of the process.

Social action. This is a way of changing social institutional policies and the distribution of power. An example might be civil rights groups that attempt to gain social and economic equity for disenfranchised groups of people. They may use confrontational approaches that create antagonisms but are often effective. Saul Alinsky was a famous social activist in Chicago who used very unique techniques to help many diverse groups. When the city of Chicago was unresponsive to hiring people of color for positions they were qualified to perform, Alinsky threatened to occupy every bathroom stall and urinal in the Chicago airport, thereby causing a true crisis. Another time, Alinsky threatened to have a "bean in" before a concert performed by the Chicago Symphony; he would then give donated tickets to the people attending the event to cause what some have called a "gas in." These unique tactics of social activism should not be seen as frivolous because the problems encountered were very real and were allowed to continue because of an unresponsive city government.

Social planning. This is used by government and large public bureaucracies to rationally determine resource allocation. Social planning also uses technical methods, including research and systems analysis. Although social action is always exciting and may stimulate popular movements, by far the most frequently used means of community change is social planning because it is done on such a large scale and with so many governmental and private organizations.

The following case is an example of the serious problems that sometimes affect communities in America. Social workers are often hired to help identify the cause of community problems, develop helping solutions, supervise the helping process, and then evaluate the results. We call these social workers *community organizers*; their work is community organization and community development. Social workers who work with communities may be employed by public coalitions of concerned citizens, corporations concerned about community problems that affect the business climate, or the government trying to resolve problems that affect healthy community life.

A Community Develops a Youth Violence Prevention Program With Teeth

Parts of this case first appeared in my book on youth violence in children younger than age 12 (Glicken, 2004b, pp. 122–123).

Jamestown, a moderately sized city of 250,000 in the southeastern part of the country, had a serious outbreak of youth violence in the early 1990s when violence nationally was reaching a peak. Much of the violence was the result of two community problems: gangs and racial conflicts. The violence was becoming so significant that police officers were sent to local elementary and secondary schools to search lockers for guns and other weapons, something more common today but very controversial in Jamestown, a community that prided itself on good racial relations and civility. To complicate matters, the two community high schools were closed during the middle of the semester because of gang and racial violence. In one episode of violence, a lunchroom incident turned into a gang fight with hundreds of students involved. Damage to the school was over a million dollars.

Community leaders were brought together to discuss a way of resolving the problem, including leaders from the opposing racial groups involved in the disturbance. A local university social work professor with group leadership skills and a background in community organization was asked to help organize and run the meetings. At first, tensions were so high it didn't appear likely that anything would be resolved. Members of the group came to meetings with armed guards, and there were frequent "walkouts" when problems became too difficult to resolve. With patience, with much talk and with the help of the social work community organization specialist, the group began to devise a plan to calm tensions in Jamestown and to resolve youth violence. The plan was very comprehensive and included considerable time and money spent to correct the social inequities affecting the two major racial minority groups involved in much of the youth violence. There were promises that were kept of new jobs for minority adults and youth, and more access to better education. There were promises made and kept that a tight lid would be placed on potential sources of violence. A violence mediation team was organized and trained by the social work community organizer, whose purpose was to immediately deal with violence when it seemed likely to become a problem. The school system promised to quickly correct inequities in the quality of education received by the two minority groups. Individual families with problems of family violence and drug abuse were identified and the local child welfare agency sent social workers out to begin the long and difficult task of correcting these problems.

The police department agreed to a mandatory arrest policy for domestic violence and child abuse since both problems often cause violence in young child victims, and began enforcing the policy immediately. Everyone felt a sense of urgency to reopen the schools since youth crime was escalating; many children who were out of school began committing crime while their parents were at work.

Because gangs may exist as a way of venting racial tensions, the police force and its community relations department began a concerted effort to modify gang behavior. Meetings were held with gang members, agreements were reached, and trust began to develop. There was an agreement that gangs could exist but that illegal or violent behavior was intolerable. Facilities were provided for gang meetings. Suggestions were made for more socially helpful gang behaviors. Gang recruitment of new members at school was eliminated, and gang members agreed not to wear gang colors or write gang signs in and around schools. Schools agreed that bullying and intimidation were preludes to violence and began cooperating with the police to modify this behavior through treatment or, if that didn't work, through more formal involvement with the juvenile court. Uses of substances were considered intolerable. Stiff penalties were provided for anyone supplying minors with alcohol and drug laws were strictly enforced, particularly the selling of drugs near school grounds.

Social workers trained in the treatment of violence were hired by the school system with help from community funding to provide treatment to children and adolescents showing signs of potential violence. The social workers had the right to include parents in treatment sessions as a mandatory aspect of the child continuing in school. The school board issued a "No tolerance for violence policy" that included sanctions for bullying, intimidation of other students and school faculty and staff, and fighting. Conflict resolution experts were brought in to teach children and adolescents the essence of conflict management. Guidelines were sent to parents suggesting limits on watching violence on TV, video games, and in films, and suitable alternatives to violent programs were suggested.

The program began working and within a year, Jamestown had returned to a peaceful and cooperative, if not a more cautious, community. Once having experienced violence, the community was unwilling to become complacent and continues on with one of the most successful and comprehensive violence control programs in the country. Like too many American communities, violence rates are still much too high for any community to feel completely safe, but the upswing in youth violence has been reduced and today's violence is often the result of economic factors that leave young adult minority males out of work with little hope for the future. On that score, Jamestown has not fared well and like many communities with high youth and young adult unemployment, Jamestown has more than its share of preventable drug- and alcohol-related domestic violence, automobile accidents, and random violence.

A Dialogue: Individuals or Larger Issues? Where Should We Put Our Energies?

This is a distillation of discussions I've had throughout the years with colleagues who are very successful social work psychotherapists in private practice. They argue that it's difficult to help individuals and families and still have time to change the communities they live in.

Me (M):   You can't really change people without changing the environments they live in. Toxic environments with high crime rates, few job opportunities, the high availability of drugs, poor housing, low educational standards in schools, unsafe streets, and dysfunctional families—all of this makes any real gain in the emotional and social functioning of our clients very difficult. We should be putting our energies as social workers into improving life in neighborhoods, communities, and our society.

Colleague (C):   Isn't it enough that we become good social workers with individuals and their families and that we read and apply the clinical research, stay up to date on the latest findings, attend timely workshops and conferences, and do careful work? Don't people need the best help they can get to deal with their serious emotional problems? Community change isn't something I'm trained to do or, in fact, do very well. Shouldn't my time be spent doing what I do well?

M: Yes, but why not spend a few hours a week helping communities, working with your professional organizations, or advising community leaders on conditions that negatively affect your clients and offering your opinion about how those conditions can be improved?

C: I'd like to, but who has the time? I see 40 patients a week individually and run three groups. I work a 60-hour week as it is. Many of the hours I work are free, and many of the clients I see are really troubled. Whether the society contributes to their problems or not, someone has to be there for them. That's my contribution. I contribute my expertise in my individual work with clients and their families. Working with communities and organizations isn't something I do very well.

M: How can you say you're not good at working outside of clinical settings? You lead groups with clients who have serious problems. You get them to talk, to problem solve, and to move in positive directions. Why couldn't you do the same thing with community groups who want to improve the quality of the neighborhoods and cities they live in?

C: It's not the same thing. Community groups are made up of healthy people who don't need anyone to help them communicate. There are many nonprofessionals who can do that. They surely don't want a therapist because everyone would start wondering if the reason a therapist is leading the group is because they have emotional problems.

M: You work with the results of child abuse. Don't you think you have a responsibility to stop it?

C: Of course, but writing letters and being on committees doesn't stop it; helping troubled families stops it. That's what I do best, I help families. The abuse stops and it doesn't continue in future generations. Isn't that a major contribution?

M: Of course it is, but perhaps by having better institutions and a more proactive response by our child welfare organizations, we'd be able to do even better.

C: Maybe, but damage has been done, and even the best child welfare agency can't undo that damage just by making sure that child abuse is caught sooner and even prevented. There is serious psychological damage done to children by poor parental modeling and by adult verbal responses to children that are emotionally harmful. Who works with that? I do. That's my contribution.

M: Don't you think that telling people how bad behavior by adults has a negative effect on children would sensitize people to child abuse? Don't you think your expertise could prevent child abuse?

C: I don't know. What I *do* know is that I'm working myself into the ground and that a few more hours of community work will reduce my effectiveness with clients. I have a responsibility to my clients to stay fresh and not to get burned out. And I have a family that complains that they hardly ever see me. Where do my personal obligations get taken care of if I work even more hours?

M: I guess we have a fundamental disagreement. I believe you should take a few hours a week and use it for the work that needs to be done to make our community a better place to live. It shouldn't be an either/or choice. It should be an obligation of every helping professional to work toward creating healthy communities and societies. If we don't do that, who will?

C: Someone, I suppose, and I applaud your idealism, but to be honest, I'm happy doing what I do. I've gone to community meetings and to my professional organizations, and I find it a contentious and ineffective way of resolving problems. I vote for socially progressive candidates and donate my money to effective social organizations. I refer clients to the best places I can find for them to get help, and I write positive and supportive letters to clinicians and agencies that, in my judgment, do a good job. That, I think, is a socially responsible act by any clinician.

M: Your absence at important meetings, your lack of direct contact with community leadership, and your feelings about the social change process make you invisible. The more invisible we become in social work, the less our community leaders see our importance. As our significance dwindles, we lose political clout, which can affect clients when the services we offer are reduced.

C: My heavy workload would suggest that you're wrong. If anything, I'm busier than ever, and although services are being cut, people continue to seek help, and they look for the best help possible.

M: But at least you'll think about what I've said.

C: Absolutely.

You Be the Social Worker

1. You've read both arguments: my argument for helping people and changing the environments we live in and my colleague's argument that we just don't have the time or energy to do both. Which argument do you find more appealing, and why?

2. Isn't it enough to have people who are experts in changing communities and people who are experts at working with individuals, families, and groups? Why do social workers have to be all things to all people?

3. Doesn't it strike you as odd that someone like my colleague would choose to do private psychotherapy? Doesn't the word *social* in social work suggest that our emphasis should be on social action, social change, and community development rather than on psychotherapy?

4. Do you think it's right for a profession to expect its members to have liberal social change philosophies, or should we expect many social workers to have more conservative social change philosophies? How would you define liberal and conservative social change philosophies? Which do you prefer, and why?

5. My arguments sound pretty idealistic. Is there anything wrong with idealism? Just thinking about yourself, define idealism and decide whether you are or are not idealistic, and why.

Summary

This chapter discusses the larger systems work done by social workers and provides arguments in favor of achieving healthy communities. A case study shows how community development can help a troubled community with a serious youth violence problem. Also, a practitioners' dialogue regarding where social work should put its energies, in large systems change or in work with individuals and their families, is provided to show two different points of view.

Questions to Determine Your Frame of Reference

1. We value freedom in America, even when freedom means we make decisions that aren't always good ones for communities. Do you think a central planning commission with ultimate power to decide what's best for communities would result in healthier community life?

2. It's true that violence, traffic congestion, and poor air quality are problems in American cities. Aren't they likely to occur in any large city in the world because of the serious problems linked with high population density? Look at crime rates, pollution, and traffic congestion rates in London, Paris, Athens, and Berlin and compare them with New York, Chicago, Los Angeles, and Boston.

3. Do you think it's realistic that social workers can actually change a community when there are so many forces and people who want to keep things as they are?

4. How can a healthy community actually increase a person's happiness?

5. Doesn't it stand to reason that a person's health is much more influenced by his or her level of income than by the health of the community? Isn't it true that people with money can afford better health care, better nutrition, and have a better standard of life?

Internet Sources

Rate your community's pollution level with the Environmental Defense (2004). Next, Kenyon (2003) writes on healthy community practices, and Flower (1993) discusses the healthy communities movement. Finally, Walls (1994) explains more on the concept of community organizing.

1. Environmental Defense. (2004). *The 50 most polluted communities in America.* Retrieved from http://www.environmentaldefense.org/dangerousdays.cfm?subnav=aiyc_50cities

2. Kenyon, P. (2003). *Healthy community checklist.* Retrieved July 28, 2005, from www.ingham.org/ce/CED/inthe works/healthy_community_checklists.htm

3. Flower, J. (1993). *Healthier communities: A compendium of best practices.* Retrieved March 15, 2005, from http://www.well.com/user/bbear/hc_compendium.html

4. Walls, D. (1994). *Power to the people: Twenty years of community organizing.* Retrieved July 27, 2005, from www.sonoma.edu/sociology/dwalls/commun.html

The Impact of Religion and Spirituality on the Social and Emotional Lives of Americans

21

Religiously Affiliated Social Service Institutions and the Role of Social Work

While promoting the 10th anniversary DVD release of *Schindler's List*, his film about the Holocaust during World War II, Steven Spielberg told host Katie Couric on the *Today Show* in March 2004 that he didn't keep any of the profits:

> I didn't take a single dollar from the profits I received from *Schindler's List*. When I first decided to make *Schindler's List* I said, if this movie makes any profit, it can't go to me or my family, it has to go out into the world and that's what we try to do here at the Shoah Foundation. We try to teach the facts of the past to prevent another Holocaust in the future.

And then he gave Couric a Hebrew lesson:

> We have a thing we say in Hebrew, tikkun olam, which means, the world always needs fixing, and we as Jews, we as all people, have a responsibility

to help fix things when they're broken and I think *Schindler's List* and the Shoah Foundation does exactly that.

We live in a time when there has been a revival in the importance of religious involvement and spirituality. Many social issues are driven by that involvement, including gay marriage, abortion rights, family values, and public monies used by religious organizations to help people with social and emotional problems. It is certainly true that a great deal of the psychotherapy and counseling done in America, and the case management to the frail, elderly, disabled, and mentally ill, is done through agencies with religious affiliations. I was the executive director of a large Jewish family service agency serving thousands of clients in Tucson, Arizona, where only a tenth or less of our clients were Jewish. Religiously affiliated organizations run hospitals, family service agencies, charitable organizations, nursing homes, and other services that provide help to all citizens, regardless of their religious beliefs and affiliations.

Some of us believe very strongly in our religion or have deeply spiritual beliefs that help guide us through our lives. A number of studies suggest that spirituality and religious involvement may have a positive impact on health and mental health, even though the helping professions, including social work, have generally believed that they can work in religiously sponsored agencies, maintain their professional identities, and separate themselves from religious beliefs and ideologies. Despite this sense that spirituality and religious involvement are issues that somehow lie outside of what social workers do in their professional practice, a number of researchers and social work practitioners agree that religion and spirituality have been neglected areas of social work practice (Canda, 1988).

This chapter discusses the impact of religion and spirituality on physical and mental health. It also considers the religiously sponsored organizations that employ social workers and the role of social work in dealing with issues of religious and spiritual beliefs. A case study is provided to help explain the relationship between religion, spirituality, and social work practice. Once again, you assume the role of a social worker, this time with a terminally ill patient who has unresolved life issues that include fear of the afterlife if he doesn't show contrition for past behavior.

Definitions of Spirituality and Religious Involvement

George, Larson, Koenig, and McCullough (2000) report work by the National Institute of Aging to define spirituality and religious involvement. They found the following common elements in the definitions of both:

1. Religious/Spiritual Preference or Affiliation: Membership in or affiliation with a specific religious or spiritual group.

2. Religious/Spiritual History: Religious upbringing, duration of participation in religious or spiritual groups, life-changing religious or spiritual experiences, and "turning points" in religious or spiritual participation or belief.

3. Religious/Spiritual Participation: Amount of participation in formal religious or spiritual groups or activities.

4. Religious/Spiritual Private Practices: Private behaviors or activities, including but not limited to prayer, meditation, reading sacred literature, and watching or listening to religious or spiritual radio or television programs.

5. Religious/Spiritual Support: Tangible and intangible forms of social support offered by the members of one's religious or spiritual group.

6. Religious/Spiritual Coping: The extent to which and ways in which religious or spiritual practices are used to cope with stressful experiences.

7. Religious/Spiritual Beliefs and Values: Specific religious or spiritual beliefs and values.

8. Religious/Spiritual Commitment: The importance of religion/-spirituality relative to other areas of life and the extent to which religious or spiritual beliefs and practices serve to affect personal values and behavior.

9. Religious/Spiritual Motivation for Regulating and Reconciling Relationships: Most measures in this domain focus on forgiveness, but other issues may be relevant as well (e.g., confession, atonement).

10. Religious/Spiritual Experiences: Personal experience with the divine or sacred, as reflected in emotions and sensations. (p. 105)

Does Spirituality and Religious Involvement Have a Positive Impact on Physical and Mental Health?

George et al. (2000) found that religious involvement reduced the likelihood of disease and disability in 78% of the studies they reviewed. Religion had a particularly positive impact on preventing or limiting coronary disease and heart attacks, emphysema, cirrhosis, and other varieties of liver disease (Comstock & Partridge, 1972; Medalie, Kahn, Neufeld, Riss, & Goldbourt, 1973), hypertension (Larson, Koenig, Kaplan, & Levin, 1989; Levin &

InfoTable 21.1	The Extent of Religious Involvement in America

The majority of Americans indicate that they believe in God (Yntema, 1999), and seven out of ten say they attend church or synagogue (Loewenberg, 1988). Religion is regarded as highly important in the lives of older Americans (McFadden, 2000), whereas active religious and spiritual participation have been shown to positively influence overall health (Ellison & Levin, 1998). Meystedt (1984) reports that 75% of the people sampled in rural areas feel confidence in organized religion. The majority of older persons (76% nationwide) regard religion as highly important in their lives (McFadden, 2000). The same study revealed that 52% of all older adults attend weekly religious services (McFadden, 2000). Research conducted by Gallup and Castelli in 1989 (Sheridan, Wilmer, & Atcheson, 1994) found that religion and spirituality continue to be important factors in the lives of most Americans. The survey revealed that 74% of the respondents stated that their primary mechanism for coping with stress was prayer. A more recent study reinforces these figures. The majority of Americans believe in God, and those aged 55 to 64 were found to be the most devout (Yntema, 1999). Of the respondents aged 55 to 64, 72% said that, without a doubt, they believe in God (Glicken, 2004a).

Vanderpool, 1989), and disability (Idler & Kasl, 1992, 1997). In these studies, "The strongest predictor of the prevention of illness onset is attendance at religious services" (George et al., 2000, p. 108). The authors also point to a relationship between religious observance and longevity, noting that "multiple dimensions of religion are associated with longevity, but attendance at religious services is the most strongly related to longevity" (p. 108).

Ellison, Boardman, Williams, and Jackson (2001) found that: (a) there is a positive relationship between church attendance and well-being, and an inverse association with distress; (b) the frequency of prayer is inversely related to well-being and only slightly positively related to distress; (c) a belief in eternal life is positively related to well-being but unrelated to distress; (d) church-based support networks are unrelated to well-being; and (e) "there is limited evidence of stress-buffering effects, but not stress-exacerbating effects, of religious involvement" (p. 215).

Gartner, Larson, and Allen (1991) comprehensively reviewed more than 200 psychiatric and psychological studies and concluded that religious involvement has a positive impact on physical and mental health. In another review of the literature, Ellison et al. (2001) concluded that "there is at least some evidence of mental health benefits of religion among men and women, persons of different ages and racial and ethnic groups, and individuals from various socioeconomic classes and geographical locations. Further, these salutary effects often persist even with an array of social, demographic, and health-related statistical controls" (p. 215).

Baetz, Larson, Marcoux, Bowen, and Griffin (2002) studied the level of religious interest of psychiatric inpatients to determine whether religious commitment had an impact on selected outcome variables. In the study,

InfoTable 21.2	The Impact of Church Attendance on African American Youth

Available empirical evidence suggests a relationship between socialization experiences emanating from the African American church and a number of positive developmental outcomes. For example, Brown and Gary (1991) found that self-reports of church involvement were positively related to educational attainment among African American adults. In an interview study of African American urban male adolescents, Zimmerman and Maton (1992) found that youths who left high school before graduation and were not employed, but who attended church, had relatively low levels of alcohol and drug abuse. In a questionnaire administered to African American adults (Seaborn-Thompson & Ensminger, 1989), 74 percent responded "very often" or "often" to the statement, "The religious beliefs I learned when I was young still help me." On the basis of data from the 1979-80 National Survey of Black Americans, Ellison (1993) argued that participation in church communities is positively related to self-esteem in African American adults. (Haight, 1998, p. 215)

88 consecutive adult patients (50% men) admitted to an inpatient facility were interviewed about their religious beliefs and practices. Patients with a Beck Depression score of 12 or more were included for outcome analysis. The researchers report the following results: frequent worship attendees had fewer symptoms of depression, had shorter hospital stays, were more satisfied with their lives, and had much lower rates of current or lifetime use of alcohol when compared to participants with less frequent or nonexistent worship attendance. Consequently, worship may protect against greater severity of symptoms and longer hospital stays, increase satisfaction with life, reduce the severity of symptoms, and enhance the quality of life among psychiatric patients.

Kissman and Maurer (2002) report that "people with strong faith, regardless of religious persuasion, live longer, experience less anxiety, cope better with stressful life events, have lower blood pressures and stronger immune systems" (p. 43). Krucoff and Crater (1998) found that coronary surgery patients who were prayed for by congregations had a better recovery rate when compared with patients in a control group where prayer was not used. George et al. (2000) report that religious involvement and spirituality have been shown to reduce the onset of illness. Once the illness is present, recovery is faster and longevity is greater than in those who are not involved with religion or spirituality. The authors believe that healthy religious involvement may positively affect the course of an illness and lead to longer survival after heart transplants (Harris, Dew, & Lee, 1995); lower mortality rates after cardiac surgeries (Oxman, Freeman, & Manheimer, 1995); reduced risk of repeated heart attacks, which might be fatal or nonfatal (Thoresen, 1990); reduced death rates among women with breast cancer (Spiegel, Bloom, & Kraemer, 1989); and increased ability to cope with pain (Kaczorowski, 1989; Landis, 1996; O'Brien, 1982), and may prove to be the most significant reason for better medical recoveries and outcomes (George et al., 2000).

Religious involvement appears to be associated with faster and more complete recovery from mental illnesses, substance abuse/dependence, and depression (George, 1992; Koenig, George, Cohen, Hays, Larson, & Blazer, 1998). Compared to patients who report no or low levels of religious involvement, those who report stronger religious involvement are more likely to recover and to do so more quickly. Evidence indicating a relationship between religious or spiritual involvement with recovery from substance abuse is based upon studies of Alcoholics Anonymous (AA) and other 12-step programs (Emrick, 1987; Montgomery, Miller, & Tonigan, 1995; Project MATCH Research Group, 1997). According to George et al. (2000), "A central component of these programs is the belief that we have no personal control over the addiction, but that there is a higher power who can help the individual to conduct it" (p. 109). The authors indicate that all of the studies cited control for multiple variables and that longitudinal studies following participants over a long period of time confirm the existence of a relationship between spirituality and religious involvement and better recovery for mental illness, depression, and substance abuse.

Some Reasons Why Spirituality and Religious Involvement May Improve Physical and Mental Health

Ellison and Levin (1998) suggest three reasons for the beneficial impact of religious involvement and spirituality.

CONTROLLING HEALTH-RELATED RISKS

Some religions have specific prohibitions against poor health behaviors. These prohibitions may include the use of tobacco and alcohol, premarital sexual experiences and other risky sexual activity, the use of foods that may contribute to high cholesterol and heart problems, and the use of illegal drugs. Many religions encourage good health practices. The Mormons, Seventh-Day Adventists, and other religious groups with strict prohibitions concerning health-related behaviors are healthier and live longer, on average, than members of other faiths and those who are uninvolved in religion (Enstrom, 1978, 1989; Gardner & Lyon, 1982; Lyon, Klauber, & Gardner, 1976; Phillips, Kuzma, & Beeson, 1980). However, George et al. (2000) indicate that strict prohibitions on health-related behaviors only explain 10% of the reasons that religious and spiritual beliefs have a positive impact on physical and mental health.

SOCIAL SUPPORT

A second possible reason why religion may affect health is the fellowship, support, and friendships developed among people who are religiously affiliated. When compared to their nonreligious peers, people who regularly attend religious services report: (a) larger social networks, (b) more contact with those social networks, (c) more help received from others, and (d) more satisfaction with their social support network (Ellison & George, 1992; Zuckerman, Kasl, & Ostfeld, 1984). Despite this, social support provides only a 5% to 10% explanation of the relationship between religion and health (Idler, 1987; Zuckerman et al., 1984).

LIFE MEANING OR THE COHERENCE HYPOTHESIS

A third explanation for the health benefits of religion is that people who are religious understand "their role in the universe, the purpose of life, and develop the courage to endure suffering" (George et al., 2000, p. 110). The authors call this the "coherence hypothesis" and believe that the connection between a sense of coherence about the meaning of life and one's role in the universe affects 20% to 30% of a client's physical and mental health, largely because it buffers clients from stress (Antonovsky, 1980; Idler, 1987; Zuckerman et al., 1984).

Other writers have noted the positive impact of spirituality and religious belief when serious illness is present. Kubler-Ross (1997) suggests that coping with the possibility of death and disability often leads to life-changing growth and new and more complex behaviors that focus on the meaning of life. Greenstein and Breitbart (2000) write, "Existentialist thinkers, such as Frankl, view suffering as a potential springboard, both for having a need for meaning and for finding it" (p. 486). Frankl (1978) believed that life meaning could be found in our actions, our values, and in our suffering. Commenting on the meaning of suffering, Frankl (1978) wrote that even while facing imminent death, there is still the opportunity to find meaning in the experience: "What matters, then, is that the stand he takes in his predicament . . . the attitude we choose in suffering" (p. 24). However, Balk (1999) believes that three issues must be present for a physical or mental health crisis to create coherence: "The situation must create a psychological imbalance or disequilibrium that resists readily being stabilized; there must be time for reflection; and the person's life must forever afterwards be colored by the crisis" (p. 485).

Should Issues of Religion and Spirituality Be Included in the Work Done by Social Workers?

The prior research indicates that religious involvement and spirituality may have a positive impact on physical and mental health. However, there is a lack of agreement about whether social workers and other helping professionals should learn about religious involvement and spirituality or even include either in their work with clients. In a study of 53 social work faculty members, Dudley and Helfgott (1990) found that those opposed to a course on spirituality were concerned about conflict with the mission of social work, about problems stemming from the separation of church and state, and that religious and spiritual material in the curriculum would conflict with the personal beliefs of faculty members and students. Sheridan et al. (1994) asked educators from 25 schools of social work questions regarding the inclusion of religious and spiritual content in social work programs. The majority (82.5%) supported inclusion in a specialized elective course.

Sheridan (2000) found that 73% of the social workers surveyed had generally positive attitudes about the appropriateness of discussing religion and spirituality in practice. Of the respondents, 43% said that religion played a positive role in the lives of their clients, whereas 62% said that spirituality played a positive role in the lives of clients. Spirituality was reported to play a harmful role in their clients' lives only 12% of the time, whereas religion was reported detrimental to client functioning 21% of the time (Sheridan, 2000). A majority of the social workers responding said that they had used spiritually and religiously based interventions with clients even though most (84%) reported little or no prior instruction in graduate school. However, more than half of the respondents had attended workshops and conferences on religion and spirituality after their professional training was completed.

Amato-von Hemert (1994) believes that we should include material on religious involvement and spirituality in graduate training and writes, "Just as we train and evaluate how workers address issues of class, gender, and race, we must maintain our professionalism by training workers to deal with religious issues" (p. 16). Tobias, Morrison, and Gray (1995) state that "today's multiethnic America encompasses a wide-ranging spiritual orientation that is, if anything, diverse" (p. 1), whereas Dudley and Helfgott (1990) suggest that "understanding spirituality is essential to understanding the culture of numerous ethnic groups that social workers help" (p. 288).

In seeking a definition of practice that includes religious and spiritual content, Boorstein (2000) reports that a study by Lajoie and Shapiro (1992) found more than 200 definitions of transpersonal (spiritual) psychology. However, the authors summarized those definitions by writing that "transpersonal psychology is concerned with the study of humanity's highest potential, and with the recognition, understanding, and realization of intuitive, spiritual, and transcendent states of consciousness" (p. 91).

Boorstein (2000) indicates that the difference between traditional psychotherapy and spiritually based psychotherapy is as follows: (a) traditional psychotherapy is pessimistic, as when Freud stated that psychoanalysis attempts to convert "neurotic misery to ordinary misery" (p. 413); (b) spiritually based psychotherapy tries to help clients gain awareness of the existence of joy, love, and happiness in their lives; and (c) spiritually based therapy is concerned with life meaning and not just symptom removal.

Religious Social Service Organizations and the Role of Social Work

A number of social service agencies are sponsored by religious organizations and are among the oldest continual social service organizations in America. They include Catholic Charities, the Association of Jewish Children and Family Services, Lutheran Social Service, and social services sponsored by the Church of Jesus Christ of Latter-day Saints (the Mormons), among a number of other religiously affiliated social service agencies. Many of these organizations offer a range of services, including case management for elderly clients, homemaker services, counseling and psychotherapy for clients experiencing social and emotional problems, emergency food and shelter, assistance with emergency medical care, adoptions, help with immigration, referral to nursing homes, supervision of frail elderly clients in their homes, and arranging transportation needs for poor and frail elderly or disabled clients.

Some churches, synagogues, and mosques have a direct social service function and may hire social workers to provide social services directly to the congregation. Some priests, ministers, and rabbis offer direct counseling services to congregants in what is called pastoral counseling. It is not unusual for many of these people to have degrees in social work. This is particularly true of the Salvation Army, which has a long history of training its workers in social work.

Some Randomly Chosen Mission Statements From Religiously Sponsored Social Service Agencies

JEWISH FAMILY SERVICE

- Mission statement: Helping families, children, and individuals in transition and adversity.
- Services available: Comprehensive Services for Senior Adults, Buz-A-Bus and Call-A-Car Transportation, Counseling and Social Services, Career Resources, Emergency Assistance, Interest Free Loans for

Student and General, Immigration and Acculturation Assistance, English as a Second Language Classes, and Jewish Family Life Education. (Collat Jewish Family Services, 2004)

CATHOLIC CHARITIES

- Mission statement: Catholic Charities is in the work of transforming lives. The organization strives to empower the working poor to move beyond basic survival living to a state of meaningful, quality living through economic, family and emotional stability. Catholic Charities assists individuals and families to establish in their lives the anchors required to break the cycle of poverty. These anchors include housing, employment, education and emotional health.
- Services available: Despite the economic prosperity, there are social and economic issues that still plague the community, particularly for the working poor. Affordable housing, steady employment with livable wages, at-risk behavior intervention and prevention, caregiver support, immigrant and refugee acculturation are critical needs—among many others—facing the working poor. To address these complex needs, Catholic Charities employs integrated services designed to address the multiple factors that impact one's ability to be self-sufficient and stable. Also because these issues have intergenerational impact, Catholic Charities programs are geared to reach families and across age groups: at-risk youth and their parents, older adult caregivers and caregivers of older adults, single parents, individuals, and newly arrived immigrants and refugees. (Catholic Charities, 2002))

THE SALVATION ARMY

- Mission statement: The Salvation Army, an international movement, is an evangelical part of the universal Christian Church. Its message is based on the Bible. Its ministry is motivated by the love of God. Its mission is to preach the gospel of Jesus Christ and to meet human needs in His name without discrimination.
- Services available: Adult rehabilitation centers are among the most widely known of all Salvation Army services and comprise the largest resident substance abuse rehabilitation program in the United States. Individuals with identifiable and treatable needs go to these centers for help when they no longer are able to cope with their problems. There they receive adequate housing, nourishing meals, and necessary medical care, and they engage in work therapy, spiritual guidance, and skilled counseling in clean and wholesome surroundings.

Residents may be referred or be remanded by the courts. Donated material, such as furniture, appliances, or clothing, provides both needed work therapy and a source of revenue through the Army's thrift stores. More than 120 adult rehabilitation centers offer these programs in the United States. Free temporary shelter is available to homeless men and women in severe financial need. Low-cost housing also is available to men and women living on pensions or social security. (Salvation Army, 2004)

A Social Worker Helps Two Terminally Ill Clients

This case first appeared in my book on the strengths perspective (Glicken, 2004a, pp. 68-69), in which the impact of religion and spirituality on physical and mental health and the role of social work in religious and spiritual issues is examined in greater detail.

Sam is a 46-year-old lawyer who recently discovered that he had advanced prostate cancer that had spread to his bladder and kidneys. Sam has been told that his chances of living much more than a year are unlikely. Sam was born a Catholic and lived in a religiously observant family who received great spiritual joy for their religious involvement. However, Sam found Catholicism overly restricting and slowly moved away from his religious background seeking, instead, secular explanations of life. He was highly active in political and civic affairs before his illness and had been cited on many occasions for his positive contributions to the community. Sam's personal life, however, had been highly chaotic. He was married and divorced three times. He often drank to excess and admits to using drugs to stay alert. He has three children whom he seldom sees and whom he thinks dislike him. "I've been a lousy father," he told the hospital social worker. "What can I say?"

Sam is afraid of dying and is deeply angry at God for letting this happen to him at such an early age. He frequently vents his anger at the hospital chaplain, who tries to console him. On several occasions, Sam has thrown pillows or vases at the chaplain, who sadly walks away, discouraged and hurt that Sam has such anger at God. One of Sam's roommates in the hospital is an older man by the name of Ed, who studied for the priesthood but didn't complete his ordination because he had serious doubts about the nature of his beliefs. Like Sam, he is also angry at God. Together, they rail against religious beliefs.

And yet, as they try and cope with their terminal illnesses, a rapport has developed between them. Late in the evening, the hospital social worker comes by to say goodnight only to find them deep in conversation about the meaning of life and the finality of death. He often sits and listens to the two men and feels a remarkable calmness come over both of them. During the day, they are as cantankerous as ever, but at night, during the quiet of the evening when the hospital is still and they are left alone, both men discuss their lives and search for meaning.

A transformation has begun to come over them. They seem to be developing a joy in life and a sudden acceptance of death. Visiting one evening, the social worker remarked about the change. Sam said that he has a lot of unfinished business before he dies and is

(Continued)

(Continued)

intent on "squaring" things with his kids and his ex-wives. "I was a jerk most of my life," he says, "and I regret it. The only thing I can do now is to apologize with all of my heart." Ed nods appreciatively and wonders if the staff connived to place both men together, and then realizes that hospitals never run that efficiently and thinks that maybe some things are divinely inspired. "You put two fallen away Catholics together," he says, "and you either blow the place up or you start looking for contrition and absolution. Death has a way of bringing out the important questions about life, and Sam here helped me at a time when I was so full of hatred, I couldn't feel anything but sorry for myself."

Both men lived the next year having frequent contact with one another. They died at roughly the same times and didn't live longer than they were expected to live. Wondering if there were other beneficial effects of their search for meaning, the hospital social worker asked the hospital staff. Both men were much easier to work with, the staff told him, and both became very giving people. A nurse who knew them both told the social worker, "The amazing thing about our Sam and the 'Rev,' as we called him, was that almost to the end of their lives, neither used pain medication to any extent. I mean the pain must have been severe, but both said that they had an inner pharmacy and that it was much better than any medication we could give them."

In trying to understand the movement of Sam and Ed from antagonism toward the spiritual and the religious, an interview by Eric Gamalinda (2002) with the noted poet Agha Shahid Ali, himself dying of a terminal brain tumor, might be instructive. Commenting on his deep sense of spirituality as he approached his own death, the poet said: "Where do you turn to in the hour of uncertainty? You turn to the realm that goes beyond the rational or undercuts the rational. And that's where religion, or spiritual elements of religion can help . . . people have been finding in medical history that many people respond to treatment if they also have a deep spiritual base" (Gamalinda, 2002, p. 50).

Some Opposing Views

It should be pointed out that although the evidence presented thus far suggests a positive relationship between church attendance and physical and mental health benefits, Rauch (2003) reports that the proportion of people who say they never attend religious services has increased 33% from 1973 to 2000. To further confuse the relationship between religious attendance and physical and mental health benefits, Rauch quotes theology professor John G. Stackhouse, Jr., as saying, "Beginning in the 1990's, a series of sociological studies has shown that many more Americans tell pollsters they attend church regularly than can be found in church when teams actually count. In fact, actual church going may be half the professed rate" (p. 34). This suggests that the validity of research on church attendance and positive physical and mental health benefits may be in doubt.

Rather than answering life meaning issues so important to good physical and mental health, Rauch (2003) finds that many people have only a vague notion of the theology of their religion and then are tolerant of other people's belief to such a degree that Rauch has coined the term *apatheist* to describe someone "who cares little about one's own religion and has an even stronger disinclination to care about other people's" (p. 34).

Although the vast majority of studies indicate a positive benefit from religious and spiritual involvement, there is some evidence that certain religious beliefs may cause harm. Simpson (1989) found that a sample of Christian Scientists died at younger ages than their peers, whereas Asser and Swan (1998) studied child deaths in families refusing medical care in favor of faith healing and found much higher rates of death. Both sets of authors believe that there are healthy and unhealthy uses of spirituality and religious involvement, but have thus far been unable to determine precisely what they are and how physical and mental health are affected.

In a dissenting view of the inclusion of religious and spiritual issues in practice, Sloan and Bagiella (2001) conclude that although interest in the impact of religious involvement and spirituality on health is great, "The empiric support required to convert this interest into recommendations for health practice is weak and inconclusive at best, with most studies having numerous methodological shortcomings. Even if there were methodologically solid findings demonstrating associations between religious and spiritual activities and health outcomes, problems would still exist" (p. 33). The authors point out the following methodological problems in trying to demonstrate a positive relationship between religious and spiritual involvement and improved health benefits.

First, Sloan and Bagiella (2001) state that "we have no idea, for example, whether recommending that patients attend religious services will lead to increased attendance and, if so, whether attendance under these conditions will lead to better health outcomes" (p. 34). Many factors influencing health are beyond the scope of practice. Although marital status is often associated with good health, most practitioners would "recoil" at recommending marriage because of its positive relationship to health. Furthermore, "Recommending religion to patients in this context may be coercive" (p. 34) because it creates two classes of people: those who comply and those who don't. This may lead to the implication that poor health may be linked to insufficient spiritual or religious involvement. The authors conclude that "the absence of compelling empiric evidence and the substantial ethical concerns raised suggest that, at the very least, it is premature to recommend making religious and spiritual activities adjunctive treatments" (p. 34).

Not all of the research to date has been positive or has found a relationship between positive health and religious involvement. In a review of the available correlational studies that attempt to link religion with positive mental health, Batson and Ventis (1982) write that being more religious is associated with poorer mental health, with greater intolerance of people who are different from ourselves, and with no greater concern for those in need. The evidence being more religious is not associated with greater mental health or happiness or with greater social compassion and concern. Quite the contrary, there is strong evidence that suggests that religion is a negative force in human life, one we would be better off without. (p. 306)

You Be the Social Worker

A terminally ill patient in a Catholic-sponsored hospital is being seen by a social worker to help the patient with unfinished business. This consists of many financial and practical concerns but also includes resolving conflict with members of his family, loved ones, and friends and colleagues. Richard, our patient, is 59 years old and dying of stomach cancer, an agonizingly painful form of cancer. Richard is very difficult and has spent much of his adult life responding to people with outbursts of anger and hostility to people when he believes they interfere in his life. Richard can be like a runaway train when he's out of control, and most of the important people in his life have disowned him.

Richard is worried about the afterlife and believes that if he doesn't apologize to the people he's offended, he might be sent to a place he doesn't want to go to when he dies. He's not a devout person, but he's had an opportunity to talk to the hospital chaplain, who says that contrition is the best way to cleanse the soul. So, he and the social worker practice what he will say to the many people whom he wants to see. The sessions are going badly. Richard just can't grasp how to be nice to people or show a caring and warm side, so the worker has taken to turning the role plays around so that Richard plays the person he's offended while the social worker plays Richard. Slowly, he's getting the hang of it and has started practicing being nice to hospital staff. "Amazing," he says. "They actually give me better service when I'm nice." During a 2-week period of time, the worker has helped Richard improve his communication skills. Richard no longer thinks he's "sucking up" to people as he originally did and now feels a genuine desire to apologize. The social worker arranged for a number of people to visit Richard in the hospital. Many were reluctant, but the worker was very persuasive. The first person who saw Richard sat as far away as possible as Richard bumbled his way through an apology. When silence set in and both people became uncomfortable, the worker said, "Richard feels badly about the things that happened years ago and wants to apologize from the core of his heart. He loves you and he wants to say goodbye as he begins passing from this place to the next." The friend was thoroughly moved by what the worker said and came over and hugged Richard. Both men were crying and, after the friend left, Richard asked if the worker could talk for him because he was so much better at it. What would you do if you were the social worker?

Questions

1. Isn't it better to have Richard talk directly to others with whom he has unfinished business instead of the worker? Doesn't it help Richard practice apologies and isn't it a more honest form of apology?

2. Richard is apologizing to people whom he has offended because he thinks he'll end up in "hell" if he doesn't. Does this suggest a legitimate reason for the apologies? Is it coming from the heart, a good place, or from fear, a bad place?

3. There is much to be learned about life when people have a terminal illness. Many writers believe that we gain more insight into ourselves and have more opportunity to answer important life issues than at any other time in our life. Can you think of ways to help Richard apologize for alienating people that not only come from the heart, but adds to his sense of fulfillment as a person?

4. Richard is learning that being nice to others has a very positive impact on the hospital staff. Do you think this new approach to people could prolong his life and even result in less pain and discomfort? Explain your answer.

5. It seems wasteful to spend so much time with dying people when there are so many living people who need help. Can you think of some positive reasons for helping people work through feelings about dying?

Summary

This chapter reports a number of positive studies showing a relationship between religious and spiritual involvement and better physical and mental health. Questions are raised about methodological problems and whether positive findings suggest a role for social workers in the religious and spiritual views of clients. The chapter notes the attempts to change curriculums in programs training social workers to include content on religious and spiritual beliefs and the difficult nature of the process. Even so, many professionals believe that these issues are fundamental to clients' well-being and that the effective practitioner should know about religious and spiritual beliefs and use them, in some fashion, in their work with clients. A case of social work practice with two terminally ill clients is presented, and a moral and practice issue about doing for clients what they can do for themselves, as well as the good and bad reasons for finishing unfinished business in terminally ill patients, is posed.

Questions to Determine Your Frame of Reference

1. Do you think religious and spiritual involvement actually has a positive impact on people, or do you think the studies cited are irrelevant and akin to those statistical relationships we hear about, such as the one reporting that eating bread causes crime because all criminals eat bread?

2. Spirituality is a pretty vague notion, don't you think? When you ask most people if they're spiritual, they'll say "yes" without really knowing what it means. What does the word mean to you?

3. How would you explain people who regularly attend religious services and are observant but are not "good" people (e.g., they're unethical, unhelpful to others, bigoted, self-centered, etc.)?

4. How can religions that have unhealthy beliefs about people have a healthy impact on participants?

5. How would you rate yourself on the issue of religious involvement and spirituality? High, moderate, low? Do you think that makes you more or less susceptible to physical and emotional illness?

Internet Sources

The rules that guide faith-based organizations that contract with public agencies to provide social services are described by the White House (2002). Next, a series of polls of Americans regarding their attitudes toward religion and spirituality is conducted by a number of different polling services. Finally, an article on atheism and its beliefs and values is provided.

1. White House. (2002). *Guidance to faith-based organizations partnering with the federal government.* Retrieved from http://www.whitehouse.gov/government/fbci/guidance_document.pdf

2. *Religion.* (2006). Retrieved January 17, 2006, from http://www.pollingreport.com/religion.htm

3. Wang, M. (2003). *An introduction to atheism.* Retrieved January 17, 2006, from http://www.infidels.org/news/atheism/intro.html

Achieving Social Justice Through Organizational Change

22

I submit that an individual who breaks a law that conscience tells him is unjust, and who willingly accepts the penalty of imprisonment in order to arouse the conscience of the community over its injustice, is in reality expressing the highest respect for the law.

—Martin Luther King, Jr. (1929–1968)

The NASW *Code of Ethics* says that "the primary mission of the social work profession is to enhance human well-being and help meet the basic human needs of all people, with particular attention to the needs and empowerment of people who are vulnerable, oppressed, and living in poverty. Social workers promote social justice and social change with and on behalf of clients." But in a practical sense, does that mean that *all* clients deserve our attention and that social justice is necessary and operative in every single instance when social workers help clients? Yes, it does. Much as an attorney or doctor is bound by a code of ethics to help all clients and patients whether we like them, think they're worthy people, or feel as if they have a right to our services, social workers are always bound by an obligation, an ethic, to promote social justices and social change on behalf of all of our clients.

Let's see if we can make some sense out of that statement because, at face value, it sounds completely wrong. Don't people who commit crimes and are found guilty lose some of their civil rights? Yes, they do, but they don't lose the right to be treated in a humane way, because the Constitution protects everyone in America against "cruel and unusual punishment." That includes illegal aliens, people who have committed crimes, and, most troubling of all, terrorists. Why? Because if we don't guarantee *everyone* social justice, might we begin to lose our treasured civil rights? Many people worry that acts such as the Patriot Act take away civil liberties and make it more difficult to guarantee social justice. But isn't that unlikely to happen and don't the bad guys have to worry, not those of us who are law-abiding citizens? Maybe, but still, social work is deeply concerned about social justice and wants as free a society as possible. To further understand the importance of social justice, the American Civil Liberties Union (ACLU), a controversial organization among many people in America, is an organization devoted to protecting individual rights as guaranteed by our Constitution. Let's consider the mission of the ACLU, which is to preserve all of the following protections and guarantees:

- Your First Amendment rights—freedom of speech, association and assembly. Freedom of the press, and freedom of religion supported by the strict separation of church and state.
- Your right to equal protection under the law—equal treatment regardless of race, sex, religion or national origin.
- Your right to due process—fair treatment by the government whenever the loss of your liberty or property is at stake.
- Your right to privacy—freedom from unwarranted government intrusion into your personal and private affairs. (ACLU, 2004)

The ACLU has, as one of its fundamental goals, the protection of religious freedoms and rights. Let's look at what the organization says about their mission as it relates to religion:

The right of each and every American to practice his or her own religion, or no religion at all, is among the most fundamental of the freedoms guaranteed by the Bill of Rights. The Constitution's framers understood very well that religious liberty can flourish only if the government leaves religion alone. The ACLU will continue working to ensure that religious liberty is protected by keeping the government out of the religion business. (ACLU, 2004)

Isn't it a good thing to have an organization that fights to protect our rights and to make certain that justice is done? I think it is, but then why is there such antagonism against the organization? Probably because they've defended the rights of very unpopular people such as American Nazis, members of the Communist Party, the Ku Klux Klan, and terrorists. Their justification is that when the rights of the least popular among us are protected, then we all benefit because the rights of the rest of us are also protected. I hope that makes sense to you because, although America has the right to be proud of our civil rights, we have some notable failures. Among them is the internment of more than 100,000 Japanese Americans during World War II for no other reason than their nationality. Similarly, the rights of African Americans were ignored in many parts of America when we had "Jim Crow" laws that gave black Americans a lower level of civil rights and treated them neither fairly nor equally. Some would argue that Jim Crow still exists in America given the unequal level of opportunity for many black Americans.

What Is Social Justice?

One of the problems in discussing social justice is that it has different meanings for different people. And although the standards we use to judge social justice may vary depending upon the situation, it may help to think of social justice in three ways: distributive, procedural, and retributive social justice. *Distributive* justice refers to fair outcomes, such as pay distributions. Many people believe that there is much less distributive justice for women and minority group members because they earn far less than white males for doing the same work. *Procedural* justice refers to the fairness in how decisions are made. Examples might be ways to resolve conflicts or to determine allocations of resources. Many people believe that a small group of people run America. C. Wright Mills called them the *power elite*, and they usually attend the same universities and colleges and come from generations of wealth and social priveledge. Mills believed that the power elite generally allocate resources to help the wealthiest among us to maintain their privaleges. An unfair tax system that taxes the middle class more than the rich might be an example of procedural justice. *Retributive* justice refers to fair punishment and how severe it should be. If you consider sentencing outcomes between white and black felons, you will find that black felons serve longer jail sentences for commiting the same crimes and with the same prior criminal records. Obviously, retributive justice is different for white and black people in America. Here are some examples of popular beliefs regarding the the state of social justice in America:

- The rich get richer and the poor get poorer.
- There is a shrinking middle income group.
- Decent health care is available only for the most wealthy among us.
- Single mothers feel the greatest economic and social strains.
- Will you have a job when you graduate?
- Poor people and middle incomes pay a disproportionately higher amount of taxes
- Many of us believe that we have little impact on the way our government works.
- Our political representatives are overly influenced by pressure and lobbying groups who contribute huge amounts of money to their campaigns.

- Politicians don't represent most Americans.
- The laws are made to benefit rich people.
- The country is run by a small group of influential people (the power elite).

I could go on, but do any of these statements upset you? Do you think that any of these statements pertain to you or are true? If so, then you have identified a social justice issue you think needs to be challenged and changed. Social workers would agree with many of these statements and would probably have clients who have been affected by one or more of these issues. How, then, would we define social justice?

The Catholic Church has defined social justice and the responsibilities it places on congregants (Office of Social Justice, 2004) in a way that I find very instructive. The major issues that define social justice are as follows:

Dignity of people. The foundation of social justice is the belief in the inherent dignity of all people.

Common good and community. We achieve our dignity and rights through our interactions with others in the community. How we organize our society—in economics and politics, in law and policy— directly affects human dignity and the capacity of individuals to grow in the community. Everyone has a responsibility to contribute to the common good of the whole society.

Option for the poor. The moral test of a society is how it treats its most vulnerable members. The deprivation and powerlessness of the poor wounds the whole community.

Rights and responsibilities. Human dignity can be protected and a healthy community can be achieved only if human rights are protected and responsibilities are met. Every person has a fundamental right to

---

InfoTable 22.1   Overemphasizing the Needs of the Individual?

Seligman believes that we have overemphasized the needs of the individual in the helping professions at the expense of healthy, flourishing, and just community life (Sandage & Hill, 2001) and argues that we should be shifting psychology's paradigm away from its narrow focus on pathology, victimology, and mental illness toward positive emotions, virtue, strength, and the positive institutions that increase people's level of happiness. Seligman believes that clinicians have ignored the importance of virtue, religion, and philosophy in the lives of people and suggests 6 core virtues that define the healthy person and which should provide direction for helping professionals in our work with clients. They are: 1) Wisdom and knowledge; 2) courage; 3) love and humanity; 4) justice; 5) temperance; and 6) spirituality and transcendence. (Glicken, 2004a, p. 308)

life and a right to those things required for human decency—starting with food, shelter, clothing, employment, health care, and education. Corresponding to these rights are duties and responsibilities—to one another, to our families, and to our country.

The role of government. Government is a way of promoting human dignity, protecting human rights, and building the common good. All people have a right and a responsibility to participate in political institutions so that government can achieve its proper goals. When people's needs cannot adequately be met by other means, then it is not only necessary but imperative that higher levels of government intervene.

Economic justice. The economy must serve people, not the other way around. All workers have a right to productive work, to receive decent and fair wages, and to function in safe working conditions. They also have a fundamental right to organize and join unions. People have a right to economic initiative and private property, but these rights have limits. No one should be allowed to amass excessive wealth when others lack the basic necessities of life.

Promotion of peace and disarmament. Peace requires mutual respect and confidence among nations and requires agreements and working together to maintain peaceful solutions to problems. Peace is the end result of justice.

Participation. All people have a right to participate in the economic, political, and cultural life of society. It is a fundamental demand of justice and a requirement for human dignity that all people should be ensured a minimum level of participation in the community. It is wrong for a person or a group to be excluded unfairly or to be unable to participate in society.

Global solidarity and development. We are one human family. Our responsibilities to each other cross national, racial, economic, and ideological differences. Authentic development must be full human development. It must respect and promote personal, social, economic, and political rights, including the rights of nations and of peoples.

Novak (2000) believes that we must understand that the term *social justice* is *social* in two ways. First, it requires us to inspire, work with, and organize others to accomplish together a work of social justice. He writes, "Citizens who take part commonly explain their efforts as attempts to 'give back' for all that they have received from the free society, or to meet the obligations of free citizens to think and act for themselves" (p. 1). The second characteristic is that it aims to provide justice for everyone, not just the individual. Novak suggests, as did Mills, that societies "can be virtuous in the same way that individuals can be" (p. 1), and that although good can come from attempts to provide social justice, bad can come as well. He writes,

Careless thinkers forget that justice is by definition social. Such carelessness becomes positively destructive when the term "social" no longer describes the product of the virtuous actions of many individuals, but rather the utopian goal toward which all institutions and all individuals are "made in the utmost degree to converge" by coercion. In that case, the "social" in "social justice" refers to something that emerges not organically and spontaneously from the rule-abiding behavior of free individuals, but rather from an abstract ideal imposed from above. (Novak, 2000, p. 1)

The Center for Economic and Social Justice (2005, p. 1) notes that the term *social justice* suggests economic justice as well. They define social justice as the following:

The virtue which guides us in creating those organized human interactions we call institutions. Social institutions, when justly organized, provide us with access to what is good for the person, both individually and in our associations with others. Social justice also imposes on each of us a personal responsibility to work with others to design and continually perfect our institutions as tools for personal and social development. Economic justice encompasses the moral principles which guide us in designing our economic institutions. These institutions determine how each person earns a living, enters into contracts, exchanges goods and services with others and otherwise produces an independent material foundation for his or her economic sustenance. The ultimate purpose of economic justice is to free each person to engage creatively in the unlimited work beyond economics, that of the mind and the spirit. (p. 1)

In this definition of social and economic justice, you can see that the institutions we create to provide for all of us, but particularly for those at risk, must contain the goals we have set for serving people but at the same time must run efficiently yet fairly. This is an area where social welfare organizations have often been accused of being negligent. The institutions we develop to help others in times of crisis are often slow to respond, biased, and unfair. They sometimes create rules that have no logical reasons to exist other than to distance the organization from the service and people they are to provide for. Hurricane Katrina created a sense among many people that our organizations work least well for those who are the most needy, and that the slow response of government to provide needed services was racially motivated. Another way of viewing this is to look at the writings of Piven and Cloward (1971), who argue that social welfare institutions work only well enough (i.e., poorly) because they exist as a limited deterrent against the potential mass uprising of poor people against the power structure or, in the words of Mouzelis (1967), "to maintain the status quo and the privilege of the ruling class" (p. 9).

The type of organizations we develop to ensure social justice has often been thought of as being heavily bureaucratic, at least in our large public and child welfare organizations. This means that careful service often translates into slow and laborious service that is so dysfunctional in nature that some people describe the functioning of bureaucracies as *bureaupathic*. The primary characteristic of bureaupathic organizations is that they avoid providing services by instituting complex and meaningless rules that often "drive workers to avoid meaningful contact with clients through compulsive defending behavior" (Wasserman, 1971, p. 89). In the aftermath of Hurricane Katrina, when many governmental institutions failed to work, one heard endless statements from many layers of government about how rules limited certain important actions, or claims that the government was actually doing an exceptional job, when television viewers of the storm could see thousands of stranded people in New Orleans begging for help 5 and 6 days after the storm and subsequent flood. Although we need to understand the elegance of social justice, at the same time we need to recognize that the institutions we develop often thwart social justice through their incompetence, and we need to recognize the reasons. Incompetent organizations do not promote social and economic justice even if they say they do. They promote class and racial differences and hostilities. In the next section, we will turn to organizational change and the need to develop organizations that are truly the instruments of social and economic justice.

You Be the Social Worker

Les Maslow is a non–social worker corrections officer for the department of correction in a rural area of a Midwestern state. Les has been counseling a rapist named Daniel, who has brutally raped and mutilated a number of women without any seeming feelings of remorse. Les thinks that rapists are "scum" and that Daniel is the worst of the lot. He uses their sessions to continually berate Daniel for his terrible behavior. Daniel is used to hearing others berate him. He feels nothing about what people say about him and has graphic fantasies of sexually abusing women during therapy. One day, however, Daniel had enough of Les's behavior and attacked him in the therapy room. Before the guards could help, Daniel had bitten and gouged Les. As a result of the attack, Les lost vision in one eye and has some serious scars on his face. Daniel was placed in solitary confinement for the incident and has permanently lost the last of his privileges.

In trying to determine what happened, Les's supervisor interviewed Daniel and discovered what Les had been doing in their sessions. Les had called Daniel an "animal," "a scumbag," a "dirtball" and any number of other words which seemed quite inappropriate for anyone trying to help another human being. When the supervisor interviewed Les, he not only didn't deny using those words but proudly said that

(Continued)

(Continued)

he was the voice of the women who had been so horribly abused by Daniel, and that he wanted Daniel to feel their pain every day of his life. By getting Daniel to feel something, Les argued, he'd reached inside that impenetrable shell of Daniel's and had, for once, made Daniel angry enough to experience emotion. Even though Daniel had harmed him, Les felt he'd been successful with Daniel. "He knows what we think of him," Les said, "and frankly, as a corrections officer, I represent the society that Daniel ignores. If I don't remind Daniel of the pain he's caused, who will? He lives in a prison where the people he's harmed provide him with room, and board, and a comfortable life. He doesn't have to worry about traffic, or high prices at the gas pump, or any of the stresses we all have to worry about. Instead of punishing him for what he's done to those poor women, he's been rewarded. If I had my way, he'd be whipped every day just to make my insults hurt even more."

Questions

1. Do rapists like Daniel deserve social justice, or is it reserved for "good people?"

2. Do you think Les is right that helping professionals represent society and that our job is to remind people of the harm they've caused others?

3. Do you think that Les is correct about berating Daniel and that making him hurt emotionally finally gets an otherwise uncaring human being to start experiencing some of the pain he's caused others?

4. Social justice means that we value all human beings, but how can we value someone like Daniel?

5. Do you think prisons should be places to punish or rehabilitate people? Explain what rehabilitation and punishment mean to you.

Social Work and Organizational Change to Achieve Social Justice

McNamara (2004) believes that when social workers are involved in organizational change, it's for the purpose of organization-wide change, not smaller changes such as adding a new person or modifying a program. The examples of organizational change he provides include a change in mission, restructuring, new technologies, mergers, major collaborations, "rightsizing," new programs such as Total Quality Management, reengineering, and so forth. This may also be called organizational transformation because it designates a fundamental and radical reorientation in the way the organization operates.

Organizational change often takes place because of outside forces, including cuts in funding, poor quality of service, poor public relations, or a sense that the organization may be doing harm to people. An example of this might be the concern many child welfare agencies have that foster homes chosen for children when their own homes are involved in abuse and neglect may be no better and perhaps even worse than a child's actual home. In California, deaths of children by abusive foster home parents have provoked widespread concern for organizational change to provide much better and safer foster homes.

Social workers often become involved in organizational change when an organization is failing to provide clients with their basic human rights. Many examples can be found in the history of social welfare agencies, including the unequal social services provided to black clients by public agencies in various parts of the country in the early years of public social welfare services. At one point, social workers were required to do "midnight raids" on homes where mothers were receiving public aid for their children to find fathers who should have been providing child support. This led to a professional revolt, and the practice was soon stopped because it was unprofessional and offensive to workers and clients.

Often, there is strong resistance to change because many people in the organization may think things are already just fine and don't understand the need for change, or they may be cynical about change because they hear the word used so often when nothing really changes. Many workers may even doubt that it's possible to accomplish change because of entrenched problems in the organization that have lasted for long periods of time and seem resistant to change. And organizational change often goes against the values people strongly believe in. For this reason, organizational change sometimes involves shifts in members' values and beliefs and in the way they enact them.

Criticism of Social Service Management

Social service organizations often fail to achieve their goal of providing services to those in need because of poorly thought-through management theories and organizational structures that isolate workers from management. The following are some general criticisms of social service management and supervision found in the literature that may create problems when organizational change is attempted. Tulgan (2004), for example, says that one of the leading concerns about supervision is that workers are undersupervised. "The under-managed worker," he writes, "struggles because his supervisor is not sufficiently engaged to provide the direction and support he needs. His manager is not informed about his worker's needs and, therefore, is unable to help with resources and problem-solving. This manager cannot judge what expectations are reasonable, and he cannot set goals and deadlines that are ambitious but still meaningful" (p. 119). In the meantime, the undersupervisor gets caught in a downward spiral where problems are dealt with after they happen, and spends increasing amounts of time putting out fires while allowing workers to make the same mistakes for weeks and even months before the mistake is rectified.

The journal *TechRepublic* (2003) warns supervisors that their negative feedback to workers often undermines self-esteem and reduces the quality of work. They blame the lack of sensitivity to others partly on a condition that seems particularly similar to that in the human services: Workers with excellent practice skills are promoted to managerial positions but often lack leadership skills and haven't been trained to provide effective supervision of workers.

Stensaker, Meyer, Falkenberg, and Haueng (2001) argue that bad supervision often occurs when management institutes "excessive change" and requires supervisors to make certain that change takes place which is often detrimental to the organization and its workforce. The authors describe excessive change as "change [that] creates initiative overload and organizational chaos, both of which provoke strong resistance from the people most affected" (p. G6). Situations that lead to excessive change include change when change isn't needed, change for the sake of change, and change where one element of the organization is changed but others aren't. The result is stress on the supervisor, unhappiness in workers, and a general decline in the quality of services. Many human service workers complain that regulations and policies change so frequently they cannot keep up, and consequently blame supervisors and upper management for creating a workplace in which workers never have sufficient knowledge of the job because the policies that govern their work are always changing. Workers also argue that they are frequently left out of the decision-making process and feel neglected and ignored by supervisors.

Ghoshal (2005) complains that too many management theories used in supervision view organizations and workers in a highly negative way, suggesting an ideology that is "essentially grounded in a set of pessimistic assumptions about both individuals and institutions—a 'gloomy vision' that views the primary purpose of social theory as one of solving the 'negative problem' of restricting the social costs arising from human imperfections" (p. 76). The result of this pessimistic view of workers and organizations, according to Ghoshal, is that management has virtually no impact on whether an organization functions well or badly. Citing a review of 31 studies of organizational leadership by Dalton, Daily, Ellstrand, and Johnson (1998), the researchers found no difference in organizational performance based upon who occupied leadership roles. The reason for this is that most labor is performed at much lower levels and that organizational health is in the hands of workers, not managers. When workers are well treated and feel a part of the organization, performance is predictably better. Although it may seem counterintuitive that good managers have no better results than bad managers, Ghoshal points to the number of corporate scandals since 1998 and reminds us that most of the managers involved were thought to not only be good managers, but great ones.

One of the reasons for poor managerial impact on the performance of organizations is the way managers are chosen. Cook and Emler (1999) looked at the issue of technical skills versus integrity (moral qualities suggesting ethical behavior and sensitivity to the feelings of others) and found that top-to-bottom hiring (hiring done at the highest level with minimal impact from subordinates) focused on technical competence with only low to moderate concern for the integrity of the manager. Bottom-to-top decision-making (subordinates choosing managers) was made with a high level of concern for managerial integrity and only moderate concern for technical competence. Subordinates worried that a manager lacking in integrity would mistreat them, whereas upper management worried that high levels of integrity might interfere with getting the job done. The authors write, "If the effectiveness of managers is a function of how they treat their subordinates and whether they will be treated fairly, that promises to them will be kept, that their welfare will be considered, that they will be told the truth—then conventional top-down methods of selection will systematically under-select the best potential performers" (p. 439).

Menzel (1999) suggests that an important criticism of American management is that from CEOs to supervisors to low-level bureaucrats, many workers in the public and private nonprofit sectors have developed a "morally mute" position where they fail to act in ways that help the organization and instead stay mute when it comes to issues that trouble organizations, particularly those involving the unethical behavior of higher-ups. In describing this atmosphere of moral muteness, Mitchell (1999) writes,

> Not much impartial scientific method is to be discerned in our administrative practices. The poisonous atmosphere of city government, the crooked secrets of state administration, the confusion, sinecurism, and corruption ever and again discovered in the bureau at Washington forbid us to believe that any clear conceptions [of public management] are as yet very widely current in the United States. (p. 16)

Although Menzel (1999) believes that precious little has been done to make managers more aware of ethical behavior, he notes that legislation to enforce morally positive behavior has produced dubious results. According to Menzel, there is even the suggestion that by stating in law or policies what are punishable offenses, this has allowed us to define ethics as "behaviors and practices that do not break the law." Rohr (1989) calls this the "low road" to ethics because it features compliance and adherence to formal rules and "meticulous attention to trivial questions" (p. 63) that often mask far more serious ethical lapses.

Pfeffer (2005) worries that what is taught in schools with management specializations tends to create a reduced level of ethical behavior in students. Williams, Barrett, and Brabston (2000) report that "the link between firm size and corporate illegal activity becomes stronger as the percentage of top *management* team members possessing an MBA degree . . . rises" (p. 706). McCabe and Trevino (1995) found that business school students placed "the least importance on knowledge and understanding, economic and racial justice, and the significance of developing a meaningful philosophy of life" (211) and that "business majors report almost 50% more [cheating] violations than any of their peer groups and almost twice as many violations as the average student in our study" (p. 210). Pfeffer (2005) notes that an Aspen Institute study in 2001 found that during their 2 years in the MBA program, students became more interested in shareholder value than customer and employee satisfaction.

Bielous (2005) believes that supervisors routinely make disciplinary mistakes that undermine their effectiveness, and writes, "Perhaps supervisors don't know enough of what is right and what is wrong to become effective disciplinarians. Or maybe, we just wing it! This method can often damage a supervisor's credibility forever" (p. 16). In the human services, supervisors come from practice where telling people what's wrong with them is usually not a typical or constructive behavior. According to the author, the following are typical disciplinary mistakes:

Praising too much or too little. Praise should be attached to the level of performance and the importance of the worker's contribution. Inconsistent praise leaves workers feeling demeaned and unclear. Ultimately it tends to make workers believe that the supervisor isn't certain about how best to provide feedback or what he or she is looking for in a worker's performance.

Losing your temper. Poor performance should be handled quietly, firmly, and rationally, with a plan developed to improve a worker's job performance. Losing one's temper only results in anger and hurt feelings and the potential for a shouting match.

Avoiding disciplinary action entirely. Although there aren't always good models of how to discipline a worker, avoiding the response altogether just reinforces a worker's likelihood of continuing the unwanted behavior. The longer the behavior continues unchecked (poor attendance comes to mind), the more likely it is to continue.

Playing therapist. This is something human service supervisors do all too often, and it leads to workers becoming clients rather than effective workers. Although we use our skills to resolve conflict, we also have to remember that a job needs to be done and the offending parties need strong, firm direction of the sort that therapists often can't give. When supervisors assume therapy stances, it can be very demeaning to workers who expect direct, firm, fair, and consistent behavior from supervisors, not treatment. And when supervisors are particularly bad at providing therapy to workers, it can seem as if they are being treated like children.

Being unfair. One of the most critical aspects of supervision is fairness. When supervisors are unfair and inconsistent, it undermines worker confidence in the supervisor and it makes workers think that the supervisor is being selective and choosing favorites, a particularly ineffective form of behavior for anyone managing people.

Successful Organizations

Successful organizations, according to McNamara (2004), must involve top management and a change agent (often a social worker in nonprofit and public agencies) whose role is to develop a realistic plan and carry it out as a team-wide effort. McNamara gives the following major approaches to organizational change:

The balanced scorecard. Focuses on four indicators including the client's perspective, more efficient business practices to make the organization more effective and efficient, business processes, and team building to understand the need for change and to carry out change strategies and monitoring progress.

Benchmarking. Using standard measurements in a social welfare organization to compare productivity of workers against standards of most other social welfare organizations. For example, there are emerging standard benchmarks for child welfare agencies, schools, and medical social work regarding how many clients should be seen, timely interventions, and average outcomes.

Organizational process reengineering. Increases organizational performance by radically redesigning the organization's structures and processes, including starting over from the ground up.

Continuous improvement. Focuses on improving client satisfaction through planned changes that are incremental and are measured every step of the way.

Cultural change. Cultural change involves changing the basic values, norms, beliefs, and so forth among members of the organization for the purpose of not only improving organizational effectiveness, but also transforming the agency so that it redefines and carries out its mission more completely.

Knowledge management. Focuses on the collection and management of critical information in an organization to increase its capacity for achieving results, and often includes extensive use of computer technology.

Learning organization. Focuses on improving the "people aspects" of organizational life so that a better quality of service is provided with more compassion and concern for clients.

Outcome-based evaluation. Outcome-based evaluation is increasingly used to improve the impact of services to clients. Impact to clients may go beyond simple indicators of client change and may also evaluate family functioning and other indicators of improved client functioning that have importance to communities, the workplace, and the larger society. For example, questions we might ask related to helping a client may also include whether they vote and their participation in community life.

Program evaluation. Program evaluation is a research approach to objectively determine whether a social program is performing its function and, if so, at what level.

King, Fowler, and Zeithaml (2001) believe that successful social service organizations can be defined by five characteristics: (a) they have a proven way of sharing work-related competencies with all workers so that high-level practice is sustained, (b) worker competencies are retained during organizational and management changes, (c) competencies are not lost when key workers or managers leave the organization, (d) competencies are maintained and utilized when the nature of the service provided changes, and (e) the values and mission of the organization are strengthened during periods of organizational change. The authors note that many organizations undervalue the competencies of individual workers and promote a type of faceless practice that is neither easy to utilize or effective. Instead, management needs to identify the competencies that lead to good practice and high organizational delivery of service, note those workers and supervisors who function competently, and move the organization in a direction that is defined by high-level practice, using highly competent practitioners and supervisors to teach others the necessary skills.

Sheaffer and Mano-Negrin (2003) indicate that crisis-prepared and crisis-prone organizations differ in the way that they approach potential crises, including funding problems, changes in the services offered, increased caseloads, political pressures, and excessive worker turnover. Organizations that are crisis-prepared are typified by frequent evaluations of services and organizational strength audits, formal actions in place that are tried and true for dealing with crises, and policies geared to forecasting the impact and actions required by an organizational crisis. The authors further note that organizations that deal with crisis share information with all employees, ask for feedback and ideas, are flexible, and clearly identify work roles. In contrast, organizations that are crisis-prone develop faulty presumptions about why they are in crisis and generally are very defensive, are overly confident, are optimistic and arrogant, fail to rethink their *theory* of organizational health, are insensitive to criticism, are unwilling to listen, are unempathic, and have an organizational mentality that is overly competitive and seldom cooperative.

Stanley (2002) argues that many management theorists believe that organizations that are underperforming need change that can be "wrenching, revolutionary and extremely painful" (p. 12). He says that this is the wrong way to go and instead suggests that effective managers, or what he calls architects of change, must

> take the go-slow approach. They are steady, well-grounded and do not rush to embrace the latest fad. They change in order to bring about meaningful improvements that will increase productivity and profitability. Effective change is managed with attention toward making full use of all resources. When change is undertaken with an eye toward increased efficiency, it can be a gigantic motivating force. Architects of Change bring a down-to-earth decision making process to the multifaceted challenges that face every organization today. (p. 12)

But change isn't always needed and can have a negative impact on the organization and the services provided. Stensaker et al. (2001) argue that unneeded change takes place when it isn't required to provide quality service, when it takes place for the sake of change, or when one aspect of a program is changed without other aspects of the program changing accordingly. Outside pressures can force unneeded changes when, for example, accrediting bodies so interfere with the basic structure of the organization that it's never the same. One of the unwanted consequences of accreditation and certification procedures, if intrusive, is a loss of top management and key workers because of the stress placed on them by the process. Social work educational programs sometimes take 2 years for accreditation and at the end of the process, faculties are tired and students sometimes see either little improvement or actual decline in the quality of the program. So change that isn't needed or done badly can have negative repercussions. Noting the impact of unnecessary change on staff and management, the authors write,

> We found that excessive change directly and indirectly influenced individual reactions, coping mechanisms, organizational consequences and performance. . . . This suggests that the organization may enter into a negative spiral as employees choose to ignore change initiatives and more and more

projects fail to be implemented. Finally there is evidence that the organizational consequences result in both implementation failure and loss of effectiveness. (p. G5)

How would you approach change in a social service organization that was underperforming in a time of crisis? Would you take the go-slow approach that is thoughtful and patient, rationally analyzing the reasons and carefully testing the possible remedies, or would you shake things up and make drastic changes that could positively change the performance of the organization or, as a decided risk, completely demoralize the workers and thus fail to provide the needed service for clients? How important would worker morale be, or is the bottom line whether the client is being served? These are practical questions that all managers must deal with when faced by nonperforming organizations. In the following case study, a school district deals with school violence by hiring a social work organizational change agent to help the district reduce school violence and improve learning.

InfoTable 22.2   Using Critical Thinking to Create Organizational Change

The following ways of thinking about an organization's problems are useful in accepting varied feedback from workers and in understanding that the way we perceive problems is influenced by the way we think about problems and about their solutions.

1. Effective thinking: This skill involves solving immediate problems and producing results. It zeroes in on the vital question of what needs to be done now. There is a qualitative measurement as it is based on facts and data.

2. Strategic thinking: It is sometimes termed hypothetical thinking as it deals with possible future actions. It is broad based and takes a longer view about the external scenarios like future events and occurrences that would have a major effect on strategic decisions endorsed by an organization.

3. Systematic thinking: This involves looking at influencing factors that affect our thinking and decision-making. One has to know and analyze the past, present and future influencing conditions to be able to look beyond the immediate context of the situation and consider the larger picture.

4. Demonstrative thinking: Practitioners describe it as "an emotional way of thinking" because it looks into our spontaneous, more instinctive ways of knowing. This type of thinking skill considers the many facets of human emotion that contribute to the ways in which we communicate, make decisions, solve problems, and generally do things in life.

5. Parallel thinking: This thinking skill propels us to consider a range of unknown possibilities that will encourage us to explore an altogether different path to solve our issues. ("Thinking Critically," 2003, pp. 17–18)

Organizational Change Reduces School Violence

After the beating and rape of a sixth-grade teacher by one of her 12-year-old students, one of a series of violent crimes to plague the school district, the Petofsky School Board voted to bring in a social work organizational change specialist to help resolve school violence. After studying the problem of school violence, the organizational change specialist suggested a series of innovative approaches for the prevention and treatment of school violence, which the school board accepted. The district initiated a no-tolerance policy on violence, but one with a heart. All incidents of violence, either committed or prevented, were to be assessed and, if possible, treated. This policy was adopted as threats were called in daily of school bombings that effectively closed down all of the schools in the district, including the K-6 elementary schools. A chance break helped authorities find the caller of the bomb threats, who was identified as an 11-year-old male Caucasian youth with an unremarkable school record and no history of prior acting-out behavior.

The child, whose name is Robert, is one of the invisible children who act out against classmates because they perceive themselves as being disliked and picked on by classmates. This was certainly the case with Robert, who has been the object of ridicule since kindergarten because of a severe cleft palate and speech problems. Many of the children have been unmerciful in their bullying and taunting of Robert, who has a deep sense of rage at the hurtful behavior he has had to endure. Robert has had his clothes taken away in the boy's shower, his picture posted all over the school with derogatory statements, his hair forcibly cut Marine fashion, and an endless number of hurtful, ego-deflating, and damaging acts of violence. He is full of anger and seeks to take it out by disrupting the school and frightening his classmates. Robert is a very intelligent child and has been able to computer-enhance his voice so that his bomb threats have a robot-like quality that frighten the secretaries and the school-aged helpers who answer the phones.

Robert's parents are very angry at the school for not controlling the teasing and bullying he has had to endure. They have done everything to protect their child but without any help from the school, which sympathizes with Robert's plight but says that it is too understaffed to do much about it. When the school board discovered the reason for the bomb threats, they created a policy that makes taunts and humiliating statements as serious as actual acts of violence. Three boys and a girl in Robert's fifth-grade class were suspended with mandatory treatment. Robert was also suspended for a semester, but he was provided very high-level treatment and then transferred to a charter school with a good reputation for controlling mean-spirited behavior among its students.

Since instituting the no-taunting or bullying policy, Petofsky has experienced a sharp decline in school violence. As the violence has been reduced, the level of achievement of the children has gone up significantly. Petofsky recognizes that children do badly in violent environments and has made a concerted effort to prevent violence at all costs and, when it does take place, to find out the cause, provide expert treatment, and recognize that children who act out in school do so for reasons that may be preventable and treatable. The suspended children are all in empathy training classes and continue on in treatment. Children who force other children to the brink of violence are dangerous and need the same help as the offenders they taunt and abuse into violence.

In evaluating her work with the Petofsky School District, the social work organizational change specialist said, "There are always reasons organizations perform badly, and

(Continued)

(Continued)

this organization was certainly not doing its job in controlling violence. The culture of the school district was to deny that any problem even existed and that everything was going along well. When I came in and did an evaluation of the school district, it was clear that teachers had opted out of disciplining students and that classes were so chaotic and children so out of control that serious episodes of violence were frequently taking place. The teachers were demoralized by what they felt was a demeaning attitude by the school board, suggesting that what they did could be done by anyone and that teachers were expendable. When teachers tried to point out student problems, they were told that the problem was with the teacher who couldn't control his or her class. Referrals to school social workers dropped to almost nothing as badly troubled children went untreated. The school board had members who were ideologically opposed to public education and who supported voucher systems to send children to private schools, some of them religious. Funding for new facilities and programs were turned down by the voters, who felt the school district was doing badly and didn't want to support new school initiatives.

"I came in and shared these findings with teachers and the school board. Over time, they began to communicate and develop an overall plan. I helped in this process, but once they began the work, it went smoothly and quickly. The new environment of cooperation resulted in much less violence, better student scores on state tests, and higher levels of teacher and school board morale. My job was to facilitate change by getting the different groups to talk to each other and to set new directions and procedures for the school. The social workers now have full loads and violence is down to a trickle. The entire process took almost 2 years to reach its current level of effectiveness, but when you think that this school district includes almost 50,000 children and over 2,000 teachers and other school personal, that's pretty fast change in my view. Social justice, in my view, is the provision of equal education for all children. I think this example of organizational change is an example of how social workers assure people of social justice by getting their organizations to work much more effectively.

"Organizational transformation almost always results in social justice, in my view, when the process is democratic and the views of all the people involved are included. The job of the organizational change specialist is to take those various perceptions of what's wrong and how to right it, and to get people to work together for a common goal. The teachers, administration, school board, and parents and students were able to do this, and the common goal—better functioning schools—was achieved. I may have come up with a plan and facilitated people working together, but in the best example of how democracy works, they worked out solutions cooperatively, and look at how great the results are."

Summary

This chapter on social justice discusses the meaning of social justice, how it applies to our lives, the commitment social work has to social justice, and the complex but necessary task of ensuring social justice for everyone, even those whom we often think of as less than optimal people. The chapter provides an opportunity for you to decide on the behavior of a helping professional who takes the role of societal representative to extremes, and it also points out the important work we do as organizational change agents by making organizations more responsive to the needs of citizens. A case example is provided that shows the ways social workers help organizations function more effectively and how positive outcomes often improve services to clients and communities.

Questions to Determine Your Frame of Reference

1.   There is a serious debate in our country regarding the treatment of suspected terrorists who are being held in military jails. What is your belief about the way suspected terrorists should be treated and if various forms of torture are acceptable? If so, under what circumstances and how far would you consider going?

2.   The ACLU is an organization that protects civil liberties but is also unpopular. Ask people you know their opinion of the ACLU, visit their website, and determine your personal opinion of the organization in a small group discussion.

3.   We often hear about organizations getting new leadership and the great changes that will follow. Often, the leader tries, but organizations resist change. Why do you think this happens, particularly when everyone in the organization knows it's an unhealthy and nonproductive place to work?

4.   Do you think a free economy provides for more or less civil liberty than a government-controlled economy such as those that may be found in socialist countries? Explain your position.

5.   Social work has often been tied to public agencies with some degree of public antagonism (e.g., public welfare and child protective services). Do you think the reason the organizations are unpopular is (a) the service provided (e.g., taking children away from parents), (b) because the quality of the service isn't as good as it might be, (c) because public services are often unpopular with most Americans, (d) because of antagonism to the idea of social services, (e) because most people have a misconception of social work, (f) all of the above, or (g) none of the above?

Internet Sources

Social justice is explained in an article appearing in Wikipedia. Michael Novak then explains social justice from his unique point of view. Izumi and

Taylor explain planned organizational change, whereas Scholl provides models of organizational change.

1. Wikipedia. (2006). *Social justice.* Retrieved January 17, 2006, from http://en.wikipedia.org/wiki/Social_justice

2. Novak, M. (2000). Defining social justice. *First Things.* Retrieved January 17, 2006, from http://www.firstthings.com/ftissues/ft0012/opinion/novak.html

3. Izumi, H., & Taylor, D. M. (1998). *Planned organizational change.* Retrieved January 17, 2006, from http://www.esc.edu/ESConline/across_esc/forumjournal.nsf/3cc42a422514347a8525671d0049f395/1f36661906ca98d9852567b0006beb07?OpenDocument

4. Scholl, R. W. (1981). An analysis of macro models of organizations: The goal and political models. *Administration & Society, 13*(3), 271–298. Retrieved January 17, 2006, from http://www.cba.uri.edu/Scholl/Papers/Macro%20_Models.html

Potential Social Problems in the 21st Century and the Future Directions for Social Welfare and Social Work

23

The belief that we can rely on shortcuts to happiness, joy, rapture, comfort, and ecstasy, rather than be entitled to these feelings by the exercise of personal strengths and virtues, results in legions of people who, in the middle of great wealth, are starving spiritually. Positive emotion alienated from the exercise of character leads to emptiness, to inauthenticity, to depression, and, as we age, to the gnawing realization that we are fidgeting until we die.

—Martin Seligman (quoted in ABCNews.com, 2002)

Problems of the 21st Century

Although no one knows for certain at this early stage in the new millennium what our future social problems will be, I've gone to the literature and found what I think are some concerns of people whom I consider to be serious social thinkers. We believe that there will be four major American social problems in the 21st century that will directly affect social work and social welfare organizations.

SOCIAL ISOLATION

Robert Putnam (Stossel, 2000) believes that we have become so focused on ourselves in the absence of creating connections to the community that we are producing a country without a sense of social connectedness where "supper eaten with friends or family has given way to supper gobbled in solitude, with only the glow of the television screen for companionship" (p. 1). According to Putnam,

> Americans today have retreated into isolation. Evidence shows that fewer and fewer contemporary Americans are unionizing, voting, rallying around shared causes, participating in religious services, inviting each other over, or doing much of anything collectively. In fact, when we do occasionally gather—for twelve-step support encounters and the like—it's most often only as an excuse to focus on ourselves in the presence of an audience. (Stossel, 2000, p. 1)

To put Putnam's work in perspective, union membership has declined by more than half since the mid-1950s. PTA membership has fallen from 12 million in 1964 to 7 million. Since 1970, membership in the Boy Scouts is down by 26% and membership in the Red Cross is off by 61% (Stossel, 2000, p. 1). Putnam believes that the lack of social involvement negatively affects school performance and physical and mental health, increases crime rates, reduces tax responsibilities and charitable work, and decreases productivity and "even simple human happiness—all are demonstrably affected by how (and whether) we connect with our family and friends and neighbors and coworkers" (Stossel, 2000, p. 1).

InfoTable 23.1	An Obsession With Wealth Destroys Social Cohesion

We are seeing increasing social breakdown, stress, depression, drug abuse, suicide, litigation, decay of communities, rural decline, and loss of social cohesion. Attitudes toward the poor, the homeless, and the unemployed are hardening. It has become a divided, winner-take-all society, with many now classified as "excluded." The rich, including the upper-middle class, which does the top managerial and legal work for the corporations, and the professionals are rapidly increasing their wealth and have no interest in calling for change. Inequality and polarization are accelerating.

All this is sociologically appalling. Damage is being done to social cohesion, public spirit, trust, good will, and concern for the public interest. You cannot have a satisfactory society made up of competitive, self-interested individuals all trying to get as rich as possible! In a satisfactory society there must be considerable concern for the public good and the welfare of all, and there must be considerable collective social control and regulation and service provision to make sure all are looked after, to maintain public institutions and standards, and to reinforce the sense of social solidarity whereby all are willing to contribute to the good of all. (Trainer, 2003)

A LOSS OF CIVIL LIBERTIES

Many people worry that terrorism and our concerns for further terrorist attacks will lessen our civil rights. Because many of you have lived during times of political stability in the United States, you may think that we have nothing to worry about and may not know about the many times civil rights have been in jeopardy in America. I grew up during one of those times: the period after World War II, when we went through what is now referred to as the Red Scare, or the deep concern for the spread of communism. During the early years of the Red Scare, the U.S. House of Representatives held hearings on un-American activities in many sectors of American society, including the movie industry. Many famous writers and directors were accused of being, or having been, Communists, and their careers were ruined, even though any Communist activity had long since ceased for some of them.

If you grew up during that time, were Jewish, and your parents came from Russia, as mine did, there was an automatic assumption that you were a Communist. My parents warned me repeatedly not to speak out, as difficult then as it is now, or my name would be placed in the record. For them, the record was something kept by the secret police in Russia, and it was very real. A number of famous civil rights activists, including Martin Luther King, were not surprised to discover that they were being spied on by the FBI. Others discovered that the FBI kept files on them because they wrote about, encouraged, or were active in the civil rights movement.

For these reasons, new laws such as the Patriot Act that remove some of our civil rights and liberties because of concerns over terrorism are troubling. Speaking about the Patriot Act, noted linguist and social activist Noam Chomsky says,

> It is doubtful that the current attack on civil liberties has much to do with security. In general, one can expect the state to use any pretext to extend its power and to impose obedience on the population; rights are won, not granted, and power will seek any opportunity to reduce them. The current incumbents in Washington are at an extreme of reactionary jingoism and contempt for democracy. The question we should ask, I think, is how far citizens will allow them to pursue their agendas. So far, they have been careful to target vulnerable populations, like immigrants, though the laws they have passed have much broader implications. (Epaminondas & Chomsky, 2002)

The point for us to remember is that civil liberties should not be taken for granted. One way to make certain our civil rights are not jeopardized is to be active in government, to know the issues, to know who represents us, and to vote. The number of Americans not voting is so high that many people worry our precious liberties are being eroded, not by unscrupulous politicians or a greedy corporate environment, but because Americans

InfoTable 23.2	The Erosion of Civil Liberties

Virtually all civil liberties have been eroded by war, the preparation for it, and other kinds of crises, such as depressions. These have been particularly effective in de-sensitizing people to encroachments on their freedom. Responses to crises have brought censorship, conscription, new and higher taxes, and control of transportation, industry, and agriculture. When those crises ended, most new controls were removed and taxes were reduced—but government power never shrunk back to its pre-crisis level (the "ratchet effect"). The people were left with new and permanent state impositions in their lives. What's more, they were effectively trained to accept further "necessary" assaults on their liberties when the next crisis arrived. (The Independent Institute, 2003, p. 1)

have handed over a large number of rights without so much as a challenge through inertia, disinterest, and apathy. Find out the facts for yourself. Evaluate them in a rational way, and make informed decisions about the type of government you want and who you believe is best able to lead us.

A DECLINING MIDDLE CLASS AND INCREASING NUMBERS OF PEOPLE IN POVERTY

This book has provided a great deal of data regarding increases in the absolute number of lower income people and the negative impact of poverty. I believe that as well-paying jobs become scarcer and many higher level jobs are outsourced to foreign countries, the threat of a dwindling middle class is a distinct possibility. What this means, unfortunately, is that education as the great influence on creating a large number of middle-class Americans will have less impact and that more and more highly educated people in our society will find that they can only be employed in jobs for which they are overqualified. The first group to feel this effect will be older workers, whereas younger workers may find that available jobs pay less than they did even a few years ago. In many ways, this is good news for those of you who want to choose social work as a career, because social work is a service field that can't be outsourced; however, it's bad news for those of you thinking about careers in business and technical fields, which are currently being outsourced. I hope I'm wrong about this, but the trends seem very clear.

A dwindling middle class means that, increasingly, those with money will wield enormous political and economic power. If President Bush is correct that 20% of Americans pay 80% of the taxes, you begin to see the economic imbalance in the country. It stands to reason that those who pay the most taxes will also be the most listened to, and that their issues will dominate the political discourse to an even greater extent in the future.

You may also begin to see a decline in the amount of money spent on public education and medical care. The social safety net will be changed, and people at risk—those who have lost jobs or people needing medical care because they lack insurance—will be less well cared for than they are at present. Writing in *Forbes,* a politically conservative finance magazine, Shilling (2004) reports that John Edwards was right about us dividing into two countries: one rich and the other poor. He reports that the share of the top 20% of incomes in America has risen from 43% to 50% of the total income in America, whereas all other incomes have fallen because of outsourcing, and that the loss of manufacturing jobs has increased from 11% to 28% at present.

Shilling provides three reasons for the reduction in the middle class: (a) upper middle income brackets are decreasing as more highly skilled professional jobs are being outsourced to other countries, where salaries are much lower; (b) many technical jobs are dependent on a manufacturing sector, such as computers, which are increasingly being made in other countries or where software has possibly gone well beyond the needs of most computer users; and (c) because many lower income people borrow to pay the difference between what they earn and what they need, causing the cost of loans to increase and thereby making it difficult to buy new goods, particularly cars and homes. Shilling says that defaults on mortgages and loans and personal bankruptcies are at an all-time high and that middle-income people "may not be able to keep borrowing much longer" (p. 228). This means that having one's own home and new cars will be increasingly unlikely for many people in America. Whether a more liberal political majority can reverse these trends is difficult to say because these changes have been taking place over a number of years.

Whether a nation that has grown to expect unprecedented wealth and consumer goods beyond anyone's imagination will be able to cope with the changing distribution of income is anyone's guess. My sense is that as jobs become more scarce and competition for work becomes more fierce, foreign-born workers will be less welcome in America and resistance to the entry of illegal immigrants will become more vocal. These episodes of anti-immigrant sentiment get repeated in America as the job market becomes more competitive, and one can sadly expect more hate crimes and violence against immigrant groups in the future. I sincerely hope I'm wrong about this, but the development of anti-immigrant sentiment and laws in Europe makes me believe otherwise. In France, for example, wearing traditional headgear and clothing for Muslims and Jews has been outlawed in public schools, and a Sheikh child was recently arrested for wearing a turban. These are not promising signs.

TWO AMERICAS

In the first chapter of this book, I mentioned the difference between conservative and liberal political orientations. The idea of two Americas,

InfoTable 23.3	The Declining Middle Class

The Economic Policy Institute has shown that the fastest-growing industries are low-wage ones, like hotel and food services, while shrinking industries are high-wage ones, like information services and manufacturing. The explanation for all of this is that we're living in an economy where the forces that should benefit average workers are overwhelmed by policies and practices that benefit corporations and the wealthy, like trillion-dollar tax cuts.

It's easy to see the effect of an economy where workers have trouble meeting their families' needs. Since the beginning of the 2001 recession, corporate profits have expanded by an astonishing 57.5 percent. Meanwhile, total wages and salaries have actually shrunk by 1.7 percent.

More and more, full-time workers are wondering how they're going to get by on their paycheck alone. Health-care costs are through the roof. For workers that dream of sending their kids to college, tuition and fees at four-year public universities are soaring, increasing by 14 percent last year alone. If all this weren't enough, average gas prices hit $2 this month, for the first time ever (and have escalated by more than 50 cents since).

From one point of view, the good times are starting to roll again: profits are up. But for most Americans, caught in the middle-class squeeze, it feels a lot more like they're getting rolled. (Miller, 2004, p. 16B)

a theme of the John Edwards Presidential Campaign in 2004, is a traditional concern for those on the more liberal side of the political spectrum. In this view, "There are two Americas . . . one privileged, the other burdened . . . one America that does the work, another America that reaps the rewards. One America that pays the taxes, another America that gets the tax breaks" (Edwards, 2005). John Cannon said something very similar, if perhaps more strident, in a speech to the 1948 Socialist Workers Party Convention:

> For there are two Americas—and millions of the people already distinguish between them. One is the America of the imperialists—of the little clique of capitalists, landlords, and militarists who are threatening and terrifying the world. This is the America the people of the world hate and fear.
>
> There is the other America—the America of the workers and farmers and the "little people." They constitute the great majority of the people. They do the work of the country. They revere its old democratic traditions—its old record of friendship for the people of other lands, in their struggles against kings and despots—its generous asylum once freely granted to the oppressed.

On the other side of the argument, writing for the conservative think tank, the Heritage Foundation, Rector and Hederman (2004) reject the idea of two Americas by saying that "class warfare has always been a mainstay of liberal politics" and that the top fifth of U.S. households (with incomes above $84,000) remain perennial targets of class-warfare enmity. These families, however, perform a third of all labor in the economy. They contain the best educated and most productive workers, and they provide a disproportionate share of the investment needed to create jobs and spur economic growth. Nearly all are married-couple families, many with two or more earners. Far from shirking the tax burden, these families pay 82.5 percent of total federal income taxes and two-thirds of federal taxes overall. By contrast, the bottom quintile pays 1.1 percent of total federal taxes.

How might we respond to these two notions of America: one with concern for the poor and the other perhaps disparaging of this group as being nonproductive and taking more than they return? This is a key issue for social work. Most of us in social work would take the position that the data showing the difference in taxes and income paid are a poor indicator because they are biased against hard physical labor that pays poorly. People who do the hardest work—the farm, factory, and construction workers—are also the lowest paid and the most likely to be laid off and injured. Their salaries and taxes are a poor indication of their worth, and Rector and Hederman (2004) do an injustice to blue-collar workers. In their view, white-collar workers reign supreme because they earn more and pay more taxes. But do they contribute more or work harder?

InfoTable 23.4	John Edwards on Two Americas

We know the difference between right and wrong. And it's right to talk about the two different Americas we still live in. We've got one for those who have been blessed and have lived the American Dream. And another for those who are struggling to get by.

Do we believe that any child in our country should go without health care just because their parents can't afford to go to the doctor? That's not what we believe in. We have to strengthen our health care system.

Do we believe one child should go to a school with computers while another goes to a school without enough books? That's not what we believe in. We have to strengthen our schools. We can start by expanding early childhood education and treating our teachers and those who work in our schools with the dignity and the respect that they deserve.

Do we believe in an America that is satisfied with two economies—one for wealthy insiders and one for the rest of us? That's not what we believe in. I'll tell you what's right. It's right to want to build one economy that honors work, not just wealth.

You know all of my life I have seen the power and dignity that comes from hard work. In the mills, the post office, and in our schools. I grew up believing that there are two important things we can give to each other—our love and our labor.

I believe there is dignity in work. It goes beyond the numbers on any paycheck. The men and women in my hometown—and yours—feel stronger and better when they know their hard work always—always—can provide for their families. (Edwards, 2005)

InfoTable 23.5	A Response to John Edwards

In one sense, John Edwards is correct: There is one America that works a lot and pays a lot in taxes, and there is another America that works less and pays little. However, the reality is the opposite of what Edwards suggests. It is the higher-income families who work a lot and pay nearly all the taxes. Raising taxes even higher on hard-working families would be unfair and, by reducing future investments, would reduce economic growth, harming all Americans in the long run. (Rector & Hederman, 2004)

I've been a blue-collar worker and find the comparison between the contribution of white-collar and blue-collar workers indicative of the class warfare that Rector and Hederman (2004) define as a liberal malady. We all contribute. We are a united country . . . one America, each of us contributing to the country in our own way. If it were up to me, blue-collar workers would be the highest-paid workers. They suffer the illnesses of the fields, where insecticides destroy their lungs and cardiovascular systems. Construction workers fall from roofs and scaffolds and suffer high rates of paralysis. Factory workers mutilate their bodies in industrial accidents and are the first to be laid off if a company decides that it's too costly to produce a product in America and moves elsewhere. For me, the issue is clear, and the conservative side of the debate, albeit worth considering and understanding, does not tell a true picture of life in America for blue-collar workers and less-educated people. Not all of us will go to college or make a great deal of money. If you grow up in a poor family, your chances of going to college are minimized. If that family is abusive, the chances of higher education dwindle. Although it's nice to think that we can all pull ourselves up by our bootstraps and become educated, affluent, and high-salaried, the reality is that the burdens of childhood poverty and unsympathetic and unsupportive environments weigh heavily on people, and the motivation to succeed may not be as strong as it is in those Americans who grow up in highly motivating and supportive families.

We live in a time of unprecedented affluence in America. For most of us, life is good, but for a growing number of Americans, life is very difficult. The taxes not paid in money are too often paid in the breakdown of the body and the spirit because of unbelievably hard work. So yes, we do have two Americas . . . one for most of us, and one for the remainder. And if the number for the remaining Americans is 15% to 20%, that's far too many, and we should not forget our fellow Americans who live in humble and impoverished circumstances. If we aren't concerned about our fellow citizens who haven't done well in life, then what good is our affluence? If the end result of education and high income is a hard-hearted and self-centered perspective on life, what are we as a people?

Problems Facing Social Work and Social Welfare Institutions

SERIOUS UNATTENDED TO PRACTICE ISSUES

Some authors, myself included, believe that social work and social welfare institutions have avoided dealing with some very serious problems in America. For example, even though men are doing badly these days, little notice is given to male problems in our professional literature. In reporting data from the University of Michigan's Institute for Social Research, Gupta (2003) notes that "men outrank women in all of the 15 leading causes of death, except one: Alzheimer's. Men's death rates are at least twice as high as women's for suicide, homicide and cirrhosis of the liver" (p. 84). Slater (2003) indicates that 900,000 black males are in prison as compared to 600,000 black males attending college, junior college, or vocational training programs, or half the number of African American females attending American colleges and universities. The discrepancy between black male and female college attendance will result in such an imbalance of college-educated men to women that, according to Roach (2001), it will alter the "social dynamics" of the African American community.

Epidemic increases in male juvenile crime suggest another serious problem for men. Commenting on the significance of the increase in male-dominated juvenile crime, Osofsky and Osofsky (2001) write, "The homicide rate among males 15–24 years old in the United States is 10 times higher than in Canada, 15 times higher than in Australia, and 28 times higher than in France or Germany" (p. 287). Yet social work seems to have very limited interest in antisocial and violent clients. In fact, in my recent book on violence in children younger than age 12 (Glicken, 2004b), I noted the highly discouraging attitudes many helping professionals have about working with violent children and, more troubling, whether there is even a role for the helping professions in work with violent children. As examples, Rae-Grant, McConville, and Fleck (1999) write, "Because exclusive individual clinical interventions for violent conduct disorders do not work, the child and adolescent psychiatrist must seek opportunities to be a leader or team member in well-organized and well-funded community prevention efforts" (p. 338). Elliott, Hamburg, and Williams (1998) believe that counseling has no positive effect on the problems of antisocial and predelinquent youth. Steiner and Stone (1999) suggest widespread pessimism among helping professionals regarding effective clinical work with violent youth. And writing about why clinicians have such a poor track record with gang members, Morales (1982) believes that worker bias about the intractability of gang members is based on a number of erroneous beliefs, including the following: (a) antisocial personality disorders and/or gang members are untreatable; (b) a fear of violent people and a belief that all gang members are violent; (c) a belief that poor or uneducated people lack the capacity for insight, a cohort sometimes associated with gang activity; (d) a belief that the only way people change is through treatment; (e) the opposite belief that gang members are untreatable, manipulative, and dishonest; and (f) the belief that therapists need to control the interview because they have ultimate power.

Even though most social workers are quick to point out the damage done by child abuse, in a book review of *Treatment of Child Abuse* edited by Robert M. Reece (2000), Lukefahr (2001) writes, "Although there is a very strong effort throughout to base findings and recommendations on the available evidence, these chapters highlight the reality that this young, evolving specialty remains largely descriptive" (p. 36). Kaplan, Pelcovitz, and Labruna (1999) write that treatment effectiveness of child abuse "has generally not been empirically evaluated." In a review of treatment research for physically abused children, Oates and Bross (1995) cite only 13 empirical studies between 1983 and 1992 meeting even minimal research standards (p. 1218). Given the hundreds of thousands of child welfare workers in America and the billions of dollars spent on child abuse, how would any of this be possible if helping professionals were seriously involved in efforts to learn more about how we can best help and prevent child abuse?

And although the number of older Americans is growing each year, many with treatable social and emotional problems, this book has examined the services offered to older adults who suffer from anxiety and depression and finds that many older adults are denied needed help because helping professionals often believe that older Americans cannot benefit from treatment. Because older Americans, when suicidal, have an extremely high completion rate, it seems very important that we learn more about them and the services we might provide to help growing numbers of depressed and anxious older adults.

The Future of Social Work and Social Welfare

The U.S. Department of Labor (2004) estimates a growth in social service/ residential care jobs between the years 2000 and 2010 of half a million new jobs, with the average salary for all social workers at $42,000 a year. Although the future for social work is very bright and those choosing a career in social work can expect to be well rewarded, the work itself may change somewhat. Krauth (1996, p. 10) predicts that psychotherapy and counseling will be used less often and, in their place, educational approaches may predominate with a focus on prevention. He also believes that we will know enough about the effective approaches to use with clients that, much like medicine, we will have treatment protocols utilizing best evidence from research literature. Smith and Reynolds (2002) predict that social workers will use the Internet to help clients in the future and that chat rooms, e-mails, and Internet webpages will augment face-to-face treatment.

In further predictions of the future, Norcross, Hedges, and Prochaska (2002) studied psychotherapy during the past several decades and, based on the results of their most recent study, they conclude that four trends will emerge: (a) the economic realities of payment for services will result in the quickest therapies, the least-expensive therapist, and the least-expensive therapeutic techniques; (b) therapists will be rewarded who utilize best evidence provided by the research evidence; (c) new therapy approaches will evolve, but it will be a gradual evolution—new approaches will build on, rather than break with, current approaches; and (d) the helping approaches most likely to emerge in the future include those that can be done at home such as homework assignments, use of the Internet to locate resources and to find out more about solutions to problems, and self-help groups. The study also predicted that there will be an increase in

> short-term treatments (e.g., problem solving, cognitive restructuring, solution-focused, and skill training). Techniques predicted to decrease precipitously were those that are part of long-term therapies (e.g., free association, analysis of resistance, transference, and dream interpretations). (p. 320)

Reynolds and Richardson (2000) suggest that the future of psychotherapy will be similar to that of medicine, with more resources placed into research efforts that will ultimately lead to increased and improved services to clients. They believe that social workers will have a basis for making better judgments about the use of resources and that effectiveness research will significantly increase. To provide direction to social work practitioners, the authors call for well-controlled studies providing research evidence that practitioners can accept and use with confidence with a diverse population of clients.

You Be the Social Worker

Much has been made about managed care and the quality of health services. This short vignette appears in my book about clinical work with men (Glicken, 2005, pp. 115–116) and describes an experience a male client had with a therapist working in a health maintenance organization (HMO). In HMOs, most services are provided by physicians and helping professionals employed by the HMO. Options for mental health services are often very limited. In this short piece, the client describes his experiences in an HMO with a therapist (not a social worker, we're happy to say).

(Continued)

(Continued)

The Case

I retired early because I was really burned out on my job. All I could think about was quitting. I'd written resignation letters on the computer for many years. They were categorized by how angry I was, and some of them were real doozies. I finally quit when I had enough money saved but without a retirement plan. After 4 months of feeling great, I started missing work, or at least something to occupy my time. I've been divorced a long time, my children live pretty far away, I don't have hobbies, and I've never been good at filling spare time, so as far as finding work, it was really hurtful after all the years I've spent successfully working to be turned down for jobs. The more I got turned down, the more anxious and depressed I became. I don't like the idea of medication for down moods. I talked to my primary care doctor, who suggested therapy. I reluctantly went, but I didn't feel very optimistic because I don't think most therapists know the first thing about men and particularly older men.

The therapist I saw made a joke out of what I was going through and said she knew lots of men who would be "tickled pink" to be in my shoes. She suggested a group called "Getting Off Your Rockers." Most of the people were easily 15 years older than me and did activities I really dislike, like square dancing and going to cheap places with these huge salad bars where everyone pigs out on food.

And as far as having relationships with women my age, it's been a dismal experience and I've pretty much given up looking for anyone. Most of the women I go out with are still angry at their ex-husbands or want to show me how tough they are by treating men like insects. I told this to the therapist, who said that I hadn't been trying hard enough to meet anyone and I should find out more about women. She even gave me the names of two books about women, which were full of male bashing jokes and put downs. I was insulted.

I saw her twice and decided she was making me more upset than I was before I first came in. I mean, a side of me knows there are better therapists, but it just makes me mad that I did something that's so hard for me to do and the results were worse than doing nothing. I don't think I have the energy to go back and try someone else. Most of the therapists in my HMO are women and, from what I can see in the waiting room, almost all of the clients are women. I don't think the therapists know what to do with older men in my place in life, and I doubt if they see retirement the same way most successful men do. I've used work to put off dealing with my nonexistent personal life. I would think that would be evident to any therapist in five minutes. For me, retirement is about getting old. Being turned down for other jobs just reinforces that feeling. Not to be taken seriously is just plain hurtful. I don't know who I'm more angry at: therapists for being incompetent, or me for getting myself in this situation and going for help when I knew it wouldn't work in the first place.

Questions

1. The client says that female therapists don't know much about men. Do you think this may be true because most clients in therapy are women and men seldom use therapy unless forced to, or might gender bias be involved?

2. Do you think in HMOs that mental health has a low priority? Explain your answer.

3. The client has some negative things to say about dating older women. In your experience, is he accurate in his description of older women and their attitudes toward men?

4. Being alone after a certain age can be very difficult. What do you think we can do to help men and women who live alone to be more connected to others in their community?

5. Do you think that this client might have stayed with his job or at least changed to more satisfying work had he initially seen a sympathetic and caring worker when he first considered retirement? Why?

Summary

This chapter discusses the problems facing America in the future, the role of social welfare organizations, and the future of professional social work. The advent of HMOs and the lack of funding social services make it more apparent than ever that certain populations are underserved, including men, those with problems of violence, the elderly, and abused children. Questions related to an older man's feelings about the poor quality of service he received from a helping professional are presented.

Questions to Determine Your Frame of Reference

1. Using the Internet to provide services seems full of potential. What might be some positives and negatives of using the Internet to provide services to clients?

2. What is your salary expectation when you graduate, and 10 years after you graduate? Compare your expectations with that of your peers and see if you note any trends by gender, race, or ethnicity.

3. Do you agree with the John Edwards notion of two Americas, or do you think that those who make the most money should also have the most privileges?

4. There seems to be a growing anti-immigrant sentiment in America. Why do you think this is the case? If you agree, what should be done about it?

5. There's nothing wrong with being poor but respectable. If more people had less money it would make us a harder working country with better values and more concern about our religious, spiritual, and community lives. Do you agree or disagree with this, and why?

Internet Sources

Apfel and Panetta (1999) provide a thoughtful and timely article on the future of social security. Next, the Center on Budget and Policy Priorities (1998) reports on the strength of the social safety net for poor and at-risk clients. Robbins (2005) discusses the future of social work and the need to pay much more attention to the problems of older adults, whereas Press brings up the problem of our declining middle class. Finally, Smith and Reynolds (2002) contemplate the future of "cyberpsychotherapy."

1. Apfel, K., & Panetta, L. (1999, November 30). *Issues forum on the future of social security.* The Panetta Institute for Public Policy. Retrieved from http://www.panettainstitute.org/ss.html

2. Center on Budget and Policy Priorities. (1998). *Strength of the safety net.* Retrieved from http://www.cbpp.org/snd98-rep.htm

3. Robbins, L. (2005, February 28). *Strengthening for the future of social work.* Aging Invitational Talk, CSWE Annual Program Meeting, New York. Retrieved from http://depts.washington.edu/geroctr/Center2/2005AgingInvitational_LRobbins.pdf

4. Press, E. (2004, November 8). Straight down the middle. *The Nation.* Retrieved January 18, 2006, from http://www.thenation.com/docprint.mhtml?i=20041108&s=press

5. Smith, S. D., & Reynolds, R. (2002). *The future of cyberpsychotherapy.* Retrieved October 15, 2005, from http://www.americanpsychotherapy.com/ce-marapr-2002-CyberPsychotherapy.php

Appendix

Code of Ethics of the National Association of Social Workers

Approved by the 1996 NASW Delegate Assembly and revised by the 1999 NASW Delegate Assembly

Found on the Internet September 13, 2005 at: http://www.naswdc.org/pubs/code/code.asp

Preamble

The primary mission of the social work profession is to enhance human well-being and help meet the basic human needs of all people, with particular attention to the needs and empowerment of people who are vulnerable, oppressed, and living in poverty. A historic and defining feature of social work is the profession's focus on individual well-being in a social context and the well-being of society. Fundamental to social work is attention to the environmental forces that create, contribute to, and address problems in living.

Social workers promote social justice and social change with and on behalf of clients. "Clients" is used inclusively to refer to individuals, families, groups, organizations, and communities. Social workers are sensitive to cultural and ethnic diversity and strive to end discrimination, oppression, poverty, and other forms of social injustice. These activities may be in the form of direct practice, community organizing, supervision, consultation, administration, advocacy, social and political action, policy development and implementation, education, and research and evaluation. Social workers seek to enhance the capacity of people to address their own needs. Social workers also seek to promote the responsiveness of organizations, communities, and other social institutions to individuals' needs and social problems.

The mission of the social work profession is rooted in a set of core values. These core values, embraced by social workers throughout the profession's history, are the foundation of social work's unique purpose and perspective:

- service
- social justice
- dignity and worth of the person
- importance of human relationships
- integrity
- competence.

This constellation of core values reflects what is unique to the social work profession. Core values, and the principles that flow from them, must be balanced within the context and complexity of the human experience.

Purpose of the NASW Code of Ethics

Professional ethics are at the core of social work. The profession has an obligation to articulate its basic values, ethical principles, and ethical standards. The *NASW Code of Ethics* sets forth these values, principles, and standards to guide social workers' conduct. The *Code* is relevant to all social workers and social work students, regardless of their professional functions, the settings in which they work, or the populations they serve.

The *NASW Code of Ethics* serves six purposes:

1. The *Code* identifies core values on which social work's mission is based.

2. The *Code* summarizes broad ethical principles that reflect the profession's core values and establishes a set of specific ethical standards that should be used to guide social work practice.

3. The *Code* is designed to help social workers identify relevant considerations when professional obligations conflict or ethical uncertainties arise.

4. The *Code* provides ethical standards to which the general public can hold the social work profession accountable.

5. The *Code* socializes practitioners new to the field to social work's mission, values, ethical principles, and ethical standards.

6. The *Code* articulates standards that the social work profession itself can use to assess whether social workers have engaged in unethical

conduct. NASW has formal procedures to adjudicate ethics complaints filed against its members.* In subscribing to this *Code,* social workers are required to cooperate in its implementation, participate in NASW adjudication proceedings, and abide by any NASW disciplinary rulings or sanctions based on it.

The *Code* offers a set of values, principles, and standards to guide decision making and conduct when ethical issues arise. It does not provide a set of rules that prescribe how social workers should act in all situations. Specific applications of the *Code* must take into account the context in which it is being considered and the possibility of conflicts among the *Code's* values, principles, and standards. Ethical responsibilities flow from all human relationships, from the personal and familial to the social and professional.

Further, the *NASW Code of Ethics* does not specify which values, principles, and standards are most important and ought to outweigh others in instances when they conflict. Reasonable differences of opinion can and do exist among social workers with respect to the ways in which values, ethical principles, and ethical standards should be rank ordered when they conflict. Ethical decision making in a given situation must apply the informed judgment of the individual social worker and should also consider how the issues would be judged in a peer review process where the ethical standards of the profession would be applied.

Ethical decision making is a process. There are many instances in social work where simple answers are not available to resolve complex ethical issues. Social workers should take into consideration all the values, principles, and standards in this *Code* that are relevant to any situation in which ethical judgment is warranted. Social workers' decisions and actions should be consistent with the spirit as well as the letter of this *Code.*

In addition to this *Code,* there are many other sources of information about ethical thinking that may be useful. Social workers should consider ethical theory and principles generally, social work theory and research, laws, regulations, agency policies, and other relevant codes of ethics, recognizing that among codes of ethics social workers should consider the *NASW Code of Ethics* as their primary source. Social workers also should be aware of the impact on ethical decision making of their clients' and their own personal values and cultural and religious beliefs and practices. They should be aware of any conflicts between personal and professional values and deal with them responsibly. For additional guidance social workers should consult the relevant literature on professional ethics and ethical decision making and seek appropriate consultation when faced with ethical dilemmas. This may involve consultation with an agency-based or social work organization's ethics committee, a regulatory body, knowledgeable colleagues, supervisors, or legal counsel.

---

*For information on NASW adjudication procedures, see *NASW Procedures for the Adjudication of Grievances.*

Instances may arise when social workers' ethical obligations conflict with agency policies or relevant laws or regulations. When such conflicts occur, social workers must make a responsible effort to resolve the conflict in a manner that is consistent with the values, principles, and standards expressed in this *Code*. If a reasonable resolution of the conflict does not appear possible, social workers should seek proper consultation before making a decision.

The *NASW Code of Ethics* is to be used by NASW and by individuals, agencies, organizations, and bodies (such as licensing and regulatory boards, professional liability insurance providers, courts of law, agency boards of directors, government agencies, and other professional groups) that choose to adopt it or use it as a frame of reference. Violation of standards in this *Code* does not automatically imply legal liability or violation of the law. Such determination can only be made in the context of legal and judicial proceedings. Alleged violations of the *Code* would be subject to a peer review process. Such processes are generally separate from legal or administrative procedures and insulated from legal review or proceedings to allow the profession to counsel and discipline its own members.

A code of ethics cannot guarantee ethical behavior. Moreover, a code of ethics cannot resolve all ethical issues or disputes or capture the richness and complexity involved in striving to make responsible choices within a moral community. Rather, a code of ethics sets forth values, ethical principles, and ethical standards to which professionals aspire and by which their actions can be judged. Social workers' ethical behavior should result from their personal commitment to engage in ethical practice. The *NASW Code of Ethics* reflects the commitment of all social workers to uphold the profession's values and to act ethically. Principles and standards must be applied by individuals of good character who discern moral questions and, in good faith, seek to make reliable ethical judgments.

Ethical Principles

The following broad ethical principles are based on social work's core values of service, social justice, dignity and worth of the person, importance of human relationships, integrity, and competence. These principles set forth ideals to which all social workers should aspire.

Value: *Service*

Ethical Principle: *Social workers' primary goal is to help people in need and to address social problems.*

Social workers elevate service to others above self-interest. Social workers draw on their knowledge, values, and skills to help people in need and to address social problems. Social workers are encouraged to volunteer some portion of their professional skills with no expectation of significant financial return (pro bono service).

Value: *Social Justice*

Ethical Principle: *Social workers challenge social injustice.*

Social workers pursue social change, particularly with and on behalf of vulnerable and oppressed individuals and groups of people. Social workers' social change efforts are focused primarily on issues of poverty, unemployment, discrimination, and other forms of social injustice. These activities seek to promote sensitivity to and knowledge about oppression and cultural and ethnic diversity. Social workers strive to ensure access to needed information, services, and resources; equality of opportunity; and meaningful participation in decision making for all people.

Value: *Dignity and Worth of the Person*

Ethical Principle: *Social workers respect the inherent dignity and worth of the person.*

Social workers treat each person in a caring and respectful fashion, mindful of individual differences and cultural and ethnic diversity. Social workers promote clients' socially responsible self-determination. Social workers seek to enhance clients' capacity and opportunity to change and to address their own needs. Social workers are cognizant of their dual responsibility to clients and to the broader society. They seek to resolve conflicts between clients' interests and the broader society's interests in a socially responsible manner consistent with the values, ethical principles, and ethical standards of the profession.

Value: *Importance of Human Relationships*

Ethical Principle: *Social workers recognize the central importance of human relationships.*

Social workers understand that relationships between and among people are an important vehicle for change. Social workers engage people as partners in the helping process. Social workers seek to strengthen relationships among people in a purposeful effort to promote, restore, maintain, and enhance the well-being of individuals, families, social groups, organizations, and communities.

Value: *Integrity*

Ethical Principle: *Social workers behave in a trustworthy manner.*

Social workers are continually aware of the profession's mission, values, ethical principles, and ethical standards and practice in a manner consistent with them. Social workers act honestly and responsibly and promote ethical practices on the part of the organizations with which they are affiliated.

Value: *Competence*

Ethical Principle: *Social workers practice within their areas of competence and develop and enhance their professional expertise.*

Social workers continually strive to increase their professional knowledge and skills and to apply them in practice. Social workers should aspire to contribute to the knowledge base of the profession.

Ethical Standards

The following ethical standards are relevant to the professional activities of all social workers. These standards concern (1) social workers' ethical responsibilities to clients, (2) social workers' ethical responsibilities to colleagues, (3) social workers' ethical responsibilities in practice settings, (4) social workers' ethical responsibilities as professionals, (5) social workers' ethical responsibilities to the social work profession, and (6) social workers' ethical responsibilities to the broader society.

Some of the standards that follow are enforceable guidelines for professional conduct, and some are aspirational. The extent to which each standard is enforceable is a matter of professional judgment to be exercised by those responsible for reviewing alleged violations of ethical standards.

1. Social Workers' Ethical Responsibilities to Clients

1.01 Commitment to Clients

Social workers' primary responsibility is to promote the well-being of clients. In general, clients' interests are primary. However, social workers' responsibility to the larger society or specific legal obligations may on limited occasions supersede the loyalty owed clients, and clients should be so advised. (Examples include when a social worker is required by law to report that a client has abused a child or has threatened to harm self or others.)

1.02 Self-Determination

Social workers respect and promote the right of clients to self-determination and assist clients in their efforts to identify and clarify their goals. Social workers may limit clients' right to self-determination when, in the social workers' professional judgment, clients' actions or potential actions pose a serious, foreseeable, and imminent risk to themselves or others.

1.03 Informed Consent

(a) Social workers should provide services to clients only in the context of a professional relationship based, when appropriate, on valid informed consent. Social workers should use clear and understandable language to inform clients of the purpose of the services, risks related to the services, limits to services because of the requirements of a third-party payer, relevant costs, reasonable alternatives, clients' right to refuse or withdraw consent, and the time frame covered by the consent. Social workers should provide clients with an opportunity to ask questions.

(b) In instances when clients are not literate or have difficulty understanding the primary language used in the practice setting, social workers should take steps to ensure clients' comprehension. This may include providing clients with a detailed verbal explanation or arranging for a qualified interpreter or translator whenever possible.

(c) In instances when clients lack the capacity to provide informed consent, social workers should protect clients' interests by seeking permission from an appropriate third party, informing clients consistent with the clients' level of understanding. In such instances social workers should seek to ensure that the third party acts in a manner consistent with clients' wishes and interests. Social workers should take reasonable steps to enhance such clients' ability to give informed consent.

(d) In instances when clients are receiving services involuntarily, social workers should provide information about the nature and extent of services and about the extent of clients' right to refuse service.

(e) Social workers who provide services via electronic media (such as computer, telephone, radio, and television) should inform recipients of the limitations and risks associated with such services.

(f) Social workers should obtain clients' informed consent before audiotaping or videotaping clients or permitting observation of services to clients by a third party.

1.04 Competence

(a) Social workers should provide services and represent themselves as competent only within the boundaries of their education, training, license, certification, consultation received, supervised experience, or other relevant professional experience.

(b) Social workers should provide services in substantive areas or use intervention techniques or approaches that are new to them only after engaging in appropriate study, training, consultation, and supervision from people who are competent in those interventions or techniques.

(c) When generally recognized standards do not exist with respect to an emerging area of practice, social workers should exercise careful judgment and take responsible steps (including appropriate education, research, training, consultation, and supervision) to ensure the competence of their work and to protect clients from harm.

1.05 Cultural Competence and Social Diversity

(a) Social workers should understand culture and its function in human behavior and society, recognizing the strengths that exist in all cultures.

(b) Social workers should have a knowledge base of their clients' cultures and be able to demonstrate competence in the provision of services that are sensitive to clients' cultures and to differences among people and cultural groups.

(c) Social workers should obtain education about and seek to understand the nature of social diversity and oppression with respect to race, ethnicity, national origin, color, sex, sexual orientation, age, marital status, political belief, religion, and mental or physical disability.

1.06 Conflicts of Interest

(a) Social workers should be alert to and avoid conflicts of interest that interfere with the exercise of professional discretion and impartial judgment. Social workers should inform clients when a real or potential conflict of interest arises and take reasonable steps to resolve the issue in a manner that makes the clients' interests primary and protects clients' interests to the greatest extent possible. In some cases, protecting clients' interests may require termination of the professional relationship with proper referral of the client.

(b) Social workers should not take unfair advantage of any professional relationship or exploit others to further their personal, religious, political, or business interests.

(c) Social workers should not engage in dual or multiple relationships with clients or former clients in which there is a risk of exploitation or potential harm to the client. In instances when dual or multiple relationships are unavoidable, social workers should take steps to protect clients and are responsible for setting clear, appropriate, and culturally sensitive boundaries. (Dual or multiple relationships occur when social workers relate to clients in more than one relationship, whether professional, social, or business. Dual or multiple relationships can occur simultaneously or consecutively.)

(d) When social workers provide services to two or more people who have a relationship with each other (for example, couples, family members), social workers should clarify with all parties which individuals will be considered clients and the nature of social workers' professional obligations to the various individuals who are receiving services. Social workers who anticipate a conflict of interest among the individuals receiving services or who anticipate having to perform in potentially conflicting roles (for example, when a social worker is asked to testify in a child custody dispute or divorce proceedings involving clients) should clarify their role with the parties involved and take appropriate action to minimize any conflict of interest.

1.07 Privacy and Confidentiality

(a) Social workers should respect clients' right to privacy. Social workers should not solicit private information from clients unless it is essential to providing services or conducting social work evaluation or research. Once private information is shared, standards of confidentiality apply.

(b) Social workers may disclose confidential information when appropriate with valid consent from a client or a person legally authorized to consent on behalf of a client.

(c) Social workers should protect the confidentiality of all information obtained in the course of professional service, except for compelling professional reasons. The general expectation that social workers will keep information confidential does not apply when disclosure is necessary to prevent serious, foreseeable, and imminent harm to a client or other identifiable person. In all instances, social workers should disclose the least amount of confidential information necessary to achieve the desired purpose; only information that is directly relevant to the purpose for which the disclosure is made should be revealed.

(d) Social workers should inform clients, to the extent possible, about the disclosure of confidential information and the potential consequences, when feasible before the disclosure is made. This applies whether or not social workers disclose confidential information on the basis of a legal requirement or client consent.

(e) Social workers should discuss with clients and other interested parties the nature of confidentiality and limitations of clients' right to confidentiality. Social workers should review with clients circumstances where confidential information may be requested and where disclosure of confidential information may be legally required. This discussion should occur as soon as possible in the social worker-client relationship and as needed throughout the course of the relationship.

(f) When social workers provide counseling services to families, couples, or groups, social workers should seek agreement among the parties involved concerning each individual's right to confidentiality and obligation to preserve the confidentiality of information shared by others. Social workers should inform participants in family, couples, or group counseling that social workers cannot guarantee that all participants will honor such agreements.

(g) Social workers should inform clients involved in family, couples, marital, or group counseling of the social worker's, employer's, and agency's policy concerning the social worker's disclosure of confidential information among the parties involved in the counseling.

(h) Social workers should not disclose confidential information to third-party payers unless clients have authorized such disclosure.

(i) Social workers should not discuss confidential information in any setting unless privacy can be ensured. Social workers should not discuss confidential information in public or semipublic areas such as hallways, waiting rooms, elevators, and restaurants.

(j) Social workers should protect the confidentiality of clients during legal proceedings to the extent permitted by law. When a court of law or other legally authorized body orders social workers to disclose confidential or privileged information without a client's consent and such disclosure could cause harm to the client, social workers should request that the court withdraw the order or limit the order as narrowly as possible or maintain the records under seal, unavailable for public inspection.

(k) Social workers should protect the confidentiality of clients when responding to requests from members of the media.

(l) Social workers should protect the confidentiality of clients' written and electronic records and other sensitive information. Social workers should take reasonable steps to ensure that clients' records are stored in a secure location and that clients' records are not available to others who are not authorized to have access.

(m) Social workers should take precautions to ensure and maintain the confidentiality of information transmitted to other parties through the use of computers, electronic mail, facsimile machines, telephones and telephone answering machines, and other electronic or computer technology. Disclosure of identifying information should be avoided whenever possible.

(n) Social workers should transfer or dispose of clients' records in a manner that protects clients' confidentiality and is consistent with state statutes governing records and social work licensure.

(o) Social workers should take reasonable precautions to protect client confidentiality in the event of the social worker's termination of practice, incapacitation, or death.

(p) Social workers should not disclose identifying information when discussing clients for teaching or training purposes unless the client has consented to disclosure of confidential information.

(q) Social workers should not disclose identifying information when discussing clients with consultants unless the client has consented to disclosure of confidential information or there is a compelling need for such disclosure.

(r) Social workers should protect the confidentiality of deceased clients consistent with the preceding standards.

1.08 Access to Records

(a) Social workers should provide clients with reasonable access to records concerning the clients. Social workers who are concerned that clients' access to their records could cause serious misunderstanding or harm to the client should provide assistance in interpreting the records and consultation with the client regarding the records. Social workers should limit clients' access to their records, or portions of their records, only in exceptional circumstances when there is compelling evidence that such access would cause serious harm to the client. Both clients' requests and the rationale for withholding some or all of the record should be documented in clients' files.

(b) When providing clients with access to their records, social workers should take steps to protect the confidentiality of other individuals identified or discussed in such records.

1.09 Sexual Relationships

(a) Social workers should under no circumstances engage in sexual activities or sexual contact with current clients, whether such contact is consensual or forced.

(b) Social workers should not engage in sexual activities or sexual contact with clients' relatives or other individuals with whom clients maintain a close personal relationship when there is a risk of exploitation or potential harm to the client. Sexual activity or sexual contact with clients' relatives or other individuals with whom clients maintain a personal relationship has the potential to be harmful to the client and may make it difficult for the social worker and client to maintain appropriate professional boundaries. Social workers—not their clients, their clients' relatives, or other individuals with whom the client maintains a personal relationship—assume the full burden for setting clear, appropriate, and culturally sensitive boundaries.

(c) Social workers should not engage in sexual activities or sexual contact with former clients because of the potential for harm to the client. If social workers engage in conduct contrary to this prohibition or claim that an exception to this prohibition is warranted because of extraordinary circumstances, it is social workers—not their clients—who assume the full burden of demonstrating that the former client has not been exploited, coerced, or manipulated, intentionally or unintentionally.

(d) Social workers should not provide clinical services to individuals with whom they have had a prior sexual relationship. Providing clinical services to a former sexual partner has the potential to be harmful to the individual and is likely to make it difficult for the social worker and individual to maintain appropriate professional boundaries.

1.10 Physical Contact

Social workers should not engage in physical contact with clients when there is a possibility of psychological harm to the client as a result of the contact (such as cradling or caressing clients). Social workers who engage in appropriate physical contact with clients are responsible for setting clear, appropriate, and culturally sensitive boundaries that govern such physical contact.

1.11 Sexual Harassment

Social workers should not sexually harass clients. Sexual harassment includes sexual advances, sexual solicitation, requests for sexual favors, and other verbal or physical conduct of a sexual nature.

1.12 Derogatory Language

Social workers should not use derogatory language in their written or verbal communications to or about clients. Social workers should use accurate and respectful language in all communications to and about clients.

1.13 Payment for Services

(a) When setting fees, social workers should ensure that the fees are fair, reasonable, and commensurate with the services performed. Consideration should be given to clients' ability to pay.

(b) Social workers should avoid accepting goods or services from clients as payment for professional services. Bartering arrangements, particularly involving services, create the potential for conflicts of interest, exploitation, and inappropriate boundaries in social workers' relationships with clients. Social workers should explore and may participate in bartering only in very limited circumstances when it can be demonstrated that such arrangements are an accepted practice among professionals in the local community, considered to be essential for the provision of services, negotiated without coercion, and entered into at the client's initiative and with the client's informed consent. Social workers who accept goods or services from clients as payment for professional services assume the full burden of demonstrating that this arrangement will not be detrimental to the client or the professional relationship.

(c) Social workers should not solicit a private fee or other remuneration for providing services to clients who are entitled to such available services through the social workers' employer or agency.

1.14 Clients Who Lack Decision-Making Capacity

When social workers act on behalf of clients who lack the capacity to make informed decisions, social workers should take reasonable steps to safeguard the interests and rights of those clients.

1.15 Interruption of Services

Social workers should make reasonable efforts to ensure continuity of services in the event that services are interrupted by factors such as unavailability, relocation, illness, disability, or death.

1.16 Termination of Services

(a) Social workers should terminate services to clients and professional relationships with them when such services and relationships are no longer required or no longer serve the clients' needs or interests.

(b) Social workers should take reasonable steps to avoid abandoning clients who are still in need of services. Social workers should withdraw services precipitously only under unusual circumstances, giving careful consideration to all factors in the situation and taking care to minimize possible adverse effects. Social workers should assist in making appropriate arrangements for continuation of services when necessary.

(c) Social workers in fee-for-service settings may terminate services to clients who are not paying an overdue balance if the financial contractual arrangements have been made clear to the client, if the client does not pose an imminent danger to self or others, and if the clinical and other consequences of the current nonpayment have been addressed and discussed with the client.

(d) Social workers should not terminate services to pursue a social, financial, or sexual relationship with a client.

(e) Social workers who anticipate the termination or interruption of services to clients should notify clients promptly and seek the transfer, referral, or continuation of services in relation to the clients' needs and preferences.

(f) Social workers who are leaving an employment setting should inform clients of appropriate options for the continuation of services and of the benefits and risks of the options.

2. Social Workers' Ethical Responsibilities to Colleagues

2.01 Respect

(a) Social workers should treat colleagues with respect and should represent accurately and fairly the qualifications, views, and obligations of colleagues.

(b) Social workers should avoid unwarranted negative criticism of colleagues in communications with clients or with other professionals. Unwarranted negative criticism may include demeaning comments that refer to colleagues' level of competence or to individuals' attributes such as race, ethnicity, national origin, color, sex, sexual orientation, age, marital status, political belief, religion, and mental or physical disability.

(c) Social workers should cooperate with social work colleagues and with colleagues of other professions when such cooperation serves the well-being of clients.

2.02 Confidentiality

Social workers should respect confidential information shared by colleagues in the course of their professional relationships and transactions. Social workers should ensure that such colleagues understand social workers' obligation to respect confidentiality and any exceptions related to it.

2.03 Interdisciplinary Collaboration

(a) Social workers who are members of an interdisciplinary team should participate in and contribute to decisions that affect the well-being of clients by drawing on the perspectives, values, and experiences of the social work profession. Professional and ethical obligations of the interdisciplinary team as a whole and of its individual members should be clearly established.

(b) Social workers for whom a team decision raises ethical concerns should attempt to resolve the disagreement through appropriate channels. If the disagreement cannot be resolved, social workers should pursue other avenues to address their concerns consistent with client well-being.

2.04 Disputes Involving Colleagues

(a) Social workers should not take advantage of a dispute between a colleague and an employer to obtain a position or otherwise advance the social workers' own interests.

(b) Social workers should not exploit clients in disputes with colleagues or engage clients in any inappropriate discussion of conflicts between social workers and their colleagues.

2.05 Consultation

(a) Social workers should seek the advice and counsel of colleagues whenever such consultation is in the best interests of clients.

(b) Social workers should keep themselves informed about colleagues' areas of expertise and competencies. Social workers should seek consultation only from colleagues who have demonstrated knowledge, expertise, and competence related to the subject of the consultation.

(c) When consulting with colleagues about clients, social workers should disclose the least amount of information necessary to achieve the purposes of the consultation.

2.06 Referral for Services

(a) Social workers should refer clients to other professionals when the other professionals' specialized knowledge or expertise is needed to serve clients fully or when social workers believe that they are not being effective or making reasonable progress with clients and that additional service is required.

(b) Social workers who refer clients to other professionals should take appropriate steps to facilitate an orderly transfer of responsibility. Social workers who refer clients to other professionals should disclose, with clients' consent, all pertinent information to the new service providers.

(c) Social workers are prohibited from giving or receiving payment for a referral when no professional service is provided by the referring social worker.

2.07 Sexual Relationships

(a) Social workers who function as supervisors or educators should not engage in sexual activities or contact with supervisees, students, trainees, or other colleagues over whom they exercise professional authority.

(b) Social workers should avoid engaging in sexual relationships with colleagues when there is potential for a conflict of interest. Social workers who become involved in, or anticipate becoming involved in, a sexual relationship with a colleague have a duty to transfer professional responsibilities, when necessary, to avoid a conflict of interest.

2.08 Sexual Harassment

Social workers should not sexually harass supervisees, students, trainees, or colleagues. Sexual harassment includes sexual advances, sexual solicitation, requests for sexual favors, and other verbal or physical conduct of a sexual nature.

2.09 Impairment of Colleagues

(a) Social workers who have direct knowledge of a social work colleague's impairment that is due to personal problems, psychosocial distress, substance abuse, or mental health difficulties and that interferes with practice effectiveness should consult with that colleague when feasible and assist the colleague in taking remedial action.

(b) Social workers who believe that a social work colleague's impairment interferes with practice effectiveness and that the colleague has not taken adequate steps to address the impairment should take action through appropriate channels established by employers, agencies, NASW, licensing and regulatory bodies, and other professional organizations.

2.10 Incompetence of Colleagues

(a) Social workers who have direct knowledge of a social work colleague's incompetence should consult with that colleague when feasible and assist the colleague in taking remedial action.

(b) Social workers who believe that a social work colleague is incompetent and has not taken adequate steps to address the incompetence should take action through appropriate channels established by employers, agencies, NASW, licensing and regulatory bodies, and other professional organizations.

2.11 Unethical Conduct of Colleagues

(a) Social workers should take adequate measures to discourage, prevent, expose, and correct the unethical conduct of colleagues.

(b) Social workers should be knowledgeable about established policies and procedures for handling concerns about colleagues' unethical behavior. Social workers should be familiar with national, state, and local procedures for handling ethics complaints. These include policies and procedures created by NASW, licensing and regulatory bodies, employers, agencies, and other professional organizations.

(c) Social workers who believe that a colleague has acted unethically should seek resolution by discussing their concerns with the colleague when feasible and when such discussion is likely to be productive.

(d) When necessary, social workers who believe that a colleague has acted unethically should take action through appropriate formal channels (such as contacting a state licensing board or regulatory body, an NASW committee on inquiry, or other professional ethics committees).

(e) Social workers should defend and assist colleagues who are unjustly charged with unethical conduct.

3. Social Workers' Ethical Responsibilities in Practice Settings

3.01 Supervision and Consultation

(a) Social workers who provide supervision or consultation should have the necessary knowledge and skill to supervise or consult appropriately and should do so only within their areas of knowledge and competence.

(b) Social workers who provide supervision or consultation are responsible for setting clear, appropriate, and culturally sensitive boundaries.

(c) Social workers should not engage in any dual or multiple relationships with supervisees in which there is a risk of exploitation of or potential harm to the supervisee.

(d) Social workers who provide supervision should evaluate supervisees' performance in a manner that is fair and respectful.

3.02 Education and Training

(a) Social workers who function as educators, field instructors for students, or trainers should provide instruction only within their areas of knowledge and competence and should provide instruction based on the most current information and knowledge available in the profession.

(b) Social workers who function as educators or field instructors for students should evaluate students' performance in a manner that is fair and respectful.

(c) Social workers who function as educators or field instructors for students should take reasonable steps to ensure that clients are routinely informed when services are being provided by students.

(d) Social workers who function as educators or field instructors for students should not engage in any dual or multiple relationships with students in which there is a risk of exploitation or potential harm to the student. Social work educators and field instructors are responsible for setting clear, appropriate, and culturally sensitive boundaries.

3.03 Performance Evaluation

Social workers who have responsibility for evaluating the performance of others should fulfill such responsibility in a fair and considerate manner and on the basis of clearly stated criteria.

3.04 Client Records

(a) Social workers should take reasonable steps to ensure that documentation in records is accurate and reflects the services provided.

(b) Social workers should include sufficient and timely documentation in records to facilitate the delivery of services and to ensure continuity of services provided to clients in the future.

(c) Social workers' documentation should protect clients' privacy to the extent that is possible and appropriate and should include only information that is directly relevant to the delivery of services.

(d) Social workers should store records following the termination of services to ensure reasonable future access. Records should be maintained for the number of years required by state statutes or relevant contracts.

3.05 Billing

Social workers should establish and maintain billing practices that accurately reflect the nature and extent of services provided and that identify who provided the service in the practice setting.

3.06 Client Transfer

(a) When an individual who is receiving services from another agency or colleague contacts a social worker for services, the social worker should carefully consider the client's needs before agreeing to provide services. To minimize possible confusion and conflict, social workers should discuss with potential clients the nature of the clients' current relationship with other service providers and the implications, including possible benefits or risks, of entering into a relationship with a new service provider.

(b) If a new client has been served by another agency or colleague, social workers should discuss with the client whether consultation with the previous service provider is in the client's best interest.

3.07 Administration

(a) Social work administrators should advocate within and outside their agencies for adequate resources to meet clients' needs.

(b) Social workers should advocate for resource allocation procedures that are open and fair. When not all clients' needs can be met, an allocation procedure should be developed that is nondiscriminatory and based on appropriate and consistently applied principles.

(c) Social workers who are administrators should take reasonable steps to ensure that adequate agency or organizational resources are available to provide appropriate staff supervision.

(d) Social work administrators should take reasonable steps to ensure that the working environment for which they are responsible is consistent with and encourages compliance with the NASW Code of Ethics. Social work administrators should take reasonable steps to eliminate any conditions in their organizations that violate, interfere with, or discourage compliance with the Code.

3.08 Continuing Education and Staff Development

Social work administrators and supervisors should take reasonable steps to provide or arrange for continuing education and staff development for all staff for whom they are responsible. Continuing education and staff development should address current knowledge and emerging developments related to social work practice and ethics.

3.09 Commitments to Employers

(a) Social workers generally should adhere to commitments made to employers and employing organizations.

(b) Social workers should work to improve employing agencies' policies and procedures and the efficiency and effectiveness of their services.

(c) Social workers should take reasonable steps to ensure that employers are aware of social workers' ethical obligations as set forth in the NASW Code of Ethics and of the implications of those obligations for social work practice.

(d) Social workers should not allow an employing organization's policies, procedures, regulations, or administrative orders to interfere with their ethical practice of social work. Social workers should take reasonable steps to ensure that their employing organizations' practices are consistent with the NASW Code of Ethics.

(e) Social workers should act to prevent and eliminate discrimination in the employing organization's work assignments and in its employment policies and practices.

(f) Social workers should accept employment or arrange student field placements only in organizations that exercise fair personnel practices.

(g) Social workers should be diligent stewards of the resources of their employing organizations, wisely conserving funds where appropriate and never misappropriating funds or using them for unintended purposes.

3.10 Labor-Management Disputes

(a) Social workers may engage in organized action, including the formation of and participation in labor unions, to improve services to clients and working conditions.

(b) The actions of social workers who are involved in labor-management disputes, job actions, or labor strikes should be guided by the profession's values, ethical principles, and ethical standards. Reasonable differences of opinion exist among social workers concerning their primary obligation as professionals during an actual or threatened labor strike or job action. Social workers should carefully examine relevant issues and their possible impact on clients before deciding on a course of action.

4. Social Workers' Ethical Responsibilities as Professionals

4.01 Competence

(a) Social workers should accept responsibility or employment only on the basis of existing competence or the intention to acquire the necessary competence.

(b) Social workers should strive to become and remain proficient in professional practice and the performance of professional functions. Social workers should critically examine and keep current with emerging knowledge relevant to social work. Social workers should routinely review the professional literature and participate in continuing education relevant to social work practice and social work ethics.

(c) Social workers should base practice on recognized knowledge, including empirically based knowledge, relevant to social work and social work ethics.

4.02 Discrimination

Social workers should not practice, condone, facilitate, or collaborate with any form of discrimination on the basis of race, ethnicity, national origin, color, sex, sexual orientation, age, marital status, political belief, religion, or mental or physical disability.

4.03 Private Conduct

Social workers should not permit their private conduct to interfere with their ability to fulfill their professional responsibilities.

4.04 Dishonesty, Fraud, and Deception

Social workers should not participate in, condone, or be associated with dishonesty, fraud, or deception.

4.05 Impairment

(a) Social workers should not allow their own personal problems, psychosocial distress, legal problems, substance abuse, or mental health difficulties to interfere with their professional judgment and performance or to jeopardize the best interests of people for whom they have a professional responsibility.

(b) Social workers whose personal problems, psychosocial distress, legal problems, substance abuse, or mental health difficulties interfere with their professional judgment and performance should immediately seek consultation and take appropriate remedial action by seeking professional help, making adjustments in workload, terminating practice, or taking any other steps necessary to protect clients and others.

4.06 Misrepresentation

(a) Social workers should make clear distinctions between statements made and actions engaged in as a private individual and as a representative of the social work profession, a professional social work organization, or the social worker's employing agency.

(b) Social workers who speak on behalf of professional social work organizations should accurately represent the official and authorized positions of the organizations.

(c) Social workers should ensure that their representations to clients, agencies, and the public of professional qualifications, credentials, education, competence, affiliations, services provided, or results to be achieved are accurate. Social workers should claim only those relevant professional credentials they actually possess and take steps to correct any inaccuracies or misrepresentations of their credentials by others.

4.07 Solicitations

(a) Social workers should not engage in uninvited solicitation of potential clients who, because of their circumstances, are vulnerable to undue influence, manipulation, or coercion.

(b) Social workers should not engage in solicitation of testimonial endorsements (including solicitation of consent to use a client's prior statement as a testimonial endorsement) from current clients or from other people who, because of their particular circumstances, are vulnerable to undue influence.

4.08 Acknowledging Credit

(a) Social workers should take responsibility and credit, including authorship credit, only for work they have actually performed and to which they have contributed.

(b) Social workers should honestly acknowledge the work of and the contributions made by others.

5. Social Workers' Ethical Responsibilities to the Social Work Profession

5.01 Integrity of the Profession

(a) Social workers should work toward the maintenance and promotion of high standards of practice.

(b) Social workers should uphold and advance the values, ethics, knowledge, and mission of the profession. Social workers should protect, enhance, and improve the integrity of the profession through appropriate study and research, active discussion, and responsible criticism of the profession.

(c) Social workers should contribute time and professional expertise to activities that promote respect for the value, integrity, and competence of the social work profession. These activities may include teaching, research, consultation, service, legislative testimony, presentations in the community, and participation in their professional organizations.

(d) Social workers should contribute to the knowledge base of social work and share with colleagues their knowledge related to practice, research, and ethics. Social workers should seek to contribute to the profession's literature and to share their knowledge at professional meetings and conferences.

(e) Social workers should act to prevent the unauthorized and unqualified practice of social work.

5.02 Evaluation and Research

(a) Social workers should monitor and evaluate policies, the implementation of programs, and practice interventions.

(b) Social workers should promote and facilitate evaluation and research to contribute to the development of knowledge.

(c) Social workers should critically examine and keep current with emerging knowledge relevant to social work and fully use evaluation and research evidence in their professional practice.

(d) Social workers engaged in evaluation or research should carefully consider possible consequences and should follow guidelines developed for the protection of evaluation and research participants. Appropriate institutional review boards should be consulted.

(e) Social workers engaged in evaluation or research should obtain voluntary and written informed consent from participants, when appropriate, without any implied or actual deprivation or penalty for refusal to participate; without undue inducement to participate; and with due regard for participants' well-being, privacy, and dignity. Informed consent should include information about the nature, extent, and duration of the participation requested and disclosure of the risks and benefits of participation in the research.

(f) When evaluation or research participants are incapable of giving informed consent, social workers should provide an appropriate explanation to the participants, obtain the participants' assent to the extent they are able, and obtain written consent from an appropriate proxy.

(g) Social workers should never design or conduct evaluation or research that does not use consent procedures, such as certain forms of naturalistic observation and archival research, unless rigorous and responsible review of the research has found it to be justified because of its prospective scientific, educational, or applied value and unless equally effective alternative procedures that do not involve waiver of consent are not feasible.

(h) Social workers should inform participants of their right to withdraw from evaluation and research at any time without penalty.

(i) Social workers should take appropriate steps to ensure that participants in evaluation and research have access to appropriate supportive services.

(j) Social workers engaged in evaluation or research should protect participants from unwarranted physical or mental distress, harm, danger, or deprivation.

(k) Social workers engaged in the evaluation of services should discuss collected information only for professional purposes and only with people professionally concerned with this information.

(l) Social workers engaged in evaluation or research should ensure the anonymity or confidentiality of participants and of the data obtained from them. Social workers should inform participants of any limits of confidentiality, the measures that will be taken to ensure confidentiality, and when any records containing research data will be destroyed.

(m) Social workers who report evaluation and research results should protect participants' confidentiality by omitting identifying information unless proper consent has been obtained authorizing disclosure.

(n) Social workers should report evaluation and research findings accurately. They should not fabricate or falsify results and should take steps to correct any errors later found in published data using standard publication methods.

(o) Social workers engaged in evaluation or research should be alert to and avoid conflicts of interest and dual relationships with participants, should inform participants when a real or potential conflict of interest arises, and should take steps to resolve the issue in a manner that makes participants' interests primary.

(p) Social workers should educate themselves, their students, and their colleagues about responsible research practices.

6. Social Workers' Ethical Responsibilities to the Broader Society

6.01 Social Welfare

Social workers should promote the general welfare of society, from local to global levels, and the development of people, their communities, and their environments. Social workers should advocate for living conditions conducive to the fulfillment of basic human needs and should promote social, economic, political, and cultural values and institutions that are compatible with the realization of social justice.

6.02 Public Participation

Social workers should facilitate informed participation by the public in shaping social policies and institutions.

6.03 Public Emergencies

Social workers should provide appropriate professional services in public emergencies to the greatest extent possible.

6.04 Social and Political Action

(a) Social workers should engage in social and political action that seeks to ensure that all people have equal access to the resources, employment, services, and opportunities they require to meet their basic human needs and to develop fully. Social workers should be aware of the impact of the political arena on practice and should advocate for changes in policy and legislation to improve social conditions in order to meet basic human needs and promote social justice.

(b) Social workers should act to expand choice and opportunity for all people, with special regard for vulnerable, disadvantaged, oppressed, and exploited people and groups.

(c) Social workers should promote conditions that encourage respect for cultural and social diversity within the United States and globally. Social workers should promote policies and practices that demonstrate respect for difference, support the expansion of cultural knowledge and resources, advocate for programs and institutions that demonstrate cultural competence, and promote policies that safeguard the rights of and confirm equity and social justice for all people.

(d) Social workers should act to prevent and eliminate domination of, exploitation of, and discrimination against any person, group, or class on the basis of race, ethnicity, national origin, color, sex, sexual orientation, age, marital status, political belief, religion, or mental or physical disability.

References

Aaron, R. (2003, July 27). Taking car keys from elderly is tough—I know firsthand. *San Antonio Express–News*, p. K3.

ABCNews.com. (2002). *Authentic happiness: Using our strength to cultivate happiness*. Retrieved October 14, 2002, from http://abcnews.go.com/sections/gma/goodmorningamerica/ gmaa020904authentic_happiness_excert.html

Abrams, M. S. (2001). Resilience in ambiguous loss. *American Journal of Psychotherapy, 2*, 283–291.

AIRNow. (2004). *Air Quality Index (AQI)*. Retrieved from www.airnow.gov

Akbar, N. (1991). *The chains and images of psychological slavery*. Jersey City, NJ: New Mind Productions.

Albert, G. (1998, May/June). *Recovery by design: City voices*. Retrieved March 1, 2005, from http://www.newyorkcityvoices.org/may98c.html

Alemi, F., Mosavel, M., Stephens, R., Ghaidri, A., Krishnaswamy, J., & Thakkar, H. (1996). Electronic self-help and support groups. *Medical Care, 34*(10), S32–S44.

Almanac of Policy Issues. (2002). *Unemployment compensation*. Retrieved December 14, 2004, at http://www.policyalmanac.org/social_welfare/archive/unemploy ment_compensation.shtml

Amato-von Hemert, K. (1994). Point/counterpoint: Should social work education address religious issues? Yes! *Journal of Social Work Education, 30*, 7–11.

American Association of Retired Persons. (1997). *Future growth*. Retrieved December 5, 2004, from http://research.aarp.org/general/profile97.html

American Civil Liberties Union. (2004, October 20). Retrieved from http://www.aclu.org/

American Management Association. (1994). *65th Annual Human Resources Conference on-site survey*. San Francisco: Author.

American Psychiatric Association. (1994). *Diagnostic and statistical manual of mental disorders* (4th ed.). Washington, DC: Author.

American Psychological Association. (1998). *Hate crimes today: An age-old foe in modern dress*. Retrieved January 26, 2006, from http://www.apa.org/publicinfo/hate.html

American Psychological Association. (2002, June). *Is youth violence just another fact of life?* Retrieved from http://www.apa.org/ppo/issues/pbviolence.html

American Psychological Association. (2004, May 8). *Psychological problems of older adults*. Retrieved from http://www.apa.org/pi/aging/older/psychological.html

Americans with Disabilities Act. (2004, October 21). Retrieved from http://www.usdoj.gov/crt/ada/adahom1.htm

Ames, C. (1992). Classrooms: Goals, structures, and student motivation. *Journal of Educational Psychology, 84*(3), 261–271.

Anderson, K. M. (1997). Uncovering survival abilities in children who have been sexually abused. *The Journal of Contemporary Human Services, 78*, 592–599.

Anthony, W. A. (1993). Recovery from mental illness: The guiding vision of the mental health service system in the 1990's. *Psychosocial Rehabilitation Journal, 16*, 12–23.

Antonovsky, A. (1980). *Health, stress, and coping.* San Francisco: Jossey-Bass.

Arkow, P. (1996). The relationships between animal abuse and other forms of family violence. *Family Violence and Sexual Assault Bulletin, 12*, 29–34.

Ascione, E. R. (1993). Children who are cruel to animals: A review of research and implications for developmental psychology. *Anthrozoös, 6*, 226–247.

Ascione, E. R. (1998). Battered women's reports of their partner's and their children's cruelty to animals. *Journal of Emotional Abuse, 1*, 119–133.

Ash, P., Kellerman, A., Fuqua-Whitley, D., & Johnson, D. (1996). Gun acquisition and use by juvenile offenders. *Journal of the American Medical Association, 275*, 1754–1758.

Asmundson, G. J. G, Coons, M. J., Taylor, S., & Katz, J. (2002). PTSD and the experience of pain: Research and clinical implications of shared vulnerability and mutual maintenance models. *Canadian Journal of Psychiatry, 47*(10), 930–938.

Asser, S. M., & Swan, K. (1998). Child fatalities from religion-motivated medical neglect. *Pediatrics, 101*, 625–629.

Atkinson, R. (1995). Treatment programs for aging alcoholics. In T. Beresford & E. Gomberg, *Alcohol and Aging* (pp. 186–210). New York: Oxford University Press.

AVERT. (2005, July). *The world wide AIDS epidemic.* Retrieved July 5, 2005, from http://www.avert.org/worlstatinfo.htm

Avison, W. R. (2004). The health consequences of unemployment. *Health Canada Online.* Retrieved May 9, 2004, from http://www.hc-sc.gc.ca/main/nfh/web/publicat/execsumm/avison.htm

Axelson, J. A. (1985). *Counseling and development in a multicultural society.* Monterey, CA: Brooks/Cole.

Baca Zinn, M. (1980). Gender and ethnic identity among Chicanos. *Frontiers, 2*, 18–24.

Backer, K. L., & Walton-Moss, B. (2001, October). Detecting and addressing alcohol abuse in women. *Nurse Practitioner, 26*(10), 13–22.

Baekeland, F., & Lundwall, L. (1975). Dropping out of treatment: A critical review. *Psychological Bulletin, 82*, 738–783.

Baetz, M., Larson, D. B., Marcoux, G., Bowen, R., & Griffin, R. (2002). Canadian psychiatric inpatient religious commitment: An association with mental health. *Canadian Journal of Psychiatry, 47*(2), 159–167.

Bagdikian, B. H. (2005). *The media monopoly.* Retrieved September 16, 2005, from http://eserver.org/filmtv/media-monopoly.txt

Baldwin, A. L., Baldwin, C., & Cole, R. E. (1990). Stress-resistant families and stress-resistant children. In J. Rolf, A. Masten, D. Cicchetti, K. Neuchterlein, & S. Weintraub (Eds.), Risk and protective factors in the development of psychopathology (pp. 257–280). New York: Cambridge University Press.

Balk, D. E. (1999). Bereavement and spiritual change. *Death Studies, 23*(6), 485–493.

Barkan, E. R. (1996). *And still they came: Immigrants and American society, 1920 to the 1990's.* Wheeler, IL: Harlan Davidson.

Batson, C. D., & Ventis, W. L. (1982). *The religious experience: A social-psychological perspective.* New York: Oxford University Press.

Baumeister, R. F., Smart, L., & Boden, J. M. (1996). Relation of threatened egotism to violence and aggression: The dark side of high self-esteem. *Psychological Review, 103*(1), 5–33.

Baumrind, D. (1966). Effects of authoritative control on child behavior. *Child Development, 37*, 887–907.

Beers, C. W. (1910). *A mind that found itself.* New York: Longmans, Green, & Co.

Bender, W. N. (1999, April). *Violence prevention in the school.* An invited workshop presented at the Doylestown Public School Board of Education, Doylestown, PA.

Bender, W. N., Shubert, T. H., & McLaughlin, P. J. (2001, November). Invisible kids: Preventing school violence by identifying kids in trouble. *Intervention in School and Clinic, 37*(2), 105–111.

Bergin, A. E. (1971). The evaluation of therapeutic outcomes. In A. E. Bergin & S. Garfield (Eds.), *Handbook of psychotherapy and behavior change* (pp. 217–270). New York: John Wiley.

Bertone, A. (2000). Sexual trafficking in women international: Political economy and the politics of sex. *Gender Issues, 18*(1), 4–23.

Bidstrup, S. (2000). *Homophobia: The fear behind the hatred.* Retrieved January 13, 2006, from bidstrup.com/phobia.htm

Bielous, G. A. (2005, February). The five worst disciplinary mistakes (and how to avoid them). *Supervision, 66*(2), 16–19.

Bien, T. J., Miller, W. R., & Tonigan, J. S. (1993). Brief interventions for alcohol problems: A review. *Addictions, 88*(3), 315–335.

Biernacki, P. (1986). *Pathways from heroin addiction: Recover without treatment.* Philadelphia: Temple University Press.

Bisman, C. (1994). *Social work practice: Cases and principles.* Belmont, CA: Brooks/Cole.

Bisson, J., Nadeau, L., & Demers, A. (1999, May). The validity of the CAGE scale to screen heavy drinking and drinking problems in a general population. *Addiction, 94*(5), 715–723.

Bisson, J. I., McFarlane, A. C., & Rose, S. (2000). Psychological debriefing. In E. B. Foa, T. M. Keane, & M. J. Friedman (Eds.), *Effective treatments for PTSD* (pp. 39–59). New York: Guilford.

Blundo, R. (2001). Learning strengths-based practice: Challenging our personal and professional frames. *Families in Society, 82*(3), 296–304.

Bly, R. (1996). *The sibling society.* Boston: Addison-Wesley.

Boorstein, S. (2000). Transpersonal psychotherapy. *American Journal of Psychotherapy, 54*(3), 408–423.

Borduin, C. M. (1999). Multisystemic treatment of criminality and violence in adolescents. *Journal of the American Academy of Child and Adolescent Psychiatry, 38*, 242–249.

Borg, M. G. (1998). The emotional reactions of school bullies and their victims. *Educational Psychology, 18*, 433–444.

Bostwick, J. M., & Pankratz, V. S. (2000). Affective disorders and suicide risk: A re-examination. *American Journal of Psychiatry, 157*, 1925–1932.

Brager, G., & Specht, H. (1973). *Community organizing.* New York: Columbia University Press.

Braithwaite, D. O. (1996). Exploring different perspectives on the communication of persons with disabilities. In E. B. Ray (Ed.), *Communication and disenfranchisement: Social health issues and implications* (pp. 449–464). Hillsdale, NJ: Lawrence Erlbaum.

Brent, D. A. (1998, February). Psychotherapy: Definitions, mechanisms of action, and relationship to etiological models. *Journal of Abnormal Child Psychology*. Retrieved from http://www.findarticles.com/cf_0/m0902/n1_v26/20565425/print.jhtml

Breslau, N., Davis, G. C., Andreski, P., & Peterson, E. (1991). Traumatic events and posttraumatic stress disorder in an urban population of young adults. *Archives of General Psychiatry, 48,* 216–222.

Brewin, C. R., Andrews, B., & Valentine, J. D. (2000). Meta-analysis of risk factors for posttraumatic stress disorder in trauma-exposed adults. *Journal of Consulting Clinical Psychology, 68,* 748–766.

Brookings Institution, The (2005). *Future of children.* Retrieved June 29, 2005, from http://www.futureofchildren.org/information3134/information_show.htm?doc_id=78865

Brown, D. R., & Gary, L. E. (1991). Religious socialization and educational attainment among African Americans: An empirical assessment. *Journal of Negro Education, 3,* 411–426.

Brown, J., & Brown, G. (1997). Characteristics and treatment of incest offenders: A review. *Journal of Aggression, Maltreatment and Trauma, 1*(1), 335–354.

Bumb, J. (2005). *Dorthea Dix.* Retrieved August 5, 2005, from http://www.webster.edu/~woolflm/dorotheadix.html

Caffrey, T. A. (2000). The whisper of death: Psychotherapy with a dying Vietnam veteran. *American Journal of Psychotherapy, 54*(4), 519–530.

California Department of Corrections. (2004). *Restitution.* Retrieved August 21, 2004, from http://www.corr.ca.gov/VictimServices/Helpng%20Crime%20Victims/Helping_Crime_Victims.asp#RESTITUTION

Canadian Revenue Service. (2005). *Your Canada child tax benefit.* Retrieved January 26, 2006, from www.cra-arc.gc.ca/E/pub/tg/t4114/t4114-e.html# p161_9469

Canda, E. R. (1988). Spirituality, religious diversity, and social work practice. *Social Casework, 69,* 238–247.

Cannon, J. P. (1948, July 1). *Two Americas.* The keynote address to the 13th National Convention of the Socialist Workers Party. Retrieved March 10, 2005, from http://www.marxists.org/archive/cannon/works/1948/twoamer .htm

Caplan, M., Weissberg, R. P., Grober, J. S., Sivo, P. J., Grady, K., et al. (1992). Social competence promotion with inner-city and suburban young adolescents: Effects on social adjustment and alcohol use. *Journal of Consulting Clinical Psychology, 60,* 56–63.

CARE. (2004, May). *Facts about health and poverty.* Retrieved May 14, 2004, from http://www.careusa.org/features/rhealth/facts.asp?source=http://www.careusa.org/features/rhealth/facts.asp?source=170440050000

Carpenter, J. (2002). Mental health recovery paradigm: Implications for social work. *Health & Social Work, 27*(2), 86–94.

Catholic Charities. (2002). Retrieved August 23, 2004, from www.ccsj.org

Centers for Disease Control. (2004). *Youth Risk Behavior Survey.* Retrieved January 27, 2006, from www.cdc.gov/mmwr/pdf/ss/555302.pdf

Center for Economic and Social Justice. (2005). *Defining social and economic justice.* Retrieved September 21, 2005, from cesj.org/thirdway/economic justice_defined.htm

Center for Immigration Studies. (2003). *Illegal immigration*. Retrieved January 27, 2006, from www.cis.org/topics/illegalimmigration.html

Center for Medicare and Medicaid Services. (2004). *CMS programs and information*. Department of Health and Human Services, Baltimore. Retrieved January 26, 2006, from www.cms.hhs.gov/default.asp

Chang, S. C. (1982). The self: A nodal issue in culture and psyche: An eastern perspective. *American Journal of Psychotherapy, 36*(1), 67–81.

The changing American family: A report of the task force of the American Academy of Pediatrics. (2003). *Pediatrics: The Journal of the American Academy of Pediatrics, 3*(6), 1541–1572.

Chatterji, P., & Markowitz, S. (2000). *The impact of maternal alcohol and illicit drug use on children's behavior problems: Evidence from the children of the National Longitudinal Survey of Youth* (Working Paper No. 7692). Cambridge, MA: National Bureau of Economic Research.

Chicago Tribune. (1994, May 15). Sect. 7, p. 1.

Chinman, M. J., Weingarten, R., Stayner, D., & Davidson, L. (2001). Chronicity reconsidered: Improving person-environment fit through a consumer-run service. *Community Mental Health Journal, 37*(3), 215–229.

CNN.com. (2003, November). *Hate crimes decrease in 2002*. Retrieved January 27, 2006, from http://www.cnn.com/2003/law/11/12/hate.crimes.ap/

CNN.Money. (2003, October 23). *250 nabbed at Wal-Mart stores*. Retrieved August 26, 2004, from http://money.cnn.com/2003/10/23/news/companies/walmart_worker_arrests/

Coleman, L. M. (1997). Stigma: An enigma demystified. In L. J. David (Ed.), *The disability studies reader* (pp. 216–231). New York: Routledge.

Coley, R. (2001). *Differences in the gender gap: Comparisons across racial/ethnic groups in education and work*. Princeton, NJ: Educational Testing Service, Policy Information Center. Available from http://www.ets.org/research/pic

Collat Jewish Family Services. (2004). Retrieved August 23, 2004, from www.cjfsbham.org

Committee for Children. (1997). *Second step: Violence prevention curriculum*. Seattle, WA: Author.

Compton experiencing record homicide rates. (2005, July 23). *Los Angeles Times*, p. A1.

Comstock, G. W., & Partridge, K. B. (1972). Church attendance and health. *Journal of Chronic Diseases, 25*, 665–672.

Conlin, M. (2003, May 26). The new gender gap. *Business Week, 17*, 74–81.

Connecticut PTA. (2005, May 27). Tracking the issues: Vouchers. Retrieved June 30, 2005, from http://www.ctpta.org/legislative/vouchers.htm#smalltool

Connors, G. J., Walitzer, K. S., & Demen, K. H. (2002, October). Preparing clients for alcoholism treatment: Effects on treatment participation and outcomes. *Journal of Consulting and Clinical Psychology, 70* (5), 1161–1169.

Conrad, M., & Hammen, C. (1993). Protective and risk factors in high and low risk children: A comparison of children with unipolar, bipolar, medically ill, and normal mothers. Development and Psychopathology, 5, 593–607.

Cook, T., & Emler, N. (1999, December). Managerial potential: An experimental study. *Journal of Occupational & Organizational Psychology, 72*(4), 423–440.

Coulson, A. J. (2005). *Vouchers*. Retrieved June 30, 2005, from http://www.school-choices.org/roo/vouchers.htm

Council on Judicial Affairs. (1990). Black and white disparities in health care. *Journal of the American Medical Association, 263*(17), 2344–2346.

Council on Social Work Educational Policy and Accreditation Standards. (2001). Retrieved January 26, 2006, from www.cswe.org/

Craig, W. M., & Pepler, D. J. (1997). Observations of bullying and victimization in the schoolyard. *Canadian Journal of School Psychology, 13*, 41–60.

Cromley, J. (2006, January 16). The buzz at the office. *Los Angeles Times*, p. F2.

Crowley, C. F. (2001, January 17). Vet's victory: Syndrome exists. *Eagle Tribune*, pp. 1–2. Retrieved December 11, 2004, from http://www.eagletribune.com/news/stories/20010117/FP_004.htm

Crown, W. H., Leavitt, T. D., & Rix, S. E. (1996, November 26). *Underemployment and the older worker: How big a problem?* Washington, DC: American Association of Retired Persons, Public Policy Institute.

Currie, E. (1993). *Reckoning: Drugs, the cities, and the American future*. New York: Hill and Wang.

Dahl, D., & Lochner, L. (2005). The impact of family income on child achievement. Retrieved September 19, 2005, from http://irp.wisc.edu/publications/dps/dpabs2005.htm#DP1305–05

Dalton, D. R., Daily, C. M., Ellstrand, A. E., & Johnson, J. L. (1998). Meta-analytic reviews of board composition, leadership structure, and financial performance. *Strategic Management Journal, 19*, 269–290.

Davidson, L., Chinman, M., Moos, B., Weingarten, R., Stayner, D. A., et al. (1999). Peer support among individuals with severe mental illness: A review of the evidence. *Clinical Psychology: Science and Practice, 6*, 165–187.

Davidson, M. J., & Cooper, C. L. (1992). *Shattering the glass ceiling: The woman manager*. London: Paul Chapman.

DeAngelis, T. (2004). *Social workers help military families*. Retrieved August 2, 2004, from http://www.naswdc.org/pressroom/events/peace/helpFamilies.asp

DePanfilis, D., & Salus, M. (1992). *Child Protective Services: A guide for caseworkers*. National Center for Child Abuse and Neglect. McLean, VA: The Circle, Inc.

de Shazer, S. (1985). *Keys to solution in brief therapy*. New York: Norton.

de Shazer, S. (1988). *Clues: Investigating solutions in brief therapy*. New York: Norton.

de Shazer, S. (1994). *Words were originally magic*. New York: Norton.

Dixon, L., Krauss, N., & Lehman, A. L. (1994). Consumers as service providers: The promise and challenge. *Community Mental Health Journal, 30*, 615–625.

Dodge, K. A., Bates, J. E., & Pettit, G. S. (1990). Mechanisms in the cycle of violence. *Science, 250*, 1678–1683.

Druss, B. G., Marcus, S. C., Rosenheck, R. A., Olfson, M., Tanielien, T., et al. (2000). Understanding disability in mental and general medical conditions. *American Journal of Psychiatry, 157*(9), 1485–1491.

Dudley, J. R., & Helfgott, C. (1990). Exploring a place for spirituality in the social work curriculum. *Journal of Social Work Education, 26*(3), 287–294.

Duffy, A. (2000). Toward effective early intervention and prevention strategies for major affective disorders: A review of risk factors. *Canadian Journal of Psychiatry, 45*(4), 340–349.

Early, T. J., & GlenMaye, L. F. (2000, March). Valuing families: Social work practice with families from a strengths perspective. *Social Work, 45*(2), 118–130.

Edlund, M. J., Wang, P. S., Berglund, P. A., Katz, S., Lin, E., et al. (2002). Dropping out of mental health treatment patterns and predictors among epidemiological survey respondents in the United States and Ontario. *American Journal of Psychiatry, 159*(5), 845–851.

Edmunson, E. D., Bedell, J. R., Archer, R. P., & Gordon, R. E. (1982). Integrating skill building and peer support in mental health treatment: The early intervention and community network development projects. In A. M. Jeger & R. S. Slotnick (Eds.), *Community mental health and behavioral ecology: A handbook of theory, research and practice.* New York: Plenum.

Education Trust West. (2005). *Short changing poor and minority schools.* Retrieved June 30, 2005, from http://www.hiddengap.org/faq/

Edwards, J. (2005, February 5). *Remarks by Senator Edwards to the 100 Club Dinner New Hampshire.* Retrieved March 9, 2005, from http://www.one americacommittee.com/100-club.asp

Egley, A., Jr. (2002). *National youth gang survey trends from 1996 to 2000.* Washington, DC: U.S. Department of Justice, Office of Juvenile Justice and Delinquency Prevention.

Elias, M. (2004, July 1). Many Iraq veterans fighting an enemy within. *USA Today,* p. D10.

Elizur, Y., & Ziv, M. A. (2001, Summer). Family support and acceptance, gay male identity formation, and psychological adjustment: A path model. *Family Process, 40,* 125–144.

Elliott, D. S. (1994). Serious violent offenders: Onset, developmental course, and termination. *Criminology, 32*(1), 1–21.

Elliott, D. S., Hamburg, B., & Williams, K. R. (1998). *Violence in American schools: A new perspective.* Boulder, CO: Center for the Study and Prevention of Violence.

Ellison, C. G., & Levin, J. S. (1998). The religion-health connection: Evidence theory and future directions. *Health Education and Behavior, 25,* 700–720.

Ellison, G., Boardman, J. D., Williams, D. R., & Jackson, J. S. (2001). Religious involvement, stress and mental health: Findings from the 1995 Detroit area study. *Social Forces, 80*(1), 215–235.

Emrick, C. D., Tonigan, J. S., Montgomery, H., & Little, L. (1993). Alcoholics Anonymous: What is currently known. In B. S. McCardy & W. R. Miller (Eds.), *Research on Alcoholics Anonymous: Opportunities and alternatives* (pp. 41–75). New Brunswick, NJ: Rutgers Center for Alcohol Studies.

Emrick, C. D. (1987). Alcoholics Anonymous: Affiliative processes and effectiveness as treatment. *Alcoholism: Clinical and Experimental Research, 12,* 416–423.

Enstrom, J. E. (1978). Cancer and total mortality among active Mormons. *Cancer, 42,* 1913–1951.

Enstrom, J. E. (1989). Health practices and cancer mortality among active California Mormons. *Journal of the National Cancer Institute, 81,* 1807–1814.

Epaminondas, D., & Chomsky, N. (2002, July 3). *Chomsky interview.* Retrieved July 17, 2004, from http://www.zmag.org/content/showarticle.cfm?Section ID=36&ItemID=2068

Estes, R. (1992). *Internationalizing social work education: A guide for a new century.* Philadelphia: University of Pennsylvania School of Social Work. Retrieved from http://caster.ssw.upenn.edu/~restes/intl.html

Ewing, C. P. (1990). Crisis intervention as a brief psychotherapy. In R. A. Wells & V. J. Giannetti (Eds.), *Handbook of brief psychotherapies* (pp. 277–294). New York: Plenum.

Fagan, J. (1997, June 19–21). *Continuity and change in American crime: Lessons from three decades.* Paper presented at the Symposium of the 30th Anniversary of the President's Commission on Law Enforcement and the Administration of Justice, Washington, DC.

Federal Highway Administration Office of Operations. (2002). *Annual person-hour highway delay per person.* Retrieved January 2006 from www.dts .gov/publications/national_transportation_statistics/2002/html/table_01_63.html

Federal Interagency Forum on Child and Family Statistics. (2003). *America's children: Key national indicators of well-being.* Retrieved May 19, 2004, from http://www.childstats.gov/

Federal Register. (2005, February 18). *70* (33), 8373–8375.

Federation for American Immigration Reform. (2004, August 25). *The estimated cost of illegal immigration.* Retrieved from http://www.fairus.org/ ImmigrationIssueCenters/ImmigrationIssueCenters.cfm?ID=2382&c=13

Fein, H. (2004, May). *Genocide.* Retrieved May 14, 2004, from http://encarta .msn.com

Feller, J. (1992). *Working with the courts in child protection.* National Center on Child Abuse and Neglect. McLean, VA: The Circle, Inc.

Felton, C. J., Stastny, P., Shern, D., Blanch, A., Donahue, S. A., et al. (1995). Consumers as peer specialists on intensive case management teams: Impact on client outcomes. *Psychiatric Services, 46,* 1037–1044.

Finkelhor, D., Hotaling, G., & Sedlack, A. (2000). *Missing, abducted, runaway and throwaway children in America. First report: Numbers and characteristics.* Washington, DC: U.S. Department of Justice, Office of Juvenile Justice and Delinquency Prevention.

Finn, J. (1999). An exploration of helping processes in an online self-help group focusing on issues of disability. *Health & Social Work, 24*(3), 220–231.

Firestone, J. M., Harris, R. J., & Lambert, L. C. (1999). Gender role ideology and the gender based differences in earnings. *Journal of Family and Economic Issues, 20,* 191–215.

Fisher, D. B. (2005). *An empowerment model of recovery from severe mental illness.* Retrieved March 1, 2005, from http://namiscc.org/Recovery/2005/ EmpowermentModel.htm

Fitzpatrick, K. M. (1999, October). Violent victimization among America's school children. *Journal of Interpersonal Violence, 14*(10), 1055–1069.

Flaherty, J. A., & Meagher, R. (1980). Measuring racial bias in inpatient treatment. *American Journal of Psychiatry, 137,* 679–682.

Fleming, M., & Manwell, L. B. (1998). Brief intervention in primary care settings: A primary treatment method for at-risk, problem, and dependent drinkers. *Alcohol Research and Health, 23*(2), 128–137.

Fleming, M. F., Barry, K. L., Manwell, L. B., Johnson, K., & London, R. (1997). Brief physician advice for problem alcohol drinkers: A randomized controlled trial in community-based primary care practices. *JAMA, 277*(13), 1039–1045.

Foa, E. B., & Meadows, E. A. (1997). Psychosocial treatments for post-traumatic stress disorder: A critical review. In J. Spence, J. M. Darley, & D. J. Foss (Eds.),

Annual Review of Psychology. Palo Alto, CA: Annual Reviews, Inc., Vol. 48, pp. 449–480.

Foa, E. B., Dancu, C. V., Hembree, E. A., Jaycox, L. H., Meadows, E. A., et al. (1999). A comparison of exposure therapy, stress inoculation training, and their combination in reducing posttraumatic stress disorder in female assault victims. *Journal of Consulting and Clinical Psychology, 67,* 194–200.

Foa, E. B., Hearst-Ikeda, D., & Perry, K. J. (1995). Evaluation of a brief cognitive-behavioral program for the prevention of chronic PTSD in recent assault victims. *Journal of Consulting & Clinical Psychology, 63,* 948–955.

Foa, E. B., Rothbaum, B. O., Riggs, D., & Murdock, T. (1991). Treatment of post-traumatic stress disorder in rape victims: A comparison between cognitive-behavioral procedures and counseling. *Journal of Consulting and Clinical Psychology, 59,* 715–723.

Fox, J. A., & Zawitz, M. W. (2002). *Homicide trends in the United States: Crime data brief.* Washington, DC: Bureau of Justice Statistics, U.S. Department of Justice. Retrieved June 17, 2004, from http://www.ojp.usdoj.gov/bjs/homicide/homtrnd.htm

Frankl, V. E. (1978). *Psychotherapy and existentialism: Selected papers on logotherapy.* New York: Touchstone Books.

Franklin, A. J. (1992). Therapy with African American men. *Families in Society: The Journal of Contemporary Human Services, 26*(6), 350–355.

Furuto, S. M., Biswas, R., Chung, D., Murase, K., & Ross-Sheriff, F. (Eds.). (1992). *Social work practice with Asian Americans.* Newbury Park, CA: Sage.

Galanter, M. (1988). Zealous self help groups as adjuncts to psychiatric treatment: A study of Recovery, Inc. *American Journal of Psychiatry, 145*(10), 1248–1253.

Galea, S. (2002). Psychological sequelae of the September 11 terrorist attacks in New York City. *New England Journal of Medicine, 346*(13), 982–987.

Gallo, J. J., Marino, S., Ford, D., & Anthony, J. C. (1995). Filters on the pathway to mental health care, II: Sociodemographic factors. *Psychological Medicine, 25,* 1149–1160.

Gambrill, E. (1999, July). Evidence-based practice: An alternative to authority-based practice source. *Families in Society: The Journal of Contemporary Human Services, 80*(4), 341–350.

Gambrill, E. (2000, October). *Evidence-based practice.* A handout to the dean and directors of schools of social work, Huntington Beach, CA.

Gardner, J., & Lyon, J. L. (1982). Cancer in Utah Mormon men by lay priesthood level. *American Journal of Epidemiology, 116,* 243–257.

Garretson, D. J. (1993). Psychological misdiagnosis of African Americans. *Journal of Multicultural Counseling and Development, 21,* 119–126.

Gartner, J., Larson, D. B., & Allen, G. D. (1991). Religious commitment and mental health: A review of the empirical literature. *Journal of Psychology and Theology, 19,* 625.

Gatto, J. T. (2001). *The underground history of American education: An intimate investigation into the problem of modern schooling.* New York: Oxford Village Press.

Gaw, A. C. (1993). Psychiatric care of Chinese Americans. In A. Gaw (Ed.), *Culture, ethnicity, and mental illness* (pp. 245–280). Washington, DC: American Psychiatric Press.

Gentilello, L. M., Donovan, D. M., Dunn, C. W., & Rivara, F. P. (1995). Alcohol interventions in trauma centers: Current practice and future directions. *JAMA, 274*(13), 1043–1048.

George, L. K. (1992). Social factors and the onset and outcome of depression. In K. W. Schaie, J. S. House, & D. G. Blazer (Eds.), *Aging, health behaviors, and health outcomes* (pp. 137–159). Hillsdale, NJ: Erlbaum.

George, L. K., Larson, D. B., Koenig, H. G., & McCullough, M. E. (2000). Spirituality and health: What we know, what we need to know. *Journal of Social and Clinical Psychology, 19*(1), 102–116.

Ghoshal, S. (2005, March). Bad management theories are destroying good management practices. *Academy of Management Learning & Education, 4*(1), 75–92.

Gist, R., & Devilly, G. J. (2002). Post-trauma debriefing: The road too frequently traveled. *Lancet, 360*(9335), 741–743.

Gladwell, M. (2002, August 12). Political heat. *The New Yorker*, pp. 76–80.

Glicken, A. J. (2002). Building on our strengths. *Park Record, 122*(59), A15.

Glicken, A. J. (2005). Volunteering as a social responsibility. In M. D. Glicken (Ed.), *Improving the effectiveness of the helping profession* (pp. 310–311). Thousand Oaks, CA: Sage.

Glicken, M. (1977). *A regional study of the job satisfaction of social workers.* Unpublished doctoral dissertation, University of Utah, Salt Lake City.

Glicken, M. (1986a, January/February). A clinician's guide to stress management. *EAP Digest, 16*, 15–18.

Glicken, M. (1986b, September/October). The after-shock of on the job accidents. *EAP Digest, 16*, 12–14.

Glicken, M. (1986c, October). Identifying worker burnout. *Personnel Management: Policies and Practices, 1*, 1–6.

Glicken, M. (1986d, October). Treating worker burnout. *Personnel Management: Policies and Practices, 2*, 1–7.

Glicken, M. (1986e). Work related accidents which lead to post traumatic stress reactions. *Labor Relations: Occupational Safety and Health, 6*, 7–10.

Glicken, M. (1988, January 24). Resolving office conflict. *National Business Employment Weekly, 14*, 7–9.

Glicken, M. (1996, February). Dealing with workplace stress. *National Business Employment Weekly, 22*, 20–23.

Glicken, M. D. (2003). *A simple approach to social research.* Boston: Allyn & Bacon.

Glicken, M. D. (2004a). *Using the strengths perspective in social work practice: A positive approach for the helping professions.* Boston: Allyn & Bacon.

Glicken, M. D. (2004b). *Violent young children.* Boston: Allyn & Bacon.

Glicken, M. D. (2005). *Improving the effectiveness of the helping professions: An evidence based approach to practice.* Thousand Oaks, CA: Sage.

Glicken, M. (2006). *Lessons from resilient people.* Thousand Oaks, CA: Sage.

Glicken, M., & Ino, S. (1997). *Workplace violence: A description of the levels of potential for violence.* Unpublished manuscript.

Glicken, M. D., & Sechrest, D. (2003). *The role of the helping professions in treating victims and perpetrators of violence.* Boston: Allyn & Bacon.

Golan, N. (1978). *Treatment in crisis situations.* New York: The Free Press.

Goldstein, H. (1990). Strength or pathology: Ethical and rhetorical contrasts in approaches to practice. *Families in Society, 71*, 267–275.

Gong-Guy, E. (1987). *California Southeast Asian mental health needs assessment.* Oakland, CA: Asian Community Mental Health Association.

Gong-Guy, E., Cravens, R. B., & Patterson, T. E. (1991). Clinical issues in mental health service delivery to refugees. *American Psychologist, 46*(6), 642–648.

Gonzalez, M. J. (2000, October). *Provision of mental health services to Hispanic clients.* Retrieved from http://www.naswnyc.org/d16.html

Granfield, R., & Cloud, W. (1996, Winter). The elephant that no one sees: Natural recovery among middle-class addicts. *Journal of Drug Issues, 26,* 45–61.

Grant, B. F., & Dawson, D. A. (1997). Age at onset of alcohol use and its association with *DSM-IV* alcohol abuse and dependence: Results from the national longitudinal alcohol epidemiologic survey. *Journal of Substance Abuse, 9,* 103–110.

Greenstein, M., & Breitbart, W. (2000). Cancer and the experience of meaning: A group psychotherapy program for people with cancer. *American Journal of Psychotherapy, 54*(4), 486–500.

Greenwood, P., Model, K. E., Rydell, P. C., & Chiesa, J. (1996). *Diverting children from a life of crime: Measuring costs and benefits.* Santa Monica, CA: RAND.

Griffin, G. (1987). Childhood predictive characteristics of aggressive adolescents. *Exceptional Children, 54,* 246–252.

Gupta, S. (2003). Why men die young. *Time, 161*(19), 84.

Haight, W. L. (1998, May). "Gathering the spirit" at First Baptist Church: Spirituality as a protective factor in the lives of African American children. *Social Work, 43*(3), 213–221.

Hamblen, J. (2004). *What are the traumatic stress effects of terrorism?* National Center for PTSD Studies, U.S. Veterans Affairs Administration. Retrieved August 21, 2004, from http://www.ncptsd.org/facts/disasters/fs_terrorism .html

Hamilton, G. (1940). *Social casework.* New York: Columbia University Press.

Hanifan, L. J. (1916). The rural school community center. *Annals of the American Academy of Social Science, 67,* 130–138.

Hansen, W. B., & Graham, J. W. (1991). Preventing alcohol, marijuana, and cigarette use among adolescents: Peer pressure resistance training versus establishing conservative norms. *Preventative Medicine, 20,* 414–430.

Harding, C. M., Brooks, G. W., Ashikaga, T., Strauss, J. S., & Breier, A. (1986a). The Vermont longitudinal study of persons with severe mental illness: I. Methodology, study sample, and overall status 32 years later. *American Journal of Psychiatry, 144,* 718–725.

Harding, C. M., Brooks, G. W., Ashikaga, T., Strauss, J. S., & Breier, A. (1986b). The Vermont longitudinal study of persons with severe mental illness: II. Long-term outcome of subjects who retrospectively met *DSM-II* criteria for schizophrenia. *American Journal of Psychiatry, 144,* 727–735.

Hardwig, J. (2000). Spiritual issues at the end of life: A call for discussion. *The Hastings Center Report, 30*(2), 28–30.

Harris, J. (1999). History of army social work. In J. Daley (Ed.), *Social work practice in the military* (pp. 3–22). Binghamton, NY: Haworth.

Harris, R. C., Dew, M. A., & Lee, A. (1995). The association of social relationships and activities with mortality: Prospective evidence from the Tecumseh Community Health Study. *American Journal of Epidemiology, 116,* 123–140.

Harrison, J., Chin, J., & Ficarrotto, T. (1988). Warning: Masculinity may be dangerous to your health. In M. S. Kimmel & M. A. Messner (Eds.), Men's lives (pp. 271–285). New York: Macmillan.

Hawkins, J. D., Catalano, R. F., Morrison, D. M., O'Donnell, J., & Abbott, R. D. (1992). The Seattle Social Development Project: Effects of the first four years on protective factors and problem behaviors. In J. McCord & R. Tremblay (Eds.), *The prevention of antisocial behavior in children*. New York: Guilford.

Haynes, B. (1998, July 25). Barriers and bridges to evidence based clinical practice. *British Medical Journal, 317,* 273–276.

Henggeler, S. W., Schoenwald, S. K., Bordin, C. M., & Rowland, M. D. (1998). *Multisystemic treatment of antisocial behavior in children and adolescents: Treatment manual for practitioners.* New York: Guilford Press.

Henry, D. L. (1999, September). Resilience in maltreated children: Implications for special needs adoptions. *Child Welfare, 78*(5), 519–540.

Hensley, L. G. (2002). Treatment for survivors of rape: Issues and interventions. *Journal of Mental Health Counseling, 24*(4), 331–348.

Herman, M. (2000). Psychotherapy with substance abusers: Integration of psychodynamic and cognitive behavioral approaches. *American Journal of Psychotherapy, 54*(4), 574–579.

Herrenkohl, R. C., & Russo, M. J. (February, 2001). Abusive early child rearing and early childhood aggression. *Child Maltreatment, 1,* 3–16.

Herrenkohl, T., Huang, I., Kosterman, B., Hawkins, R., David, J., et al. (2001, February). A comparison of social development processes leading to violent behavior in late adolescence for childhood initiators and adolescent initiators of violence. *Journal of Research in Crime & Delinquency, 38*(1), 45–63.

Hetherington, E. M. (1989). Coping with family transitions: Winners, losers and survivors. *Child Development, 60,* 1–14.

Higginbotham, P. (2004). *The poor laws.* Retrieved August 12, 2005, from users.ox.ac.uk/~peter/workhouse/poorlaws/poorlaws.html

Hingson, R., Scotch, N., Day, N., & Culbert, A. (1980). Recognizing and seeking help for drinking problems. *Journal of Studies on Alcohol, 41,* 1102–1117.

Ho, M. K. (1987). *Family therapy with ethnic minorities.* Newbury Park, CA: Sage.

Hochschild, J. (1995, April 29). *The New Yorker,* p. 69.

Hoff, D. J. (2002). A year later, the impact of 9/11 lingers. *Education Week, 22*(2), 1–3.

Hojat, M., Gonnella, J. S., Erdmann, J. B., Rattner, S. L., Veloski, J. J., et al. (2000). Gender comparisons of income expectations in the USA at the beginning of medical school during the past 28 years. *Social Science and Medicine, 50,* 1665–1672.

Horowitz, M. A. (2000, Summer). Kids who kill: A critique of how the American legal system deals with juveniles who commit homicide. *Law and Contemporary Problems, 63*(3), 133–177.

Horowitz, M. J. (1976). *Stress response syndromes.* New York: Aronson.

Houk, V., & Warren, R. (1991). Forum on youth violence in minority communities: Setting the agenda for prevention. *Public Health Reports, 106,* 225–280.

Hsu, F. L. K. (1983). *Rugged individualism reconsidered: Essays in psychological anthropology.* Knoxville: University of Tennessee Press.

Huber, G., Gross, G., & Schuttler, R. (1975). A long-term follow up study of schizophrenia: Psychiatric course of illness and prognosis. *Acta Psychiatrica Scandinavica, 52,* 49–57.

Hughes, M. J. (June, 1997). An exploratory study of young adult black and Latino males and the factors facilitating their decisions to make positive behavioral changes. *Smith College Studies in Social Work, 67*(3), 27–35.

Human Rights Watch. (2001). *Hatred in the hallways.* Retrieved January 27, 2006, from www.hrw.org/reports/pdf/c/crd/usalbg01.pdf

Humphreys, K. (1998). Can addiction-related self-help/mutual aid groups lower demand for professional substance abuse treatment? *Social Policy, 29*(2), 13–17.

Humphreys, K., & Moos, R. H. (1996). Reduced substance-abuse-related health care costs among voluntary participants in Alcoholics Anonymous. *Psychiatric Services, 47,* 709–713.

Humphreys, K., & Ribisl, K. M. (1999). The case for partnership with self-help groups. *Public Health Reports, 114*(4), 322–329.

Humphreys, K., Mavis, B. E., & Stoffelmayr, B. E. (1994). Are twelve step programs appropriate for disenfranchised groups? Evidence from a study of post-treatment mutual help involvement. *Prevention in Human Services, 11*(1), 165–179.

Independent Institute, The. (2003). *On civil liberties.* Retrieved December 6, 2004, from http://www.onpower.org/crises_civil.html

Idler, E. L. (1987). Religious involvement and the health of the elderly: Some hypotheses and an initial test. *Social Forces, 66,* 226-238:

Idler, E. L., & Kasl, S. V. (1992). Religion: Disability, depression, and the timing of death. *American Journal of Sociology, 97,* 1052–1079.

Idler, E. L., & Kasl, S. V. (1997). Religion among disabled elderly persons II: Attendance at religious services as a predictor of the course of disability. *Journal of Gerontology: Social Sciences,* S306–S316.

Ino, S. M., & Glicken, M. D. (1999, June). Treating Asian American clients in crisis: A collectivist approach. *Smith College Studies in Social Work, 69*(3), 525–540.

Ino, S. M., & Glicken, M. D. (2002). Understanding and treating the ethnically Asian client: A collectivist approach. *Journal of Health and Social Policy, 14*(4), 37–48.

Ionia Community Mental Health. (2005). *Services we offer.* Retrieved July 10, 2005, from http://www.ioniacmhs.org/services.asp

Issacs, D., & Fitzgerald, D. (1999, December 18). Seven alternatives to evidence based medicine. *British Medical Journal, 319,* 1619.

Jacobs, S., & Prigerson, H. (2000). Psychotherapy of traumatic grief: A review of evidence for psychotherapeutic treatments. *Death Studies, 24*(6), 479–496.

Jamison, K. R. (1995). *An unquiet mind.* New York: Alfred A. Knopf.

Johnson, D. L. (1990). The Houston parent-child development center project: Disseminating a viable program for enhancing at-risk families. *Prevention in the Human Services, 7,* 89–108.

Judicial Council of California. (2005). *Guide to California courts.* Retrieved June 29, 2005, from http://www.courtinfo.ca.gov/reference/guide-juvenile.htm

Kaczorowski, J. M. (1989). Spiritual well-being and anxiety in adults diagnosed with cancer. *Hospice Journal, 5,* 105–126.

Kann, L. (2001). Commentary. *Journal of Drug Issues, 31*(3), 725–727.

Kaplan, S. J., Pelcovitz, D., & Labruna, V. (1999, October). Child and adolescent abuse research: A review of the past ten years: Physical and emotional abuse. *Journal of the American Academy of Child and Adolescent Psychiatry, 38*(10), 1214–1222.

Katz, N. (2004). *Sexual harassment charges, EEOC & FEPAs combined: FY 1992–FY 2002.* Retrieved May 8, 2004, from http://womensissues.about.com/library/blsexharassmentstats.htm

Kaufman, C. (1995). The self help employment center: Some outcomes from the first year. *Psychosocial Rehabilitation Journal, 18,* 145–162.

Kazdin, A. E., Holland, L., Crowley, M., & Breton, S. (1997). Barriers to treatment participation scale: Evaluation and validation in the context of child outpatient treatment. *Journal of Child Psychology and Psychiatry, 38*(8), 1051–1062.

Keane, T. M., Fairbank, J. A., Caddell, J. M., & Zimering, R. T. (1989). Implosive (flooding) therapy reduces symptoms of PTSD in Vietnam combat veterans. *Behavior Therapy, 20,* 245–260.

Keaveny, T. J., & Inderrieden, E. J. (2000). Gender differences in pay satisfaction and pay expectations. *Journal of Managerial Issues, 12,* 363–379.

Keith-Lucas A. (1972). *Giving and taking help.* Chapel Hill: University of North Carolina Press.

Kennedy, D. (1999). The future of Navy social work. In J. Daley (Ed.), *Social work practice in the military* (pp. 317–327). Binghamton, NY: Haworth.

Kennedy, M. (1990, July 17). *Psychiatric hospitalization of Growers.* Paper presented at the Second Biennial Conference on Community Research and Action, East Lansing, MI.

Kesler, J. T. (2000). The healthy communities movement: Seven counterintuitive next steps. *National Civic Review, 89*(3), 271–284.

Kessler, D. B., & Hyden, P. (1991). Physical, sexual and emotional abuse of children. *Clinical Symposia, 43,* 1.

Kessler, R. C., Sonnega, A., Bromet, E., Hughes, M., & Nelson, C. B. (1995). Posttraumatic stress disorder in the National Comorbidity Survey. *Archives of General Psychiatry, 52,* 1048–1060.

Kids count data book. (2002). Baltimore: Annie E. Casey Foundation.

King, A. W., Fowler, S. W., & Zeithaml, C. P. (2001). Managing organizational competencies for competitive advantage: The middle-management edge. *Supervision, 15*(2), 107.

King, M. L., Jr. (1967, December 24). *A Christmas sermon on peace.* Ebenezer Baptist Church, Atlanta, GA.

Kirst-Ashman, K. K., & Hull, G. H., Jr. (1999). *Understanding generalist practice* (2nd ed.). Belmont, CA: Brooks/Cole.

Kissman, K., & Maurer, L. (2002). East meets west: Therapeutic aspects of spirituality in health, mental health and addiction recovery. *International Social Work, 45*(1), 35–44.

Klein, J. (2005, September 12). Listen to what Katrina is saying. *Time,* p. 27.

Koenig, H. G., George, L. K., Cohen, H. J., Hays, J. C., Larson, D. B., & Blazer, D. G. (1998). The relationship between religious activities and cigarette smoking in older adults. *Journal of Gerontology: Medical Services, 53A,* M426–M434.

Kogan, J. N., Edelstein, B. A., & McKee, D. R. (2000). Assessment of anxiety in older adults: Current status. *Journal of Anxiety Disorders, 14*(2), 109–132.

Kogan, M. J. (2000, October). The pressure men feel to live up to the macho image is literally making them sick. *Monitor on Psychology, 31*(9), 48–49.

Kolko, D. J., & Kazdin, A. E. (1991). Aggression and psychopathology in match playing and fire setting children: A replication and extension. *Journal of Clinical Child Psychology, 20,* 191–201.

Kopta, M. S., Lueger, R. J., Saunders, S. M, & Howard, K. I. (1999). Individual psychotherapy outcome and process research: Challenges leading to greater turmoil or positive transition. *Annual Review of Psychology, 50,* 441–469.

Kraemer, S. (2000). The fragile male. *British Medical Journal, 321*, 1609–1612.

Kramer, S. H., & Rosenthal, R. (1998). Meta-analytic research synthesis. In A. S. Bellack, M. Hersen, & N. R. Schooler (Eds.), *Comprehensive clinical psychology: Vol. 3—Research and methods* (pp. 351–368). Oxford, UK: Pergamon.

Krauth, L. D. (1996, May/June). Providers confront the future. *Behavioral Health Management, 16*(3), 10–14.

Krucoff, M., & Crater, S. (1998, June 17). *The impact of prayer in recovery from heart attacks.* Paper presented at the American Heart Association National Meeting, Dallas, TX.

Kruger, A. (2000). Schizophrenia: Recovery and hope. *Psychiatric Rehabilitation Journal, 24*, 29–37.

Kübler-Ross, E. (1997). *On death and dying.* New York: Touchstone.

Kulka, R. A., Schlenger, W. E., Fairbank, J. A., Hough, R. L., Jordan, B. K., et al. (1990). *Cognitive behavioral therapies for trauma.* New York: Brunner/Mazel.

Kuperman, S., Schlosser, S. S., Kraemer, J. R., Bucholz, K., Hesselbrock, V., et al. (2001, April). Risk domains with adolescent alcohol diagnosis. *Addiction, 96*, 629–637.

Kurtz, L. F. (1988). Mutual aid for affective disorders: The manic depressive and depressive associations. *American Journal of Orthopsychiatry, 58*(1), 152–155.

Kyrouz, E., & Humphreys, K. (1996). Do psychiatrically disabled people benefit from participation in self-help/mutual aid organizations? A research review. *The Community Psychologist, 29*, 21–25.

La Monde Diplomatique. (1998, March). *When our "friend" Saddam was gassing the Kurds.* Retrieved May 14, 2004, from http://mondediplo.com/1998/03/04iraqkn

Lajoie, D. H., & Shapiro, S. Y. (1992). Definitions of transpersonal psychology: The first twenty-three years. *Journal of Transpersonal Psychology, 24*(1), 79–98.

Landesman, P. (2004, January, 25). Sex slaves on main street. *New York Times,* pp. 30–61.

Landis, B. J. (1996). Uncertainty, spiritual well-being, and psychosocial adjustment to chronic illness. *Issues in Mental Health Nursing, 27*, 217–231.

Lang, A. J., & Stein, M. B. (2001). Anxiety disorders. *Geriatrics, 56*(5), 24–30.

Lara-Cinisomo, S., Pebley, A. R., Vaiana, M. E., Maggio, E., Berends, M., et al. (2004, Fall). *RAND Corporation report: A matter of class: Educational achievement reflects family background more than ethnicity or immigration.* Retrieved July 1, 2005, from http://www.rand.org/publications/randreview/issues/fa112004/class.html

Larson, D. B., Koenig, H. G., Kaplan, B. H., & Levin, J. S. (1989). The impact of religion on men's blood pressure. *Journal of Religion and Health, 28*, 265–278.

Laszloffy, T. A., & Hardy, C. B. (2000). Uncommon strategies for a common problem: Addressing racism in family therapy. *Family Process, 39*, 35–50.

Lauriello, J., Bustillo, J., & Keith, S. J. (1999). A critical review of research on psychosocial treatment of schizophrenia. *Biological Psychiatry, 46*, 1409–1417.

Lawson, E. J., & Sharpe, T. L. (2000, July). Black men and divorce: Implications for culturally competent practice. *Minority Health Today.* Retrieved from http://www.findarticles.com/cf_0/m0HKU/5_1/66918338/print.jhtml

Lawton, M. P. (1977). The impact of the environment on aging and behavior. In J. E. Birren & K. W. Schaie (Eds.), *Handbook of the psychology of aging* (pp. 276–301). New York: Van Nostrand Reinhold.

Lawton, M. P., & Nahemow, L. (1973). Ecology and the aging process. In C. Eisdorfer & M. P. Lawton (Eds.), *The psychology of adult development and aging* (pp. 619–674). Washington, DC: American Psychological Association.

Lee, E. (1996). Asian American families: An overview. In M. McGoldrick, J. Giordana, & J. Pearce (Eds.), *Ethnicity and family therapy* (2nd ed.). New York: Guilford.

Leigh, G., Ogborne, A. C., & Cleland, P. (1984). Factors associated with patient dropout from outpatient alcoholism treatment services. *Journal of Studies on Alcohol, 45*, 359–362.

Leong, F. T. L. (1986). Counseling and psychotherapy with Asian-Americans: Review of the literature. *Journal of Counseling Psychology, 33*(2), 196–206.

Levin, J. S., & Vanderpool, H. Y. (1989). Is religion therapeutically significant for hypertension? *Social Science and Medicine, 29*, 69-78.

Lewis, O. (1998). The culture of poverty. *Society, 35*(2), 7–10.

Lewis, T. (2005, December). *FBI releases 2004 hate crime statistics.* Retrieved January 16, 2006, from http://www.civilrights.org/issues/hate/details.cfm?id=38513

Liberto, J. G., & Oslin, D. W. (1995). Early versus late onset of alcoholism in the elderly. *International Journal of Addiction, 30*(13–14), 1799–1818.

Lindeman, E. (1921). *The community: An introduction to the study of community leadership and organization.* New York: Association Press.

Lindsay, J. (2005). *Public education:* Views of a concerned parent. Retrieved June 30, 2005, from http://www.jefflindsay.com/Education.shtml

Link, B., Phelan, J., Bresnahan, M., Stueve, A., Moore, R., et al. (1995). Lifetime and five-year prevalence of homelessness in the United States. *American Journal of Orthopsychiatry, 65*(3), 347–354.

Lloyd-Williams, M. (2001). Screening for depression in palliative care patients: A review. *European Journal of Cancer Care, 10*(1), 31–36.

Lochner, L., & Moretti, E. (2002, March 3). *JCPR Working Paper No. 287.* Retrieved September 19, 2002, from JCPR.org/wp/wpprofile.cfm?ID=341

Lockett, G. (1999). The future of Army social work. In J. Daley (Ed.), *Social work practice in the military* (pp. 307–316). Binghamton, NY: Haworth.

Lockwood, R., & Church. A. (1998). Deadly serious: An FBI perspective on animal cruelty. In R. Lockwood & F. R. Ascione (Eds.), *Cruelty to animals and interpersonal violence: Readings in research and application* (pp. 241–245). West Lafayette, IN: Purdue University Press.

Loewenberg, F. M. (1988). *Caring and responsibility: Crossroads between holistic practice and traditional medicine.* Philadelphia: University of Pennsylvania Press.

Loewenberg, F. M., & Dolgoff, R. (1996). *Ethical decisions for social work practice* (5th ed.). Itasca, IL: F. E. Peacock.

Lopez, S. (2005, August 3). Officials bicker as mentally ill wither. *Los Angeles Times*, pp. A1, A6.

Luft, M. (2005). *Jane Addam's Hull House.* Retrieved August 4, 2005, from http://www.hullhouse.org/about.asp

Lukefahr, J. L. (2001). Treatment of child abuse. *Journal of the American Academy of Child and Adolescent Psychiatry, 40*(3), 383.

Lyon, L., Klauber, M. R., & Gardner, J. Y. (1976). Cancer incidence in Mormons and non-Mormons in Laah, 1966–1970. *New England Journal of Medicine, 294*, 129–133.

Mahoney, J. S. (2003). *Defining social problems*. Retrieved September 15, 2005, from http://www.people.vcu.edu/~jmahoney/define.htm#Defining%20Social

Manfred-Gilham, J. J., Sales, E., & Koeske, G. (2002). Therapist and case manager perceptions of client barriers to treatment participation and use of engagement strategies. *Community Mental Health Journal, 38*(3), 213–221.

Manske, J. (2005, July 29). 30% of troops mentally stressed after Iraq. *Los Angeles Times*, p. A4.

Markowitz, F. E. (1998). The effects of stigma on the psychological well-being and life satisfaction of persons with mental illness. *Journal of Health & Social Behavior, 39*(4), 335–347.

Martin, B. A. (1989). Gender differences in salary expectations when current salary information is provided. *Psychology of Women Quarterly, 13,* 87–96.

Mayer, G. R. (1995). Preventing antisocial behavior in the schools. *Journal of Applied Behavior Analysis, 28,* 467–478.

McCabe, D. L., & Trevino, L. K. (1995). Cheating among business students: A challenge for business leaders and educators. *Journal of Management Education, 19,* 205–218.

McClain, C. S, Rosenfeld, B., & Breitbart, W. (2003). Effect of spiritual well-being on end-of-life despair in terminally-ill cancer patients. *Lancet, 361*(9369), 1603–1608.

McCubbin, H. I., McCubbin, M. A., Thompson, A. I., Han, S. Y., & Allen, C. T. (1997, June 22). Families under stress: What makes them resilient. The 1997 *American Association of Family and Consumer Sciences* (AAFCS) commemorative lecture, Washington, DC. Retrieved August 4, 2004, from http://www.cyfernet.org/research/resilient.html

McCubbin, M. A., & McCubbin, H. I. (1993). Family coping with health crises: The resiliency model of family stress, adjustment and adaptation. In C. Danielson, B. Hamel-Bissell, & P. Winstead-Fry (Eds.), *Families, health, and illness.* New York: Mosby.

McCubbin, M. A., & McCubbin, H. I. (1996). Resiliency in families: A conceptual model of family adjustment and adaptation in response to stress and crises. In H. I. McCubbin, A. I. Thompson, & M. A. McCubbin (Eds.), Family assessment: Resiliency, coping and adaptation—Inventories for research and practice (pp. 1–64). Madison: University of Wisconsin System.

McFadden, S. (2000). *The importance of religion in the lives of older adults.* Retrieved April 9, 2000, from http://www.lutersem.edu/cars/newsletters/Artus.htm

McKay, J. R., Alterman, A. I., McLellan, A. T., & Snider, E. C. (1994). Treatment goals, community of care, and outcomes in a day hospital substance abuse rehabilitation program. *American Journal of Psychiatry, 15*(2), 254–259.

McKeel, A. J. (1999). *A selected review of research of solution-focused brief therapy.* Retrieved November 4, 2004, from http://www.enabling.org/ia/sft/Review%20McKeel.htm

McNamara, C. (2004). *Broad overview of various programs and movements to improve organizational performance.* Retrieved November 18, 2004, from http://www.mapnp.org/library/org_perf/methods.htm

Meadows, E. A., & Foa, E. B. (1998). Intrusion, arousal, and avoidance: Sexual trauma survivors. In V. Follette, I. Ruzek, & F. Abueg (Eds.), *Cognitive-behavioral therapies for trauma* (pp. 100–123). New York: Guilford.

Medalie, J. H., Kahn, H. A., Neufeld, H. N., Riss, E., & Goldbourt, U. (1973). Five-year myocardial infarction incidence II: Association of single variables to age and birthplace. *Journal of Chronic Disease, 26,* 329–349.

Media Bias Basics. (2005). *Media Research Center.* Retrieved September 16, 2005, from http://secure.mediaresearch.org/news/MediaBiasBasics.html

Mendel, R. A. (1995). *Prevention or pork? A hard-headed look at youth-oriented anti-crime programs.* Washington, DC: American Youth Policy Forum.

Menzel, D. C. (1999, Winter). The morally mute manager: Fact or fiction? *Public Personnel Management, 28*(4), 515–528.

Meystedt, D. M. (1984). Religion in the rural population. *Social Casework, 65*(4), 219–226.

Miller, G. (2004, June 16). A wonderful life if you're on top good numbers, bad results: Many still struggling to get by. *Pittsburgh Post-Gazette,* p. A16.

Miller, K. E. (2001). Can two questions screen for alcohol and substance abuse? *American Family Physician, 64,* 1247.

Miller, L. (1999, Summer). The impact of child abuse. *Victim Advocate, 6,* 28–34.

Miller, W. R., & Rollnick, S. (1991). *Motivational interviewing: Preparing people to change addictive behavior.* New York: Guilford.

Miller, W. R., & Sanchez, V. C. (1994). Motivating young adults for treatment and lifestyle change. In G. S. Howard & P. E. Nathan (Eds.), *Alcohol use and misuse by young adults* (pp. 55–81). Notre Dame, IN: University of Notre Dame Press.

Mills, T. L., & Henretta, J. C. (2001). Racial, ethnic, and socio-demographic differences in the level of psychosocial distress among older Americans. *Research on Aging, 23*(2), 131–152.

Mitchell, C. E. (1999). Violating the public trust: The ethical and moral obligations of government officials. *Public Personnel Management, 28,* 27–38.

Moffitt, T. E. (1994). Adolescence-limited and life-course persistent antisocial behavior: A developmental taxonomy. *Psychological Review, 100,* 674–701.

Monteleone, J. (2004, May 17). Five decades after the Brown decision, the journey continues. *The Idaho Statesman,* p. 8.

Montgomery, H. A., Miller, W. R., & Tonigan, J. S. (1995). Does Alcoholics Anonymous involvement predict treatment outcome? *Journal of Substance Abuse Treatment, 22,* 241–246.

Monti, P. M., Colby, S. M., Barnett, N. P., Spirito, A., Rohsenow, D. J., et al. (1999). Brief intervention for harm reduction with alcohol-positive older adolescents in a hospital emergency department. *Journal of Consulting and Clinical Psychology, 67*(6), 989–994.

Morales, A. (1982). The Mexican American gang member: Evaluation and treatment. In R. Becerra, M. Karno, & J. Escolar (Eds.), *Mental health and Hispanic Americans: Clinical perspective.* New York: Grune and Stratton.

Mothers & More. (2004). Retrieved October 20, 2004, from http://www.mothersandmore.com/Advocacy/advocacy_and_action.sht

Mouzelis, N. P. (1967). *Organizations and bureaucracy.* Chicago: Aldine.

Moxley, D. P., & Olivia, G. (2001). Strengths-based recovery practice in chemical dependency: A transperson perspective. *Families in Society, 82*(3), 251–262.

Moynihan, D. P. (1969). *Maximum feasible misunderstanding.* New York: The Free Press.

Mueller, T. I., Leon, A. C., Keller, M. B., Solomon, D. A., Endicott, J., et al. (1999). Recurrence after recovery from major depressive disorder during 15 years of observational follow-up. *American Journal of Psychiatry, 156,* 1.

Murray, C. J., & Lopez, A. D. (1997). Alternative projections of mortality and disability by cause 1990–2020: Global burden of disease study. *Lancet, 349,* 1498–1504.

Murray, J. (1997). *The social work history on-line time line.* Retrieved July 17, 2005, from http://www.gnofn.org/~jill/sehistory/

Myers, M. K. (1993). Organizational factors in the integration of services for children. *Social-Service-Review, 67*(4), 547–575.

A nation at risk: The imperative for educational reform. (1983, April 1). A report to the Nation and the Secretary of Education, the U.S. Department of Education by the National Committee on Excellence in Education. Retrieved June 27, 2006, from http://www.ed.gov/pubs/NaAtRisk/risk.html

National Association of Social Workers. (1996). *Code of ethics.* Retrieved from http://www.naswdc.org/pubs/code/code.asp

National Center for Injury Prevention and Control. (2004). *Facts about violence among youth and violence in schools,* NCIPC, Atlanta, Georgia. Retrieved June 14, 2005, from http://www.cdc.gov/ncipc/cmpfact.htm

National Center on Elder Abuse. (1998, September). *National elder abuse incidence study: Final report.* Washington, DC: U.S. Department of Health and Human Services, Administration for Children and Families and Administration on Aging.

National Clearing House on Child Abuse and Neglect Information, US Dept of Health and Human Services. (2004). *Administration for children and families.* Retrieved May 10, 2004, from http://nccanch.acf.hhs.gov/pubs/factsheets/canstats.cfm

National Education Association. (2005). *Vouchers.* Retrieved June 30, 2005, from http://www.nea.org/vouchers/index.html

National Fire Protection Association. (1999). *Statistics on the national fire problem.* Retrieved July 8, 2002, from http: //www.fema.gov/nfpa/

National Institute of Alcohol Abuse and Alcoholism. (2000). Alcohol alert. *NIAAA,* p. 49.

National Institutes of Health, National Institutes of Health News. (2004, September 8). *New research shows air pollution can reduce children's lung function.* Retrieved November 12, 2004, from http://www.nih.gov/news/pr/sep2004/niehs-08a

National Institute of Mental Health. (1999). *Schizophrenia.* Retrieved May 23, 2004, from http://www.nimh.nih.gov/publicat/schizoph.htm

National Institute of Mental Health. (2001a). *Bi-polar disorder.* Publication 01–3679, Bethesda, MD. Retrieved October 13, 2002, from http://www.nimh.nih.gov/publicat/bipolar.cfm#intro

National Institute of Mental Health. (2001b). *The impact of mental illness on society.* Retrieved July 10, 2005, from http://www.nimh.nih.gov/publicat/burden.cfm

National Institute of Mental Health. (2001c). *The numbers count.* Retrieved August 24, 2004, from http://www.nimh.nih.gov/publicat/numbers.cfm

National Institute of Occupational Safety and Health. (1992). *Homicide in U.S. workplaces: A strategy for prevention and research.* Morgantown, WV: U.S. Department of Health and Human Services, Public Health Service, Centers for Disease Control, National Institute for Occupational Safety and Health. (DHHS [NIOSH] Publication No. 92-103)

National Institute of Occupational Safety and Health. (1993). *Fatal injuries to workers in the United States, 1980–1989: A decade of surveillance; national profile.* (DHHS [NIOSH] Publication No. 93-108) Cincinnati, OH: U.S. Department of Health and Human Services, Public Health Service, Centers for Disease Control and Prevention, National Institute for Occupational Safety and Health.

National Institutes of Health. (2003, October). *HIV infection and AIDS: An overview.* Prepared by the National Institutes of Health, Bethesda, MD. Retrieved March 10, 2005, from http://www.niaid.nih.gov/factsheets/hivinf.htmhttp://www.niaid.nih.gov/factsheets/hivinf.htm

National Mental Heath Association. (2005). *NMHA and the history of the Mental Health Movement.* Retrieved July 10, 2005, from http://www.nmha.org/about/history.cfm

National School Safety Center. (1996, March). *National School Safety Center newsletter.* Malibu, CA: Author.

Natvig, G. K., Albrektsen, G., & Qvarnstrom, U. (2001). School-related stress experience as a risk factor for bullying behavior. *Journal of Youth & Adolescence, 30*(5), 561–575.

Norcross, J. C., Hedges, M., & Prochaska, J. O. (2002, June). The face of 2010: A delphi poll on the future of psychotherapy. *Professional Psychology: Research and Practice, 33*(3), 316–322.

Norris, F. H. (2002). *The range, magnitude, and duration of the effects of natural disasters: A review of the empirical literature.* A National Center for PTSO fact sheet. Retrieved from www.ncptsd.org/facts/disasters/fs%5frange.html

Novak, M. (2000, December). *First things.* Retrieved September 21, 2005, from http://www.firstthings.com/ftissues/ft0012/opinion/novak.html

O'Connor, R. (2001). Active treatment of depression. *American Journal of Psychotherapy, 55*(4), 507–530.

O'Donnell M. (1997). *A skeptic's medical dictionary.* London: BMJ Books.

O'Hara, A., & Miller, E. (2000). *Priced out in 2000: The crisis continues.* Boston: Technical Assistance Collaborative, Inc.

Oates, R. K., & Bross, D. C. (1995). What have we learned about treating child physical abuse? A literature review of the last decade. *Journal of Child Abuse & Neglect, 19,* 463–473.

O'Brien, M. E. (1982). Religious faith and long-term adjustment to hemodialysis. *Journal of Religion and Health, 21,* 68–80.

Office of Social Justice. (2004). *Major themes from Catholic social teaching: Archdioceses of St. Paul and Minneapolis.* Retrieved November 15, 2004, from http://www.osjspm.org/cst/themes.htm

Older Women's League. (2004). *Suicide.* Retrieved December 5, 2004, from http://www.owl-national.org/mentalhealthweek/statistics.html

Olds, D. L., Henderson, C. R., Tatelbaum, R., & Chamberlin, R. (1988). Improving the life-course development of socially disadvantaged mothers: A randomized trial of nurse home visitation. *American Journal of Public Health, 78,* 1436–1444.

Olweus, D. (1997). Bully/victim problems in school: Facts and intervention. *European Journal Psychology and Education, 12*(4), 495–510.

Osofsky, H. J., & Osofsky, J. D. (2001, Winter). Violent and aggressive behaviors in youth: A mental health and prevention perspective. *Psychiatry, 64*(4), 285–295.

Oxman, T. E., Freeman, D. H., & Manheimer, E. D. (1995). Lack of social participation or religious strength and comfort as risk factors for death after cardiac
surgery in the elderly. *Psychosomatic Medicine, 57*(1), 5–15.

Ozer, E. J., Best, S. R., Lipsey, T. L., & Weiss, D. S. (2003). Predictors of posttraumatic stress disorder and symptoms in adults: A meta-analysis. *Psychological
Bulletin, 129*(1), 52–73.

Parikh, S. V., Wasylenki, D., Goerung, P., & Wong, J. (1996). Mood disorders:
Rural/urban differences in prevalence, health care utilization, and disability
in Ontario. *Journal of Affective Disorders, 38*, 57–65.

Peele, S. (1989). *The diseasing of America: Addiction treatment out of control.*
Lexington, MA: Lexington Books.

Pena, J. M., Bland, I. J., Shervinton, D., Rice, J. C., & Foulks, E. F. (2000, February 1).
Racial identity and its assessment in a sample of African-American men in
treatment for cocaine dependence. *American Journal of Drug and Alcohol
Abuse.* Retrieved from http://www.findarticles.com/cf_0/PI/search.jhtml?
magR=all+magazines&key=psychotherapy+%2B+race

Pennington, H., Butler, R., & Eagger, S. (2000, May). The assessment of patients
with alcohol disorders by an old age psychiatric service. *Aging and Mental
Health, 4*(2), 182–184.

Petersen, G. J., Pietrzak, D., & Speaker, K. M. (1998, September). The enemy
within: A national study on school violence and prevention. *Urban
Education, 33*(3), 331–359.

Pfeffer, J. (2005, March). Why do bad management theories persist? A comment
on Ghoshal. *Academy of Management Learning & Education, 4*(1), 96–101.

Phillips, R. L., Kuzma, J., & Beeson, W. L. (1980). Influence of selection versus
lifestyle on risk of fatal cancer and cardiovascular disease among Seventh Day
Adventists. *American Journal of Epidemiology, 712*, 296–314.

Pisani, V. D., & Fawcett, J. (1993). The relative contributions of medication adherence and AA meeting attendance to abstinent. *Journal of Studies on Alcohol,
54*(1), 115–120.

Piven, F. F., & Cloward, R. A. (1971). *Regulating the poor: The functions of public
welfare.* New York: Pantheon.

Poussaint, A. (1993, February). Enough already. *Ebony, 48*(4), 86–89.

Poverty, 1997–2004. (2004). *Microsoft® Encarta® online encyclopedia.* Retrieved
May 22, 2004, from http://encarta.msn.com

Powell, T. J., Yeaton, W., Hill, E. M., & Silk, K. R. (2001). Predictors of psychosocial
outcomes for patients with mood disorders. *Psychiatric Rehabilitation
Journal, 25*(1), 3–12.

Pratt, L. A., Ford, D. E., Crum, R. M., Armenian, H. K., Gallo, J. J., et al. (1996).
Depression, psychotropic medication, and risk of myocardial infarction:
Prospective data from the Baltimore ECA follow-up. *Circulation, 94*, 3123–3129.

Project MATCH Research Group. (1997). Matching alcoholism treatments to
client heterogeneity: Project MATCH posttreatment drinking outcomes.
Journal of Studies on Alcohol, 58, 7–29.

Public Agenda. (2005). *Education at glance.* Retrieved June 30, 2005, from
http://publicagenda.org/issues/overview.cfm?issue_type=education

Pulkkinen, L., & Tremblay, R. E. (1992). Patterns of boy's social adjustment in two
cultures: A longitudinal perspective. *International Journal of Behavior, 15*(4),
527–533.

Putnam, R. D. (2000). *Bowling alone.* New York: Touchstone Books.

Quinn, J. F., & Downs, B. (1995). Predictors of gang violence: The impact of drugs and guns on police perceptions in nine states. *Journal of Gang Research, 2*(3), 15–27.

Rae-Grant, N., McConville, B. J., & Fleck, S. (1999, March). Violent behavior in children and youth: Preventive intervention from a psychiatric perspective. *Journal of the American Academy of Child and Adolescent Psychiatry, 38*(3), 235–241.

Raines, J. C., & Foy, C. W. (1994, December). Extinguishing the fires within: Treating juvenile fire setters. *Families in Society: The Journal of Contemporary Human Services, 75*(10), 596–607.

Randall, V. R. (1996). *Slavery, segregation and racism: Trusting the health care system ain't always easy! An African American perspective on bioethics.* (15 St. Louis U. Pub.L.Rev. 191)

Rauch, J. (2003). Let it be. *Atlantic Monthly, 291*(4), 34.

Rector, R., & Hederman, R., Jr. (2004, August). *Two Americas: One rich, one poor? Understanding income inequality in the United States.* Washington, DC: The Heritage Foundation. Retrieved March 9, 2005, from http://www.heritage.org/Research/Taxes/bg1791.cfm

Rees, D.W. (1986). Changing patient's health beliefs to improve compliance with alcohol treatment. *Journal of Studies on Alcohol, 47,* 436–439.

Regehr, C., Cadell, S., & Jansen, K. (1999). Perceptions of control and long-term recovery from rape. *American Journal of Orthopsychiatrty, 69,* 110–114.

Reid, J. (1993). Prevention of conduct disorder before and after school entry: Relating interventions to developmental findings. *Development and Psychopathology, 5*(1/2), 243–262.

Reidy, A. (1992). Shattering illusions of difference. *Resources, 4,* 3–6.

Reich, M., & Tannenbaum, A. (2001, Fall). *From charitable volunteers to architects of social welfare: A brief history of social work.* Retrieved July 22, 2005, from http://www.ssw.umich.edu/ongoing/fa112001/briefhistory.html

Remick, R. A. (2002). Diagnosis and management of depression in primary care: A clinical update and review. *Canadian Medical Association Journal, 167*(11), 1253–1261.

Rennison, C. (2000, August). *Criminal victimization 1999, changes 1998–99 with trends 1993–99.* Retrieved June 27, 2006, from http://www.ojp.gov/bjs/pub/press/cv00pr.htm

Resnick, H., Acierno, R., Holmes, M., Kilpatrick, D., & Jager, N. (1999). Prevention of post-rape psychopathology: Preliminary findings of a controlled acute rape treatment study. *Journal of Anxiety Disorders, 13,* 359–370.

Reynolds, R. & Richardson, P. (2000). Evidence based practice and psychotherapy research. *Journal of Mental Health, 9*(3), 257–267.

Ricardo, D. (1817). *On the principles of political economy and taxation* (3rd ed.). London: John Murray.

Richman, J. (2000). Introduction: Psychotherapy with terminally ill patients. *American Journal of Psychotherapy, 54*(4), 482–486.

Richters, J. E., & Martinez, P. E. (1993). Violent communities, family choices, and children's chances: An algorithm for improving the odds. *Development and Psychopathology, 5,* 609–627.

Riding, A. (1989). *Distant neighbors: A portrait of the Mexicans.* New York: Vintage.

Riessman, F. (1965). The helper-therapy principle. *Social Work, 10,* 27–32.

Riessman, F. (1997). Ten self-help principles. *Social Policy, 30*(4), 6–11.

Roach, R. (2001). Where are the black men on campus. *Black Issues in Higher Education.* Retrieved May 10, 2001, from http://www.findarticles.com/cf_0/m0DXK/6_18/75561775/print.jhtml

Robert, S. A., & Li, L. W. (2001). Age variation in the relationship between community socioeconomic status and adult health. *Research on Aging, 23*(2), 233–258.

Roberts, A. R. (1990). *Crisis intervention handbook: Assessment, treatment, and research.* Belmont, CA: Wadsworth.

Robinson, J. L. (1996). *10 facts every employer and employee should know about workplace violence: It may save your life!* Retrieved from http://www.smartbiz.com

Rogler, L., & Magaldy, R. (1987). What do culturally sensitive mental health services mean? The case of Hispanics. *American Psychologist, 42,* 565–570.

Rohr, J. A. (1989). *Ethics for bureaucrats: An essay on law and values* (2nd ed.). New York: Marcel Dekker.

Roizen, R., Cahalan, D., Lambert, E., Wiebel, W., & Shanks, P. (1978). Spontaneous remission among untreated problem drinkers. In D. Kandel (Ed.), *Longitudinal research on drug use.* Washington, DC: Hemisphere.

Root, M. (1993). Guidelines for facilitating therapy with Asian American clients. In D. Atkinson, G. Morten, & D.W. Sue (Eds.), *Counseling American minorities: A cross-cultural perspective* (pp. 349–356). Madison, WI: Brown and Benchmark.

Rosenhan, D. L. (1973, January). On being sane in insane places. *Science, 179,* 250–258.

Rothbaum, B., Olasov, C., & Schwartz, A. C. (2002). Exposure therapy for posttraumatic stress disorder. *American Journal of Psychotherapy, 56*(1), 59–75.

Rothbaum, B. O., Meadows E. A., Resick, P., & Foy, D. W. (2000). Cognitive-behavioral therapy. In E. B. Foa, M. Friedman, & T. Keane (Eds.), *Effective treatments for posttraumatic stress disorder: Practice guidelines from the International Society for Traumatic Stress Studies* (pp. 60–83). New York: Guilford.

Rubinbach, A. (1992). Is case management effective for people with serious mental illness? A research review. *Health & Social Work, 17*(2), 138–150.

Rugala, F. A., & Issacs, A. R. (Eds.).(2003).*Workplace violence.* Quantico, VA: U.S. Department of Justice. Retrieved January 2006 from www.fbi.gov/publications/violence.pdf

Rush, A. J., & Giles, D. E. (1982). *Cognitive therapy: Theory and research in short term psychotherapies for depression.* New York: Guilford.

Rutter, M. (1987, July). Psychosocial resilience and protective mechanisms. *American Journal of Orthopsychiatry, 57*(3), 316–331.

Sackett, D. L., Richardson, W. S., Rosenberg, W., & Haynes, R. B. (1997). *Evidence-based medicine: How to practice and teach EMB.* New York: Churchill Livingstone.

Sackett, D. L., Rosenberg, W. M. C., Muir Gray, J. A., Haynes, R. B., & Richardson, W. S. (1996, January 13). Evidence based medicine: What it is and what it isn't. *British Medical Journal, 312,* 71–72. Retrieved from http://bmj.com/cgi/content/full/312/7023/71?ijkey=JflK2VHyVI2F6

Sakheim, G. A., & Osborn, E. (1999). Severe vs. nonsevere fire setters revisited. *Child Welfare, 78*(4), 411–434.

Saleebey, D. (1985). In clinical social work practice, is the body politic? *Social Service Review, 59,* 578–592.

Saleebey, D. (1992). *The strengths perspective in social work practice*. White Plains, NY: Longman.

Saleebey, D. (1994). Culture, theory, and narrative: The intersection of meanings in practice. *Social Work, 39,* 352–359.

Saleebey, D. (1996). The strengths perspective in social work practice: Extensions and cautions. *Social Work, 41*(3), 296–305.

Saleebey, D. (2000, Fall). Power to the people; strength and hope. *Advancements in Social Work, 1*(2), 127–136.

Salgado de Snyder, V. N. (1990). Gender and ethnic differences in psychological stress and generalized distress among Hispanics. *Sex Roles, 22*(7\8), 441–453.

Salvation Army. (2004). Retrieved August 23, 2004, from www.salvation-armyusa.org

SAMSHA. (2001). *The CMHS approach to preventing violence*. U.S. Department of Health and Human Services. Retrieved May 14, 2005, from http://alt.samhsa.gov/grants/content/2002/YouthViolence/need.htm

Samuelson, R. J. (1997, April 30). The culture of poverty. *Newsweek*, p. A21.

Sanders, D. S. (1977). Developing a graduate social work curriculum with an international cross-cultural perspective. *Journal of Education for Social Work, 13*(3), 76–83.

Sartorius, N., Jablensky, A., Ernberg, G., Korten, A., & Gulbinat, W. (1987). Course of schizophrenia in different countries: Some result in WHO international comparative follow up. In H. Hafner, W. F. Gattaz, & W. Janzarik (Eds.), *Search for schizophrenia* (pp. 107–113). New York: Springer.

Satcher, D. (1999). *Mental health: A report of the Surgeon General*. Retrieved from http://www.mentalhealth.org/features/surgeongeneralreport/chapter8/sec1.asp #ensure

Satcher, D. (2001). *Mental health: Culture, race, and ethnicity*. Retrieved from http://www.surgeongeneral.gov/library/mentalhealth/cre/release.asp

Saunders, C. S. (2000, June 15). Where are all the men? *Patient Care*. Retrieved from http://www.findarticles.com/cf_0/m3233/11_34/63602907/print.jhtm

Schlenger, W. E., Kulka, R. A., Fairbank, J. A., Hough, R. L., Jordan, B. K., et al. (1992). The prevalence of post-traumatic stress disorder in the Vietnam generation: A multimethod, multisource assessment of psychiatric disorder. *Journal of Traumatic Stress, 5,* 333–363.

Schlosberg, C. (1998, January 12). *Not-qualified immigrants' access to public health and emergency services after the welfare law*. Retrieved November 24, 2004, from http://www.healthlaw.org/pubs/19980112immigrant.html

Schwartz, W. (1996, October). An overview of strategies to reduce school violence. *ERIC Clearing House on Urban Education, 115.* (EDO-UD-96-4)

Seaborn-Thompson, M., & Ensminger, M. E. (1989). Psychological well-being among mothers with school age children: Evolving family structures. *Social Forces, 67,* 715–730.

Seattle Youth Risk Survey Results. (1995). *Summaries of Youth Risk Behavior Survey*. Retrieved from http://www.safeschoolscoalition.org/safe.html

Sechrest, D. (1991). The effects of density on jail assaults. *Journal of Criminal Justice, 19*(3), 211–223.

Sechrest, D. (2001). *Juvenile crime: A predictive study*. Unpublished document.

Sedlack, A. (1997). Risk factors for the occurrence of child abuse and neglect. *Journal of Aggression, Maltreatment and Trauma, 1*(1), 149–181.

Seligman, M. (1992). *Learned optimism: How to change your mind and your life.* New York: Pocket Books.

Seligman, M. E. P. (1995). The effectiveness of psychotherapy: The consumer's report study. *American Psychologist, 50*(12), 965–974.

Seligman, M. E. P. (2002). *Authentic happiness: New positive psychology to realize your potential for lasting fulfillment.* New York: The Free Press.

Shah, A. (2004, April 28). *Causes of poverty.* Retrieved May 15, 2004, from http://www.globalissues.org/TradeRelated/Facts.asp

Sheaffer, Z., & Mano-Negrin, R. (2003, March). Executives' orientations as indicators of crisis management policies and practices. *Journal of Management Studies, 40*(2), 573–607.

Sheridan, M. J. (2000). *The use of spiritually-derived interventions in social work practice.* 46th Annual Program Meeting of the Council on Social Work Education, 1-22.

Sheridan, M. J., Wilmer, C. M., & Atcheson, L. (1994). Inclusion of content on religion and spirituality in the social work curriculum. *Journal of Social Work Education, 30*(3), 363–377.

Shilling, A. G. (2004, November 1). Carriage trade. *Forbes, 174*(9), 228.

Showers, J., & Pickrell, E. (1987). Child fire setters: A study of three populations. *Hospital and Community Psychiatry, 38,* 495–501.

Shworles, T. R. (1983). The person with disability and the benefits of the microcomputer revolution: To have or to have not. *Rehabilitation Literature, 44*(11/12), 322–330.

Simon, L. (2001). Media violence. *Offsprings, 1,* 12–16.

Simons, R. L., Johnson, C., & Conger, R. D. (1994). Harsh corporal punishment versus quality of parental involvement as an explanation of adolescent maladjustment. *Journal of Marriage and the Family, 56,* 591–607.

Simpson, W. F. (1989). Comparative longevity in a college cohort of Christian Scientists. *Journal of the American Medical Association, 262,* 1657–1658.

Skiba, R. J., Peterson, R. L., & Williams, T. (1997). Office referrals and suspensions: Disciplinary intervention in middle schools. *Education and Treatment of Children, 20,* 295–315.

Slater, E. (2003, June 23). Democratic candidates skewer Bush in appeal to black voters. *Los Angeles Times,* p. A13.

Sloan, R. P., & Bagiella, E. (2001). Spirituality and medical practice: A look at the evidence. *American Family Physician, 63*(1), 33–34.

Smith, D. & Reynold, C. (2002). *Cyber-psychotherapy.* Retrieved June 14, 2005, from http://www.americanpsychotherapy.com/ce-marapr-2002-CyberPsycho therapy.php

Smith, S. S., Sherrill, K. A., & Celenda, C. C. (1995). Anxious elders deserve careful diagnosing and the most appropriate interventions. *Brown University Long-Term Care Letter, 7*(10), 5–7.

Snow, M. (1973). Maturing out of narcotic addiction in New York City. *International Journal of the Addictions, 8*(6), 932–938.

Sobell, L., Sobell, M., Toneatto, T., & Leo, G. (1993). What triggers the resolution of alcohol problems without treatment? *Alcoholism: Clinical and Experimental Research, 17*(2), 217–224.

Solomon, A. (1992). Clinical diagnosis among diverse populations: A multicultural perspective. *Families in Society, 73,* 371–377.

Solomon, D. A., Keller, M. B., Leon, A. C., Mueller, T. L., Lavori, P. W., et al. (2000). Multiple recurrences of major depressive disorder. *American Journal of Psychiatry, 157*, 229–233.

Solomon, P., & Draine, J. (1995). The efficacy of a consumer case management team: Two year outcomes of a randomized trail. *Journal of Mental Health Administration, 22*, 135–146.

Speakers discuss Rx for health insurance ills. (2004, May 22). *University Times, 35*(14). Retrieved from http://www.pitt.edu/utimes/issues/35/030320/ 10.html

Spiegel, D., Bloom, J. R., & Kraemer, H. C. (1989). Effect of psychosocial treatment on survival of patients with metastatic breast cancer. *Lancet, 142*, 888–897.

Spieker, S. J., Larson, N. C., Lewis, S. M., Keller, T. E., & Gilchrist, L. (1999). Developmental trajectories of disruptive behavior problems in preschool children of adolescent mothers. *Child Development, 70*, 443–458.

Spock, B., & Rothenberg, M. B. (1985). *Baby and child care* (8th ed.). New York: E. P. Dutton.

Sprague, J. R., & Walker, H. M. (2000, Spring). Early identification and intervention for youth with antisocial and violent behavior. *Exceptional Children, 66*(3), 367–379.

Stall, R., & Biernacki, P. (1989). Spontaneous remission from the problematic use of substances. *International Journal of the Addictions, 21*, 1–23.

Stanley, T. L. (2002, October). Architects of change: A new role for managers. *Supervision, 63*(10), 10–14.

Stein, M. B. (2002). Taking aim at posttraumatic stress disorder: Understanding its nature and shooting down myths. *Canadian Journal of Psychiatry, 47*(10), 921–923.

Steiner, H., & Stone, L. A. (1999, March). Introduction: Violence and related psychopathology. *Journal of the American Academy of Child and Adolescent Psychiatry, 38*(3), 232–234.

Stensaker, I., Meyer, C., Falkenberg, J., & Haueng, A.-C. (2001). Excessive change: Unintended consequences of strategic change. *Academy of Management Proceedings*, pp. G1–G7.

Stewart, K. B., & Richards, A. B. (2000). Recognizing and managing your patient's alcohol abuse. *Nursing, 30*(2), 56–60.

Stossel, S. (2000, September 21). Lonely in America [Interview with Robert Putnam]. *Atlantic Unbound*. Retrieved June 12, 2002, from www.theatlantic .com/unbound/interviews/ba2000-09-21.htm

Straus, M. A., & Gelles, R. J. (1990). *Physical violence in American families: Risk factors and adaptations to violence in families*. New Brunswick, NJ: Transaction Publishers.

Strengthening American families: Reweaving the social tapestry. (2000, September 21–23). Final report of the Ninety-Seventh American Assembly, Washington, DC. Retrieved May 19, 2004, from www.americanassembly.org/programs/ uas_families_TOC.htm

Stroebe, M. S. (2001). Bereavement research and theory: Retrospective and prospective. *American Behavioral Scientist, 44*(5), 854–865.

Studer, J. (1996, February). Understanding and preventing aggressive responses in youth. *Elementary School Guidance and Counseling, 30*, 194–203.

Suberri, K. (2004). *What is solution focused therapy.* Retrieved November 4, 2004, from http://www.enabling.org/ia/sft/Intro.htm

Substance Abuse and Mental Health Services Administration. (2005). *Answering questions about homelessness*. Retrieved September 20, 2005, from http://www.nrchmi.samhsa.gov/facts/facts_question_1.asp

Sue, S., & Morishima, J. K. (1982). *The mental health of Asian Americans: Contemporary issues in identifying and treating mental problems*. San Francisco: Jossey-Bass.

Susser, E. S., Herman, D. B., & Aaron, B. (2002). Combating the terror of terrorism. *Scientific American, 287*(2), 70–78.

Sussman, L. K., Robins, L. N., & Earls, F. (1987). Treatment-seeking for depression by black and white Americans. *Social Science Medicine, 24*, 187–196.

Tallant, S. H., & Ryberg, R. A. (2004). *Social work in the military: Ethical dilemmas and training implications*. Retrieved May 3, 2004, from http://www.usafa.af.mil/jscope/JSCOPE00/Tallant00.html

Tapia, E. H. (1971). Children who are cruel to animals. *Child Psychiatry and Human Development, 2*, 70–77.

Tarpley, A. (1999). The future of Air Force social work. In J. Daley (Ed.), *Social work practice in the military* (pp. 329–342). Binghamton, NY: Haworth.

Tatara, R. (1997, November). Reporting requirements and characteristics of victims. *Domestic Elder Abuse Information Series 3*. Washington, DC: National Center on Elder Abuse.

TechRepublic. (2003, October 23). *Stop negative management talk before it damages your staff*. Retrieved August 11, 2005, from http://techrepublic.com.com/5102-10878-5076323.html

Ten questions to Andrew Stern. (2005, August 6). *Time, 166*(6), 6.

Terkel, S. (1974). *Working: People talk about what they do all day and how they feel about it*. New York: Random House.

Texas Department of Child Protective Services. (2005). *Investigations*. Retrieved June 29, 2005, from http://www.dfps.state.tx.us/Child_Protection/About_Child_Protective_Services/investigation.asp

Theuninck, A. (2000). *The traumatic impact of minority stressors on males self-identified as homosexual or bisexual*. Unpublished master's thesis, University of the Witwatersrand, Johannesburg.

Thinking critically and creatively to achieve business goals. (2003, December 7). *New Straits Times*, pp. 14–28.

Thoresen, C. E. (1990). *Long-term 8-year follow-up of recurrent coronary prevention* (monograph). Uppsola, Sweden: International Society of Behavioral Medicine.

Thornberry, T. P., Smith, C. A., Rivera, C., Huizina, D., & Stouthamer-Loeber, M. (1999, September). *Family disruption and delinquency*. Washington, DC: Office of Juvenile Justice and Delinquency Prevention, U.S. Department of Justice.

Timmermans, S., & Angell, A. (2001). Evidence-based medicine, clinical uncertainty, and learning to doctor. *Journal of Health & Social Behavior, 42*(4), 342.

Tingle, D., Barnard, G. W., Robbins, G., Newman, G., & Hutchinson, D. (1986). Childhood and adolescent characteristics of pedophiles and rapists. *International Journal of Law and Psychiatry, 9*, S103–S116.

Tobias, M., Morrison, J., & Gray, B. (Eds.). (1995). *A parliament of souls*. San Francisco: KQED Books.

Today Show. (2004, March 18). Retrieved January 17, 2006, from http://msnbc
.msn.com/id/4548509

Torrey, E. F., & Zdanowicz, M. T. (1999, July 9). Deinstitutionalization hasn't
worked. *Washington Post.* Retrieved from http://www.coc.cc.ca.us/depart
ments/english/davis_d/deinstitutionalization.html

Trainer, T. (2003). *The simpler way: Our global situation.* Retrieved December 6,
2004, from http://futurepositive.synearth.net/

Trice, H., & Roman, P. (1970). Delabeling, relabeling, and Alcoholics Anonymous.
Social Problems, 17, 538–546.

Tsuang, M. T., Woolson, R. F., & Fleming, M. S. (1979). Long term outcome of
major psychoses. *Archives of General Psychiatry, 36,* 1295–1301.

Tulgan, B. (2004, October). The under-management epidemic. *HR Magazine,
49*(10), 119–123.

Turner, F. (2002). *Diagnosis in social work.* Toronto: Allyn & Bacon.

Tuskegee Syphilis Experiment, The. (2004). Retrieved May 24, 2004, from http://
www.infoplease.com/ipa/A0762136.html

Tyler, K. A., & Hoyt, D. R. (2000). The effects of an acute stressor on depressive
symptoms among older adults. *Research on Aging, 22*(2), 143–164.

Tyndall, C. (1997). Current treatment strategies for sexually abused children.
Journal of Aggression, Maltreatment and Trauma, 1(1), 291.

Uba, L. (1994). *Asian Americans: Personality patterns, identity, and mental health.*
New York: Guilford.

U.S. Department of Labor. (2004). *Workplace violence.* Retrieved January 27, 2006,
from http://www.osha.gov/SLTC/workplaceviolence/

U.S. Census Bureau. (2003). *Data on income.* Retrieved May 22, 2004, from
http://www.census.gov/Press-Release/www/2003/cb03-153.html

U.S. Census Bureau. (2005). *Census data for 2003.* Retrieved June 8, 2005, from
http://www.census.gov/statab/www/pop.html

U.S. Department Equal Opportunity Employment Commission. (2004, May).
Laws administered by the OEO Commission: Title 7. Retrieved January 27,
2006, from http://www.eeoc.gov/policy/vii.html

U.S. Department of Defense. (2004). *Military social work.* Retrieved May 14, 2004,
from http://www.iseek.org/sv/12120.jsp?id=111

U.S. Department of Health and Human Services, Administration for Children and
Families. (2004). *Temporary Assistance for Needy Families (TANF) program:
Summary of final rules.* Retrieved May 19, 2004, from http://www.acf.hhs
.gov/programs/ofa/exsumcl.htm

U.S. Department of Health and Human Services. (2002). *National household
survey on drug abuse.* Retrieved October 13, 2002, from http://www.samhsa
.gov/oas/dependence/chapter2.htm

U.S. Department of Health and Social Services. (2005). *2004 national survey on
drug and alcohol use in health.* Office of Substance Abuse and Mental Health
Services. Retrieved January 27, 2006, from www.oas.samsha.gov/nsduh/
2k4overhead/2k4overhead.htm#toc

U.S. Department of Housing and Urban Development. (2001). *A report on worst
case housing needs in 1999.* Washington, DC: Economic Policy Institute.

U.S. Department of Justice, Bureau of Justice Statistics. (1998, July). *Workplace
safety.* Washington, DC: Author. (NCJ 168634)

U.S. Department of Labor. (2004). *Industry employment.* Retrieved November 8, 2004, from http://stats.bls.gov/opub/ooq/2001/winter/art04.pdf

U.S. Department of Labor. (2004, March 21). *Social workers.* Retrieved June 29, 2005, from http://stats.bls.gov/oco/ocos060.htm

U.S. Department of Veterans Affairs. (2004). *How social workers help veterans.* Retrieved January 12, 2005, http://www.va.gov/socialwork/page.cfm?pg=3

U.S. Department of Veterans Affairs. (2004). *Social work in the department of veterans affairs.* Retrieved January 12, 2005, http://www.va.gov/socialwork/page.cfm?pg=2

U.S. Federal Bureau of Investigation. (2004). *Hate crimes.* Retrieved January 25, 2005, http://www.fbi.gov/ucr/cius_04/offenses_reported/hate_crime/index.htm

U.S. Office of Family Assistance. (2004). *Highlights of the TANF program.* U.S. Department of Health and Human Services Administration for Children and Families. Retrieved September 20, 2005, from acf.hhs.gov/opa/fact_sheet/TANF_factsheet.html

Vaillant, G. E., & Mukamal, K. (2001). Successful aging. *American Journal of Psychiatry, 158*(6), 839–847.

van Emmerik, A. P., Kamphuis, J. H., Hulsbosch, A. M, & Emmelkamp, P. M. (2002). Single session debriefing after psychological trauma: A meta-analysis. *Lancet, 360*(9335), 766–772.

Van Wormer, K. (1999). The strengths perspective: A paradigm for correctional counseling. *Federal Probation, 63*(1), 51–58.

Veterans Administration. (2004). Retrieved January 26, 2006, from www.va.gov

Veterans Administration Office of Academic Affairs. (2002, February 7). Retrieved January 26, 2006, from www.va.gov.oaa/

Veterans Administration Workforce Statistical Data Report. (2001). Retrieved January 26, 2006, from www.va.gov/orm/reports/orm/2003/pdf

Viney, W., & Zorich, S. (1982). Contributions to the history of psychology XXIX: Dorothea Dix. *Psychological Reports, 50,* 211–218.

Wagner, L., & Lane, L. (1998). *Juvenile justice services: 1997 report.* Eugene, OR: Lane County Department of Youth Services.

Waldorf, D., Reinarman, C., & Murphy, S. (1991). *Cocaine changes: The experience of using and quitting.* Philadelphia: Temple University Press.

Walker, H. M., Colvin, G., & Ramsey, E. (1995). *Antisocial behavior in school: Strategies and best practices.* Pacific Grove, CA: Brooks/Cole.

Walker, H. M., & Severson, H. H. (1990). *Systematic screening for behavior disorders.* Longmont, CO: Sopris West.

Waller, M. A., & Patterson, S. (2002). Natural helping and resilience in a Dine (Navajo) community. *Families in Society, 83*(1), 73–84.

Wallis, M. A. (2000). Looking at depression through bifocal lenses. *Nursing, 30*(9), 58–62.

Walls, D. (1994). *Power to the people: Twenty years of community organizing.* Retrieved July 27, 2005, from www.sonoma.edu/sociology/dwalls/commun.html

Walsh, F. (1998). *Strengthening family resilience.* New York: Guilford Press.

Walsh, F. (2003). Family resilience: A framework for clinical practice—Theory and practice. *Family Processes, 42,* 1–18.

Warren, C. S. (2001). Book review. *Psychotherapy Research, 11*(3), 357–359.

Wasserman H. (1971). The professional social worker in a bureaucracy. *Social Work, 16,* 89–95.

Weick, A., Rapp, C., Sullivan, W. P., & Kisthardt, W. (1989). A strengths perspective for social work practice. *Social Work, 34,* 350–354.

Weikart, D. P., Schweinhart, L. J., & Larner, M. B. (1986). A report on the High/Scope preschool curriculum comparison study: Consequences of three preschool curriculum models through age 15. *Early Child Research, 1,* 15–45.

Weil, D. S., & Knox, R. C. (1996). Effects of limiting handgun purchases on interstate transfer of firearms. *JAMA, 22,* 1759–1761.

Weiss, D. S., Marmar, C. R., Schlenger, W. E., Fairbank, J. A., Jordan, B. K., et al. (1992). The prevalence of lifetime and partial post-traumatic stress disorder in Vietnam theater veterans. *Journal of Traumatic Stress,* 5, 365–376.

Werner, E., & Smith, R. (1982). *Vulnerable but invincible.* New York: Adams, Bannister, and Cox.

Werner, E. E., & Smith, R. S. (1992). *Overcoming the odds: High risk children from birth to adulthood.* New York: Cornell University Press.

Whaley, A. L. (2001). Cultural mistrust: An important psychological construct for diagnosis and treatment of African Americans. *Psychology: Research and Practice, 32*(6), 555–562.

What causes post-traumatic stress disorder: Two views. (2002). *Harvard Mental Health Letter, 19*(4), 8.

White, P., & Faustman, W. (1989). Coexisting physical conditions among inpatients with post-traumatic stress disorder. *Military Medicine,* 154, 66–71.

Widom, C. S. (1989). Does violence beget violence? A critical evaluation of the literature. *Psychology Bulletin, 106,* 3–28.

Widom, C. S. (1992, October). *The cycle of violence* (National Institute of Justice Research in Brief). Washington, DC: U.S. Department of Justice.

Williams, O. J. (1992, December). Ethnically sensitive practice to enhance treatment participation of African American men who batter. *Families in Society,* pp. 588–595.

Williams, R. J., Barrett, J. D., & Brabston, M. (2000). Managers' business school education and military service: Possible links to corporate criminal activity. *Human Relations, 53,* 691–712.

Williams, J. H., Ayers, C. D., Abbott, R. D, Hawkins, J. D., & Catalano, R. F. (1996). Structural equivalence of involvement in problem behavior by adolescents across racial groups using multiple group confirmatory factor analysis. *Social Work Research, 20*(3), 168–178.

Winick, C. (1962). Maturing out of narcotic addiction. *Bulletin on Narcotics, 6,* 1.

Witte, E. (1955, August 15). *Reflections on the beginning of social security.* Remarks delivered at the observance of the 20th Anniversary of the Social Security Act by the Department of Health, Education and Welfare, Washington, DC. Retrieved July 27, 2005, from http://www.socialsecurity.gov/history/witte4.html

Wolfgang, M. E. (1972). *Delinquency in a birth cohort.* Chicago: University of Chicago Press.

Wolfgang, M. E. (1987). *From boy to man, from delinquency to crime.* Chicago: University of Chicago Press.

Work in America. (1973). Cambridge: MIT Press.

World Fellowship for Schizophrenia and Allied Disorders. (2002). *Schizophrenia.* Retrieved May 23, 2004, from http://www.world-schizophrenia.org/publications/20-warnings.html

World hunger facts. (2004, May 14). Retrieved from http://www.worldhunger.org/articles/Learn/world%20hunger%20facts%202002.htm

World Health Organization. (2002). *World report on violence and health.* Retrieved May 14, 2004, from http://www.Amnestyusa.org/women

Wyman, P. A., Cowen, E. L., Work, W. C., & Parker, G. R. (1991). Developmental and family milieu correlates of resilience in urban children who have experienced major life stress. American Journal of Community Psychology, *19*(3), 405–426.

Wyman, R. A., Cowen, E. L., Work, W. C., Raoof, A., Gribble, P. A., et al. (1992). Interviews with children who experienced major life stress: Family and child attributes that predict resilient outcomes. *Journal of the American Academy of Child and Adolescent Psychiatry, 31*(5), 904–910.

Yntema, S. (Ed.). (1999). *Americans 55 and older* (2nd ed.). New York: New Strategist Publications.

Zimmerman, M. A., & Maton, K. I. (1992). Life-style and substance use among male African American urban adolescents: A cluster analytic approach. *American Journal of Community Psychology, 20,* 121–138.

Zimring, F. E., & Hawkins, G. (1997). *Crime is not the problem: Lethal violence in America.* New York: Oxford University.

Zucchino, D. (2005, July 31). Marine to Marine. *Los Angeles Times,* pp. A1, A24–25.

Zuckerman, D. M., Kasl, S. V., & Ostfeld, A. M. (1984). Psychosocial predictors of mortality among the elderly poor: The role of religion, well-being, and social contacts. *American Journal of Epidemiology, 179,* 410–423.

Zuniga, M. E. (1992, January). Using metaphors in therapy: Dichos and Latino clients. *Social Work,* 55–60.

Additional
Recommended Readings

ABCNews.com. (2002). *Authentic happiness: Using our strengths to cultivate happiness.* Retrieved October 14, 2002, from http://abcnews.go.com/sections/GMA/GoodMorningAmerica/GMA020904 Happiness_feature.html

Aboramph, O. M. (1989). Black male-female relationships: Some observations. *Journal of Black Studies, 19*(3), 320–342.

Abromovitz, M. (1988). *Regulating the lives of women: Social welfare policy from colonial times to the present.* Cambridge, MA: South End Press.

Alexander, L. B. (1976). *Organizing the professional social worker: Union development in voluntary social work, 1830–1850.* Unpublished doctoral dissertation, Bryn Mawr College.

American Psychological Association. (1993). *Violence and youth: Psychology's response* (Vol. 1). Washington, DC: Author.

Appleby, J. (2002, September 30). 1.4 million lost their medical coverage in '01. *USA Today.* Retrieved May 19, 2004, from http://www.usatoday.com/news/nation/2002–09–30-uninsured_x.htm

Arnold, S. E. (1970). *The song celestial: A poetic version of the Bhagavad-Gita.* Wheaton, IL: Theosophical Publishing House.

Babor, T. F., & Higgins-Biddle, J. C. (2000, May). Alcohol screening and brief intervention: Dissemination strategies for medical practice and public health. *Addiction, 95*(5), 677–687.

Bagley, C. (1990). Development of a measure of unwanted sexual contact in childhood, for use in community mental health surveys. *Psychological Reports, 66,* 401–402.

Barnard, N. D. (1999, November). *The psychology of abuse.* Retrieved from www.perm.org

Beck, J. G., & Stanley, M. A. (1997). Anxiety disorders in the elderly: The emerging role of behavior therapy. *Behavior Therapy, 28,* 83–100.

Becvar, D. S. (1997). *Soul healing: A spiritual orientation in counseling and therapy.* New York: Basic Books.

Beekman, A. T., et al. (1998). Anxiety disorders in later life: A report from the Longitudinal Aging Study Amsterdam. *International Journal of Geriatric Psychiatry, 12*(10), 717–726.

Bell, A. P. (1978). Black sexuality: Fact and fancy. In R. Staples (Ed.), *The black family: Essays and studies* (pp. 78–80). Belmont, CA: Wadsworth.

Bell, C. A. (1991). Female homicides in United States workplaces, 1980–1985. *American Journal of Public Health, 81(6)*, 729–732.

Bellush, J., & Bellush, B. (1984). *Union power and New York: Victor Gotbaum and District Council 37*. New York: Praeger.

Bender, W. N. (1999, April). *Violence prevention in the school*. An invited workshop presented at the Doylestown Public School Board of Education, Doylestown, PA.

Bender, W. N., Shubert, T. H., & McLaughlin, P. J. (2001). Invisible kids: Preventing school violence by identifying kids in trouble. *Intervention in School and Clinic, 37(2)*, 105–111.

Berg-Weger, M., Rubio, D. M., & Tebb, S. S. (2001). Strengths-based practice with family caregivers of the chronically ill: Qualitative insights. *Families in Society, 82(3)*, 263–272.

Blatt, S. J., Zuroff, D. C., Bondi, C. M., & Sanisolow, C. A., III. (2000). Short and long-term effects of medication and psychotherapy in the brief treatment of depression: Further analyses of data from the NIMH TDCRP. *Psychotherapy Research, 10*, 215–234.

Blazer, D. G. (1993). *Depression in late life* (2nd ed.). St. Louis, MO: Mosby.

Blazer, D. G., Hughes, D. C., & George, L. K. (1987). The epidemiology of depression in an elderly community population. *Journal of the American Geriatric Society, 27*, 281–287.

Boorstein, S. (Ed.). (1996). *Transpersonal psychotherapy*. Albany: SUNY.

Brent, D. A., Holder, D., Kolko, D., Birmaher, B., Baugher, M., et al. (1999). A clinical psychotherapy trial for adolescent depression comparing cognitive, family, and supportive therapy. *Canadian Psychologist, 40*, 289–327.

Brians, P., Gallwey, M., Hughes, D., Hussain, A., Law, R., et al. (1999). *Reading about the world* (Vol. 2). New York: Harcourt Brace Custom Books.

Bross, D., Krugman, R., Lenherr, M., Rosenberg, D., & Schmitt, B. (1988). *The new child protection team handbook*. New York: Garland.

Bureau of Justice Statistics. (1997). *Criminal victimization, 1973–95*. Washington, DC: Government Printing Office.

Burge, S. K., Amodei, N., Elkin, B., Catala, S., Andrew, S. R., et al. (1997). An evaluation of two primary care interventions for alcohol abuse among Mexican-American patients. *Addiction, 92(12)*, 1705–1716.

Burke, K. J. (1999). Health, mental health, and spirituality in chronically ill elders. *Social Work Abstracts, 14*, 141–142.

Burtscheidt, W., et al. (2002, September). Alcoholism, rehabilitation and comorbidity. *Acta Psychiatrica Scandinavica, 106(3)*, 227–233.

Bush, D. E., Ziegelstein, R. C., Tayback, M., Richter D., Stevens, S., et al. (2001). Even minimal symptoms of depression increase mortality risk after acute myocardial infarction. *American Journal of Cardiology, 88*, 337–341.

Bustillo, J. R., Lauriello, J. H., Keith, W. P., & Samuel, J. (2001). The psychosocial treatment of schizophrenia: An update. *American Journal of Psychiatry, 158(2)*, 163–175.

California Department of Justice, Office of the Attorney General. (1993). *Child abuse prevention handbook*. Sacramento: Author.

Canda, E. R. (1989). Religious content in social work education: A comparative approach. *Journal of Social Work Education, 25(36)*, 15–24.

Canda, E. R., & Phaobtong, T. (1992). Buddhism as a support system for Southeast Asian Refugees. *Social Work, 37*(1), 61–67.

Cannon, A., Streisand, B., & McGraw, D. (1999, May). *Why?* Retrieved October 1999 from www.usnews.com

Carson, M. (1990). *Settlement folk: Social thought and the American Settlement Movement.* Chicago: University of Chicago Press.

Casey, D. A. (1994). Depression in the elderly. *Southern Medical Journal, 87*(5), 559–564.

Castillo, D. N., & Jenkins, E. L. (1993). Industries and occupations at high risk for work-related homicides. *Journal of Occupational Medicine, 36,* 125–132.

Centers for Disease Control. (1991). Attempted suicide among high school students—United States, 1990. *Journal of the American Medical Association, 266,* 1911–1912.

Centers for Disease Control and Prevention. (1999). *National summary of injury mortality data, 1981–1997.* Atlanta, GA: Centers for Disease Control and Prevention, National Center for Injury Prevention and Control.

Chambers, C. A. (1963). *Seedtime of reform: American social service and social activism, 1918–1933.* Minneapolis: University of Minnesota Press.

Chambers, C. A. (1986, March). Women in the creation of the profession of social work. *Social Service Review,* 1–33.

Chambless, D. L., & Hollon, S. D. (1998). Defining empirically supported therapies. *Journal of Consulting and Clinical Psychology, 66,* 7–18.

Chambless, D. L., & Ollendick, T. H. (2001). Empirically supported psychological interventions: Controversies and evidence. *Annual Review of Psychology, 52,* 685–716.

Chang, G., Wilkins-Haug, L., Berman, S., & Goetz, M. A. (1999). Brief intervention for alcohol use in pregnancy: A randomized trial. *Addiction, 94*(10), 1499–1508.

Chapman, S. G. (1986). *Cops, killers and staying alive: The murder of police officers in America.* Springfield, IL: Charles C Thomas.

Chatterji, P., & Markowitz, S. (2000). *The impact of maternal alcohol and illicit drug use on children's behavior problems: Evidence from the children of the National Longitudinal Survey of Youth* (Working Paper No. 7692). Cambridge, MA: National Bureau of Economic Research, Inc.

Clark, R. (1970). *Crime in America: Observations on its nature, causes, prevention and control.* New York: Simon & Schuster.

Clifford, P. R., Maisto, S. A., & Franzke, L. H. (2000). Alcohol treatment research follow-up and drinking behaviors. *Journal of Studies on Alcohol, 61*(5), 736–743.

Clifford, P. R., Maisto, S. A., Franzke, L. H., Longabaugh, R., & Beattie, M. C. (1997). *Alcohol treatment research protocols and treatment outcomes.* Paper presented at the annual conference of the Research Society on Alcoholism, San Francisco.

Cloud, J. (1999, May). Just a routine school shooting. *Time.* Retrieved October 1999 from http://www.time.com

Cohen, J. A. (1998, September). Summary of the practice parameters for the assessment and treatment of children and adolescents with posttraumatic stress disorder. *Journal of the American Academy of Child and Adolescent Psychiatry, 37*(10).

The condition of American family life. (2000, June). *Pediatrics, 111*(6), 1541–1572.

Connors, G. J., Walitzer, K. S., & Demen, K. H. (2002, October). Preparing clients for alcoholism treatment: Effects on treatment participation and outcomes. *Journal of Consulting and Clinical Psychology, 70*(5), 1161–1169.

Cose, E. (1993, November 15). Rage of the privileged. *Newsweek,* pp. 52–63.

Craig, W. M., & Pepler, D. J. (1997). Observations of bullying and victimization in the schoolyard. *Canadian Journal of School Psychology, 13,* 41–60.

Critical Incident Response Group. (1999). *The school shooter: A threat assessment perspective.* Quantico, VA: FBI Academy, National Center for the Analysis of Violent Crime.

Crocker, R. H. (1992). *Social work and social order: The settlement movement in two industrial cities, 1889–1930.* Chicago: Illinois University Press.

Crow, W. J., & Erickson, R. (1989). *The store safety issue: Facts for the future.* Alexandria, VA: National Association of Convenience Stores.

Crowe, T. (1991). *Habitual offenders: Guidelines for citizen action and public responses.* Washington, DC: Office of Juvenile Justice and Delinquency Prevention, U.S. Department of Justice.

Crowe, T. (1995, January). *Youth crime and community safety.* Paper presented at the Eugene City Club, Eugene, OR.

Currie, E. (1990). Violence is increasing. In J. Rohr (Ed.), *Violence in America* (pp. 17–23). San Diego, CA: Greenhaven Press.

Dahlgren, L., & Willander, A. (1989). Are special treatment facilities for female alcoholics needed? *Alcoholism, Clinical and Experimental Research, 13,* 499–504.

Danner, D. D., Snowdon, D. A., & Friesen, W. V. (2001). Positive emotions in early life and longevity: Findings from the nun study. *Journal of Personality and Social Psychology, 80*(5), 804–813.

Daro, D. (1988). *Confronting child abuse.* New York: The Free Press.

Davis, A. F. (1963). *Spearheads for reform: The social settlements and the Progressive Movement, 1890–1914.* Oxford University Press.

Davis, D. R., & Jansen, G. C. (1998). Making meaning of AA for social workers: Myths, metaphors and reality. *Social Work, 43*(2), 169–182.

Davis, H. (1987). Workplace homicides of Texas males. *American Journal of Public Health, 77(10),* 1290–1293.

Davis, H., Honchar, P. A., & Suarez, L. (1987). Fatal occupational injuries of women, Texas 1975–84. *American Journal of Public Health, 77(12),* 1524–1527.

Deblinger, E., McLeer, S. V., & Henry, D. (1990). Cognitive behavioral treatment for sexually abused children suffering from post-traumatic stress: Preliminary findings. *Journal of the American Academy of Child & Adolescent Psychiatry, 29,* 747–752.

Denton, W. H., Walsh, S. R., & Daniel, S. S. (2002). Evidence-based practice in family therapy: Adolescent depression as an example. *Journal of Marital and Family Therapy, 28*(1), 39–45.

Department of Justice. (2001). *Elder abuse and neglect.* Retrieved December 7, 2004, from http://www.ojp.usdoj.gov/ovc/ncvrw/2001/stat_over_7.htm

Derezotes, D. S. (1995). Spirituality and religiosity: Neglected factors in social work practice. *Arête, 20*(1), 1–15.

DiClemente, C. C., Bellino, L. E., & Neavins, T. M. (1999). Motivation for change and alcoholism treatment. *Alcohol Research and Health, 23*(2), 86–92.

DiIulio, J. J., Jr. (1996a, February 28). *Fill churches, not jails: Youth crime and super predators.* Statement before the U.S. Senate Subcommittee on Youth Violence. Retrieved from http://www/brook.edu/pa/hot/diiulio.htm

DiIulio, J. J., Jr. (1996b, July 13). Stop crime where it starts. *New York Times.* Retrieved from http://www.brook.edu/pa/hot/arttoppics/diiulio.htm

Doogan, D. P., & Caillard, V. (1992). Sertraline in the prevention of depression. *British Journal of Psychiatry, 160,* 217–222.

Dossey, L. (1997). *Prayer is good medicine: How to reap the healing benefits of prayer.* San Francisco: Harper.

Dwyer, K. P., Osher, D., & Warger, W. (1998). *Early warning, timely response: A guide to safe schools.* Washington, DC: U.S. Department of Education. (ERIC Document Reproduction Service No. ED418372)

Ebeling, N., & Hill, D. (1975). *Child abuse: Intervention and treatment.* Acton, MA: Publishing Sciences Group, Inc.

Ehrenkranz, S., et al. (1989). *Clinical social work practice with maltreated children and their families.* New York: New York University Press.

Ehrenreich, J. H. (1985). *The altruistic imagination: A history of social work and social policy in the United States.* New York: Cornell University Press.

Elkin, I., Shea, T., Watkins, J. T., Imber, S. D., Sotsky, S. M., et al. (1989). National Institute of Mental Health Treatment of Depression Collaborative Research Program: General effectiveness of treatments. *Archives of General Psychiatry, 46,* 971–982.

Ellis, A. (1963). *Reason and emotion in psychotherapy.* New York: Lyle Stuart.

Ellison, C. G., & George, L. K. (1992). Religious involvement, social ties, and social support in a southeastern community. *Journal for the Scientific Study of Religion, 33,* 46–6l.

Enkin, M., Keirse, M. J. N., Renfrew, M., & Neilson, J. (1995). *A guide to effective care in pregnancy and childbirth* (2nd ed.). New York: Oxford University Press.

Environmental Defense. (2004). Retrieved October 20, 2004, from http://www .environmentaldefense.org/dangerousdays.cfm?subnav=aiyc_50cities

Epstein, M. H., & Sharma, J. (1998). *Behavioral and emotional rating scale.* Austin, TX: PRO-ED.

ERIC Digest. (2002). *Gender differences in educational achievement within racial and ethnic groups.* Retrieved May 18, 2004, from http://www.ericdigests.org/2002–1/gender.html

Fagan, J. (1996). *Recent perspectives on youth violence.* Paper presented at the Northwest Conference on Youth Violence, Seattle, WA.

Faller, K. (1981). *Social work with abused and neglected children.* New York: The Free Press.

Felix-Ortiz, M., Salazar, M. R., Gonzalez, J. R., Sorensen, J. L., & Plock, D. (2000). Addictions services: A qualitative evaluation of an assisted self-help group for drug-addicted clients in a structured outpatient treatment setting. *Community Mental Health Journal, 36*(4), 339–350.

Finn, J. (1999). An exploration of helping processes in an online self-help group focusing on issues of disability. *Health & Social Work, 24*(3), 220–231.

Fisher, J. (1980). *The response of social work to the Depression.* Thorndike, ME: G. K. Hall.

Foa, E. B., & Rothbaum, B. O. (1998). *Treating the trauma of rape: A cognitive behavioral therapy for PTSD.* New York: Guilford.

Frasure-Smith, N., Lesperance, F., & Talajic, M. (1995). Depression and 18 month prognosis after myocardial infarction. *Circulation, 91,* 999–1005.

Freeman-Longo, R., & Wall, R. V. (1986, March 20). Changing a lifetime of sexual crimes. *Psychology Today,* 58–64.

Frieden, T. (2003). INS: 7 million illegal immigrants in United States: *Mexicans make up nearly 70 percent of total, figures show.* Retrieved May 13, 2004, from http://www.cnn.com/2003/US/01/31/illegal.immigration/

Furlong, M. J. (1994). Evaluating school violence trends. *National School Safety Center News Journal, 3,* 23–27.

Gallagher-Thompson, D., Hanley-Peterson, P., & Thompson, L. W. (1990). Maintenance of gains versus relapse following brief psychotherapy for depression. *Journal of Consulting and Clinical Psychology, 58,* 371–374.

Gang violence in Los Angeles County. (2005, May 7). Retrieved June 28, 2005, from http://www.lapdonline.org/general_information/crime_statistics/gang_stats/2005_gang_stats/05_05_sum.htm

Gilgun, J., & Connor, T. (1989, May). How perpetrators view child sexual abuse. *Social Work,* 249–251.

Gilliland, B. E., & James, R. K. (1993). *Crisis intervention strategies.* Belmont, CA: Brooks/Cole.

Glicken, M. (1986a, September–October). The after-shock of on the job accidents. *EAP Digest, 23,* 41–42.

Glicken, M. (1986b, March 20). A manager's guide to stress management. *Executive Action Report, 12,* 20–23.

Glicken, M. (1986c). Post-traumatic stress syndrome and work: Treatment considerations. *EAP Journal, 6,* 33–34.

Glicken, M.D. (1986d). Work related accidents which lead to post traumatic stress reactions. *Labor Relations: Occupational Safety and Health, 3,* 12–14.

Glicken, M. (1995). *Understanding and treating male abusive behavior.* Unpublished monograph.

Glicken, M. D. (2005). *Working with troubled men: A contemporary practitioner's guide.* Mahwah, NJ: Lawrence Erlbaum.

Glicken, M. D., & Garza, M. A. (1996, October). *Crisis intervention with newly immigrated Latino clients.* Paper presented at the California Conference for Latino Social Workers, Sacramento.

Goldner, J. C. (1949). *Resolution of major crisis situations in the New York City Department of Welfare, 1939–1949.* Unpublished master's thesis, New York School of Social Work, Columbia University.

Gordon, L. (1988). *Heroes of their own lives: The politics and history of family violence; Boston, 1880–1960.* New York: Viking.

Gordon, L. (1994). *Pitied but not entitled: Single mothers and the history of welfare.* New York: The Free Press.

Gordon, L. (Ed.). (1990). *Women, the state and welfare.* Madison: University of Wisconsin Press.

Gottfredson, D. C. (1998). School-based crime prevention. In L. Sherman, D. Gottfredson, D. Mackenzie, J. Eck, P. Reuter, et al. (Eds.), *Preventing crime: What works, what doesn't, what's promising* (pp. 5–74). College Park, MD: Department of Criminology and Criminal Justice. (ERIC Document Reproduction Service No. ED423321)

Gredon, J. F. (2001). The burden of disease in treatment-resistant depression. *Journal of Clinical Psychiatry, 62,* 26–31.

Greenwood, P. (2000, May 5). *Three strikes sentencing: RAND Corporation study.* Paper presented at the Association for Criminal Justice Research, California.

Grier, W. H., & Cobbs, P. M. (1965). *Black rage.* New York: Basic Books.

Hale, G., Duckworth, J., Zimostrad, N., & Scott, D. (1988). Abusive partners: MMPI profiles of male batterers. *Journal of Mental health Counseling, 10,* 214–224.

Hammil, P. (1996). Mike Tyson. *Esquire,* p. 101.

Haney, L. (1996, October). Homeboys, babies, men in suits: The state and the reproduction of male dominance. *American Sociological Review, 61,* 759–778.

Hanson, R. R., Steffy, R. A., & Gauthier, R. (1993). Long term recidivism child molestors. *Journal of Consulting and Clinical Psychology, 61,* 646–652.

Harrington, R., & Clark, A. (1998). Prevention and early intervention for depression in adolescence and early adult life. *European Archives of Psychiatry in Clinical Neuroscience, 248,* 32–45.

Harris, I. (1990). Media myths and the reality of men's work. In M. Kimmel & M. Messner (Eds.), *Men's lives* (pp. 225–231). New York: Macmillan.

Haug, L. E. (1998). Including a spiritual dimension in family therapy: Ethical considerations. *Contemporary Family Therapy, 20*(2), 181–194.

Hawkins, D., & Catalano, R. (1992). *Communities that care.* San Francisco: Jossey-Bass.

Haynes, J. E. (1975, Winter). The "rank and file movement" in private social work. *Labor History, 16*(1), 78–98.

Herbert, E. A. (1950). *A Confucian notebook.* London: Butler & Tanner, Ltd.

Herman, M. (2000). Psychotherapy with substance abusers: Integration of psychodynamic and cognitive-behavioral approaches. *American Journal of Psychotherapy, 54*(4), 574–579.

Hetherington, E. M. (1989). Coping with family transitions: Winners, losers and survivors. *Child Development, 60,* 1–14.

Higgins-Biddle, J. C., Babor, T. F., Mullahy, J., Daniels, J., & Mcree, B. (1997). Alcohol screening and brief interventions: Where research meets practice. *Connecticut Medicine, 61,* 565–575.

Himmelfarb, S., & Murrell, S. A. (1984). Prevalence and correlates of anxiety symptoms in older adults. *Journal of Psychology, 116,* 159–167.

Hinshaw, S. P. (1987). On the distinction between attentional deficits/hyperactivity and conduct problems/aggression in child psychopathology. *Psychological Bulletin, 101,* 443–463.

History of Medicaid and Medicare. (2003, September 23). Retrieved May 23, 2004, from http://www.cms.hhs.gov/about/history/CMS/HCFAHistory

Hogarty, G. E. (1989). Metaanalysis of the effects of practice with the chronically mentally ill: A critique and reappraisal of the literature. *Social Work, 34,* 363–373.

Holmes, M. (1987). *Protective services for abused and neglected children and their families.* Washington, DC: Department of Health, Education and Welfare.

Holmes, R. M. (1991). *Sex crimes.* Newbury Park, CA: Sage.

Horowitz, M. J., & Solomon, G. F. (1975). A prediction of delayed stress response syndromes in Vietnam veterans. *Journal of Social Issues, 31,* 67–80.

Howell, J. C. (Ed.). (1995). *Guide for implementing a comprehensive strategy for serious, violent and chronic juvenile offenders.* Washington, DC: Office of Juvenile Justice and Delinquency Prevention.

Huffman, G. B. (1999). Preventing recurrence of depression in the elderly. *American Family Physician, 59*(9), 2589–2591.

Humphreys, K. (1998, Winter). Can addiction-related self-help/mutual aid groups lower demand for professional substance abuse treatment? *Social Policy, 29*(2), 13–17.

Individuals With Disabilities Education Act Amendments of 1997, Pub. L. No. 105–17, 105th Cong. (ERIC Document Reproduction Service No. ED419322)

Ino, S. (1985a). *Close relationships: Their subjective construction and contribution to the sense of self.* Ann Arbor, MI: University Microfilms International.

Ino, S. (1985b, August 22). *The concept of an Asian American collective self.* Paper presented at the Pacific/Asian American Research Methods Workshop (P/AAMHRC), Ann Arbor, MI.

Ino, S. (1987, August 27). *The sense of collective self in Asian American psychology.* Paper presented at the Asian American Psychological Association National Convention, New York.

Ino, S. (1991, August 16–20). *The sense of collective self in Asian American psychology.* Paper presented at the American Psychological Association (APA) 99th Annual Convention, San Francisco.

Institute for the Study of Poverty and Homelessness at the Weingart Center. (2005). *Selected readings on poverty.* Retrieved September 20, 2005, from http://www.weingart.org/institute/cf_files/parseResults.cfm

Iraqi Coalition casualty count. (2004). Retrieved October 31, 2004, from http://icasualties.org/oif/

Jenkins, E. L., Layne, L. A., & Kisner, S. M. (1992). Homicide in the workplace: The U.S. experience, 1980–1988. *American Association of Occupational Health Nurses Journal, 40*(5), 215–218.

Jimenez, M. A. (1988). Chronicity in mental disorders: Evolution of a concept. *Social Casework, 69,* 627–633.

Johnson, L. (1999, August). Understanding and responding to youth violence: A juvenile corrections approach. *Corrections Today, 61*(5), 62–64.

Johnson, L., & Schwartz, C. (1991). *Social welfare.* Needham Heights, MA: Simon & Schuster.

Juvenile Crime Bulletin. (1997, May). 1999 National Report Series NCJ-180753.

Katz, M. B. (1986). *In the shadow of the poorhouse: A social history of welfare in America.* New York: Basic Books.

Kauffman, J. M. (1997). *Characteristics of emotional and behavioral disorders of children and youth* (6th ed.). Upper Saddle River, NJ: Merrill.

Kennedy, G. J., & Tannenbaum, S. (2000). Psychotherapy with older adults. *American Journal of Psychotherapy, 54*(3), 386–407.

Kirchner, J. E., et al. (2000, August). Predictors of patient entry into alcohol treatment after initial diagnosis. *Journal of Behavioral Health Services & Research, 27*(3), 339–347.

Knight, C. (1990, May). Use of support groups with adult female survivors of sexual abuse. *Social Work,* 202–208.

Kocka, J. (1980). *White collar workers in America, 1890–1940: A socio-political history in international perspective.* Thousand Oaks, CA: Sage.

Koening, H. (1998). *The healing power of faith.* New York: Simon & Schuster.

Kolko, D. J. (1985). Juvenile fire setting: A review and methodological critique. *Clinical Psychology Review, 31,* 345–376.

Kopta, M. S., Lueger, R. J., Saunders, S. M., & Howard, K. I. (1999). Individual psychotherapy outcome and process research: Challenges leading to greater turmoil or a positive transition? *Annual Review of Psychology, 50,* 441–469.

Korman, H. (2001). *Solution focused therapy.* Retrieved November 4, 2004, from http://www.enabling.org/ia/sft/Tips_from_SFT.htm

Koven, S., & Michel, S. (Eds.). (1993). *Mothers of a new world: Maternalist politics and the origins of welfare states.* New York: Routledge.

Kraus, J. F. (1987). Homicide while at work: Persons, industries, and occupations at high risk. *American Journal of Public Health, 77*(10), 1285–1289.

Kretzmann, J. P., & McKnight, J. L. (1993). *Building communities from the inside out.* Evanston, IL: Northwestern University, Center for Urban Affairs and Policy Research.

Kubler-Ross, E. (1975). *Death: The final stage of growth.* Englewood Cliffs, NJ: Prentice Hall.

Kunzel, R. G. (1993). *Fallen women, problem girls: Unmarried mothers and the professionalization of social work, 1890–1945.* Boston: Yale University Press.

Kuperman, S., Schlosser, S.S., Kramer, J.R. Bucholz, K., Hesselbrock, V., et al. (2001, April). Risk domains associated with adolescent alcohol dependence diagnosis. *Addiction, 96*(4), 629–637.

Lang, R. A., Pugh, G. M., & Langevin, R. (1988). Treatment of incest and pedophilic offenders: A pilot study. *Behavioral Science and the Law, 6,* 239–255.

Lanyan, R. I. (1986). Theory and treatment in child molestation. *Journal of Consulting and Clinical Psychology, 54*(2), 176–182.

Lee, C., Gavriel, H., Drummond, P., Richards, J., & Greenwald, R. (2002). Treatment of PTSD: Stress inoculation training with prolonged exposure compared to EMDR. *Journal of Clinical Psychology, 58*(9), 1071–1089.

Leiby, J. (1978). *A history of social welfare and social work in the United States.* New York: Columbia University Press.

Leighninger, L. H. (1987). *Social work: Search for identity.* Westport, CT: Greenwood Press.

Lennox, R. D., & Mansfield, A. J. (2001, May). A latent variable model of evidence-based quality improvement for substance abuse treatment. *Journal of Behavioral Health Services & Research, 28*(2), 164–177.

Lenze, E. J., et al. (2002). Combined pharmacotherapy and psychotherapy as maintenance treatment for late-life depression: Effects on social adjustment. *American Journal of Psychiatry, 159*(3), 466–468.

Leone, P. E., Rutherford, R. B., & Nelson, C. M. (1991). *Special education in juvenile corrections.* Reston, VA: The Council for Exceptional Children. (ERIC Document Reproduction Service No. ED333654)

Lie, G. Y., & Inman, A. (1991, September). The use of anatomical dolls as assessment and evidentiary tools. *Social Work, 36*(5), 396–399.

Loeber, R., & Farrington, D. P. (1998). *Serious and violent juvenile offenders: Risk factors and successful interventions.* Thousand Oaks, CA: Sage.

Loeber, R., Dishion, T. J., & Patterson, G. R. (1984). Multiple gating: A multistage assessment procedure for identifying youths at-risk for delinquency. *Journal of Research in Crime & Delinquency, 21,* 7–32.

Lu, M., & McGuire, T. G. (2002). The productivity of outpatient treatment for substance abuse. *Journal of Human Resources, 37*(2), 309–335.

Lukefahr, J. L. (2001). Treatment of child abuse. *Journal of the American Academy of Child and Adolescent Psychiatry, 40*(3), 383.

Lynam, D. (1996). Early identification of chronic offenders: Who is the fledgling psychopath? *Psychological Bulletin, 120,* 209–234.

Maier, M. H. (1987). *City unions: Managing discontent in New York City, 1954–1973.* Brunswick, NJ: Rutgers University Press.

Malmquist, C. P. (1996). *Homicide: A psychiatric perspective.* Washington, DC: American Psychiatric Press.

Manheimer, R. J. (Ed.). (1994). *Older Americans almanac.* Detroit: Gale Research.

Marin, P. (1991, July 8). The prejudice against men. *Nation, 253*(2), 46–51.

Marshall, W. L. (1996). Assessment, treatment and theorizing about sexual offenders. *Criminal Justice and Behavior, 231*(1), 162–199.

Mason, M. A. (1991, September). The McMartin case revisited: The conflict between social work and criminal justice. *Social Work, 36*(5), 391–395.

Mason, M. A. (1992 January). Social workers as expert witnesses in child sexual abuse cases. *Social Work, 37:1,* 30–34.

May, R. (1973). *Man's search for himself.* New York: Delta.

McColloch, M. (1983). *White collar workers in transition: The boom years, 1940–1970.* Westport, CT: Greenwood Press.

McFarlane, A. C., Atchison, M., Rafalowicz, E., & Papay, P. (1994). Physical symptoms in post-traumatic stress disorder. *Journal of Psychosomatic Research, 38,* 715–726.

McGaugh, J. L., & Cahill, L. (1997). Interaction of neuromodulatory systems in modulating memory storage. *Behavioral Brain Research, 83,* 31–38.

McMillen, C., Zuravin, S., & Rideout, G. (1995). Perceived benefit from child sexual abuse. *Journal of Consulting and Clinical Psychology, 63,* 1037–1043.

Medline Plus Health Information. (2004). *Schizophrenia.* Retrieved May 23, 2004, from http://www.nlm.nih.gov/medlineplus/schizophrenia.html

Mendes, R. (1974). *The professional union: A study of the Social Service Employees Union of the New York City Department of Social Services.* Unpublished doctoral dissertation, Columbia University.

Menninger, J. A. (2002, Spring). Source assessment and treatment of alcoholism and substance-related disorders in the elderly. *Bulletin of the Menninger Clinic, 66*(2), 166–184.

Minorities lack proper mental health. (2001, August 27). Retrieved from http://www.cnn.com/2001/HEALTH/08/26/mental.health/Report

Money, J. (1979). Sexual dictatorship, dissidence, and democracy. *International Journal of Medicine and Law, 1,* 11–20.

Morell, C. (1996). Radicalizing recovery: Addiction, spirituality and politics. *Social Work, 41*(3), 306–312.

Mullison, M. B., & Dudley, J. R. (1990). The importance of spirituality in hospice work: A study of hospice professionals. *The Hospice Journal, 6*(3), 63–79.

Mulvey, E. P., & Repucci, M. D. (1981). Police crisis intervention training: An empirical investigation. *American Journal of Community Psychology, 9,* 44–51.

Mulvihill, D., Tumin, M., & Curtis, L. (1969). *Crimes of violence: A staff report to the National Commission on the Causes and Prevention of Violence.* Washington, DC: U.S. Government Printing Office.

Murray, B. A., & Myers, M. A. (1998, April). Conduct disorders and the special-education trap. *The Education Digest, 63*(8), 48–53.

Myers, S. L., Jr. (1983). Estimating the economic model of crime: Employment versus punishment effects. *Quarterly Journal of Economics, 88,* 157–166.

Myles, B. S., & Simpson, R. L. (1998, May). Aggression and violence by school-age children and youth: Understanding the aggression cycle and prevention/intervention strategies. *Intervention in School and Clinic, 33*(5), 259–264.

Myss, C. (1996). *Anatomy of the spirit: The seven stages of power and healing.* New York: Three Rivers Press.

Nasar, S. (1998). *A brilliant mind: The life of mathematical genius and Nobel Laureate John Nash.* New York: Simon & Schuster.

Nash, A. (1979, Spring). Local 1707, CSAE: Facets of a union in the non-profit field. *Labor History, 20*(2), 256–277.

National Center for Injury Prevention and Control. (2001). *Facts about violence among youth and violence in schools.* Atlanta, GA: Author. Retrieved from http://www.cdc.gov/ncipc/cmpfact.htm

National Center on Child Abuse and Neglect. (1979). *Caregivers of young children: Preventing and responding to child maltreatment.* Washington, DC: U.S. Department of Health and Human Services.

National Institute on Aging/Fetzer Institute Working Group. (1997). *Measurement scale on religion, spirituality, health, and aging.* Bethesda, MD: Author.

National Institute on Drug Abuse. (1999). *Principles of drug addiction treatment: A research-based guide.* Rockville, MD: Author.

Neuman, E. (1995, Winter). Trouble with domestic violence. *Critic, 2*(1), 67–73.

New York City Police Department. (1990). *Safety tips for the taxi driver and the for-hire vehicle driver.* New York: Author.

Northrup, C. (1994). *Women's bodies, women's wisdom: Creating physical and emotional health and healing.* New York: Bantam Books.

O'Neill, R. E., Horner, R. H., Albin, R. W., Sprague, J. R., Newton, S., et al. (1997). *Functional assessment and program development for problem behavior: A practical handbook* (2nd ed.). Pacific Grove, CA: Brooks/Cole.

Obiakor, F. E., Merhing, T. A., & Schwenn, J. O. (1997). *Disruption, disaster, and death: Helping students deal with crises.* Reston, VA: The Council for Exceptional Children. (ERIC Document Reproduction Service No. ED403709)

Olasov, B., & Schwartz, A. C. (2002). Exposure therapy for posttraumatic stress disorder. *American Journal of Psychotherapy, 56*(1), 59–75.

Old Age Depression Interest Group. (1993). How long should the elderly take antidepressants? A double blind placebo controlled study of continuation/prophylaxis therapy with dothiepin. *British Journal of Psychiatry, 162,* 175–182.

Orten, J. D., & Rich, L. L. (1988, December). A model for assessment of incestuous families: Social casework. *The Journal of Contemporary Social Work, 7,* 72–89.

Ouimette, P. C., Finney, J. W., & Moos, R. H. (1997). Twelve-step and cognitive-behavioral treatment for substance abuse: A comparison of treatment effectiveness. *Journal of Consulting and Clinical Psychology, 65*(2), 230–240.

Owen, G., & Williams, J. (1989). *Incest offenders after treatment: A follow-up study from the transitional offenders program at Lino Lakes correctional facility.* St. Paul, MN: Wilder Foundation.

Paniati, J. (2002, November 19). *Traffic congestion and sprawl.* Retrieved September 12, 2004, from http://www.fhwa.dot.gov/congestion/congpress.htm

Pargament, K. I. (1997). *Theory, research, practice: The psychology of religion and coping.* New York: Guilford.

Pargament, K. I., Smith, B. T., Koenig, F. G., & Perez, L. (1998). Patterns of positive and negative religious coping with major life stressors. *Journal for the Scientific Study of Religion, 37*(4), 710–724.

Parloff, M. B. (1979). Can psychotherapy research guide the policymaker? A little knowledge may be a dangerous thing. *American Psychologist, 34,* 296–306.

Patten, S., et al. (1989, May). Post-traumatic stress disorder and the treatment of sexual abuse. *Social Work,* 197–202.

Patten, S. B. (2000). Incidence of major depression in Canada. *Canadian Medical Association Journal, 163,* 714–715.

Patterson, G. R. (1992). Developmental changes in antisocial behavior. In R. D. Peters, R. J. McMahon, & V. L. Quinsey (Eds.), *Aggression and violence throughout the life span* (pp. 52–82). Newbury Park, CA: Sage.

Patterson, G. R., Reid, J. B., & Dishion, T. J. (1992). *A social interactional approach: Antisocial boys.* Eugene, OR: Castalia Press.

Peebles, J. (2000, November). The future of psychotherapy outcome research: Science or political rhetoric? *Journal of Psychology, 134*(6), 659–670.

Peltier, M. J. (Director), & Shapiro, A. (Producer). (1991, July). *Scared silent* [Utah public television broadcast].

Pennington, H., Butler, R., & Eagger, S. (2000, May). The assessment of patients with alcohol disorders by an old age psychiatric service. *Aging & Mental Health, 4*(2), 182–185.

Peterson, A. L., & Halstead, T. S. (1998). Group cognitive behavior therapy for depression in a community setting: A clinical replication series. *Behavioral Therapy, 29,* 3–18.

Peterson, R. L., & Skiba, R. (2001). Creating school climates that prevent school violence. *The Clearing House, 74*(3), 155–163.

Pitman, R. K., Sanders, K. M., Zusman, R. M., Healy, A. R., Cheema, F., et al. (2002). Pilot study of secondary prevention of posttraumatic stress disorder with propranolol. *Biological Psychiatry, 51,* 189–192.

Piven, F. F., & Cloward, R. A. (1993). *Regulating the poor: The functions of public welfare* (Rev. ed.). New York: Vintage.

Pressley, S. A. (1999, May). Six wounded in Georgia school shooting. *Washington Post.* Retrieved October 1999 from www.washingtonpost.com.

Prien, R. F., & Kupfer, D. J. (1986). Continuation drug therapy for major depressive episodes: How long should it be maintained. *American Journal of Psychiatry, 143,* 18–23.

Princeton Religion Research Center. (1996). *Religion in America.* Princeton, NJ: Gallup Poll.

Quincy, V. L. (1977). The assessment and treatment of child molestors: A review. *Canadian Psychological Review, 18,* 204–220.

RAND Corporation. (2004, Fall). *Educational achievement reflects family background more than ethnicity or immigration.* Retrieved July 1, 2005, from http://www.rand.org/publications/randreview/issues/fa112004/class.html

Resick, P. A. (1992). Cognitive treatment of a crime-related PTSD. In R. D. Peters, R. J. McMahon, & V. L. Quinsey (Eds.), *Aggression and violence throughout the life span* (pp. 171–191). Newbury Park, CA: Sage.

Resick, P. A., Nisith, P., Weaver, T. L., Astin, M. C., & Feuer, C. A. (2002). A comparison of cognitive-processing therapy with prolonged exposure and a waiting condition for the treatment of chronic posttraumatic stress disorder in female rape victims. *Journal of Consulting and Clinical Psychology, 70*(4), 867–879.

Resick, P. A., & Schnicke, M. K. (1992). Cognitive processing therapy for sexual assault victims. *Journal of Consulting and Clinical Psychology, 60,* 748–756.

Resick, P. A., & Schnicke, M. K. (1993). *Interpersonal violence: The practice series* (Vol. 4). Newbury Park, CA: Sage.

Reynolds, R., & Richardson, P. (2000). Evidence based practice and psychotherapy research. *Journal of Mental Health, 9*(3), 257–267.

Rioux, D. (1996). Shamanic healing techniques: Toward holistic addiction counseling. *Alcoholism Treatment Quarterly, 14*(1), 59–70.

Rosenfeld, A., et al. (1986). Determining incestuous contact between parent and child: Frequency of children touching parents' genitals in a non-clinical population. *Journal of American Academy of Child Psychiatry, 25*(4), 481–484.

Roth, J. A. (1994, February). *Understanding and preventing violence.* Washington, DC: U.S. Department of Justice, Office of Justice Programs, National Institute of Justice.

Rubin, A. (1986). Review of current research on chronic mental illness. In A. Rubin & J. Bowker (Eds.), *Studies on chronic mental illness: A new horizon for social work, researchers* (pp. 5–28). New York: Council on Social Work Education.

Rubin, A. (1989). Research on the long-term care of mental illness: A challenge and opportunity for social work. In K. E. Davis, R. Harris, R. Farmer, J. Reeves, & F. Segal (Eds.), *Strengthening the scientific base of social work education for services to the long-term seriously mentally ill* (pp. 39–74). Richmond: Virginia Commonwealth University.

Ryff, C. D., & Singer, B. (1998). The contours of positive human health. Psychological Inquiry, 9, 1–28.

Sandage, S. T., & Hill, P. C. (2001). The virtue of positive psychology: The rapprochement and challenge of an affirmative postmodern perspective. *Journal of the Theory of Social Behavior, 31*(3), 241–260.

Sautter, R. (1995, January). Standing up to violence. *Phi Delta Kappan, 76,* 1–2.

Schuerger, J. M., & Reigle, N. (1988). Personality and biographic data that characterize men who abuse their wives. Journal of Clinical Psychology, 44(1), 75–81.

Seigel, B. S. (1998). *Love, medicine and miracles.* New York: Harper/Perennial.

Seligman, M. E. P. (1994). *What you can change and what you can't.* New York: Knopf.

Seligman, M. E. P. (1999). The president's address. *American Psychologist, 54,* 559–562.

Shaw, S. J. (1996). *What a woman ought to be and to do: Black professional workers during the Jim Crow era.* Chicago: University of Chicago Press.

Sheldon, T. A., & Freemantle, N. (1993). Examining the effectiveness of treatments for depression. *Journal of Mental Health, 2*(2), 141–157.

Sheridan, M. J., & Amato-von Hemert, K. (1999). The role of religion and spirituality in social work education and practice: A survey of student views and experiences. *Journal of Social Work Education, 15*(1), 125–141.

Sheridan, M. J., Bullis, R. K., Adcock, C. R., Berlin, S. D., & Miller, P. C. (1992). Practitioners' personal and professional attitudes and behaviors toward religion and spirituality: Issues for social work education and practice. *Journal of Social Work Education, 28*, 190–203.

Shon, S., & Ja, D. (1982). Asian Families. In M. McGoldrick, J. Pearce, & J. Giordano (Eds.), *Ethnicity and family therapy* (pp. 208–229). New York: Guilford.

Shubert, T. H., Bressette, S., Deeken, J., & Bender, W. N. (1999). Analysis of random school shootings. In W. N. Bender, G. Clinton, & R. L. Bender (Eds.), *Violence prevention and reduction in schools* (pp. 97–101). Austin, TX: PRO-ED.

Sickmund, M., Snyder, H. N., & Poe-Yamagata, E. (1997). *Juvenile offenders and victims: 1997 update on violence.* Washington, DC: Office of Juvenile Justice and Delinquency Prevention, U.S. Department of Justice. (ERIC Document Reproduction Service No. ED416287)

Siegel, L. J., & Senna, J. J. (1994). *Juvenile delinquency: Theory, practice, and law* (5th ed.). St. Paul, MN: West.

Skeesis, A. (2000, January). *Monsters among us . . . The tragedy at Columbine High; The victims/the heroes: Could it have been prevented?* Retrieved June 2002 from www.angelfire.com

Skocpol, T. (1992). *Protecting soldiers and mothers: The political origins of social policy in the United States.* Boston: Harvard University Press.

Smith, E. D. (1995). Addressing the psycho-spiritual distress of death as reality: A transpersonal approach. *Social Work, 40*(3), 402–413.

Solinger, R. (1992). *Wake up little Susie: Single pregnancy and race before* Roe v. Wade. New York: Routledge.

Spano, R. (1982). *The rank and file movement in social work.* Washington, DC: University Press of America.

Spergel, I. (1995). *The youth gang problem: A community approach.* New York: Oxford University Press.

Spieker, S. J., Larson, N. C., Lewis, S. M., Keller, T. E., & Gilchrist, L. (1999). Developmental trajectories of disruptive behavior problems in preschool children of adolescent mothers. *Child Development, 70*, 443–458.

Spungen, C., et al. (1989, March). Child personal safety: Model program for prevention of child sexual abuse. *Social Work*, 127–131.

Stanley, M. A., & Novy, D. M. (2000). Cognitive-behavior therapy for generalized anxiety in late life: An evaluative overview. *Journal of Anxiety Disorders, 14*(2), 191–207.

Staples, R. (1986). Stereotypes of black male sexuality: The facts behind the myths. In M. Kimmel & M. Messner (Eds.), *Men's lives* (pp. 432–438). New York: Macmillan.

Stark, E. (1985). The battering syndrome: Social knowledge, social therapy and the abuse of women. Unpublished doctoral dissertation, SUNY–Binghampton.

Stark, E., & Flitcraft, A. (1985). Woman-battering, child abuse, and social heredity. In N. Johnson (Ed.), Marital violence (pp. 147–171). London: Routledge and Kegan-Paul.

Stark, K., Rouse, L., & Livingston, R. (1991). Treatment of depression during childhood and adolescence: Cognitive-behavioral procedures for the individual and family. In P. C. Kendall (Ed.), *Child and adolescent therapy* (pp. 165–206). New York: Guilford.

State of Florida. (1991). *Study of safety and security requirements for at-risk businesses.* Tallahassee, FL: Office of the Attorney General.

Stein, T. (1981). *Social work practice in child welfare.* Englewood Cliffs, NJ: Prentice Hall.

Stephens, R. D. (1995). *Safe schools: A handbook for violence prevention.* Bloomington, IN: National Education Service.

Stevens, R. (1995, April 26). Increasing violence in schools. In W. N. Bender & R. L. Bender (Eds.), *Teachers' safety.* Bishop, GA: Teacher's Workshop.

Straus, M. A. (1978). Sexual inequality, cultural norms, and wife beating. Victimology: An International Journal, 1, 54–70.

Straus, M. A., & Gelles, R. J. (1990). *Physical violence in American families: Risk factors and adaptations to violence in families.* New Brunswick, NJ: Transaction Publishers.

Strean, H. (1988, September-October). Effects of childhood sexual abuse on the psychosocial functioning of adults. *Social Work,* 465–467.

Sugai, G., Sprague, J. R., Horner, R. H., & Walker, H. M. (2000). Preventing school violence: The use of office discipline referrals to assess and monitor school-wide discipline interventions. *Journal of Emotional and Behavioral Disorders, 8,* 94–101.

Tatem-Kelly, B., Loeber, R., Keenan, K., & DeLamatre, M. (1997, December). *Developmental pathways in boys' disruptive and delinquent behavior: Juvenile Justice Bulletin.* Washington, DC: U.S. Office of Juvenile Justice and Delinquency Prevention.

Taylor, J. (1993). *Poverty and niches: A systems view.* Unpublished manuscript.

Taylor, S. (1999). *Anxiety sensitivity: Theory, research, and treatment of the fear of anxiety.* Mahwah, NJ: Lawrence Erlbaum.

Taylor, S. (2000). *Understanding and treating panic disorder: Cognitive-behavioural approaches.* Chichester, UK: Wiley.

Teske, R. H. C., & Parker, M. L. (1983). *Spouse abuse in Texas.* Huntsville, TX: Criminal Justice Center, Sam Houston State University.

Thornberry, T. P., Huizinga, D., & Loeber, R. (1995). The prevention of serious delinquency and violence: Implications from the program of research on the causes and correlates of delinquency. In J. C. Howell, B. Krisberg, J. D. Hawkins, & J. J. Wilson (Eds.), *A sourcebook: Serious, violent, and chronic juvenile offenders* (pp. 213–237). Thousand Oaks, CA: Sage.

Tice, K. C. (1998). *Tales of wayward girls and immoral women: Case records and the professionalization of social work.* Chicago: University of Illinois Press.

Tiet, Q. Q., Bird, H., & Davies, M. R. (1998, November). Adverse life events and resilience. *Journal of the American Academy of Child and Adolescent Psychiatry, 37*(11), 1191–1200.

Tobin, T., Sugai, G., & Colvin, G. (2000, May). Using discipline referrals to make decisions. *NASSP Bulletin.*

Tower, C. (1989). *Understanding child abuse and neglect.* Boston: Allyn & Bacon.

Trattner, W. I. (1989). *From poor law to welfare state: A history of social welfare in America* (4th ed.). New York: The Free Press.

Trolander, J. (1975). *Settlement houses and the Great Depression.* Detroit, MI: Wayne State Press.

The 2004 Department of Health and Human Services Poverty Guidelines. (2004, February 13). *Federal Register, 69*(30), 7336–7338.

U.S. Advisory Board on Child Abuse and Neglect. (1991, September 15). *Creating caring communities: Blueprints for an effective federal policy on child abuse and neglect* (Second Report). Washington, DC: Administration for Children and Families, U.S. Department of Health and Human Services.

U.S. Department of Education. (1998). *National educational goals panel report.* Washington, DC: Author.

U.S. Department of Health and Human Services. (1988). *Study of the national incidence and prevalence of child abuse and neglect: 1988.* Washington, DC: Author.

U.S. Department of Health and Human Services. (2000). *Healthy people 2010: With understanding and improving health and objectives for improving health* (2 vols.). Washington, DC: U.S. Government Printing Office.

U.S. Department of Health, Education and Welfare. (1977). *Child abuse and neglect programs: Practice and theory.* Washington, DC: U.S. Government Printing Office.

U.S. Department of Justice and U.S. Department of Education. (1998). *First annual report on school safety.* Washington, DC: Author.

Van Hasselt, V. B., Morrison, R. L., Bellack, A. S., & Hersen, M. (1988). *Handbook of family violence.* New York: Plenum Press.

Vance, J., Fernandez, G., & Biber, M. (1998). Educational progress in a population of youth with aggression and emotional disturbance: The role and risk of protective factors. *Journal of Emotional and Behavioral Disorders, 6,* 214–221.

Wagner, K. D., & Lorion, R. P. (1984). Correlates of death anxiety in elderly persons. *Journal of Clinical Psychology, 40,* 1235–1241.

Wagner, L., & Lane, L. (1998). *Lane County Department of Youth Services: 1997 report.* Eugene, OR: Department of Youth Services.

Walker, H. M., & Severson, H. H. (1990). *Systematic screening for behavior disorders.* Longmont, CO: Sopris West.

Walker, H. M., Block-Pedego, A. E., Todis, B. J., & Severson, H. H. (1991). *School archival records search (SARS): User's guide and technical manual.* Longmont, CO: Sopris West.

Walker, H. M., Colvin, G., & Ramsey, E. (1995). *Antisocial behavior in school: Strategies and best practices.* Pacific Grove, CA: Brooks/Cole.

Walker, H. M., Horner, R. H., Sugai, G., Bullis, M., Sprague, J. R., Bricker, D., & Kaufman, M. J. (1996). Integrated approaches to preventing antisocial behavior patterns among school-age children and youth. *Journal of Emotional and Behavioral Disorders, 4,* 194–209.

Walker, H. M., Irvin, L. K., & Sprague, J. R. (1997). Violence prevention and school safety: Issues, problems, approaches, and recommended solutions. *OSSC Bulletin.*

Walker, H. M., Shinn, M. R., O'Neill, R. E., & Ramsey, E. (1987). A longitudinal assessment of the development of antisocial behavior in boys: Rationale, methodology and first year results. *Remedial and Special Education, 8*(4), 7–16, 27.

Walkowitz, D. J. (1990, October). The making of a feminine professional identity: Social workers in the 1920s. *American Historical Review, 95*(4), 1051–1075.

Walkowitz, D. J. (1999). *Working with class: Social workers and the politics of middle-class identity.* Chapel Hill: University of North Carolina Press.

Weil, A. (1998). *Natural health.* New York: Houghton Mifflin.

Weiss, D. S., & Marmar, C. R. (1997). The Impact of Event Scale–Revised. In J. P. Wilson & T. M. Keane (Eds.), *Assessing psychological trauma and PTSD: A practitioner's handbook* (pp. 399–411). New York: Guilford Press.

Weiss, D. S., Marmar, C. R., Metzler, T. J., & Ronfeldt, H. M. (1995). Predicting symptomatic distress in emergency services personnel. *Journal of Consulting and Clinical Psychology, 63,* 361–368.

Wenocur, S., & Reich, M. (1989). *From charity to enterprise: The development of American social work in a market economy.* Chicago: Illinois University Press.

Widom, C. S. (1999). The cycle of violence. In F. R. Scarpitti & A. L. Nielson (Eds.), *Crime and criminals: Contemporary and classic readings* (pp. 332–334). Los Angeles: Roxbury.

Wilber, K. (1998). *The eye of the spirit: An integral vision for a world gone slightly mad.* Boston: Shambhala.

Wilk, R. J., & McCarthy, C. R. (1986, January). Interventions in child sexual abuse: A survey of attitudes. *Social Casework, 27, 106–118.*

Will, G. F. (2001, July 9). In Jedwabne. Newsweek, p. 68.

Wilson, J., & Howell, J. (1993). *A comprehensive strategy for serious, violent, and chronic juvenile offenders.* Washington, DC: Office of Juvenile Delinquency Prevention, U.S. Department of Justice. (ERIC Document Reproduction Service No. ED365925)

Wirth, D. P. (1995). The significance of belief and expectancy with the spiritual healing encounter. *Social Science & Medicine, 41*(2), 249–260.

The World Bank Group. (2004, May). *Measuring poverty.* Retrieved May 14, 2004, from http://www.worldbank.org/poverty/mission/up2.htm

Yu, E. (1989). Chinese collective orientation and need for achievement. *International Journal of Social Psychiatry, 26*(3), 184–189.

Zigler, E., Taussig, C., & Black, K. (1992). Early childhood intervention: A promising preventative for juvenile delinquency. *American Psychologist, 47,* 997–1006.

Internet Sources

America's Second Harvest: http://www.secondharvest.org

Assessing the New Federalism: http://newfederalism.urban.org/

Center on Budget and Policy Priorities: http://www.cbpp.org

Commonwealth Fund: http://www.cmwf.org/

Free the Slaves: http://www.freetheslaves.net/home.php

http://aspe.hhs.gov/hsp/hspincpov.htm

http://aspe.hhs.gov/poverty/figures-fed-reg.shtml

http://aspe.os.dhhs.gov/poverty/contacts.shtml#a

http://econ.worldbank.org/

http://www.brookings.edu/dybdocroot/es/urban/publications/jargowsky-poverty.pdf

http://www.cbpp.org/6–1-05pov.pdf

http://www.cbpp.org/SAFETY.htm

http://www.census.gov/hhes/www/income/income.html

http://www.census.gov/hhes/www/poverty.html

http://www.census.gov/prod/2002pubs/p60–219.pdf

http://www.census.gov/prod/2004pubs/p60–226.pdf

http://www.epinet.org/studies/Pulling_Apart_2002.pdf

http://www.iwpr.org/

http://www.nccp.org/media/cpc02-text.pdf

http://www.poverty.smartlibrary.org

http://www.urbanpoverty.net/

http://www.wider.unu.edu/wiid/wiid.htm

http://www.worldbank.org/data/

Inter-university Consortium for Political and Social Research: http://www.icpsr.umich.edu/

Joint Center for Poverty Research, Northwestern University/University of Chicago: http://www.jcpr.org/

Let's Invest in Families Today (LIFT): http://lift.nccp.org/wizard/wizard.cgi

Mathematica Policy Research, Inc.: http://www.mathematica-mpr.com/

National Center for Children in Poverty: http://www.nccp.org/

National Center on Poverty Law: http://www.povertylaw.org/

National Institute for Social Science Information (NISSI): http://www.nissi.org/

National Law Center on Homelessness and Poverty: http://www.nlchp.org/

National Low Income Housing Coalition (NLIHC): http://www.nlihc.org/

National Priorities Project (NPP): http://www.nationalpriorities.org/

National Priorities Project Database: http://database.nationalpriorities.org/

Population Studies Center: http://www.psc.isr.umich.edu/

Index

About the Author

 **Morley D. Glicken** is the former dean of the Worden School of Social Service in San Antonio; the founding director of the Master of Social Work Department at California State University, San Bernardino; the past director of the Master of Social Work Program at the University of Alabama; and the former executive director of Jewish Family Service of Greater Tucson. He has also held faculty positions in social work at the University of Kansas and Arizona State University. Dr. Glicken received his BA in social work with a minor in psychology from the University of North Dakota, holds an MSW from the University of Washington, and earned the MPA and DSW from the University of Utah. He is a member of Phi Kappa Phi Honorary Fraternity.

Dr. Glicken published two books for Allyn & Bacon/Longman Publishers in 2003: *The Role of the Helping Professions in the Treatment of Victims and Perpetrators of Crime* (with Dale Sechrest) and *A Simple Guide to Social Research;* and two additional books for Allyn & Bacon/Longman in 2004: *Violent Young Children* and *Understanding and Using the Strengths Perspective.* He published *Improving the Effectiveness of the Helping Professions: An Evidence-Based Approach to Practice* in 2005 for Sage and *Working with Troubled Men: a Guide to Contemporary Practice* for Lawrence Erlbaum, also in 2005. Sage published *Learning From Resilient People: Lessons We Can Apply to Counseling and Psychotherapy* in 2006 and will publish *A Competency Based Approach to Supervision for the Helping Profession*s in 2007.

Dr. Glicken has published more than 50 articles in professional journals and has written extensively on personnel issues for Dow Jones, publisher of the *Wall Street Journal.* He has held clinical social work licenses in Alabama and Kansas, and is a member of the Academy of Certified Social Workers. He is currently Professor Emeritus in Social Work at California State University, San Bernardino, and Executive Director of the Institute for Positive Growth: A Research, Treatment and Training Institute in Los Angeles, California. The Institute's website may be found at *morleyglicken.com,* and Dr. Glicken can be reached online at *mglicken@msn.com.*